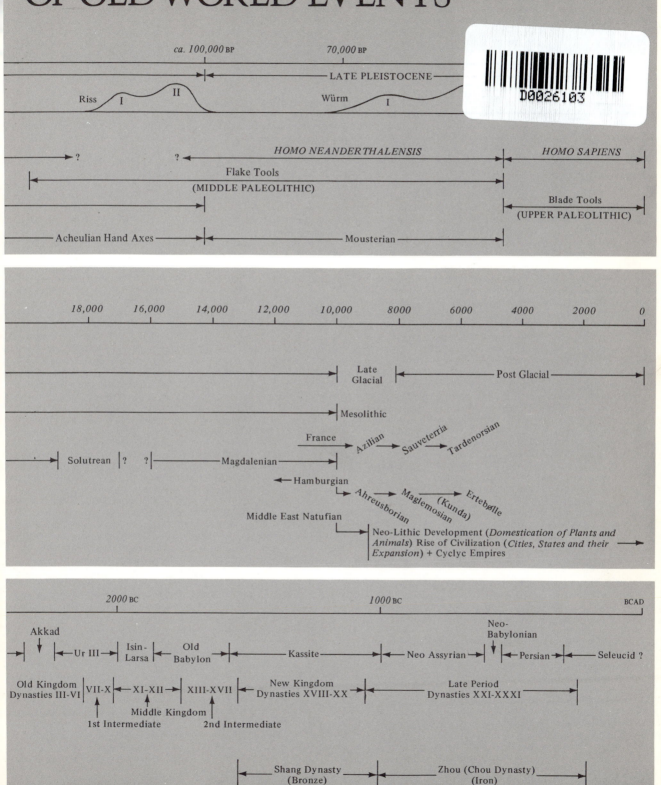

Introduction to Archaeology

SECOND EDITION

James J. Hester
University of Colorado at Boulder

James Grady
The Colorado College, Colorado Springs

2ND EDITION

INTRODUCTION TO ARCHAEOLOGY

HOLT, RINEHART AND WINSTON

New York   Chicago   San Francisco
Philadelphia   Montreal   Toronto   London
Sydney   Tokyo   Mexico City
Rio de Janeiro   Madrid

Acquisitions Editor: David Boynton
Project Editor: Marina Barrios
Production Manager: Annette Mayeski
Design Supervisor: Robert F. Kopelman

Illustration credits appear at end of book.

Library of Congress Cataloging in Publication Data

Hester, James J.
   Introduction to archaeology.

   Includes bibliographies and indexes.
   1. Archaeology.   I. Grady, James, 1931–
II. Title.
CC165.H45   1981   930.1   81-6843
ISBN 0-03-046291-6   AACR2

CBS COLLEGE PUBLISHING
Holt, Rinehart and Winston
The Dryden Press
Saunders College Publishing

Contents

v

PART III
CULTURAL DATA REVEALED BY ARCHAEOLOGY: THE OLD WORLD
125

Preface to the Second Edition

The writing of this second edition of *Introduction to Archaeology* has been easier than the first attempt. For one reason, we had available criticisms and comments concerning the first edition and it was therefore relatively easy to isolate areas and topics that needed better coverage. Secondly, it was possible to amend those sections with greater authority since Dr. James Grady had agreed to serve as co-author. He was initially selected because of his expertise in the archaeology of the Old World. However he has also contributed much knowledge of graphics in archaeology, especially aerial photography. His collaboration not only provided additional expertise in those areas but also permitted us to parcel out the work by chapters and or topics. One favorable result was that this edition took only two and a half years to prepare in contrast to the first version which took five years. Therefore we feel confident that this edition is more up to date. A second benefit from having a collaborator was the opportunity to discuss together how to respond to our critics and how to present specific topics. Although we will undoubedly still have our critics we believe most of our differences will be the intentional result of intellectual decisions rather than omissions or errors in fact.

Critics of the first edition stressed the need for more comprehensive geographic coverage, the need for the basic content to be more up to date, and the need to include a range of theoretical constructs rather than focusing too narrowly on cultural historical reconstruction. Finally the intent of the illustrations in the first edition was to provide a source of information additional to that in the text. Most reviewers considered this attempt to represent information overload and confusing because the illustrations were not specifically keyed to passages in the text.

In response to those criticisms we have rewritten the text wherever we felt we could improve on the original. This then is not just a warmed-up version of the original but a completely revised and rewritten new edition. We have added sections on new dating techniques, recently developed theoretical and methodological constructs, the archaeology of Afghanistan and the Far East, and the need for conservation archaeology. The coverage of Mesoamerica and Peru has been restructured by cultural stage — Preclassic, Classic, and Postclassic, as a means of more clearly presenting the development of New World civilizations. Finally we have keyed the illustrations to the text and wherever possible replaced the original illustrations with others we felt were of better quality or more appropriate. As a result approximately half of the illustrations are new.

Our goal in preparing this edition has been to provide a text for the beginning college course in archaeology or world prehistory. We provide a balanced survey of world prehistory plus introductory material on archaeological methods, theory, and applications. It is designed to reconstruct prehistoric lifeways by geographic area and time period so that each chapter can be the focus of one week's consideration. We have sought to avoid professional disputes by introducing the student to the basic data of archaeology without advocating any particular theoretical approach. We hope our efforts will meet the needs of both professors and students.

James J. Hester

PART I

THE NATURE OF ARCHAEOLOGY

To the average person archaeology is a thinly disguised "treasure hunt," a quest for ancient objects made of precious materials, or for the remains of humans of extinct physical types. Much of the popular press continues to emphasize these aspects, and one has only to reflect on the popularity of the Tutankhamen exhibit or the current smash hit, the Search for Alexander, an exhibit of objects associated with Alexander the Great and his era, to know that these motives affect us all. To the specialist, however, archaeology is a set of techniques perfected to recover information from evidences of former human occupation. These evidences are for the most part fragmentary; they are buried, having been discarded long before written records existed. Thus if we attempt to understand the nature of archaeology as a sci-

1

entific discipline we must focus on the nature of the objects to be found, and these include not just royal treasures but the lowly potsherd, stone-flaking debris, and splintered food bones as well. In the section which follows we will describe some of the more common artifacts and the kinds of information that they have the potential to yield.

The excavation of archaeological materials is governed by a set of techniques that has evolved over several hundred years. Developing at the same time as excavation techniques were attitudes toward the objects found. After all, the location of bones of extinct animals and of previously unknown tools and implements might conceivably be explained in a number of ways, including magic, "spontaneous generation," and other nonscientific explanations. We shall therefore detail, in a brief history of the development of archaeology, how archaeological finds were integrated into the contemporaneously evolving concepts of biological and cultural evolution.

We will then proceed to describe how the modern archaeologist finds sites, excavates them, records and dates the finds made, and then goes on to interpret these in terms of past behavioral patterns. Modern archaeology then goes beyond the description of finds and attempts to interpret and explain them. Such interpretations and explanations are based on a scientific methodology and a set of theoretical orientations. We believe that you, the beginning student, must have some understanding of these in order to better comprehend how we have derived what we present later as the best explanations possible, to date, of how our ancestors lived, what they looked like, their mode of subsistence, and all the other aspects of human prehistory which each of us find fascinating. Join with us then in this brief review of history, methods, analytical techniques, and theoretical orientations.

■ Archaeology is a scientific discipline not a "treasure hunt."

1

The Science of Archaeology

In the conception of most people the archaeologist is a privileged "treasure hunter" who is paid to search the exotic parts of the world for the oldest and most spectacular objects, tombs, and ruins of ancient cities. If the finds are of gold, silver, or precious stones, so much the better. In contrast, archaeologists consider themselves to be scientists to whom the lowly potsherd may be just as important as the king's scepter. ■ Actually, the archaeologist is a combination of all these things and more; and we seek here to introduce you to the development of archaeology as a scientific discipline so that you may understand how and why the archaeologist does what he or she does.

The development of archaeology as a discipline is recent, most of its current form, interests, and methods having originated within the past 100 years. On the other hand, interest in the past is common to all human societies. Evidence of such interest (Hole and Heizer 1969: 5) dates back to the last days of Babylon (555–538 B.C.)* The earliest known excavations in search of ancient artifacts were conducted by Nabonidus, the last king of Babylon, who dug at Ur. How, then, do we differentiate modern archaeology from its historical antecedents, and if we do so, to what purpose?

Perhaps this question can be answered by defining what the archaeologist does, besides finding ancient objects, that is unique. The modern archaeologist would draw a distinction between the simple collector of antiquities and the ar-

*All dates shown as B.C. are general dates obtained by one or another dating technique. Radiocarbon dates shown with a plus or minus factor and an uppercase B.C. or A.D. have been recalibrated. Uncalibrated dates are shown with a lowercase b.c. or a.d. See Chapter 3 for a discussion of the recalibration problem.

> ● Archaeology studies past cultural behavior.
> ▲ Digging is hard work and often boring.

chaeologist. Further, the modern archaeologist would define some students of ancient objects as philologists, others as epigraphers, and still others as art historians. What, then, are the criteria by which we define and differentiate archaeology? Practically every archaeologist has attempted to create definitions, so we will not quote here an exhaustive series of them. One *usable* definition, however, is that of Grahame Clark (1957):

> Archaeology may be simply defined as the systematic study of antiquities as a means of reconstructing the past. For his contributions to be fruitful the archaeologist has to possess a real feeling for history, even though he may not have to face what is perhaps the keenest challenge of historical scholarship, the subtle interplay of human personality and circumstance. Yet he is likely to be involved even more deeply in the flow of time. The prehistoric archaeologist in particular is confronted by historical changes of altogether greater dimensions than those with which the historian of literate civilizations is concerned, and has to face demands on his historical imagination of a commensurate order; further, at a purely technical level he is likely to be met with much greater difficulties of decipherment, difficulties which can as a rule only be surmounted by calling on scientists and scholars practiced in highly specialized branches of knowledge.

At this point it is in order to offer a definition of archaeology as we view it. ● We consider archaeology to be the study of past cultural behavior within the specific historical and ecological frameworks in which it occurred. The methodology includes the finding of evidences of the past cultural activity and then establishing the relationship of these findings to the temporal and spatial locale in which they occurred. Also of importance is the fact that these findings are not, of themselves, cultural behavior but are the result of behavioral patterns; and thus the behavioral patterns themselves must be inferred. For example, the presence of a potsherd on a site provides a major opportunity for such inferences. The sherd may be painted, the interior showing scraping marks; and the clay from which it was made may have a distinctive temper (the crushed rock, sand, or other material used to inhibit cracking as the pot dries). From the painted decoration we learn something of the design style. We may even be able to infer that the design is symbolic, since it may have religious, calendrical, or mnemonic meaning. The interior scraping will be typical of either handmade or wheel-made pottery. Furthermore, the temper may be identifiable to a specific place where the material was obtained, meaning that trips were made to that place to acquire the tempering substance. The design style would probably have chronological significance, and the direction in which the coils of clay were laid up in the manufacturing process might lead to the inference that the maker was right- or left-handed. The form of the sherd may suggest the shape of the vessel that it is from, which may lead us to infer possible uses of the vessel.

If we can learn so much from a single potsherd, then what possibilities await the study of the other remnants of our past? Here lies the core of interest that makes archaeology so appealing to young and old alike. Beneath the next layer of dirt may lie something hitherto unknown to history, an object the like of which no person today has ever seen before. We have thus bound up in one field, the glamour of a treasure hunt, a sense of creativity equal to that of the artist, and the exploratory vision of the scientist. It is the excitement of the treasure hunt which so appeals to most people. Everywhere the archaeologist goes, he or she is greeted by "How fascinating, I'm sure your work must be exciting!" The truth of the matter is that, frequently, archaeology is not all that exciting. ▲ It has its share of drudgery, because digging is hard work, often carried out in hot, dusty caves, in the rain, or in a cloud of gnats—all of which contribute to making one's existence somewhat less than ideal. Normally, the research archaeologist is too busy labeling sample bags, drawing profiles, or taking photographs to notice everything that comes out of the trenches. Therefore it is easy to lose, or at least temporarily forget, the excitement which is so typical of the nonprofessional. However, there are times when the excitement suddenly returns, accompanied by the realization that one is a "treasure hunter" after all, only somewhat disguised by scientific motives and methodology.

The senior author of this text recalls excavating a Clovis-age (9,000-year B.C.) mammoth killsite in New Mexico: In the trench wall of the Clovis level a workman had exposed what in profile looked like a human skull. Immediately I planned what steps to take; I would first obtain a highway patrolman to guard the find and then would notify the press of this momentous find—the earliest human found to date in the New World. Fortunately, I dug just a little bit more around the skull to be sure what it was and it turned out to be a large turtle shell!

Fig. 1-1 Typical pair of sandstone columns found along the ancient Roman road. (Hester, Hobler, and Russell 1970:Fig. 3.)

Fig. 1-2 Map showing location of Roman road in southern Egypt. (Hester, Hobler, and Russell 1970:Fig. 1.)

In another instance:

While working in the Egyptian desert south of Aswan Dr. Philip Hobler and I were driving across an open sandy plain some 5 or 6 miles west of the Nile. Suddenly, we noticed two cut stone columns, each about a foot in diameter and 5 feet in height, lying on the sand (Fig. 1-1). They were obviously of some antiquity, but we were unable to understand why they were at that particular place. We photographed them and then drove on. A day later in the same area we found another set of columns. This time we realized their presence was not accidental. We drove in a straight line toward the first set we had located and began to find additional sets at intervals of about one mile (Fig. 1-2). Obviously, they were some kind of road markers. We eventually traced the former road for about 30 miles,

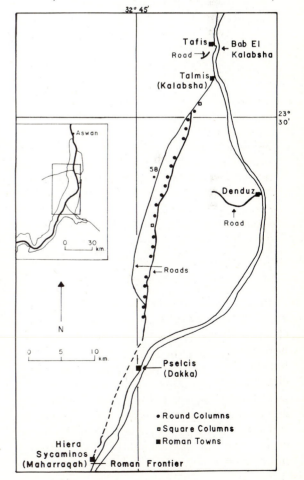

> ■ Archaeology is made possible by preservation.

finding 22 sets of columns en route. We found that some of the markers had Roman numerals on them and that the interval between sets was about 4,800 feet, the distance of the Roman mile. We had discovered the first Roman roads known in southern Egypt; such roads had been long known in Libya but not in Egypt.

The important point here is that *an exciting discovery had been made* but not recognized as such until later.

We have established that the archaeologist studies remains of past cultures and from these remains attempts to infer the nature of prior human behavioral patterns. The subject thus includes a methodology for the recovery of objects and other kinds of information, a body of already known data with which new finds may be compared, a set of concepts to organize the data in cultural terms, and a variety of ancillary techniques of laboratory analysis, such as radiocarbon dating, paleomagnetic studies, and so on. Specific details of each of these portions of archaeology will be considered in later chapters.

■ The entire study of archaeology is made possible by accidents of preservation. Durable items, such as stone tools, pottery, or stone architecture, are usually preserved, even if broken or disarranged. Items of perishable materials also may be preserved in certain kinds of environments of deposition. Dry caves and sites below the water table are both excellent environments for the preservation of fibers, wood, cloth, leather, and other perishable materials (Fig. 1-3). The preserved cultural materials are always fragmentary in the sense that it is never possible to recover all the remains of a specific culture. Often the items found are preserved through some unique circumstance, such as a volcanic eruption or the accidental loss of a ship at sea. In addition, most finds are items that were broken

in antiquity and discarded by their users. Our task in archaeology is thus made more difficult. We must reconstruct the nature of past cultures from those remnants which have been preserved, no matter how fragmentary or incomplete are the specimens. However, we do not mean to suggest that archaeological remains are rare; for they occur almost everywhere, even on the continental shelves now below sea level and in deserts now completely uninhabited. The problem is that archaeological sites, wherever they occur, and no matter what their size, contain only a portion of the material culture of the people who occupied that site. A major portion of the original materials has been destroyed by burning, erosion, organic decay, or chemical alteration. Therefore, the archaeologist's task is twofold: to reconstruct the original nature of the objects found, and to infer the role of these objects in a former society. A helpful device is the recording of the position of each item found in a site. The relationship of items to each other may give clues as to their former uses and associations. By such means we may learn that items of vastly different forms were used together in the past. An example would be the parts of a composite tool, such as a harpoon. The harpoon head might be slotted for the insertion of a chipped stone point. We could infer from a slotted harpoon head that it had possessed a point, but finding one example with a point in place would constitute archaeological "proof" that the two items were associated in their use. A more abstract example would be a cluster of small items utilized in a religious ceremony. By their form there might be no way in which we could guess that they had ever been used together. Finding them in a group suggests that they were used together in the past. An outstanding example of this is the series of figurines in human form made of jade found at the Olmec site of LaVenta on the east coast of Mexico (Fig. 1-4). These figurines had been placed vertically in a semicircle. Facing the semicircular group was a single figurine. From the association, the exca-

Fig. 1-3 Wooden furnishing from the tomb of the pharoah Tutankhamen, illustrating examples of excellent preservation. (Photographs by Harry Burton, Metropolitan Museum of Art.)

● Archaeology has many specialties.

▲ The earliest archaeology dates back to early Babylon.

■ The collector was a product of the Renaissance.

vators postulated that the group had been purposefully buried in that position to represent some specific past ceremony.

Although the field techniques for the recovery of archaeological materials are fairly standardized, the types of intellectual inquiry possible through examination of archaeologically obtained specimens are infinitely variable. Obvious divisions include those governed by the major time-space considerations. Some special

interests depend upon study of the techniques used, such as in weaving or pottery manufacture. Historical concerns afford another approach, such as the development of specific architectural features in cities or the development of social systems associated with specific economies.

● These problems or interest areas have culminated in a series of specialties within archaeology. As a result, the archaeologist of today usually does not attempt to master the entire body of knowledge relative to past human cultural activity but instead specializes in one or more areas. The archaeologist may also specialize in a specific technique or method for the recovery of data. For example, there are archaeologists who specialize in dating techniques, ceramic analyses, tracing of ancient trade routes, the decipher-

Fig. 1-4 Human figurines of jade found within a pyramid at La Venta, Tabasco, Mexico. Their arrangement suggests a prehistoric ceremony. (Hester photograph, courtesy Mexican National Museum of Anthropology.)

ing of ancient languages, verification of the Bible, underwater archaeology, and many more endeavors.

In summary, an *archaeologist* is anyone who studies the remains of the past collected through the use of scientific field methods. These methods are more or less standardized, whereas the point of view of the archaeologist toward the remains studied varies according to the particular bias or interest. Thus we perceive that the unifying elements binding these rather diverse studies together are (1) the study of the remains of ancient cultures and (2) the collection of these remains through the use of standardized scientific archaeological methods.

A Brief History of the Development of Archaeology

We have already narrowed our field of interest by stating that archaeologists study ancient remains as a means of reconstructing past cultural behavior. This limitation has by no means always been in effect. Archaeology has evolved over the past 2,500 years, and during this interval the study of antiquities has had a number of different emphases. The first concern with objects from the past was displayed by tomb robbers. Tomb robbing is a long-standing tradition in Egypt, and one which continues to the present. We have no idea when the earliest such occurrence took place, but we do know that by 1120 B.C. the practice was so widespread that an investigation was held by the ancient Egyptians.

▲ At a somewhat later date Nabonidus excavated at Ur, brought his findings back to Babylon, and placed them in a museum (Hole and Heizer 1973: 41). Other early incidents involving the planned or accidental finding of antiquities are known. In most cases these demonstrate only a limited concern for the past and frequently the motivation was the procurement of objects for sale.

In the fifth century B.C. the Athenians opened some graves which they adjudged to be Carian as these included artifacts which were similar to those still used by the Carians. Julius Caesar's soldiers sold bronze vessels which they pilfered from graves at Corinth. Another Roman emperor collected ancient Greek coins, but even that practice was centuries ahead of its time. (The collecting of antiquities as a special interest did not develop until the fifteenth century.) It is difficult to apply a term to this early historic period. Tomb robbing was a major aspect, and occasionally there were other concerns, but these could be categorized as curiosity rather than true interest in the antiquities themselves. And, certainly, there was as yet little interest in the lives of ancient peoples.

■ With the Renaissance in Europe came the development of interest in the collecting of art treasures. This practice began in Italy during the fifteenth century A.D. and rapidly became a widespread custom among wealthy individuals and officials of the church, who decorated their homes and establishments with ancient statuary. Alexander VI, who was pope between 1492 and 1503, initiated the practice of excavating in search of such treasures. Pompei and Herculaneum were principal sources of these objects and were "mined" in an extractive sense rather than being excavated for purposes of collecting scholarly information. The collector's spirit spread to other parts of Europe, especially to England, where wealthy persons, such as Thomas Howard, made periodic visits to Italy to purchase antiquities. Soon this practice included the remains of other ancient civilizations, especially those of the Middle East and Egypt. Claudius Rich was one such collector. Residing in Bagdad as part of Britain's diplomatic corps, Rich was an assiduous collector of ancient coins, manuscripts, and clay tablets for 25 years (Daniel 1967). (After Rich's death in 1821, 7,000 pounds of these antiquities were deposited in the British Museum.) Another Englishman, Henry Creswick Rawlinson, traveled the length and breadth of Iran in the search

● Napoleon's invasion of Egypt initiated the study of Egyptology.

▲ The prehistory of Britain becomes important.

■ God created the world in 4004 B.C.

for examples of ancient writing. He then spent years in the decipherment of cuneiform script. Of special help in Rawlinson's quest were the inscriptions on Behistun rock in three languages: Old Persian, Babylonian, and Susian (Fig. 1-5). He worked on the texts from 1835 to 1847, at which time he was able to publish a full translation.

● An interest in Egyptian antiquities became widespread after Napoleon's invasion of Egypt in 1789. With the French troops were archaeological specialists, and from this initial contact the French Institute in Cairo developed. The most important find was the Rosetta stone (in 1799) which, after the British victory in 1801, was transported to the British Museum. (It was the Rosetta stone which eventually provided the means of deciphering the ancient Egyptian hieroglyphs.)

Giovanni Belzoni (1778–1823) was the most famous collector of Egyptian antiquities. An Italian, Belzoni was in Egypt to work on irrigation projects, but when this pursuit failed he went to work for the British Consul collecting antiquities. A former circus "strong man," Belzoni collected papyri, mummies, statues, and anything else portable. In 1820 he held an exhibition in the Egyptian Hall in Piccadilly. He also published a book, *Narrative of the Operations and Recent Discoveries within the Pyramids, Temples, Tombs and Excavations in Egypt and Nubia*, one of the earliest (1820) works devoted to antiquities.

In general, collectors of this period specialized in antiquities derived from the great civilizations and sought them to resell to art lovers. Men like Rawlinson, who maintained serious scholastic interest in the objects they obtained, were rare; looters like Belzoni were more common. By categorizing periods of interest we do not intend to imply a neat sequence of steps in the evolution of archaeology. The collecting phase is still with us (e.g., J. Paul Getty's [1965] *The Joys of Collecting*). However, it is usually possible to attribute the efforts of individuals to the specific intellectual interests of the times in which they lived.

▲ In seventeenth- and eighteenth-century England several individuals developed a strong interest in the cultures of ancient Britain. For the first time in history the inquiry shifted from the nature of the ancient objects to the nature of their makers. The outstanding pioneer in this field was William Camden, a school headmaster (1551–1623) who traveled over England studying antiquities. In 1586 Camden published *Britannia*, the first general guide to the archaeology of England, containing descriptions and illustrations of the antiquities. Camden's writings included not only descriptions of the barrows (prehistoric burial mounds) and other architectural remains but sought to explain why these were constructed as they were.

John Aubrey (1626–97), writing between 1659 and 1670, was another of the English antiquarians. The following description by Aubrey (Daniel 1967: 37) indicates that intellectual inquiries were becoming increasingly discerning:

> Let us imagine then what kind of countrie this was in the time of the Britons. By the nature of the soil, which is sour woodsere land, very natural for the production of oakes especially, one may conclude that this North Division was a shady dismal wood; and the inhabitants almost as savage as the Beasts whose skins were their only rayment.

Edward Lhwyd (1660–1708), the first keeper of the Ashmolean Museum at Oxford, published a catalogue of fossils and, in 1707, the first volume of *Archaeologia Britannica*, which presents the histories and customs of the original inhabitants of Great Britain. One of Lhwyd's major

Fig. 1-5 Sir Henry Creswicke Rawlinson deciphered Mesopotamian writing through the study of this text on Behistun rock. The inscription was carved in three ancient languages in 516 B.C. by order of Darius I. (Cottrell 1960: Plate 25.)

concerns was to lay to rest the myth that stone implements were shot from the sky by elves. As Lhwyd states, "but for my part I must crave leave to suspend my faith, until I see one of them descend" (Daniel 1967: 39). Other antiquaries, Henry Rowlands (1655–1723) and William Stukeley (1697–1765) were deeply concerned with the nature of pre-Roman Britain, especially the Druid cult and the sites of Avebury and Stonehenge.

However, prehistoric archaeology had almost insurmountable intellectual problems to overcome before it could consider questions concerning the antiquity of humans and their works. This was because seventeenth-century Christianity provided the only acceptable answer to questions of human origins. Everyone knew that God had created humans in his own image, but the question was *When* did this occur? ■ In 1650 James Ussher, archbishop of Armagh, pub-

● Ancient stone tools were thought to be thunderbolts.

▲ The first archaeological site report.

■ The three-age system.

lished the *Annals of the Ancient and New Testament*, in which it was declared that creation took place in 4004 B.C. This date was added to the margins of the Bible, and to question it was regarded as the same as questioning the validity of the Bible (Daniel 1962: 24). Dr. Charles Lightfoot, master of St. Catherine's College and vice chancellor of Cambridge University refined Archbishop Ussher's dating (Daniel 1967: 25) by declaring that "heaven and earth, centre and circumference, were created all together in the same instinct . . . this took place and man was created by the Trinity on October 23, 4004 B.C. at nine o'clock in the morning." (By some strange coincidence the Cambridge University academic year also began on October 23, at nine o'clock in the morning!)

With this impossibly short chronology the only acceptable explanation for the existence of humans and for the variety found in the plant and animal kingdoms was instantaneous creation, wherein each species was the result of a specific act of creation. The problem posed by a biblically based short chronology was not resolved until the 1830s, when catastrophist explanations of the fossil record were replaced by uniformitarianist concepts. (The uniformitarianist-catastrophist debate is described later in this chapter.)

Despite biblical arguments as to when creation took place, what we now know to be prehistoric stone tools had long been known, and as Daniel (1962: 47) describes:

they had been explained away as thunderbolts, fairy arrows, elfshot. Ulisses Aldrovandi in the mid-seventeenth century described stone tools as "due to an admixture of a certain exhalation of thunder and lightning with metallic matter,

chiefly in dark clouds, which is coagulated by the circumfused moisture and conglutinated into a mass (like flour with water) and subsequently indurated by heat, like a brick," and these rather surprising words were written by a man who has been described as the greatest zoologist of the Renaissance period. ● Tollius, at about the same time, claimed chipped flints to be "generated in the sky by a fulgurous exhalation conglobed in a cloud by the circumposed humour." . . . Others, however, had already more intelligent views of the nature of stone tools. Mercati, as early as the end of the sixteenth century, had agreed that the so-called thunderbolts were the weapons of a primitive folk ignorant of a knowledge of metallurgy.

The controversy over the nature of these stone tools was still strong in 1766, when Charles Lyttelton, bishop of Carlisle, read a paper on stone hatchets to the Society of Antiquaries of London in which it was stated that "there is not the least doubt of these stone instruments having been fabricated in the earliest times and by barbarous people, before the use of iron or other metals was known" (Daniel 1962: 49).

At the end of the seventeenth century a London apothecary and antique dealer by the name of Conyers reported finding what was described as a stone axe made by ancient Britons who did not know the use of metal. Although the axe was found in association with the bones of an elephant, Conyers's report was received with ridicule and certainly was not accepted by the scientific community at large. In 1715 a friend of Conyers, John Bagford, undertook to resolve the dispute over Conyers's find. The problem as Bagford saw it was simple: How do you explain the presence of an elephant in London? (Accepted was the association of the axe and the elephant.) There was, of course, a historic reference to elephants in London: The Roman emperor Claudius was supposed to have brought four of the creatures with him when he came to celebrate the conquest of Britain. Thus the association of the elephant and the axe was interpreted as the result of some poor Briton defending hearth and home against the onslaught of the Romans (Daniel 1962: 49).

Bagford had thus developed a perfectly rational explanation for the association. This rationale represented current knowledge — what we today would call "state-of-the-art" thinking. The only problem was that the explanation was incorrect, and therein lies a lesson for us. We, too, explain things in light of our existing knowledge, and who knows how strange our explanations will seem 200 years hence?

In 1797 John Frere wrote a letter to the secretary of the Society of Antiquaries in which were described flint implements found at Hoxne, Suffolk, the stratigraphic sequence at Hoxne, and the fact that the implements were associated with extinct fauna. Frere even drew scientific conclusions about this association. In other words, John Frere wrote the *first* archaeological site report. Noted were the following:

▲ "They are, I think, evident weapons of war, fabricated and used by a people who had not the use of metals. They lay in great numbers at the depth of about twelve feet, in a stratified soil, which was dug into for the purpose of raising clay for bricks.

"The situation in which these weapons were found may tempt us to refer them to a very remote period indeed; even beyond that of the present world: but, whatever our conjectures on that head may be, it will be difficult to account for the stratum in which they lie being covered with another stratum, which, on that supposition, may be conjectured to have been once the bottom, or at least the shore, of the sea."

"If you think the above worthy the notice of the Society you will please to lay it before them.

I am, Sir,
with great respect,
Your faithful humble Servant,
John Frere"

The foundations of the scientific discipline of archaeology were established in the first half of the nineteenth century with two major developments, one in Denmark and the other in England. The Danish contribution, known as the *three-age system*, was a method developed to categorize artifacts into periods or ages according to their characteristic components — tools of stone, bronze, or iron. The English contribution was in the field of stratigraphic geology: the principle of *uniformitarianism*, defined and linked with new concepts about the true age of earth strata.

■ The three-age system was the first truly archaeological theory, for it predicted that one could determine the relative age of an artifact merely by knowing the material of which it was made, without any other kind of corroborative information. The foundations of this approach date back to the writings of P. F. Suhm (1776), Skuli Thorlacius (1802), and L. S. V. Simonsen (1813–16).

Daniel (1967: 90–91) has quoted from Simonson:

"At first the tools and weapons of the earliest inhabitants of Scandinavia were made of stone or wood. Then the Scandinavians learnt to work copper and then to smelt it and harden it . . . and then latterly to work iron. From this point of view the development of their culture can be divided into a Stone Age, a Copper Age and an Iron Age. These three ages cannot be separated from each other by exact limits for they encroach on each other. Without any doubt the use of stone implements continued among the more impoverished groups after the introduction of copper, and similarly objects of copper were used after the introduction of iron. . . . Artifacts of wood have naturally decomposed, those of iron are rusted in the ground; it is those of stone and copper which are the best preserved.

The theoretical statements concerning the stone-copper-iron sequence were further implemented by practical application. In 1806 Professor Rasmus Nyerup of the University of Copenhagen proposed the establishment of a Danish national museum for antiquities. The following year the Danish government set up a royal committee to establish such a museum. In 1816 Christian Jurgensen Thomsen was appointed its

- ● Uniformitarianism: The present is the key to the past.
- ▲ An alternative explanation: catastrophism.
- ■ First axes in the Somme terraces.
- ● Swiss lake dwellings

first curator. He set to work arranging the exhibits on the basis of the three-age system and the museum was opened in 1819. The first systematic description of artifacts classified according to this system was published in a guidebook to the National Museum in 1836. Shortly thereafter the museum staff was augmented by the addition of Jens Jacob Asmussen Worsaae (1821–85), who may properly be termed the first professional archaeologist. His monumental *The Primeval Antiquities of Denmark*, first published in 1843 (when Worsaae was only 22 years old), contained several major concepts basic to the development of a true discipline of archaeology. In this work he detailed the need for the three-age scheme of classification. He also outlined the use of the comparative method of analysis and methods of excavation and stressed the need for a public awareness of the values of archaeology.

The importance of Worsaae's work was recognized in Scandinavia, and from that time it is appropriate to speak of a true archaeological discipline. However, the significance of these writings was slow to influence the efforts of researchers elsewhere in Europe. In England and France other developments independently formed the antecedents of a true archaeological tradition. Foremost among these were the concepts of the new geology. ● Based on the concept of *uniformitarianism*, the principle that the present is the key to the past, this view of the antiquity of the earth stressed that all geologic features are the result of geological processes at work in the present. Therefore the variety and great thickness of geologic sediments can only be explained by extremely minute causal factors acting over long periods of time. An integral aspect of these ideas was the concept of *stratigraphy*, which states that the layers of the earth were laid down sequentially and that unless there subsequently has been dramatic tectonic action the oldest layers are those on the bottom of each sequence, each layer therefore being somewhat younger than the one immediately beneath it. ▲ An alternative view was that termed "catastrophism." First proposed by Georges Cuvier (1769–1832) and derived from studies of fossil vertebrates, this theory emphasized the catastrophic destruction of one fauna and the subsequent creation of another. The publication of Charles Lyell's *Principles of Geology* (1830–33) led to public acceptance of uniformitarianism and the rejection both of Ussher's biblical interpretation and of catastrophism. These important events preceded the papers delivered in 1858 and 1859 by Darwin and Wallace at the Royal Society, the Linnean Society, and the Society of Antiquaries of London, which outlined the principles of evolution. One of the ramifications of the concept of evolution, as perceived by Darwin, was that it also could be used to explain human origins.

At approximately the same time, major finds of artifacts led to increased interest in our past as well as speculations concerning the manner in which these implements came to be deposited. In 1849 J. C. Boucher de Perthes first published accounts of his findings at Abbeville, France. ■ Within undisturbed beds of sand and gravel in the Somme river terraces stone implements were found in association with extinct mammals. The major facts revealed were that these items were undoubtedly artifacts of deliberately manufactured form. They were in undisturbed strata and were associated with animals now extinct; therefore they must have great antiquity. In addition to numerous field trips on which Boucher de Perthes convinced colleagues of the importance of these finds, the findings were also interpreted by geologists. In 1863 Sir Charles Lyell published *The Geological Evidences of the Antiquity of Man*, in which the available prehistoric evidence was reviewed. Included were the Somme tools as well as a Neanderthal skeleton which had been found near Düsseldorf, Germany, in 1857.

Another outstanding find was made during the very dry winter of 1853–54 in Switzerland. A. Morlot, professor of geology at the Academy of Lausanne and Dr. Ferdinand Keller of Zurich examined the remains of ancient peoples revealed by the lowering of lake levels. They found that along the shores of these lakes were former villages which had been built on pilings. ● The remains of these villages, which included stone axes, antler artifacts, pottery, and so forth, revealed that the three-age sequence de-

veloped in Scandinavia could be adapted to the Swiss remains.

We may thus conclude that by 1870 there existed in several parts of Europe an intellectual tradition which may be termed "archaeological." Major theoretical and methodological advances were yet to come, but the discipline itself had been established. The final third of the nineteenth century featured widespread efforts by European archaeologists to extend their knowledge through the systematic excavation and documentation of the remains of ancient civilizations. It is in this period that discovery of the unknown past became a common profession with increasingly rigorous methodologies. During this period there were the excavations at Troy by Schliemann (Fig. 1-6), the discovery of

Fig. 1-6 Schliemann recording the walls at Troy after excavation. (Originally published in Schliemann's 1884 report, Fig. 19.)

▲ Petrie begins scientific excavations in Egypt.

■ Thomas Jefferson was the first American archaeologist.

● Humboldt studies the antiquities of Peru.

▲ Squier maps the mounds of the Mississippi Valley.

■ Stephens and Catherwood discover the Mayan ruins.

paleolithic cave art in France and Spain, the beginnings of scientific excavations in Mesopotamia (with Layard's work at Nimrud), Fiorelli's excavations at Pompei, excavations by Flinders Petrie in Egypt in which the famous sequence dating of graves originated, and General Pitt-Rivers's work on Roman and ancient British remains in England. Some of the latter's statements on methods are as pertinent today as when they were written:

> Excavators, as a rule, record only those things which appear to them important at the time, but fresh problems in archaeology and anthropology are constantly arising, and it can hardly fail to have escaped the notice of anthropologists, especially those who, like myself, have been concerned with the morphology of art, that on turning back to old accounts in search of evidence, the points which would have been most valuable have been passed over from being thought uninteresting at the time. Every detail should, therefore, be recorded in the manner most conducive to facility of reference, and it ought at all times to be the chief object of an excavator to reduce his own personal equation to a minimum. . . . I have endeavoured to record the results of these excavations in such a way that the whole of the evidence may be available for those who are concerned to go into it. . . . [Daniel 1967: 238]

Pitt-Rivers also had designed special medals which were dated and inscribed "Opened by A. Pitt-Rivers, F.R.S." These were placed in the bottom of test pits to inform future excavators that a particular site had already been investigated.

Sir Flinders Petrie, whose professional life spanned not only the last third of the nineteenth century but the first 40 years of the twentieth, is credited with a number of "firsts" in archaeological techniques. In 1877 he delineated the practice of precise measurements of ancient earthworks and architecture, in this case remains in southern England. ▲ In 1880 Petrie went to Egypt to measure the pyramids and there found his life's work. In excavations conducted almost annually until 1926, he pioneered the use of potsherds in dating, demonstrated that systematic excavation could lead to a rigorous interpretation of past events, and set up the sequence dating of graves at Naqada. Petrie also trained workmen to dig with professional care, stressed the cultural importance of minor objects ignored by treasure hunters, had the materials of which various objects were made carefully analyzed, and in every way pioneered the development of a rigorous science of archaeology.

We have described in some detail the history of archaeology in Europe. To some degree, there was a separate development of archaeology in the United States. ■ In America an outstanding pioneer was the third president of the United States, Thomas Jefferson. In 1780, overcome with curiosity as to the constitution of some mounds on his plantation, Jefferson caused one of them to be trenched (Jefferson 1944: 222–225). These findings, published in *Notes on the State of Virginia*, noted that the mound was probably of recent Indian manufacture and had been built up as a sequence of four layers deposited at different times. This work was descriptively sound and was equivalent to excavation techniques utilized a century later. Unfortunately, however, Jefferson's findings went largely unnoticed at the time and made little contribution to the development of archaeology as a discipline. A second pioneer, William Henry Harrison, examined the mounds near Cincinnati in 1793 and later (1838) wrote *A Discourse on the Aborigines of the Valley of Ohio* for the Historical Society of Ohio. This approach was less descriptive and more philosophical than Jefferson's, one of the major differences being that Harrison ascribed great antiquity to the mounds.

In 1799 Baron Alexander von Humboldt received from King Charles IV of Spain the right of unlimited access to the Spanish colonies in the New World in order to engage in scientific investigations. Everything was of interest: the geography, climate, flora, fauna, people, and the antiquities. ● Humboldt's five-year trek extended across South America, Cuba, Mexico, and part of the United States. Later, in 1814, a scientific work detailing this expedition was published. It contained numerous illustrations and descriptions of pyramids, codices, and stone sculpture. Much more influential than either Jefferson's or Harrison's work, Humboldt's book stimulated later scholars of American antiquities, including John Lloyd Stephens, William H. Prescott, the abbé Brasseur de Bourbourg, and Edward Seler. Humboldt investigated pictographs in the Amazon, the Archaic-period occupation sites (now termed "Formative") in the Valley of Mexico, the pyramids at Teotihuacan, Inca masonry and roads, and calendrical inscriptions in Colombia. Although his interests were only partially devoted to antiquities, Humboldt's efforts were nevertheless the earliest to awaken other students to America's past.

Perhaps the first American professional archaeologist was E. George Squier (1821–88). ▲ Squier's efforts, in collaboration with E. H. Davis, consisted of a monumental survey of ancient mounds in the eastern United States. *Ancient Monuments of the Mississippi Valley*, published by the Smithsonian Institution in 1848, described the hundreds of mounds Squier and Davis had personally investigated, mapped, and measured, with illustrations of the artifacts they had recovered. The approach of these investigators was descriptive and pragmatic, ruling out any reliance on conjecture as to origins. Soon after its publication, their book came to the attention of William H. Prescott, the famous his-

torian of the conquests of Mexico and Peru. With Prescott's help, Squier was appointed U.S. chargé d'affaires for Central America in 1849. This position permitted the study of the antiquities of Central America and later those of Peru. Once his assigned duties were taken care of, Squier set off on an eighteen-month journey covering most of Peru, with the mission of describing, photographing, excavating, and surveying sites. This included the mapping of the massive ancient city of Chan Chan, a project which only today is being completed. Squier's book *Peru Illustrated. Incidents of Travel and Exploration in the Land of the Incas*, published in 1877, was the capstone of a distinguished career.

John Lloyd Stephens was a traveler and explorer whose book on Arabia and the Holy Land was a best-seller in 1837. Among potential new fields to explore, it was only natural that Central America, with its reputed lost stone cities, attracted Stephen's attention. With Frederick Catherwood, an English architect and draftsman, Stephens landed in British Honduras in 1839. ■ The goal of their quest was the ruins of the ancient Mayan city of Copan. Their first glimpse of Copan is described in *Incidents of Travel in Central America, Chiapas, and Yucatan* (1843):

> The massive stone structures before us had little the air of belonging to a city, the intrenchment of which could be broken down by the charge of a single horseman.... The wall was of cut stone, well laid, and in a good state of preservation. We ascended by large stone steps, in some places perfect, and in others thrown down by trees which had grown up between the crevices, and reached a terrace, the form of which it was impossible to make out, from the density of the forest in which it was enveloped. Our guide cleared a way with his machete, and we passed, as it lay half buried in the earth, a large fragment of stone elaborately sculptured, and came to the angle of a structure with steps on the sides, in form and appearance, so far as the trees would enable us to make it out, like the sides of a pyramid. Diverging from the base, and working our way through the thick woods, we

came upon a square stone column, about fourteen feet high and three feet on each side, sculptured in very bold relief, and on all four of the sides, from the base to the top. The front was the figure of a man curiously and richly dressed, and the face, evidently a portrait, solemn, stern, and well fitted to excite terror. The back was of a different design, unlike anything we had ever seen before, and the sides were covered with hieroglyphics (Fig. 1-7). This our guide called an Idol; and before it, at a distance of three feet, was a large block of stone, also sculptured with figures and emblematical devices, which he called an altar. The sight of this unexpected monument put at rest at once and forever, in our minds, all uncertainty in regard to the character of American antiquities, and gave us the assurance that the objects we were in search of were interesting, not only as the remains of an unknown people, but as works of art, proving, like newly-discovered historical records, that the people who once occupied the continent of America were not savages.

Equal to and even surpassing the quality of Stephens's prose were Catherwood's illustrations. In beauty and clarity these are outstanding. Photographic in detail, they combine artistic beauty with precise objectivity in such a way that the inscriptions, unintelligible to Catherwood, can nonetheless be deciphered today. This attention to detail is remarkable, as numbers of other European-trained artists presented with the opportunity to paint American aborigines portrayed them with European physical traits and, in some cases, even in allegorical scenes drawn from Greek mythology.

The Central American journeys of Stephens and Catherwood, as described in Stephens's books, were popular fare and were reprinted in many different editions. America was becoming aware of its archaeological past; and with the pattern of exploration of Central America and the Yucatan established by Stephens and Squier, the latter half of the nineteenth century witnessed numerous expeditions of discovery. The general pattern was the penetration of the jungle by explorers in search of a reported ruin, which, upon occasion, was found. This process is still being continued, the most outstanding recent find being the painted temple at Bonampak, located in 1947.

A contrasting approach to Mayan archaeology was that of Edward H. Thompson, who purchased a plantation which included the ruined

Fig. 1-7 Stelae in the central plaza at Copan. Stephens and Catherwood were the first Europeans to view these magnificent ancient American sculptures, which at the time were totally overgrown with jungle vegetation. (Hester photograph.)

city of Chichen Itza and began its systematic exploration. Thompson's most outstanding feat was the dredging of the sacred cenote a limestone sinkhole used as a well into which offerings were thrown. He recovered quantities of gold ornaments, jade, human skeletal remains, and copal incense. These finds were spectacular in themselves, but more important was the fact that Thompson undertook the dredging to determine if the ancient legends of human sacrifice were true—a demonstration of motives that were scientific as well as object-oriented.

During the last half of the nineteenth century other areas elicited increasing archaeological interest. The moundbuilder sites in the eastern United States received attention with the beginning of full-scale excavations of some mound groups. Frederick W. Putnam (1839–1915), curator of the Peabody Museum of American Archaeology and Anthropology at Harvard, excavated the Turner Mound group at Moundsville, Ohio, as well as numerous other Ohio mounds. Putnam was also personally responsible for the preservation of Serpent Mound, Ohio, as a state park. The wealth of artifacts in these mounds stimulated extensive excavation by Fowke, Moorehead, and others for the recovery of effigy stone pipes, cutout decorations of mica and copper, engraved shell, and thousands of freshwater pearls.

Geographical exploration of the American Southwest by the Hayden Survey also led to archaeological discoveries. These exploration trips, first organized and directed by Ferdinand V. Hayden, later became the U.S. Geological Survey. Beginning in 1870, Hayden's survey crew of the Yellowstone country included William Henry Jackson, a pioneer photographer of the American West. Four years later, guided by a local prospector, Jackson and others visited Mancos Canyon in southwestern Colorado and became the first persons in recent history to explore the ancient Puebloan cliff dwellings. ● Back in Washington, after Jackson's return Hayden viewed the photographs and descriptions of the ruins with interest and dispatched Jackson

back to the Southwest in 1875 and again in 1876 and 1877. The result was the constant acquisition of information about these cliff houses in a scientific manner, with this knowledge in turn going to the Smithsonian Institution and the Bureau of American Ethnology, two pioneer scientific institutions concerned with American antiquities.

Ernest Ingersoll, a correspondent for the *New York Tribune*, was with Jackson in 1874 at the first discovery of a cliff dwelling. His description bears repeating:

There seven hundred measured feet above the valley, perched on a little ledge only just large enough to hold it, was a two-story house made of finely cut sandstone, each block about 14 by 6 inches, accurately fitted and set in mortar now harder than the stone itself. The floor was the ledge upon which it rested, and the roof of the overhanging rock. There were three rooms upon the ground floor, each one 6 by 9 feet, with partition walls of faced stone. Between the stories was originally a wood floor, traces of which still remained, as did also the cedar sticks set in the wall over the windows and door.... Each of the stories was six feet in height, and all the rooms, upstairs and down, were nicely plastered and painted what now looks a dull brick-red color, with a white band along the floor like a baseboard. There was a low doorway from the ledge into the lower story, and another above, showing that the upper chamber was entered from without. The windows were large, square apertures, with no indication of any glazing or shutters. They commanded a view of the whole valley for many miles. Near the house several convenient little niches in the rock were built into better shape, as though they had been used as cupboards or caches; and behind it a semicircular wall inclosing the angle of the house and cliff formed a water-reservoir holding two and a half hogsheads.... Searching further in this vicinity we found remains of many houses on the same ledge, and some perfect ones above it quite inaccessible. The rocks also bore some inscriptions—unintelligible hieroglyphics for the most part.... All these facts were carefully photographed and recorded. [Quoted in Deuel 1967]

▲ Anthropology provides the scientific framework for archaeology.

It was not until 1888 that the nearby, more spectacular ruins in the Mesa Verde were discovered. Richard Wetherill, a local rancher, and a cousin were pursuing stray cattle when they came upon the remains of an ancient village, now part of Mesa Verde National Park. Their name, Cliff Palace, was appropriate because the site contained two hundred rooms and twenty-three kivas, circular ceremonial rooms. The Wetherills found Spruce Tree House the following day, and public recognition of their finds revived interest in southwestern ruins.

During the 1890s numerous eastern museums sent expeditions to the Southwest to locate and excavate ruins and bring their finds back to the East for exhibit. Men such as A. F. Bandelier, J. W. Fewkes, W. H. Holmes, Walter Hough, Victor Mindeleff, George H. Pepper, Byron Cummings, and Baron Gustav Nordenskiold began the systematic recovery of information which provided the background of our present knowledge of southwestern archaeology.

Archaeology in the Americas does not seem to have undergone the long period of intellectual development which it experienced in Europe. This was due in part to transatlantic intellectual contacts; for example, John Lloyd Stephens had traveled in the Holy Land and Egypt prior to the American explorations, and undoubtedly he had discussed these interests with Europeans intrigued with remains of the past. On the other hand, the American remains were also of different character from European ones; those of most interest at an early date were spectacular architectural monuments which were impossible to ignore and, as with the mounds of Ohio, sufficient in themselves to stimulate excavation simply to satisfy one's curiosity. Less spectacular remains, such as Stone Age, Iron Age, or Bronze Age implements and Paleolithic hand axes found in European river gravels, required greater intellectual skills in order to interpret their relevance to human prehistory. Also of importance to the development of American archaeology was the influence of the historian William H. Prescott. With Prescott as a guide, later investigators had little difficulty in relating their archaeological findings in Mexico and Peru to the ancient civilizations of the Aztecs and Incas. Although some of these associations were in error, there was now at least an intellectual framework into which archaeological findings could fit.

Another major intellectual development occurred nearly simultaneously in both England and the United States. The writings of E. B. Tylor and Lewis H. Morgan laid the groundwork for the science of anthropology, a discipline concerned with the development of cultural patterns in all human societies, past and present. In Tylor's *Anthropology* (1881), the first text by that name, the author states:

> The student who seeks to understand how mankind came to be as they are, and to live as they do, ought first to know clearly whether men are newcomers on the earth, or old inhabitants. Did they appear with their various races and ways of life ready-made or were these shaped by the long, slow growth of ages? . . .

On the American side of the Atlantic, Morgan published in 1877 *Ancient Society or Researches in the Lines of Human Progress from Savagery through Barbarism to Civilization.* In this work he presented a series of definitions which he viewed as necessary steps in human evolution (and not patterns of behavior, as these terms often signify today):

I. Lower Status of Savagery
II. Middle Status of Savagery
III. Upper Status of Savagery
IV. Lower Status of Barbarism
V. Middle Status of Barbarism
VI. Upper Status of Barbarism
VII. Status of Civilization

pieces of pottery (after its invention). Probably next in frequency are bone tools, whereas wooden implements, cordage, basketry, gourds, and other perishable items are less common. ■ In most sites, even more common than tools are discarded bones, shells, plant parts, and other food remains. Perhaps next in importance are structural remains; these vary from the least permanent — slight indentations in the ground with, sometimes, an associated firepit or post holes — to multistory buildings of cut stone. The grouping of individual structures or the clustering of contiguous rooms can be segregated into types, and these types then form the basis of inferences as to the size and social organization of the family, band, or tribe.

● In addition to the objects themselves, another order of data may be obtained by precisely recording the association of the objects to one another. Associational data provide a means whereby we may infer that several separate objects which do not fit together, at least in form, were utilized together in a particular cultural practice. (A modern example would be finding together a tin can and a can opener.)

There are other situations in which archaeological inferences may be made. For example, large stones occurring in fine-grained lacustrine sediments (which obviously could not have been placed there by water action or other geological processes) may well be the result of human activity, even though the stones themselves show no modification, pattern, or even any evidence of use. Obviously, human footprints or handprints constitute another category of data (Leakey 1979).

Finally, archaeologists rely in great part on data recorded by scientists in other disciplines. Geologists, paleontologists, botanists, palynologists, geochronologists, and others study the natural as well as cultural materials recovered from archaeological sites (Wilson 1974; Georgi 1978). These results aid in estimating the age of sites as well as understanding the nature of the environment being occupied at the time, providing clues

as to how a particular group of people modified and adapted to their environment.

All archaeological data are dependent upon the degree of preservation in terms of weathering, corrosion, or other modification. In addition, there may have been alterations in the physical association of the objects with one another, brought about through erosion and other geological processes. ▲ Before we can make valid interpretations about the nature of archaeological sites, we must have some knowledge of geological processes in order to properly attribute the association of objects to either cultural or natural causes. Archaeological remains are not randomly distributed over the earth's surface but are concentrated in those areas which formerly provided the optimum conditions for human occupation. In addition, with the refinements in cultural technology that have been effected through time, humans have been able to gradually expand into more hostile or marginal environments.

Finally, we must concede that knowledge is in part limited by the extent of prior archaeological investigations. During the combined Prehistoric Expedition's work in 1963–65 (part of the Aswan Dam Salvage program) hundreds of sites in the Egyptian Sahara were found in an area which today is uninhabited. Until this work was undertaken, the area had not been investigated for archaeological evidence (Wendorf 1968). Another outstanding example is the very ancient Mayan remains recently excavated in Belize by Norman Hammond which we discuss in a later chapter. There is no doubt that many such areas, archaeologically unknown at present, will reveal major evidence of past occupation once they have been studied.

Artifacts

Artifacts are a primary form of cultural evidence. They are the specific implements that were used and often were manufactured according to an intentional and preconceived form

■ Artifacts include tools manufactured for use as well as those shaped by use.

● Human-made tools are distinctive in form.

prior to use. Once identified as an artifact, a specimen provides primary evidence as to manufacturing processes, material, sources, use, function, wear, association, and post-use disposal. Artifacts are of many different types and materials. The most common are of stone, pottery, bone, wood, and shell.

Stone Tools

Tool use is not limited to humans but is also a characteristic of some anthropoids as well as the sea otter and certain other animals. Human-made implements of stone are the most common cultural items found on sites. Their study is of importance to the archaeological record from early to late; and for many sites, they are the only cultural material preserved. ■ Stone tools may be classified as (1) pieces of stone selected for use which, as a result, possess evidence of battering or dulling; (2) pieces of stone that have been modified to a specific form prior to use; and (3) pieces that were imported to sites but show no evidence of use, the latter category being termed "manuports."

Because of their archaeological importance stone tools have been subjected to detailed analysis to determine, if possible, how they were made and the functions they performed. Critical to such studies is the distinction between naturally broken stones, which can resemble authentic implements, and those deliberately broken by humans to be manufactured into tools. This is the most confusing factor in archaeology for the nonarchaeologist to comprehend, and the question most frequently asked is "How can you *tell* that this piece of stone is a tool?" In answer, the following quote from Kenneth Oakley's *Man the Tool-Maker* clarifies this issue most effectively:

Wherever it was available to him, Stone Age man made tools of flint or flint-like rock. Flint and similar hard homogeneous rocks break somewhat after the fashion of glass. A sharp blow directed vertically at a point on the surface of a slab of glass or flint knocks out a solid cone (resembling a limpet-shell in shape), with the apex or origin at a point of impact. . . . Fracture of this type is called conchoidal (from Greek for shell). When a blow is directed obliquely near the edge of a slab of material which breaks conchoidally, a chip or *flake* is detached. . . . The fractured face of the flake looks like a mussel-shell; it has a half-formed *cone of percussion* at the point of impact, passing into a salient, or swelling, called the *positive bulb of percussion*, followed by low concentric ripples. There is a corresponding rippled hollow, or *flake-scar*, with *negative bulb of percussion*, on the parent lump, or *core*. . . . The bulb of percussion on a large flake struck by a sharp blow commonly shows a miniature scar or *eraillure*, near the centre. . . .

● We can therefore identify the distinctions between human-made stone artifacts and naturally broken flints (Fig. 2-1):

Human-made stone tools possess

1. A positive bulb of percussion on the flake.
2. A negative bulb of percussion on the core.
3. Evidence, on the flake, of a striking platform.
4. Radiating lines of force in a concentric pattern from the point of impact.
5. Flake scars on the dorsal surface of a flake, which show evidence of prior removal of flakes from the core.

Naturally broken flints possess

1. No prepared striking platform.
2. Random flake scars.
3. Lines of force ripples, which are concentric around a central point.
4. Flakes which are often round in outline.
5. Scratched flake surfaces and battered flake edges.

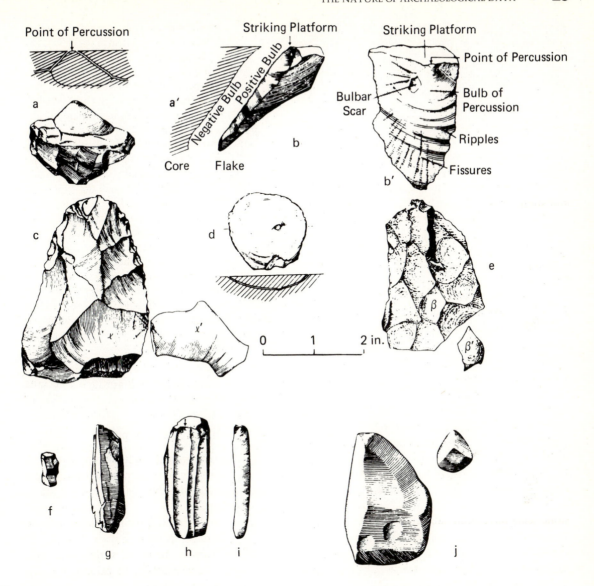

Fig. 2-1 Characteristics of humanly worked flints vs. natural forms sometimes mistaken for artifacts. (*a*) Complete cone of percussion in flint. (*b*, *b'*) Flint flake struck by humans (two views). (*c*) Flint hand axe (Palaeolithic Core Tool Tradition), and one of the waste flakes. (*d*) Flake scar with negative bulb of percussion, a'-waste flake with positive bulb). (*d*) Rounded spall of flint ("pot-lid") split from nodule by frost action. (*e*) Lump of flint pitted by the intersecting scars of frost spalls (e.g. B'). (*f*) Shrinkage prism of starch. (*g*) Flint showing prismatic or starch fracture. (*h*) Prismatic core of volcanic glass from which blades (such as i) have been struck; Chalcolithic, Crete. (*j*) Ventifacts of dreikanter type; pebbles of jasper faceted by wind-blown sand; Carnac, Brittany. (Oakley 1972:Fig. 4.)

▲ Tools may be classified by type.

■ Pottery is our most informative kind of artifact.

● Bone tools were also used by our earliest ancestors.

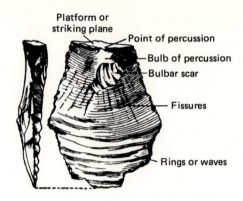

Fig. 2-2 The ideal flake, in which all the conchoidal features are clearly visible. (After Watson 1968: 28.)

Whereas naturally broken flints may possess a bulb of percussion, they do not possess the other landmarks of percussion apparent on human-made implements. Another bit of evidence is that naturally broken flints often exhibit scars of flakes that were removed at different times by various processes such as heat, frost, the battering of stones in stream beds, and wave action on beaches.

Material from Olduvai Gorge in East Africa, dated by the potassium-argon radio-active-decay method to as early as 2 million years ago, has been named "Oldowan" by its finders, the Leakeys. What is demonstrated is that the Oldowan stone industry is not simple; in fact, most of the implements are battered pebbles and utilized flakes which can be divided into 10 or more distinct form categories (Leakey 1967: 417–446). This suggests the possibility that there was an even earlier and simpler use of stones such as that at Lake Turkana described in Chapter 7. Thus the search for the earliest stone tools goes on.

Identification of a stone fragment as being of human manufacture is only the first step in the analysis (Fig. 2-2). Subsequent steps include the classification of objects into the major categories of tools and debitage (waste flakes). The tools are then divided into form classes — core tools versus flake tools — which are in turn subdivided by morphology according to their overall shape, shape of edge, type and amount of retouch, and so forth. In some cases a form is given a specific name which implies a function (e.g., knife, scraper, point, etc.). In other cases the name is descriptive (e.g., truncated flake or denticulate), without function being implied. ▲ The classification of stone tools by type provides one means whereby we may describe specific assemblages (e.g., 14.4 percent of the tools may be side scrapers). Comparison of the tool types present at several sites helps determine the degree of similarity among site collections.

Another procedure is to identify the specific manufacturing techniques and the order in which they were used. Through such studies, archaeologists attempt to reconstruct every manufacturing step, from the quarrying of the original raw material to the completion of the finished artifact. This technological approach provides another method of describing ancient cultural practices.

Pottery

Pottery appears much later in the cultural record than tools of stone, wood, bone, or shell. ■ Where pottery is present, no other source is as informative, with the exception of written records. (Even in the latter instance the first writing was on clay tablets.) Different kinds of information provided by pottery include the details of the manufacturing processes and the sources of the clay utilized. Design styles provide insight into cultural beliefs. These styles also establish a means of chronological ordering because once invented, pottery proved such a flexible medium that its form and decoration were constantly being modified. Since continuous changes through time are characteristic of pottery, we can identify archaeological periods on the basis of these changes. (Such sequence dating is called *seriation* and is described in greater detail in Chapter 3.) Another outstanding characteristic of pottery is its virtual indestructability. Entire vessels are fragile and easily broken, but once broken, the smaller potsherds are likely to be preserved as they can only be destroyed by severe erosion. Fire merely changes their color, and they are almost impervious to chemical decay (Frankel 1979).

The characteristics (or attributes) of pottery are numerous. In some cases as many as 60 or 70 separate attributes can be identified within a specific assemblage of potsherds. The basic features include shape and method of manufacture (either the coiling method, the paddle-and-anvil method, or the wheel method). Base color is determined by the clay and by whether the object was fired in a reducing or an oxidizing atmosphere; the base color may be covered with a thin wash of clay called a "slip," or it may be painted on with a variety of colors. Further decoration may be added by pinching, punching, incising, engraving, or by appliqué (small pieces of clay pressed onto the surface). Pottery also may be cast in molds. In some cases, such as the Mochica culture of Peru, most of what we know about a people's past cultural practices has been learned from portrayals on its pottery.

Bone Artifacts

Artifacts of bone are less informative than those of pottery or stone because they are usually utilitarian objects of simple form. However, bone is durable, and due to our ancestors' early reliance on game animals for food was easily available. The earliest presumed bone tools are those termed the "Osteodontokeratic culture." ● These are objects of bone, teeth, and horn which

according to their describer, Raymond Dart, were used as simple tools by the earliest hominids, the Australopithecines of South Africa. In most cultures items of bone are relatively unimportant; however, in a few, such as that of the Eskimo (where other materials suitable for tool manufacture are rare), bone was widely used, replacing stone or wood. In bone we perceive the earliest human artistic expressions, small carvings of humans and animals made in the Upper Paleolithic period some 20 to 30 thousand years ago. Bone tools can also be studied to determine what functions they performed and the manufacturing methods employed: cutting, grinding, engraving, and so on (Semenov 1957; 1964) (Fig. 2-3). Tools of bone were frequently combined with portions of wood or stone to form composite tools. In normal instances bone tools are small and usually of a size to be conveniently hand held. Rarely, large bones are used; for example, whale bones are used in the construction of Eskimo houses. The most common occurrence of bone is as food debris.

Fig. 2-3 Upper Paleolithic antler and bone projectile heads: (*1-2*) single and double bevelled points: (3) split-base; (4) forked base; (5) lozenge-shaped points; (6-7) barbed harpoonhead (biserial and uniserial). (Clark 1977: Fig. 38.)

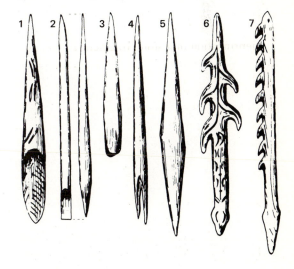

▲ Although perishable, many unique specimens of wood have been preserved.

Wooden Objects

Tools of wood were undoubtedly among the very first implements to be used by humans. We know, for example, that the simplest use of tools by modern apes consists of the picking up or tearing off of tree limbs, then stripping off the leaves and twigs and using the stick as a club, missile, or digging tool. There can be no doubt that such tools have been in use since the dawn of culture. Unfortunately, wood is a perishable material and these early tools have not been preserved except in unusual instances such as Little Salt Spring in Florida, where wooden implements have been found in quantity dating back to 10,000 B.C. (Clausen et al. 1979). To our knowledge, the earliest wooden implements found to date are from from Kalambo Falls in Zambia. These are at least 55,000 years old, and new work indicates appreciably earlier dates. They have been identified as digging sticks, a throwing stick, and the point of a spear (Cole 1965: 158). These particular specimens were recovered from a waterlogged level, where bacterial decay was inhibited. However, another major depositional environment where wood may be preserved is within dry caves. Any environment which is alternately subject to wetting and drying will result in the decay of wood and other perishable materials. Such decay is a major limitation to archaeology, as most environments are of this type rather than being either waterlogged or totally dry. One other technique for recovering the form of wooden objects, where they have rotted away, is by making a plaster cast. In rare circumstances while dig-

Fig. 2-4 Reconstruction of Sumerian harp found at Ur, achieved by pouring plaster of paris down holes left from the rotting away of the wooden harp frame. (Hole and Heizer 1973: 105.)

Fig. 2-5 Excavation of the ancient ship burial at Sutton Hoo, England. The ship was found in 1939 and dates to the seventh century A.D. The wooden ship had rotted away but left in the soil were the impressions of the planks as well as the nails used to secure them. (Trustees of the British Museum [Natural History] 1959.).

ging, one encounters holes in the soil which are the result of wood having rotted away. Usually such holes are post holes, but occasionally they are the result of the decay of wooden artifacts. The most famous such find was the ancient Sumerian harps which Sir Leonard Wooley recovered by pouring plaster into the holes (Fig. 2-4). Imagine his delight, after the excavation of the hardened plaster cast, to find attached to the plaster the metal ornaments that had originally decorated the harps.

Most wooden items were either simple tools or the hafts of tools such as spears, knives, axes, and so forth. It is only within the past few thousand years that major constructions of wood (i.e., ships, forts, houses, pile villages, etc.) have been built. ▲ In rare instances examples of these have been recovered archaeologically. The Sutton Hoo ship (Fig. 2-5) can be reconstructed from its impression in the earth, and the warship *Vasa*, which sunk on its maiden voyage, has been salvaged. The Swiss lake dwellings are another example of preserved structures of wood. The most outstanding recovery of ancient furniture is from the tombs of Egyptian royalty, particularly the tombs of Queen Hetaphares, the mother of Cheops, builder of the great pyramid, and from the tomb of the boy-king Tutankhamun (Edwards 1972).

One of the most important uses of wood in archaeology is in dating. Radiocarbon analysis is possible with both wood and charcoal, and some wood specimens can be dated through study of their tree rings.

■ The site—the place where ancient humans lived and obtained their living.

● There are many different types of sites.

Shell Objects

Items of shell are rare in early sites—from which we infer that they do not seem to have been important to Paleolithic peoples. Later, however, shells were used for ornaments, such as beads, pendants, and bracelets. The utilitarian use of shells seems to have been a late development, with shells being used for cutting implements, horns, fish hooks, and, occasionally, as currency. The great majority of shells occur in sites as food debris, therefore providing information about prehistoric diet.

Other Items

A wide variety of other materials have been utilized by ancient cultures. These include pearls, metal, pitch, amber, glass, precious stones, quartz crystals, mica, and many other exotic and unusual substances. Foremost in importance among these is metal because it is malleable and may be hammered or cast into any form. Metal is also fairly durable. It will rust or corrode, but in many cases such decay has not completely destroyed the item; and through the use of specialized techniques these items may be recovered and restored. The archaeological record includes many other unique forms of evidence; for example, netting (Fig. 2-6) and human footprints (Fig. 2-7) both remained preserved through unusual conditions of burial.

Types of Sites

The recovery of individual specimens is only part of the archaeologist's concern. ■ The larger context in which the items are found is espe-

Fig. 2-6 Prehistoric netting from a cemetary on the western coast of Peru. The excellent preservation is due to the extremely arid climate. (Hester photograph.)

cially important because the sites are the remains of ancient communities and specialized-use areas. The *site* is the basic unit of interest (Willey and Phillips 1958), and the archaeologist attempts to learn everything possible about a particular site—its size, type, plan, the architectural style of the buildings, relationships that existed between units of the site, the position of every artifact recovered, and, lastly, the relationships of that site to the local environment and to similar sites in the region.

● Types of sites are myriad; however, there are only a few major categories. The largest subdivisions are *open sites* and *cave sites*. Open sites occur on the surface of the natural landscape and often have architectural remains ranging from the smallest storage bin to elaborate cities. Cave sites pertain to those caves or rock shelters that were used for human occupancy. Open sites are subdivided into the lesser categories which follow.

A *sherd area* is any area in which potsherds occur on the surface. In some cases buried structures may be present. In other cases, the evidence of prior occupation is entirely on the surface, either because the site was not occupied for long or because subsequent erosion has removed the soil.

A *Lithic scatter* possesses stone artifacts and waste flakes on the surface. Many such sites were occupied for only a brief period of time and often represent the locale of a specialized activity such as seed collecting or processing.

A *killsite* is any location at which an animal was killed and butchered. Killsites are of several varieties. The stampede was a favorite hunting technique in ancient times, and the animals were either forced into some type of natural trap (a swamp, pond, creek, or draw) or were driven over a cliff. The result consists of a welter of bones or dismembered carcasses on the top of the pile with more articulated and occasionally whole carcasses toward the bottom of the bone pile. Ambush was another hunting technique; the ancient hunters hid near waterholes, salt licks, game trails, or other natural points of animal concentration, and as the animals ap-

Fig. 2-7 Human footprints some 5,000 years of age on the shores of Lake Nicaragua. Originally soft volcanic mud, the deposit has since solidified into stone. (Hester photograph.)

▲ Some sites include houses and other structures.

proached they were speared, clubbed, or shot, and then butchered on the spot. The pit trap was another hunting method utilized.

A *campsite* is any place where the inhabitants lived for any length of time; this was a place where humans prepared and ate their food, manufactured tools, and carried out everyday activities. Frequently, killsites occur at some distance from a campsite, the meat having been carried back to the base camp for consumption. Occasionally people camped at the killsite, and thus we have two kinds of evidence at the same place. Both open sites and cave sites were used as campsites or habitation sites. However, it is rare that a kill is found to have taken place within a cave.

A *quarry site* is the place at which suitable stone for the manufacture of tools was acquired. Frequently, preliminary shaping of the selected stone was accomplished at the quarry. A *workshop*, being somewhat different in nature, was

where the tools were manufactured from the selected quarry material. In some cases workshops occur in isolation; in other cases they occur at the quarry or on the campsite. The archaeologist identifies the kinds of activities carried out at each site through detailed analyses of that site's particular components. This involves the study of the percentages of each type of stone tool, the frequency and type of waste flakes, the occurrence of fire hearths, food bones, and other forms of evidence.

Sites with architecture form one of the largest categories. Although an inclusive classification of all possible kinds of structures is beyond the scope of this book, it is possible to describe the more common types of units and the ways in which they are grouped together in communities.

Miscellaneous site types include rock faces decorated by pecking or painting. Termed *petroglyphs* and *pictographs*, according to whether they are pecked or painted, this rock art is commonly found where suitable natural rock exposures occur (Fig. 2-8).

Another category consists of sites that occur underwater. The sites are of many different

Fig. 2-8 Record of an expedition of pharonic ships up the Nile. The exact date is unknown, but it could possibly be that of Harkhuf about 3200 B.C. (Hester photograph.)

types and are underwater for a variety of reasons. Such sites include shipwrecks, ancient harbours, sites on fossil beaches now submerged by a rising sea level, wells or springs into which offerings were tossed, and situations where earthquakes caused a local change in sea level. Underwater sites are classed together not because they are similar in nature, but because similar excavation techniques are used in their study.

Structures

▲ Individual house units are the most common architectural elements. These vary in size from a tiny hut or single room to extended longhouses of up to 100 feet in length by 30 feet in width. The size of the individual house unit is dependent, in part, upon the environment. For example, the availability of certain building materials may limit house size. A second variable is the social organization of the group which builds the houses. Those with a nuclear family pattern (parents with children) most likely would build smaller units than a group with an extended family pattern (which includes grandparents and unmarried relatives).

House types include the following:

1. *Pithouses.* These are excavated subterranean or semisubterranean rooms of either round or square form, with walls of poles or logs and either a flat or beehive-shaped roof made of logs.

2. *Masonry structures.* Units of masonry may be of any shape, although a rectangular form is most common. Walls frequently have window or door openings with stone or wooden lintels. Roofs are commonly of logs or planks, although stone slabs are also used. Most masonry units are above ground, although a few specialized structures, such as kivas, or chambered graves, may be subterranean. Masonry units were easily added onto or subdivided by construction of cross walls; as a result, masonry is one of the major building materials used in larger structures. A major variable in masonry structures is the pattern of the stonework itself (Fig. 2-9). Walls may be with or without mortar; and they may or may not be plastered. In some cases the walls are layered, having cut-stone facing

Fig. 2-9 Massive masonry walls at the Inca fortress of Sacsahuaman near Cuzco, Peru. (Hester photograph.)

■ Burials reveal physical type and evidence of cultural practices.

on the interior and exterior and a core of loose rubble. Although masonry units are usually well preserved, the archaeologist has to reconstruct their original height and configuration, because usually the wooden beams have decayed, walls have collapsed, and the cut-stone facing may have been stolen for use in later buildings.

3. *Adobe*. Walls of adobe may be either of sun-dried-mud brick or of puddled or poured courses of mud, called "tapia." The bricks may be of almost any form, contrary to what one might have thought. They are usually rectangular, but may also be round, conical, or shaped like a loaf of bread. The actual shape of the bricks is made immaterial through the use of ample mortar. Tapia walls are laid up in courses, the mud being patted into shape. The mud is put up in as dry a form as possible and can be piled to a height of from 12 to 15 inches. Above that height the weight of the wet mud causes it to slump. Therefore, each course must be allowed to dry before the next can be added. The use of adobe permits the construction of units of any form, and remodeling is easy. One has only to cut a hole for a new window or door. In dry environments adobe is an excellent building material as it will last for hundreds of years if kept dry. (Fig. 2-10).

4. *Wood* is a common building material. Wherever it is present it is used, even in the Arctic, where the only available variety is driftwood. Houses of wood are most often of logs, although plank structures are also common. An interesting variant is the earth lodge, consisting of a beehive-shaped unit of logs, covered over with grass and earth. Wood is more often used for single-

Fig. 2-10 Sculptured adobe walls at the famous north coast Peruvian site of Chan Chan. (Hester photograph.)

family dwellings than for communal structures, although such were used by the Iroquois and tribes of the Northwest Coast (British Columbia). The Swiss lake dwellings represent one of the most elaborate uses of wood, with the entire village being built on wooden pilings.

5. *Jacal*, also called "wattle and daub," is a building type consisting of walls made of poles interwoven with twigs or grass and plastered with mud. Typical of dry climates, jacal is most common in individual family units because it is not particularly strong and is seldom used for long walls. Another common usage is for dividing walls within structures.

6. *Thatch* houses are common the world over. Made of grass, palm fronds, or other pliable materials woven over a pole framework, they probably represent one of the most frequent prehistoric house types. Unfortunately, such structures are almost never preserved. What may be found archaeologically are the scattered remains of the poles which have usually been preserved by having been burned, as charcoal is resistant to decay and the mud plaster has hardened by being fired.

Normally, house units are grouped near one another or are physically connected. Such a grouping consists of the settlement-type, or prehistoric, community. Modern archaeologists are interested in settlement patterns, since both the nature of the specific communities and their distribution within the natural environment provide information about the social organization and environmental adaptation of the specific culture. The basic types of settlements include (1) individual houses; (2) small house clusters; (3) small agglutinated villages (with the individual rooms or houses tied together into one unit); (4) nucleated villages (groups of houses or housing units united by streets or other connective devices); (5) towns (larger nucleated settle-

ments); and (6) cities (urban centers with a high population and reciprocal relationships with outlying communities).

Special-use areas are set apart on the basis of function. These may occur within the confines of a village, town, or city; or they may be located adjacent to or separate from any of the latter. Such use areas include cemeteries, fields, terraces, roads, wells, irrigation canals, and sacred places. The latter range from places where offerings were deposited (for spirits presumed to reside there) to complex ceremonial centers. In the case of the latter, temples, residences of priests, altars, and other sacred structures may be grouped within a restricted area of the community or may instead be built as separate communities.

Burials

■ Finally, archaeological data include human burials. Physical type is evidenced by the skeletons or mummies found; and cultural practices are revealed by the mutilation or alteration of the bodies (either before or after death). The method of burial (inhumation, cremation, bundle burial, group burial, etc.) and the cultural objects placed with the bodies provide evidence of beliefs connected with the afterlife. Objects are also frequently informative in determining the individual's role in life (whether farmer, warrior, priest, weaver, potter, or whatever). Group burials may also be indicative of family structure or of other details of nonmaterial culture (e.g., warfare).

Ecofacts

Ecofacts are those items of archaeological data that include all the environmental items that are either preserved within a site or that form part of the specific environment in which the site occurs. Specifically, ecofacts are not artifacts,

● Ecofacts provide evidence of diet and the nature of the environment.

▲ Features are nonportable artifacts.

■ Provenience: the location of each specimen in the site.

● Transforms: the changes that have occurred since the site was occupied.

but they possess cultural information. The most typical examples include food debris: bones, shells, fiber, seeds, bark, skins, and other remnants of plants or animals utilized for food. ● Other site components, including soil, charcoal, rock fragments, chemical fractions, and so forth, also contribute to our understanding of past cultural practices and climatic events that occurred during human occupation of the site. In order to be meaningful these ecofacts must be collected in a scientific manner and tied into the stratigraphy established for the site. Then in the laboratory the ecofact samples must be identified as to species, measured, and studied to ascertain their environmental information. In the case of food debris, the nature of the utilization by the ancient society must also be established (Brothwell and Higgs 1970). (To demonstrate the importance of ecofacts, it is sufficient to note that in prehistoric shell middens the ecofacts often make up 99 percent of the midden and artifacts only 1 percent. The term shell midden refers to the mound of discarded shells left over from the consumption of shellfish which includes all the other evidences of occupation—charcoal, bones, fish scales, artifacts and so forth.)

Features

Features include any and all cultural manifestations which are neither artifacts nor structures. Actually, during the excavation process anything can be labeled a feature, since one is often unaware what a particular manifestation may be. For example, a charcoal-stained area may turn out to be a hearth, a burial, a storage pit, or some other unit. Most features, in contrast to artifacts, constitute the kind of evidence of past cultural activity which cannot be easily removed but which can be excavated, photographed, drawn, and described in detail. Features are additional guides to the everyday life of ancient peoples, and they are just as important in their own way as structures. ▲ Another way of describing features is to term them "nonportable artifacts," since they cannot be removed intact from their original position. The shared characteristic of features and artifacts is that they often have a specific function. Features and structures have in common the fact that often the soil within them contains a record of utilization over a period of time.

Associational Data

The site context—its soil, layering, and other constituents—forms the matrix within which artifacts occur. Such contextual information is additional to that gained from studying the artifacts in isolation. For example, loose beads found within a midden could denote the ancient breaking of a string of beads, some of which were lost through mixing with occupation debris. On the other hand, the finding of beads with a burial often indicates not only that they were intentionally buried but also provides information as to the manner in which they were worn in life. ■ Such associational information has led to the development of the cornerstone concept of archaeological excavation methodology: *provenience.* This term refers to the exact location of every single artifact and ecofact found. Records of these locations permit the archaeologist, once back in the laboratory, to evaluate how and why the individual specimens came to be associated with one another. Such an understanding in turn leads to more accurate reconstructions of past cultural practices. If we may contrast the difference between the looter and the archaeologist, the looter digs simply to find objects for sale, whereas the archaeologist digs not only to recover objects but also to collect and record all possible information associated with them.

Transforms

● The term *transformational data* refers to the evidences of the processes that have affected the sites since their time of occupation (Schiffer 1976). We have in the transforms the history of what has happened to the site over the years since it was abandoned by its prehistoric inhabitants. There is a long list of causes that can effect such postdepositional changes. The most universal are the geologic processes of erosion and deposition. Other factors are chemical and bacterial decay and the actions of burrowing animals, scavengers, and so forth. Furthermore, we certainly cannot ignore the actions of later peoples (and there were looters in antiquity just as there are today). Then there are natural catastrophic events, such as earthquakes and volca-

noes, and the equally catastrophic effects of warfare. There is reoccupation of sites, rebuilding of structures, reburial or the disruption of previously existing burials, trash removal, reuse of building stone, and so on. All these events, both natural and cultural, lead to transformations in the nature of the archaeological data. It is part of the task of the archaeologist to decipher this site history in order to accurately infer the nature of past behavioral practices. Not to do so will lead to errors and ridiculous interpretations (e.g., the assumption that ancient people lived in peat bogs because we find their remains within bogs today).

It is not our purpose here to present a catalog of archaeological data, the variety and variability of which are almost infinite. We have summarized the most common kinds of data, but other kinds which we have not mentioned are also important (e.g., samples for dating or pollen analysis, or information about resources locally available to the prehistoric inhabitants). What is important to bear in mind is that the archaeologist is not particularly interested in the *specific* items found except as a means of reconstructing the cultural patterns of prehistoric peoples and of relating these to their ancient environments.

3

Stratigraphy, Chronology, and Dating Techniques

■ Stratigraphy: the sequence of layers in a site.

● The archaeologist must be aware of ancient site disturbances.

▲ Stratigraphy: the result of geologic processes and cultural activity.

Stratigraphy

When a find has been made, the question most often asked the archaeologist is, "How old is it?" This is the same question the archaeologist asks as well. Unfortunately, it is seldom easy, and sometimes impossible, to date prehistoric finds. In response to this need, over the years archaeologists have developed a wide range of dating techniques. The most basic of all of these has been the study of site stratigraphy. In one way or another, all other dating techniques must be tied to the stratigraphy of the site in order to be meaningful.

Stratigraphy is one of the cornerstones of archaeological methodology (Smiley 1955). Without an understanding of the natural sequence of strata in a site there would be no framework to which we could relate the objects found there. ■ In its simplest definition, *stratigraphy* is the sequence of layers in a site, each of which is older than the layer above it. Once this principle is understood, it is possible to describe the sequence of accretion at individual places of former occupation. The sequence of strata provides a historical record which permits the archaeologist to describe the order of events, both cultural and environmental, which occurred at that particular site. Without any other means of dating, the archaeologist can determine from the strata a *relative* sequence. We know which items occur in which levels, and thus we can estimate the age of each specimen relative to that of other specimens from the same site. At this point we have no knowledge of their exact age in terms of years, but it is possible to order their occurrence from early to late. We also assume that all items found within a given layer were deposited there during the formation of that unit; therefore, those items within that layer are of approximately the same age. However, at the same time, we must always be alert to the possibility of earlier or later specimens being introduced into a layer. Several factors can contribute to the overturning of entire layers, which results in *inverted* stratigraphy in which the oldest levels are those on the top. One of the most common causes of this situation is prior excavation of a site by an archaeologist or artifact hunter—unknown, of course, to the current investigator. As the earlier excavator piled the earth by the side of the excavation pit, each older layer was placed on top of "younger" material previously removed from the pit. After a short time the rearranged layers thus came to resemble an undisturbed stratigraphic sequence, the only difference being that the sequence of layers is now reversed. A similar situation could also have occurred in antiquity with the excavation of a burial pit, especially if the pit was dug into midden debris or other cultural strata. Erosion is another means whereby strata may be rearranged and redeposited. In this case, however, the true age of the strata can usually be recognized through study of the included fossils or artifacts, which can be dated by some chronological method. However, it is common for the artifacts in such a deposit to be derived from several sources of different ages; therefore, the resultant grouping of artifacts is chronologically mixed. If we do not already have some knowledge of the age of the artifact types present, we may incorrectly assume that because they were found together in the same layer they are of the same age.

It is also common for objects to be accidentally introduced into strata of an older age. One of the most common culprits in this action is the lowly gopher; however, artifact introduction can also occur through the movement of specimens into and down cracks in the soil or into cavities formed by the decay of tree roots. ● The archaeologist is always alert to the possibility of such postdepositional alteration of a site, because finding a single artifact in a layer where it should not occur can literally cause mental anguish in the attempt to reconstruct the sequence of events that occurred at the site.

▲ The development of layers in a site is the result of two factors: geologic processes and cultural activity. The layers themselves vary from natural, noncultural deposits to cultural ones. However, most layers in a site are the result of both factors in operation at the same time. The deposition of layers may have been either continuous, as in lakes or bogs, or interrupted by periods of nondeposition or erosion. Erosion frequently causes the development of an *erosion surface*. Such a surface could have lying upon it all those objects which were too large to have been swept away by water or wind. If some later deposition were to cover this erosion surface, the objects found on that surface might all be estimated to be of the same age, which might be an erroneous assumption. It is therefore important for the archaeologist to record every detail of the strata in order to interpret correctly how they and the associated artifacts come to be deposited. Interruptions in cultural deposition may occur simply because at some point the inhabitants moved elsewhere.

One contrast between natural and cultural stratigraphy is that the latter is normally restricted to a small area. One technique is to put down test pits beyond the site to reveal the sequence of layers due to natural causes. Such tests can then aid in the interpretation of the cultural sequence. In situations where natural stratigraphic layers are not easily followed, the archaeologist may excavate the site by arbitrary levels (for example, each level may be 10 cm in thickness). Such levels provide a means whereby the individual objects can be assigned provenience to a specific level. This methodology achieves a *relative* sequence for purposes of dating the objects found. (Figures 3-1 and 3-2 provide an example of the development of stratigraphic layers in a site.)

▲ Chronology provides a temporal framework for the individual finds.

■ The index fossil: a chronological tool.

● Artifacts are classified into types.

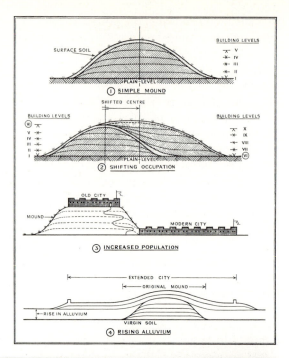

Fig 3-1 Sequences of accumulation of layers to form mounds of similar outward shapes but differing stratigraphic histories. (Lloyd 1963: Fig. 10.)

Fig. 3-2 The tell of Erbil, Mesopotamia, showing the continuing use of an ancient site location. Compare this illustration with the third stage in Lloyd's sequence of mound accumulation diagrams (Fig. 3-1.). Courtesy of Aerofilms Ltd.

Chronology

The study of chronology is essential to understanding how old cultures are and what has been their sequence of development. The establishment of a sequence of cultures for a region is therefore one of the major tasks of archaeology. Once established, these regional sequences may then be correlated to provide area-wide (areal) or even continent-wide (continental) chronologies. ▲ Critical to archaeological chronology is the ability to date individual objects and the levels within which they occur. However, prior to the discovery of various dating techniques, which provide dates in terms of years, archaeologists had to devise methods which permitted the establishment of chronologies or cultural sequences in the absence of exact dates. The techniques so developed are basic to all archaeology and are still in use.

We have previously discussed the role of stratigraphy in the formulation of *relative sequences*. ■ Another basic archaeological tool is the concept of the *index fossil*. Derived from paleontology, this usage relies on three related principles: 1) certain fossils or artifacts are distinctive in form; 2) they are widespread in their distribution; and 3) they were in existence for a short period of time. One of the first things early archaeologists noticed was that certain prehistoric implements were of distinctive form. During the earliest excavations it was apparent that objects of certain forms were common in some levels and did not occur in others. This is the underlying principle which led to the development of the three-age scheme of classification of ancient cultures into the Stone, Bronze, and Iron ages. With such a concept available, it was only a small step further to utilize index fossils in crossdating. If an object was utilized during a brief span of time, it can be used for dating, wherever it is found, even if it is rare in its occurrence. However, it must occur in primary association with other objects and not have been secondarily deposited at a later date through geologic or other causes.

We have briefly reviewed the use of the archaeological index fossil. ● The definition of an index fossil is based upon the *type* concept. Prehistoric objects are considered as having been made according to a preconceived idea on the part of the maker. This is what Deetz (1967) terms the "mental template," which is defined as the form the maker had in mind during the manufacturing process. As a result, items of the same artifactual class, such as projectile points, scrapers, and so forth, will have a similar form. Although these items will not be identical, they will feature a central core of shared attributes. This modal tendency is typical for a particular group of related artifacts, even though no single specimen may possess exactly the same attributes as the idealized type description. The concept is useful in providing a means of assigning individual objects to form classes. This assignment provides one method of categorizing items from a particular level (e.g., 45 percent of the projectile points may be type A and 25 percent may be type B). In addition, if the types are distinctive, the presence of a single example may indicate the relative age of a level. However, form is not the only relative criterion: for example, angle of cutting edges and flaking style are other characteristics which could provide the core attributes of a type.

Stratigraphy is the primary tool for the construction of regional sequences. Once established, the individual regional sequences are then crossdated through the use of index fossils. Chronology is frequently confused by the nonprofessional with techniques of dating. Although the two are related they are not synonymous. *Chronology* consists of the construction of a conceptual framework with space-time dimensions into which the specific content of cultural levels can be fitted. Chronologies in archaeology have traditionally been based on the correlation of cultural levels through the comparison of included artifacts. Increasingly chron-

▲ Not all archaeological dates are equally precise.

■ Relative dates indicate that a specimen is older or younger than another specimen.

● Seriation—a method for dating continually changing specimens.

ologies are based on geologic sequences, pollen diagrams, or deep sea cores all of which contain evidence of climatic changes which have been correlated in age by means of C-14 (radiocarbon) dates. An example: the correlation of glacial sequences and the pollen record, both on shore and from cores taken from the ocean floor which extends 75,000 years back for the U.S. Pacific Northwest (Stuiver et al. 1978).

On the other hand, dating techniques provide chronological *data* in the sense that dates can be assigned to individual specimens or levels. We will now discuss how each of the major dating techniques works.

Dating Techniques

Techniques utilized in dating may be classified by the types of dates obtained. A simple classification includes periodization, relative dates, and absolute dates (Michels 1973: 10). ▲ By no means are all dates the same: Some are given in terms of years, others in years with a probable error stated, others as "older than" or "younger than" a particular level or item, and, finally, some as age estimates which are not true dates at all.

Periodization is the simplest dating technique. It refers to the classification of cultural levels on the basis of content alone. When two cultural levels are quite different in content, the archaeologist feels secure in the belief that these units date to different eras. The three-age system developed by Thomsen and Worsaae owes its initial delineation to the fact that tools found were of three differing materials—stone, bronze, and iron. Archaeologists believed these tools dated to different time periods, respectively, and later excavations proved them to be right. The inherent limitation of periodization is that, used alone, it provides no clues to the true age relationships between differing cultures. However, an initial step in the latter direction is gained through the use of relative dating.

Relative Dating

■ All those techniques which provide information about the age of an object or a level as compared with the age of some other object or level provide *relative dates*. Thus, according to this system, dates are older, younger, or contemporaneous. Chronological sequence building is one of the major applications of relative dating. If, for example, we have excavated three sites and have identified levels in these sites according to their diagnostic artifacts, then we may compare and arrange their respective levels into a relative sequence (Fig. 3-3).

The chronology to be established would include levels 0, 1, 1A, 2, 3, 4, 5 in the order given, from late to early. Note, for example, that level 1A occurs between levels 1 and 2 and is therefore bracketed in time; its relative age has been established. Level 0 is later than 1, as it is statigraphically superimposed above 1. However, from the stratigraphic evidence we have no knowledge of how *much* of a time gap existed between levels 0 and 1, or, for that matter, how much elapsed time is represented by any two of the other levels, considered consecutively.

Seriation

Cultures are continually changing, and as they change their artifact assemblages alter in form and in frequency of occurrence. Archaeologists have utilized this general cultural tendency in the attempt to establish relative dates for occupation levels at sites. The basic assumption is

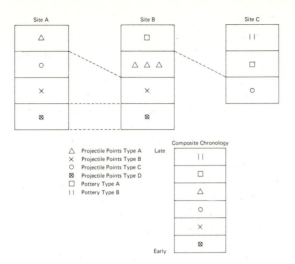

Fig. 3-3 Model illustrating the method of archaeological-sequence building, where site levels are correlated on the basis of included artifacts of distinctive form. The total sequence established is thus an abstraction, not precisely represented at any single site, but assumed to be representative of the culture sequence of the region.

that the more alike two cultural units are in their content, the closer they are to each other in time. This assumption is supported by the fact that after artifact types appear in a culture they follow a normal pattern of occurrence: They initially increase in frequency, reach a peak of popularity, then decline in frequency and eventually disappear. Analysis of these changes through time is a type of study termed seriation. The method requires first the identification of the frequency of occurrence of each artifact type in each component. The next step requires the comparison of the composition of each component with all other components. This pattern easily lends itself to measurement and plotting in graphic form. Chronological utilization of seriation depends upon the staggered (sequential) appearance of different artifact types. ● Even though similar traits may occur in different components (a component is a distinctive cultural level within a site), their seria-

tion normally will indicate which is the later or earlier, since the artifact types in common will either be increasing in one and decreasing in another or vice versa. A further step requires stratigraphic analysis to determine which types occur earlier or later in the entire sequence. Another assumption employed in seriation is that artifact types are earliest at their point of origin and then spread to other sites over time. Expressed in spatial terms, the farther from its point of origin, normally the later in time is the appearance of a specific trait.

Seriation has been most commonly applied to analyses of collections of potsherds. Sherds are easily identifiable or assignable to types. Further, change in pottery types is frequent, making fine chronological distinctions between components possible. For example, potsherds have a large number of constituent attributes such as paint color, line width, design style, slip, paste, temper, and so forth. As these change through time, lines become wider or narrower, paint changes from one, to two, to several colors, design styles change from naturalistic to geometric, and so on. Specific features change, of course, at different rates. However, by examining the totality of attributes present in a particular potsherd we can usually assign it to a position on the total cultural continuum of which it forms a part. Once so ranked, it may then be used as an index fossil. A further refinement in seriation consists of quantifying in percentile terms the occurrence of items in a given level. Once this has been done, it is possible to *arbitrarily* subdivide cultural sequences on the basis of changes in these frequencies. For example, at a point where the pottery type Mancos Black on White becomes less common than Mesa Verde Black on White, we can state that there has been a transition to the Mesa Verde period. Such a demarcation of the archaeological record should be recognized as arbitrary, but it is nonetheless useful for subdividing a regional chronology into easy space-time units.

Figure 3-4 illustrates a typical use of seriation in a chronological study based on pottery.

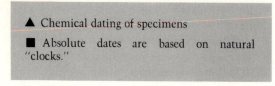

▲ Chemical dating of specimens

■ Absolute dates are based on natural "clocks."

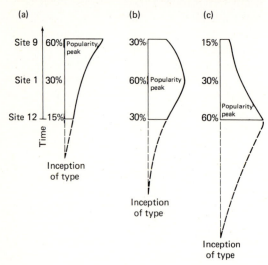

Fig. 3-4 Example of the seriation of ceramics of three different types, illustrating the change in their frequency of occurrence through time. (Michels 1973:Fig. 3.)

Intracomponent Associations

Properly speaking, with the exception of index fossils, the association of specimens together in the same layer does not provide a means of dating. However, a number of methods have been developed which can demonstrate whether or not different specimens from the same level are contemporary with one another. ▲ Such tests include the chemical dating of bone (the nitrogen test, the fluorine test, and the uranium test), radiological and optical dating of bone, and patination of stone (Michels 1973). What all these techniques have in common is that they permit the discrimination between two specimens as to whether they are of similar ages or different ages. If the two differ in age, then we may suspect that their occurrence together is due to some action which occurred after the site was occupied. (Such actions include secondary geological deposition, intrusion due to burrowing animals or human burials, differential alterations in chemistry as a result of groundwater action, and other such events.) We now turn to a description of how association techniques are utilized.

Buried bones gradually absorb fluorine from the local groundwater (depending, of course, on the composition of the latter). Inasmuch as the quantity of absorption depends on the length of time the bone has been buried, it is possible to measure the fluorine in two bones from the same deposit and determine if there is any significant difference in their relative ages. (The amount of fluorine can be determined either through chemical analysis or by the x-ray crystallographic method.)

The nitrogen test, used on skeletal remains, provides another measurement of relative age. Unlike fluorine, nitrogen in bone decreases with the length of time bone has been buried. The principle involved is that the rate of protein loss in bone is affected by the chemistry of the soil in which it has been buried. Thus the quantity of nitrogen present (along with carbon and chemically bound water) permits bones to be compared with one another. Differences in the amounts of these components suggest that the bones have been buried for different lengths of time. The nitrogen and fluorine techniques utilized together can provide critical information as to the relative age of bone specimens. Such techniques are especially important when we wish to establish whether all the bone specimens in a level are of the same age or whether they may be of different ages (and therefore, whether their association in the level is due to secondary deposition). The most illustrious example of the use of these chemical dating techniques was in the exposé of the famous Piltdown hoax. In this case the nitrogen test demonstrated that a lower jaw, previously thought to have been very ancient, and a modern-looking human skull found supposedly in association, were the modern mandible of a female orangutan (which had been deliberately altered) and a comparatively recent human skull, probably from the Bronze Age.

The uranium test works similarly to the fluorine and nitrogen tests. As a result of contact with groundwater, uranium is deposited in bones in exchange for calcium. The longer the bone has been buried, the more uranium it will contain. Measurement of the uranium present is done with a counter which calculates the amount of radioactivity.

Other changes in bone are the result of mineralization and alterations in the microstructure of the bone itself. Techniques for analyzing such changes include x-ray absorption, x-ray diffraction, and optical methods, including the index of refraction and the absorption of light. Again, the purpose is to discern whether or not the specimens are contemporary with one another.

Stones, either buried or lying on the ground's surface for a length of time, accumulate a chemical coating, termed *patination*. The patina usually consists of a milky colored layer on the surface of the stone. Flints that have lain on the ground with the same side uppermost through time may be heavily patinated on the bottom and only lightly patinated on the upper surface. Whatever the causes of patination, it is a local phenomenon which is not useful for regional dating. However, when comparing objects from different levels in a single site or comparing different objects from the surface of a site, differences in degree of patination, if present, may be assumed to represent differences in relative age. What we must bear in mind is that all such associational techniques refer to the relative age of the *specimen* rather than the age of the level from which it was collected.

Chronometric Dating

Chronometric dating refers to the *quantitative* (versus relative) measurement of time. In using this technique, there must be a referent to measure the time against, and this is the calendar.
■ According to Michels (1973: 14) all chronometric techniques "are based on natural phenomena that undergo progressive change at uniform rates through time. By knowing the rate of change and the amount of change, the number of years that have elapsed since the process of change began can be computed." Techniques that yield dates in years include dendrochronology, archeomagnetic dating, radiocarbon dating, potassium-argon dating, fission-track dating, thermoluminescence dating, obsidian-hydration-dating, and amino-acid racemization.

Such dates are of 2 separate categories. Those which are stated in terms of years in our calendar are true *absolute* dates. (Many techniques yield dates expressed in years but with an associated-probability factor.) Other dates are referred to as a floating chronology which has yet to be correlated with our calendar. Only the first category yields dates that may be termed absolute. Absolute dates may be derived from tree rings, ancient calendrical systems, coins, and varves, where traced directly back in time from the present. What is essential for a true absolute date is that there must be no equivocation: The date must be exactly correct to the year, and it must be exactly correlated with our present calendar. As we shall see, such accuracy is seldom available to the archaeologist. A final caveat is that even if a specimen can be dated to a specific year we must then prove that its archaeological association is correct — that it in fact can be used to date an occupation or level.

DENDROCHRONOLOGY

Tree-ring dating (another name for *dendrochronology*) is possibly our best example of absolute dating. Trees sensitive to fluctuations in

● Tree rings provide dates exact to a specific year.

▲ Tree-ring dates possess limitations.

rainfall or other climatic factors form annual growth rings of varying widths. Over a period of 25 to 50 years such a sequence of ring widths establishes a pattern which is not exactly duplicated by any other such sequence of rings. This sequence can then be correlated with a master chronology of ring widths extending from the present backward in time (Fig. 3-5). ● Such correlation can thus provide a date for the year in which the last ring on our specimen was laid down. This is a specific and absolute date. However, we must bear in mind that the outermost ring on the specimen may not represent the year the tree was cut or died, because the exterior may be eroded, may have been removed when the log was modified for use, or may have been burned or otherwise altered.

Another inherent limitation of the tree-ring method is that in years of severe climatic stress no ring may be deposited, or it may be of microscopic size. This leads to "missing" rings in the chronology, or to rings that are termed "locally absent" because they occur on only a portion of the circumference of the specimen. Careful dating of such specimens should provide the correct date, but careless analysis can provide a date in error by one or more years. It is also true that the date pertains to the last year in which the particular specimen was growing. For a variety of reasons, such a date cannot automatically be applied to the archaeological site from which the specimen was obtained. The log may have been salvaged from an earlier dwelling and reused, or the tree may have stood dead for a number of years before being cut and used. What must be established before the date can be utilized is the archaeological provenience of the specimen: In what way was the log used, and what was its association in the site? For example, if all the roof beams in a room date to within one or two years

Fig. 3-5 Example of chronology building, using tree-ring samples. (*a*) sample cut from a living tree. (*b-j*) Specimens taken from old houses and successively older ruins. In this way a chronology may be extended from the present backward into the prehistoric period. (Bannister in Brothwell and Higgs 1969: Fig. 33.)

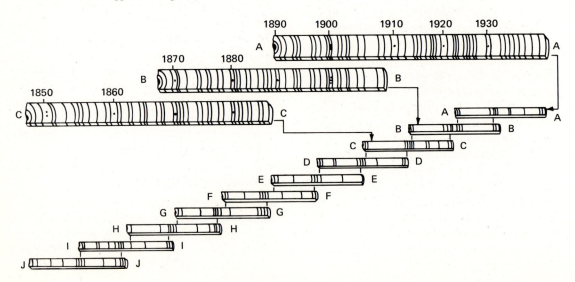

of one another, then we may assume that those dates bracket the period of construction. On the other hand, one conspicuously early date in such a group would suggest the reuse of an older beam. It is possible to determine the sequence of room building from wall abutments. If the associated tree-ring dates are in a similar sequence, then it is possible to rely on those dates with greater confidence, even if there are only one or two dates per room. Dates obtained from charcoal in a firepit or from burned logs lying on a floor may also be correlated with the room's use, its abandonment, and eventual filling with trash.

The development of a tree-ring chronology is dependent upon the presence of the correct tree species — species which produce annual rings in sensitivity to some climatic factor such as temperature or rainfall. Secondly, the climate must be variable in order to cause the formation of rings of varying widths. Regions such as the Hawaiian islands or the coast of British Columbia have climates that are too constant, thus producing unvarying, or "complacent," ring widths. Areas which are too desertic, too wet, or too cold are also eliminated. However, many of the temperate regions of the world have suitable conditions, and tree-ring chronologies have been developed for some of these.

▲ Although the tree-ring chronology is capable of producing absolute dates for certain regions, the use of such dates is dependent upon our understanding of the position of the dated specimens in the sequence of events recorded at the specific site. The method is accurate, but its application also depends on the accuracy of observations made in the field and on the skill by which the specimens have been excavated. A further limitation is that the master chronology must be established by working backward in time from living trees. If this reconstruction is based only on archaeologically obtained specimens, it will be a "floating" chronology, which must then be correlated with our calendar by some other independent means, such as radiocarbon dating.

Tree-ring chronologies have been developed for Alaska, northern Mexico, Germany, Norway, Great Britain, and Switzerland (Michels 1973: 126). The technique has also been applied in other portions of the United States, Turkey, Egypt, Japan, Russia, and northern Chile. However, it is in the southwestern United States that the use of this technique has been the greatest for archaeological dating. Most spectacular has been the backward extension of the tree-ring chronology of the American Southwest to beyond 6000 B.C., based on specimens of bristlecone pine, both living and dead, found near timberline. The bristlecones are slow-growing and extremely long-lived trees, individual specimens of which provide a continuous record several thousand years in length. Its utility has extended beyond the dating of ancient wood from archaeological sites, as the bristlecone-pine chronology has been used to check the accuracy of the radiocarbon chronology, a scientific breakthrough which we shall later discuss.

RADIOCARBON DATING

The radioactive decay of the isotope carbon-14 (C-14) provides another method of dating. The dates are expressed in years, with a statistical notation as to the amount of probable error. For example, the expression 2250 b.c. ± 200 means that the true date in question is 2250 years b.c. plus or minus 200 years, with a reliability of one standard deviation, or sigma. Translation of this statistical expression means that in 67 percent of such cases the true date would fall between 2050 and 2450 b.c. If we wish to be more exact we can utilize 2 sigma, in which case there is a 95 percent probability that the true date falls between 1850 and 2650 b.c. Three sigma would provide a 99 percent probability that the true date would fall between 1650 and 2850 b.c. It must also be pointed out that there are no limits within which the true age lies with *absolute* certainty. (This should dispel any impression that simply because radiocarbon dates are published in terms of years they are true absolute dates.)

■ Radiocarbon — a technique useful in dating any remains of a previously living organism.

● Samples may be contaminated and thus yield erroneous dates.

The principle behind the radiocarbon method is that neutrons produced by cosmic radiation enter the earth's atmosphere and react with the isotope nitrogen 14. This reaction produces the isotope of carbon, C-14, which readily mixes with the oxygen in the atmosphere. From the atmosphere the C-14 isotope eventually enters all living organisms as part of the oxygen-exchange process. The individual organism continues to incorporate C-14 as long as it is living. ■ After the organism dies it no longer receives atoms of C-14, but instead begins the process of radioactive decay. The C-14 is continually being reduced at a fixed rate, or *half-life*. Such a reduction is described as the length of time necessary for the radioactive substance to lose one-half of its radioactive isotopes. The half-life of C-14 has been calculated by counting the number of beta emissions per minute per gram of samples of known age. A wide variety of specimens of known age were counted initially in order to establish the C-14 half-life at 5568 ± 30 years. Samples included wood and mummified flesh from pharaonic tombs, dated tree-ring specimens, living trees, and other materials of known age. Such a demonstration that dates obtained by a counting of C-14 isotopes could be correlated with objects of known age proved that this method had value. However, the half-life so established had only theoretical significance, as it was still only an average of determinations. In addition, the entire concept depends upon several major assumptions:

1. The rate of cosmic radiation has remained constant through time.
2. C-14 is evenly distributed throughout the atmosphere and all living matter.

3. The concentration of C-14 in the reservoir of exchangeable carbon on the earth and in the atmosphere has not changed.

Research has demonstrated that the natural concentration of C-14 in the atmosphere has varied for certain periods, the primary variable seemingly being variation in solar activity (Stuiver and Quay 1980). Since this variation has not yet been adequately explained by theoretical considerations, scientists have had to check the veracity of the C-14 dates by systematic dating of dated tree-ring specimens. The result has suggested that the original computation of C-14 half-life was in error and that a figure of 5730 ± 40 years is more nearly correct.

The actual counting of the samples was accomplished first by Willard Libby, the inventor of the method, by converting the organic sample to elemental carbon, which was then smeared on the inner surface of a steel cylinder. The cylinder was surrounded by a ring of Geiger counters in order to record the emissions from the sample. Since cosmic radiation reaching the counters would also be recorded, this "background count" was therefore screened out by enclosing the entire counting mechanism in a thick-walled lead vault. The method had drawbacks in that it was time-consuming and the possibilities for error were relatively high. Within a few years more modern techniques were developed in which the carbon is changed to a gas (either carbon dioxide, acetylene, or methane), which is then counted in a proportional counter. The gas method is more reliable inasmuch as the sample is not handled after it has been prepared for conversion to gas. A second advantage of the gas method is that reliable dates may be obtained from smaller samples. (The currently recommended minimum sample sizes are listed in Table 3-1.) Other carbonaceous materials suitable for dating include soot; any preserved vegetal material, such as grass, twigs, or bark; burned bone; antler or tusk; calcareous tufa; lake mud; parchment; dung; flesh; hide; hair; and any other substance from a once-living organism. The material collected need not represent the remains of a single organism; for example, a number of small shells could be dated as one sample. The sample may also combine particles found separately; for example, some of the most valuable dates have been obtained by the painstaking picking of tiny charcoal flecks scattered throughout a stratigraphic layer. A date so derived would represent an average age for that geologic unit.

● A serious concern of both the archaeologist and the radiocarbon-dating analyst is the possibility of *sample contamination*. Samples may be contaminated while in the ground, during the collection process, or in the dating laboratory.

We will not attempt to outline in detail all of the possible sources of contamination, as this is a highly complex subject. Contamination may result in a date being either too "young" or too "old." For example, an older date may be obtained by dating shells which have incorporated inactive (radioactively dead) carbon during their growth. Both younger and older dates may be the result of groundwater activity. Leaching of carbon from a sample would yield an older date, whereas enrichment could occur if there is a nearby source of more recent carbon. Samples may contain recent rootlets, another source of younger carbon. Sample collection requires care, as contamination may be introduced by the wrapping material used (e.g., cotton). The coat-

TABLE 3-1
Suggested Amount of Material to Be Collected for Radiocarbon Dating

Description	Dry (1) Weight		Comments
	Absolute Minimum	Desirable	
Materials Generally Suitable			
Wood—clean or rotten	5 gm	25–30 gm	
Charcoal	2 gm	10–20 gm	Rich, black flakes
	5–10 gm	50–100 gm	Sandy, brown
			Whole shell specimens:
Shell—carbonate	20 gm	100 gm	Hard, shiny surface
	30 gm	150–200 gm	Powdery, soft surface
Shell—conchiolin (shell protein)	500 gm	1,000–2,000 gm	
Grass, leaves	5 gm	35–50 gm	
Flesh, skin, hair	5 gm	45–60 gm	Fresh weight
Paper, cloth	3 gm	25–30 gm	
Peat, gyttja	30 gm	80–120 gm	Dark brown
	60 gm	150–200 gm	Light gray-brown
Bone—carbonate	300 gm	800 gm	Seldom yields a valid date.
Bone—collagen (bone protein)	300 gm	800–1500 gm	Up to 10,000 years old
Bone—charred	600 gm	1,500–3,000 gm	Up to 36,000 years old
Materials for Special Projects Only			
Soil—organic matter	N.A.	2–5 kgm	As research projects only
Soil—carbonate		100–500 gm	
Ceramics, plaster, and mortars	(?)	(?)	Subject to research

(From *Australian Archaeology*, edited by D. J. Mulvaney, p. 93 [Australian Institute of Aboriginal Studies, Canberra, 1972].)

▲ Radiocarbon is our best dating method for the last 50,000 years.

■ Dating the North Acropolis at Tikal—an archaeological test.

ing of fragile specimens with preservatives, such as shellac, can introduce modern carbon, which is almost impossible to remove in the laboratory. In recent years dating laboratories have become increasingly conscious of contamination problems. As a result, they now routinely prepare the samples by a rigorous cleaning. Samples are picked under a microscope, then washed in strong acid and alkali solutions, and then burned. Once prepared, samples are stored in tight containers for several weeks before dating in order to permit the decay of tritium and other radioactive isotopes with a short half-life.

▲ The radiocarbon technique is the single most effective method available for dating specimens of ages within the past 50,000 years, which is the practical limit of the technique. However, with elaborate preparation methods, it is possible to enrich the quantity of isotopes available for dating within a sample. This technique pushes back the theoretical limit of the process to 75,000 years (Grootes 1978). Isotopic enrichment deals with the concentration of very small amounts of C-14. Therefore, the introduction of only a very small percentage of modern carbon would result in serious contamination, making the date erroneous.

If contamination is such a problem, then how is it possible to use radiocarbon dates with confidence? The most important fact to bear in mind is that radiocarbon dates are archaeological dates. They are based on samples collected from archaeological sites and their isolation, recovery, and identification to provenience are the result of standard archaeological methods. Reused beams, intrusions such as burials into earlier levels, and so on are all archaeological problems which must be deciphered from excavation

notes before a radiocarbon sample is submitted for dating. Therefore, if we have obtained one date from each of eight successive stratified levels, it is assumed that these dates would form a single sequence from early to late. Any deviation from this sequence would have to be explained. Presented with an anomalous date, the archaeologist can date other samples from the same level or reexamine the site excavation notes in order to determine whether some feature, such as a burial pit, missed during excavation, might be the cause of the inappropriate date. In some cases it is also possible that the archaeologist has had an age estimate in mind for a level which C-14 has shown to be erroneous. In such cases the archaeologist may simply have refused to believe that the C-14 date is accurate, since it does not support a prior bias. (After all, scientists are only human, with the usual human failings.)

■ An excellent example of the resolution of an archaeological problem through the use of radiocarbon dates is the dating of the sequence of construction of the North Acropolis at Tikal (Fig. 3-6) (Stuckenrath, Coe, and Ralph 1966). In this case the archaeological problem was simple: the dating of the long constructional sequence of a major architectural feature in a classic Mayan ceremonial center. The resolution, however, was far from simple, as the researchers demonstrated. Twenty-five radiocarbon dates were obtained, primarily on samples of charcoal collected from the constructional fill between finished platform surfaces. The researchers describe the North Acropolis, its constructional sequence, and the problems attendant with sample collection as follows:

It [the North Acropolis] consists essentially of a series of great superimposed platforms, each of which sustains various buildings of a ceremonial nature. The majority of radiocarbon samples considered here are charcoals recovered from the fills employed in construction. Such charcoals occur in fill as randomly as potsherds and other cultural material. The true source of this charcoal is diffi-

Fig. 3-6 The North Acropolis at Tikal, Guatemala. This massive, overbuilt sequence of architectural units has been dated in detail by radiocarbon. (Hester photograph.)

cult if not impossible to isolate. This is basically true of the actual fills. We assume that the cultural detritus and charcoal found in such fills ultimately derive from household middens, workshop scrap, and from other accumulations of trash resulting from daily living at Tikal. The fill matrix ranges from limestone rubble, to demolished prior constructions, marl scraped from bedrock, and earths and clays. A serious drawback in assessing sources is the extent to which the old was demolished to make way for the new at Tikal. . . .

Specific dating problems posed by the charcoal samples are identified as follows (Stuckenrath, Coe, and Ralph 1966: 372–374):

1. Post-sample error — this is the interval of time between the "death" of the organic source of the sample and the "death" of the organic matrix of the source. A common example is the differential age between pith wood and the cambial layer, in some cases a difference of several hundred years.
2. Placement history — the interval between the death carbonization of the source and the final archaeological placement of the sample. This gap must be assessed through archaeo-

logical means — the range of variation in age of associated artifacts, stratigraphy, etc. Of importance is the fact that the PH gap may range from nonexistent to as much as 1000 years.
3. Average death-rate — if the sample is made up of mixed botanical elements, the date assigned represents an average age.
4. Contamination — rootlets, groundwater leaching, etc., are problems inherent to all radiocarbon samples.
5. Sigma — the true age, as we have discussed earlier, lies within a statistical range of the ± factor given; i.e., the exact age lies within the ± factor (1 sigma) given in only 2 out of 3 cases. The chances are that even 2 sigmas from the mean includes only 19 out of 20 true ages.
6. Half-life — the exact half-life used will affect the dates assigned. The Tikal dates are based on a 5568 year half-life, whereas 5730 is now more commonly used. The 5730 figure would result in dates some 240 years earlier.

The dating of the North Acropolis was facilitated through the exact placement of the sam-

51

● Radiocarbon years are not exactly equivalent to calendar years.

ples in the constructional sequence (Fig. 3-7). The next step was the assigning of expected ages to the levels, based on ceramic crossdating of the associated potsherds, the stratigraphic sequence, the contemporaneity of specific samples, and the estimated age of the architectural features. These estimated ages are plotted in Figure 3-7 by the symbol X; departures from this expected age are plotted as circles. The significance of the technique employed is obvious. Only about one-half of the dates are reasonably close to their predicted ages. The authors resign themselves to

these facts: The samples are no better than any other archaeological remains; their stratigraphic location is the result of numerous factors, many of which are chronologically significant. The authors (Stuckenrath, Coe, and Ralph 1966: 383) state:

> The point is that somewhat less than 50% of the North Acropolis samples make the depositional sense expected of all. This may be a useful statistic; it may be that at other complex sites half the results on charcoal are merely useful for detecting error in the other half.

In conclusion, the authors also point out that even with samples which they personally excavated and for which they found no evidence of archaeological error, the dated results clearly in-

Fig. 3-7 Radiocarbon chronology of the North Acropolis, Tikal, Guatemala. *(Left)* X's are C-14 dates; O's, expected dates. For reasons not adequately revealed by the archaeology, many of the C-14 dates differ from the expected dates. *(Right)* Stratigraphy, showing the layers of construction. (Stuckenrath, Coe, and Ralph 1966:375.)

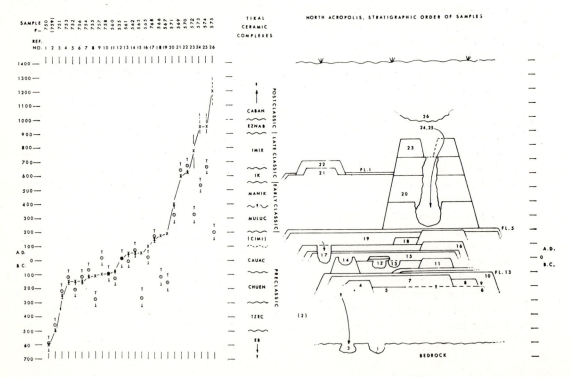

dicate that a substantial PH (placement history) error was in fact present. Thus an interval exists between the age of the sample and the time of its burial in the site layer. The results are humbling for all those interested in dating the events of the past.

The early efforts at radiocarbon dating were derived from theoretical assumptions concerning the rate of radioactive decay of C-14. The decay rate was based on the rate of cosmic radiation reaching the earth, which was assumed to have been constant through time. Proof of these assumptions could be obtained only through the radiocarbon dating of specimens of known archaeological age. Tests were run on ancient specimens from pharaonic Egypt, specimens attributed to specific dynasties of a known age, and the radiocarbon dates agreed with the archaeological data. It could therefore be assumed that the radiocarbon chronology was accurate: One radiocarbon year was equivalent to one calendar year. Further refinement of this relationship has been made possible in recent years by the radiocarbon dating of tree-ring samples, each of 10-year length, covering the last 8000 years (Ferguson 1972). ● When these precisely dated tree-ring specimens were dated in a series of 312 radiocarbon runs, it was determined that *radiocarbon years* were not exactly equivalent to *calendar years* but in fact fluctuated through time by being either too young or too old, depending on the age of the specimen (Fig. 3-8). The results are of extreme importance to all the historical sciences. We now know more precisely the true age of samples dated by radiocarbon, and we further have verified that cosmic radiation has fluctuated through time.

Of extreme importance to archaeology is the fact that the recalibration of C-14 dates provides a means of refining the known chronology of almost every known prehistoric culture. While radiocarbon years have been proven not to be identical to calendar years, we now have a method available for reducing the error between the two.

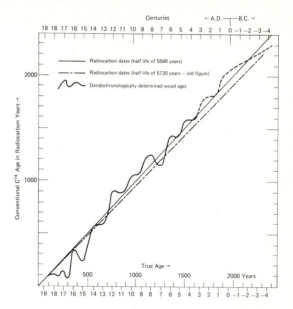

Fig. 3-8 Graph of correlation between radiocarbon years and calendar years, showing the results of recalibration. The difference between the dendrodates and the expected radiocarbon age revealed that some C-14 dates were either too old or too young. These errors were due to fluctuations in atmospheric carbon in the past. (Suess 1965:Fig. 4.)

CALENDARS

Ancient calendrical systems would appear capable of yielding exact dates which can be correlated with our present calendar. The occurrence of calendars is limited in archaeology, as their development is associated with a high level of cultural attainment. The ancient civilizations of Greece, Rome, Egypt, Carthage, Mesopotamia, and the Maya of Yucatan are examples. Most of the cultures studied by archaeologists are prehistoric, having developed neither calendrical observations nor writing, and thus other methods of dating must be employed. For those cultures which possessed calendars, several qualifications must be noted. All calendars of archaeological concern are subject to slight modifications due to the difference between the astronomical year

▲ All calendars must be correlated with our present calendar.

■ All objects with a calendrical date must be interpreted on the basis of their archaeological provenience.

● K/A dating — a method useful for dating the oldest sites.

and the 365-day tropical year. ▲ Such a correlation is handled in our present Gregorian calendar by the addition of an extra day every fourth year. Early calendars coped with such variations in a number of ways and it is necessary to know which method was used in order to make an exact correlation with our present system. It is also possible to have an exact calendar which, because its use was discontinued in antiquity, forms a floating chronology. The ancient Mayan calendar is such an example. It contained two systems: the extremely accurate Long Count system, correct to the day over 374,440 years (Fig. 3-9), and the abbreviated and much less accurate Short Count system, correct only within 256 1/4 years. By the time of European contact only the Short Count system was still in use. Therefore, we have short-count dates for which corresponding Gregorian equivalents are known. However, the next step of correlating the Mayan Short Count with the Mayan Long Count has led to two different correlations. Termed the "Goodman, Thompson, Martinez (GMT) correlation," and the "Spinden correlation" (after those who described them), they differ in their alignment with our present calendar by 260 years. In recent years, the correlation controversy has abated due to the radiocarbon dating of wooden door lintels which had dates in the Mayan Long Count system carved on them. The result suggested that the GMT correlation is the more accurate. Thus, finally, Mayan calendrical dates may be assigned modern equivalents.

■ Probably the major restriction on the use of calendrical dates is that they are inscribed on objects subject to all the vicissitudes of time encountered by all other archaeological specimens. If the date is struck on a coin, then the presence of that coin in a site does not necessarily date the site to that year. After all, coins are in circulation for a number of years after being minted, so the dated coin would provide only a *minimal* date for that level in the site. (That is, the introduction of the coin into the level could not have occurred *earlier* than its mint date.) Application of archaeological methods is again in order, as the position of dated specimens in a site must be

Fig. 3-9 An example of a date recorded in the Mayan long count system. The inscription from the east side of Stela E at Quirigua, Guatemala, records not only the date but also lunar records and glyphs of deities. (Morley and Brainerd 1956: Fig. 25.)

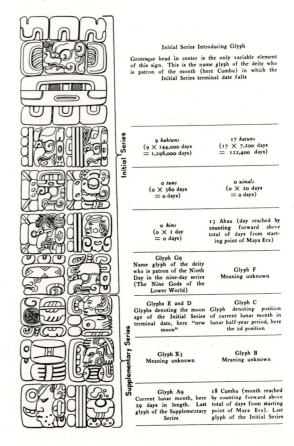

explained in terms of site accretion as determined by excavation. Coins occurring in groups with closely clustered dates provide stronger evidence that their presence in the site dates to shortly after the latest date in the group. Occasionally, freshly minted coins are found in hoards, which makes it possible to assume that their presence in the site is the result of an event which occurred almost immediately after minting. Other dated objects such as stelae (carved stone slabs), building blocks, and so forth, must also be viewed with some reserve. (Were the stones introduced into a structure on the date inscribed? Was the building begun or completed on that date?) One has only to consider the construction history of European medieval cathedrals to realize that a dated stone might differ considerably in age from the completion date of the building to which it belongs. Thus calendars can provide exact dates for specimens, but their chronological relation to the history of a site must be assessed in the context of the total body of archaeological information available.

POTASSIUM ARGON DATING

Radioactive decay is a principle that provides a mechanism for the dating of many kinds of specimens. To be of value to archaeology, the isotopes being counted must have a half-life of a time span capable of providing dates applicable to human prehistory. Some isotopes decay in a matter of hours or days — obviously, too short a time to be of value. ● One usable ratio is that resulting from the decay of potassium-40 into the gas argon-40. The half-life of K-40 (1.3 million $\pm$ 40 million years) greatly extends the chronology possible with C-14, and so far the potassium-argon method has yielded dates ranging from 500 B.C. back to 4.5 billion years. With the K/A method, the age of rocks, including chronological marker beds (such as volcanic ash falls) can be measured. Stone artifacts found in a site should not be dated by this method, however, as the age of the rock probably is much greater

than the time of its use as an implement. What must be dated are rock crystals that were formed at the time of their deposition. The principal application of the method is in dating volcanic beds which occur in a stratigraphic sequence containing human cultural materials. In such a case the K/A age relative to the cultural items can be established. It is through the use of this method that the oldest dates associated with human remains have been obtained.

The potassium-argon method is based on the following principles. During rock formation the isotope argon-40, being a gas, will escape. After formation of the rock, the isotope potassium-40 decays as follows: 89% decays into calcium-40 and 11% into argon-40. Therefore, any argon-40 present in the rock at the time of its measurement is the result of the postformational radioactive decay of potassium-40.

According to Evernden and Curtis, who developed the applicability of the method to archaeological problems, K/A dates are acceptable if they meet the following criteria (Michels 1973: 172–173):

1. Two different crystal types from the same tuff yield essentially the same age.
2. The sample is a volcanic flow (basalt, trachyte, etc.), and the problem of argon loss is not insurmountable.
3. Several samples from the same horizon at scattered localities yield the same age.
4. The primary nature of the tuff can be established.

According to the same authorities, criteria for the rejection of dates are the following:

1. There is the possibility of the deposit having been reworked.
2. There is the possibility of there being admixed detrital components of different age.
3. Different concentrates of the same mineral from the same tuff yield markedly different ages.

▲ Paleomagnetic dating—a method for dating clay floors and hearths fired in antiquity.

■ Paleomagnetic reversals—a different kind of natural clock.

The K/A method has been of extreme importance in the dating of early hominids. Evernden and Curtis, working on samples from Olduvai Gorge, Tanzania, have dated the earliest living floors there and the associated fossil hominids (in this case the genus *Homo*) at about 1.75 million years of age. Since dates on multiple ash falls both above and below these living floors provide a consistent sequence without any anomalies, we feel confident that the dates are reasonably correct. A different situation is present at the East Rudolf locality in northern Kenya.

At East Rudolf (Lake Turkana) the initial dating of the KBS tuff (a specific layer of volcanic ash) by the K/A method yielded dates of about 2.5 million years. These dates were of critical importance, since the KBS tuff lies above the occurrence of stone tools, remains of Australopithecines, and even more importantly, the surprisingly modern-appearing 1470 skull assigned to the genus *Homo*. More recent dates on the KBS tuff are in the vicinity of 1.6–1.8 million years (Walker and Leakey 1978). While the research continues and the controversy is far from resolved, it is possible that the different dates may be due to inherent problems in the K/A method. For example, the Potassium-40 may not be uniformly distributed throughout the sample dated. Furthermore, the sample treatment to remove the contaminant atmospheric argon-40 can also cause some loss of the argon-40 resulting from the radioactive decay—the very fraction that is measured to obtain the date.

PALEOMAGNETIC DATING

Through time the angle of declination between magnetic north and true north fluctuates due to changes in the earth's magnetic field. Such fluc-

tuations vary in a systematic way which can be plotted as a series of curves whose position changes with time. What is needed to date a specimen within a particular cycle is to have preserved information as to the direction of magnetic north at the time the specimen was in use. ▲The key to this method is the fact that an item of fired clay has, fixed permanently by the firing process, the declination of magnetic north as it was when the specimen was fired. The principle is based on the fact that minerals in clay are realigned to magnetic north at the time they are heated. Different clay minerals are realigned as they reach what is called the "blocking temperature," which, according to the specific mineral, ranges from room temperature to 675 degrees centigrade. The result is termed *thermoremanent magnetism*.

The field techniques employed in collecting a paleomagnetic sample are relatively easy. The sample, usually a portion of a fire hearth or burned floor, is isolated as a small block in place. It is then surrounded with plaster of paris, which, as it is setting, has inscribed upon it magnetic north and true north. After these determinations have been made and the plaster has set, the specimen is removed from the ground. Back in the laboratory, the permanent magnetism in the specimen is measured with a magnetometer. This enables the plotting of the magnetic declination as it was at the time when the specimen was fired. This measurement, after its position on a known secular variation curve has been identified, yields a date.

Known curves of secular variation have been built up by measuring the magnetic declination of archaeological samples of known age. These are fired-clay specimens which came from levels dated by radiocarbon, tree rings, or other chronometric methods. To date, such curves have only been developed for England, Germany, France, Japan, and the southwestern United States. The latter is the most comprehensive, covering the last 2000 years (Fig. 3-10). The other curves are of shorter duration. (For example, the English curve is based on actual mea-

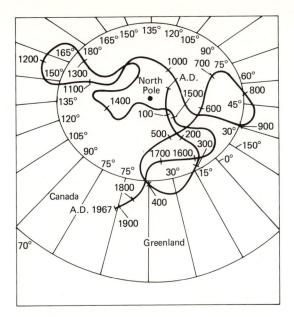

Fig. 3-10 Graph illustrating the wandering of the geomagnetic pole over the past 2,000 years. (National Geographic Magazine.)

surements of declination and dip in London over the past 400 years.) So far this, the directional method of archaeomagnetic dating, has received the most attention, and according to one of its developers, Robert DuBois, once a secular variation curve has been established, dates can be obtained with an accuracy to within 50 years (Michels 1973: 141). As with any dating method, there are, of course, problems. Errors may be caused by subsequent heating of the sample, even by the sun, which can lead to remagnetization of the low-temperature-sensitive particles. (This is called *viscous magnetism*, and it can be removed through laboratory treatment of the sample.) Other sources of error include chemical change, which is not common in well-fired clays, and the action of strong magnetic fields. For example, lightning causes isothermal-remanent magnetism; however, this contaminant magnetism can also be removed in the laboratory.

Selection of the samples to be collected is also important. As an example, the following classi-

fication of sample types according to quality has been developed by the Archaeological Research Laboratory in England (Michels 1973: 135):

> Category I (good): structures containing a substantial floor of well-baked clay.
> Category II (average): kilns and ovens having an intact circumference of solid wall, not less than a foot in height; well-built clay hearths.
> Category III (poor): unsubstantial hearths, kilns with incomplete walls, patches of burning, iron-smelting sites.
> Category IV (very poor): stone structures, poorly fired tile, and brick ovens.

A second method of paleomagnetic dating is the *intensity method*. It is based on differences in the dip of a needle toward the magnetic pole over time. While research on this technique lags behind that of the directional method, a secular intensity-variation curve has been worked out for Czechoslovakia (Fig. 3-11).

■ On an entirely different time scale, extending back to a potential 75 million years, is another form of paleomagnetic dating based on geomagnetic reversals of the earth's magnetic field. This change in polarity produces a shift from a normal state to a reversed state. (The result, if you had a compass, is that the needle would point south instead of north.) Study of such phenomena indicates there have been about 10 such reversals since the oldest living

Fig. 3-11 Curve illustrating variation in secular intensity, a promising technique which may be useful for dating in the future. (Cambridge University Press.)

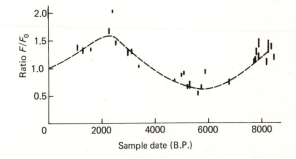

● Dating the time of formation of natural glasses.

▲ Thermoluminescence — a method for dating pottery.

■ Dating obsidian tools.

floors at Olduvai Gorge were occupied. This method is currently in the experimental stage (Cox 1969) and probably has greater potential for geology than for archaeology. However, in critical questions concerning the age of ancient sediments associated with early hominids, it may be a method useful in the settling of dating controversies unresolved by other methods.

FISSION-TRACK DATING

In the same manner as potassium-argon dating, fission-track dating relies for its samples on rock which was newly formed at the time of its deposition. ● The technique is based on the principle that many minerals and natural glasses, such as obsidian, contain a small quantity of uranium. Over time, as the uranium decays its atoms occasionally undergo spontaneous fission. This fission occurs at a constant rate of 10^{-16} per year, leading to the passing of energy-charged particles through the material. The resulting ionization of the particles adjacent to the path of the charged particles causes positive ions to be repulsed, forcing them into the chemical "lattice" of the matrix. Such an event leaves permanent damage trails, or *tracks*. Fission tracks can be seen under high magnification such as is possible with an electron microscope. The tracks accumulate as the uranium decays, and dating can therefore be achieved by counting the density of tracks per square centimeter. Since samples with few tracks are difficult to date, the slow rate of decay means that samples at least 100,000 years of age must be selected for dating. An exception is artificial glass which, owing to a high concentration of uranium can be dated (even though the samples are of very recent age) within the past 200 years.

In dating, after the original track density caused by natural decay has been counted the sample is then irradiated and the new resultant track density is counted. The age of the specimen is computed on the basis of the ratio of the natural tracks to the induced tracks. Counting the tracks is made simpler by etching the samples in hydrofluoric acid, which enlarges the tracks so that they are visible with an optical microscope. Comparison of fission-track dates with those obtained by other chronometric methods indicates the reliability of the method (Fig. 3-12). Errors in this method are due primarily to postdepositional heating rather than to chemical variation in the rock. The technique may therefore be used to cross-check the dating of samples by the potassium-argon method. On the other hand, heating causes the tracks to alter and even to disappear. Thus the method cannot be used on any materials which have come in contact with fire. (This eliminates the fission-track method for dating all hearth stones, fired clay, ceramics, and so on.)

Fig. 3-12 Comparison of ages based on fission-track dating with ages obtained by other methods. (Science, 149:383–393 © 1965.)

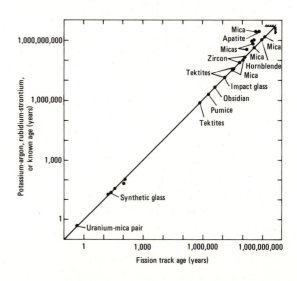

THERMOLUMINESCENCE

▲ The principle of thermoluminescent dating is that pottery or stones, which have been heated in the past, will release energy in the form of light when reheated. The amount of light emitted by a specimen depends on the amount of time which has elapsed since the specimen was last fired. In addition, the glow curve also permits the measurement of the temperature at which the specimen was originally fired.

First announced by two physicists, Kennedy and Knopff (1960), the method seemed theoretically sound. It was received with enthusiasm by archaeologists because the primary material to be dated was potsherds, the most important artifact class previously used for sequence building. It was reasoned that if the relative sequences established with potsherd seriation could be tied to absolute dates, the entire chronological foundations of archaeology could be dramatically improved. Furthermore, it was suggested that with the thermoluminescent technique the dating of an individual sample would be relatively inexpensive.

In order for the method to be applied the specimen must have been fired in antiquity to a temperature in excess of 750°C. This firing would drive off any prior thermoluminescence acquired as a result of geologic processes. As a result, subsequent measurement of the light emitted when the specimen was reheated in the laboratory would be the result of energy accumulated in the specimen since its original firing. Problems with the method involve different light emissions from different-sized particles. However, this can be eliminated by separating the particles to be measured according to grain size. Testing of the different-sized fractions for both natural thermoluminescence and alpha-induced artificial thermoluminescence permits an age formula to be developed. Tests on pottery specimens of known ages covering the last 3500 years indicate that an accuracy within ± 10 percent is achievable (Aitken 1968). Promising indications notwithstanding, work on this technique is progressing slowly and few laboratories are presently equipped to do such dating.

OBSIDIAN HYDRATION

A freshly broken surface of obsidian exposed to the atmosphere will absorb water, forming a visible surface layer. Termed a *hydration layer*, it increases in thickness at a fixed rate. We thus have available another natural clock for the measurement of elapsed time. ■ Inasmuch as a great many stone implements were made from obsidian, the potential of such a method is indeed considerable. Its application is relatively simple. First a small, thin section is removed from the specimen with a diamond lapidary saw; the sample is then mounted on a microscope slide and examined with a polarizing petrographic microscope. The polarized light makes the hydration layer visible, and its thickness in microns can be directly measured. Two techniques are used for measurement. The first consists of measurement by eye through the use of an image-splitting eyepiece. In the second technique, a photograph of the sample is taken and then the negative is placed on a scanning densitometer. Identification of the boundaries of the hydration layer is thus enhanced, and measurement is made easier. The results of both techniques are similar.

It is not possible to compare the measurement of any one hydration layer with any universal thickness standard, as hydration does not occur at the same rate in every region. There seems to be a correlation with temperature and other environmental factors, which suggests that regional rates of hydration are possible. Lists of dates have been prepared for various selected areas, and these give promise of an acceptable reliability. Thousands of specimens have been dated, covering a time range of at least the past 16,000 years. The method has been applied in many regions of North and South America as well as in Europe, Africa, the Middle East, Japan, and New Zealand. Problems limiting the method are (1) the variable chemical composition of different obsidians and (2) modification

● Varves—dating the sequence of glacial sediments.

▲ "Guess dates" may be used where no other dating method can be employed.

in the surface of the obsidian by burning, sand blasting, surface exposure, and frequent variations in temperature and precipitation. A final problem is posed by the reuse of obsidian implements. The method has merit in spite of these limitations, however, when the specimens dated are of a similar variety of obsidian and have been buried in a similar environment since use.

Perhaps the best advantage of obsidian dating is the fact that it pinpoints the time of manufacture of the artifact. Few archaeological dating methods so specifically date cultural materials. The method is continually being improved by the construction of regional hydration rates based upon the measurement of hydration layers of specimens from sites of known age.

AMINO ACID RACEMIZATION

Amino acids used by living organisms to synthesize complex proteins are of the L configuration. *L*, or *Levo*, refers to the tendency of these compounds to rotate, when in solution, the polarization plane of polarized light to the left as the observer views the light source. Over a period of time, in fossil bone, some of the L-configured amino acids will interconvert, or racemize, into a D, or Dexter, configuration (one that rotates to the right when viewed in polarized light). Consequently, fresh or living bone will have only L-configured acids, but as the bone ages it will acquire more and more D-configured acids. In other words, the older the bone the greater the proportion of D to L. If the rate of change from L- to D-configured amino acids can be determined then, of course, one has an absolute dating technique. (For dates within the time range 5,000 to 100,000 years, aspertic acid is the most useful.)

Certain problems have precluded widespread acceptance of the amino acid method by archaeologists. As Bada and Helfman (1975: 160–173) point out, racemization is a chemical process, and as such it is temperature-sensitive. In other words, the amount of D-configured amino acids present in a fossil specimen is not only dependent on time but also on temperature. In this case the higher the temperatures, the greater the ratio of D to L.

Moisture, which easily penetrates porous bone, also affects the method, since amino acids are easily leached away by excessive water. Additionally, smaller bones are more affected than larger ones, and there is also the possibility that leaching rates may vary by species (Hare 1974). This means that the archaeologist must know in some detail the climatic history of the area under study in order to successfully date fossil bone by this method.

At present there are simply too many "ifs" for the archaeologist or prehistorian to rely heavily on this method, but this does not preclude its future use as an absolute dating technique.

VARVES

● *Varves* are laminated layers of sediments which have been deposited in lakes near a glacial margin. Each varve is made up of two layers: a coarse, thicker, usually lighter-colored layer on the bottom and a thin, fine-grained, darker-colored layer on top. The two layers together represent the deposition resulting from one year's glacial melt. The coarse layer may be correlated with the summer melt and the thin layer with the winter's runoff. Varves are variable in thickness, but this is not a problem in their use in dating. Major restrictions are that varves occur only in glaciated regions and therefore are absent in most parts of the world. Their most outstanding occurrence is in Scandinavia, where they have been traced continuously backward in time from the present to 17,000 years ago. Varve sequences were first described on the basis of the Scandinavian evidence (DeGeer 1912: 1940).

Subsequently, varve analysis has been applied to certain areas of North America, South America, and Africa. In these regions varve sequences are not continuous, due to the intermittent presence of glaciers in the past; thus we have had the description of floating varve chronologies. Ernst Antevs has worked in both Scandinavia and North America and has attempted a correlation of these two sequences. Antev's work probably has suitable accuracy, but what is more of a drawback is the fact that varve sequences can seldom be correlated with an archaeological site. In recent years the varve sequences have been further dated by the radiocarbon technique.

Age Estimates

▲ In certain situations where no other dating techniques have been applicable, archaeologists have relied on simple guesses termed *age estimates*. This method has little to recommend it, although there are unique situations in which such "guesses" were later shown to be reasonably correct. One of the most outstanding was the age assigned to the Folsom bison killsite. When first discovered in 1927, this previously undocumented association of humans with animals now extinct in North America was "guessdated" at approximately 10,000 years of age. In recent years, C-14 determinations on samples of Folsom age reveal that such dates concentrate at between 8,200 and 7,800 b.c. — quite a remarkable accuracy for a guess date! On the other hand, in introductory courses in archaeology taught 20 years ago, the age of the earliest humans was guessdated at about 500,000 to 1,000,000 years. The recent K-A dates at Olduvai Gorge and at East Rudolf now suggest that human antiquity is two to three times this earlier estimate.

Rather than choose a date at random and assign it to a site or cultural level, archaeologists

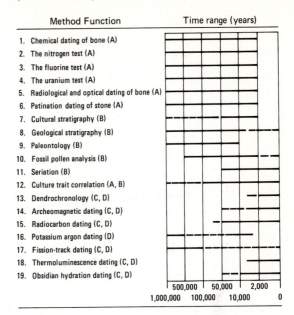

Fig. 3-13 Summary of dating techniques, illustrating the time ranges for which they may be used. The methods are further segregated by type as follows. A: intracomponent associations; B: relative dating; C: chronometric dating of artifacts; D: chronometric dating of components. (Michels 1973: Fig. 1.)

have long used a somewhat more rigorous method. By assuming a certain rate of deposition in a site, such as one foot per thousand years, they have attempted to quantify site accumulation. While several attempts have been made (Cosgrove and Cosgrove 1932: 100–103; Gifford 1916; Cook 1946; Vaillant 1935: 166–167, 257–258), especially with cave deposits and shell middens, the results have not always agreed with dates obtained by other methods. In short, archaeological deposits accumulate at different rates, and no standard is universally applicable.

A summary of the various dating techniques we have discussed, with the time ranges for which they are applicable, is shown in Figure 3-13.

4

Techniques in Archaeological Investigation

■ Every site, no matter how small, can yield cultural information.

● How to find a site

▲ Site-survey techniques

How does the archaeologist find the sites to study? To answer this question we must first define what the archaeologist looks for when field work begins. The basic unit is the *site*, which may be defined as any location which exhibits evidence of past human activity. While such a definition may seem too general, we must have a term equally adequate for areas on which a few potsherds occur (perhaps as the result of the accidental breaking of a single pot) to those of the size and complexity of a city of several hundred thousand inhabitants. By keeping the definition of a site flexible, the archaeologist thus reserves the right to study any evidence of past culture. The concept of *site* embodies not only content but location and relationship to environmental features. ■ Therefore sites of even minimal content can yield information about past cultural utilization of the landscape. It is for these reasons that the archaeologist may record every manifestation as a "site," even down to the occurrence of single isolated artifacts. (Thus, every item may be recorded, no matter how small its concentration.) On the other hand, the archaeologist's interest may pertain only to sites having a certain level of complexity (e.g., those with architecture). With a general approach to site definition, the archaeologist remains free to study whatever is of interest concerning past cultural practices.

Site Survey

The next most common questions that puzzle the nonarchaeologist are How can you tell that you have found a site? and How did you know where to look in the first place? Sites are unique in character. They are places containing evidence of past human activity. The site area commonly will have either stone tools or pottery fragments, or both, lying on the surface. Buried sites may be revealed in the eroded banks of streams. Another technique is to examine closely those areas which previous experience has indicated to be the most frequently occupied (for example, the edge of a bluff overlooking a river valley). Once one has discovered which specific portions of an area most commonly have sites, it is not difficult to find other sites. Another valid method of site location used by the archaeologist is simply to look everywhere. ● If nothing is known about an area then the first step is to start looking until just a few sites are found. Once these have been located, the archaeologist notes carefully the features of the terrain in which they occur and then searches similar locales for other sites. Sites are also indicated by evidence of human modification of the local environment. A particular area may have been cleared of vegetation (in prehistoric times) and therefore its modern vegetation differs from that adjacent to it. There also may be ruined walls or other architectural features present. Mounds may be the result of human activity, and even holes will show up as depressions of regular form. (Forms which are not natural in nature are most likely cultural remains) and the latter most frequently reveal the presence of former pit-house villages.

▲ Once the site has been located the archaeologist normally makes out a survey form (Fig. 4-1). The location of the site is recorded on a map; and all the features of the site (such as the presence of pottery, architecture, stone tools, and other surface manifestations) are described (Table 4-1). The site's size and depth are recorded, provided these can be determined. Other pertinent factors include the site situation: its location relative to local topographic features and the location of resources, such as stone, arable land, water, hunting areas, or areas of potential plant harvests. Normally, the site is photographed and a sketch map drawn. The site is also given a number, which is used to identify all notes or materials obtained therefrom.

A final step in the survey is the collection of artifacts from the surface of the site. This collection may be random or may be a statistical sample. The latter technique requires collecting all the material from the surface of selected squares (normally 1 to 5 meters in size) laid out in a systematic pattern in order to provide a sample from every portion of the site. Such sampling enables the archaeologist to compare the material collected from one site with that from another.

Site surveys are variable because they are structured in response to logistical considera-

Fig. 4-1 Survey form illustrating the categories of information to be recorded by the archaeologist during site survey. (Courtesy of the Office of the Colorado State Archaeologist.)

ARCHAEOLOGICAL SURVEY OF COLORADO
INVENTORY SHEET

Site No. ____, ____ County, ____ State ____ Drainage

1. Prior No./Name ____ Used By ____

2. Elevation ____ 3. ____ U.S.G.S. Quad 4 Other Map ____

5. LOCATION ____

____, ____ of U.T.M. Grid ____ SEC. ____ TOWNSHIP ____, RANGE ____

6. Owner ____ 7. Address ____

8. Tenant ____ 9. Prior Owner(s) ____

10. Informant ____ 11. Address ____

12. NEAREST WATER ____ permanent ____, season ____

13. Distance to 12 ____ 14 Elevation of 12 ____

15. LOCALE VEGETATION ____

16. SITE TYPE ____ 17. Cultural Affiliation (if known) ____

18. Description ____

19. Size ____ 20. Faces to (cardinal direction) ____

21. Depth & Character of Deposits ____

22. Material Observed or Reported ____

23. Material Collected ____

24. Condition ____

25. RECOMMENDATIONS ____

26. Photograph Nos. ____ 27. Recorded By ____

28 Date ____

SEND TO — Office of the State Archaeologist
5-A Ketchum Hall
University of Colorado
Boulder, Colorado 80302

Site No. ____, County, ____ State ____ Drainage ____ SEC ____, T ____, R ____ Page l of ____ tions, the nature of the sites being studied, and the research interests of the archaeologist. Logistical factors include topography, time available, distance from sources of supply, available field transportation, and so forth. Archaeological surveys have been carried out on foot, on horseback, camel, by jeep, boat, plane, helicopter, and by every other known mode of transportation. Whatever transport is most reasonable is utilized. For example, while site surveying on the Nile, Phillip Hobler and James Hester chartered a freight felucca (an Egyptian sailing vessel) and spent 4 days on board, doing all cooking, eating, and sleeping in the space between decks (some

TABLE 4-1
Categories of Information for Site-Survey Forms

General Category	Specific Information
1. Site designation	Number, name, previous designations
2. Site location	Political unit (state, county, city, or town, township)
	Map coordinates (latitude and longitude, Universal Transverse Mercator, township-range)
	Verbal description
3. Previous investigation	Professional, amateur, vandalism
4. Ownership	Present owner, previous owner, tenants
	Attitude toward intensive investigation
5. Environment description	General environment (vegetation and soil zones, drainage system, landforms)
	Specific environment (flora, soil, slope, elevation, hydrology)
	Present land use (cultivation, housing, pasture, etc.)
6. Archaeological description	Artifacts observed and collected
	Dimensions (surface area and depth)
	Structure (surface concentrations and stratification)
	Relation to other sites
7. Cultural classification age estimate	Ethnic affiliation of recent occupants
	Cultural tradition, phase, or period
	Time period
	Function
8. Survey method	Personnel (field workers, record keepers)
	Sponsor (individual, organization, institution)
	Date of visit(s)
	Informants
	Survey conditions
9. References	Artifact catalog
	Photographs
	Field-notebook pages
	Published references
10. Evaluation	Condition of site; recommendation for future intensive investigation
11. Map	Small-scale of area with site location marked
	Large-scale showing specific features of site

3 1/2 feet, vertically) without any built-in facilities. When they first saw the felucca they described its fly-filled interior as a "Black hole of Calcutta." Several days later, however, they had come to consider their "ship" reasonably comfortable.

Owing to distance from a source of supply, the survey may necessarily be limited in ways detrimental to data collection. Ideally, all sites in an area should be recorded, but if this is not possible the archaeologist records as much as possible in the time available. While site surveying in the Egyptian desert, Bahay Issawy and James Hester, with a crew of eight men, wished to record sites in an area near Bir Sheb and Bir Nakhlai, some 150 miles west of Aswan. Accordingly, two pickup trucks were loaded with food for 10 days and water sufficient for three days. Plans were for a 10-day survey; however, water had to be found at Bir Nakhlai in order to make a 10-day stay possible. None of the party had ever been to Bir Nakhlai, and the latest previous expedition to that oasis had been in 1927, at which time a water flow of about 5 gallons per hour had been reported. The water was found, and the party was able to proceed according to plan. Although it was impossible to find every site in the area in the short time available, surveyors located a sample of the sites present. Such a survey in which it is not intended either to locate or record all sites, or even a statistically selected sample, is termed an *archaeological reconnaissance*.

Site survey may also be limited by the research interests of the archaeologist. The researcher is under no commitment to locate *every* site, only those relevant to the problem being investigated. If you are interested in sites with rock art, then those are looked for and recorded. A famous example is the search made by Walter Taylor for a dry cave site in the American Southwest. The expedition's goal was a site with Pueblo Indian remains and a long continuous profile with numerous preserved ecological specimens, especially plant materials. The survey lasted the entirety of one summer, and although many sites were investigated the ideal example was never found—primarily because the best ones had already been excavated. Most surveys are more general in nature, with all sites being recorded. However, it is possible to restrict one's problem orientation. Good examples are surveys for irrigation canals or terraces, rock-art sites, locales of a particular time period, or sites along the periphery of an area which might define an archaeological "boundary." With our present concern for prehistoric cultural inventories and site protection from construction or vandalism, it is the archaeologist's responsibility to record all sites found, even if they do not fit the defined problem.

Surveys are normally conducted before an excavation is initiated; however, it is also possible to resurvey an area, once certain problems have been isolated, for further study. For example, after several seasons of excavation in an area it may be possible to construct a regional chronology. This chronology may reveal that no excavation units pertain to a certain time period or periods, and at that time it would be reasonable to initiate a resurvey in order to locate sites to fill the missing periods.

Once the sites in an area have been surveyed, the survey notes are reviewed in detail; this enables the archaeologist to determine the kinds of sites which occur in the region, the frequency of occurrence, and the size range. By studying the collections we learn which cultural periods are represented and the different kinds of activities that were carried out at each site. At this point the archaeologist is ready to decide which sites should be excavated. A model of how these different survey methods may be used in a regional research design is presented in Figure 4-2.

Site Sampling

So far we have discussed site survey as a means of locating sites and recording surface data in

■ Site survey is a research technique, not just a means of finding sites.

● Site sampling—a technique for learning more from less.

order to identify sites for excavation. ■ Site survey may also be carried out as a research technique in itself wherein the site locations and distribution of surface artifacts will provide the basic data necessary for the study. The reasons for this approach include (1) the frequent occurrence of sites which have no depth and (2) the need to learn as much about sites in an area when neither time nor money is sufficient to excavate every site. ● Both reasons have led to the development of survey techniques designed to

obtain as much information as possible without excavation. Most of these methods depend upon site sampling, proceeding from the premise that since cultural remains are *patterned* in their occurrence (reflecting the nature of patterns of past behavior) it should be possible to record only a portion of the surface remains in a systematic manner, inferring from that sample the entire pattern of past use. Several methods of sampling are used, including simple random sampling (Fig. 4-3), systematic sampling, and stratified sampling. Each has its advantages and limitations.

Simple random sampling, contrary to what one might assume, is not a haphazard, "grab-bag" approach. *Random sampling* means that the units to be collected (normally, 1- to 5-meter squares) are selected in a scientifically random

Fig. 4-2   A regional multistage field research design, demonstrating how the focus of the investigation narrows from stage 1 to stage 4. (Dancey 1981: Fig. 3-8.)

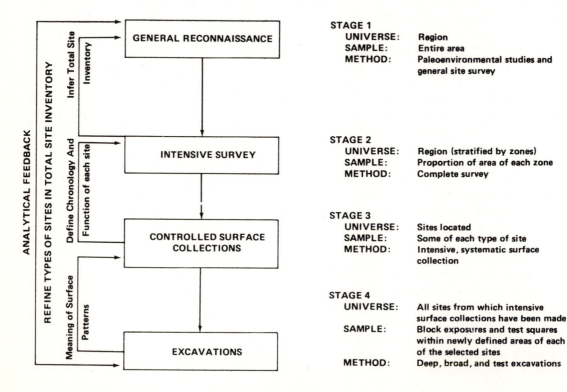

STAGE 1
UNIVERSE: Region
SAMPLE: Entire area
METHOD: Paleoenvironmental studies and general site survey

STAGE 2
UNIVERSE: Region (stratified by zones)
SAMPLE: Proportion of area of each zone
METHOD: Complete survey

STAGE 3
UNIVERSE: Sites located
SAMPLE: Some of each type of site
METHOD: Intensive, systematic surface collection

STAGE 4
UNIVERSE: All sites from which intensive surface collections have been made
SAMPLE: Block exposures and test squares within newly defined areas of each of the selected sites
METHOD: Deep, broad, and test excavations

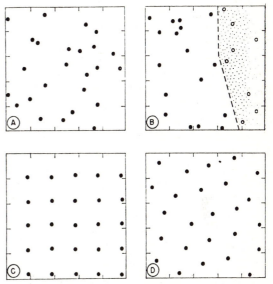

Fig. 4-3 Collecting environmental data by means of a pollen core. (Hester photograph.)

Fig. 4-4 Alternative sampling designs. A: random; B: stratified random; C: systematic; and D: stratified systematic unaligned. (Haggett 1965.)

manner. The site is gridded, and each unit is given a number. In the next step a number of units are selected for collection by referring to a table of random numbers or by some other means of random selection. This selection permits a series of sample units to be collected which are then assumed to be representative of the entire site (Fig. 4-4). Simple random sampling is normally used when the site is believed to be uniform (without internal variation) or simply when little is known about the site. When it is known that a site possesses internal variation then other sampling techniques are used (King 1978: 82).

Systematic sampling is based on the selection of the first unit to be sampled by some random method. After the first unit has been selected, then all subsequent sample units are selected at a specified interval. Such sampling is often, at least in the Western United States, based on section lines. The convenience of this method lies not only in being able to use units of standardized size, but in addition the units to be surveyed are already plotted on United States Geological Survey (U.S.G.S.) maps and thus through the aid of benchmarks (permanently marked section corners) can be easily located on the ground. Where systematic sampling is to be conducted within a single site, then its design may be a function of the size sample desired. For example, if you wish to collect 10 percent of the site surface then you may grid the site and collect every 10th square. Systematic sampling reduces the risk of missing any unique portion of the site, which could happen if simple random sampling were employed. On the other hand,

▲ Site sampling permits statistical comparison.

■ Sites may be located and mapped from the air or underwater.

systematic sampling cannot be employed if the site features a regular pattern of features. In the latter case it would be possible for systematic sampling to miss every example of a regular pattern spaced between the sample units (King 1978: 82).

Stratified sampling (King 1978: 83) is utilized when the desired sample is to be taken from a site or region possessing known internal variation. The key is to first identify the variation within the area to be sampled. The sample units are then subdivided into *sampling strata* which correspond to the differing phenomena to be sampled. For example, on a coal-lease survey in northwestern New Mexico it was decided that a stratified random sample could provide the originating federal agency with the information needed for budgeting the archaeological salvage required before strip-mining the area for coal. The stratified portion of the sampling design was based on known differences in soil type. These soil types had been mapped and therefore formed the basis for the selection of the sample units. The sample units were then selected randomly within each soil zone. The sample units were one square mile in size, and the total units selected made up 9 percent of the land in the area to be mined. The number of units selected could have been either proportional or disproportional. Proportional sampling would require that if 15 percent of the area was made up of soil-type A, then 15 percent of the sample units must be selected from the area containing soil-type A. Disproportional sampling would occur when the sample units were selected either randomly or systematically from the entire universe.

A final technique used in site sampling includes the use of transects (Judge, Ebert, and Hitchcock 1975: 98–100). *Transects* are lines of survey laid out across the landscape to be surveyed. These lines are useful because they permit easy identification of the areas to be surveyed in the field. They further may be utilized with any of the above methods — simple random sampling, systematic sampling, and stratified sampling. Research at Chaco Canyon, New Mexico with a variety of these methods indicated that stratified transects provided the best return for the effort expended.

▲ The techniques of site sampling may be both probabilistic and nonprobabilistic. *Probabilistic sampling* means that a sample is obtained in such a way as to allow prediction about the nature of the larger universe from which the sample was derived. *Nonprobabilistic sampling*, on the other hand, lacks this predictive ability but is also of value, since unique data may be recorded by its use. (The archaeologist should never ignore unique data which lie outside the sample units being surveyed. To do so is to restrict scientific inquiry to mechanical methods — a self-limiting procedure.)

A final concern is that of sample-unit size. The problem here consists of site density or, in the case of an intrasite survey, artifact density. The sample unit must be of sufficient size to reasonably be expected to include an example of the data sought. As an impracticable example, several years ago a federal agency advertised a contract to sample several hundred thousand acres with 10-acre sample units. Since the known site density in that region was about 1 site per square mile, the chances that a site would lie within a specific 10-acre tract were minimal (actually, 1/64). For sample units to be effective they must be of a size appropriate to the site density being sampled.

Remote Sensing

Archaeological survey has often benefited from the use of techniques of *remote sensing*. First developed by the military, remote sensing initially

Fig. 4-5 Roman fortifications revealed by aerial photography at Glen Lochar, Kirkcudbright-shire, Scotland. (Courtesy of J.K.S. St. Joseph and the Committee for Aerial Photography, University of Cambridge.)

included the use of aerial photography in the identification of ground features such as airfields, munitions plants, and so forth (Deuel 1973). ■ Adapted to archaeology, aerial photography permits the identification of surface features and of subsurface ones as well (Fig. 4-5). The latter are visible due to color changes in the soil, vegetational differences due to differing soil conditions, and the presence of groundwater (St. Joseph 1966). Two kinds of photos are used: verticals and obliques. Vertical photographs are used for mapping since they permit exact measurements anywhere on the photographic print. All that is required to make an exact map is to have one feature in the photo be of a known dimension. A common practice in the establishment of ground control is to place an X in white cloth on the ground prior to making the photo-mapping flight. The X, which can vary in size depending on scale, permits the measurement of any other dimension on the photo. The mapping

of archaeological sites through air photography normally requires a scale of less than 1/10,000. Such a scale is large enough to permit prehistoric structures to be identified and mapped. Smaller scales of up to 1/60,000 may be useful in the plotting of regional land-use patterns, which can then be linked with the known archaeological sites in the region (Stone 1960). Aerial reconnaissance is most useful in those regions where vegetation is limited and where prehistoric peoples constructed houses, roads, pyramids, canals, and other major structures which are visible from the air.

Oblique photos are taken at an angle and show major features well, and often minor ones, due to the intensification of relief provided by long shadows. Oblique photos are not useful in mapping, however, since measurements taken from the photo would be in error due to foreshortening. The primary utilization of oblique photos is in site discovery and in the illustration

● Excavation techniques reveal buried cultural information.

▲ A grid layout provides horizontal control.

of sites in reports (St. Joseph 1972: personal communication).

In archaeological work where the area of interest is small (such as an individual site) much use has been made of photos taken from tethered balloons and kites. Photography from above is one of the best ways to quickly record complex features such as a bone bed in a butchering site (Whittlesey 1967, 1970, 1975).

The majority of aerial photo mapping in archaeology has relied on the use of ordinary black-and-white film. Special techniques, such as image enhancement, have also been employed in order to make certain features more readily visible. The technique relies on the use of overlapping stereo pairs of prints which, when viewed through a stereo viewer, permits the objects on the landscape that has been photographed to be seen in relief. The flight lines are flown with an overlap of 40 percent forward and 60 percent to the sides. This compensation is necessary in order for the stereo viewing to be properly used.

Owing to the nature of the electromagnetic spectrum, the visible sector represents only a portion of the potential wavelengths which may be recorded. Infrared and ultraviolet film have also been successfully utilized to record or enhance features not easily visible on black-and-white film. There is also heat-sensing film, which can detect underground reservoirs of heat (some of which are archaeological features). Radar is also useful in remote sensing, especially side-looking airborne radar (SLAR), which is useful in mapping ground features covered by heavy vegetation, such as the Mayan drainage canals recently discovered in the Peten of Guatemala (Adams 1980). The utility of remote

sensing with longer wavelengths, such as those used in radio, is as yet unknown in archaeological reconnaissance.

Another category of remote sensing includes the use of a wide variety of instruments in the recording of subsurface phenomena. A *magnetometer* is often used for identifying magnetic anomalies which, when mapped, can often indicate the position of buried archaeological features. Magnetometers are also used in underwater prospecting for sunken vessels. Another instrument, the *sensitivity detector*, measures subsurface electrical currents. Differences in the current measured often permit the identification and mapping of subsurface archaeological features. There has even been an adaptation of *radar* to the mapping of subsurface features. The principle employed is that the ground-penetrating radar beams pulses into the earth which are reflected off the subsurface features, returning as measurable echoes. A final remote-sensing technique applied underwater is that of *side-scanning sonar*. Again the principle of recording echoes is employed to locate underwater obstructions, some of which are ancient shipwrecks or other cultural features.

In our work at the Mayan site at Copan, Honduras, using black-and-white and infrared airborne photography, we discovered a previously unknown ball court and a possible moat. In addition, we were able to map a major series of residential mounds which are now covered by tropical forest, map a causeway connecting the residential unit with the ceremonial center, and plot the location of former channels of the Copan River.

The future of remote sensing in archaeology seems bright indeed. Efforts, to date, are promising, having yielded much data not visible to the eye and often at much less time and cost than on-the-ground survey. And prospects look even brighter when we consider that remote-sensing technology is still in the early stages of development.

Excavation Techniques

● Archaeological excavation is a complex system of techniques for gathering data which the archaeologist uses to answer specific research questions. These techniques provide information in different ways. For example, chronological information is obtained from deep-stratified test pits or trenches while horizontal identification of data on the surface or within a single level can reveal information about differential-use areas. Naturally, these techniques will be adapted to the different kinds of sites being excavated. We will, of course, discuss some specialized techniques, but first it is appropriate to describe those techniques of almost universal applicability. There are numerous references on excavation techniques (for example, Hester, Heizer, and Graham [1975] and Barker [1977]).

Excavation Layout

The first duty of the archaeologist is to maintain precise control of the data recovered. This is accomplished through the use of horizontal and vertical controls, enabling each specimen to be precisely located as to original position. *Horizontal control* is provided by a grid system which divides the surface of the site into equal-area squares. The grid system is laid out with N-S and E-W lines at equal distances. These grid systems are expressed in either the English or metric system of measurement, although currently there is greater emphasis on the latter system (Milisaukas 1973). Each square, usually 2 meters on a side, is given an identifying number (Fig. 4-6). Site excavation is usually a sampling process, as only rarely are entire sites excavated. ▲ The grid system thus provides a means of indicating where on the site the individual specimens were obtained. On the other hand, the grid system does not limit the excavation, as any combination of squares may be selected for excavation.

A variety of sites are better suited to other types of excavation layout. For example, in the American Southwest any sites for which there are identifiable prehistoric-site divisions (e.g., rooms, plazas, specialized structures, and so on) can be excavated with those structures as the excavation units. In some cases the sites are so simple that a specialized grid system would be superfluous. An example would be a small cave within which the position of any object could be obtained by triangulation from two or more points established on the cave wall.

Fig. 4-6 Excavations in progress at Lamb Springs site, Colorado. The field techniques include use of two meter grids and the leaving of balks to provide vertical control and to show the site stratigraphy. (Grady photograph.)

■ Provenience — the key to excavation techniques.

● Many different excavation techniques may be employed.

▲ Many different tools may be used for excavation.

■ All features and strata exposed are mapped.

■ Once excavation begins it is necessary to define the vertical provenience of each specimen within the site. One means is to set up an arbitrary datum level, either by using a line level on a string or using a surveying instrument, and then plot the exact depth of every object below this arbitrary datum. The preferred system is to define the *natural* levels of deposition within the site and then segregate all specimens from each. Where natural levels cannot be identified, another method consists of establishing a series of arbitrary levels — all of the same thickness (e.g., 6 in., 10 cm, etc.). Provenience of specimens is then indicated by square and level (e.g., square 1 East, level 4, 30 to 40 cm). The exact location of the item within the grid and level may or may not be more precisely identified than this. It is possible to combine these methods, with most specimens being lumped by level and the unique items being exactly located by horizontal and depth measurements. The provenience-measuring systems are not intended to restrict site sampling but only serve as a means of data recording.

While excavation of the entire site is often a desirable goal, this is not often practicable. Limitations of time, personnel, and funds usually allow only a portion of a site to be excavated. Occasionally it is impossible to excavate all of a site because only a part may be owned by parties willing to give their permission. In other cases the site may be too large and complex; for example, excavations have been carried out on an annual basis at Monte Alban, Mexico and Sakkara, Egypt for over 40 years, yet much remains untouched. What is desirable in excavation is the intelligent selection of the best areas of the site for obtaining preserved information.

Site sampling in excavation can best be provided by a series of test pits or test trenches. It is possible to dig test pits on a random basis or systematically (e.g., every fifth square, or some other arbitrary number). A common technique is to put in two test trenches that cross each other at right angles. The resultant wall profiles permit the examination of a cross section of the entire site stratigraphy. Other methods include the dividing of the site into quadrants and completely excavating one quadrant, which is then considered a sample of the whole.

The archaeologist's goal is the recovery of information, which means that the primary objective is not simply the removal of a certain percentage of the dirt in a site. For example, in a site with architecture it is possible to excavate a trench around the interior of the room walls. Such a trench provides exact information on the height, width, composition, and abutments of the walls as well as information about the location and composition of room floors. From this sampling it is possible to work out the *sequence* of room construction. The excavations may remove only 20 percent or so of the entire earth fill present, yet the information recovered may be 50 percent of that potentially available.

The broadside is another frequently utilized method. In this approach a large excavation face is opened and then systematically cut back into a bank or hillside. The method is most appropriate when the area to be excavated is on a slope and rigorous arbitrary levels would be unusable. Another reason for the broadside is when the site is covered with so much overburden that no other excavation method is feasible. Tell Judaidah is an example of this situation (Fig. 4-7).

● In no way should the use of any of these methods be considered restrictive or mutually exclusive. The archaeologist is interested in data recovery, and excavation techniques should be modified whenever it is believed that some

Fig. 4-7 Excavations by means of a step trench at Tell Judaidah. The trench intercepts 70 levels of occupation dating from the 4th millennium B.C. to the 7th century A.D. (Courtesy of the Oriental Institute, University of Chicago.)

other kind of sampling will better provide the information sought. Frequently, test pits will be put in around the site, in addition to the main excavation units, in order to be certain that nothing vital is being overlooked. If some important information is so located, then a more complete excavation of that area will be initiated. Since what is found buried is often not apparent from the surface, it often occurs that excavation of a small unit thought to require only a few days may reveal time-consuming complexities. A common cause of such incidents is the discovery of unexpected burials, which require careful excavation.

Excavation techniques are also governed by the kinds of labor and equipment locally available. ▲ When practicable, it is often possible to use road maintainers, bulldozers, tractors with a backhoe, or other mechanized equipment. The decision to use such equipment is based on availability, cost, and the nature of the site. If large quantities of overburden are present, power equipment is essential. On the other hand, it may be that the site is so delicate that only hand tools may be used, in order to avoid destroying valuable data. For example, while we were working at the Blackwater Draw site there was an excellent opportunity to use power equipment. The site is a commercial gravel pit, and bulldozers and payloaders were available for use at no charge. The site consisted of numerous sand and silt layers, in some cases 12 feet thick, overlying bone beds of ancient killsites. The available machinery provided a remarkable opportunity to cut away the overburden efficiently

and quickly. Surprisingly, the bulldozers were able to cut within two to three inches of a bone bed without causing damage.

Other considerations governing the use or nonuse of power equipment include cost and logistics. If local labor is cheap, it may also be the case that large machinery is nonexistent or very expensive. Some areas are too remote, too rocky, or too marshy for heavy machinery to be transported or used. The decision of the archaeologist, in such instances, is always to use the most practical alternative.

■ In addition to measuring the depth of individual specimens, it is important to map the individual site strata. If the site has been sectioned with cross trenches this consists of simply mapping the exposed trench walls. If the site is being excavated in sections it is frequently necessary to map the walls of each pit separately. The construction of a site cross section is then accomplished in the laboratory, after the dig has been completed, by correlating the cross sections of each pit. Another method consists of the leaving of balks (standing remnants of original site fill) between the excavation units. The balks can then be mapped on profile drawings. The popular press, in articles on archaeology, stresses the exactness and care with which archaeological excavations are carried out. The archaeologist is pictured as an expert who specializes in the extremely careful recovery of delicate specimens. This conceptualization has been somewhat overdone. Although it is true that on occasion it is necessary to excavate with great care, most of the time the major task at hand is to get the ob-

● Laboratory procedures are used to preserve specimens.

▲ Excavation procedures are geared to what is being recovered.

■ Everything in the site is important as a potential source of cultural or environmental data.

structive dirt out in an orderly fashion and record the provenience of the specimens found. The single most important task of the archaeologist is to keep accurate records of everything found.

The preservation of specimens is accomplished in the ground by natural forces prior to removal and by the archaeologist in the laboratory. ● There are two major aspects of archaeological preservation: (1) cleaning the specimen and (2) strengthening the specimen by using preservatives to replace ground-accumulated moisture which had "cemented" together its various fibers or pieces. Mechanical strengthening is also possible through binding with a wrapping of string or coating with plaster of paris. Field treatment is often kept as simple as possible, the primary goal being removal of the delicate specimen so that excavation will not be delayed. Later, in the laboratory, there is time available for careful cleaning and the application of repeated coats of preservative. The processes employed are too complex to describe in detail here. Several of the more routine are: (1) Strengthening charcoal samples for tree-ring dating by soaking in a solution of gasoline and paraffin; the former evaporates, leaving the paraffin as a strengthening agent. (2) Strengthening perishable wood, bark, or other materials by soaking in a solution of fish glue or polyethylene glycol. (3)

Fig. 4-8 Excavations to reveal the details of butchered bone at a bison killsite, the Jones-Miller site, Colorado. Balks are left between excavation units, and planks are laid between the balks to provide a surface to rest upon when excavating. The final cleaning of the excavated units is then accomplished through use of industrial-size vacuum cleaners. (Hester photograph.)

Preservation of bone by impregnation with a thin solution of water and white glue, acetone and alvar, or shellac and alcohol.

In each of the above examples the thinner evaporates after having carried the glue deep into the specimen. It should be noted that preservatives create problems as well as solve them. For example, a specimen which is to be dated by the radiocarbon method must be cleaned of all organic preservatives. A second problem is that the preservatives may also cause the specimen to shrink, thus altering its original form. This can be rectified by measuring the item *prior* to coating or soaking, or at least before it dries, as most size changes occur in the drying process.

▲ Excavation procedures appropriate to the recovery of items consist of whatever methods are feasible and possible at the time. The tools used can range in size from bulldozers to dental picks. As excavation proceeds and a delicate item is located, or is suspected, the archaeologist switches to more careful techniques and more delicate tools. The item may first be cleared off from above with a shovel. If its outline can be determined it is possible to isolate the specimen on a "pedestal" by cutting around it. Excavation can then proceed with a trowel and whisk-broom. If greater care is required, finer tools are employed, including grapefruit knives, ice picks, dental picks, small paintbrushes, and small syringes. The earth is carefully dislodged with the picks and then brushed or blown away. It is usually possible to find one part of the item which is less delicate, or still earth-covered, and the loose earth can be brushed away over this part without injury to the specimen. It is also possible to remove the loose soil with industrial vacuum cleaners (Fig. 4-8). Final exposure of the item for photography can be accomplished by brushing or by washing with water or spraying with air from a syringe. The removal of delicate items is easier if the specimen is removed encased in a block of earth. In the final analysis, what is really important is the documentation of the nature of the find. If a specimen is too delicate to be removed, or if the proper materials are not available for its preservation, it is still possible to uncover the item, photograph or draw it, and take measurements or samples for chemical analyses. Beyond these efforts the specimen may not be recoverable, but at least considerable information has been obtained. In Egypt, for example, when we were excavating burials (some of which, at 14,000 years of age, were the oldest found in that country) the skeletons were embedded in a sand-dune formation cemented by groundwater activity. The result was that the bones were softer than the matrix in which they occurred. Our solution was to remove the skulls in plaster "jackets" and simply measure the lengths of the other bones in the ground, as it was impossible to remove them intact.

Sampling of Environmental Remains

Items of interest to modern archaeologists include not only tools or manufactured objects but all discarded food remains, waste materials discarded in the manufacturing process, and even the soil itself. Chemical analysis of soil provides evidence of the geologic processes in effect since the site was abandoned. ■ We can learn much about the paleoecology (former environment) of the site and the area from included fossils, such as pollen grains, snails, diatoms, and small animal bones. These interests have led to the development of a variety of sampling techniques (Table 4-2). However, no single technique is applicable to all sites, nor is there a single standard-sized soil sample. For example, samples rich in preserved pollen can provide hundreds of pollen grains in a teaspoonful of soil, whereas if no pollen is preserved the size of the sample is immaterial. If we are interested in the recovery of small-mammal bones, a suitable sample, in the richest deposits, consists of perhaps 100 pounds

TABLE 4-2
Types of Ecological Samples

Type of Sample	Comments
Midden	
Column	Small midden material samples taken from a column with specific dimensions.
Miscellaneous	Small midden material samples taken from a pit or trench wall, by real or arbitrary levels.
Large	Huge midden samples, taken to correct for bone bias. Weighing up to 100 pounds each, these may be taken by real or arbitrary levels.
Specimen	
Shell	Taken from real levels only. The purpose is to get whole shells of all species possible for species identification and age-ring dating. At least 15 shells per level are needed.
Bone	Taken from real levels only. The purpose is to get as many specimens as possible for species identification and possible chemical analysis.
Pocket	Taken from each naturally or culturally occurring pocket or lens requiring content identification.
Feature	Wood, stone, etc., fragments from cultural features requiring chemical analyses or special examination.
Soil	
Site	Soil from the site's real levels, taken apart from the midden samples for purposes of the standard soil chemistry tests; includes burial area soils.
Nonsite	From a nonsite pit, to determine the area's natural soil horizons and history. May be chemically examined.
Dating	
Charcoal	For dating by radiocarbon laboratories only; collected where found or desired, if amount needed is present.
Shell	For radiocarbon and oxygen -18/oxygen-16 testing; can be collected by anyone. Collect as many thick bivalve-shell fragments as possible.
Pollen	Collected by a palynologist using an auger or in spot samples taken from pit walls. The specific amount needed varies and care must be taken not to contaminate the sample.
Chemical	Small vials of soil collected at intervals from a continuous vertical profile; 40-gram vials collected at 10-cm vertical intervals are sufficient.

of soil. In less rich deposits up to 1,000 pounds of soil must be washed and sifted in order to produce one identifiable bone. Chemical samples may be of small size, from 5 to 40 grams.

The adequate sampling of a site for materials of the kind described requires that several different series of different-size samples be collected from each level of the site. In addition, close-interval samples may be needed for some of these profiles, while a single bulk sample from each level is sufficient for other needs. Several factors are important in sampling. The samples must be clearly identified as to provenience on a profile drawing, and the samples must also be identified by level and sample number. As nearly as possible, the individual profiles must be correlatable with one another, as it is a waste of time to collect several suites of samples if their chronological relationships to each other cannot be established. One approach to this problem is to collect the largest samples first and then remove the smaller samples from these, a method which provides an exact correlation. Such samples are usually processed in the laboratory, although some separation can be accomplished in the field through the use of wet or dry screening.

For artifacts, sampling is usually somewhat less complex, as the standard method is to dry-screen all debris from a test pit by level (either natural or arbitrary) and bag all recovered artifacts by level. This method is fast and yields a statistically valid sample which provides a quick means of assessing the artifactual changes level by level.

Sampling is thus inherent in practically every kind of archaeology. It is seldom possible to excavate an entire site or even to collect everything from the surface. Therefore, we utilize specific sampling techniques in the site survey, in the excavation of portions of sites, and in the collection of samples for laboratory analysis from the respective levels within the site. These techniques provide scientifically verifiable, methodically correlated information, and they also aid in the identification of site characteristics without the necessity of excavating the entire site.

Laboratory Analysis

Work in the laboratory includes the washing, cleaning, and preserving of specimens, and the labeling of them with site and level numbers so that their specific provenience can always be identified. Artifacts are measured, described, photographed, and drawn, when necessary, for purposes of illustration in reports. Broken artifacts are mended and restored when possible. All the artifacts are then sorted into types. Even broken items, such as potsherds, can be typed, and the frequency of occurrence of each type aids in the description of each level and the changes in the culture at that particular site through time. For the most part, the kinds of laboratory analysis performed by the archaeologist are not elaborate, nor do they require expensive equipment. Laboratory work is time-consuming, however, and therefore much of it is carried out at the home institution rather than in the field. For example, the restoration of a pot requires time for the mended piece to set before the next piece is glued on. There are also other aspects of restoration requiring the exercise of care, which the field situation does not permit. Even standard facilities, such as electricity and running water, may not be available in the field; thus the general rule is that all operations which can be postponed until the archaeologist is back at the home lab are deferred until then. Environmental samples, especially, require laboratory techniques of some complexity. Pollen analysis requires the centrifuging and boiling of the samples in hydrochloric and hydrofluoric acid. Radiocarbon analysis utilizes expensive equipment which must also be exactly calibrated by the frequent processing of radioactively dead samples. The sifting and washing of soil samples

● Laboratory analysis of specimens is the first step in the preparation of the final report.

are routine laboratory tasks but are also time-consuming. It is often possible to collect in one day on the site enough such samples to require a month of laboratory processing.

In recent years increasing archaeological attention has been focused upon the characteristics of the environmental components, the waste flakes, and the evidences of wear on artifact surfaces and edges (Fig. 4-9). One versatile tool used in studying such materials is a low-power (10 to 50X) binocular microscope. In previous years it was thought sufficient to examine artifacts and other items with a 10-power hand lens. Today the microscope has come into widespread use because it provides greater magnification and in turn is a means of measuring the details of artifacts. (Another function of the microscope is photomicroscopy of small objects for illustration in reports.)

Laboratory-analysis techniques can be almost infinitely variable, as any technique developed in the physical sciences may be applicable, (e.g., the thin sectioning of potsherds, use of a sonic

generator for specimen cleaning, and so on). An innovation currently employed in large projects is the use of a computer terminal in the field. All laboratory descriptions for each specimen are "fed" into the computer, which transmits these back to the home institution. There, analysis through use of a computer program is possible. Archaeological laboratory analysis is concerned with the cleaning, labeling, preservation, and study of the objects recovered through excavation. ● Therefore, laboratory analysis includes the first steps in the preparation of the final archaeological report (Fig. 4-10).

Fig. 4-10 A flow chart illustrating laboratory analysis utilizing numerical taxonomy. (Clarke 1969: Fig. 118.)

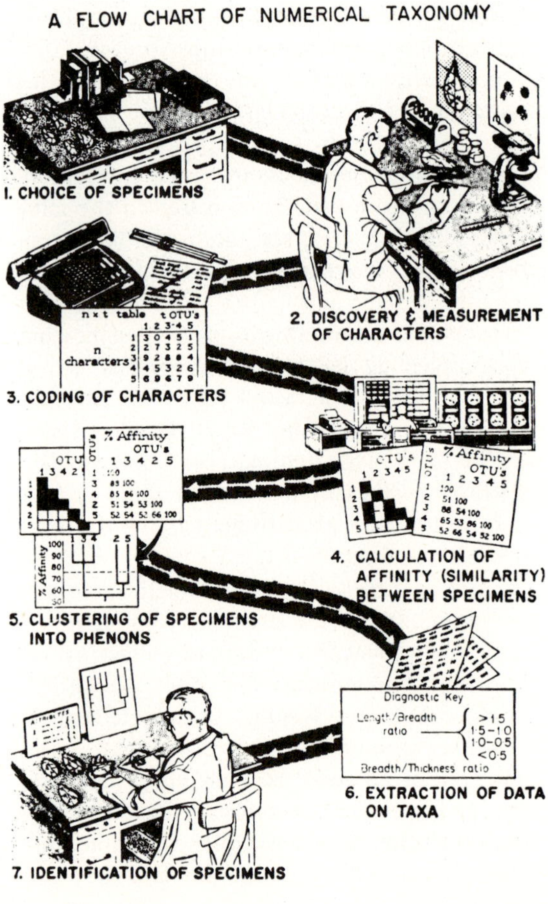

Fig. 4-9 Photomicrograph of the edge of a flaked artifact, illustrating edge battering. (Grady photograph.)

5

Archaeological Concepts and Theoretical Frameworks

Foremost among the concepts utilized in archaeology is the one we term "culture." Briefly, *culture* is "the learned patterns of thought and behavior characteristic of a population or society" (Harris 1971:629). A more inclusive definition is that of Tylor (1871:1): "Culture . . . is that complex whole which includes knowledge, belief, art, morals, law, custom, and any other capabilities and habits acquired by man as a member of society." ■ The archaeologist, in the study of culture (or cultures), seeks to understand the patterns of past behavior. Archaeological methodology permits inferences as to the nature of past cultures through reference to the patterned remains left by those cultures.

The evolution of culture is less constrained by environmental factors than biological evolution, since culture provides a protective buffer between humans and their environment. Clothing, fire, languages, and other cultural innovations all provide means of shielding ourselves from environmental stresses. Therefore, culture frees us to some degree from direct biological selection, in the Darwinian sense, although at the same time it imposes its own selective pressures.

Biological inheritance, being genetically based, is slow to change. By contrast, culture, with its learned patterns of behavior, can be transmitted directly from one individual or group to another without waiting for gene flow to occur. Those cultural practices that are viewed as attractive may be transmitted within an amazingly short period of time. (The use of the frisbee is an amusing example.) The relevance of these observations to archaeology is that there is no genetically or otherwise predetermined sequence of evolution for culture. Cultural evolution does have direction, but it can either exhibit change from simple to complex

STYLISTIC ATTRIBUTES

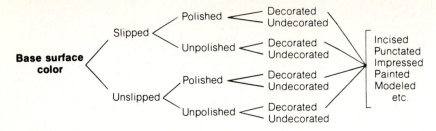

FORM ATTRIBUTES

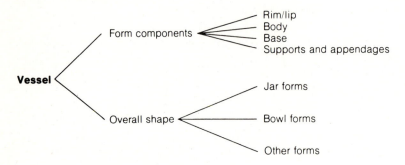

TECHNOLOGICAL ATTRIBUTES

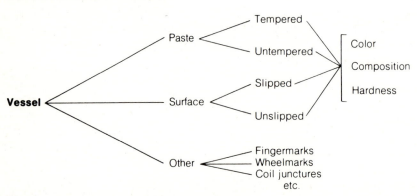

Fig. 5-1 Classification illustrating attributes studied in the analysis of pottery (left). (Sharer and Ashmore 1979: Fig. 8-7.)

(or vice versa) or it can continue for long intervals of time with little alteration. In general, through time culture has become increasingly complex, but this is not true for every area at every period in the past. Cultural traits can also be introduced rapidly from one society to another. (One has only to observe the worldwide distribution of Coca Cola and the transistor radio to understand this phenomenon.) Cultural traits may also be independently "invented" in more than one area. Convergent development can also occur: Differing evolutionary traditions can produce similar end results. In order to categorize these characteristics of culture, archaeologists have developed a series of concepts to explain the processes involved in cultural change.

Archaeological concepts may be viewed as a system of building blocks which may be recombined in various ways. There is nothing immutable about these building blocks, as they are arbitrarily defined and are subject to continuing revision. The concepts which have been devised can be organized into a series of categories. These include descriptive units, cultural units, spatial units, chronological units, and integrative units. We will describe each of these.

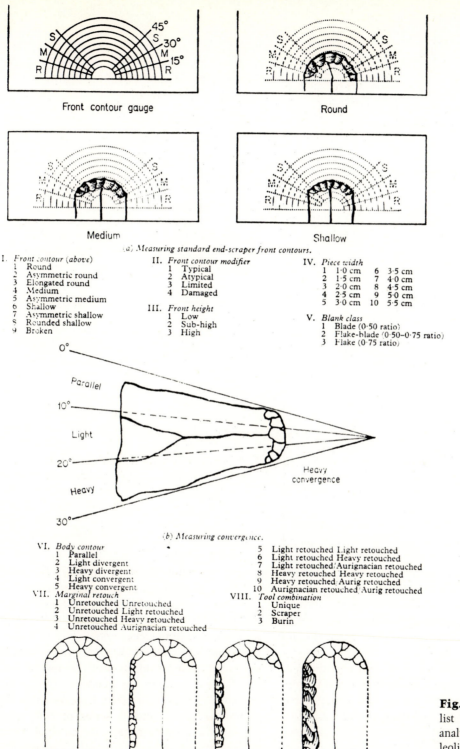

Front contour gauge

Round

Medium

Shallow

(a) Measuring standard end-scraper front contours.

I. *Front contour (above)*
  1 Round
  2 Asymmetric round
  3 Elongated round
  4 Medium
  5 Asymmetric medium
  6 Shallow
  7 Asymmetric shallow
  8 Rounded shallow
  9 Broken

II. *Front contour modifier*
  1 Typical
  2 Atypical
  3 Limited
  4 Damaged

III. *Front height*
  1 Low
  2 Sub-high
  3 High

IV. *Piece width*
  1 1·0 cm   6 3·5 cm
  2 1·5 cm   7 4·0 cm
  3 2·0 cm   8 4·5 cm
  4 2·5 cm   9 5·0 cm
  5 3·0 cm 10 5·5 cm

V. *Blank class*
  1 Blade (0·50 ratio)
  2 Flake-blade (0·50–0·75 ratio)
  3 Flake (0·75 ratio)

(b) Measuring convergence.

VI. *Body contour*
  1 Parallel
  2 Light divergent
  3 Heavy divergent
  4 Light convergent
  5 Heavy convergent

VII. *Marginal retouch*
  1 Unretouched Unretouched
  2 Unretouched Light retouched
  3 Unretouched Heavy retouched
  4 Unretouched Aurignacian retouched

  5 Light retouched Light retouched
  6 Light retouched Heavy retouched
  7 Light retouched/Aurignacian retouched
  8 Heavy retouched Heavy retouched
  9 Heavy retouched Aurig retouched
 10 Aurignacian retouched Aurig retouched

VIII. *Tool combination*
  1 Unique
  2 Scraper
  3 Burin

Unretouched   Light   Heavy   Aurignacian

(c) Marginal retouch.

Fig. 5-2 Attribute list utilized for the analysis of Upper Paleolithic blade end scrapers (opposite).

● Cultural units are descriptions of past societies.

▲ Cultures inhabit space; therefore a system is needed to describe units of space.

Descriptive Units

ATTRIBUTES

Those elements which form consistent features characteristic of an artifact are termed *attributes.* Any identifiable element can be considered an attribute (e.g., painted-line width in pottery [Fig. 5-1] or the presence of retouch on a blade [Fig. 5-2]). The attribute is the smallest or most detailed cultural element which can be described archaeologically; and its notation, description, and statistical frequency afford the component elements of the next larger cultural concept, the artifact type.

ARTIFACT TYPE

An *artifact type* is defined as "a particular kind of artifact (for example, arrow-point, house floor, metate, scraper, bone awl, and so on) in which several attributes combine or cluster with sufficient frequency or in such distinctive ways that the archaeologist can define and label the artifact and can recognize it when he sees another example" (Hole and Heizer 1967:167). In addition, it is usually assumed that the types existed as concepts in the minds of their prehistoric makers. The archaeologist, in the study and definition of types, is thus reconstructing certain prehistoric cultural patterns. This is the concept termed the "mental template" by Deetz (1967:45).

There is another point of view, namely that types are "artifacts" of the archaeologist, the result of arbitrary decisions by the latter which form useful descriptive categories for analysis but which are not true evidence of past cultural patterns. These two viewpoints depict the archaeologist as either "discovering" prehistoric artifactual types or "inventing" types to suit specific purposes of analysis. Both points of view have merit.

ARTIFACT CLASSES

Artifacts may further be grouped into larger categories based on general similarities in form or function. These *classes* include examples such as scrapers (a functional category) and bifaces (a category based on form and flaking patterns). Grouping by classes is useful to the archaeologist in several ways. In the preliminary sorting of artifacts it is easier and quicker to first sort the implements into classes from which specific artifact types may then be isolated. Another major use is in the descriptive report where the types are grouped by artifact class. The result is a standardization of style which facilitates the comparison of archaeological reports with one another.

TYPOLOGY

A *typology* constitutes all the recognized and described types of artifacts characteristic of a particular archaeological culture, or "industry." The typology is a classification which seeks to objectively unite all artifacts from a particular site or level into meaningful categories on the basis of form.

TECHNOLOGY

An opposing system to typology is the description of the prehistoric technology. In the *technology* it is the manufacturing processes and their sequence that are emphasized. Technology includes the selection and preparation of stone for future use (for example, the removal of trimming flakes from cores, the removal of primary flakes from cores, and the later modification of the flakes into tools). A detailed study of these preparation steps, extending through final retouch, edge grinding, and so on, provides a history of the manufacture of the finished specimen.

Cultural Units

● *Cultural units* are those descriptive categories which are designed to be synonymous with prehistoric cultural entities. Actually, owing to the inadequate preservation of archaeological data, it is impossible for such units to occur in their entirety, since any prehistoric culture will have possessed numerous nonmaterial items which are *not* preserved. When we speak of an "archaeological culture" we are normally referring to those items which have been *preserved* and *recorded* through the use of archaeological methods. We shall now describe some commonly defined cultural units.

ASSEMBLAGE

The *assemblage* is that grouping of artifacts normally occurring in a single site or cultural level. By definition, an assemblage is too insufficient a sample to be representative of a *total* prehistoric culture. It is assumed that evidence of a prehistoric culture must be identified in more than one location or level for it to be proven to possess distinctive characteristics due to *cultural factors* rather than to chance. The assemblage is thus a group of implements utilized by a prehistoric culture at a *particular time and place*, but which may not necessarily be representative of the total material culture of that particular prehistoric people.

INDUSTRY

The *industry* is that cluster of artifact *types* which are believed to represent the remains of a true prehistoric society. The usual case is that similar assemblages have been located on several sites. These assemblages can be assigned to one larger overall grouping, the industry, which, due to its repetitive occurrence, is indicative of a past pattern practiced by a specific group of people.

The above definitions of descriptive cultural units have been based solely upon content of these units. However, some archaeologically defined concepts are based on spatial or temporal considerations, and we will discuss these next.

Spatial Units

Since the total amount of space in the units defined below is variable, the amount of space which equals any unit is arbitrarily defined. It is also true that the space requirements of any particular prehistoric culture varied with its economy, population, and other factors. ▲ If spatial units are arbitrarily defined by archaeologists, then how do we reach agreement? One set of definitions that is widely used is those proposed by Willey and Phillips in their 1958 text *Method and Theory in American Archaeology*:

> A *site* is the smallest unit of space dealt with by the archaeologist. . . . About the only requirement ordinarily demanded of the site is that it be fairly continuously covered by remains of former occupation, and the general idea is that these pertain to a single unit of settlement, which may be anything from a small camp to a large city. [1958:18]
>
> A *locality* is a slightly larger spatial unit, varying in size from a single site to a district of uncertain dimensions; it is generally not larger than the space that might be occupied by a single community or local group. [1958:18]
>
> A *region* is a considerably larger unit of geographical space usually determined by the vagaries of archaeological history. Quite often it is simply the result of concentrated research by an individual or group. Rightly or wrongly, such a region comes to be thought of as having problems of its own that set it apart from other regions. [1958:19]
>
> An *area* is a geographical unit very considerably larger than a region; it corresponds roughly to the culture area of the ethnographer. . . . They tend to coincide with major physiographic divisions. . . . [1958:20]

The use of spatial units is properly a convenience for the archaeologist in analytic studies. While the regions and areas may have constrained prehistoric societies in certain ways,

> ■ Culture is a continuum, but it is arbitrarily divided into temporal segments.
>
> ● Cultural units are characteristic of a specific time and place.
>
> ▲ Horizon: cultural traits that are widespread and occur within a brief time span.
>
> ■ A tradition: the persistence of cultural traits through time.

primitive peoples often overcame these environmental limitations through technological innovations.

Temporal Units

The archaeologist is acutely aware of time both in its immensity and in its passage. Time is a continuum which must be subdivided, for practical reasons, into uniform and meaningful units. ■ For example, our culture's concept of a century consists of a definite temporal unit, the extent of which is arbitrarily defined. The Maya relied upon time units of 20 years each, and the Aztec upon a 52-year cycle.

In archaeology the length of time assigned to each chronological unit is variable; it may vary from sequence to sequence and within a single sequence. The reason for this is that the criterion used to separate one cultural period from another is change in the form of artifact types. When a sufficient change in form of diagnostic artifacts has occurred, we designate a new cultural period. This is the basic unit of archaeological chronology termed the *phase*. We emphasize the importance of the phase since its dimensions include not only time but space and cultural content. The chronological utility of the phase and other units of cultural content is their arrangeability into a sequence. Willey and Phillips distinguish the following types of these sequences (1958: 24–25): "The *local sequence* in its purest form is a series of components found in vertical stratigraphic succession in a single site. . . . The local sequence may, therefore, be defined as a *chronological series of components, phases, or subphases, within the geographical limits of a locality. . . .*" Willey and Phillips define the *regional sequence* as "*a chronological series of phases or subphases within the geographical limits of a region. . . .*"

Integrative Units

The integrative nature of culture is such that its form and pattern are expressed in every cultural manifestation, from the attribute (the smallest unit) to the entire culture area (the largest unit). These aspects change through time in their form and in the space they occupy. We thus must view culture not only in its temporal and spatial dimensions but also in terms of continuity versus change, contact versus isolation, and independent invention versus diffusion. These multivariate aspects require that the archaeologist, in order to fully understand the development of culture through time, devise conceptual units that accurately reflect these configurations. These conceptual units are called *integrative units.*

● The basic integrative unit is the *phase*, the smallest whole cultural component with which we can deal. Willey and Phillips (1958:22) define *phase* as "an archaeological unit possessing traits sufficiently characteristic to distinguish it from all other units similarly conceived, whether of the same or other cultures or civilizations, spatially limited to the order of magnitude of a locality or region and chronologically limited to a relatively brief interval of time."

The phase has three basic dimensions: It has (1) a specific cultural content, (2) temporal dimension, and (3) spatial dimensions (Fig. 5-3). You have undoubtedly noticed that we have set no precise limits on any of these dimensions; there is no specific amount of culture, time, or space mentioned in the definition. This is the

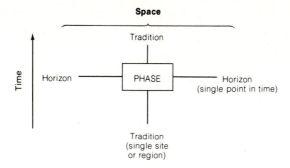

Fig. 5-3 Diagram illustrating the integration of time and space through the concepts of tradition, horizon, and phase. (Sharer and Ashmore 1979: Fig. 13-7.)

value of the phase concept: It is the most flexible, and hence the most useful, basic integrative unit devised to date.

Horizon

The *horizon* is a concept which is limited to a cluster of culture traits or to some other portion of an entire culture. "The horizon, then, may be defined as a primarily spatial continuity represented by cultural traits and assemblages whose nature and mode of occurrence permit the assumption of a broad and rapid spread" (Willey and Phillips 1958:33). While horizon markers and index fossils *may* be the same, typically, the index fossil is a single artifact type of known age; the horizon *style*, on the other hand, tends to be a *complex of traits* occurring together. An example is the complex of feline traits represented in pottery, stone sculpture, metalwork, and other media that is known as the Chavin horizontal style. We will describe the Chavin style in more detail later. ▲ Horizons may not be precisely dated, but due to their broad geographical spread over a brief time span, they can be utilized for chronological correlation.

Tradition

■ As archaeologically defined, a *tradition* is a cultural trait or pattern which persists through time. Traditions may be manifest in every aspect of culture, from the individual attribute to an entire societal way of life. Traditions vary in complexity, in their rate of change, and in the direction in which they change. A group of archaeologists studying the nature of traditions arrived at the following set of definitions (Haury et al. 1955: 43–44):

A Direct Tradition is characterized by an essentially unchanging continuity. . . .

A Converging Tradition describes the segment in which two or more traditions come together. Convergence may result in a merger of the traditions into a single tradition. Sometimes one of the traditions is absorbed. On the other hand, convergence may mean that the traditions impinge on one another for a time, without the submergence of either. . . .

A Diverging Tradition is in many respects the opposite of a Converging Tradition and refers to the segment in which a single tradition splits into two or more distinguishable traditions. . . .

An Elaborating Tradition is characterized by an increasing complexity resulting from the addition

● Culture area: an area within which a common cultural pattern exists.

Tradition is characterized by an increasing simplification through loss of traits and perhaps in time of a less complex organization. . . . (Fig. 5-4)

of traits or attributes which are integrated in a single line of development. Not only quantity and variety of traits are involved, but also their organization and embellishment. . . .

A Reducing Tradition is in some ways the opposite of an Elaborating Tradition. The Reducing

Culture Area

The concept of culture area is borrowed wholeheartedly from cultural anthropology. ● In its simplest form, the *culture area* consists of a

Fig. 5-4 Diagrams illustrating different forms of archaeological tradition segments. (Haury et al. 1955: Fig. 1.)

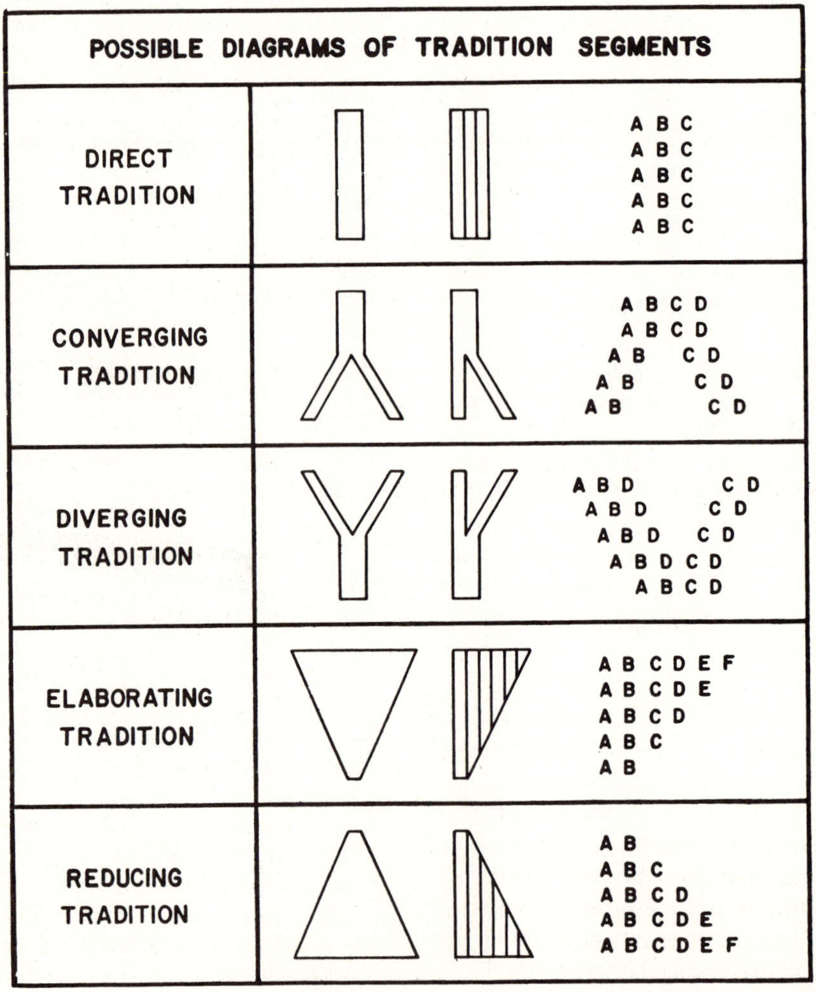

POSSIBLE DIAGRAMS OF TRADITION SEGMENTS		
DIRECT TRADITION		A B C A B C A B C A B C A B C
CONVERGING TRADITION		A B C D A B C D A B C D A B C D A B C D
DIVERGING TRADITION		A B D C D A B D C D A B D C D A B D C D A B C D
ELABORATING TRADITION		A B C D E F A B C D E A B C D A B C A B
REDUCING TRADITION		A B A B C A B C D A B C D E A B C D E F

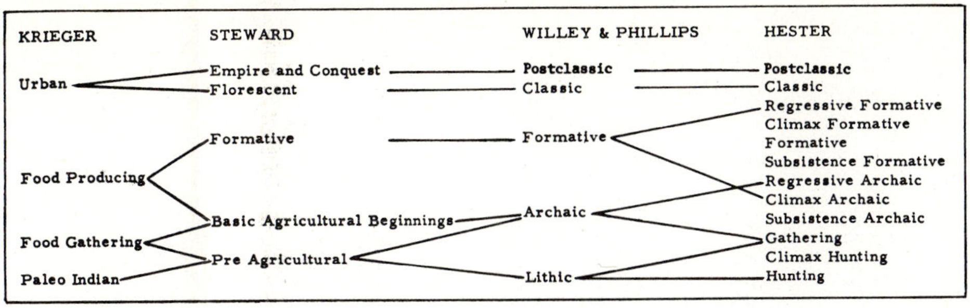

Fig. 5-5 Comparison of New World stage classifications by different authors. (Hester 1962: Fig. 4.)

Fig. 5-6 Development stages as outlined by Willey and Phillips, showing the technological, social, and ideological attributes they define for each stage. (Sharer and Ashmore 1979: Fig. 13-7.)

DEVELOPMENTAL STAGES (Time ↑)	ATTRIBUTES: *Technological*	*Social*	*Ideological*
Postclassic:	Metallurgy	Complex urbanism; militarism	Secularization of society
Classic:	Craft specialization Beginnings of metallurgy	Large ceremonial centers; beginnings of urbanism	Developed theocracies
Formative:	Pottery, weaving, developed food production	Permanent villages and towns; first ceremonial centers	Beginnings of priest class (theocracy)
Archaic:	Diversified tools; groundstone utensils beginnings of food production	Beginnings of permanent villages	?
Lithic:	Chipped stone tools	Nonsettled hunters and gatherers	?

major physiographic province (the area as defined by Willey and Phillips) which has had developed within it a series of similar cultural manifestations due to similar economies and historical factors. An ethnographic example would be the area inhabited by the North American Plains Indians. The great utility of the culture-area concept is that it provides a framework well suited for the organization of data for teaching purposes.

▲ Stages are levels of cultural development.

■ Cultural climax: a period of cultural intensity.

● Diffusion is the transmission of cultural traits.

▲ Archaeologists order their data in time and space and seek to explain cultural processes that were in effect in the past.

■ Archaeology is not just the finding of interesting objects.

Cultural Stage

The stage concept is more widespread and all encompassing than that of culture area. Stages are defined in developmental terms, and they are not tied to any specific environment or time period. ▲ What is important here is the *level* of cultural development or attainment. Stages are high-level abstractions, and they may be applied to cultures with different technologies or other major cultural differences. Alex Krieger (1953: 247) defines *stage* as "a segment of a historical sequence in a given area, characterized by a dominating pattern of economic existence."

Stages are useful for broad-level synthesis. To illustrate their scope, it can be pointed out that Willey and Phillips have ordered all New World archaeological cultures into five stages. (These will be described in detail in a later chapter [Figs. 5-5, 5-6]).

Culture Climax

The *climax* [italics added] may be defined as the *type or types of maximum intensity and individuality of an archaeological horizon or tradition.* This is necessarily a value judgement, but only in relation to the horizon or tradition involved. ■ In whole cultural terms the climax becomes *the phase or phases of maximum intensity and individ-*

uality of a culture or civilization. [Willey and Phillips 1958:39]

The concept of *climax* is useful in understanding the developments within a single cultural tradition. However, comparison of the climax in one tradition with the climax in another tradition may be nonproductive, as different causal factors may have been in effect.

Cultural Origination and Transmission

Cultures are seldom transmitted from one area to another as entire units. ● More frequently, single traits or trait complexes are the items conveyed. The standard term for this transmission is *diffusion*. The traits transmitted, if they do not threaten existing cultural patterns too seriously, will either be adopted intact or modified to fit existing cultural patterns. In some cases actual traits or objects may be transmitted, whereas in others the *idea* of how these are to be manufactured and used may be conveyed. The latter procedure is termed *stimulus diffusion*. The presence in an archaeological site of a trait identified as having been introduced from another culture is termed *trait intrusion*. The alternative, of course, to introductions is the "independent invention" of traits by the indigenous culture.

Occasionally, whole peoples and their cultures move from one location to another, and this phenomenon is called *migration*. Migrations are difficult to establish on the basis of archaeological data because most of the evidence consists of traits which *could be* the result of diffusion. Occasionally, however, it is possible to identify an entire site representative of a culture foreign to the area in which it is located — an enclave identical in culture content to a culture located elsewhere. This situation, when identified archaeologically, is evidence of migration and is termed *site-unit intrusion*.

Archaeological Concepts: A Summary

Archaeological concepts have been developed as a means of describing and understanding cultural manifestations and of ordering them historically. ▲ The study of archaeology may be divided into three major subdivisions: (1) observation—the collection of data in the field; (2) description—the outlining of formal characteristics of the data, and its ordering in time and space (termed "culture-historical integration" by Willey and Phillips); and (3) explanation—the drawing of inferences which seek to explain the cultural processes that have been in effect (processual interpretation).

Archaeology has not been hesitant to adopt concepts developed in other disciplines (e.g., the stratigraphic concepts first pioneered in geology). And moreover, new concepts, such as the *phase*, have been developed by archaeologists to meet their specific needs. For most of its theoretical framework archaeology can operate easily within the conceptual structure provided by cultural anthropology. However, in those aspects requiring the description and correlation of objects, archaeology has had to forge its own methods and theories. In one other aspect—chronology—archaeology has had to be innovative. In the absence of written records keyed to a calendar, archaeological data have had to be examined in terms of their constituent elements and these then related to cultural change through time. The result provides us not only with dates for past events but also with information about the rate and causal factors involved in culture change. Thus we perceive archaeology as not only a means for verifying cultural inferences and theoretical constructs derived from cultural anthropology, but also as a discipline originating new data and concepts in its own right. Archaeology is capable of providing a record of unique cultural events of the past, as well as providing its own explanation of the processes involved in these developments. The concepts defined in

this chapter may thus be viewed as having been developed to categorize the various aspects of archaeology—its distribution in time and space, its unique cultural content, its sequential development, its transmission, and the processes of cultural change involved in all the foregoing. These concepts form the basis of archaeological *description*. The theoretical orientations basic to the *explanations* of cultural events and processes will be examined in the section which follows.

Theoretical Frameworks

■ Modern archaeology is no longer primarily concerned with the discovery of sites and objects. In contrast to the lingering public conception of archaeology as a thinly disguised treasure hunt, modern archaeologists are dedicated to placing their finds into theoretical frameworks in order to explain how past societies came to behave as they did. No longer do the burning questions concern what ancient peoples looked like but instead *how* and *why* they lived as they did. Prior to 1960 archaeologists were interested primarily in documenting the history of culture and the nature of its manifestations within specific time and space frameworks. This was the orientation that led to the formulations of the culture-descriptive units just discussed; and these units—cultural, spatial, temporal, and integrative—all form concepts utilized in the scientific paradigm, or model, which we call the "cultural-historical approach." (A paradigm is simply a body of scientific thought which is self-reinforcing and which all of its scientific practitioners accept without serious question.)

Over the past two decades archaeology has experienced new methods and objectives. New interests in Old World archaeology have been for the most part topical rather than theoretical; as a result, Old World archaeologists have been concerned with the technological analysis of stone tools, wear-pattern studies, human paleontology, environmental studies, ancient land-

- The cultural-historical method—the inductive approach.

▲ Cultural items are the product of shared cultural beliefs.

■ At best, the cultural-historical method is primarily descriptive.

- The cultural-processual method is a deductive approach.

scapes, and also with the great ancient civilizations of the Mediterranean world. We thus find that the twentieth century has been a time of innovation in archaeological theories and methods, many of which have originated in American archaeology. Since the earliest of these theories developed was the cultural-historical approach, we shall begin there.

The Cultural-Historical Method

- *Cultural-historical reconstruction* embodies an inductive research methodology plus a normative view of culture. The use of the inductive method grew out of American cultural anthropology as influenced by Franz Boas. Boas and his students, reacting to the unilinear cultural evolutionary school initiated by Tylor and Morgan, established that the available evidence was insufficient proof that all human societies went lockstep fashion through the various stages from savagery to civilization. These researchers in fact claimed evidence to the effect that some societies did not fit such a model. In their reaction they applied the inductive method of the natural sciences to archaeology, wherein descriptive data are gathered first and then the models of cultural change and continuity are developed from a chronological and spatial ordering of these data.

The final step in the cultural-historical approach, that of interpretation, relies on the use of analogies drawn from ethnology and history.

These analogies may be either specific, where the prehistoric event is essentially identical to an ethnographic or historic example, or general, where the similarities may not imply a direct historical connection but may be due to a similar general level of adaptation. (An example of a specific analogy would be the finding of ancient kiva mural paintings portraying gods which can be identified today by living Pueblo Indians.) The final goal in cultural-historical interpretation is a chronicle of past events expressed in terms of general patterns of cultural change and continuity.

▲ The *normative view of culture*, which is also a major tenet of the method, holds that *cultural items are the product of shared cultural beliefs and norms*. The maker of a tool or an artifact had these norms in mind during the manufacturing process. Therefore, the archaeologist is free to utilize all data as *examples* of cultural patterns, attempting to describe these data in terms of typical patterns which then become the basis of the described cultural units. The resultant descriptions are then *considered* to be *reconstructions* of the past behavioral patterns.

The inductive approach was the new scientific paradigm in the first half of the twentieth century. The inductive approach featured a rigorous search for data, and an equally rigorous system of comparison of cultural data, seeking to justify the organizational framework for the data that was developed. The inductive approach replaced the earlier unilinear evolutionary scheme which sought to fit the data to a *predetermined* set of cultural stages. Once initiated as a methodology, this approach was utilized by two generations of American archaeologists in their attempts to categorize all New World cultural manifestations. The long-term result was a network of time-space units which encompassed the entire history of the New World. Fig. 5-7 presents an example of such a framework from one culture area, the American Southwest. By the middle of the twentieth century the rigorous inductive approach had led to the development of cultural sequences for every region in the New World and the time was ripe for the rise and acceptance of a new paradigm.

Criticisms of the Cultural-Historical Method

■ An inherent difficulty of the cultural-historical approach is that cultural forms may be similar but may have differing historical causes. The major reason is that cultural change may come about in several ways, either as similar cultures evolving in similar ways (parallel evolution) retaining their similarity, or different cultures may come to be similar through convergence — they independently adapt in the same way, or they may become similar through diffusion. Such change as a result of *diffusion* is often impossible to separate from internal change, at least in the comparison of individual artifacts. This deficiency of the method requires exhaustive research into cultural antecedents in order to be sure that the proper cause is identified, and frequently such evidence has not been preserved.

Another controversy has been the debate over whether artifact types are actually discovered or whether they are "imposed" by the archaeologist. This argument is somewhat circular, since either view can be substantiated; and most artifact distributions in fact form a continuum in which one artifact type is gradational to another. The same is true of the division of the cultural continuum at a site into phases, since the boundaries between phases represent a somewhat arbitrary subdivision. Thus we perceive that the cultural-historical reconstruction is not a mirror image of a past culture but in fact an arbitrarily organized and sequenced interpretation of one developed by the archaeologist.

A final criticism concerns the inductive nature of the cultural-historical method. Critics state that if one cannot ask questions *prior* to collecting the data, then the method is nonscientific because all subsequent questions are biased by the data collected. The same critics argue for a *deductive* approach, in which the scientific questions are posed first and then the data are collected to test the hypotheses posed. This shift in intellectual orientation has led to the formulation of a new paradigm, the cultural-processual method, to be discussed next.

The Cultural-Processual Method

It is fair to state that the cultural-processual approach probably could not have been developed until after cultural historians had ordered cultures in time and space. The reason for this is that the cultural-processual approach is concerned with the causes of cultural processes, that is, with why cultures change as they do. This concern had to await the time-space ordering, since only by application of that method was it possible to determine how cultures had changed through time. Studies of the processes involved in change had to be postponed until it had been determined what was the cultures' subsequent form. For example, it could not simply be assumed that the more complex societies were later and that all simpler societies were earlier. Only through use of the cultural-historical method, with its step-by-step approach, was it possible to document the long and involved development of cultures through time and demonstrate which cultural traits antedated others.

● The *cultural-processual method* is a simple one based on a deductive-research methodology. The first step in the research is the formulation of hypotheses, or tentative explanations, to be tested. Such hypotheses are based on a model of the past cultural change as it was *believed* to have occurred. The next step is to outline the kinds of archaeological data that will support or refute each of the specific working hypotheses. In a sense the hypotheses developed compete with each other, since an attempt is made to provide all possible explanations and it is not assumed that all hypotheses being tested will be

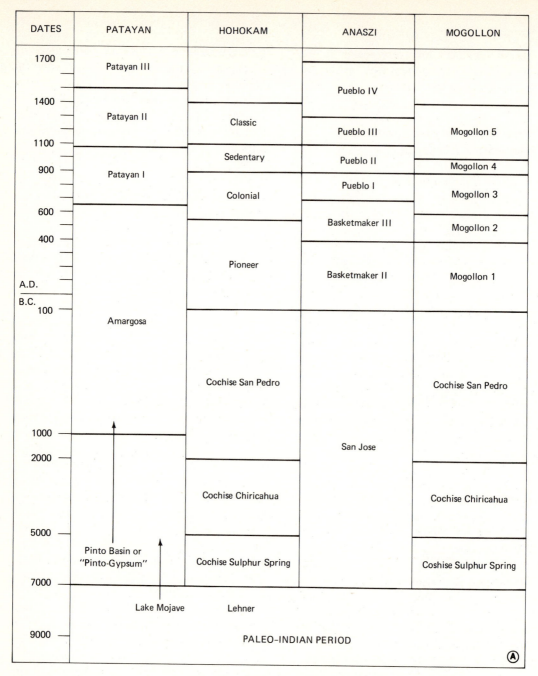

Fig. 5-7 The organization of culture history into a time-space framework. (*a*) Culture chronology of the various regions of the American Southwest. (*b*) Map illustrating the geographic extent of those regions. (Willey 1961: Figs. 4-6 and 4-1.)

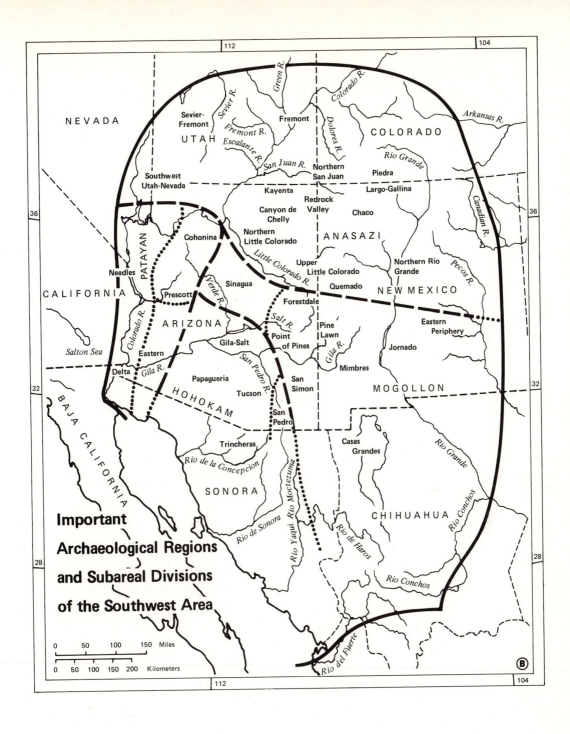

Important
Archaeological Regions
and Subareal Divisions
of the Southwest Area

NEVADA

UTAH

COLORADO

CALIFORNIA

ARIZONA

NEW MEXICO

BAJA CALIFORNIA

SONORA

CHIHUAHUA

PATAYAN

ANASAZI

MOGOLLON

HOHOKAM

Sevier-Fremont

Fremont

Southwest Utah-Nevada

Cohonina

Needles

Prescott

Eastern

Delta

Papagueria

Tucson

Trincheras

Northern San Juan

Kayenta

Canyon de Chelly

Northern Little Colorado

Sinagua

Gila-Salt

Point of Pines

San Simon

San Pedro

Piedra

Largo-Gallina

Chaco

Redrock Valley

Upper Little Colorado

Quemado

Northern Rio Grande

Forestdale

Pine Lawn

Mimbres

Jornado

Eastern Periphery

Casas Grandes

Green R.

Sevier R.

Fremont R.

Escalante R.

San Juan R.

Dolores R.

Colorado R.

Arkansas R.

Rio Grande

Canadian R.

Pecos R.

Little Colorado R.

Verde R.

Colorado R.

Salton Sea

Gila R.

Salt R.

Gila R.

San Pedro R.

Rio de la Concepcion

Rio de Sonora

Rio Yaqui

Rio Moctezuma

Rio de Haros

Rio Conchos

Rio Grande

Rio Conchos

Rio del Fuerte

0   50   100   150 Miles

0   50   100   150   200 Kilometers

Ⓑ

▲ The cultural-processual method seeks scientific proof.

■ The method seeks explanations as to how the culture came to be as it was.

supported. Those hypotheses that are supported are then tested again and made more specific by reference to the data in order to identify those factors that were causal in the initiation of cultural change. In this method *synthesis* refers to the testing of the hypotheses, while *interpretation* consists of the phase of hypothesis refinement (Sharer and Ashmore: 1979). The reason for this is that the goal of the method is not, as in the case of the cultural-historical method, the definition or description of cultural data but the delineation of the cultural processes that were involved in the past.

It is also basic to this method that the hypotheses be based on like phenomena. This requirement has led to the development of three categories of hypotheses: those based on relationships between artifacts and ancient behavior, those based on relationships between features and sites and past behavior, and finally, those based on relationships among all factors—sites, artifacts, features, and past behavioral patterns. Testing of the hypotheses is based on the degree of fit between what has been predicted and the data examined. ▲ The more closely the data fit the prediction of the hypothesis, the more confidence we have in that explanation. Other criteria utilized in the selection of the most probable of competing hypotheses include:

1. The least complicated explanation (i.e., the one requiring the least complex set of circumstances) is favored.
2. The most comprehensive explanation of the data is favored.
3. The most unified and internally self-reinforcing explanation is favored.

We have referred earlier to the fact that the hypotheses developed to be tested are based on a working model of the past culture. Whereas there are a number of models which could be used as part of the method, several have been most commonly utilized. These include a *systems model*, an *ecological model*, and the *multilinear evolutionary model*. ■ These do not have to be mutually exclusive; whatever the model, it is based on how the culture functions today or has functioned in the recent past.

A summary of how the approach differs from culture history is presented in Figure 5-8. Whereas the cultural-processual approach has been termed the "new archaeology," it is in fact nothing more than a new *scientific paradigm*—*"an overall strategy with its own unique research methods, theory, and goals"* (Sharer and Ashmore 1979:532–533). (The appearance of a new paradigm or model within a scientific discipline does not invalidate the old, but simply provides a different methodology which leads to alternative explanations of reality.) Neither does the "new archaeology" necessarily provide a better understanding of the past than the cultural-historical approach. The distinction, then, is not between right and wrong or between good and better, but instead simply represents a change in emphasis. Meltzer (1979) goes even further, stating that the "new" is simply an expansion in methodology.

Criticisms of the Cultural-Processual Method

As stated earlier, part of the cultural-processual method incorporates the testing, or fitting, of the data to general cultural laws. Some archaeologists have failed in their attempts to use this approach, owing to the difficulties associated with the following:

1. The definition of general laws (i.e., sufficiently specific but with wide enough applicability to be useful).
2. Demonstration that all behavior can in fact be predicted on the basis of general laws.

Whereas cultural-processual archaeology embodies an approach, not all archaeologists utilize it in its entirety, but tend instead to choose those research methods in which they have confidence or which offer the best resolution to the particular problem they are researching.

A second criticism of the method concerns its reliance on statistical manipulations of the data (by factor analysis, for example). Critics cite instances in which, after the statistical analysis has "proven" something to be the case, common sense dictates another explanation. In one such example, a study attempted to identify factors influencing site location. Based on factor analysis, the interpretation was that none of the nine factors identified and tested were causal and that not even in various combinations could they be demonstrated to have been more influential

Fig. 5-8 Diagram illustrating how the inductive and deductive research strategies in archaeology are utilized to reconstruct culture history and culture process. (Sharer and Ashmore 1979: 532–34.)

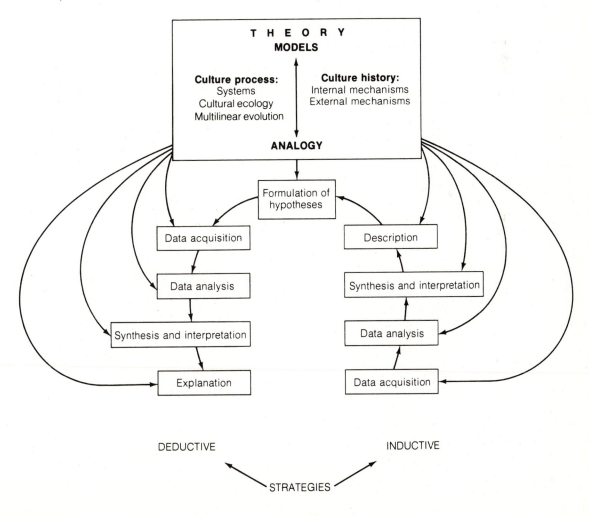

● Settlement patterns provide a way to study ancient societies.

▲ Ecology — human-environmental relationships.

■ Does the environment permit or cause cultural change?

than chance. On the other hand, the sites were selective in their occurrence, being situated on ridges with excellent views. Common sense suggests that there were selective choices made by the ancient people, even though factor analysis failed to demonstrate this. In another case, excavation pits were situated on sites on the basis of reference to a table of random numbers. In theory such locations should provide an adequate sample of the prehistoric manifestations, permitting a "scientific sample" of data and changes through time. In fact, the pits failed to locate the prehistoric structures, which were also present and invisible on the surface but infrequent.

A final criticism concerns the problem of the investigator's own cultural bias; how can we frame culture-free hypotheses with respect to another culture when we are the product of our own culture's inherent biases?

Settlement Archaeology and Spatial Analysis

● Among the other approaches to archaeological data, interest in settlement patterns is a comparatively recent phenomenon. The publication in 1953 of Gordon R. Willey's *Prehistoric Settlement Patterns in the Viru Valley, Peru*, provided the first explicit statement dealing with the study of settlement patterns, which Willey (1953:1) defined as follows:

The term "settlement pattern" is defined here as the way in which man disposed himself over the landscape on which he lived. It refers to dwellings, to their arrangement, and to the nature and disposition of other buildings pertaining to community life (Willey 1953:1)

This pioneer work sparked a proliferation of settlement studies. By the early 1960s two basic trends had emerged. The first, a descriptive approach, was a continuation of Willey's method. The second approach, a hierarchical approach, is described by Chang (1958), who distinguished between settlement pattern and community pattern in the following manner:

Settlement pattern is the manner in which human settlements are arranged over the landscape in relation to physiographic environment, while community pattern is the manner in which the inhabitants arrange their structures within the community and their communities within the aggregate.

Trigger (1968:79) described three levels of settlement organization: the individual house, the site or community, and the total landscape distribution. This third level, total landscape distribution, added a new factor — the determinant he defined as "those classes of factors that interact with each other to produce spatial configurations of a social group" (1968:53).

It would seem, then, that there are four main aspects of settlement archaeology: (1) the settlement can be studied descriptively; (2) it can be studied at different levels of organization; (3) it can be studied as a system with subsystems; and (4) it can be studied as a process.

Ecological Approaches to the Study of Archaeological Site Location

▲ An *ecological approach* to the study of culture implies an interrelationship between the environment and the culture as represented by the site within its specific environmental setting. Thinking on the subject has diverged into two points of view.

The first view tends to consider the environment as a "permissive and limiting" factor. For example, Meggers (1954) proposed a deterministic theory about the inhibiting effects of tropical-lowland forests, and Wittfogel (1955) views the rise of despotic states as a need to control large-scale irrigation projects in semiarid regions. In 1964, M. D. Coe and K. V. Flannery focused attention on the role of the *microenvironment*, which is the specific environmental zone being exploited at any particular time. Steward, in 1938, already provided the general model of microenvironmental exploitation. Steward's study (1938) showed that the Great Basin people seasonally exploited both vertically and horizontally differentiated sets of environments. This model underlies much current thinking on hunter-gatherers. Testing and confirmation of this model has been conducted in Thomas's Reese River Ecological project (1972, 1973) and in Grady's (1980) Piceance Basin project. In the latter it was demonstrated that in summer people harvested mule deer at the higher elevations, that in the fall they exploited pinon nuts in the pinon-juniper zone at lower elevations, and that in the spring they utilized the resources in the lowland valley bottoms.

It is within microenvironments that humans have consistently found the critical resources which enable them to survive. Yet, although most site reports contain both an ecological and subsistence statement, until recently little effort has been made to relate site location to specific environmental factors. In one attempt to accomplish such a correlation, the Southwestern Anthropological Research Group (SARG) has devised a three-step program to tie archaeological sites to environmental factors. This approach focuses on the following:

1. Locating the site as accurately as possible, either through the use of careful mapping techniques or through aerial photography (Plog and Hill 1971).
2. Relating site location to a set of agreed-upon environmental factors (landform, drainage, plant community, etc.) through use of simple statistical tests.
3. Formulation of an explanatory statement to account for the known distribution of sites.

The second ecological approach to the study of factors influencing site location (and hence cultural differences and change) is essentially economic in outlook. This approach assumes that the environment provides opportunities which will be rationally exploited to economic advantage depending, of course, on the level of the available technology. Change is believed to occur when existing resources are stressed, primarily through overpopulation. Under these circumstances new resources must be added to the existing inventory, or old resources must be more efficiently exploited, or a combination of both must happen. The leading exponents of this point of view are Higgs (1972, 1975), Vita-Finzi and Higgs (1970), and Clark (1952, 1953, 1972).

■ It should not be surprising that the two divergent ecological approaches also offer differing explanations to account for cultural change. The first approach, that of the "permissive and limiting" school, sees cultural change occurring because of changes within the environment. In either case—environmental change or resource stress—the typical cultural response is the development of new technology and new patterns of behavior for coping with new environmental conditions.

Geographical Approaches to Site Location

The influence of geographical thinking and techniques upon archaeological research is a comparatively recent phenomenon. With the 1968 publication of David Clarke's *Analytical Archaeology*, names of geographers like Chorley and Haggett became familiar to the archaeologist. Certainly, Haggett's book *Locational Analysis in Human Geography* (1965) and the Chorley and Haggett *Models in Geography* (1967) have had a major impact on archaeological thinking. Within this geographic literature two general trends are discernible.

● The theoretical approach constructs a model of where sites are expected to occur.

▲ Roman settlement fits a theoretical model.

■ Site location is the result of conscious choices.

THEORETICAL APPROACH

The first is the theoretical approach, which is of current interest to the new generation of geographers and archaeologists. The theoretical view is based on Christaller's 1933 studies of central places in southern Germany. ● In Christaller's approach, theories are developed regarding the nature of "ideal" distributions of places. Evidence is then collected to illustrate that the reality conforms to these theoretical patterns. This view centers on what the patterns should be rather than what they really are, and there is the

Fig. 5-9 Use of Thiessen polygons around Romano-British walled centers to illustrate the area served by each center. (Hodder 1972: Fig. 23-6.)

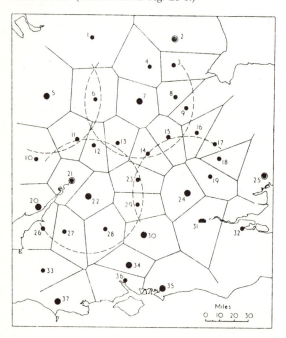

overall goal of building a model which can explain site locations. The ultimate question is Why are archaeological sites located where they are?

Archaeology in general has not made extensive use of the ideas and methods of the theoretical geographer. However, a theoretical model has been applied to Romano-British settlement patterns with interesting results (Fig. 5-9) (Hodder 1972). ▲ Hodder was able to determine that the Roman settlement of lowland Britain closely approximated that predicted by the Christaller concept. Settlement was hierarchically arranged along Christaller's transport principle, and therefore centers which could only be identified as "Roman" could, by use of the model, be assigned a hierarchical position. Marcus (1973) has also used the method in an analysis of Mayan settlement patterns.

Another technique, the Thiessen polygon, involves the building up of a lattice through the geometrical construction of polygons or boundaries around known sites. The resulting polygons may possibly indicate the economic catchment area (resource area) supporting the central site. In addition, the shapes and sizes of the polygons can often be useful in defining anomalies within the existing data base and thus can lead the archaeologist to search for additional data to fill the gaps. Hammond (1972) has done this in the Mayan area.

ECONOMIC APPROACHES

Contrary to the theoretical approach to the problem of site location are concepts developed by economists and economic geographers. These approaches have been set forth by Greenhut (1956) and Weber (1957), and their focus concerns all factors which have influenced or determined industrial plant location. ■ A specific plant site is thus the result of *choosing*, among alternative locations, the one which is most *desirable* in terms of minimizing cost and maximizing profits (Chisholm 1968). By analogy, the location of an archaeological site can also be considered to be the result of just such a design to minimize effort while maximizing some desired return, such as food getting. This approach, termed a *mini-max strategy* (Clarke 1968), could possibly provide a method of linking sites to their respective resource bases in a consistent and comprehensive manner. However, so far economic approaches have yet to impinge on archaeological thinking.

CRITICISMS OF THE THEORETICAL GEOGRAPHIC METHOD

Geographic theories tend to be formulated in mathematical and algebraic terms which require a considerable degree of expertise for comprehension. Consequently, the uses of such theory are restricted to experts. Secondly, mathematical models and mathematical expressions of data require a high degree of abstraction with the associated risk that some of the assumptions may be dubious. (Factors to which numerical values cannot be assigned are ignored.) Finally, it is impossible to take into account all phenomena, and "exceptions" always occur. Therefore, any general theory is to some extent unrealistic when compared to the real world. This is not a serious drawback, however, since we recognize that theories are only the best approximation of reality at a given time. Advantages of such theories are that they offer simplicity and clarity because the elements possess only those properties explicitly assigned to them. On the other hand, in the real world behavior is often due to causes so involved that they cannot be traced.

Conclusions

To date, archaeological use of theoretical geographic models seems to have been most successful when dealing with a cultural landscape and entities where hierarchical organization is apparent (Hodder 1972; Hammond 1972). However, the usefulness of such models in dealing with hunting-gathering societies also seems promising. Using such techniques as nearest-neighbor analysis and Thiessen-polygon construction on a series of Paleo-Indian sites on the Llano Estacado and in the Rio Grande Valley, Hester and Grady (1977) were able to provide insights into site territoriality and function, and into the interrelationship between campsites and killsites. For example, killsites were less frequent than campsites. All sites became more frequent the later they were in time. Finally, band territory was estimated at a radius of 90 to 120 miles and site polygons had a radius of 3.6 to 18.6 miles (Hester and Grady 1977:89, 94).

Of all of the concepts described above, the SARG approach comes closest to providing a methodology for studying the nature of the relationship between humans and their environment. Unfortunately, little effort has been expended in the implementation of the SARG design, and even less has been devoted to relating site location to specific environmental factors. What is clear, however, is that archaeology is an evolving field of inquiry in which new methodological techniques and theories continue to appear.

PART II

PLEISTOCENE ENVIRONMENTS AND HOMINID EVOLUTION

The search for human origins is conducted using evidence so fragmentary that we know that often our interpretations must be subject to significant errors. We know that humans have evolved from a generalized primate ancestor to a generalized human ancestor (hominid) but the exact step-by-step progression of that evolution leading to modern humans is obscured as we are forced to study fragmentary remains (the only ones available to us). There has often been doubt as to which fossil hominids lie in the direct line of ancestry leading to *Homo sapiens sapiens*, the modern human species, and we are sometimes also in doubt as to which fossil forms are separate species and which may only be males and females of the same species. Similarly, there is the question of which fossil hominids used tools and which did not. Yet out of all

101

this uncertainty paleoanthropologists have developed explanations of the human evolutionary path. These explanations disagree with one another in many significant ways, yet we are confident that over a period of time new finds will permit us to better understand how our ancestors evolved physically and culturally over the immensely long period of time—some 3 million years or so—from which we have evidence of that evolution. (And lack of absolute proof notwithstanding, all of these interpretations are interesting in their own right.)

What we do know is that 2 to 3 million years ago some of our ancestors walked erect, used tools, and had already begun the long evolutionary journey from primate to human. How, when, and where these events came about will be the subject of this section. In addition, we are not concerned merely with the time when these evolutionary events occurred but also with the nature of the climate, flora, and fauna—the makeup of the specific environments inhabited by our ancestors. What is most unique about the environment of human evolution is that it coincided with one of the most unique periods in geological history—the Pleistocene epoch—which was characterized by sequential glacial periods interspersed with glacial retreats (the interglacials). This sequence of glacial events provides the chronological framework for those events that antedate written history. In addition, Pleistocene climatic events structured the very nature of human evolution, both physical and cultural. Finally, with the development of scientific techniques in the earth and biological sciences, we can identify the plants and animals utilized by our ancestors for food, we can date their occupation levels by several separate techniques, and we can correlate this specific information with long-term climatic episodes. All of this will be summarized in the section which follows. Join us for a tour of environments and events different from those that now exist in order to understand how our ancestors coped with them. Had they failed we might not be here today.

6

Setting the Stage for Human Evolution

A burning question in Paleolithic archaeology is How long have humans been manufacturing tools? Continuing research on the earliest evidences of culture has pushed back the chronological horizons of our cultural ancestry to close to 2 million years ago at Olduvai Gorge, Tanzania, increasing the known use of tools by at least 1 million years in the past two decades. Furthermore, recent research by Clark Howell, Richard Leakey, and Karl Butzer indicates that tool using in the Omo region of southern Ethiopia has an even greater antiquity. L. S. B. Leakey has gone even further in his assertion that *Ramapithecus wickeri*, a Miocene primate some 15 million years of age, also utilized stone tools.

The Lower Paleolithic, or Early Stone Age, was the period during which those primates we term hominids developed a system of tool manufacture and use which was passed on from generation to generation. ■ The development of such a system, or culture, distinguished these hominids from their primate ancestors and contemporaries because it provided a shield between them and the environmental hazards they faced. With tools, they could protect themselves and secure an advantage over prey animals. Thus with the establishment of tool use and manufacture as a learnable cultural tradition, our ancestors had taken the most important single step in their evolution.

The latter point is important to grasp, because it is crucial to our understanding of prehistory; it is not tool use per se that distinguishes humans from higher primates. (Certain modern apes utilize a variety of implements for specified purposes, and we may assume that their ancestors did likewise.) Nor is it tool *manufacture*

● Culture is transmitted from one generation to the next.

▲ Early evidence is often inadequate.

■ All evidence must be placed in a chronological framework.

● The Pleistocene epoch was unique in climatic composition.

that distinguishes us, since chimpanzees also prepare sticks for use. ● It is the *transmission* of both of these practices through learned and shared behavior patterns from one generation to the next, with the reliance on culture, that distinguishes us as unique.

Our investigation of early cultural beginnings must take into account our primate nature. Early humans probably functioned like modern primate bands with a pattern of *male dominance* in social relationships and a social structure in which the strongest ties are between females and their offspring. Band territoriality was expressed in the quest for food conducted within a known area. Group cooperation probably consisted of defense, the communication of danger, and a tradition of band solidarity and cohabitation. To this primate background we must add the conscious making of tools and the transmission of the techniques of manufacture and use to other members of the band through example and symbolic speech (language) (Falk 1980: 72–78). With respect to these innovations, it is appropriate to ask ourselves: At what point in human evolution did tool use and speech begin to qualitatively change our way of life? These questions cannot be easily answered with the evidence at hand. Because certain other primates are tool users, we assume that tool using was practiced by our early hominid ancestors and that through time this facility became more developed. According to this view, culture, or at least tool using, was a gradual development, not a dramatic change at a particular time.

Speech also may have developed slowly (Washburn 1978). In addition, we have no assurance that the development of speech was synchronous with the development of other aspects of culture. However, symbolic speech would have been a great asset in the transmission of cultural knowledge. On the other hand, since the archaeological record indicates that early industries were simple and changed slowly through time, we can assume that speech also was slow to change, with early humans probably having a very limited vocabulary. (According to Washburn [1978], the most logical order of human evolution was first walking, next tool use, then food sharing, cooperative hunting, and, finally, an increase to a larger brain size.)

Our assessment of the influence of culture suffers from the fact that little evidence other than living floors, killsites, and stone tools has been preserved to indicate early human behavioral patterns. We do know that implements were initially hand-held and that they provided their users with superior skills in cutting and scraping. However, they were not adequate in themselves to afford the users much of an advantage in direct confrontations with large carnivores. Implements aided in the killing and butchering of animals already trapped or surrounded, or in the utilization of scavenged remains, but they did not add to human speed or agility. It is also clear that early humans were at a disadvantage in the hunt because they did not possess the means to kill animals at a distance. Other limitations included less acuity of smell and hearing than that possessed by the prey animals. Advantages on the human side were prehensile hands, stereoscopic vision, and *superior intellectual ability*.

▲ The basic problem in our study of the beginnings of the Lower Paleolithic (the initial period of stone tool use) lies in the inadequacy of the archaeological record. We may find chipped flints or split and broken animal bones in an ancient stratum, but these must be of patterned form in their shape or distribution for us to infer that humans (rather than animals or the forces of nature) were the agents. The earlier and presumably less patterned these remains are, the less evidence we have for attributing them to human activity. Thus while the search for the earliest cultural remains continues, enthusiasm and judgment must be tempered by our insistence upon scientific proof of human influence. What is most often revealed is the later, more clearly patterned remains, which constitute the core of material we term "Lower Paleolithic." It is these stone industries, living floors, piled or scattered food debris, and such, that make up the items we collect, identify, and study in our search for knowledge of our past.

Chronology of Pleistocene Events

In order to comprehend the meaning inherent in these early remains, we first need to understand the environments inhabited by early humans. ■ We must also understand, as best we can, the physical capabilities of these ancestors (from the incomplete fossil record), and we must learn something of the time frame within which to integrate these diverse elements.

Our understanding of human evolution, both cultural and physical, is ordered by the presence of artifacts and fossils in specific strata. These strata are correlated one with another on the basis of stratigraphic position, faunal content, artifactual content, and age as established by independent dating techniques. These studies have enabled geologists and prehistorians to construct relative sequences of geologic events and cultural and evolutionary phenomena. However, all such chronologies are subject to reinterpretation, since the levels and finds that are so correlated are widely separated in time and space. Furthermore, these strata frequently differ in included fossils so that a true correlation is not possible, and new finds continually bring about the revision of such attempts. Nonetheless, this framework is the basis to which all Pleistocene studies must be referred. (See Figure 6-1 for an example of such a correlation.)

Human evolution, both physical and cultural, occurred during the Pleistocene epoch.

This period was one of the more unique in geologic history. ● Whereas most of the rest of geologic time (2 billion years) typically featured a warm, unglaciated climate, the Pleistocene had, alternatively, both a warm and a cold climate. It was a time marked by the formation of large continental glaciers. Forming in the subarctic and temperate regions, especially in Europe and North America, these glacial masses advanced outward from numerous centers, then went through a series of minor fluctuations: advances (called *stades*) interspersed with halts or temporary retreats (called *interstadials*). The period between two continental glacials is defined as an *interglacial*. This entire process was repeated at least four times, and the major glacial periods in Alpine Europe from early to late have been termed Günz, Mindel, Riss, and Würm. Interspersed between these glacials were the interglacials, termed Cromerian, Hoxnian, and Eem (Table 6-1). To further complicate the overall picture, differing terminology is used for different regions, and the terminology used in one region is not always comparable to that used in another. Yet even this scheme is too simplistic, since there were a number of advances and retreats within each of these glacial events. Additionally, some areas, including most of Africa, southeast Asia, and central Alaska, remained unglaciated. Even though Africa was unglaciated, there is evidence for a series of wet periods (*pluvials*) separated by dry periods (*interpluvials*). The extent to which the African pluvials may

TABLE 6-1
The European Glacial Sequence

Epoch	Glacials	Postglacial	Interglacials
Late Pleistocene	Würm		
			Eem
	Riss		
Middle Pleistocene			Hoxnian
	Mindel		
			Cromerian
Villafranchian	Günz		
	Period of minor climatic fluctuations		

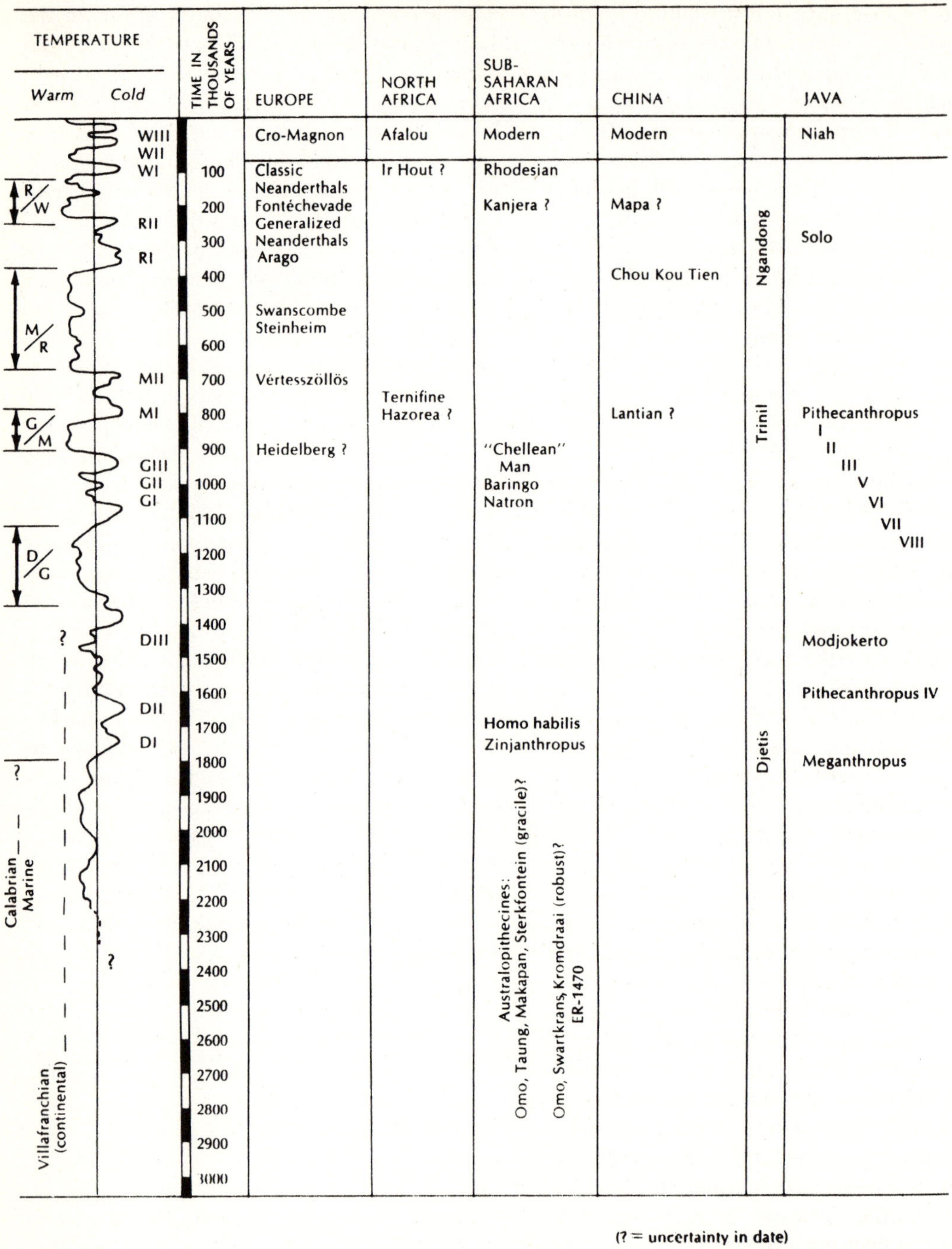

TEMPERATURE (Warm / Cold)	TIME IN THOUSANDS OF YEARS	EUROPE	NORTH AFRICA	SUB-SAHARAN AFRICA	CHINA	JAVA
WIII / WII / WI		Cro-Magnon	Afalou	Modern	Modern	Niah
WI	100	Classic Neanderthals	Ir Hout ?	Rhodesian		
RII	200	Fontéchevade Generalized		Kanjera ?	Mapa ?	
	300	Neanderthals				Solo
RI	400	Arago			Chou Kou Tien	
	500	Swanscombe				
	600	Steinheim				
MII	700	Vértesszöllös				
MI	800		Ternifine Hazorea ?		Lantian ?	Pithecanthropus I, II
	900	Heidelberg ?		"Chellean" Man		III
GIII GII GI	1000			Baringo		V
	1100			Natron		VI, VII, VIII
	1200					
	1300					
	1400					
DIII	1500					Modjokerto
	1600					Pithecanthropus IV
DII	1700			Homo habilis		
DI	1800			Zinjanthropus		Meganthropus
	1900					
	2000					
	2100					
	2200			Australopithecines: Omo, Taung, Makapan, Sterkfontein (gracile)?		
	2300					
	2400					
	2500					
	2600			Omo, Swartkrans, Kromdraai (robust)? ER-1470		
	2700					
	2800					
	2900					
	3000					

Temperature oscillation markers (left margin): R/W, M/R, G/M, D/G. Cultural/stratigraphic labels: Calabrian Marine; Villafranchian (continental). China column right-side labels: Ngandong, Trinil, Djetis.

(? = uncertainty in date)

Fig. 6-1 Correlation of Pleistocene events and the occurrence of specific fossil hominid forms. (Birdsell 1975: Fig. 9-5.)

▲ The effects of glaciation

■ The best early evidence of human evolution is from Africa.

be synchronized with the northern-hemisphere glacial periods has yet to be determined.

A further note on chronology concerns the use of the terms *Villafranchian*, *Lower Pleistocene*, *Middle Pleistocene*, and *Upper Pleistocene*. Most workers, instead of referring to the "Lower Pleistocene," use the term *Villafranchian* (after the Villafranca d'Asti, Piedmont, a site in Italy famous for its early Pleistocene fauna) to denote that portion of the Pleistocene between the end of the preceding Pliocene period and the first glacial period (Günz) of the Pleistocene. The Middle Pleistocene period includes the Günz, Mindel, and Riss glaciations, while the Late Pleistocene starts at the end of the Riss glaciation, continues through the entire Würm glaciation, and ends with the beginning of the Postglacial period (ca. 8000 B.C.).

▲ The effects of glaciation were many: (1) the total area of habitable land was greatly reduced; (2) the major vegetational zones were compressed toward the equator; (3) rainfall and temperature patterns were also altered as atmospheric circulation was influenced by the glacial masses. One way to visualize the effects of the glaciers is to plot their geographic distribution. Another method of assessing glaciation is to compare graphs of temperature changes, with one end of the graph reflecting "modern" temperatures. Emiliani (1966) has constructed one such temperature graph based on data derived from the analysis of deep-sea cores. (This graph, correlated with the North American and European glacial chronologies, is presented in Figure 6-1.) The deep-sea-core graph presents a smoothed profile because as each layer is formed, ocean floor organisms churn up the sediments, thus blurring the record. Still another analysis of glacial effect relies on changes in the isotopic composition of glacial ice. The ice-core data is the most sensitive climatic record available to date. Unfortunately, it only covers the last 100,000 years.

With glaciers covering the higher latitudes and elevations, areas suitable for the evolution of humans were somewhat limited. ■ Our best evidence of early humankind is from Africa, although this does not mean that Africa was the only possible hearth for human development. (Early remains are also known from southern Europe and from Southeast Asia.) However, it is Africa which provides us with the greatest quantity of early cultural evidence. The tropical savanna zone with its warm climate, adequate rainfall, and wealth of plants and animals was most favorable for human early development. The other major world environmental zones—the Arctic ice, tundra, temperate forest, grasslands, deserts, subtropical forests, the cold dry steppes, and the tropical rain forests—all provide less in the way of easily acquired foods, as well as requiring more specialized adaptations for survival. In the tropical savanna an amazing wealth of diverse forms inhabited every ecological niche, taking advantage of the high biomass-carrying capacity (as illustrated in Table 6-2). Other features included tremendous concentrations of herd-dwelling species and a major emphasis on giantism. Toward the end of the Pleistocene, (about 8000 B.C.), a majority of these species became extinct. The extinction of these exotic forms was an outstanding feature of the Late Pleistocene, and it has been suggested that human predation was the cause. Whether or not humans were responsible for the extinction of specific species, our ancestors were, at least by Middle Pleistocene times, efficient predators. Humans were also influential in altering other aspects of their environments through fire, dispersal of plants, and exploitation of specific resources. However, during the Lower Paleolithic, the primary influence of humans on their environment was seen in their predation on animal species.

● Human evolution—a controversial subject

▲ The Australopithecines, the earliest known culture-bearing hominids

Human Evolution: The Fossil Record

● Probably no field of thought has generated more heated debate than the topic of human evolution. This controversy exists at two very different levels. The first level concerns the arguments, pro and con, dealing with human evolution itself. Here we find scientifically derived evidence of gradual evolutionary change pitted against supernatural creation as specified in the Bible. Since the adherents on one side argue from physical evidence and those on the other from faith, this argument is unresolvable.

At the second level, debate is not centered on evolution per se but on the evolutionary implications of specific fossil specimens. In this sector there are two current anthropological points of view. The most widely accepted of these recognizes a basic four-stage evolutionary sequence leading to the modern human species. In this progression the Australopithecine stage *(Aus-*

tralopithecus sp.) is followed sequentially by the Pithecanthropine *(Homo erectus)*, Neanderthal *(Homo sapiens neanderthalensis)*, and the modern *(Homo sapiens sapiens)* stages. The other perspective, strongly advocated by the late Louis Leakey and his son Richard Leakey, argues for the great antiquity and separate evolution of *Homo sapiens sapiens.* The Leakeys argue that *Australopithecus, Homo erectus,* and *Homo sapiens neanderthalensis* cannot be related to the modern species since there are fossil remains that support an earlier ancestral life for the species *Homo sapiens sapiens.* As evidence, particular importance is attributed to fossils recovered at Steinheim in Germany, Swanscombe in England, and Fontechevade in France. These specimens, which predate the Neanderthal remains, are interpreted as being ancestral *Homo sapiens sapiens* (the modern species). Proponents of the four-stage approach tend to view these specimens as being intermediate forms falling between *Homo erectus* and early varieties of *Homo sapiens neanderthalensis.* Since proponents of both arguments accept the basic sequence outlined above, the question is one of interpretation.

Because it is the more generally accepted, we shall follow the four-stage theory, briefly describing each stage, but first a cautionary note:

TABLE 6-2
Ungulate Biomasses of Certain Environments

Vegetation Type	Locality	Species Number	Biomass (kg/sq km)
Rain Forest	Ghana	3	5.6
Thorn Forest	Zimbabwe	15	4,900
Savanna Parkland	Congo; Uganda	5–11	5,950–19,540
High-Grass Savanna	Kenya; Transvaal	17–19	1,760–16,560
Low-Grass Savanna	Kenya; Tanzania	over 15	5,250
Semidesert Grassland	Chad	4	83
Desert Shrub	Rio de Oro; Mauretania	2	0.3–189
Temperate Grassland	Eurasian Steppe; Great Plains		350–3,000
Deciduous Forest	Scotland		ca. 1,000
Mixed Forest	Carpathians		ca. 500
Tundra	Northern Canada		ca. 800

(Butzer 1971:150)

In reviewing the literature the reader must bear in mind the fact that fossil finds are usually fragmentary and are seldom found in chronological order. (More typically, they appear as unrelated bits of a jigsaw puzzle.) A second problem is that the paleoanthropologist, in describing a find, may exaggerate the differences between it and some specimen found previously in order to justify a new species or generic name. As time passes, the known forms are restudied and the inappropriate names dropped, which makes an understanding of the subject more difficult for the nonspecialized student. Finally, since new fossils are being recovered at a fantastic rate and old finds are being reinterpreted in light of the new ones, this field of study is constantly in a state of flux.

Early Hominids

The earliest hominid fossils are known from numerous finds in East Africa and South Africa. ▲ Dated (by the potassium-argon method) at approximately 3.5 million to 1 million years ago,

these hominids have been termed the *Australopithecine subfamily*. This group is divided into two separate lineages, a gracile form and a robust form. The robust forms have been assigned to two species, *Australopithecus boisei* and *Australopithecus robustus*. Features in common between these species are heavy brow ridges, a sagittal crest (a bony ridge down the center line of the skull), no forehead, small incisors and canines, and large molars and premolars. The major difference between the two is that the molars and premolars of the *boisei* form are especially large. It is presumed that the large molar development of both forms was an adaptation for the crushing and chewing of tough vegetal foods. (Some authorities place both *boisei* and *robustus* within the same species.)

The gracile form, *Australopithecus africanus*, was smaller in size, possessed something of a forehead, and lacked a sagittal crest (Figs. 6-2 and 6-3). The contrast in size between the cutting and grinding teeth was less marked than in the *robustus* forms. This feature presumably reflects an omnivorous diet. Both subgenera possessed a

Fig. 6-2 Reconstructed skull of *Australopithecus* from the cave deposits at Sterkfontein, South Africa. (Courtesy British Museum [Natural History].)

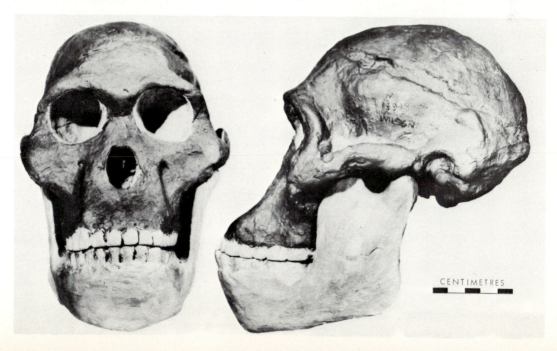

CENTIMETRES

■ *Homo habilis* — the connecting link

● The East African Australopithecines lived along streams and lakes.

▲ The South African Australopithecines lived in caves.

cranial capacity of about 500 cc and habitually walked erect. The robust form possessed a body weight of 120 to 150 pounds, whereas the gracile form probably weighed somewhere in the 50-to-100-pound range. Differences among the various *Australopithecus* forms may be attributed to differing ecological adaptations, allometry (differential evolution of the various body parts), variation among populations, differences in age (these finds cover 2.5 million years or so), and sexual dimorphism (male-female differentiation). The Australopithecine forms also now in-

Fig. 6-3 Reconstruction of the *Australopithecus* child from Taung by A. Forestier. (Copyright *The Illustrated London News.*)

clude the recently defined gracile species *Australopithecus afarensis*, which dates to 3.0 million years, was 1.2 meters in height, and was well adapted to bipedal locomotion (Harris 1980). According to Johanson and White (1979), *afarensis* is directly ancestral to *africanus*. Further, they see *A. africanus* and *A. robustus* as not in the line leading to humans. Instead, the lineage they outline considers *A. afarensis* as ancestral to both *A. africanus* and *Homo habilis* (the gracile tool-using form from Olduvai Gorge), with *Homo habilis* being ancestral to *Homo erectus*.

Most authorities currently view the Australopithecines as in part ancestral to humans and in part as a related evolutionary dead end. In either case, their various evolutionary characters and their use of tools make them of central importance to our understanding of human origins.

Sites with Australopithecines are known only from East and South Africa and from environments which today are either semiarid or semihumid. The chronology of the finds suggests that *A. africanus* (2.5–3.0 million years) occurs earlier than *A. robustus* (1.5–2.0 million years; Day 1965; Harris 1980). *Australopithecus afarensis* dates to even earlier: 2.9 to 3.8 million years ago (Johanson and White 1979). The chronologically most recent gracile form evolved in East Africa. ■ Originally found in Bed I at Olduvai Gorge, this early hominid, termed *Homo habilis*, appears to be the connecting link between the Australopithecines and true humans. Its age is in the 1.5–2.0-million-year range. Sites with *H. habilis* remains contain both tools and food debris and will be described in further detail later.

As we have noted, the Leakeys (Leakey and Leakey 1978) reject the Australopithecines as being directly ancestral to *Homo sapien sapiens*. They feel that *Homo habilis* and the recently discovered 1470 skull from Lake Turkana represent a separate line leading to the modern human species. According to their view, this eliminates the Australopithecines from the direct line of evolution leading to *Homo sapien sapiens*. Skull 1470 has a larger brain capacity than the original *H. habilis* find but is of about the same age (1.6–1.8 million years). The crux of the matter centers on a simple question: If both *H. habilis* and *Australopithecus* coexisted simultaneously, are they separate species or are they related? The Leakeys' position is obvious. On the other hand, if *Homo habilis* and *Australopithecus* are related, then the next question is When did *H. habilis* split off from the general Australopithecine line, and for how long after this did *Australopithecus* continue to survive?

Ecology of the Australopithecine Environments

The ecology of the sites in which these Australopithecines have been found is of two principal types. ● In East Africa, sites are typically located along the edges of streams or lakes. The occupation sites were selected for their proximity to watering places frequented by ungulates (cloven-hoofed mammals). The fauna preserved in the sites suggests that nearby were open uplands and fringes of trees along the water courses (Fig. 6-4). The sites represented camping spots located in the open, often in places that were seasonally inundated.

▲ In contrast to sites in East Africa, the South African remains are primarily located in cave fills. After deposition, the sediments within the caves were cemented together with carbonates, resulting in the formation of breccia, a soft rock including large quantities of bone. Although differences in the cave deposits have been interpreted as indicative of climatic changes, Butzer (1971: 424) contends that these interpretations are improbable in that materials of different ages were washed into the caves, with the breccia formation being carried out under one specific climatic regimen. He infers that the climate at the time was drier than that of today, or at least featured a less well-distributed rainfall. The habitat

Fig. 6-4 Reconstruction of an adult *Australopithecus* troop engaged in scavenging and the hunting of small or young animals. (Courtesy the British Museum [Natural History].)

requirements of the included fauna suggest the presence of an open grassland. Perhaps most important is the fact that both robust and gracile Australopithecines are known from the same sites, and their geographic ranges overlapped to a considerable degree. Another consideration is the possibility that the gracile forms may have preyed upon their vegetarian relatives. The opportunities afforded the *A. africanus* and *H. habilis* forms by their omnivorous diets permitted them to exploit a wider range of habitats than the *robustus* forms and may therefore have insured them a greater chance of survival. On the other hand, Peters (1979) suggests that wet-season environments favored the greatest variety of

■ Characteristics of *Homo erectus*

age and sex groups, whereas the stress of semi-arid intervals would have favored the hyperrobust forms.

Homo erectus

Major finds now classified as *Homo erectus* (originally termed *Pithecanthropus erectus* by Dubois, the discoverer) are those from the Djetis and Trinil beds in Java and those (originally termed *Sinanthropus pekinensis* from Zhou Koudian (Choukoutien) near Peking, China. In marked contrast to the tropical distribution of the Australopithecines, the *Homo erectus* finds, although comparatively few in number, are widespread in both the tropical and temperate regions of the Old World. A modern list of the more important localities featuring *H. erectus* is reproduced below (Butzer 1971: 443; and deLumley 1979: 54–59).

Important *Homo erectus* finds are the following:

1. Early Lower Pleistocene
   a) Olduvai: Upper Bed II. *Homo* cf. *erectus* ("Chellean Man") and one or more Australopithecines.
   b) Swartkrans: *Homo erectus* ("Telanthropus") and *Australopithecus robustus*.
   c) Sangiran and Modjokerto, Java: Djetis fauna. *Homo* cf. *erectus* ("Meganthropus paleojavanicus") and *Homo erectus* ("Pithecanthropus").
2. Late Lower Pleistocene
   a) Heidelberg-Mauer, Germany: *Homo* cf. *erectus* ("Palaeanthropus") of post-Cromerian but pre-Elster age.
   b) Verteszollos, Hungary: *Homo* cf. *sapiens* of Elster age.[1]

   c) Ternifine, Algeria: *Homo erectus* ("Atlanthropus").
   d) Koro Toro, Chad: *Homo* cf. *erectus* ("Tchadanthropus"), a poorly preserved fossil of uncertain age.
   e) Sangiran and Trinil, Java: Trinil fauna. *Homo erectus* ("Pithecanthropus").
   f) Tautavel, France: *Homo erectus* ("Tautavelensis").
3. Uncertain, early to Mid-Pleistocene
   a) Olduvai: Bed IV. *Homo erectus*.
   b) Zhou Koudian (Choukoutien) I, near Peking, China: *Homo erectus* ("Sinanthropus pekinensis") of Holstein age or from an earlier interglacial or interstadial.
   c) Landian (Lantian) China: *Homo erectus* ("Sinanthropus lantianensis") of Holstein age, or more probably, from an earlier interglacial.

The above list reflects the confusion caused by the coining of new generic and specific names by paleontologists at the finding of a new bone or even a single tooth. In this introductory work we will not review each *H. erectus* find in detail. ■ General characteristics of the species include primitive teeth with large roots, large canine teeth, a sharp backward slope to the forehead, a very thick cranial vault (1 cm), heavy brow ridges, postorbital constriction, a cranial capacity ranging from 775 cc to 1,225 cc, and marked sexual dimorphism (Fig. 6-5).

The original type site of *Homo erectus* was found by Eugene Dubois, a Dutch physician, on the banks of the Solo River near Trinil in Central Java. In 1891 Dubois located a skull cap and in 1892 a femur which led to his terming the find *Pithecanthropus erectus* ("the ape man that walked erect"). After the finds at Zhou Koudian[2] (Choukoutien) by Davidson Black in 1927 and

---

[1] Although labeled *Homo* cf. (which means compare with or comparable to) *sapiens* species by the author of this list, the Verteszollos find is placed within the list of *Homo erectus* finds. This is simply another example of the confusing nomenclature of early fossil finds.

[2] We have opted to use the Chinese government's official romanized transliterations of place names (known as Pinyin) in place of the traditional Wade Giles transliterations. In this chapter and in Chapters 15 and 16 the first version given will be Pinyin and the second, in parentheses, will be the Wade Giles version.

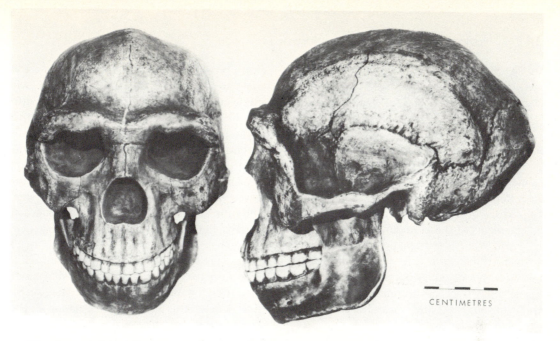

CENTIMETRES

Fig. 6-5 Model of the restored skull of the Peking fossil hominid. Originally termed *Sinanthropus pekinensis*, these hominids are now assigned to the species *Homo erectus*. (Courtesy British Museum [Natural History].)

Fig. 6-6 Reconstruction of the life-style of the Peking hominids. The life-style included the use of fire, the manufacture of stone tools, hunting, and the use of caves as dwelling places. (Courtesy British Museum [Natural History].)

● Characteristics of Neanderthals

▲ The discovery of Neanderthal specimens

1928 (Fig. 6-6), the true nature of the species became clear, since the Trinil finds had been too fragmentary to permit reconstruction. Finds at Zhou Koudian (Choukoutien) include portions of 14 skulls; 14 lower jaws, including 148 teeth; and fragments of the postcranial skeleton. During World War II the original Peking finds were lost, but fortunately for science, casts of the originals were preserved. A surprising fact is that Dubois failed to accept the *Sinanthropus* finds as similar to those at Trinil, regarding the former as a degenerate Neanderthal type.

Neanderthal Man: Homo sapiens neanderthalensis

Most of us have heard of the Neanderthals and have some impression of their general characteristics. To many nonprofessionals, they are the archetype of the beetle-browed cave dweller portrayed in cartoons and comic strips. In scientific fact, the Neanderthals constitute something of an enigma, for they form a physically varied group, especially during the last 5,000 years of their existence, the period of transition to *H. sapiens sapiens* some 35,000–40,000 years ago (Trinkaus and Howells 1979). The Neanderthals concern us because although some are of primitive form, they must lie directly within our line of ancestry.

● The "classic" Neanderthal possessed massive brow ridges, a lower and flatter skull than *Homo s. sapiens*, and a large cranial capacity (1,350 to 1,723 cc), which slightly exceeds that of the latter (Fig. 6-7). The large cranial size is achieved by a bulging out of the sides and rear of the skull rather than through an increase in skull height, the latter being a characteristic of *Homo sapiens sapiens*. The nasal bones are prominent, and the nasal aperture large. The

chin ranges from "weak" to absent. The cheekbones are prominent. The molars are large, with strong cusp development and deep pulp cavities; and the premolars and canines are similar in size to those of the modern species. The remainder of the Neanderthal skeleton indicates a short (5 feet to 5 feet 4 inches in height) but very powerful build. The limbs were short and slightly bowed, and the hands and fingers were short. The muscle attachments on the long bones are massive, indicating great physical strength. One author has suggested that these muscle attachments were necessary to support an increased fat layer of up to 60 pounds, accumulated to sustain these individuals over the winter. (Most authorities believe this human hibernation theory stretches the available data beyond the level of reasonable inference.)

Fig. 6-7 Reconstructions of an example of a Neanderthal *(Homo sapiens neanderthalensis)*, the dominant form in Europe during the time interval from 70,000 to 35,000 years ago. After that date the Neanderthals were replaced by *Homo sapiens sapiens*. (Courtesy British Museum [Natural History].)

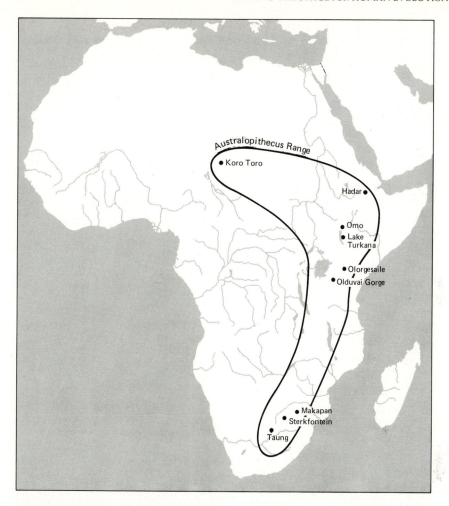

Australopithecus Range

• Koro Toro

Hadar •

• Omo
• Lake Turkana

• Olorgesaile
• Olduvai Gorge

• Makapan
• Sterkfontein
• Taung

▲ The first find of a fossil specimen — a child — occurred in 1839, in Belgium at Engis near Liège. The second find, a woman, was made at Gibraltar in 1845. Unfortunately, the significance of both finds was overlooked. The first specimen recognized as an ancestral human was found by workmen quarrying a cave deposit, Feldhofer grotto, in the Neander valley seven miles east of Düsseldorf, Germany, in 1856. A local teacher, J. C. Von Fuhlrott, recognized the importance of the find, and it was preserved. The portions of the skeleton recovered included a skull cap, one clavicle (collar bone), one scapula (shoulder blade), five ribs, two humeri (upper arm), one radius (lower arm), two ulnae (lower arm), two femora (thigh bone), and part of the pelvis (hip bone). The scientific classification of the find as that of a new fossil species termed *Homo neanderthalensis* was carried out by an Englishman named King in 1864. The Neanderthal finds antedated all other discoveries of human fossils, and thus investigators began to form impressions of our ancestry with only limited evidence — a situation in part responsible for the "caveman" impression of our ancestors held by the uninformed today. Subsequent finds of similar Neanderthal specimens were made at Spy, Belgium in 1886: two skulls

■ Differential evolution of the Neanderthals

● Appearance of *Homo s. sapiens*

and some skeletal remains; La Chapelle aux Saints, France, 1908: a complete adult skeleton; Le Moustier, France, 1908: a complete adolescent skeleton; La Quina, France, 1908–21: several skulls; and La Ferrassie, France, 1909–21: skulls (Boule and Valois 1957). Subsequent to these initial finds, Neanderthal or Neanderthal-like remains have been found in numerous parts of the world: Broken Hill, Rhodesia, 1921: a skull without mandible, with some skeletal fragments; Saldanha Bay, South Africa, 1953: a skull cap and lower-jaw fragment; Ngandong, Java, 1931–33: 11 skull caps and two tibias; Sidi-Abderrahman, Morocco, 1955: a lower jaw; Mugharet-es-Skhul, Palestine, 1931–32: parts of 10 individuals; Mugharet-et-Tabun, 1931–32: a female skeleton, a male lower jaw, other skeletal remains and teeth; Shanidar Cave, Iraq, 1951–60: nine skeletons, including those of two infants. Three sites in China, Zhang yang, Hubei (Ch'ang-yang, Hupei) Maba, Guandong (Ma-Pa, Kwangtung), and Ding cuu, Shaanxi (Ting-Ts'un, Shansi) have also produced fossil material of a Neanderthal-like nature (Howells 1977). The finds cited here are only some of the most important. Today, remains of at least 155 Neanderthal individuals are known from 68 sites in Europe, Africa, the Middle East, and Southeast Asia (Map 6-1).

As more complete skeletons were found and other hominid fossils discovered, it became apparent that the Neanderthals were anatomically closer to the modern species than had been originally believed. Another major result of the increasing number of recent finds has been a reassessment of the evolutionary position of the various Neanderthal groups. ■ The Middle Eastern specimens exhibit a variety of physical features, from those of "classic" type to some forms which are quite advanced in appearance, with reduced brow ridges and higher cranial vaults approximating those of modern types; other specimens are intermediate in form. The Middle Eastern population apparently consisted of an extremely varied gene group, some of which probably were directly ancestral to true *Homo sapiens sapiens* (described in the next sec-

Fig. 6-8 Reconstruction of hominid finds by the sculptor Maurice P. Coon. The specimens illustrate the range of variation existing among various fossils assigned to the Neanderthals or to the modern species, *Homo sapiens sapiens*. Shown with their sculptor, from *left* to *right* the finds are from: Combe Capelle; La Chapelle aux Saints; Upper Cave Male; Skhul 5; Wadjak; Cro-Magnon; Circeo 1; Steinheim. (Courtesy of Maurice P. Coon and photographer Wayland Minot.)

tion). Recent finds of Upper Pleistocene hominids in Yugoslavia, dated at 45–40,000 years of age, are morphologically intermediate between most "classic" central European Neanderthals and Upper-Paleolithic *Homo sapiens.* These data suggest that the Neanderthals were directly ancestral to *H. sapiens sapiens* (Malez et al. 1980).

How, then, do we explain the different character of the "classic" Neanderthals of Western Europe? These individuals represent a population living under severe climatic stress and thus were subjected to considerable genetic selection (Fig. 6-8). Another significant factor would be the isolation caused by the ice masses during the height of the Würm period, which would necessarily have led to inbreeding. It has been suggested that these classic Neanderthals became extinct as their environments became too cold and too severe for their continued existence. This explanation is too simplistic, however, because they had already survived previous glacial maxima and their culture was highly adaptive. More likely, a combination of factors was responsible for their extinction. Meanwhile, the other Neanderthals throughout the world provided a gene pool which has most likely been incorporated into that of modern humans. Von Koenigswald (1962) views the finds at Mt. Carmel in Palestine as representing an intermediate group which resulted from actual interbreeding between classic Neanderthals and *Homo s. sapiens.* The controversy continues, and new discoveries will give rise to new explanations in the future. (Alternative explanations of human physical evolution are expressed in Figure 6-9).

Modern Humans: Homo sapiens sapiens

● The appearance of *Homo sapiens sapiens* was not a precipitous affair but instead was contemporaneous with the later stages of Neanderthal evolution. At least this is the view held by many investigators. On the other hand, there are fossil finds at Swanscombe, Steinheim, and Fontechevade that are of Middle Pleistocene, second in-

terglacial age, which have tentatively been assigned to *Homo s. sapiens.* Only the Steinheim specimen is a reasonably complete skull, the others being skull caps without the diagnostic brow ridges. According to Brace, Nelson, and Korn (1971), these specimens show affinities closer to the Neanderthals than to the modern form. A recent find by Richard Leakey on the northeast shore of Lake Rudolf in East Africa consists of three skulls and some other skeletal parts of anatomically modern individuals *(Homo sapiens sapiens).* These materials are believed by Leakey to be some 250,000 years of age (Middle Pleistocene); however, other researchers (Butzer 1969) believe the geology of the site to be confused, with the result that the true age of the specimens lies somewhere between 30,000 years and the late Middle Pleistocene. The skeleton from Border Cave in South Africa is definitely of *Homo sapiens sapiens* type, and its age is greater than 50,000 years and is possibly as much as 115,000 years (Rightmire 1979); thus it may be our best evidence of *Homo sapiens sapiens* dated earlier than 30,000 years.

However, the argument continues as to the earliest appearance of *Homo sapiens sapiens.* This species became widespread in the interval between 30,000 and 20,000 B.C., with well-dated specimens abundant after about 23,000 B.C. By contrast, few Neanderthal specimens are assigned ages more recent than 33,000 B.C. From this date until the present, *H. s. sapiens* has been the human species on earth. During the Upper Paleolithic and more recent cultural periods, our ancestors became increasingly divergent in culture and better adapted to specific climatic regimes and environments. One response to differing environmental conditions has been the selection for those traits diagnostic of the differing human races. The amount of elapsed time necessary for such modifications is probably variable. We know, for example, that skeletons 14,000 years of age in Egypt and Sudan are robust in form, while skeletons only 4,000 to 6,000 years old in the same region are remarkably gracile. Thus change in human physical type can

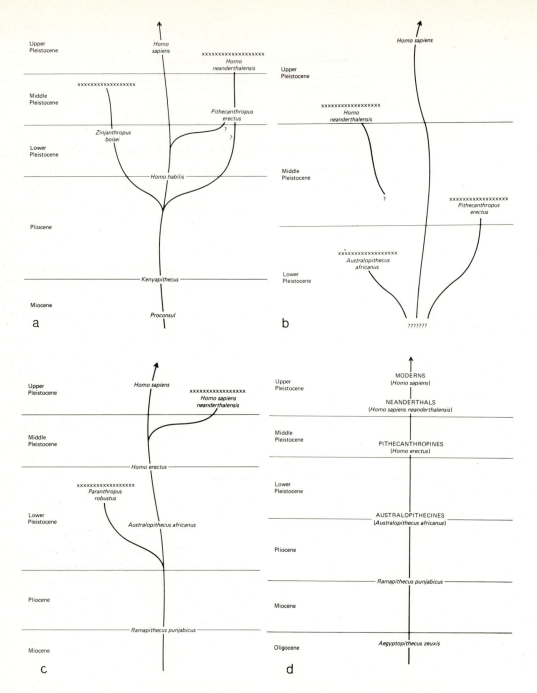

Fig. 6-9 Alternative views of hominid evolution as interpreted by Brace, Nelson, and Korn (1971:144–147). The reasons for differing explanations include doubt as to which forms are in the direct line of evolution leading to modern humans and whether individual species were evolutionary offshoots which became extinct and did not contribute their genes to the line that survived. Equally likely is the possibility that evidence is still so incomplete that none of these reconstructions is totally accurate.

▲ The Cro-Magnon find

■ Human evolution—a four-stage sequence

occur rapidly, the result not only of climatic factors but also of diet; thus culture has been a cause in continuing human physical evolution.

It is probably appropriate at this point to place in context the find termed *Cro-Magnon*. ▲ Our reason for doing so is the historical importance of the Cro-Magnon find—the earliest of an ancient example of *Homo s. sapiens*. This discovery was made in Les Eyzies, France, by the geologist L. Lartet in 1868 (Fig. 6-10). A railroad cut revealed a filled rock shelter within which were found the remains of five adults and some fragmentary infant bones. The best preserved skull is that of a male aged about 50 termed "the old man of Cro-Magnon". Associated with the skeletons were artifacts of the Aurignacian culture, an Upper-Paleolithic manifestation. Today, on the basis of the relative age of the associated culture, the remains are estimated to be approximately 20,000 years of age. Thus these skeletons are not now the earliest known *H. s. sapiens*, as more recent finds date to the interval between 30 and 35,000 years.

Dating Human Evolution

Dating of fossil materials provides points of contention among specialists, since most fossil evidence is not found in precisely dated contexts. Even those fossils that have been well dated are often challenged. In these cases, either the nature of the association between the specimen and its geologic context or the validity of the dating technique itself is disputed. ■ Despite these problems, it is still possible to delineate the following four-stage evolutionary sequence in time (see also Fig. 6-9):

1. *Australopithecus:* A long-lived genus, whose origins go back at least 3.5 to 4 mil-

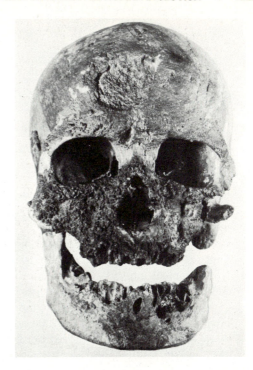

Fig. 6-10 A Cro-Magnon skull, one of the earliest finds of a fossil hominid of modern form and an example of *Homo sapiens sapiens*. (Courtesy Musée de L'Homme.)

lion years and who may have survived to less than 1 million years ago. *Homo habilis*, whether an advanced Australopithecine or an ancestral member of the genus *Homo*, fits well within the general Australopithecine time frame, with the juvenile from Olduvai Gorge dated at ca. 1.85 million years ago and Skull 1470 from Lake Rudolf at about the same age.

2. *Homo erectus:* Tenure on earth lasted from about 1.5 million years ago to as late as about 200,000 years ago. Boundaries are difficult to define, since we tend to feel that the transition from *H. habilis* to *H. erectus* was a gradual evolutionary change. The same argument is also true for the upper boundary between *H. erectus* and the pre-*sapiens* stage represented by Swanscombe

● Our primate behavioral heritage

▲ Primates use tools but do not possess culture.

■ The protohuman stage—a hypothetical reconstruction

and Steinheim, which are fairly well dated to the Mindel-Riss interglacial approximately 200,000 years ago.

3. *Homo sapiens neanderthalensis:* The Neanderthals are firmly dated to between 70,000 and 32,000 B.C. This age can be extended to about 100,000 years ago if we include Fontechevade and some other finds which date to the Riss/Würm interglacial.

4. *Homo sapiens sapiens:* Modern humans date at least 35,000 years ago to the present. One of the earliest specimens (found at Niah Cave in North Borneo) is 40,000 years of age (Harrisson 1972), and that from Border Cave (in South Africa) is greater than 50,000 years.

The Evolution of Human Behavior

We have discussed, in summary, human physical evolution, which is based on actual finds of bones located within a datable geological context. The evolution of human behavioral patterns must be reconstructed on the basis of less finite evidence. For such reconstructions we rely on the derivation of our species from a primate ancestry and on the gradual shift to tool manufacture and the transmission of culture from one generation to the next. A hypothetical sequence of human behavioral stages follows.

Nonhuman Primate Behavior

● Since human origins may be directly traced to primate ancestry, we will use this basic primate background as our starting point (Watson and Watson 1969).

All animals require protection, nourishment, and reproduction in order to survive. In the nonhuman primate these needs are met by the following anatomical and behavioral adaptations: The head is positioned so that in a sitting, standing, or walking position the animal faces forward and objects may be perceived with stereoscopic vision in color. When the animal is sitting or standing, its arms swing freely, and the unique adaptation of the opposable thumb permits articles to be grasped with the hand. The sexes are of differing sizes, with males occasionally attaining twice the size of females. Sexual activity may occur at any time during the year, with females in heat usually accepting the dominant male in the group, although occasionally they accept the other males as well. Infants are relatively helpless and require considerable maternal care and aid in locomotion. Compared to that of other animals, the primate's brain capacity is large, resulting in greater intelligence, perception, and skill in problem solving. Such primates are adaptable to a wide range of habitats.

Inadequately armed in terms of strength, teeth, and speed, primates gain protection through numbers. These primates form groups, which occupy a specific home range. Within the group, cooperative activity is structured to minimize conflict. The primary social mechanism utilized is the establishment of dominance, which permits each individual to establish his or her place in the group. Each individual also knows when to exert dominance and when to be subordinate. This pattern avoids conflict over sexual matters and the acquisition of food; and furthermore, it reduces anxiety in the individual inasmuch as each knows its rights and privileges. An additional factor is the security obtained as a result of being a group member. The individual is reinforced by behavior patterns, such as grooming, in which its psychological needs are clearly satisfied by others.

In the food quest, the individual primate operates primarily alone, consuming what is found. While some food sharing does occur, this is relatively rare, and happens only after basic hunger has been satisfied. Conflict over food is resolved through application of the principle of dominance. Another factor of relevance, since it differs from human behavior, is that food is seldom carried very far or stored for future use. Protection and food getting are further enhanced by the use of communication. Although vocalizations and gestures are interpreted by the other primates in certain ways, these responses are primarily inherited rather than learned. Thus, in no sense should primate behavior be interpreted as including a language, although primates do *symbolize* to a limited degree.

A further distinction applicable to primates is their ability to learn. The young acquire behavioral skills by observing their elders. However, there is little if any attempt to *teach* the young. ▲ Tool use among primates, while present, is limited. Sticks may be prepared for use against marauders, and twigs are peeled and inserted into termite nests to acquire the termites for food; also, stones are thrown at predators. Experiments with an orangutan resulted in the animal learning to strike flakes from a core and then use the flake to cut a string in order to open a box containing food. The importance of this experiment lies in the proof of the ability of the primate to *produce a tool through use of another object as a tool* (Kitahara-Frisch 1980). However, in a strict sense, primates do not *rely* upon tools in solving their problems of food acquisition, shelter, protection, and so forth. Thus while some nonprimates do make and use tools, this faculty is not basic to their survival.

Protohumans

■ At this stage, it is inappropriate to attempt to identify the time and place of the development of those behavioral patterns which can be termed *protohuman* (from *proto*, meaning "first"). What we are in fact describing is a stage of evolution which, while hypothetical, probably did indeed occur. Protohumans evolved to the point where they could stand and walk on two legs, which, according to Washburn (1978), probably happened between 5 and 10 million years ago. (Actual proof of bipedal locomotion is provided by the footprints found by Mary Leakey and dated to 3.7 million years [Anonymous 1979: 5].) By this time the posture reflected a shortening of the pelvis and a recurvature of the spine, internal organs having shifted to adjust to an upright posture. Arms were by now shorter than legs. Further evolution of the tongue and larynx facilitated sound production. While similar to the nonhuman primates in sexual dimorphism, these protohumans were of slightly larger size, and their life span was probably somewhat greater, being in the vicinity of 35 years.

The diet of protohumans was omnivorous and reflected a greater consumption of meat than that of nonhuman primates. Life in groups continued, but with certain major modifications, the most important of which was the development of the nuclear family. The protohuman infant was relatively helpless for a long period of time, and the mother of necessity had to devote her time to its care.

Cooperation in food gathering, food sharing, hunting, and child care, reinforced by a greater dependence on an *intentional* system of communication, are features of the protohuman family (Isaac 1978). The vocal manifestations of such communication may not have been particularly elaborate, but they were intended to facilitate sharing and cooperation. Thus the development of language was a result of the meeting of social needs.

The greater reliance on hunting among protohumans required a larger territory and more exclusive use of such an area due to the nature of the food chain. Herbivores consume large quantities of vegetal foods; thus, reliance on the herbivores for food by the protohumans required a greater area for the band than if the protohumans themselves were subsisting on vegetal foods. This expansion of exploited territory might incidentally have increased the chance for contact with other groups.

● How humans are defined

▲ The savanna—our earliest environment

■ Human evolution featured cooperation, communication, and planning.

● Culture as a protective mechanism

A major innovation relating to tool use by protohumans was that they intentionally manufactured tools for use; thus, they were capable of anticipating future needs. The gathering of food by the females to be shared back at the base camp required both planning and foresight (Isaac 1978). In addition, cooperative hunting requires planning, which is another feature indicative of *symbolization*, the intellectual quality associated with problem solving. Since such planning refers to future events, there was an increasing need for symbolic language.

Early Humans

● One definition of what is "human" is based on intelligence: Humans solve their problems of existence through the use of intellectual abilities. Our human ancestors did not overpower, outrun, or otherwise subjugate animal adversaries: They outwitted them. Crucial to this survival technique is the use of symbolic language and reliance on the cooperation of the group to carry out planned activities. While humans were larger and somewhat more modified for erect posture than protohumans, it was their intellectual attainments that distinguished them even further.

The Savanna Adaptation

▲ If, as the evidence suggests, the savanna environment was the "hearth" of human evolution, what were the unique factors that made it so? Perhaps first, in order of evolutionary priority, we should discuss the adaptations of our primate ancestors. For many years, physical anthro-

pologists have believed that because humans have prehensile hands and stereoscopic vision, their ancestors must have been forest dwellers adapted for brachiation, the method of locomotion by swinging from limb to limb (as practiced today by gibbons and Tarzan). In recent years, Sherwood Washburn (1978) has suggested that these ancestors experienced a period of knuckle walking, the four-legged ground-locomotion pattern of the modern gorilla. Such a pattern could eventually have led to the assumption of erect posture and true bipedalism. On the other hand, a knuckle-walking stage in human evolution is hypothetical rather than proven, and early humans may have shifted directly from brachiation and branch running to bipedalism (Jolly 1972: 49–50).

If these assumptions are reasonably correct, then the change from life in an arboreal environment to the savanna would have provided certain opportunities and stimuli. The greater distance between trees would have forced reliance on walking rather than on brachiation. The total vegetal productivity in a savanna is great, with a corresponding quantity and variety of animals. In contrast with a forest, the savanna would provide lesser amounts of fruits, nuts, and vegetal foods but a more than compensatory increase in animal foods. These factors would have favored a species which could subsist on an omnivorous diet.

Food getting in a savanna would probably have stimulated more cooperative activity as compared with forest life. Subsistence on vegetal foods can be an individual activity inasmuch as the foods are available for the taking and are not elusive. When early humans were faced with the acquisition of animal foods on the savanna, they had to cope with the fact that they were weaker, slower, and less keen of ear and nose than their quarry. Probably the earliest solution to this problem was the grouping together for purposes of scavenging. The group would locate a recent animal kill and then cooperate in keeping away other scavengers. Tools were used in the cutting of flesh from bones (necessary to replace the function of long canine teeth), the smashing of bones to obtain the marrow, and the hurling of missiles at other scavengers.

Hunting, as a cultural practice, could have evolved rather simply from the above example. Evidence from Olduvai Gorge indicates that small and immature animals were the preferred prey, although elephants were also killed and butchered. At Lake Turkana the prey species included hippos. The preference for small and immature prey is a situation similar to hunting by modern primates, such as baboons. Somewhat later is actual evidence of cooperative hunts, in which the group purpose was to search an area intensively for game and surround the game to limit its escape, or to dispatch an animal trapped in a bog or in some other disadvantageous situation. Only by cooperative effort could humans overcome their inherent weaknesses and subjugate animals larger, stronger, and faster than themselves. ■ This cooperation would lead to further cultural developments, primarily in the areas of defense, territoriality, social responsibility, and specialized skills used for the common good. Once developed, these behavioral patterns would provide a selective advantage of humans over their prey.

The basic structural unit in human social organization remains the family, although the recognition of relationship has been extended to several generations by means of formalized kinship systems. Thus by this extension, behavioral patterns among individuals were structured to include most if not all members of a band.

Culture as an Evolutionary Filter

Rights of inheritance, acquired status, and such are expressed in behavioral patterns keyed to the social framework of kinship. From this moment onward (once early humans had developed tool use, cooperation, and communication) in the history of human development, behavioral patterns are influenced more by cultural needs than by biological ones. In addition, the mass of accumulated knowledge that we know as culture is transmitted from generation to generation by means of symbolic language and intentional teaching. Thus by its nature, culture is accretional: It is forever increasing in quantity and variation. As a result, through time, humans create an increasingly powerful buffer between themselves and the environments they inhabit. With fire, simple and compound tools, constructed shelters, clothing, food storage, medical practices, and others in the long list of cultural traits, our ancestors protected themselves from the rigors of direct exposure to the natural elements. ● It is here that humans depart from the principles of natural selection as outlined by Darwin, for we have culture — a separate system which intercedes between us and the natural environment. The survival of the fittest, in human terms, no longer refers to the quick or the strong, but to the most adaptable culturally.

In answer to our initial question, How long have humans been using culture as their principal adaptive mechanism in survival? we now know that tool use extends over more than 2 million years. The development and transmission of culture — viewed as one whole — is at least equally as old. We know further that this process occurred during a period of dramatically fluctuating climate and that its evolution was initially slow. In part this was so because of the need for human physical evolution to occur prior to cultural evolution. In addition, since culture accumulates through time, its evolution progresses at an ever-increasing velocity.

PART III

CULTURAL DATA REVEALED BY ARCHAEOLOGY: THE OLD WORLD

Contained in the Old World — the continents of Africa, Europe, and Asia — is the long development of human cultural history. We shall devote the major portion of this text to the events of the Old World because they extended over an immense amount of time, from some 3 million to about 30,000 years ago. Prior to the latter date and the peopling of the New World, as far as can be determined, North and South America were uninhabited.

Although we shall present the Old World data in some detail, it is possible to group these findings into a limited number of cultural periods (which can typically be done for large geographic areas over long periods of time). The reason for this is the very limited change in tool types, subsistence patterns, and life styles over the immensely long period which we term the Paleolithic. This was the era which is primarily represented by stone tools, and it coincided with the evolution of hominids, from early ancestral forms to modern humans. Thus the slow evolution of tool types is undoubtedly linked to the slow development of human physical and mental capabilities. Also, as we have stated, these cultural patterns were typical over large geographic areas. It is therefore appropriate to separate our coverage into major descriptive categories. The divisions we have chosen to use are the traditional ones: Lower Paleolithic, Middle Paleolithic, Upper Paleolithic, Mesolithic, and Neolithic. This is the classification which has been typical of the archaeological literature since the late 19th century. Originally defined on the basis of changes in stone-tool types, we now view these periods not just in terms of their tool forms but more in terms of the overall cultural adaptations which characterize each. In the latter respect, it would be possible to introduce other terms for these periods, and some authors have done this. For example, the Neolithic period, or New Stone Age, has come to be recognized more for its change to food production—the raising of domesticated plants and animals—than for any changes in the form of its stone tools. Nonetheless, even if we chose to use such more appropriately descriptive terms, our needs would not totally be met since the older terms are deeply embedded in the archaeological literature. We have thus patterned our chapter headings on the more traditional grouping, not because we believe the traditional grouping to be better but because it is convenient and well known.

7

The Lower Paleolithic: Origins and Pebble Tools

The earliest cultural evidence of humankind occurs in the period prehistorians have termed the Lower Paleolithic or Old Stone Age. In spite of the neat three-part system consisting of nonhuman primates, protohumans, and early humans as outlined in the last chapter, we at times have difficulty in distinguishing these stages as represented by their archaeological remains.

A further consideration, when dealing with the archaeological record, is one of time. ■ The further we go backward in time, the harder it becomes to separate the human works from accidents of nature. The problem is that the older remains are, the less one has to work with, until, in the very oldest sites, only the most durable materials, such as stone, survive. Even stone tools are more difficult to distinguish from natural occurrences in the very early periods. Consequently, the nature and significance of this early material is often the center of controversy. For example, 50 to 100 years ago archaeologists argued for the acceptance of a class of artifacts called "eoliths," or "dawnstones," as being of human manufacture. These were naturally broken rocks which had supposedly been used as tools. Since these so-called tools do not follow any standardized pattern or form, are generally found in areas characterized by large-scale soil movement, and are often found in geological contexts of such antiquity as to preclude their manufacture by humans, modern workers no longer accept "eoliths" as being of human workmanship, and thus the term has disappeared from the recent literature (Oakley 1972:7–9).

Even under ideal circumstances and with good preservation, the material from very early sites usually consists of stone tools, bone remains

● A 15-million-year-old tool?

(either food debris or skeletal parts of individuals), and artificially introduced nonmodified stones, or manuports. A concentration of these various remains in the place originally occupied is termed a *living floor*. Living floors are our best evidence of the way of life during the Lower Paleolithic because it was at these locations that the tools, waste flakes or debitage, and food debris were actually discarded by the former inhabitants. We analyze these materials and their relationships to one another in order to derive inferences as to the original life-style of their users.

The Earliest Finds

The earliest evidence of possible tool use is that from Ft. Ternan in Kenya, excavated by L. S. B. Leakey. At this site in a level dated to the Miocene period, and approximately 15 million years of age, were found the remains of *Ramapithecus wickeri*, a small primate. In the same deposits occurred broken bones of several animal species in association with a battered stone. It is Leakey's opinion (personal communication 1970) that this find represents our earliest archaeological evidence of true tool use. He does not imply that this signifies culture or the presence of humans. ● What he does suggest is that the history of tool use has an antiquity of at least 15 million years.

The Osteodontokeratic Culture

Osteodontokeratic is a term that refers to the use of the bones, teeth, and horns of animals as tools. Raymond Dart (1955, 1957), reporting on a statistical analysis of thousands of bones recovered from the Makapansgat site in South Africa, indicates that there was a preference for certain

bones and for portions of certain bones to occur in the latter site. For example, there were 10 times as many distal ends of antelope humeri as there were proximal ends and 5 times as many humeri as femora. A high percentage of baboon skulls recovered at Makapansgat, Sterkfontein, Taung, and other early Pleistocene localities in South Africa show damage from use of a blunt object. Dart argues that the damage was inflicted by the distal end of an antelope humerus used as a club. Other points stressed by Dart are that antelope mandibles were split, the ascending rami removed, and that the sharp V-shaped teeth, still mounted in the jaw, were used as cutting implements. He also hypothesizes that many of the long bones were split by a twisting motion and that similar bones and horns were rammed into the long bones, probably to extract the marrow.

Few researchers accept the Osteodontokeratic culture as defined by Raymond Dart, as they believe many of the bones to be the result of scavenging. However, in spite of the fancifulness of some of Dart's interpretations, many workers would agree that if the Osteondontokeratic culture did not exist something very like it probably did.

Early Stone Tools in East Africa

According to Yves Coppens (1976) two East African localities, Omo in Ethiopia and East Rudolf in Kenya, have produced stone tools dated to approximately 2.0 million years ago. The Omo materials consist essentially of small pieces of quartz, with three basic groups or classes of tools having been identified. They are: angular fragments (60 percent), globular cores (10 percent), and flakes (30 percent). Bone remains and some teeth also show wear and retouch. Isaac et al. (1976) refer to this industry as the "Karari industry."

The "KBS industry" from East Rudolf is stratigraphically older than that of Omo; however, recent potassium-argon dates are 1.6 to 1.8 million years (Walker and Leakey 1978). According

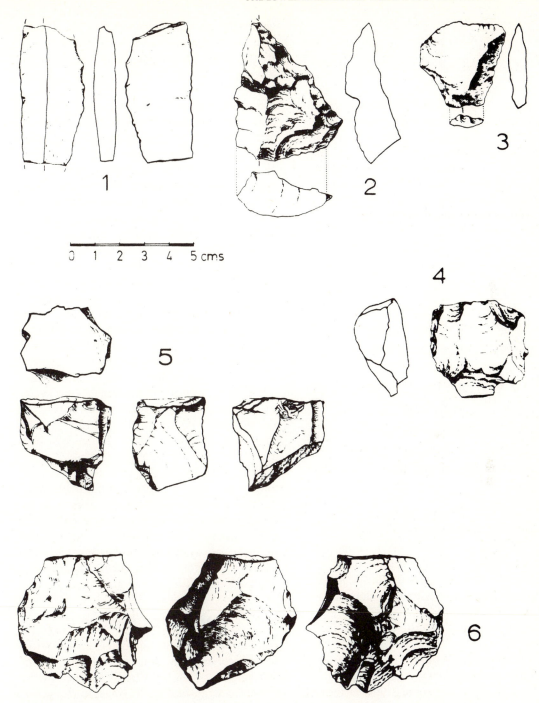

0 1 2 3 4 5 cms

Fig. 7-1 Early stone tools excavated from the KBS Tuff, East Rudolf region, East Africa. (*1*) Bladelike flake fragment with slight evidence of use. (*2*) and (*3*) Flakes. (*4*) Discoids. (*5*) and (*6*) Polyhedrons. These are among the earliest stone tools ever found. (Coppens et al. 1976.)

▲ Problems in identification of early stone tools

to Isaac et al. (1976), the KBS industry is an early component of the well-defined Oldowan industrial complex of East Africa. The KBS industry is very similar to one at site DK I in Olduvai Gorge, Tanzania, with the following exceptions: (1) The KBS industry is missing the flake scrapers and spheroids of the Oldowan and (2) overall, it tends to feature smaller implements (Fig. 7-1).

Both Omo and East Rudolf feature scattered and infrequent stone tools. While the age of these implements is still somewhat in doubt, we can perceive their affinity with the better-known Oldowan industry at Olduvai Gorge. Thus we may assume that they are at least as old as the Olduvai finds (1.75 million years) and perhaps even older.

Early Stone Tools in South Africa

In the South African sites, the problem lies not just with the location of early stone tools but in achieving agreement among the various authorities as to which specimens are in fact tools. A further problem is that the sites are not dated and can only be assigned a relative chronological position on the basis of the fauna present. Nonetheless, these sites are of extreme importance because they contain the type specimens of *Australopithecus africanus* and *Australopithecus robustus* in association with Osteodontokeratic remains and stone tools.

The earliest evidence for stone-tool making in South Africa comes from the site of Sterkfontein in the Transvaal region north of Johannesburg. Sterkfontein is today a small hill which contains the remains of small caves and sinkholes formed by solution of the local dolomite bedrock. In the breccia, a limestone-cemented deposit of bone fragments left by carnivores, a total of 286 stone

objects have been recovered, of which 97.5 percent are foreign to the site. There is the possibility that these were introduced by floodwaters of the nearby Blaauwbank River when its bed was some 30 meters higher than present. However, if such a natural cause can be ruled out, then the only other conclusion is that these rocks were carried to the site by hominids. The stones themselves have been studied by several archaeologists. R. J. Mason (1962) identified 98 as actual manufactured artifacts and the rest as natural pebbles or naturally fractured rocks. M. D. Leakey, restudying the same collection, identified only 73 as artifacts. R. G. Klein, in an unpublished study, was able to accept only 35 as artifacts. ▲ (It should by now be apparent that the study of the earliest tools poses serious problems of analysis.) The stones were randomly scattered through the upper layers of the site and thus do not indicate a living floor. The tools themselves exhibit numerous flake scars, with the detached flakes not common in the site (suggesting that they could have been manufactured elsewhere). Most of the implements are irregular rock lumps or oval pebbles which have had a few flakes removed. Three crude so-called hand axes are known, as well as one split bone point.

Who made the Sterkfontein tools? The beds contain remains of *Australopithecus africanus*, but not in association with the artifacts. In association with the implements are only three adult teeth and a juvenile palate (none of which are diagnostic as to species), which could represent remains of *Australopithecus africanus*, *Homo habilis* or even *Homo erectus*.

Olduvai Gorge

The best archaeological evidence for early tool making comes from Bed I at Olduvai Gorge, Tanzania (Fig. 7-2). Bed I has been dated by the potassium-argon method as covering the period from approximately 1.75 to 1 million years ago. At several locations within the bed (Fig 7-3, 7-6) is evidence of actual *in situ* living floors. Fur-

Fig. 7-2 Aerial view of Olduvai Gorge, Tanzania, the locale of numerous finds of early hominids and living floors. (Dexter slides, West Nyack, N.Y.)

Fig. 7-3 Map of Olduvai Gorge, showing the sites of major finds. (Jurmain et al. 1981: Fig 10-4.)

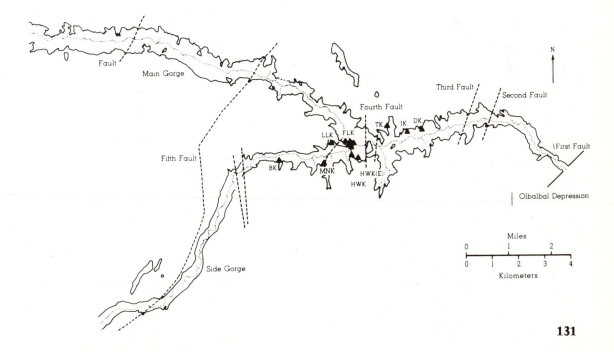

■ The Oldowan industry

thermore, the latter have been sealed in by subsequent volcanic-ash falls so that the chance of postdepositional alteration or introduction is minimal. These floors contain specific-use areas for stone-tool manufacture and food butchery, and even one ring of small boulders about 30 feet in diameter and 3 feet in width. This structure has been termed a "house," although an equally probable explanation is that the stones formed a ring of missiles ready for use against carnivores (Fig 7-4). Bone fragments indicate that the economy featured a reliance on birds, fish, snakes, small mammals, tortoises, gazelles, antelopes, pigs, and even carnivores. A final equivocal specimen here consists of remains of *Australopithecus boisei*, the famous 1959 find, initially termed a new genus, *"Zinjanthropus"* (Fig 7-6, 7-7). With the more recent finding of

Homo habilis remains in Bed I in the same sites, the Leakeys now regard *H. habilis*, the smaller gracile form, as the tool maker and site occupant and the robust *A. boisei* as a possible prey species.

The Olduvai sites are of incalculable importance as the earliest unequivocal evidence of true cultural living floors. They contain the camp debris of tool-manufacturing humans with a varied and omnivorous diet. Further, it is apparent that the species was capable of taking prey much larger than itself through reliance on cultural means. Also of importance is the fact that for the first time in the history of human culture, there is evidence of a true stone industry. The stone implements and chipping debris are indicative of a *pattern* of tool manufacture, and there is an inventory of specialized tools, including those of differing forms with presumably differing functions (Fig 7-5). ■ Termed the "Oldowan industry," this collection of stone implements has been described by M. D. Leakey

Fig. 7-4 Mary Leakey examining the stone circle found within Bed I at Olduvai Gorge. (Dexter slides, West Nyack, N.Y.)

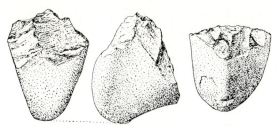

Fig. 7-5 Examples of Olduvan culture pebble tools from Olduvai Gorge. (Oakley 1972:4a.)

Fig. 7-6 (*Below*) The "Zinzanthropus" find site, located near the base of Bed I, Olduvai Gorge, underneath layers of volcanic ash dated by the potassium-argon method at 1.75 million years of age. (Dexter Slides, West Nyack, N.Y.)

Fig. 7-7 (*Right*) Reconstruction of the "Zinjanthropus" hominid, which today is considered to be a robust Australopithecine. (Courtesy British Museum [Natural History].)

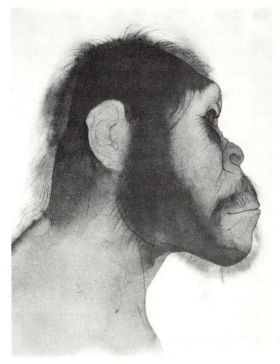

(1967). The sites from which the implements have been recovered occur from the very base of Bed I, throughout Bed I, and into the lower portion of Bed II, representing a time span of more than 1 million years (Figure 7-8). According to Leakey, the entire sequence demonstrates little evolutionary change over this enormously long period. However, the implements from the different sites differ in their frequency by type, suggesting that there was some specialization in function at various sites. The most important fact is that these early pebble tools are not simply crude lumps of rock but can be subdivided into a wide variety of categories based on form. According to M. D. Leakey, 13 types of tools—including choppers, spheroids, polyhedrons, scrapers, and discoids, as well as a variety of utilized materials—are distinguishable. By far the greatest number of tools are made on "cores," that is, on cobblestones, nodules, or blocks (M. D. Leakey 1967:420). What is surprising is the complexity and variety of tools in these earliest

● The Moroccan beach sequence

▲ European manifestations of Oldowan industries

known living floors. All of these finds, then, are extremely important to the understanding of human prehistory because they represent our earliest substantial evidence of a cultural inventory and of its maker, *Homo habilis*. This evidence is further augmented by abundant examples of the local fauna.

Immediately above the layer of wind-deposited tuff (fine-grained volcanic deposits) dividing Olduvai's Bed II into two parts, upper and lower, is the first appearance of a new culture, the Acheulean, which initially coexists with the developed Oldowan industry. Whether this new culture, normally associated with *Homo erectus*, represents an in-place development out of the simpler Oldowan culture or is the result of migration by another group with a superior technology has yet to be determined. (The Acheulean hand-axe culture will be described in detail in the next chapter.)

Fig. 7-8   The stratigraphy of Olduvai Gorge, showing the age and vertical provenience of the various hominid fossils, principal sites, and cultures. (Clark 1970: Fig. 12.)

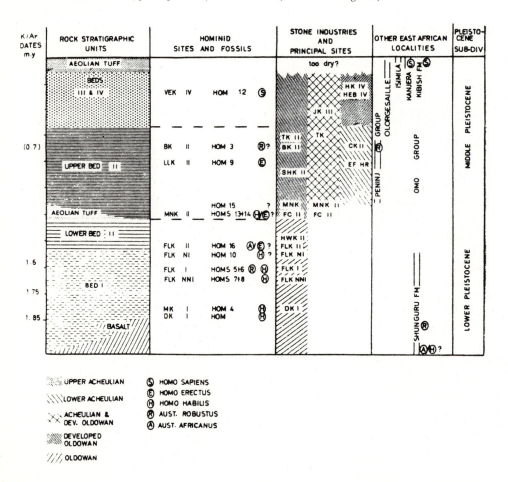

UPPER ACHEULIAN
LOWER ACHEULIAN
ACHEULIAN & DEV. OLDOWAN
DEVELOPED OLDOWAN
OLDOWAN

Ⓢ HOMO SAPIENS
Ⓔ HOMO ERECTUS
Ⓗ HOMO HABILIS
Ⓡ AUST. ROBUSTUS
Ⓐ AUST. AFRICANUS

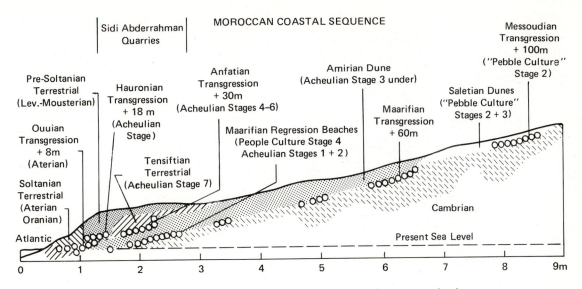

Fig. 7-9 Sequence of beach terraces on the Moroccan coast, illustrating the position of Acheulean cultural remains. (Clark 1970: Fig. 2.)

Oldowan and Evolved Oldowan Cultures outside Sub-Saharan Africa

On the northwest coast of Africa, in Morocco, is what Biberson (1961) has described as one of the most complete geologic and archaeological sequences in the Old World. In this scheme, a series of marine transgressions, or beaches, is integrated with a series of terrestrial dunes (see Table 7-1 and Figure 7-9). Found correlated with these events are stages of the local pebble-tool culture, which shows a strong similarity to the Oldowan pebble culture of East Africa. There are also eight stages of the succeeding Abbeville-Acheulean tradition. ● The Moroccan beach sequence clearly demonstrates continuity between the pebble-tool tradition and the later hand-axe tradition, which supports the contention that the hand axe evolved out of the earlier pebble-tool technology. ▲ Pebble tools typologically similar to the African examples are also known in Europe, for example, at the open-air site of

Terre Amata near Nice. (This latter site is also important for its evidence of huts, which will be described later.)

TABLE 7-1
Pleistocene Sequence at the Moroccan Beach Terraces

Marine Phase	Climatic Phase	Industries
	Soltanian	
Ouljian		Aterian
	Presoltanian	Mousterian
Harounian		Acheulean VIII
	Tensiftian	" VII
		" VI
		" V
		" IV
Anfatian		" III
		" II
	Amirian	" I
Maarifian		Pebble-culture IV
	Saletian	" III
Messaoudian		(Tardiguetian) II
	Moulouyen	" I

(Coles and Higgs 1969:170)

The oldest known Paleolithic (tool) industry in the British Isles, the Clactonian, was initially defined on the basis of its diagnostic flakes, and little attention was paid to the cores from which the flakes were detached. Recently, reanalysis of the Clactonian material has revealed it to be quite specific in its geographic and temporal occurrences. Therefore, Ohel (1979) concludes that the Clactonian may, in fact, represent only *preparatory areas* within a total Acheulean complex.

Another pebble-tool site has been found in Hungary, 50 kilometers northwest of Budapest. This is the important site of Vértesszöllös, which is known for: (1) its well-developed stratigraphy, (2) the presence of large numbers of stone tools and chipping debris (2,000 pieces), (3) evidence of the early use of fires, and (4) remains of *Homo erectus*. This site has been dated by faunal studies to the latter part of the Mindel glaciation. The tools, although small, appear related to those found at Olduvai Gorge; however, considering their later age, these, like most of the European materials, are probably part of an evolved Oldowan culture (Kretzoi and Vertes 1965).

In the Middle East the earliest evidence of the pebble-tool tradition occurs at Ubeidiya in the Jordan Valley, in Israel. Like Olduvai Gorge, the occupation at Ubeidiya represents a lakeside occurrence. The pebble culture is considered to be a variant of that found at Olduvai Bed II (Stekelis 1966).

Finds in India, Pakistan, Burma, Java, and China exhibit characteristics of a general evolved Oldowan culture. However, this does not mean that the Asian variants are direct lin-

Fig. 7-10 Excavations in progress at the site of Zhou koudian (Choukoutien), near Peking, China, the home of *Sinanthropus (Homo erectus)* for thousands of years. (Courtesy American Museum of Natural History.)

eal descendants of the Oldowan culture of East Africa. What is clear is that the relationships between the Asian Oldowan variants and the East African examples are yet to be explained. The best preserved evidence from Asia is from Zhoukoudian (Choukoutien). The site, which is a hill today (Figure 7-10), was formerly a narrow gorge, which has partially collapsed and is now filled with rubble. *Sinanthropus* camped here in small caves and under projecting rocks (Figure 6-6). The inhabitants possessed fire and manufactured chopping tools of quartz. Unfortunately, quartz is a poor material for tool manufacture, making it difficult to compare these implements with those of other industries. Bones within the cave include those of deer, pigs, antelopes, bison, horses, water buffaloes, elephants, monkeys, and rhinoceri. Hyenas were also common, suggesting that when the human occupants were not present the caves were used as lairs (Coles and Higgs 1969; Freeman 1977). Most importantly, all of the human skulls had the foramen magnum (the opening in the base of the skull for the spinal chord) enlarged, suggesting that *Sinanthropus* were cannibals. Cannibalism is also evidenced by femurs apparently having been cracked for the marrow. (*Sinanthropus* may in fact have even been headhunters.)

The implements made by *Sinanthropus* feature the bipolar technique, in which the stone core was placed on an anvil prior to the removal of flakes (Figure 7-11). As the flakes were struck off, the rebounding force of the blow from the anvil produced a secondary bulb of percussion; thus the flakes are double-ended, with a bulb at each end. Major tool types are choppers, chopping tools, scrapers, and a few bifacial, leaf-shaped tools. The Asian and Southeast Asian chopper-chopping-tool traditions were extremely long-lived and survived virtually unchanged throughout most of the Pleistocene, whereas in Europe and Africa pebble-tool cultures gave way to the succeeding biface tradition and the Middle-Paleolithic flake tradition.

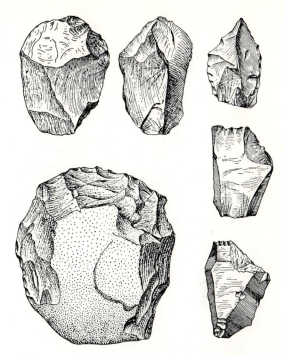

Fig. 7-11 Stone tools of *Sinanthropus* (*Home erectus*) (*a*) Quartz chopper tool. (*b*) Boulder chopper. (*c*) Pointed quartz flake. (*d*) Bipolar quartz flake. (*e*) Quartz crystal used as a tool. (Oakley 1972:49.)

Summary

The Oldowan pebble-chopper-chopping tool tradition and its associated variants clearly represent the single longest technological stage in human prehistory. This technology, crude and simple as it may have been, was obviously a successful adaptation which was widespread in Africa, Europe, and Asia (Map 7-1). This evidence suggests that the Oldowan "tool kit" was successfully utilized in a large variety of environments throughout the temperate and tropical regions of the Old World. Whereas in our discussion above we have followed numerous authors in assigning these materials to a Developed Oldowan category, we should point out that not all experts agree. For example, Stiles (1979), in studying the materials from Olduvai Gorge, states that the differences between the Acheulean and the developed Oldowan bifaces are due to differences in the raw materials and in the primary forms utilized. Such differences would not, then, support the concept of the developed Oldowan being a separate culture of its own, and thus Stiles suggests that the term "developed Oldowan" is invalid.

Map 7-1 Find Sites of Cultures with Early Pebble Tools.

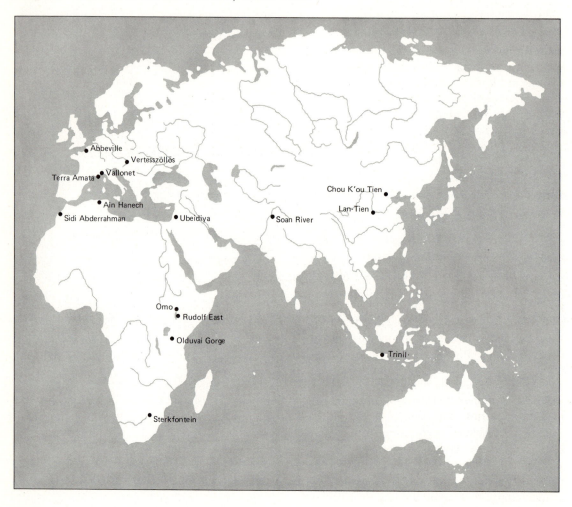

8

The Lower Paleolithic of Africa and Europe: The Acheulean Tradition

The Acheulean period covers a major unit of human prehistory. It extends over the remainder of the Lower Paleolithic, from at least 1 million years ago until as late as 100,-000 years ago. The geographic distribution of Acheulean remains is widespread, covering much of Africa and southern Europe, and extending eastward to India. The remainder of Asia featured a pebble-tool tradition. However, there seems to have been a northern limit to human occupation during this period, probably due to an inability to cope adequately with cold climates.

■ The original finds of Paleolithic materials were those made in France in 1846 by Boucher de Perthes and others. These bifacially flaked implements were termed "fist axes," or *coup-de-poing*. The earliest of such tools featured bifacial flaking only along the sides and at one end of a flat core. This resulted in a crude tool which was pointed on one end and of a size to be held in one hand. These tools were termed "Abbevillian" because they were first discovered near Abbeville. Since those initial findings, similar tools have been recovered in numerous sites from England to Africa. The stage of cultural evolution so represented has been known by a number of terms, including "Pre-Chellean," "Chellean," "Abbevillian," and "Lower Acheulean." According to Francois Bordes, one possible stage in the development from the Oldowan pebble tools to the true hand axe included the extention of edge retouch all along the circumference of the pebble, with retouch extending over both the upper and lower surfaces (Bordes 1968). Although Abbevillian implements are common, the sites in which they occur stratigraphically are rare in Europe but more frequent in Africa.

139

● The Acheulean industry

▲ Prepared flakes—a new technological tradition.

Little is known about their transition to the later main period of hand-axe use termed the "Acheulean."

In the absence of Abbevillian living floors, we are forced to define the transition from the Abbevillian to the Acheulean period in terms of the nature of the stone tools recovered. The major distinction is that the hand axes, or "bifaces" as they are frequently termed, are better made in the Acheulean period. They tend to be flaked all over, and, most importantly, there was a shift in the flaking technique from the use of hammer-stones to the use of cylinder hammers. The latter are round in cross section and are of a relatively soft material. Typical cylinder hammers are portions of mammal long bones or wood of a similar size and shape. The use of a cylinder hammer produces flatter and thinner flakes, thus giving greater control over the end product (Fig. 8-1) (Watson 1968). Hand axes may have been utilized as weapons, although they were probably more often used as skinning knives, scrapers, or as multipurpose tools. ● The hand axe is the hallmark of the Acheulean tradition.

For many years it was believed that these core tools represented a distinct tradition, with another tradition relying on flake tools existing simultaneously in Europe. In recent years, more complete excavations of *in situ* living floors have clearly indicated that the Acheulean peoples possessed a large inventory of flake tools. In his monumental studies of Lower- and Middle-Paleolithic tools, Bordes (1961) has identified a

Fig. 8-1 (*Below*) Acheulean hand axe from the gravels of the 100-foot terrace of the Thames River, England. (Courtesy British Museum [Natural History].)

Fig. 8-2 (*Right*) A Levallois core with flake removed. The core (to the *right*) exhibits scars of the preparatory flakes that were struck off prior to the removal of the Levallois flake. (Grady photograph.)

total of 63 separate implement types, most of which are present in the Acheulean. The most important core tools are the hand axe and bifacially flaked cleavers, with flake tools having been fashioned to perform a variety of cutting and scraping functions.

The Levallois Technique

At the site of Cagny, near Amiens, France, in deposits attributed to the Riss glaciation, we have the earliest documented presence of a new stone-tool manufacturing method. Termed the "Levallois technique," after the French site where these particular tools were first discovered, this procedure resulted in the manufacture of flakes that were shaped to a predetermined form before being detached from the core (Fig. 8-2). ▲ These prepared flakes were then further modified by edge chipping to form a wide variety of flake tools. The Levallois technique became the dominant tool tradition in the later Middle-Paleolithic period of Europe and North Africa and will be discussed later in greater detail (Watson 1968).

Throughout the Acheulean period, the bifaces evolved in form. Through time they became better made, flatter, thinner, and smaller. Differences in their shapes — for example, elliptical, ovoid, or teardrop — seem to bear little relationship to differences in temporal or spatial distribution.

Acheulean People

The human species most commonly associated with Acheulean remains is *Homo erectus*. However, this is not to imply that there is a precise correlation between that particular human physical type and a cultural tradition as long-lived as the Acheulean. The latest Acheulean sites are in the vicinity of 50,000–100,000 years of age, which is within the time span of *Homo sapiens neanderthalensis*. (According to some au-

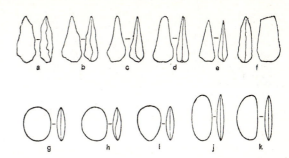

Fig. 8-3 Differing shapes of hand axes, ranging from pointed to tongue-shaped, lanceolate, heart-shaped, and even oval. (Oakley 1972: Fig. 9.)

thors, this span might even include *Homo sapiens sapiens*.)

The Nature of Acheulean Hunter-Gatherers

A striking feature of Acheulean industries is that in spite of their coverage of 500,000 to 1,000,000 years and their distribution over much of three continents, they are similar to one another. We explain this continuity of tradition in a number of ways: (1) The limited evolutionary change in Acheulean implements has been linked to the rate of evolution of the human brain: It is hypothesized that a limited industry was all that was needed at that time. (2) Because Acheulean implements are not specific as to function, adaptations to different environments could be effected by modifications in social structure rather than in the form of the tools used. (3) Where careful excavation of Acheulean sites has been carried out, artifacts of wood and bone have occasionally been recovered. Thus it is possible that artifacts of *differing* form have existed but have not been preserved. Most archaeological studies of Acheulean stone tools provide only information about their form rather than their function (Fig. 8-3).

In addition to the stone tools, we have evidence of a number of structures and evidence of the use of wooden spears, wooden digging implements, wooden clubs or throwing sticks, and

■ The Acheulean life-style

● An omnivorous diet was important to human survival.

fire. The structures are not common, although they are known from Spain, France, Italy, Nubia, Syria, and Zambia. ■ This suggests either that Acheuleans frequently camped without building any type of permanent shelter or that such structures have not been preserved.

Major food resources were the large mammals, including elephants, hippos, horses, cattle, baboons, pigs, rhinos, and occasional carnivores. Small animals were also common, with rodents, birds, and reptiles being represented in Acheulean sites. The bulk of evidence suggests that by this time early humans had become successful hunters, although our knowledge of specific hunting techniques is vague. Large animals were driven into bogs or swamps, where they were dispatched with spears, clubs, and hand axes. The use of the bolas, fire drives, and vegetable poisons, while possible, would be difficult to establish from the archaeological data at hand, although these methods may occasionally be inferred from the evidence.

With only stone tools and bones as major data, it is extremely difficult to interpret Acheulean social structure and subsistence patterns. We are therefore forced to rely on analogies with modern hunter-gatherers (Lee and DeVore 1968), which suggest that most such groups are made up of bands of 20 to 30 individuals, with a population density seldom exceeding 100 persons per 1,000 square kilometers. Such a population stabilizes at only 20 to 30 percent of the average carrying capacity of the environment, since the population size is adjusted to the season and to the years of minimal carrying capacity. The fact that in modern aboriginal groups band size is fairly stable, even in differing environments, suggests that the typical band size of 20 to 30 persons may be conditioned more by

human social factors than by environmental limitations.

The Acheulean economic pattern probably included seasonal movements in search of food, with certain favorable sites functioning as central loci to which the band returned periodically. Much of the food must have been of vegetable nature, for modern tropical hunter-gatherers rely on meat for only 20 to 40 percent of their diet. Unfortunately, the archaeological record provides little evidence of vegetal foods and may moreover provide an overrepresentation of tools used in hunting.

Sites in both Europe and Africa suggest that open savannas or grasslands were preferred, with sites being located near streams, lakes, and other sources of water. The Acheuleans did not modify their environment appreciably, and even their use of fire was probably restricted. Presumably, the Acheuleans expanded to the geographic and climatic limits permitted by their culture. Acheulean living floors are relatively common, and an example of the one from Olorgesailie, Kenya, is illustrated to demonstrate the type of evidence which has been preserved (Figure 8-4).

The Diet of the Acheuleans

Inferences as to Acheulean diet are of course limited by what has been preserved. Since plant parts are not present, the evidence consists only of food bones and their patterned occurrence within butchering sites. Evidence from a butchering site at Mwanganda (although a later Lupemban culture site [Sampson 1974:229]) may be used as a guide in our inference of Acheulean behavioral patterns. Clark and Haynes (1970:407–409) have summarized and interpreted these bone occurrences as follows:

... where a single or a minimal number of carcasses are present, slight as it is, [the evidence] suggests first, that human butchering practices generally resulted in the disarticulation, dispersal and differential fracture of the bones of the large food animals. It would seem also that they were butchered at the place where they were killed or where the carcass was found.

Secondly, the evidence suggests that Paleolithic butchering and meat processing equipment consisted predominantly of small numbers of Light Duty tools and cutting flakes and small scraping tools with few larger implements. This large tool element appears to be supplementary rather than primary to the main purpose of the equipment.

Thirdly, . . . little change can be observed in the basic pattern of these occurrences from the Lower Pleistocene right through to Holocene times.

Reviewing much the same evidence, Isaac (1971) has formulated an interpretation of Lower Paleolithic diet. ● His conclusions are that throughout the Pleistocene the hominid diet was omnivorous and specifically included meat. Further, the utilization of large animals is at-

Fig. 8-4 Acheulean living floor at the East African site at Olorgesailie, Kenya, illustrating the quantity of artifacts and manuports present. (Isaac 1977: Plate 10.)

tested to by the presence of bones of the latter in refuse of Lower Pleistocene age. The exact age of cooperative hunting is as yet unknown, although positive evidence dates back to the Middle Pleistocene. More important, according to Isaac, was the division of labor between male hunters and female gatherers, a differentiation which he believes is basic to the hominid pattern of adaptation over the past 2 million years. He stresses the fact that the omnivorous diet was of greater importance to the survival and evolution of early humans than the mere fact of predation.

An Acheulean Hunt

One of our best examples of a reconstruction of a Lower Paleolithic hunt is that of F. C. Howell, based on his excavations in the Ambrona Valley of Spain (Howell and others 1965:91–100). Such a reconstruction is hypothetical at best, owing to the variables affecting preservation of site data. For example, we have no human remains from the site so we must infer that the hunters were *Homo erectus* from the presence of their Acheulean type implements. The actual tools found were made of imported stone; thus they were carried there in preparation for the hunt. A linked inference is that since the hunt was planned in advance it took place at a specific time in the year, such as autumn when the migratory mammoth would have been moving South to warmer locations. The valley itself would have formed a natural funnel which the hunters were able to use for their ambush. The hunters would have normally consisted of bands of a few adult males and females plus their offspring; no more than 30 people at the most, at least that is the typical group size of modern primitive hunting bands and we believe the Acheulean bands were similar. If such was the case, then more than one band grouped together to provide the manpower for the Ambrona mammoth drive. The actual drive itself was conducted through use of fire by means of which

the prey were driven into boggy ground where they were killed with wooden spears and rocks. The elephants would have been hemmed in by the steep sides of the valley as well as by fires set by the hunters to cut off their escape. Howell found the charcoal and stones used in the kill as well as the bones of the mammoths in the spot where they were killed, still mired in the bog. Other specific evidence found consisted of a smashed elephant skull from which the brains were taken and a line of bones—a tusk, two femurs, and two tibias, all from the same animal but dismembered. Howell infers that these bones formed a causeway across the bog providing a means for the hunters to carry the butchered meat to dry ground (see Fig. 8-5). After the hunt there was undoubtedly a feast. Probably some of the meat and internal organs were eaten raw immediately after the kill to be followed later by more leisurely gorging around the campfires. Other activities inferred by Howell are of a social nature. We cannot prove that there was boasting about the day's successful hunt or its reenactment, but such seems probable.

At another Acheulean site, Olorgesailie in Kenya excavated by Glynn Isaac (1977), the prey species of *Homo erectus* was the giant gelada baboon. The site is located in a basin that formed as a result of tectonic activity in the Rift Valley. The baboon bones and artifacts, which included thousands of hand axes, were deposited at the time that the site formed the shore of an ancient lake in the basin. Although the baboon bones may not be in their original position, since there is evidence of deposition by water action Shipman, Bosler, and Davis (1981 p. 257), state that they believe the presence of large quantities of broken baboon bones is the direct result of butchering activities by *Homo erectus*. Supporting evidence for this view is the large number of artifacts present and the fact that all body parts of the baboons are represented. In their efforts to prove this hypothesis Shipman, Bosler, and Davis analyzed the breakage patterns of the

Fig. 8-5 Distribution of bone and artifacts in the Acheulean site of Ambrona, Spain, excavated by Clark Howell of the University of Chicago. This is the alignment of bones and tusk thought to have been used as a causeway on the boggy ground. (de Sonneville-Bordes 1967: Fig. 45.)

bones from Olorgesailie and then compared those with breakage characteristics of the baboon bones from all the nonarchaeological sites from East Turkana. Their conclusions are that the breakage patterns at Olorgesailie are so distinctive that they must be the result of butchering by humans. Their reconstruction of the butchering is that the shoulder joint was disarticulated by smashing the proximal end of the humerus, the forearm was separated by striking the humerus next to the elbow, further blows to the forearm shattered the radius and the posterior end of the ulna, the hip joint was disarticulated by forcing a lateral rotation of the femur and then chopping through the muscles and tendons. Next the femur was separated by smash-ing the acetabulum, the socket in the pelvis. The knee joint was smashed and then the foot was removed by a blow to the ankle followed by severing of the muscles and tendons. This pattern of bone breakage suggests that the hand axes were used primarily to smash through the joints rather than cut through them. Other evidence consists of the age/sex ratio. The male female ratio of the 90 individuals, of which 76 are juveniles and 14 adult, is 1:1. Since these characteristics differ from those typical of living groups of baboons, the conclusion is that the killing represents attrition rather than the killing of an entire troop at one time. This inferred pattern of the hunting of individuals rather than troops differs from the modern hunting method

145

▲ Early shelters included huts and caves.

of the Hadza of Tanzania cited by Isaac (1977) wherein the troop is encircled and then all are clubbed to death as they attempt to break out of the circle. The Acheulean pattern is thus inferred as the hunting of stray individuals or small numbers of individuals and then bringing the entire carcass back to the campsite for butchering.

Opinions differ as to why *Homo erectus* selected these giant baboons as prey. There is a strong bias toward the selection of young individuals, which would likely have been the easiest to kill, and also most likely to be caught isolated from the troop. Although there are also bovids, equids, and suids present as probable prey species at Olorgesailie it was the baboons that were preferred. Weighing up to 65 kilograms as adults, the male baboons were similar in size to modern female gorillas. Some authorities feel that primates of this size would have been easier prey animals to kill than the equids and bovids which were more fleet of foot. The opposing argument is that owing to their size and strength the giant baboons would have been formidable prey animals in their own right. In any event scientific analysis of the bone breakage patterns suggests that *Homo erectus* was able to kill numbers of these baboons seemingly without difficulty.

Habitations of the Lower Paleolithic

One of the more exciting developments in recent Lower-Paleolithic research has been the recovery of the evidence of shelters. Implications of the rock circle found at Olduvai Gorge have already been discussed. The Abbevillian site of Terre Amata ("Beloved Land") at Nice (France), however, is far more complex than the simple

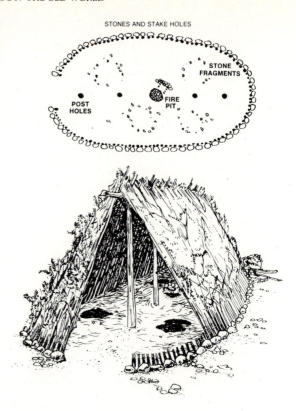

Fig. 8-6 Reconstruction of the type of Acheulean hut that was inhabited at Terra Amata near Nice, France, some 300,000 years ago. The walls were of poles some three inches in diameter. The huts ranged from 26 to 49 feet in length and from 13 to 20 feet in width. (Fairservis 1975: 62.)

living floors at Olduvai. Excavations of some 144 square yards recovered 35,000 objects, each of which has been mapped on one or more of 1,200 charts. ▲ Twenty-one huts and living floors were excavated, 6 on an ancient beach, 4 on a sand bar, and 11 on an inland dune. With an age of 300,000 years, these huts are among the oldest structures known. The hut shape in general was an elongated oval, ranging in length from 26 to 49 feet and from 13 to 20 feet in width. Down the long central hut axis were a series of postholes (approximately 1 foot in diameter) which served as central beam supports. The walls are defined by a series of stake holes approximately 3 inches in diameter. The stability of the hut walls was reinforced by a line of rocks (Figure 8-6), and there is evidence within the huts of hearths 1 to 2 feet in diameter. With Verteszollos in Hungary, Terre Amata also thus provides the earliest evidence for the use of fire in Europe.

The exact superimposition of the huts on the inland dune and the repeated use of the fire hearths tempts one to visualize the site as being used annually over several years. Pollen analysis of the associated human fecal material places this use at the end of spring and the beginning of summer.

A short distance geographically — but considerably removed in time — from Terre Amata is the Acheulean cave of Lazaret (Delumley 1969b). The site is located at Nice, just east of the commercial harbor and less than 100 meters from the sea. The grotto is a cavity 40 meters deep and 20 meters wide. In layer 5, at about 100,000 years of age, there is evidence for a tent-like structure 11 meters long and 3.5 meters wide at its middle (Figure 8-7). This site seems to have been a place of rest and shelter from the elements. Evidence of periodic cleaning of the habitation areas argues for repeated occupation. These habitation sites — the Oldowan circle, the Abbevillian Terre Amata, and the Acheulean Lazaret cave — have one thing in common: All are circumscribed by a border of large rocks.

Summary

The Lower Paleolithic is an immensely long period of human cultural history. During this interval humans adapted to the savanna in Africa, in more northern regions survived several gla-

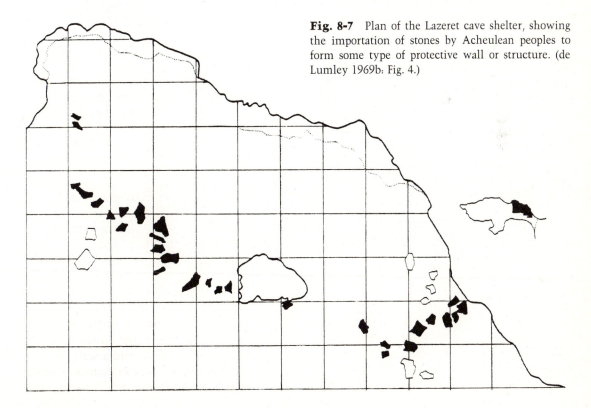

Fig. 8-7 Plan of the Lazeret cave shelter, showing the importation of stones by Acheulean peoples to form some type of protective wall or structure. (de Lumley 1969b: Fig. 4.)

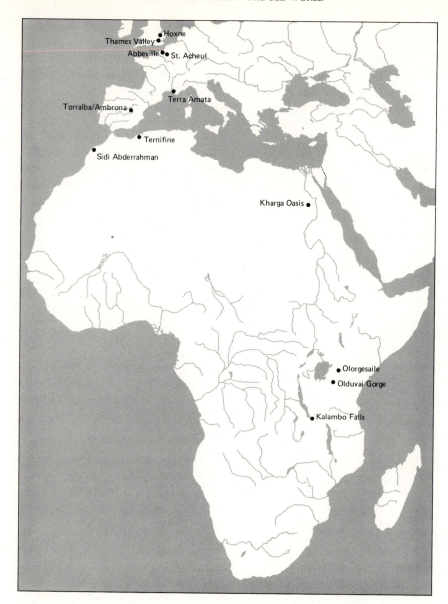

Map 8-1 Major Lower Paleolithic (Acheulian) Sites.

cial and interglacial periods, learned to control fire, developed cultural techniques for hunting, butchering, and plant gathering, and even began to diversify their tool inventory. Major tool traditions include first pebble tools, which are followed by bifaces and then by the Levalloisian technique, which came to dominate later periods of tool manufacture.

During the Lower Paleolithic our ancestors evolved physically from one of the more capable

Australopithecines into true humans. Cranial capacity increased and, concomitantly, so did the abilities to communicate, organize, and symbolize. However, at this time we have limited evidence that humans had developed much social organization or any religious beliefs. Edwards (1978) has nevertheless taken issue with these conclusions. He cites the fact that some nonutilitarian artifacts do occur in Acheulean contexts. These include lumps of red ochre at Ambrona, quartz crystals at Zhoukoudian (Choukoutien), a preponderance of skulls preserved at Zhoukoudian (Choukoutien) suggesting that there was some selection involved in their preservation, the fine flaking exhibited on the bifaces, and an engraved ox rib of Acheulean age from Pech d l'Aze. All these remains suggest that *Homo erectus* may not have been *only* interested in basic survival.

At this level, early humans were capable predators but were only on the threshold of their destiny as a major influence on their environment. Presumably, during this interval, they lived in small bands of 25 to 30 individuals, hunted and gathered, and followed a migratory way of life, accumulating few permanent possessions. Having evolved this far, our ancestors—whether they knew it or not—were ready to take a new cultural step into the Middle Paleolithic.

9

The Middle Paleolithic

The Middle Paleolithic includes those cultures which flourished during the early and middle stages of the Würm glaciation. These industries are for the most part an outgrowth of the late Acheulean culture. In Asia we perceive a continuation of the earlier pebble-tool-chopper tradition. Whereas the earliest cultures termed "Middle Paleolithic" are dated on geologic evidence from as early as 75,000 to 100,000 years ago, radiocarbon dates only go back to ca. 55,000 B.C. due to the limitations of this dating method. Securely dated Middle Paleolithic sites thus extend from 55,000 B.C. to 32,000 B.C. (Clark 1979).

During this period there was regional variation in cultural evolution, with some areas evolving more rapidly than others; and this was to be expected in a situation marked by small local groups frequently existing in relative isolation. The major cultural tradition of the Middle Paleolithic is that termed "Mousterian," after its typesite, the rock shelter at Le Moustier, France. Mousterian industries are widespread throughout the ancient world, being found not only in those regions characterized by the early Acheulean, but in regions where the Mousterian represents the earliest human occupation, such as European Russia. Mousterian sites are widespread not only in Europe but also in the Middle East, Northern Asia, and North Africa. As noted previously, the chopper-chopping-tool tradition continued in existence, forming a cultural isolate in southern Asia and China. The period is marked by the expansion of peoples into new geographic regions. ■ The environment changed with the onset of the Würm glaciation, and some Mousterian cultures became adapted to life in a cold climate. Major cultural innovations included the development of "tool kits," presumed to represent increasing adaptations to local environments. Thus the Middle Paleolithic is marked by an increasing diversification and specialization of tool inventories. There was a major emphasis on the use of caves and rock shelters as occupation sites, while sites in the open featured constructed shelters (Figure 9-1). The economy included heavy reliance on the hunting of herd-dwelling animals. Site remains indicate that the Mousterian hunters were highly proficient, as some sites contain the bones of thousands of animals. The species hunted were apparently highly selected, as some sites feature horses, others bison, and so on. Other innovations, such as intentional burial, reflect the development of a system of beliefs which may be termed "magico-religious." The human variety present during the period is predominantly Neanderthal.

● In our consideration of the Middle Paleolithic we will review the nature of the stone in-

Map 9-1 Major Neanderthal/Mousterian Sites.

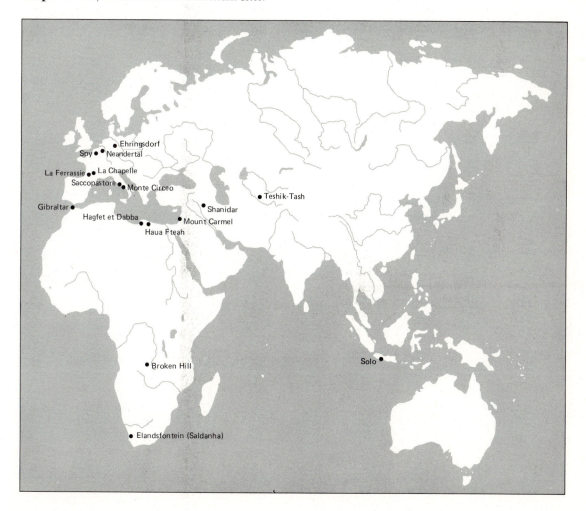

▲ Mousterian variants—a case study in interpretation.

dustries and their distribution, the Neanderthal people, the Würm environments, the growth of cultural elaboration, and, finally, the replacement of the Neanderthals by *Homo s. sapiens*.

Mousterian Industries

Mousterian industries are characterized by tools made on flakes by the Levallois technique and the discoid technique. The former, named after the Parisian working-class suburb of Le Vallois,

is a technique in which the flint knapper detaches a flake of a predetermined size and shape from a preshaped core. Discoid derived flakes, on the other hand, are not preshaped but are detached from a core and then shaped to meet the maker's needs.

Hand axes are present, in limited numbers, but these tend to be of small size. However, the *variety* of implements increases in comparison with the earlier Acheulean industries. Tool types of high frequency in the Mousterian include backed knives, a variety of end and side scrapers, burins, borers, and points. The number of variations suggests new functions for tools, such as the scraping of hides, the manufacture of clothing, and the working of wood and bone

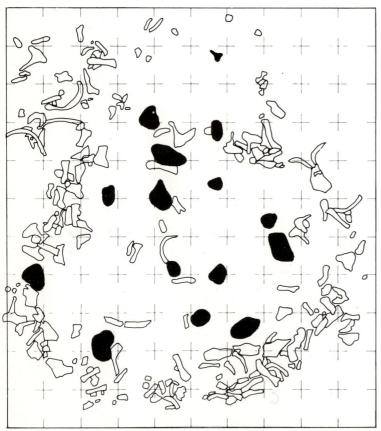

10 m

Fig. 9-1 (*Left*) Cultural remains present at the Russian site of Molodova. These mammoth hunters not only preyed upon the species but extensively utilized mammoth bones and tusks in their housing. (*Below*) Reconstruction of house type. (Freeman 1980: Figs. 12.4 and 12.5.)

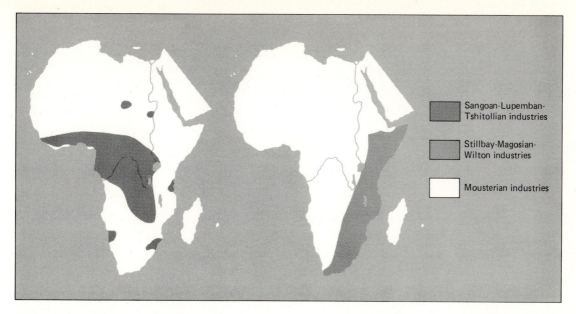

Map 9-2 Distributions of African Middle Paleo-lithic Industries. (After Cole 1963:196.)

Fig. 9-2 Mousterian implements: the prepared-platform flake technique. (*1*) struck Levallois core; (*2*) untrimmed flake tool; (*3*) edge-trimmed flake tool; (*4*) flake tool; (*5*) Levallois blade. Specimens (*6*) and (*7*) are Levallois points. (Watson 1968: Plate III.)

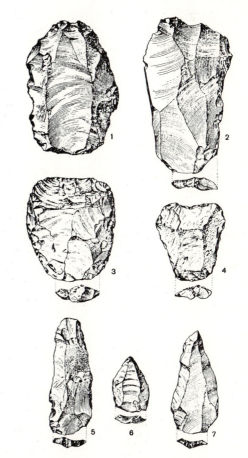

into a variety of useful objects. In summary, there is a dramatic increase in the number of tools used to make culturally useful implements.

▲ The Mousterian culture is widespread geographically and possesses distinct cultural variants. For example, the Mousterian of the Levant is somewhat different from that of North Africa and that of Europe in the frequency of occurrence and types of tools, and even in Europe alone there is widespread variation (McBurney 1950). It is in the Mousterian of Europe that we have had the greatest amount of study, enabling the delineation of four major subtraditions. These have been termed the Typical Mousterian, the Mousterian of Acheulean Tradition, the Charentian Mousterian, and the Denticulate Mousterian (Figures 9-2 to 9-5). These industries

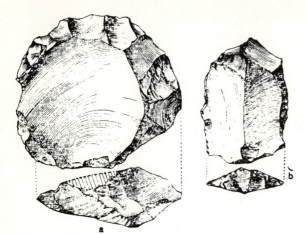

Fig. 9-3 Mousterian implements: Levallois core and flake. (*a*) Plan and profile of the core. (*b*) Plan and profile of the flake. These specimens, although not a matched set, came from the same working floor in Cyrenaica, North Africa. (Watson 1968:54.)

Fig. 9-4 Mousterian implements. (*a,b*) Side scrapers; (*c*) disc-core; (*d*) point; (*e*) small anvil or hammerstone; (*f,g*) hand axes; (*h*) oval flake tool. (*a–d*) Typical Mousterian. (*f,g,h*) Mousterian of Acheulean tradition. (Oakley 1972:57.)

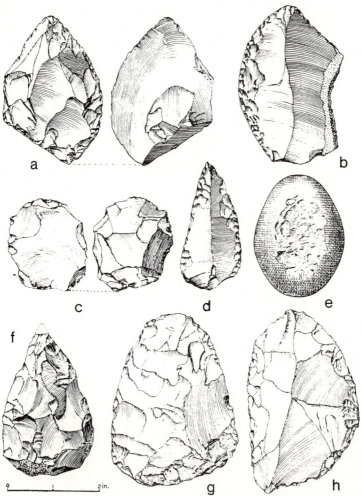

Fig. 9-5 Mousterian implements: leaf-shaped points and bifaces. (Watson 1968: Plate IV.)

may be geographical variants, although occurring in the same region and even in the same sites; furthermore, they are not entirely chronological variants, as several existed contemporaneously. At one well-known site, Combe Grenal in southern France, are 68 layers of Mousterian culture. Within these layers the Mousterian variants occur and reoccur without chronological segregation. A brief description of the salient features of each of these variants is presented below (Bordes 1968, 1972; Bordes and de Sonneville-Bordes 1970).

The *Charentian Mousterian group* is characterized by extremely high percentages of side scrapers. Hand axes and denticulates tend to be rare, but there are numbers of notched flakes. This group is further subdivided into (1) Quina type and (2) Ferrassie type, based on the absence in the former and the presence in the latter of the Levallois technique.

The *Typical Mousterian group* is characterized by a variable percentage of side scrapers, low percentages of transverse scrapers, and the absence or low percentage of Quina-type scrapers. Both hand axes and backed knives are rare. Variable percentages of Levallois flakes are present.

The *Mousterian of Acheulean Tradition group* has been divided by Bordes into two phases: type A and type B. The difference, in this case, is chronological, since type A always precedes type B. The type-A variant is present from the beginning of the Würm glaciation. Distinctive tools are the hand axes, present in frequencies of up to 40 percent. Typical hand axe forms are triangular, cordiform and subcordiform. Flake tools are varied but feature scrapers in frequencies of from 10 to 40 percent. Points are common, having thinned butts and some bifacial flaking. Denticulates are also common. Burins, end scrapers, borers, flakes, and trun-

cated blades are more common than in the other types of the Mousterian. Backed knives are rare. Type-B features fewer hand axes, at only 2 to 8 percent, and few side scrapers. Most common are denticulates and backed knives, the latter being made on elongated flakes or blades. Type B seems to date from the beginning of Würm II to the Würm II-III transition.

> ■ Different-cultures hypothesis
> ● Different-activities hypothesis
> ▲ Evolutionary hypothesis
> ■ Evaluation of the hypotheses
> ● Differences could be due to chance

The *Denticulate Mousterian group* is characterized by high percentages of denticulates and notched tools, with a low percentage of side scrapers. There are no Quina-type scrapers, no hand axes, and only on rare occasions are backed knives present. The presence of Levallois flakes is variable.

Figure 9-6 illustrates the complexity of the sequence of the various groups at the multilayered site of Combe Grenal in southwestern France. Several hypotheses have been proposed to explain this sequence; however, to date no single theory has been accepted as definitive. F. Bordes (1972) tends to interpret these variants as representing cultural differences of human groups possessing different traditions. ■ L. Binford and S. Binford (1966) using Bordes's typology, factor analysis, and the results of their own and some of Bordes's excavations, have argued that the various groups represent different specialized activities, such as living sites, hunting sites, and workshops. ● A variation of this theme would argue for seasonal activities. ▲ A third hypothesis concerns the idea of change through time. According to this argument, the Mousterian of Acheulean Tradition (with its Acheulean affinities) loses its hand axes, thus becoming Typical Mousterian, which in turn is followed by an evolved Mousterian of the Quina type.

■ The first argument, the "different-cultures" hypothesis, is difficult to sustain because it implies separate cultural entities surviving side by side, unchanged, for tens of thousands of years. The second hypothesis requires acceptance of the improbable proposition that certain sites were reserved for thousands of years for only certain activities or for seasonal occupation. The "change-through-time" argument has much to recommend it, but how do we explain a sequence in which two typical Mousterian layers are separated by a layer of the Mousterian of the Acheulean Tradition? This problem is not insurmountable if we consider that the Mousterian of Acheulean Tradition is characterized (according to Bordes 1972) by "rarely less than 8 percent handaxes," and that percentages are an internal measurement. In other words, depending upon the size of the sample, the presence or absence of a single hand axe could change the group-affiliation diagnosis.

In light of our present knowledge, perhaps the most rational answer to this problem has been provided by David L. Clarke (1972). He proposes a simple experiment in which five white and five black marbles are placed in a bag and a 60 percent sample is then drawn therefrom. ● If this is done a number of times and the number of white and black marbles is tallied for each draw, we have a situation (according to Clarke) similar to that found in the deeply stratified cave sites with their complex sequences of "groups": These so-called differentiations may be nothing more than the results of sampling error (Figure 9-7).

Cultural Elaboration in the Middle Paleolithic

For the first time in the history of cultural evolution, we find evidence that humans were concerned with more than mere subsistence. Culture is a cumulative process consisting of learned, shared behavior which is transmitted from generation to generation. Thus the Middle Paleolithic legacy of food-getting techniques which had developed during the Lower Paleolithic was now elaborated upon, and new interests unrelated to the economy developed. The shift from open sites to caves or rock shelters noted earlier (e.g., Lazaret Grotto) now became

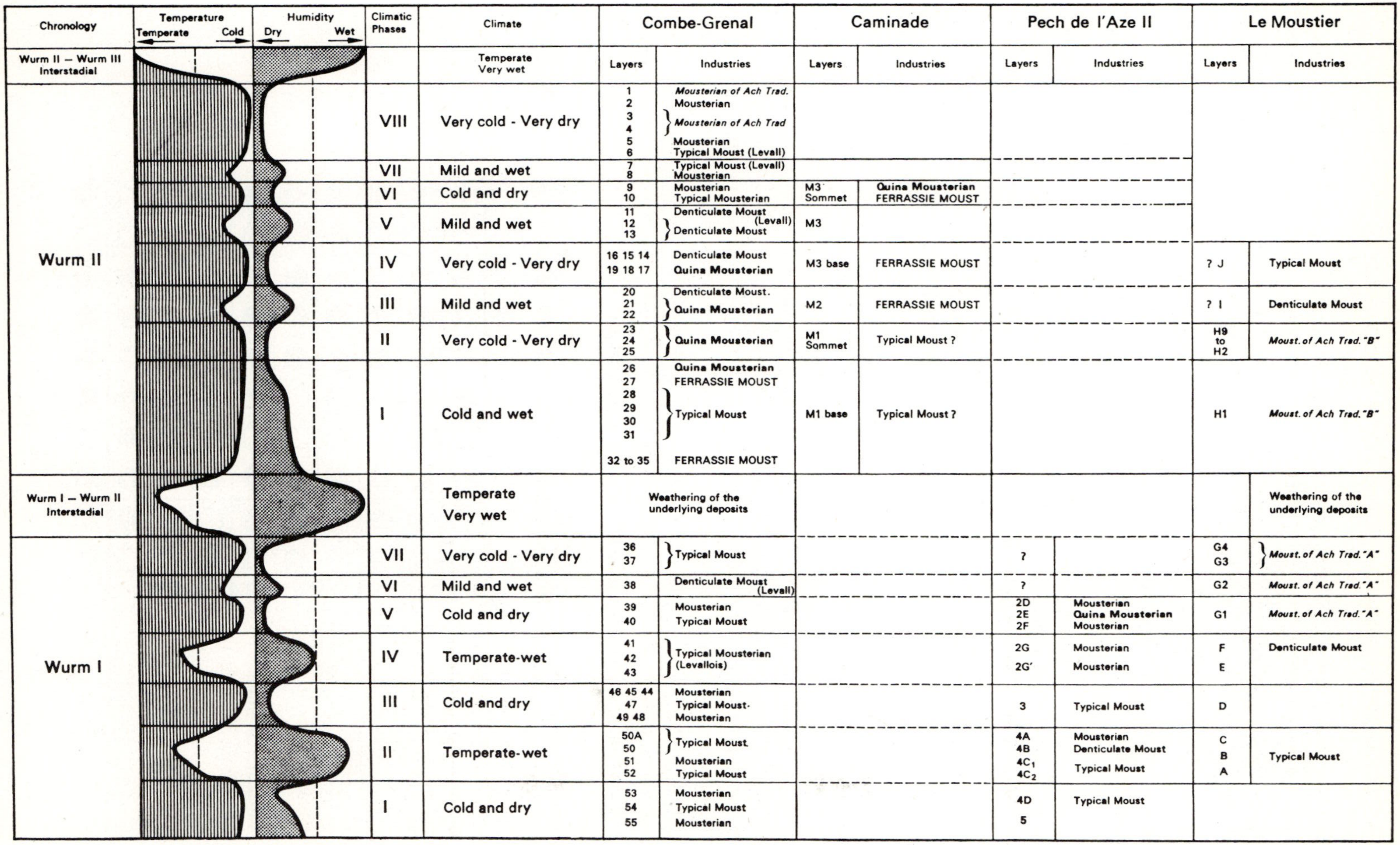

Fig. 9-6 Correlation chart of the chronology, climate, and cultural variants present in the layers at Combe-Grenal, France. (Loville 1973:325.)

▲ The Mousterian life-style

■ The earliest cemeteries

● The cave bear cult

more intense. ▲ In fact, one major change in human habits during the Middle Paleolithic was the reliance on caves and rock shelters as habitations. And even these were modified to meet human needs, as the posthole at Combe Grenal, France, clearly attests. The change in culture resulting from life in such permanent dwellings was subtle but significant. For the first time in cultural history large numbers of individuals were living together in a place which protected them from the natural environment. Thus, as people adjusted to living more closely with each other their world became more cultural and separate from the natural environment.

One of the first possible results of this heightened contact among humans would have been the intensification of social relationships. ■ Since Neanderthal burial groups have been

found with age and sex representations identical to those we would expect in the nuclear family, we can conclude that families were more closely united. For example, the cemetery at La Ferrassie, France (Fig. 9-8) contained the skeletons of two adults and four children. The adults were buried head to head, with two of the children being buried at their "mother's" feet. The graves of the other two children are unique. One, possibly a stillborn baby, was placed in the top of one of nine small mounds of earth, the remainder of which were empty. With the bones were three beautifully worked flint implements. The other child was buried beneath a triangular slab of stone hollowed out on the bottom. Artifacts with this burial included two scrapers and a point. The inclusion of implements with burials is clear evidence of some belief in an afterlife (Peyrony 1934). The La Ferrassie examples are not isolated finds. For example, in the cave at Teshik-Tash, Uzbekistan, a child was buried with the horns of six mountain goats placed to form a circle around its head. The cemetery at Mugharet-es-Skhul, Palestine, had 10 graves con-

Fig. 9-7 Chart illustrating how sampling error can affect interpretation of an excavated layer. The sample observed (shown in the center unshaded panel) is 60 percent of the total, yet the true assemblage in the layer may be considerably different from that in the 60 percent sample. This example, while useful in representing any assemblages, has particular reference to the sequence of Mousterian industries reported from Combe-Grenal. (Clarke 1972: Fig. 1-8.)

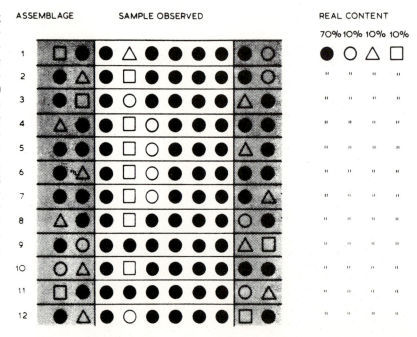

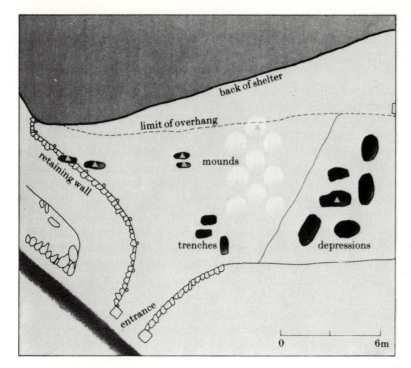

Fig. 9-8 Mousterian cemetary at La Ferrassie, France. The mounds marked with triangles contained intentional burials of Neanderthals. (Sherratt 1980: Fig. 12-6.)

taining individuals ranging in age from 3 to 50 years. In Shanidar Cave, Iraq, one group found within a single grave consisted of four individuals, one of whom was a child. Some of the nine burials present in the cave were the result of accidental death from a roof cave-in; nonetheless such recent dead were then interred with stones placed over the bones. Also present were small rodent bones—possibly the remains of a funeral feast—and even an offering of flowers. The latter is demonstrated by the recovery of pollen from the burial soil (Solecki 1963, 1971). A fire had been built over the grave, and within the ashes were found more animal bones and several stone points. In addition, the mere fact of intentional burial implies that disposal of the deceased was a matter of group planning and execution. Intentional burial further implies beliefs concerning an afterlife. Thus we have the beginnings of what may be termed "religion."

During the Middle Paleolithic, for the first time in human culture we also have the appearance of nonutilitarian objects. These are items of presumed ceremonial or decorative use, and could have performed little of direct practical importance. The site of Tata, Hungary, has yielded a polished piece of mammoth's tooth cut to an oval form. Another find at the same site, a marine invertebrate fossil with an X or cross scratched upon it, was perhaps worn as an amulet.

● In addition to burial customs, the Neanderthal's possessed a system of beliefs connected with the cave bear, *Ursus spelaeus*. We cannot define such beliefs as a religion, yet they must have been ritualistic in nature. At Drachenloch, Switzerland, there has been found a stone-lined pit in which were stacked several cave bear skulls. Another find at Drachenloch was a bear skull with the leg bones of a younger bear placed through the arches formed by the cheek bones; this arrangement had been set on top of two bones from two other bears. Such a configuration could not have been the result of chance

▲ Neanderthals were cannibals.

■ Middle Paleolithic peoples were adapted to a periglacial climate.

● Animals hunted by the Neanderthals

but represents deliberate human placement. Hunting the cave bear may have been a demonstration of prowess similar to the hunting of lion by the Masai of today; and the arrangements of bear bones were possibly trophies of such hunts. In another cave, the Drachenhohle ("Dragon's Cave") near Mixnitz, Austria, is a similar trophy of a cave bear skull with an ulna thrust through the cheek arch. Also present in

the cave were more than 30 bear skulls as well as the remains of Mousterian campfires containing charred bear bones. In this cave the bears were hunted as they tried to escape through a narrow passageway, killing being accomplished by hitting the animal on the muzzle or forehead with a sharp-pointed club. Numerous skulls show the marks of such blows (Able 1926).

Evidence from Neanderthal bones themselves also attests to cultural practices. The Neanderthal skull found at La Ferrassie possessed unusual tooth wear on the incisors. The closest similarity to a modern example is found in the Eskimo, where such wear is the result of years of chewing to soften skins. Thus we may infer that skin clothing was probably a Mousterian

Fig. 9-9 A Mousterian family of Neanderthal physical type in front of their cave home in Gibraltar some 50,000 years ago. (Courtesy British Museum [Natural History].)

culture trait (Fig. 9-9). ▲ Another proclivity of the Neanderthals was their preference for human flesh. A Neanderthal skull from Monte Circeo, Italy, has had the base broken open to permit removal of the brain. A mass of bones found at Krapina, Yugoslavia, includes wild-animal bones as well as the partial remains of a dozen Neanderthals, all treated in the same fashion. The long bones had been broken open for marrow and all were charred by fire, rather clear evidence of a cannibalistic feast.

One of the most controversial topics is that of Neanderthal speech and language. Desmond Clark states that, based on archaeological studies, "we do not presume that Neanderthal had as good a method of communication as we have, but there is also no doubt that Neanderthal had a good social setup that would be impossible without some sort of language" (Anonymous 1979:45). The linguist Philip Lieberman has attempted to reconstruct Neanderthal speech through reference to the anatomy, such as the location and form of the hyoid bone. He concludes that the Neanderthals could not articulate all of the sounds that are typical of the speech of *Homo s. sapiens.* According to Lieberman, "Neanderthal represents a stage at which speech was slightly less effective than that of modern humans, a very advanced hominid that obviously had language but lacked some human vocal capabilities" (Anonymous 1979:45).

Climate and Environment

Our knowledge of the climate and the environments inhabited by Middle Paleolithic peoples is more complete for Europe, less complete for Africa, and nearly nonexistent for most other areas of the world. Therefore, we will concentrate upon the European data.

The major environmental zones occupied by European Middle Paleolithic peoples were the forest-tundra and the cold loess steppes. Farther south in the Mediterranean region, including the North African coast, was a warmer temperate woodland, but this environment seems to have been less intensively occupied. ■ Most likely, human preference for the colder environments at this time was the result of several factors: the control of fire, skill at hunting, skin clothing, and, most importantly, the animal-carrying capacity of the low-latitude tundra. The European Middle Paleolithic peoples were primarily hunters, and the tundra was an optimum environment for the cold-adapted, herd-dwelling animals of the period.

Temperature depressions during the Würm glaciation varied according to region (Fig. 9-10). For example, southwestern England during the coldest phase had forest-tundra with July temperatures averaging 10°C, whereas today the range is from 10°C to 14°C. In southern France the Würm snow line was at 1,200 meters, about 100 meters lower than at present. Evidence of permafrost in the Alps suggests a temperature some 11°C lower during the Würm than at present. To the east, the arctic tree line probably extended as far south as Vienna; thus Würm summer temperatures were 7°C to 9°C lower than today. A further feature of the landscape would have been vegetationless, arctic barrens immediately adjacent to the glacial masses and large meltwater streams crossing the loessial plains in summer. There is evidence that the Mousterian hunters moved northward onto these plains (probably in summer), camping in the open along streams in order to take advantage of the hunting. On the other hand, the evidence from other Mousterian sites, especially caves, is that they were occupied year round, as indicated by the ages of the game killed. Thus Mousterian peoples were not universally nomadic but, where possible, were likely to be semisedentary.

● The game hunted was among the most varied of faunas known. Furthermore, there was both an interglacial and a glacial fauna. (Representative species of each are listed below.) Of significance is the value of these genera for habitat reconstructions, since only three of the genera

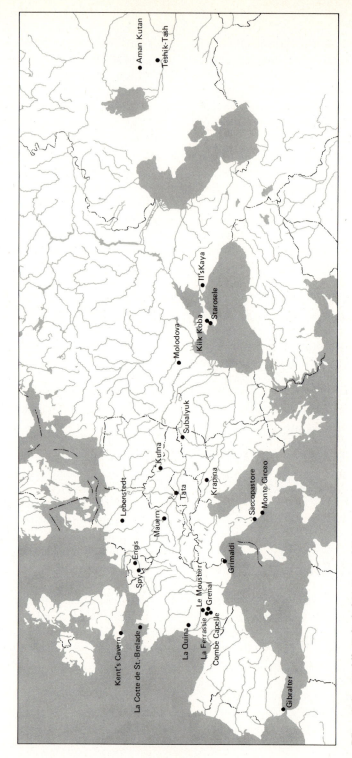

Map 9-3 Middle Paleolithic Sites of Europe.

are now extinct. Of these, the woolly mammoth and the rhinoceros have been found frozen reasonably intact in tundra soil, even to the preserved stomach contents with identified pollen grains and plant species. Thus there is excellent evidence of the tundra plant environment and of the species' dietary preferences.

The interglacial (Eem) fauna (Butzer 1971:258) includes the extinct straight-tusked woodland elephant *(Elephas antiquus)*, the extinct woodland rhino, the African hippo *(H. amphibius major)*, the boar *(Sus scrofa)*, the fallow deer *(Dama dama)*, and the roe deer *(Capreolus capreolus)*. These species were characteristic of midlatitude Europe during interglacial periods. During colder, glacial epochs they were present only in southern Europe and Africa.

The glacial fauna (Würm) consisted of several components. In southern France it contained temperate and boreal woodland forms. Other species were clearly tundra-dwelling. There were alpine forms, a cool midlatitude-steppe fauna, and special cave forms, as shown in Figure 9-11.

Fig. 9-10 Reconstruction of European environmental zones for the Würm maximum (18,000 B.C.). (Butzer 1971: Fig. 51.)

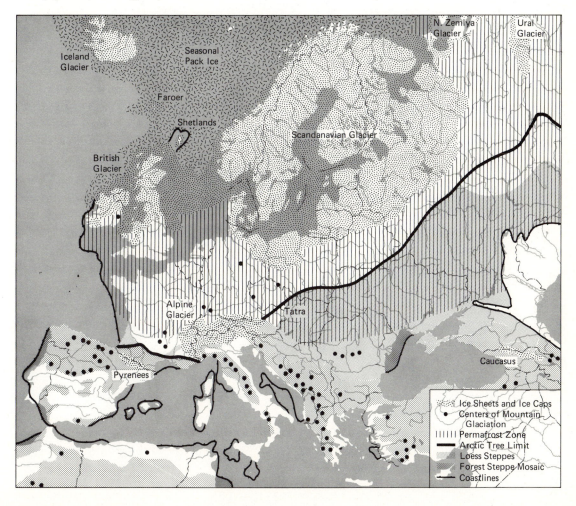

Fig. 9-11 The Upper Pleistocene megafauna of Central Europe. The species illustrated were restricted to specific environmental zones, ranging from arctic tundra to the temperate woodlands. (Butzer 1971: Fig. 49.)

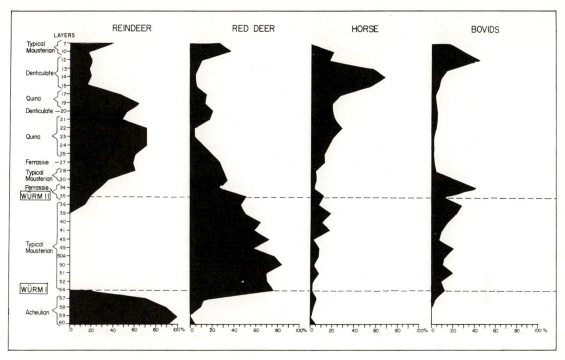

Fig. 9-12 Distribution of major fauna hunted by the Mousterian occupants of Combe-Grenal, France. (Compiled from Bordes and Prat 1966.)

An understanding of how Mousterian hunters utilized these beasts is provided by the faunal remains from the 68 levels of Combe Grenal. The graph in Figure 9-12 illustrates the changing reliance on different species by humans through time, but we should bear in mind that these data represent bone-count frequencies, which are difficult to translate into animal units. Furthermore, these animal units are of varying size. (For example, a mammoth "equals" numerous reindeer). Nonetheless, such a graph is indicative of changing Mousterian food preferences (Bordes and Prat 1966).

African Environments

In recent years research scientists have come to realize that there exists little firm evidence concerning the nature of past African environments. Current impressions based on African data are that the assumption of pan-African fluctuations in climate is not supportable. Instead, the changes in climate were regional in character. For example, the movement of European climatic zones to the south influenced North Africa, while the equatorial region was directly affected by the southeastern trade winds and the Indian monsoon. South Africa received influences from the West Wind drift and the Antarctic currents. The desert regions, the Sahara and the Kalahari, due to their continental positions, typically received little moisture from the northeastern trade winds and the dry westerly winds.

Late Pleistocene African environments may thus be described as follows. During glacial maxima there was a southward displacement of the Mediterranean flora and fauna to North Africa,

▲ African occupations were adapted to climatic fluctuations.

■ Sangoan implements

● Mousterian industry is widespread in Asia.

including the Sahara. The higher and typically more moist regions of East Africa and equatorial Africa may have experienced pluvial conditions, with some mountain glaciation (snow-line depression of from 1,000 to 1,200 meters) and temperatures 5°C to 9°C lower than those of today. During periods of glacial retreat in Europe (interstadials), the major shifts in sub-Saharan climate were controlled by the Indian monsoon, with warmer, drier conditions accompanied by savanna-woodland invasion of the Congo (formerly tropical forests) and the upslope retreat of vegetal zones in East Africa. Simultaneously, there seems to have been an expansion of the sub-Saharan savanna and thorn-scrub zones northward into the southern Sahara. These interpretations are tentative, however, because the area concerned is enormous, and for much of it there exists no paleoecological data whatever.

▲ Human and faunal migrations were closely keyed to these climatic fluctuations. One result of the monsoonal expansion into the Sahara, for example, was the territorial increase of the Ethiopian fauna: giraffes, elephants, hippos, white rhinos, antelopes, gazelles, and even a species of crocodile moved into the higher mountain ranges of the Central Sahara. The Hoggar range, for example, is more than 10,000 feet in elevation and attracted considerable rainfall, possibly as much as 150 millimeters per year. On the other hand, most evidence from the Sahara suggests that through time the typical climatic regimen there has been arid and that wetter intervals have been of brief duration.

Cultural distributions in Africa may be understood through reference to these climatic factors. The North African and Saharan Middle Paleolithic features Mousterian industries. Although these are best known from sites along the North African coast, this fact is related to the difficulty of carrying out research in the modern Sahara rather than to the original distribution of Mousterian culture. On the other hand, sub-Saharan Africa during the Middle Paleolithic was characterized by non-Mousterian, non-Levallois industries, such as the Sangoan, Lupemban, Pieterburg, Bambata, and others.

The Sangoan Culture

The Sangoan culture was a forest and woodland adaptation found within the region which today receives more than 40 inches annual rainfall. The distribution suggests a dry-period occupation of the equatorial forest region. This particular hypothesis is supported by pollen analysis of Sangoan levels at Kalambo Falls. However, at the Khami Waterworks site analysis of feldspar grain size implies a climate wetter than that of today (Sampson 1974:146–148). Thus the controversy continues. At Kalambo Falls, the Sangoan levels are dated 41,000 to 38,000 B.C. with the subsequent Lupemban industry dated 27,000 to 25,000 B.C. At the site of Mufo, Angola, radiocarbon dates indicate that the upper Lupemban lasted until as late as 12,550 B.C. ■ The basic implements, termed "picks," are elongated, steep-sided, double-ended tools. Other implements include rough hand axes, prepared cores, points, and several types of scrapers made from flakes. While the Lupemban seems to be a direct outgrowth of the Sangoan (but featuring somewhat finer and better-made implements), its distinctive element consists of well-made, laurel-leaf-shaped, bifacially flaked points. In general, the flaking technology of both the Sangoan and Lupemban features heavy, crude implements, which are less well made than those of the preceding late Acheulean. This shift is believed related to the change in the function of the implements from cutting and skinning in Acheulean times to chopping and digging during the Middle Paleolithic.

Middle Paleolithic Industries of Asia

● The Mousterian industry is widespread in Northern Asia, with sites extending from Syria, Lebanon, Turkey, and Iran eastward to northern China and Siberia. In between, Mousterian cultures are known from the Asiatic part of the U.S.S.R. south of the Caucasus Mountains, in caves and open sites on the eastern shore of the Caspian Sea, and in Central Asia in Uzbekistan. South of Samarkand, the Aman Kutan Cave contains Mousterian implements in addition to a Neanderthal femur. Northern India features an industry termed "Upper Soan," which some investigators believe shows Mousterian affinities.

South of the above areas in Southeast Asia, the Middle Paleolithic is marked by a continuation of the chopper-chopping-tool tradition. One of the best-known such industries is the Sangeran flake culture of Java, whose implements are flake tools of the Clacton type made on chalcedony. The Ngandongian culture, also from Java, includes antler picks, stingray points, bola stones, and small flakes. Another Middle Paleolithic industry, from Niah Cave in Borneo, includes bone points, stone flakes, some flake blades, and chopping tools made on river pebbles. Industries of similar types are also found in the Philippines. These and other insular Paleolithic industries are related to those of the Southeast Asian mainland, for during low-water phases of the Pleistocene many East Indian islands were connected to the mainland. The Sino-Asiatic fauna was also present in this region at the time. To the east, human distribution was blocked by the Macassar Strait between Borneo and Celebes, which was 900 fathoms in depth and thus was never bridged by land during the Pleistocene.

10

The Upper Paleolithic

■ The appearance of *Homo sapiens sapiens*

● Upper Paleolithic cultures were adapted to a periglacial climate.

▲ The Upper Paleolithic features regional cultures.

■ The Upper Paleolithic period is marked by the dominance of anatomically modern humans (*Homo sapiens sapiens*), a new stone-working technology, a heavy dependence upon the use of bone as a raw material for tool making, and the first major expression of art.

The new stone-working technology represents a revolution in manufacturing efficiency. In this period the predominant tool form was the blade. Blades are, by definition, flakes that are more than twice as long as they are wide. In practice, most blades have parallel sides and either triangular or trapezoidal cross sections. During the Upper Paleolithic, blades were the blank forms from which an incredible variety of tools were made. As a comparison of technological efficiency Butzer (1964), quoting Eiseley (1955), tabulates the following outputs of various stone-working techniques.

The table on page 169 indicates the impressive evolution of efficiency in the utilization of stone for tool manufacture. The increase in cutting edge per pound of raw material represents a technological breakthrough, the greatest difference being achieved with the Upper Paleolithic shift to blade tools. Although we tend to stress the minimal change in stone tools within the Paleolithic period, this exponential growth in technological efficiency cannot be ignored.

Climate and Fauna

● Upper Paleolithic culture began during the cool-temperate phase of the Würm II-III interstadial ca. 35,000 B.C. and continued throughout

TABLE 10-1
Production Output of Various Flint-Working Technologies

Culture (Major Implement)	Quantity of Flint	Cutting-Edge Yield	Efficiency (× Original)
Pebble-tool culture, chopper-chopping tools	1 lb	5 cm	——
Acheulean hand axes	1 lb	20 cm	4×
Middle Paleolithic flake tools	1 lb	100 cm	20×
Upper Paleolithic blade tools	1 lb	300 to 1,200 cm	60 to 240×

the entire Würm III cold maximum until ca. 9000 B.C. Environmental conditions were similar to those of the earlier Middle Paleolithic. In Europe, during the cool-temperate interstadial there occurred some northward movement of the environmental zones. The Mediterranean deciduous woodland of the south contained oak, pine, and hornbeam, while a zone of spruce, pine, birch, and fir (the forest steppe) covered most of central Europe. Surrounding the Baltic Sea was a spruce, pine, and larch forest. Farther north was a zone of spruce and birch; and north of the latter was forest tundra in northern Scandinavia. In terms of faunal adjustments, there would have been an expansion of the steppe-dwelling forms—the bison, steppe horse, woolly mammoth, and ass—with the red deer, elk, auroch, and woodland horse as the primary food species in the expanded temperate woodland. Species of the forest tundra—the reindeer, musk ox, woolly mammoth, and woolly rhino—would have had their range restricted except where they could adapt to cool steppe conditions.

After 27,000 B.C. there occurred a glacial advance during which the Würm III cold maximum lasted until 11,000 B.C. During this interval there was southward movement of the environmental zones, with a major expansion of the glaciers and tundra zone and a reduction of all other zones. Between 11,000 and 10,000 B.C. there was a warming trend accompanied by rapid glacial retreat. Upper Paleolithic cultures

in Europe apparently did not persist beyond this point. The European Upper Paleolithic consisted of a series of cultures adapted to the hunting of cool-steppe and tundra species. With the advent of post-Würm warming, the fauna were either reduced in numbers or became extinct, and Upper Paleolithic cultures were forced to modify their economies (Coles and Higgs 1969, Cornwall 1970).

Upper Paleolithic Industries

Industries of the Upper Paleolithic are numerous and varied. ▲ There are regional traditions, within which are a series of sequential forms having specific industry names. This is thus the first period in human prehistory for which archaeologists have been able to develop regional sequences or chronologies. Such sequences are based upon two major characteristics: (1) the presence of deeply stratified occupation layers in caves and (2) distinctive tool types characteristic of specific areas and periods. The tools themselves are primarily variants of knives, scrapers, points, and burins made on core-struck blades. The sequences of industries, one after another, have been preserved in the cave deposits just as they were left as occupational layers by Upper Paleolithic peoples. This has provided considerable data with which to construct the regional

■ The core-struck blade—the basic Upper Paleolithic tool type.

● Some Upper Paleolithic industries described

chronologies. In addition, these levels are well stratified and have been dated by the radiocarbon method.

Within the scope of our text it is impossible to delineate each Upper Paleolithic industry in detail, as such treatment should be reserved for an advanced course in European prehistory. However, we will describe the major features of the period. Cultures termed "Upper Paleolithic" occur throughout most of Europe, including Russia, Siberia, and eastward into Japan; and to the south, similar industries are present in the Middle East and North Africa. Furthermore, migrants to the New World crossed the Bering Strait during this period, and their tool inventories show strong Upper Paleolithic affinities. (Although we recognize this cultural continuity between the Siberian Upper Paleolithic and the New World Paleo-Indian tradition, we will reserve discussion of New World remains until a later chapter.) It was also during this period that we have the earliest known migrants to the continent of Australia. These were peoples who presumably used tools related to the chopper-chopping-tool tradition of Southeast Asia rather than to that of the European and West Asian Upper Paleolithic. South of the Sahara, African cultures evolved separately, evincing no relationships with the European blade industries. Other areas of great size, including most of Arabia, Pakistan, India, China, and Southeast Asia, have not been studied in great detail by archaeologists specializing in this period; and thus our knowledge is limited. (The major known cultures are plotted in Map 10-1.)

Industries of the Upper Paleolithic feature numerous tools made of materials other than stone. Although the stone tools tend to be those most frequently used by archaeologists as their type specimens or index fossils, the tools of other

substances are common and well made. The new materials include bone, ivory, and antler, worked by grooving and splitting, then grinding, polishing, and (frequently) engraving. Ornaments were made from these materials, as well as utilitarian objects such as spear points, harpoons, throwing sticks, and clubs. Also prepared were carved ornamental staffs or batons, termed *batons de commandemente*, which have been variously interpreted as symbols of authority or shaft straighteners. The implements used for bone splitting and carving were the stone burins which occur in enormous quantity and variety at this time. Another major innovation was the manufacture of composite tools, which were made by hafting a blade or point to a shaft. In this configuration there is (1) the haft, a wrapping of thong or cordage, (2) possibly a separate piece of wood or bone which fits between the haft and the point, termed a foreshaft, and (3) the point or harpoon to which a separate line may have been tied. Numerous specimens exhibit realistic carving and incising—the first evidences of Paleolithic art.

■ The hallmark of the Upper Paleolithic industries is, of course, the core-struck blade. These are symmetrical flint blades struck from trimmed, specially prepared cores. As each blade is struck off, it bears upon its upper face the scars of the blades struck off previously. The blades are long and slim, are rectangular to triangular in form, and have a triangular or trapezoidal cross section. They are exceptionally sharp without retouch, although a variety of implements such as end scrapers, side scrapers, backed blades, and points were made on blades by retouching the edges. Burins differ in that they are not the product of retouch but instead were made by striking off spalls from the blades in much the same fashion as the original blades were struck from their core.

Figures 10-1 to 10-5 illustrate a variety of blade tools characteristic of several of the best-known Upper Paleolithic industries. ● Following Bordes (1968), definitions of some of these industries are offered.

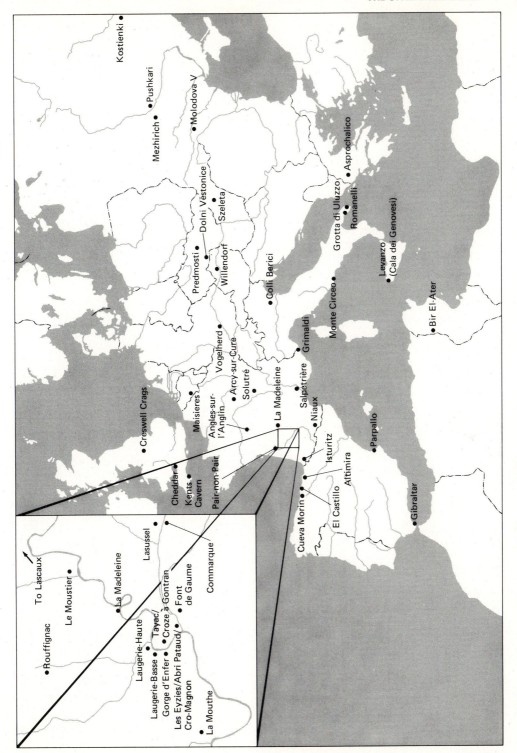

Map 10-1 Upper Paleolithic Sites of Europe.

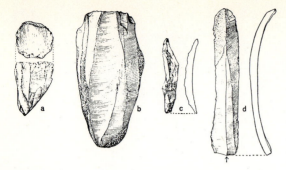

Fig. 10-1 Upper Paleolithic implements. (*a,b*) Blade cores; (*c*) rejuvenation flake; (*d*) typical blade. (Sieveking 1968:62.)

Fig. 10-2 Upper Paleolithic implements. (*a*) Chatelperronian knife point; (*b*) Gravettian knife point; (*c*) trapezoid blade; (*d*) Perigordian burin; (*e*) Aurignacoid nosed graver; (*f*) Aurignacian burin; (*g*) Magdalenian graver; (*h*) Aurignacian strangulated blade or spokeshave; (*i*) Aurignacian nosed scraper; (*j*) end scraper; (*k*) Solutrean piercer; (*l*) Magdalenian double-ended scraper; (*m*) Magdalenian blade core. (Oakley 1972:60.)

The Perigordian

The *Perigordian industry* has strong features of the Mousterian of Acheulean tradition, including scrapers, Mousterian points, Levallois flakes, and denticulates. This tradition thus bridges the gap between the Middle and Upper Paleolithic periods. Perigordian diagnostic tools include pointed blades with curved backs blunted by steep retouch (the Chatelperron knife), end scrapers on flakes, and mediocre burins (Fig. 10-2). Bone implements are few, but awls occur, as do pendants and notched (for suspension) teeth and bones. Later in the Perigordian sequence the Mousterian-type tools disappear and burin types multiply. Small implements become more common, especially backed bladelets, La Gravette points, and small foliate points. By Perigordian V we have the introduction of a new projectile point, called Font-Robert (Fig. 10-3), which featured a basal tang for use in hafting.

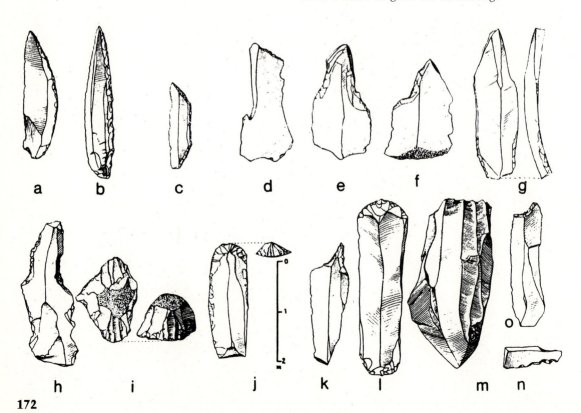

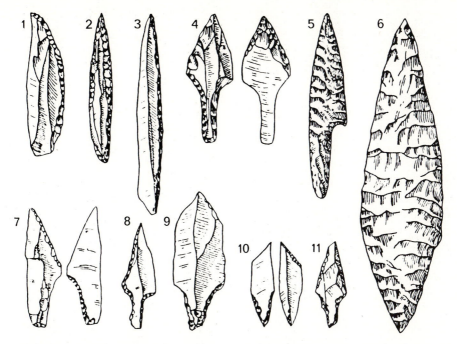

Fig. 10-3 Upper Paleolithic implements. (*1*) Chatelperron knife; (*2*) Gravettian knife; (*3*) Krems knife; (*4*) Font Robert point; (*5*) Solutrean single-shouldered point; (*6*) Solutrean laurel-leaf point; (*7*) Hamburg point; (*8*) Ahrensburg point; (*9*) Lyngby point; (*10*) Swidry point; and (*11*) Chwalibogowice point. (Clark 1977: Fig. 37.)

The Aurignacian

The *Aurignacian industry*, in contrast to the Perigordian, may represent an intrusion of new peoples into western Europe from central or eastern Europe. The tools are considerably different from those of the Perigordian culture, featuring fine blades with strong retouch forming a scraper edge on the blade end. Burins increase through time but are never as frequent as in the Perigordian. Other tools are thick-ended scrapers similar to the Quina Mousterian style, strangled blades, *batons de commandemente*, awls, and split-base bone points. Through time, the fine blades are abandoned, burins are developed, and scrapers increase in variety. Later bone points lack the split base, being either rounded or beveled at the base. Another feature is the presence of small bladelets. Bordes suggests that the Aurignacian and Perigordian peoples lived side by side in the same region without exerting much influence on one another.

The Gravettian

The *Gravettian industry* represents a culture of central and eastern Europe similar in time to the Aurignacian and Perigordian. Its primary index fossil is the La Gravette point, a small point with a convex blunted back, possibly hafted in composite tools. Other tool types include triangular points with shallow bifacial flaking, perforated needles, shaft straighteners, awls, reindeer-antler clubs, handled scoops, heavy chisels of mammoth ivory, carved human figurines of ivory, and flat bracelets. The Gravettian people were adapted to life on the steppe, camping in the open in tents and specializing in mammoth

▲ Distribution of Upper Paleolithic industries

■ African Upper Paleolithic cultures

hunting. The latter activity accounts for the wide range of implements and ornaments of ivory.

The Solutrean

Later cultures of western Europe include the *Solutrean* and *Magdalenian*. Early Solutrean projectile points are unifacial, but by Middle Solutrean times these have become bifacially worked, laurel-leaf-shaped in form, and very well flaked. Presumably they also were used as knives. Some of these points are extremely large and beautifully worked, suggesting that they were works of art rather than utilitarian tools. Pressure flaking was introduced at this time as a means of producing finer specimens. In the Upper Solutrean we have the introduction of shouldered points and stemmed points, presumably innovations for hafting. A new form, the willow leaf, also appears, and unifacial points persist. Other implements include end scrapers, borers, (rarely) burins, some Mousterian-type tools, and bone implements, such as eyed needles.

The Solutrean industry, which may have originally been intrusive into western Europe, suddenly disappears to be succeeded by the seemingly unrelated Magdalenian culture.

The Magdalenian

The early *Magdalenian* levels feature small, simple, unifacially retouched flake tools, including tanged points, star-shaped multiple borers, and little steeply retouched scrapers called raclettes.

In Magdalenian I, bone tools include needles, pierced batons, and smoothing tools (Fig. 10-4). By the Magdalenian III period, bone tools are quite common and include beveled-base bone points and decorated wands. After Magdalenian

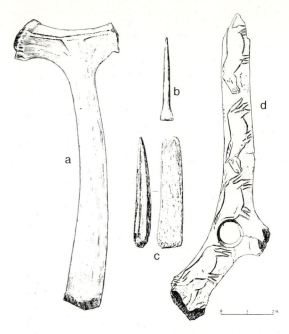

Fig. 10-4 Upper Paleolithic tools of bone and antler. (*a*) Magdalenian antler hammer; (*b*) Aurignacoid bone awl; (*c*) Magdalenian antler wedge; (*d*) Magdalenian "*bâton de commandement*" of reindeer antler. (Oakley 1972:62.)

III the major tool changes occur in the bone industry, with flint tools changing little. Bone harpoons appear and proliferate into a variety of single- and double-barbed varieties (Fig. 10-5). Other tools include awls, javelin bone points, needles, spear throwers, decorated wands, and works of art. In some of the latest levels, geometric flints appear in the form of triangles, trapezoids, and semilunates.

▲ Upper Paleolithic sites of mammoth hunters are common throughout Siberia. Locations such as Molodova, Kostienki, and Ust Kanskaiya provide evidence of the Russian Upper Paleolithic. These cultures feature some Mousterian-type tools, flake and blade tools retouched unifacially, and (rarely) bifacial points. These industries should be the antecedents of the American Paleolithic, although the details of cultural evolution in Siberia are not as well known as those of western Europe.

■ The Upper Paleolithic of North Africa is closely related to the traditions of Europe, a complicating factor being the possibility of east-to-west movements from the Middle East. Excavations by McBurney (1960, 1967) at Hagfet et Dabba (Cave of the Hyena) on the coast of Libya have revealed a sequence of occupations extending from Mousterian through levels with Upper Paleolithic-style blade tools. Termed "Dabban,"

Fig. 10-5 Upper Paleolithic bone and antler points and harpoons, all of the Magdalenian type. (*a*) Barbed point of antler; (*b*) harpoon of antler; (*c*) harpoon of antler; (*d*) spear point of antler; (*e*) bore shaft; (*i,h*) spear thrower, showing method of use. (Oakley 1972:60.)

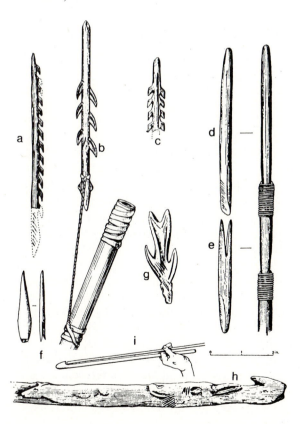

this industry is dated between ca. 38,000 and 31,150 B.C. Tool types include backed blades, gravers, end scrapers, and transverse burins. McBurney cites the presence of Middle Eastern fauna as evidence that the Dabban origins should be found in that region.

A later industry in North Africa, more widespread than the Dabban, is that termed "Aterian," after Bir el Ater, Tunisia, the type site (McBurney 1960). The Aterian is a blade industry with a strong Levalloisian tradition. Major tools feature unifacial retouch with some bifacial working at the base. Tools of stemmed form are the hallmark of the Aterian, and more than 30 forms of these points, scrapers, knives, and such have been identified. Other implements include some flake tools, scrapers, and piercers, as well as bifacially worked points, bifacially worked blades, and true Mousterian points. The Aterian is only peripherally related to the European Upper Paleolithic industries, being primarily an outgrowth of the local North African Mousterian. The Aterian extends along the entire North African coast and southward across the Sahara to Lake Chad; and presumably this culture, which is guess-dated at 15,000–20,000 years of age, flourished during a brief wetter interval.

Another related North African industry, the Khargan (Caton-Thompson 1952), features numerous multiple-use tools made on short truncated flakes. This tradition also appears to be a local derivative of the Mousterian, without much reliance on blades. The Levallois component of the technology is quite high. Age relationships between the Khargan and the Aterian are unclear, although the Khargan is presumed to be slightly the older. The Khargan is regionally restricted, having been identified only from the western desert of Egypt.

Later industries found along the North African coast, termed the "Capsian" and the "Ibero-Maurusian," feature a highly specialized blade technology. These industries are Upper Paleolithic in form, but their late age is contemporaneous with the Mesolithic or even Neolithic periods. Cultures in sub-Saharan Africa from this period are not assigned to the Upper Paleolithic. These industries are derived from the Sangoan, Lupemban, and other previously described traditions and represent a non-Levallois, non-blade-making tool culture. Presumably there was little contact between North Africa and sub-Saharan Africa, and the cultures in those regions evolved independently and remained separate. This period in East and South Africa has been assigned to the later portion of the Middle Stone Age. Extant cultural traditions are several: the Sangoan-Lupemban-Tshitolian tradition of heavy wood-working and digging implements, characteristic of central Africa; the East African Stillbay-Magosian-Wilton industrial tradition; and the South African Howiesonspoort and Nachikufan complexes. (The terms refer to historically related industries, with names given to the various individually recognized chronological variants.) The latter cultures are poorly known and have few described archaeological diagnostics.

Inskeep (1979:53–58) tends to reject the cultural names and affiliations, but he notes that in the Middle Stone Age hand axes and cleavers are absent, the Levallois technique is refined, and new tool types appear. In general, he notes a reduction in flake size and greater control in their manufacture. Freeman (1980:80), on the other hand, concedes the possibility that the Sangoan and the succeeding Lupemban culture may be typological outgrowths of the late Acheulean, but he then raises chronological questions and suggests that both the Sangoan and Lupemban may be far older than previously thought. In any case, much more work is needed in order to clarify the total sub-Saharan picture during the Middle Stone Age.

The Stillbay-Magosian-Wilton peoples were hunting groups who inhabited the eastern side of Africa from Uganda to South Africa. The Stillbay culture is characterized by pressure-chipped bifacial points made on flakes of the prepared faceted-platform type. The points were leaf-shaped or subtriangular and were probably used on lances or spears. Other implements include backed blades, lunates, and burins. One (obsidian) date on Stillbay materials is 31,000 years B.C. The Magosian industry which follows has been dated at 7550 b.c. and has elements indicative of a Mesolithic way of life which will be described in the next chapter. It is appropriate to state that so far our knowledge of these African industries of the Middle and Late Stone Age is limited.

Upper Paleolithic Art

The art of the Upper Paleolithic period in Europe is justly well known, for it not only embodies the earliest major development of esthetic creativity by humans but also is sensitive and of high quality. The art that first became known to the scientific world consisted of a number of finds of small carved objects which are called *mobilary art*. These finds first occurred in France, the earliest being a bone engraved with figures of deer, found by a notary, Brouillet, in Chaffaud Cave near Savigne in about 1834. The find, not recognized as Paleolithic at the time, was given to the Cluny Museum. Edouard Lartet was perhaps the first person to document the Paleolithic age of such finds. In 1860 he found a *baton de commandement* carved with a bear figure in the Massat Cave. In 1864 he recovered from a Paleolithic layer of the cave of La Madeleine, in the Vezere Valley, a piece of tusk engraved with the figure of a mammoth. Two features supported the age of the specimen. The clear-cut edges of the carving showed it had been done when the specimen was fresh, not fossilized. And since the engraving was of an extinct animal, the artist would have had to be contemporary with the animal. Such was the conclusive evidence that this art had been made by people of the Paleolithic age. Numerous other carvings were later found in the same region, and the Vezere Valley became recognized as a center for such art (Map 10-1).

● Throughout the latter half of the nineteenth century, finds of art were common as Paleolithic archaeology became widespread. In the summer of 1879 the Spanish nobleman Marcelino de Sautuola excavated in the cave of Altamira in the province of Santander, and his daughter noticed paintings of bison on the cave ceiling (Fig. 10-6). De Sautuola was convinced these paintings—the first of their kind ever discovered—were Paleolithic, and in 1880 he published a monograph describing them and estimating their age. The world remained unconvinced of the authenticity of these finds, but for 15 years de Sautuola persisted in his be-

Fig. 10-6 Plan of Altamira, Spain, showing the distribution of paintings and the details of the great painted ceiling. (Leroi-Gourhan 1967: Figs. 132–133.)

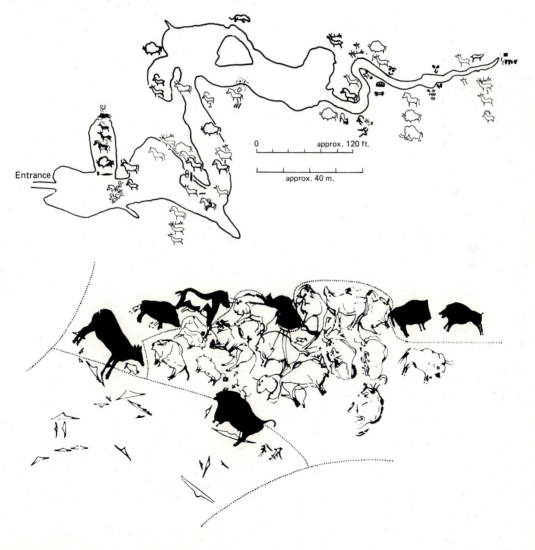

▲ Paintings and engravings on the walls of caves

■ The caves were religious sanctuaries.

liefs; and finally, in 1895, the French prehistorian Emile Rivière decided to personally examine Altamira. What he saw there led him to search caves in the Dordogne in France, where he found similar paintings. Rivière's discovery of still other paintings in the cave of La Mouthe, which had until that time been sealed, thus validated the Paleolithic origin of the cave paintings. From that date (1895) until the present, interest in Paleolithic cave art has continued to be important in European prehistory, with the result that today 110 caves and rock shelters with paintings, engravings, or sculpture are known (Map 10-1). One of the best-preserved ''galleries'' of art ever found is that of the Cave of Lascaux in France, discovered accidentally in 1940 by two boys. It is conceivable that in the future there will be found other concealed caves which have collapsed or been filled since their use by Paleolithic peoples.

Cave Art

Cave art features the depiction on cave walls and ceilings of the primarily herd-dwelling animals which were hunted by Paleolithic peoples. ▲ Some animals were engraved and some were painted, and many renderings exhibit a combination of both techniques. The animals were illustrated singly, in pairs, and in larger groups. Occasionally they are portrayed in conjunction with lines or stakes which could represent traps. In addition there are bas-relief carvings, sometimes featuring the use of rock protuberances in the caves for added dramatic effect. Also present in the caves are animal figures, primarily bears and bison, sculpted in clay and resting on the cave floor. Such figures are sizable, of up to several feet in length. Clay deposits within the caves were also decorated by engraving. A final

evidence of Paleolithic humans is footprints in the soft clay of the cave floors.

In addition to numerous and skillful renditions of reindeer, mammoths, stags, rhinos, bison, wolves, boars, ibex, bears, felines, cattle, and other animals, cave art features other symbols. There are infrequent examples of men and women, with bodies accurately portrayed but with strangely awkward and crude faces. Another major cave-art category includes geometric designs (many of which are interpreted as male or female symbols), abstract geometric forms, and lines of dots or trailing lines. The so-called tectiform designs appear to be plank houses, although there is no proof that this was their intended representation. Some recent studies suggest that these forms have symbolic meaning and thus may represent early attempts at written language (Forbes and Crowder 1979).

Cave painting was done by the light of burning torches, and the paints consisted of ochre, manganese, and charcoal mixed with animal fat. The paint was smeared on, possibly with pieces of cancellous (porous) bone being used as brushes. Charcoal was probably applied directly when in stick form or, when powdered, blown onto the surface of the cave wall. Some finger painting was also done.

Engraving was done on hard surfaces with sharp stones and burins; and in wet clay the fingers were used. Numerous small, flat pebbles have been found which have engravings on their surfaces. These engravings are difficult to decipher, as up to 10 animals of different species may be superimposed upon one another. It has been suggested that these pebbles represent practice by the artists, since the designs are identical to those on the cave walls. There are also chronological and regional styles, suggesting that the art was taught from one generation to the next. Natural accidents in the caves were frequently incorporated into the art. At Niaux, a bison sculpted in clay features natural depressions in the clay resulting from water dropping. These depressions have been used to represent wounds

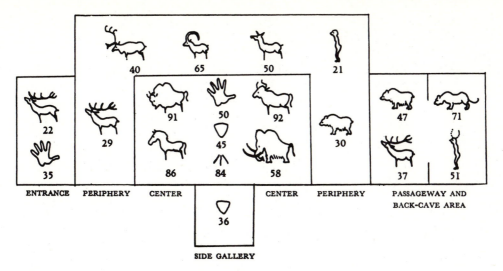

Fig. 10-7 Schematic diagram of the typical placement of painted figures within a cave sanctuary. This summary chart is based on Leroi-Gourhan's (1967:501) study of 865 paintings located in 62 caves.

in the animal. At Pech Merle a stalagmite has been modified into a mammoth.

A major feature of the art is its organization within the caves. ■ Leroi-Gourhan, in his exhaustive coverage of the subject (1967, 1968), has identified what he terms "sanctuaries"—main caves which are painted in a specific order. The cave will have a sequence of short strokes painted at each end; in between, in the deeper part of the cave, the pattern features bison next to horses, stags, and ibex, as well as women associated with bison. In addition, some combinations are repeated within the same cave. The conclusion reached is that the decoration of an entire cave was conceived as a unit. Of course, over time superposition of forms made the architectural unity of the compositions difficult to decipher. Nonetheless, Leroi-Gourhan believes it possible to identify the composition of the "ideal" sanctuary (1968) (Fig. 10-7).

Upper Paleolithic art has been divided into the following series of periods:

1. Period I, 30,000–23,000 B.C.: Early Perigordian and Aurignacian scrawls; only mobilary art was present. (No cave art dating from this period has been identified.) Major themes are the same as later but are represented only by fragments of design—animal heads, forequarters, dorsal lines, vulvar figures, dots, and strokes.

2. Period II, 23,000–17,000 B.C.: This period, associated with Upper Perigordian and Gravettian cultures, witnessed the first development of the great sanctuaries. A major feature is the animal silhouettes on the cave walls, embodying a flattened S-curve for the dorsal line. Engravings are common.

3. Period III, 17,000–13,000 B.C.: This period is marked by mastery of the painting techniques, relief sculpture, and the depiction of movement. Chronologically this was the period of Solutrean and early Magdalenian cultures.

4. Period IV, 13,000–8,000 B.C.: Late Magdalenian period. The style features finer modeling, an increase in mobilary art, and use of more conventional symbolism.

Cave art has been commonly thought to be indicative of *sympathetic magic:* the depiction of animals which the hunters wished to possess.

● Mobilary art—carvings on bone, ivory, antler, or stone.

▲ Deciphering possible Paleolithic lunar counts

However, not all of this art can be so viewed; for example, the hands outlined in red, the geometric figures, and the rows of dots are difficult to interpret as part of hunting magic. (However, it seems easy to link red-outlined hands to the bloodied hands of hunters.) A further hypothesis, based on the prevalence of paired animals and of male and female sexual symbols, holds that much of the cave art is based on the maker's concept of sexuality and its role in nature. In any event, Upper Paleolithic cave art is among the grandest expressions of art known from any period in history or prehistory.

Mobilary Art

Art carved on small objects which are either utilitarian or decorative is equally indicative of the skill of its makers. Perhaps the most famous of such objects are the so-called venuses, figures of human females carved in the round, with exaggerated hips, thighs, and breasts. These presumed fertility symbols have no known utilitarian function and are widespread in Europe, being especially common in the Gravettian-culture sites of central and eastern Europe. According to Leroi-Gourhan, these figures, typically of mammoth ivory or bone, feature a consistent set of proportions and were thus made according to a specific mental concept. While to our eyes

they may appear lumpy and poorly proportioned, we assume they fulfilled the standard of beauty held by their makers.

● Mobilary art includes (1) engraving on bone, antler, ivory, or stone; (2) carving in the round, primarily on bone or ivory; and (3) cutout profiles further elaborated with relief carving and engraving, again in ivory and bone. The elements portrayed include the full range of animals known from cave art as well as seals, snakes or eels, rabbits, birds, fish, and geometric symbols. Decorated objects include bone staffs,

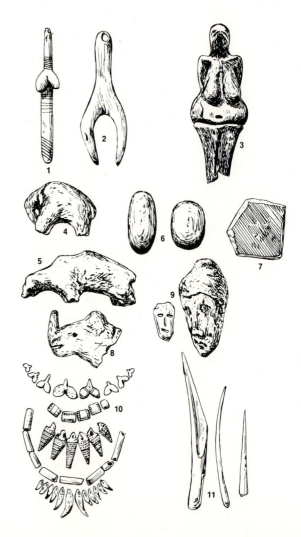

Fig. 10-8 Examples of mobilary art, ornaments, and utilitarian implements from Dolni Vestonice. (1,2) Stylized figurines in bone; (3) "Venus" figure of clay; (4,5) clay animal figurines; (6) ground stones; (7) ground-stone palette; (8) clay rhinoceros figurine; (9) carvings of deformed human faces; (10) bead necklaces of clay, bone, shell, and teeth; (11) bone needles or punches. (Fairservis 1975:84.)

antler-shaft wrenches, *batons de commande-mente*, spear throwers, half-round rods, disks, pendants, pebbles, and venuses (Fig. 10-8). Most of the decorated items were utilitarian. Some of the other objects, such as the batons and bone staffs, probably had specific functions, but we do not know what these were. Much of mobilary art is fragmentary, as many of the specimens have been broken. Other examples, such as cut-out profiles, never portrayed an entire animal.

Paleolithic Notation: A Search into the Minds of Paleolithic Peoples

As mentioned previously, much of the mobilary art in the Upper Paleolithic period features enigmatic rows of lines or dots. For years scientists had pondered the meaning of these notations, but to little avail. This situation was dramatically reversed during the 1960s by one individual, Alexander Marshack. Not an archaeologist by training, Marshack had nevertheless had a long career in scientific journalism. In connection with his responsibilities in the U.S. space program and the International Geophysical Year, he became interested in the history of human developments in science, mathematics, and astronomy. These inquiries led him to contact Ralph Solecki of Columbia University, who suggested that the authority on Upper Paleolithic art, Leroi-Gourhan, might provide further information concerning the mentality of Paleolithic peoples. Marshack wrote to Leroi-Gourhan, asking if the cave art had been painted on a seasonal basis. Leroi-Gourhan, replied that Paleolithic sanctuaries may have had a seasonal character but that there was no proof of this.

The next step in Marshack's search led him to the undeciphered bone from Ishango, a Mesolithic site, in Zaire, Africa. The bone tool, probably a knife handle, bore on one side a number of scratches or grooves in the following groups: 7, 5, 5, 10, 8, 4, 6, 3. On the opposite side

were two sets of groupings: 8, 19, 21, 11 and 19, 17, 13, 11. The excavator, Jean de Heinzelin, asserted that these grooves were not mere decoration but in fact must have a meaning, which he interpreted as "an arithmetical game of some sort, devised by a people who had a number system based on 10 as well as a knowledge of duplication and of prime numbers" (de Heinzelin 1962).

Marshack was not convinced, arguing that the Ishango bone represented some form of notation rather than an arithmetic game and thus there was need for further clarification. ▲ The first step was to assume that the markings represented some sort of count of time, possibly a lunar record. Having made this assumption, Marshack proceeded to attempt verification. Adding the numbers together, he found that the latter two columns totaled, 59 and 60, a possible count for two months. Following this lead, the sequence of grooves was aligned with a lunar sequence of the same length. The sequence of marks (days?) so arranged matched the waxing and waning of the moon. Marshack now had a hypothesis, but so far no proof. To broaden the evidence he decided to go to Europe and consult original specimens of Upper Paleolithic mobilary art. In his research at the Musée de Antiquites Nationales near Paris, Marshack found that one of the first specimens he studied, the engraved bone from the Abri Lartet, had such a sequence. The search was seemingly a success, for within that first cabinet there was obtained a strong correlation of the bone records with the lunar sequence (Marshack 1972): not only the bone from Abri Lartet but numerous others could be so interpreted.

It is not our intention here to cite all the specific details of Marshack's approach, nor will we attempt to verify the results. It is, however, sufficient to state that his attempt to interpret prehistoric mental patterns provides strong evidence that Upper Paleolithic people possessed a system of notation, that these records were made at different times and in different ways, and that

■ Upper Paleolithic peoples were specialized hunters.

● They occupied caves in winter and tents in summer.

very possibly they record lunar counts, although some archaeologists disagree. (In later studies Marshack [1979] has investigated engraved pieces of bone and ivory from Russia, and preliminary conclusions are that these specimens represent a whole new set of symbols which are yet to be understood.)

Recent research on the possible meaning of the abstract symbols common in parietal art (another term for *cave art*) indicates numerous similarities with symbols used in later systems of writing (Forbes and Crowder 1979). The possibility that Upper Paleolithic peoples possessed symbolic writing is far from proven, but this is an exciting idea worthy of further research.

The Life of Upper Paleolithic Peoples

We have given considerable coverage to the art of the late Paleolithic period because art was one of its triumphant achievements. Moreover, there exists much archaeological documentation of the life-style of the people. ■ They were hunters, specializing in the hunting of the large herd-dwelling mammals of the time. In areas such as the steppes of Russia and Siberia the mammoth and woolly rhino were most common. Hunting techniques were varied and successful. Traps and pitfalls are portrayed in the cave art, and the evidence from actual killsites

Fig. 10-9 Examples of dwellings of Upper Paleolithic mammoth hunters. *(above)* Skin tent on mammoth-bone and wooden-pole framework, Pushkari, Russia; *(below)* wooden framework covered with mammoth bone, Mezhirich, Russia. The floors were excavated slightly below the surface. Hearths were placed in a row down the center of these structures, which ranged up to 30 meters in length. Their size suggests that a number of families occupied a single dwelling. (Hawkes 1976:30.)

Fig. 10-10   Reconstruction of the life-style of Magdalenian peoples in southwest France in about 10,000 B.C. Skin clothing is shown as being worn, although the archaeological evidence of such apparel is quite limited. (Courtesy British Museum [Natural History].)

indicates that the ambush and stampede were commonly utilized techniques. At Predmost, the bones of at least 1,000 mammoths are present. The cliff-drive site at Solutre contains the bones of 100,000 horses at its base. The Magdalenian peoples were specialized reindeer hunters, living in a close symbiotic relationship with these animals, from whom they obtained almost their entire subsistence: meat, skins for clothing and tents, bone and antler for tools, sinew for thread, teeth for ornaments, and so forth. In some Magdalenian levels, reindeer comprise more than 90 percent of all bone remains. The Magdalenian peoples moved northward with the herds in summer and southward in the winter.

● Shelter was provided by the abundant caves and rock shelters of western Europe or by the skin tents common to the steppe and tundra dwellers of eastern and northern Europe. Examples of such tent villages consisted of three or more tents, some of which were as large as 40 by 12 feet (Fig. 10-9). Associated with the tents were hearths, both inside and outside, with large piles of discarded food bones between the tents. The tents had a supporting structure, probably of poles, set in postholes. Pits in the ground were used for food storage.

Other traits evidenced by the artifacts are sewn skin clothing and the wearing of ornaments (Fig. 10-10). Little is known about the clothing, however. The venuses were portrayed as nearly nude but were adorned with a type of fringed belt around the waist as well as a long apron extending down the back of the legs. Pre-

▲ Burial practices

■ The Bear Cult

● The Upper Paleolithic was a time of adaptation to a cold climate.

sumably for cold weather there was an entire inventory of full body covering of which we have little specific knowledge. Beads were especially common and were made of amber, brown coal, fish vertebrae, fired clay, and shells. Other ornaments included pendants, pins, bracelets, and anklets. The presence of amber and shells indicates trade, since items are found beyond their natural areas of origin.

▲ Specific ceremonies were carried out at death. The dead were interred fully clothed with all of their ornaments being worn. Also included were everyday tools and trophies of the hunt, such as tusks. A coating of powdered red ochre was sprinkled over the burial, possibly to restore color to the body. Whatever the reason, the placing of red ochre in burials became a widespread trait which occurs in early levels of New World cultures as well.

Spiritualism and religious practices include the major complex of the painting of the cave sanctuaries. ■ In addition, within the caves there was a continuation of the bear cult practiced by the Neanderthals. Bears were hunted in the caves as evidenced by their bones with associated skull wounds. One of the sculptured bear figures shows signs of having been utilized in rites where it was attacked, possibly by novices being initiated into the cult — at least that is one theory. Human remains were also mutilated, possibly for ceremonial reasons. Several human skulls were cut off and possibly utilized as cups. When found they were all arranged side by side on a rock deep within a French cave. Their use is problematical but ceremonial purposes seems the best answer.

Summary

The Upper Paleolithic was a time of increasing expansion by humans of the modern species, *Homo s. sapiens*, into previously unpopulated regions of the world, including the New World and Australia. ● Furthermore, humans had by

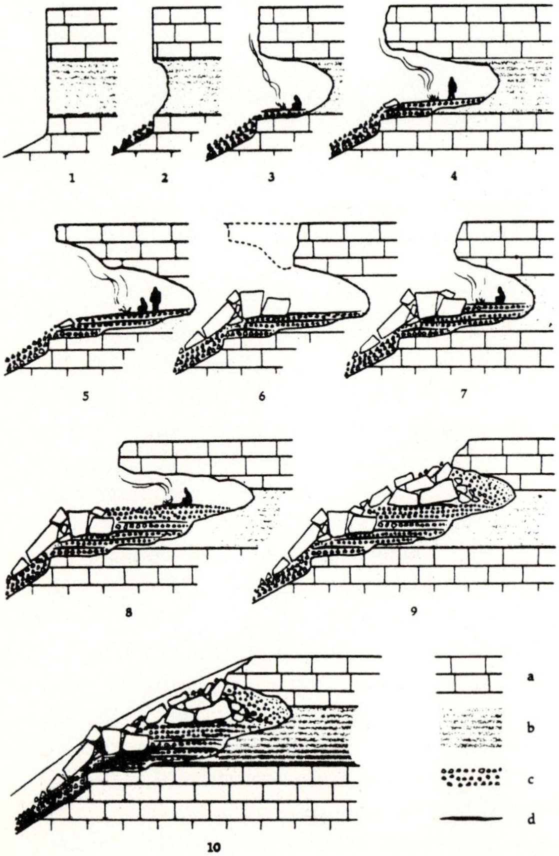

Fig. 10-11 The formation and evolution of a rock shelter. (1) The compact limestone (*a*) forms a layer resistant to erosion. The frost-sensitive limestone (*b*) erodes (2) forming a shelter deep enough for human occupation (3). Further erosion (4,5) widens and deepens the cave, eventually weakening the cave roof. Then, collapse of the roof occurs (6). The sequence may be repeated (7,8), but eventually the entry roof falls and the shelter ceases to exist (9,10). (Bordes 1972: Fig. 9.)

now clearly mastered life in the extremely cold portions of Europe, using as one adaptive technique the use of caves as shelter (Fig. 10-11). Their control of their environment permitted leisure time to paint and carve. Their use of these techniques in magic suggests that they were striving to further exert their will upon their surroundings. The period was a time of major adaptation to the late glacial environment, achieving a period of cultural climax for peoples existing as specialized hunters. With the major retreat of the glaciers, beginning in approxi-

mately 11,000 B.C., major species of the fauna, such as the woolly mammoth, woolly rhino, bison, and cave bear, became extinct. The climatic warming brought about a northward movement of environment zones which reduced the amount of cool steppe and tundra and increased the area of temperate woodland. The environment had changed to new conditions typical of the postglacial period. The nature of these changes and of the human response to them forms the subject of our next chapter, the Mesolithic.

11

The Mesolithic

The period following the last or Würmian glaciation some 12,000 years ago was a period of great environmental change, with corresponding stress on human populations. ■ The great herds of the large tundra-dwelling animals exploited by Paleolithic hunters either became extinct or survived in the north in greatly reduced numbers. Dense forests spread northward, bringing a new associated fauna. Gone were the herds of bison, mammoth, horse and rhino. In their place red deer, roe deer, and other solitary species became prevalent.

This period of change and stress was also an era of cultural crisis. Humans were forced into a totally new way of life, with survival depending upon rapid cultural adaptation to new and constantly changing environmental conditions. These changes required that humans modify their hunting techniques and hunting implements, and, almost certainly, develop new skills in food collecting. Diversification was the key to survival. During this interval, vegetal foods became more important, shellfish were gathered, fishing was important, and sea mammals, such as whales and seals, were hunted or utilized when they washed ashore.

Most of the published archaeological evidence for the Mesolithic comes from northern and western Europe, although this stage of environmental adjustment is known from other areas of the world, including Africa, the Far East, the Middle East, and North America. Archaeologically, however, the best-known sites are European, and most of our study will be based on those data, with no intent to minimize the importance of research conducted elsewhere.

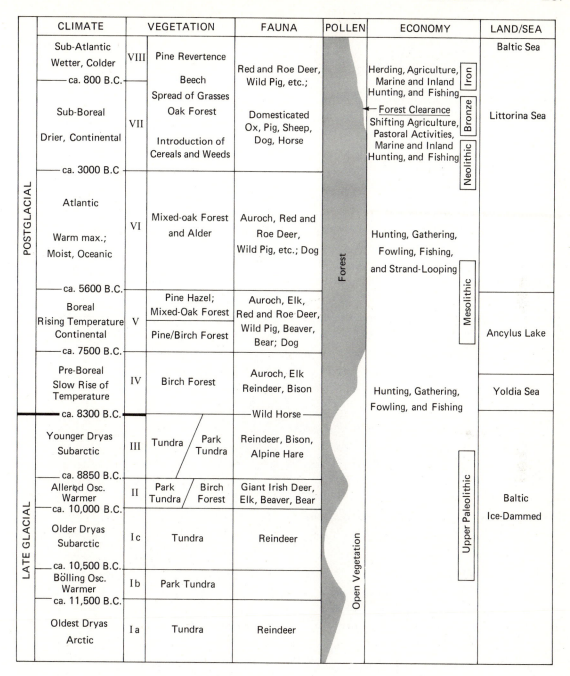

CLIMATE		VEGETATION	FAUNA	POLLEN	ECONOMY		LAND/SEA
POSTGLACIAL Sub-Atlantic Wetter, Colder — ca. 800 B.C.	VIII	Pine Revertence	Red and Roe Deer, Wild Pig, etc.;	Forest	Herding, Agriculture, Marine and Inland Hunting, and Fishing	Iron / Bronze / Neolithic	Baltic Sea
Sub-Boreal Drier, Continental — ca. 3000 B.C	VII	Beech Spread of Grasses Oak Forest Introduction of Cereals and Weeds	Domesticated Ox, Pig, Sheep, Dog, Horse		◄ Forest Clearance Shifting Agriculture, Pastoral Activities, Marine and Inland Hunting, and Fishing		Littorina Sea
Atlantic Warm max.; Moist, Oceanic — ca. 5600 B.C.	VI	Mixed-oak Forest and Alder	Auroch, Red and Roe Deer, Wild Pig, etc.; Dog		Hunting, Gathering, Fowling, Fishing, and Strand-Looping	Mesolithic	
Boreal Rising Temperature Continental — ca. 7500 B.C.	V	Pine Hazel; Mixed-Oak Forest Pine/Birch Forest	Auroch, Elk, Red and Roe Deer, Wild Pig, Beaver, Bear; Dog				Ancylus Lake
Pre-Boreal Slow Rise of Temperature — ca. 8300 B.C.	IV	Birch Forest	Auroch, Elk Reindeer, Bison — Wild Horse —		Hunting, Gathering, Fowling, and Fishing	Upper Paleolithic	Yoldia Sea
LATE GLACIAL Younger Dryas Subarctic — ca. 8850 B.C.	III	Tundra / Park Tundra	Reindeer, Bison, Alpine Hare	Open Vegetation			Baltic Ice-Dammed
Allerød Osc. Warmer — ca. 10,000 B.C.	II	Park Tundra / Birch Forest	Giant Irish Deer, Elk, Beaver, Bear				
Older Dryas Subarctic — ca. 10,500 B.C.	I c	Tundra	Reindeer				
Bölling Osc. Warmer — ca. 11,500 B.C.	I b	Park Tundra					
Oldest Dryas Arctic	I a	Tundra	Reindeer				

TABLE 11-1 *Correlation of Habitat, Biome, and Economy in the Mesolithic of Denmark.*

● A warming trend

▲ Colonization of northern Europe by forest

■ Extinction of fauna

● Adaptations to a forest economy

The Postglacial Environment

The Postglacial period was marked by warm or temperate climatic oscillations interspersed with brief colder, wetter intervals. ● The entire trend was one of warming, continuing to the present. Major features were the northward movement of biotic zones, the melting of ice, and the rise in sea level accompanied by uplift of the land formerly weighed down by ice.

These climatic oscillations are well known because we have numerous pollen profiles covering the entire period, mostly from peat bogs, the optimum environment for pollen preservation. In addition, the anaerobic environment of bogs inhibits decay of organic remains. Thus there have been preserved within bogs numerous plant parts, including whole trees. As a result, the composition of the forests of the period is accurately known. The Postglacial period of

Fig. 11-1 Reconstruction of vegetational zones of northwestern Europe during the Alleröd climatic period. (Butzer 1971:Fig. 72.)

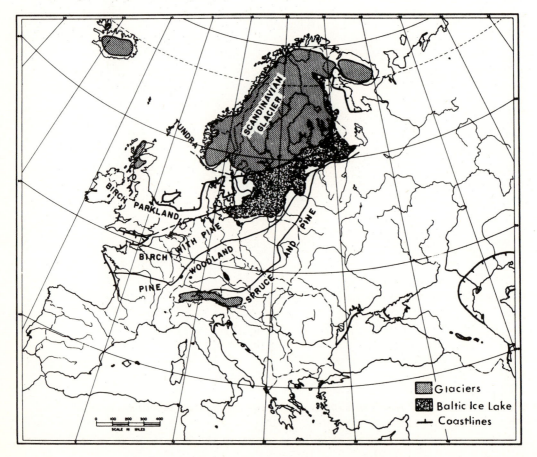

northwestern Europe has been divided into a series of pollen zones, as summarized in Table 11-1 (Clark 1952:12).

A vegetation map, (Fig. 11-1), for the Allerod period illustrates vegetal-zone changes (Zeuner 1958). The sites of Mesolithic humans are best known from the zones featuring birch parkland and birch with pine. During much of this period England was connected to continental Europe by a land bridge. A second geographic feature of major importance was the presence of a freshwater lake, the Ancyclus Lake, in the region that today is the eastern half of the Baltic Sea (Fig. 11-2). The Ancyclus Lake at times was frozen over and at times not; but in any event, it formed a major resource of fresh water (Zeuner 1958).

During the cold intervals the snowline depression was 500 to 800 meters below modern limits, and temperatures were depressed 2°C to 7°C. ▲ The sudden temperature reversals of the warmer periods resulted in rapid colonization by forest of the zones formerly occupied by ice and tundra. Johannes Iverson, the Danish palynologist, who has devoted a lifetime to the study of Postglacial floras of Europe, views the pollen record for this period as indicating a succession of species normal to forest colonization. This succession progresses from early or "pioneer" species to "climax" species. Pioneer species reproduce rapidly and have a quick rate of dispersion. These trees, which include willow, aspen, and birch, have a high need for light and thus are successful in newly vacated ground. Soon competition from the climax species is telling, however, for the pioneer species have a short life span and their seedlings must compete with the climax species, which are hardy, long-lived, and have a reduced need for light. Thus the pioneer species are crowded out by elm, oak, beech, and other deciduous hardwoods. The changes in the pollen diagrams record sequences such as juniper followed by aspen, then birch and pine. These changes are *successional* rather than *climatic*. Thus the Postglacial period experienced both a true climatic change — the shift to a modern climate — and local successional changes in flora typical of colonization followed by a climax forest.

Faunal changes were linked to both the worldwide end of the glacial epoch and the local fluctuations in floras. The tundra and steppe faunas of mammoth, rhino, reindeer, bison, horse, musk ox, and such were common in Europe until 11,000 B.C. ■ Between that date and 9000 B.C., most of these species became locally extinct in western and northern Europe. The time of greatest stress would appear to have been the warmer Allerod interval (10,000–8,850 B.C.), during which only the reindeer survived in quantity and then only in the northern areas. Local pockets of forest species, such as the woodland horse and forest bison, existed until recently in Europe, but the herd-dwelling steppe forms became extinct much earlier. The entire period of 11,000 to 7,500 B.C. was one of transition from tundra to forest, with the consequent extinction of most of the tundra and steppe species. Within this changing environmental scene the human species adapted, but most of the large Pleistocene animal species did not.

The Mesolithic Adaptation

During the Mesolithic humans became forest dwellers. ● They developed tools suitable for woodworking, axes, and adzes, and became skilled at forest clearance (Fig. 11-3). The results of their skill are even visible in the pollen diagrams, which show reduction in tree species and an increase in shrubs and herbs, indicating for the first time a pronounced effect of people upon the environment. With the trees felled, Mesolithic humans filled in bogs and swamps or stabilized their surfaces with logs, stones, and clay in order to build residences. "Houses" were rectangular huts with floors of bark. The walls were of branches tied at the top. Wood was also included in the manufacture of implements, especially for hafts. For the first time, we have ev-

BALTIC ICE LAKE

SALPAUSSELKÄ STAGE

AFTER RAMSAY and SAURAMO (MODIFIED)

A

YOLDIA SEA

AFTER SAURAMO 1929 and 1939 (MODIFIED)

6800 B.C.

7900 B.C.

B

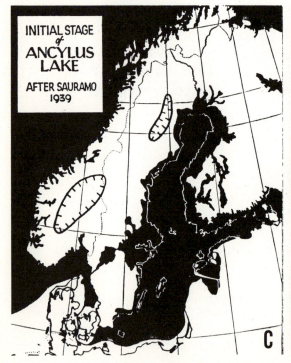

INITIAL STAGE of ANCYLUS LAKE

AFTER SAURAMO 1939

C

FIRST STAGE of LITORINA SEA

AFTER SAURAMO 1939

D

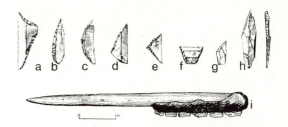

Fig. 11-3 Mesolithic implements: axes and adzes. These tools provided Mesolithic peoples with the means of modifying their environment through forest clearance. (Clark 1975: Fig. 48.)

idence of various means of transportation. There are preserved remains of dugout canoes, paddles, skis, and skin boats (Fig. 11-4). Humans no longer were solely terrestrial but could now travel on snow or water with ease. Sledges were also constructed, and since the dog had been domesticated, it is possible sleds were drawn by dog power. The development of boats may well have been an Upper Paleolithic feat, since early C-14 dates from Australia place the earliest occupation of that continent at between 30,000 and 40,000 B.C. (although some would argue for as early as 50,000 B.C.). Boats would have been required, since during the recent geologic past Australia has always been separated from the mainland by deep water. The spread of microblade industries from Japan to the mainland after 9000 B.C. can also most plausibly be explained by water transport.

The Mesolithic economy featured adjustments to the new forest environment, since it was no longer possible to utilize the Upper Paleolithic hunting techniques developed for use on herd-dwelling species. The new environment required the stalking or trapping, in dense cover, of individual animals such as the red deer, elk, roe deer, and auroch. ▲ A new implement was developed for hunting: the bow and arrow. The self-bow, of simple one-piece construction, was made of yew (Fig. 11-10). These new hunting conditions undoubtedly reduced the success of the hunter, and even on successful days the bag would be one animal instead of many.

Fig. 11-2 Evolutionary stages in the development of the Baltic Sea. (*a*) The Baltic Sea Lake, about 8800 B.C.; (*b*) the Yoldia Sea, about 7900 B.C.; (*c*) the Ancyclus Lake, about 6500 B.C.; (*d*) the Litorina Sea, about 5000 B.C. Mesolithic peoples adapted to these changing environmental conditions. (Zeuner 1958:Figs. 16–19.)

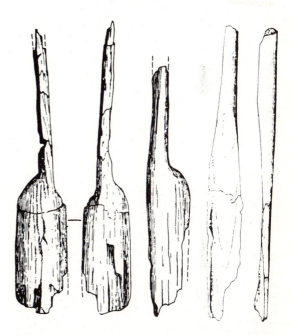

Fig. 11-4 Mesolithic implements: canoe paddles from various sites in northern Europe. Canoes and sleds were used in transporting goods and people. (Clark 1975: Fig. 20.)

Percentages of food provided by the various species hunted may be ascertained from bone remains at the sites. For example, at Star Carr, England, one of the most meticulously excavated sites from the period, the food remains were distributed as follows.

- ■ New types of game-taking devices
- ● Consequences of a more varied food supply
- ▲ The appearance of trade
- ■ We can identify the times of the year sites were occupied.
- ● Burials imply a belief in an afterlife.

TABLE 11-2
The Distribution of
Food Remains at Star Carr

Animal	Clean Carcass Weight	Average Weight of Each
160 Red Deer	67,200 lb	420 lb
66 Roe Deer	3,360 lb	50 lb
22 Elk	9,800 lb	445 lb
18 Ox	27,720 lb	1,542 lb
10 Pig	1,960 lb	196 lb
Total	Approximately 110,000 lb	

(J. G. D. Clark 1971:15)

Table 11-2 shows a preference for medium sized animals, such as red deer and roe deer, with larger and smaller species also being taken. Although both the numbers and the meat yield of these animals is impressive, it is essential to remember that Star Carr was occupied for some 300 years and that these figures represent a three-century accumulation of animal debris. The reduction in large animals available meant that everything else edible in the environment had to be exploited. Thus new devices were developed for the taking of game, which in many cases did not require the actual presence of the hunter. ■ Snare traps became common, the wooden tread trap was developed, and a variety of fishing techniques were employed. Fish were taken with hook and line, fish spears, harpoons, nets, and traps (Fig. 11-5). Late in the period the economy was extended to include the sea fauna, with seal and other marine species being taken. Stranded whales were also utilized. With the necessity of adapting to a varied economy, each element of which provided limited amounts of food, it is probable that Mesolithic peoples spent more time in the food quest than did their Paleolithic forebears.

● The shift from a relatively limited economy to a more varied one in which many resources are exploited has certain consequences:

1. There is greater nutritional security, with a multiple-food resource base providing a more stable food supply than a single, and perhaps more vulnerable, food resource.
2. There is an elaboration of the cultural inventory, with differing food resources requiring different tools and techniques for their successful exploitation.
3. The successful exploitation of multiple food resources requires specific knowledge — information as to where, when, and in what quantities given food resources are likely to be produced. This knowledge permits the making of rational exploitational choices.
4. With more time spent in the food quest less leisure time is available for other activities.

One possible result of reduced leisure time was a decrease in the quantity and quality of art, which in the Mesolithic consists of pebbles and bone and antler implements decorated with incised or painted geometric designs of lines and dots. Most naturalistic art is no longer present, although a few animals are portrayed as simple, stiff stick figures. Among the more unique objects are the Azilian painted pebbles. Named for the French site of Mas d'Azil, where they have been found in quantity, these are smooth river pebbles painted in red ochre with designs of stripes, spots, and zigzags. Some may even represent degenerate efforts at portraying the human figure; and some of the pebbles have also been broken, perhaps as part of a ceremony. Otherwise their use is unknown.

▲ Another element of the times is the appearance of trade. Items such as amber and polished stone axes were traded over long distances connected by specific trade routes. Although true craft specialists probably did not exist at this time, trade itself indicates specialized development of regional resources. And the commerce begun during the Mesolithic continued for a long time over the same routes.

Mesolithic peoples were colonizers, inasmuch as many of the areas they inhabited had formerly been covered with ice, water, or tundra. Their economic practice of multiple-resource use led to the semisedentary occupation of a series of sites over a region. ■ At Star Carr, for example, analysis of the stage of growth of the deer antlers present in the site clearly pinpointed the time of year—the late winter and early spring—during which the site was occupied. The size of the group was probably somewhat dependent upon the food resources locally available. The average site was some 12 by 20 meters, suggesting that the local group was typically not large, probably of less than 50 and per-

haps of no more than 15 or 20 persons. Grahame Clark, in the analysis of the remains at Star Carr (1971), believes that the site is similar to the area within caves occupied by Paleolithic man; thus it is estimated that group size did not increase during the Mesolithic. On the other hand, early Neolithic sites featuring food production may be as much as 100 times larger.

● Mesolithic burials indicate concern for the welfare of the individual after death. Some burials feature individual interment on the back with the legs flexed. The burials were frequently placed within an excavated pit surrounded by stone slabs set on edge (Fig. 11-6). The burial was then covered with several stag antlers. The body was dressed in a skin cloak fastened by bone pins. Another form, termed "head burial," has several skulls placed together in a pit. The skulls and attached neck bones were coated with red ochre. Associated with the bones were personal ornaments and a few microliths.

Fig. 11-5 Mesolithic implements used in fishing, (a) fish-hooks, with suggested method of attaching bait; and (b) wicker fish trap. (Clark 1952: Fig. 17; Clark 1952: Plate IIb.)

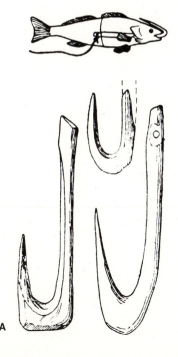

A

B

The best-known such burial (Figure 11-7), from Ofnet, in southern Germany, featured 27 skulls in one burial. It seems clear that the burial pattern was ceremonial in nature. In the modern aboriginal societies of Melanesia the skulls of ancestors are kept within the house as objects of veneration. Whether a similar form of ancestor worship is indicated by the Mesolithic head burials cannot be determined from the evidence at hand.

In many of the sites the anaerobic environment of bogs and swamps has preserved items of wood and other organic materials. Thus there is evidence of a wide variety of implements not found in Paleolithic levels. It is possible to view these finds as evidence of the *sudden* appearance

of boats, skis, etc., whereas in fact the transition to the Mesolithic way of life undoubtedly continued many earlier traditions for which we have little preserved evidence. Elaborately developed harpoons are known to have existed during the prior Magdalenian culture, and thus the Mesolithic adaptation to fishing and sealing does not represent such a dramatic shift.

An Inventory of Selected Mesolithic Industries

Major industries of Mesolithic type in Europe are placed in geographic and chronological perspective in Table 11-3. The geographic distribu-

Fig. 11-6 Mesolithic burial surrounded by stone slabs and covered with stag antlers. The individual buried was probably of high status to have warranted such elaborate treatment. (Clark 1967: Fig. 106.)

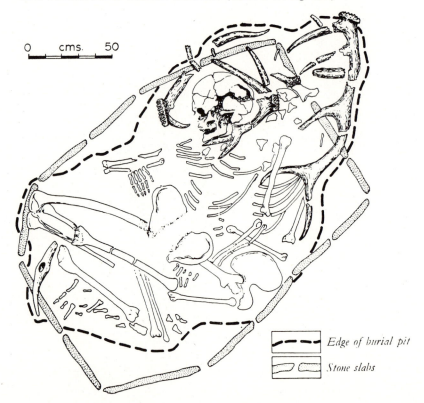

0   cms.   50

Edge of burial pit

Stone slabs

Man ♂
Woman ♀
Child ♀

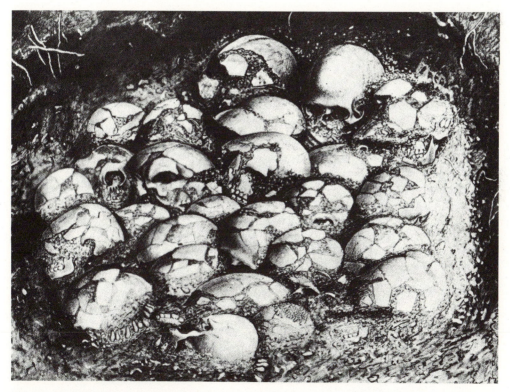

Fig. 11-7 Mass burial of skulls found at Ofnet in southern Germany. The severing of skulls and their burial as a group may well have had a ceremonial purpose; or they could have been war trophies. Four of the skulls were identified as male, 6 as female, and 15 as children. (Clark 1967: Figs. 126 and 128.)

tion of major sites is presented in Map 11-1. However, within this geographic and chronological perspective there are many variations. These represent (1) an overall adaptation to changing climatic conditions of the postglacial period, and (2) adaptation as adjustment to specific geographic areas or regions. Consequently, there is no overall uniformity to the Mesolithic period, since each region has its own variants and idiosyncratic features (Table 11-4).

Basic Tool Considerations

The Mesolithic tool makers elaborated upon several traditions which had been established during the Upper Paleolithic. Probably the most im-

TABLE 11-3
Mesolithic Chronology in Europe

Years B.P.	N.W.	Europe		S.E.
7000	Campignian			
8000	Maglemosian			
		Tardenoisian		
9000	Star Carr			
		Sauveterrian	Crvena	
10,000			Stijena	Asprochaliko
	Ahrensburgian			
11,000				
	Federmesser			
12,000		Azilian		
	Hamburgian			
13,000		Magdalenian		

(Braidwood 1967:101.)

TABLE 11-4
Diagnostic Characteristics of Selected Archaeologically Defined Cultures

Western Europe (France)

Azilian Culture

Gravers and scrapers on blades (survived from Magdalenian)
Microliths (great numbers, geometric forms)
Thumbnail scrapers
Harpoon head (made from red deer antler)
Red-painted pebbles

Sauveterrian Culture (also known as Lower Tardenoisian)

Microlithic tools (microburin manufacture technique)
Tiny blades and little pointed flakes used as blanks
Elongated triangles
Narrow, steeply battered points
Penknives (preponderantly crescent and lanceolate shapes)

Tardenoisian Culture (related to or similar in content to a number of Mesolithic cultures in Europe, ranging from the low countries to Poland and southern Russia)

Microliths
Broad-based points
Trapeze forms (most characteristic), and particularly the trapeze form with one right angle

The Northern Mesolithic Cultures

Tanged-point Cultures (Ahrensburg, Remouchamps, Swiderian, and other similar cultures of the northern European plains), derived from the Hamburgian culture of the late Upper Paleolithic)

Gravers and round-end scrapers (from Upper Paleolithic)
Microliths (not exhibiting perfect geometric forms)
Tanged points
Single points of bone and antler

Ahrensburg

Small points with hollow bases

Remouchamps

Triangles

The Lyngby Culture (Europe's oldest axe culture)

Heavy reindeer axes, adzes, and hafts

Maglemose and Kunda Cultures

Variety of woodworking, hunting, fishing, and fowling equipment, (remarkable preservation in the anaerobic bogs of Denmark)
Microliths (usually hafted in either wood or bone)
Awls, bow and arrow, axes and adzes, canoes and wooden paddles, traps, nets, basketry, fire-hardened spears, Leister prongs, and fish hooks (all extensively used)

Ertebolle Culture

More or less a continuation of the Maglemosian
Core axes and adzes (large numbers)
Coarse pottery

(After Hawkes, 1965)

▲ Florescence of composite tools

■ Development of microliths

● Appearance of axes

portant of these was a bone industry featuring hafted, barbed spears, and harpoons. ▲ Each of these implements is a composite tool consisting of several parts socketed and glued or wrapped together to form one unit. Composite tools are the hallmark of the Mesolithic.

■ A major innovation at this time was the development and use of *microliths*. These are small, geometrically shaped portions of core-struck blades of triangular, crescentic, or trapezoidal form. (The method of their manufacture is illustrated in Figure 11-8.) The microlith rep-

Fig. 11-8 Illustration of the technique of manufacturing microliths from blades. The central portions became the geometrically shaped microliths. The notched ends, termed *microburins*, were probably discarded as waste fragments. (Bordaz 1970: Fig. 42.)

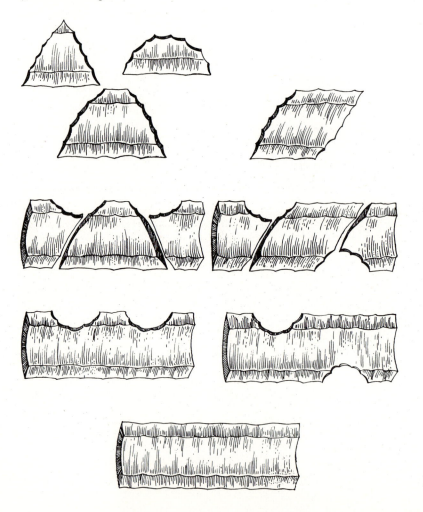

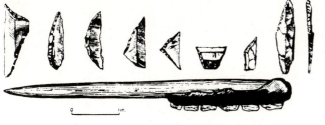

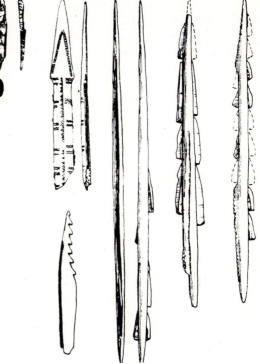

Fig. 11-9 Mesolithic implements: microliths shown individually and set in rows for use in knives and projectile points. (After Oakley [1962:69] and Clark [1975:Fig. 43].)

resents the culmination of a long trend of increasing the quantity of cutting edges prepared from a specific amount of raw material. (See Table 10-1 in Chapter 10.) The development of microliths enabled prehistoric stoneworkers to produce up to 300 feet of cutting edge from two pounds of flint (roughly the weight of one Abbevillian biface). Since microliths themselves, being from a half-inch to 2 inches in length, cannot be used efficiently if held in the hand, they were hafted in series in grooves cut in bone, antler, or wood. Mounted in this way they became exceedingly efficient cutting tools. Thus their development depended not only on the evolution of flint knapping but also on advancement in suitable hafting techniques. Microliths are the most distinctive stone tools of the Mesolithic period (Fig. 11-9), and their distribution is widespread, covering most of Europe as well as North Africa, East and South Africa, the Middle East, India, and Australia. However, our knowledge of the spread of microliths from early centers of development is unclear. In some areas they were introduced long after food production had developed within the more advanced cultures. For example, they do not appear in Australia until 3000 B.C., whereas they occur in South Africa as early as 23,000 B.C. (Sampson 1974:257). In other regions (the Nubian Nile, for example) microliths continued in use after the introduction of

agriculture, and in parts of India they are still employed today. Thus, the presence of microliths does not automatically signify that a particular site is of Mesolithic age.

Other implements of chipped stone include backed and tanged flakes and blades, serrated blades or saws, awls or borers, core scrapers, flake and blade scrapers, burins, flaked adzes and axes, and a variety of flaked utility tools. ● The earliest axes and adzes in both northwestern Europe and southwestern Asia appear about 9000 B.C. These implements feature an initial flaking to shape, then edge grinding of the bit. Later forms feature overall grinding and smoothing. A typical form, the celt, consists of a straight blade of somewhat triangular form with the bit at the widest end. The narrow tapering butt was hafted in a "sleeve" of antler which had a socket for the insertion of a wooden handle. It was after the development of the ground and polished cutting tools—celts and adzes—that Mesolithic

▲ An antler industry

■ Adaptation to hunting elk

● Adaptation to collecting shellfish

peoples became proficient in tree cutting and woodworking.

▲ The antler industry was one result of the economic shift to deer. For example, at Star Carr three types of antler were available: roe deer, red deer, and elk. Roe deer antler was not used, although the bones were used, whereas red deer antler was commonly used, but the bones were not. Both shed and unshed antlers were used as a source of material. Typical manufacturing techniques include the initial removal of the crown and tines. Longitudinal splinters were then removed from the beam by a grooving and splitting technique. The grooving was done with use of burins. The splinters were then further modified by grinding and polishing into barbed points. The points were unilaterally barbed, with the barbs ranging in number from 2 to about 30. When hafted in groups of three, these formed the Leister type of point, the elements of which spring apart slightly on contact and then contract to hold the game securely. Modern aboriginal peoples use similar spears or arrows for the taking of birds and fish. Tines were also converted into tools by grinding their tips to a beveled point. Elk antler was used for mattock heads. These feature a flat, beveled point at one end and a hafting hole cut through the rear portion of the blade. Small bone pins (bodkins), presumably for securing clothing, were made of elk bone. Other large sections of bone and antler were prepared by grinding a flat, beveled edge which was then used for scraping. The most distinctive antler artifacts were the worked stag frontlets, which are portions of the frontal bone with antlers attached. Two to four holes for attachment were drilled into the frontal bone. It is assumed that these frontlets were worn in ceremonies, perhaps by the religious practitioner,

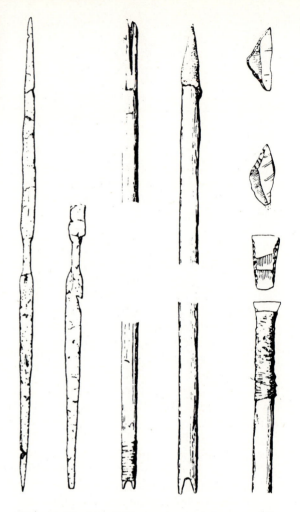

Fig. 11-10 Mesolithic implements: bows and arrows. Two methods of hafting of microlithic points are shown, one using resin and the other wrapping with fiber. The transverse mounted arrow tip *(lower right)* is the form of microlithic arrow point termed a *tranchet.* (Clark 1977: Fig. 49.)

the shaman. Such a costume is known to have been worn in recent times by tribal shamen among the Tungu. Evidence that the Star Carr frontlets were intended to be worn is suggested by the fact that they were lightened by hollowing out the backs of the beams.

Other typical objects include crude beads with holes drilled for suspension. Beads were made of amber, shale, hematite, and animal teeth. The presence of iron pyrites (crystals made of iron that look like gold) is interesting; these may have been used as strike-a-lights.

Special mention should also be made of transverse arrowheads called tranchets (Fig. 11-10). These were arrow points with a straight, sharp edge at a right angle to the arrow shaft. These points were microliths of triangular or trapezoidal form, hafted with one of the long axes as the leading edge.

It is interesting to note the differences in two of these archaeologically defined cultures. ■ For example, the Maglemosian culture tends to have a Danish inland distribution and a strong association with elk. We know that elk herds migrated northward out of Germany through Denmark into southern Scandinavia in spring and returned in the fall. Maglemosian sites are located along these ancient migration routes.

Ertebølle sites, on the other hand, have a strong coastal affiliation. ● On these sites, huge kitchen middens are found, and it is obvious that great quantities of shellfish were consumed by the Ertebølle folk. Since the Ertebølle is later in date but shows affinities with the Maglemosian culture, the Ertebølle has been described as an outgrowth of the latter. It is also true that the Ertebølle is the latest of a series of coastally oriented cultures, thus raising some interesting questions. For example, are we really dealing with two different cultures—the Maglemosian and Ertebølle—or are we in fact describing a system of *complementary resource exploitation* in which the Maglemosian represents an inland exploitation of elk in spring and fall while the Ertebølle represents a coastal occupation by the same people during summer and winters? Under this scheme, the differing tool inventories of the two cultural groups can be seen as the result of one culture exploiting two different food resources, elk and clams. The occurrence of traits by culture is plotted in Figure 11-11.

The Mesolithic Period of Eastern Europe

According to Tringham (1971) eastern Europe was also dramatically affected by the glacial retreat, and its inhabitants had to adapt to new and stress-laden conditions. However, the nature of this adaptation is not nearly as well known or understood as that of western Europe.

One of the problems is that of preservation, with much of eastern Europe covered by either sandy, alluvial soils, which are acidic in nature, or by limestone uplands with thin soils. Since both conditions are unfavorable to the survival of any sort of organic material, only chipped stone tools remain. Consequently, we have arrowheads but know nothing of the targets against which the arrows were directed. Part of this lack of information is due to the fact that most of the specimen collections are from the surface and are undated. Equally, in those comparatively few excavated sites the habitation layers tend to be quite thin, and therefore little has been preserved for study.

In general, the Mesolithic food gatherers occupied a variety of settings with river banks, lake shores, sand dunes, and mountain-foothill zones being especially preferred. On the other hand, the loess plains of central Europe were not utilized. Tools tend to be small, and when they exhibit marked geometric characteristics there is a tendency to attribute them to a general Europe-wide Tardenoisian culture. We shall restrict our detailed review of the eastern European Mesolithic culture to a single well-preserved site, Lepenski Vir.

Lepenski Vir—a Unique Site

Lepenski Vir, on the banks of the Danube in northeastern Yugoslavia, is one of those rare occurrences in archaeology—a site not similar to any other known. Overlooking the great Whirl-

▲ A Mesolithic house type

■ Mesolithic sculpture

● Mesolithic cultures in Africa exploited a wide variety of foods.

pool in the Danube, Lepenski Vir consists of four basic levels, with the topmost attributed to the Neolithic period. The earlier three levels are attributed to the Mesolithic. Levels I and II are dated between 5410 and 4610 B.C., with the Proto-Lepenski Vir level antedating both.

▲ The site itself consists of a series of trapezoidally shaped houses which are of four sizes: 5.5m², 9.5m², 17m², and 28m². The large end of each house is the segment of a circle forming an arc of 60°, and the houses exhibit a 3:1 or 4:1 proportion of length to width. Large structures, "central houses" of up to 30m², are also present, each having an open space in front of it (Srejovic 1972). The floors are plastered with a cementlike mixture of local limestone, sand, and water; and the layouts of floor features, such as post holes, hearths, etc., are virtually identical for each house (Fig. 11-12). House sites were repeatedly

Fig. 11-11 Diagram of the time span of specific culture traits known for the various Mesolithic cultures of Denmark. (Clark 1975:Fig 41.)

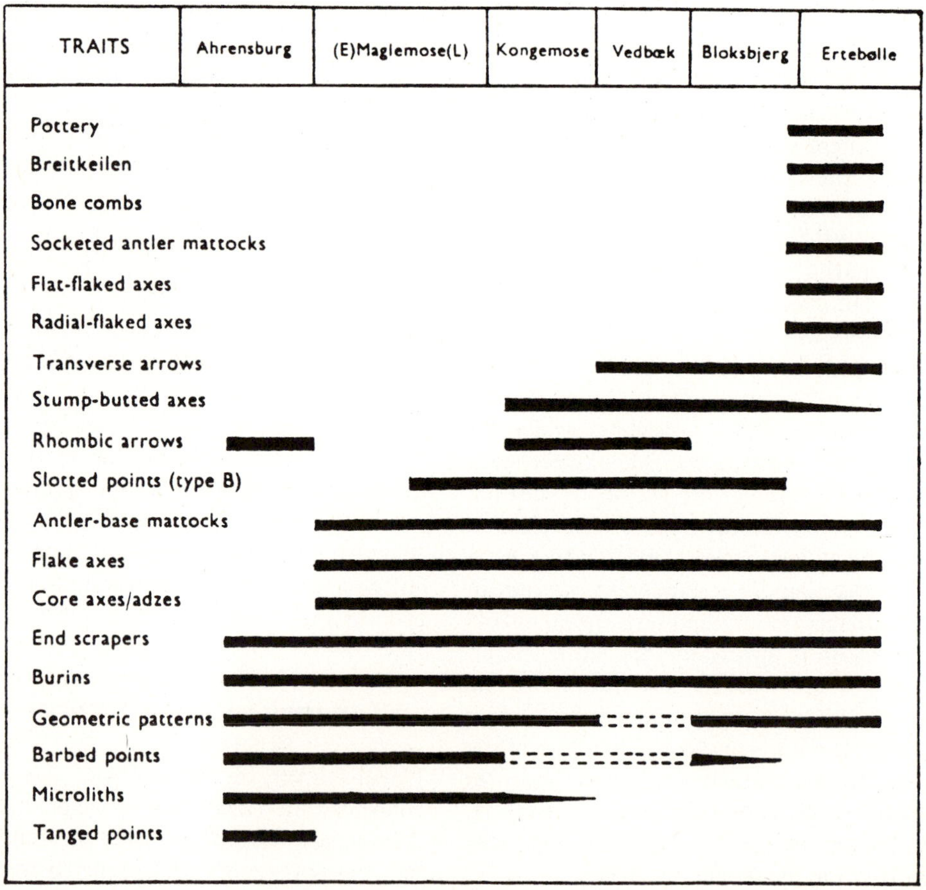

TRAITS	Ahrensburg	(E)Maglemose(L)	Kongemose	Vedbæk	Bloksbjerg	Ertebølle
Pottery						▬▬▬
Breitkeilen						▬▬▬
Bone combs						▬▬▬
Socketed antler mattocks						▬▬▬
Flat-flaked axes						▬▬▬
Radial-flaked axes						▬▬▬
Transverse arrows				▬▬▬▬▬▬		
Stump-butted axes			▬▬▬▬▬▬▬▬			
Rhombic arrows	▬▬▬		▬▬▬			
Slotted points (type B)		▬▬▬▬▬▬▬▬▬▬				
Antler-base mattocks		▬▬▬▬▬▬▬▬▬▬▬▬▬▬▬▬▬				
Flake axes		▬▬▬▬▬▬▬▬▬▬▬▬▬▬▬▬▬				
Core axes/adzes		▬▬▬▬▬▬▬▬▬▬▬▬▬▬▬▬▬				
End scrapers	▬▬▬▬▬▬▬▬▬▬▬▬▬▬▬▬▬▬▬▬					
Burins	▬▬▬▬▬▬▬▬▬▬▬▬▬▬▬▬▬▬▬▬					
Geometric patterns	▬▬▬▬▬▬▬▬ - - - - - ▬▬▬▬▬▬					
Barbed points	▬▬▬▬ - - - - - - - - ▬▬					
Microliths	▬▬▬▬▬▬▬▬					
Tanged points	▬▬▬					

reused, and the houses are arranged in a fan-shaped pattern (Wernick 1975:34–41), with the large end of each house facing the river. The total effect is one of order, precision, and centralized planning.

■ Of great interest was the discovery of life-sized monumental sculptures. Most of the pieces have human characteristics: eyes, noses, and mouths. However, the "goggle" eyes give an overall fishlike appearance (Fig. 11-13), suggesting that these sculptures possibly represent some sort of deity connected with the rich fish life of the Danube. The sculpture at Lepenski Vir is as old as any in the world and, like the site itself, seems unrelated to anything else either before or after.

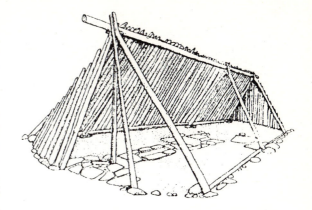

Fig. 11-12 Detail of house type found at the unique fishing village of Lepenski Vir. (Hawkes 1976: 53.)

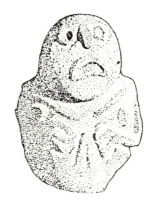

Fig. 11-13 Carved stone head found at Lepenski Vir. (Hawkes 1976:57.)

The Mesolithic in Africa

Mesolithic cultures are widespread in Africa, where they represent adaptations to environmental conditions different from those of Europe. Africa possesses several major environmental situations: the North African coast, with its Mediterranean climate; the Sahara; the equatorial rain forest; and the South African veld. Between the rain forest and the Sahara is a series of zones grading from savanna to thorn scrub. East and South Africa feature grassland to wooded savanna, primarily structured by elevation. An added feature is the Rift Valley lakes. In view of such varied environmental conditions, it is obvious that the archaeology of the period must be equally diverse.

Several items exist as constants characteristic of the Mesolithic period. ● The inhabitants were locally adapted food collectors. In North Africa, a major food source was the African land snail, available in great quantity on the scrub vegetation. In the Sahara, native grasses were collected for seeds. Along the Nile a variety of fish, freshwater mollusks, gazelle, hippo, and water birds were available. The savannas were

rich in tree and root foods. Another sign of the times was the presence of microliths. These occur over most of the continent, with the possible exception of the equatorial forest region. There is a large area, extending across North Africa southward along the Nile Valley and into the East African horn and Kenya, which may have had strong cultural interconnections. These include the Capsian culture of North Africa, the Natufian culture of Palestine, the Sebilian and related industries along the Nile, and the Kenya Capsian, Magosian, and Doian cultures of East Africa. Common features among these industries include core-struck blades and bladelets, microliths (especially the crescent-shaped lunate forms), backed blades, and burins. As yet, however, there is insufficient archaeological evidence to specifically arrange these var-

▲ Earliest grinding stones

■ Fishing in central Africa

● Exploitation of the South African coastal fauna

▲ Life in the Late African Stone Age

ious cultures into a comparative chronology. While they possess traits in common, we do not know that they are of equivalent ages; and their similarities may in fact be more apparent than real, the result of convergent evolution.

▲ In sites along the Nubian Nile grinding stones were utilized in the production of food. The cultural levels containing these have been dated at 10,000 to 12,000 B.C. Thus these specimens represent the world's oldest known grinding stones (Wendorf 1968:940–942).

Another tradition is represented in parts of East Africa, the Congo, and Sudan. ■ In this well-watered region there was the widespread taking of fish by means of barbed bone points. The wide geographic separation between this region and Europe, with the arid Sahara in between, suggests that a fishing economy in central Africa represents an independent development. Some authors disagree, claiming that harpoons were actually diffused from Africa to Europe, but more archaeological research on the Sahara is needed to resolve questions of this type.

Some stone industries of South Africa and portions of East Africa are clearly derived from prior traditions of the region. These include the cultures assigned to what has been termed the "African Late Stone Age." Such industries include the Stillbay, Magosian, and Wilton cultures. Chronologically and culturally, these are transitional groups with both a late hunting economy and a Mesolithic type of omnivorous food collecting.

● Archaeological and paleoecological evidence derived from a series of caves distributed along the coast of the Cape province of South Africa shows that the people of the African Late Stone Age in South Africa more effectively exploited their environment than their Middle Stone Age predecessors (Klein 1977:151–160). For example, at Klasies river-mouth cave, the Middle Stone Age people prior to 40,000 B.C. exploited the molluscs, mammals, and sea birds (seals and penguins) but did not engage in fishing. These latter activities were practiced by the Late Stone Age peoples. Middle Stone Age peoples did not stalk the dangerous wild pig, hunting instead the more docile eland, whereas the Late Stone Age hunters exploited both the eland and the pig (Klein 1979:151–160). Even the taking of eland by the Middle Stone Age people testifies to their hunting inefficiency. For example, most eland taken were either less than one year old or over 10 years old, which means that the age group of these prey closely matched that taken by other predators, such as the lion. Animals in prime condition seem to have been beyond the hunting capability of Middle Stone Age hunters. Late Stone Age hunters were able to take all age groups and therefore probably had more impact on the herds.

In the following summary, based on a description by J. Desmond Clark (1959, 1970:184–186), we have a reconstruction of life in the Late Stone Age in Africa. This composite is deduced not only from the archaeological remains of settlements but from perishable materials preserved in rock shelters and from paintings on the shelter walls. Further confirmation is provided by the cultural practices of the modern native peoples who lead a similar life.

▲ The social unit was a band of 20 to 30 people, who had no permanent dwellings; their possessions were thus limited to what they could carry. In the rainy season the band size could increase to 200. Hunting probably covered an area of 2,000 to 3,000 square miles. Regions were claimed by specific bands and were seasonally occupied in order to utilize food resources currently available. Caves or rock shelters were favored for occupation, and reed windbreaks were also constructed. Rock paintings illustrate band activities, such as warfare, marriage, rain ceremonies, burial, abduction of women, sexual intercourse, homicide, and theft. Trade by barter was conducted with salt, sea shells, and red and yellow ochre. Some groups may have had chiefs, for the burial scenes show individuals of unique status. Males did the hunting and made the hunting implements. Females gathered the food and made the tools they needed. The one-piece bow was used with composite arrows (probably poisoned). Throwing sticks and stabbing spears were used. Hunting disguises included the use of ostrich skins. Pit traps with or without stakes were employed, as well as spring traps and nets. Fishing was done with barbed harpoons, arrows, and through the use of tidal traps made of reed basketry. Women used the digging stick weighted with a bored stone. Bone adzes were used for skin scraping. Stone scrapers were used for woodworking and removing meat from bones. Ostrich eggshells were used for containers. Containers also were made of bark, animal bladders, turtle shells, and late in the period, pottery. Foods included meat, ants, eggs, locusts, grass seeds, berries, honey, tree caterpil-

lars, snakes, and the abdominal juices of freshly killed animals. Cooking included baking, stone boiling, and roasting; and meat was also eaten raw. According to the rock art, clothing was not worn, although there was much use of body painting and the wearing of ornaments. The people wore grass bracelets; pendants of shell, bone, and stone; beads of bone, ivory, and stone; and necklaces of seeds and berries. Burial, in which objects of personal ornamentation were included, was in a grass bed. Sometimes a windbreak was burned and thrown over the burial. After interment there was feasting. The mythical animals portrayed in the scenes of rain ceremonies suggest that a cosmology was present in these cultures. Ceremonies also included music provided by reed flutes and musical bows.

The economy of the Late Stone Age was of Mesolithic type—a mixture of hunting and food collecting. After the initiation of food production, about 8,000 years ago or earlier in the Middle East and elsewhere, and its subsequent spread to other regions during the period 5000–2000 B.C., we may view all subsequent Mesolithic peoples as being so well adapted to their environment that a change to food production offered few advantages.

12

The Neolithic Revolution as a Process

Sometime during the Mesolithic period, 10,000 or more years ago, there began a series of cultural developments that were to change the entire human life-style. This development, the change from hunting and gathering to the production of food, whether abrupt, as once thought, or more gradual, as now believed, was so significant it has been termed a revolution (Childe 1953). With food *production*, humans were no longer totally dependent upon the availability of wild game, upon their hunting ability, or upon the availability of wild plant foods in a seasonal harvest. Their new skill in food production has had widespread and profound ramifications that remain important today.

The term "Neolithic" was coined in 1865 by John Lubbock (later Lord Avebury) in his book *Prehistoric Times*. In this work, the term Neolithic or "New Stone Age" was used to describe the period characterized by the appearance of the polished stone axe. By 1925, as defined by MacCurdy, the Neolithic, as a cultural concept, had been expanded to include domestic animals and pottery as well as polished stone axes. We now know that all three of the above criteria have also been found in contexts that can only be described as Mesolithic. On the other hand, there are also sites bearing no evidence of pottery or domesticated animals which can only be classed as Neolithic due to the presence of plant cultivation. ■ Currently, archaeologists view the Neolithic change as primarily representing a change of economic activity rather than one in tool types. We feel that this change is particularly significant for the following reasons: (1) For the first time, through the production of food humans were able to restructure their relationship with their environment. No longer were they simply improving techniques used to obtain naturally occurring foods. (2) For the first time, also, our ancestors were able to modify their environment on a substantial scale. Food production was responsible for numerous cultural changes. While still subject to the deleterious effects of droughts, floods, blights, and such, people were able to nourish the food-producing plants and animals and protect them to some degree from adverse natural influences. (3) Humans were able to live in larger groups due to the increase in the average food yields resulting from cultivation. For example, the physical area occupied by individual communities increased from the Mesolithic average of 20 meters × 12 meters to a Neolithic average of 200 meters × 50 meters — a gain of more than 40 times. The population increase was probably of similar magnitude. (4) Food production also resulted in the establishment of stable permanent villages. Once people began to live in one place permanently, they began to take an increased interest in the rights of ownership. They could now afford to construct more elaborate dwellings and furnishings of a permanent nature because such possessions no longer had to be moved or abandoned during the seasonal food harvests (as had been the case with the occupational sites of hunter-gatherers). ● With food production, there occurred concomitant developments in architecture, systems of ownership rights, and crafts. (5) Food production also led to the generation of food surpluses and to food storage. (6) The widespread development of pottery occurred, the result of the alteration of malleable clay into a hard permanent form through the mechanism of firing. Pottery is brittle and friable as well as heavy, all of which are disadvantageous traits to the mobile hunter or food collector. However, with a settled way of life, pottery became extremely important because it could be made into almost any form and if broken could be easily replaced. Archaeologically, pottery is extremely important since once broken, the remnant sherds are nearly indestructible and hence provide a wealth of information about past culture. Throughout the Neolithic pottery became increasingly integral to the preparation and storage of food.

▲ With the accumulation of food surpluses, societies could afford the luxury of nonfood producers — specialists, such as potters, priests, warriors, and others, who were valued for their unique contributions in areas outside the basic economy. With the rise of these craftspeople we perceive the beginnings of the generally complex culture of today. The Neolithic is the foundation of modern society. During this period many activities which are still practiced, such as agriculture, animal husbandry, brewing, wine making, bee keeping, irrigation and the use of fertilizer, were established. In many parts of the world, only recently have societies shifted out of a basic Neolithic economy, and in other areas modern societies persist in a Neolithic way of life. The latter are the groups we term "peasant," in which subsistence is based on agriculture as practiced with hand tools and draft animals.

Theoretical Considerations and Opinions

The shift from hunting and gathering to food production and domestication has fascinated archaeologists for a long time, and much has been written on the subject. Most of these studies fall into one of two perspectives: descriptive or explanatory.

Descriptive approaches, the more traditional of the two, document when and where domestication took place and detail the steps involved in the process. In contrast, *explanatory approaches* are less concerned with when and where but more interested in how and why domestication occurred.

■ Explanations for the development of food production

● Childe's oasis theory

▲ Early sites are not known in the river valleys.

■ Braidwood's eras—an evolutionary sequence.

● Nuclear areas

■ Several explanatory hypotheses, some of which are quite recent, have been proposed to account for the development of agriculture. After all, why should people shift from hunting and gathering if these techniques provided an adequate food supply? We have little evidence that hunting-and-gathering societies suffered, or suffer, from a lack of food. In fact, modern hunting-and-gathering peoples acquire their food with less than full-time effort, and in many instances farmers actually must work longer hours to insure successful crops. It is obvious, then, that other factors must have led to food production.

The domestication hypotheses we will consider are those proposed by V. Gordon Childe, Robert J. Braidwood, Lewis R. Binford, and Kent V. Flannery. Each of these authorities approaches the problem of origins from a different perspective. All of these hypotheses were developed from archaeological research in the Middle East, and consequently they tend to project a Middle Eastern bias (with the exception of Flannery, who has also worked in Mesoamerica). This does not necessarily mean that the first steps toward domestication occurred in the Middle East. However, not only is the Middle Eastern evidence the best known, but the developments in that part of the world went on to become ancestral to the cultural heritage of our own Western civilization.

The Theory of Propinquity

Childe, who coined the term "Neolithic Revo-

lution," developed the first of the explanatory hypotheses (1929:42–49). Childe contends that the drying-out of the Middle East after the end of the last glacial period caused those plants and animals needed for human food to become increasingly concentrated in the few remaining moist regions, thereby forming a series of biotic refuges. ● The closer proximity to humans of the animals trapped in these oases made the latter more tolerant of people. This closer proximity, according to Childe, also permitted an increase in the knowledge and understanding of both plant and animal characteristics. Domestication, then, was the result of the selective elimination of less desirable individuals, both plant and animal, plus selection of the most productive plants and the most docile animals. This hypothesis includes two archaeologically testable conditions: (1) evidence of climatic change, and (2) evidence of early sites in the well-watered lowlands and river valleys.

The first condition seems to have been met. There is evidence of climatic change from Lake Zeribar in the Zagros mountains of western Iran (van Zeist 1969:35–46) and from Ghab Marsh in northwestern Syria (Wright 1977:285). At those sites the pollen diagrams indicate that beginning in 20,000 B.C. there was a dominance of *Chenopodiacaae* (low, bushy, annual plants that we would probably call weeds) and *artemisia* (sagebrush), with tree pollen being in low frequency. Trees, primarily oak and pistachio, appear between 8000 and 6000 B.C., after which the vegetation changed to that typical of today—oak forest. H. E. Wright, Jr. (1977:313) has reviewed this evidence and concludes that in the Middle East there was a strong and direct correlation between the environmental change that occurred after 8000 B.C. and the development of plant domestication.

The second part of Childe's hypothesis, however, is not so well documented. The earliest sites have not been found in the river valleys but on the "hilly flanks" zone of the Zagros mountains overlooking the river valleys. ▲ There may be several reasons for the absence of early sites in the river valleys:

1. The earliest Neolithic sites in the river valleys may underlie ancient cities and other monuments of antiquity and may either have been covered over or destroyed by such later building.
2. Both the Tigris and Euphrates rivers are meandering streams, and the early sites may have been eroded away.
3. The early sites may be covered with thick layers of alluvial silt, leaving no visible surface evidence.

Under these circumstances, recovery of early sites within river valleys would be primarily the result of chance. Whatever the reasons involved, only one of the two main criteria of Childe's propinquity hypothesis seems to have been proven thus far.

Braidwood's Descriptive System

■ The most clearly thought-out of the descriptive approaches is the stage system of R. J. Braidwood, who believes it is possible to discern a series of stages or eras leading to the development of food production. These are defined as follows.

1. Food-Gathering Stage:
   a) The Terminal Era of Food Collection, which can be equated with the Mesolithic period
2. Food-Producing Stage:
   a) The Era of Incipient Cultivation and Domestication
   b) The Era of Primary Village Farming — the full-fledged Neolithic period (Braidwood 1967:92–94)

Of the subperiods, the Era of Incipient Cultivation and Domestication is the most difficult to detect archaeologically. This is because within this period it is impossible to distinguish domesticated plants and animals from their wild relatives, since both were of identical form.

During the Paleolithic, people simply "gathered" food, wandering over large areas to scavenge or hunt in a simple way. However, during the Terminal Era of Food Collecting they restricted their wandering and adapted to the local environment in a more intensive way, seeking specific food harvests. This constituted a shift from "gathering" to "collecting," which in turn set the stage for the next period of development, the Era of Incipient Cultivation and Domestication.

The Era of Incipient Cultivation and Domestication is characterized by Braidwood as one in which the harvesters returned season after season to the same food resource. In addition, they began to keep the young of animals being hunted. All in all, this was a period of experimentation and increasing knowledge of the life-sustaining requirements of both plants and animals.

The Era of Primary Village Farming is quite well delineated, archaeologically. It is characterized by permanent villages, recognizable domesticated plants and animals, and an explosive radiation of new arts and crafts. Braidwood also sets out two conditions that must be fulfilled if domestication is to occur. The first is simple: There must be a natural environment in which plants and animals are capable of and ready for domestication. ● Environments that meet these requirements are called "nuclear areas." The best known of these was the "hilly flanks" region of the Zagros mountains, where today grow wild some of the same plants that were domesticated during the early Neolithic. Secondly, according to Braidwood, culture must be *receptive* to the potential provided by the nuclear area. (An absence of cultural receptiveness may be the reason why domestication was not attempted earlier.)

Braidwood's explanation relies on cultural rather than environmental factors. This view contends that the development of agriculture

▲ Demography as a causal factor

■ Negative and positive feedback

● The search for agricultural origins continues.

was the logical result of the evolution of groups living in the right place at the right time. In other words, the time and place were "ripe," and culture developed in the way it did simply due to qualities and characteristics inherent in human nature.

Binford's Demographic Explanation

Lewis Binford (1968) has taken strong exception to Braidwood's approach. This criticism is based on the belief that the causes of domestication were more concrete than simply "human nature." As Binford points out, there is little in the Braidwood explanation that may be tested through standard archaeological techniques. Although Binford proposes environment as one of only two possible testable factors which could have brought about the development of agriculture, he then rejects the environmental explanation as not feasible, since he considers the minor nature of the Post-Pleistocene environmental changes as not sufficient to induce domestication. ▲ Binford's explanation relies heavily on demography, and the factors cited include internal population growth as well as external pressure and the emigration of peoples into a region. He goes further, stating that the influx of peoples was from the seacoasts to the less populated inland regions. Therefore the advent of population pressure provided a stimulus to food production.

Flannery's Processual Approach

Flannery (1968) views the entire domestication process within the framework of specific rela-tionships between humans and plant and animal resources, in which the shift from nomadic hunting and gathering to a settled village life based on agriculture was a process of gradual change over a long period of time. ■ The regulating mechanisms are termed "negative feedback" and "positive feedback." Negative feedback encouraged the *status quo* and inhibited change. Food resources collected seasonally, without conflicts in the scheduling of harvests, led to the long-term, balanced use of these environmental resources and hence to nonchange, or negative feedback. On the other hand, those resources which increased in their productivity as a result of human exploitation tended to become more important through time or, in Flannery's conception, exhibited positive feedback (Fig. 12-1). An example is the wild grasses which, after humans began to utilize them, experienced a series of genetic changes, making them more productive and thus more utilized than other species (Fig. 12-2). As a result the cultivators had embarked on a course of increasing reliance on specific plants. Thus the positive-feedback cycle intensified, leading to the development of agriculture.

Other Explanations

J. Thomas Meyers (1971), in an article synthesizing all the above hypotheses, proposes that agriculture developed as a combination of causal factors—demographic stress, favorable environment, and the proper type of exploitative technology. ● However, in spite of these explanations the search for the origins of agriculture goes on unabated. For example, at the Ninth International Congress of Anthropological and Ethnological Sciences, held in 1973, nearly 30 papers were presented on the topic. Edited by Charles A. Reed and published in 1977, these writings amass more than 1,000 pages, and it is of course impossible to summarize the findings in this space. However, several authors included summary views which we will present here.

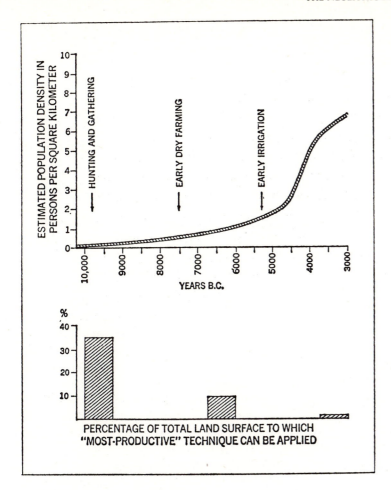

Fig 12-1 Feedback diagram illustrating the cumulative effect of food production in prehistoric Iran. Through time the percentage of land devoted to hunting and gathering, early dry farming, and early irrigation is plotted, as shown in lower graph. Upper graph illustrates the increase in population through time. Although less land was used in farming, the productivity—and therefore the population density possible—was greater. (Flannery 1971:76.)

Fig. 12-2 Illustrations of the wild and domesticated forms of einkorn wheat, emmer wheat, and barley. Originally growing wild in specific habitats in the Middle East, these grains were among the earliest of domesticated plants. Cultivation led to selection for forms which had a grain that was readily separated from the chaff and heads that did not shatter upon ripening. The forms that were selected included hybrids, other wild forms, and mutants. The result of the selection process was the identification and use of forms that were more productive and more easily harvested. (Hawkes 1976:49.)

MacNeish (1977:796) postulates that agriculture may evolve, given a center with potential domesticates, a diversity of life zones, and the possibility of early interaction among the latter. These conditions are then followed by environmental changes, which realigns human subsistence options. Finally, a village life-style will develop if (1) one of the subsistence options selected is seasonally scheduled, and (2) there is interaction among most of the life zones in the center, including both those with cultigens (cultivated plants and animals) and those with hunting-and-gathering options.

Reed (1977:941–944) stresses the importance of the presence of anatomically modern humans

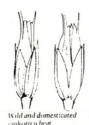

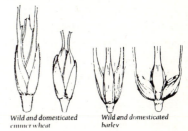

Wild and domesticated einkorn wheat   *Wild and domesticated emmer wheat*   *Wild and domesticated barley*

(*Homo s. sapiens*) and the occurrence of environmental change. He cites an attitudinal change in humans which led to the protection of animals rather than the killing of them. Furthermore, increased population density due to rising sea levels may have forced people to adopt agriculture.

▲ Multiple centers of origin

■ Actual proof of domestication is rare.

● Biological barriers to early food production

Once initiated, village life would have led to further population increase which in turn would stimulate further experiments in food production. The transition to agriculture from hunting and gathering was gradual. However, once dependent upon agriculture, Neolithic peoples could not survive without it, since their numbers now exceeded the carrying capacity of the area for hunters and gatherers. As Reed states, however, in spite of all of this scholarly attention, "many unsolved problems remain" (1977:944).

A dramatically different approach has been proposed by Cohen (1977a) to explain why plants and animals were domesticated at approximately the same time but in different places around the world. He argues that a growing population in the process of outstripping its resource base is the prime causal factor leading to domestication. Under these circumstances, hunters and gatherers are forced to readapt to the new and, often, less desirable foods in order to feed their growing numbers.

Boserup (1965) also sees continuing population growth as the main stimulus to agricultural innovation. For example, fully developed forest can be cleared with the use of a simple axe, shrubland requires a hoe, and grasslands are best broken up with a plough. A cleared forest, if given enough time, will recycle itself through a series of stages: grassland, shrubland, and, finally, reestablished tree cover. However, the need to produce increasing amounts of food leads to shortened fallow times, and new tools and techniques are needed to clear and reclaim land for farming. With each technological innovation, more food is produced and more people are fed, but each innovation also leads to increased cost per unit of food production.

Biological Aspects of Plant Domestication

According to Harlan and Zohary (1966), the specific cereal grains that were domesticated in the Middle East are found there today in a wild state but in somewhat differing environments. For example, wild barley does not tolerate extreme cold and is only occasionally found above 1,500 meters of elevation. However, wild barley has a wide ecological range and exists in a number of distinct varieties. One type is specifically adapted to the wadis of the Negev and Sinai, where it occurs at elevations of from 350 meters below sea level to 600 meters above sea level. On the other hand, wild einkorn wheat is more cold-tolerant than wild barley and occurs at up to 2,000 meters in southeastern Turkey. Wild emmer wheat is adapted to a warmer climate, and extensive stands are found today around the Sea of Galilee. ▲ This environmental evidence suggests that each plant domesticated may well have had an independent place of origin.

■ In the Middle East the actual proof of farming as evidenced by preserved plant parts is still somewhat rare, but new excavation techniques, including flotation, permit the finding of new data, such as preserved grains. These findings continue to modify prior views. The presence of agriculture is verified as much as anything by the subsequent developments of sedentism and urbanism. As Flannery suggests, the local economic mix was probably quite variable, according to which plants and animals were available and depending on the practice of seasonal movements (Figure 12-3). Only after a lengthy developmental period would the systematic planting and harvesting of a few cultigens become the pattern.

These processes are described in greater detail by Flannery (1965). He states that "collecting patterns were keyed to seasonal aspects of the wild resources of each environmental zone, with perhaps a certain amount of seasonal migration from zone to zone." The evidence from Ali Kosh

(Flannery 1965:1250) suggests that intensive collecting of wild plants may have been the predominant pattern throughout the Middle East, not just where wild wheat occurred. Flannery states further:

> . . . from an ecological standpoint the important point is not that man planted wheat but that he (i) moved it to niches to which it was not adapted, (ii) removed certain pressures of natural selection, which allowed more deviants from the normal phenotype to survive, and (iii) eventually selected for characters not beneficial under conditions of natural selection.

Flannery (1965:1251) also asks, "Was 'incipient cultivation' a fumbling attempt at cultivation or only the intensification of an already existing system of interregional exchange?"

Flannery (1965) has reviewed the nature of biological obstacles to early food production. There had to be selection of existing varieties or mutants which did not possess these biological problems before plant species could be successfully cultivated on a large scale; and there is no doubt that the necessary selection process took considerable time, probably on the order of several thousand years. ● Identified problems are as follows:

1. Wild grains have a brittle rachis which holds the seeds together in the head. Harvesting of such plants is difficult, since the seeds are adapted for easy dispersal. Thus the harvester recovers only a percentage of the grain.

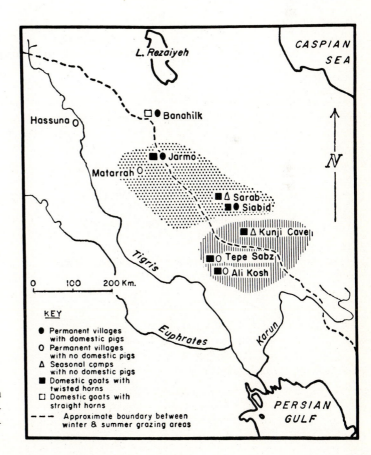

Fig. 12-3 Areas of Mesopotamia where seasonal movements were practiced to permit greater utilization of native resources. (Flannery 1965:1247.)

▲ Preconditions for domestication of animals

■ The earliest evidence for domesticated animals—the dog.

2. Primitive grains are enclosed in a tough husk which is difficult to remove, even by severe threshing.

3. Wild grains are native to hilly slopes, which are not the best locations for extensive farming from the standpoint of soil type and moisture.

According to modern botanists, a single gene controls the differences between hulled and naked barley grains; therefore, mutation followed by selection could easily have produced

Fig. 12-4 Illustrations of the wild and domesticated forms of sheep, pig, goat, and cattle. Selection practiced during domestication led to an increase in wool production, increase in milk production, increase in meat production, and a decrease in horn size. (Hawkes 1976:49.)

grains suitable for threshing. Another mutant was the six-row type of barley, a variety adapted to dry spring weather, which became the successful irrigated form grown in the Mesopotamian alluvial flood plain. Early farmers probably

TABLE 12-1
Effects of Domestication in Animals

Phenotypic Characteristic	Effect	Archaeological Visibility
Size	In general, animals become smaller.	Preservation varies. May still be within range of variation found in wild populations.
Coloration	Hair was red, black, and white pigment. Mutations (domesticates) usually lose one color and produce piebaldness (black and white) or skewbaldness (brown and white). Both are rare in nature.	Not usually preserved.
Hair	In some species, hair gets longer, whereas others become bald.	Not usually preserved.
Soft Parts	Skin becomes more flabby.	Not usually preserved.
Skeleton	*Skull:* some facial shortening and teeth become smaller. *Limb bones:* no real changes, but muscle attachments are weaker. (Limb bones may be shorter.) *Skeleton:* possible overall reduction in size, but number of bones not altered except in tail.	Preservation varies from excellent to none, depending on soil conditions (acidity). Butchering patterns influence which bones are left.

(After Zeuner 1963.)

Domesticated pig Wild pig Domesticated goat Wild bezoar goat Domesticated cow Wild auroch bull

overcame these problems (either consciously or unconsciously) by

1. Selecting for tough rachis grains
2. Roasting and grinding the grain to remove the husks
3. Selecting those varieties which had a less tough husk
4. For maximum productivity, introducing the grains into the alluvial flood plains outside their native habitat

According to Flannery, most of these changes had occurred by 7000 B.C., with the six-row form of barley first appearing about 6000 B.C. The appearance of free-threshing wheat occurred at the same time.

Biological Aspects of Animal Domestication

Like that for plants, evidence for animal domestication is unclear. There are several basic problems relative to recognizing when domestication has occurred. Since the cultivated species are the same as their wild counterparts, recognizable phenotypic differences (i.e., in size, coat, color, and so forth) due to domestication must exist before domestication per se can be perceived. Although there are several phenotypic effects of domestication, these are not normally preserved in the archaeological record (Table 12-1).

Within the domesticated varieties of animals there is a greater frequency of pathological conditions. In general, most domesticate characteristics are juvenile characteristics retained into adulthood. Some changes due to domestication had no utilitarian value. For example, as goats

became domesticated there was a change in horn shape from the scimitar to the twisted form (present by 6000 B.C.). Some other changes, however, were of obvious value, such as that from a hairy to a woolly coat in sheep.

With domestication, the butchering of young animals increased, with older animals being kept for breeding purposes. Reliance became concentrated on a few species (Figure 12-4). On the other hand, hunters take what they can get, therefore the age-sex ratio of the animals they take is similar to that of the wild population.

▲ According to Reed (1971), several preconditions governed the early cultivation of animals. The earliest domesticates were the dog, pig, sheep, goat, and cattle (see Table 12-2). Of these species, the dog and pig were food competitors with humans, requiring an omnivorous diet. According to Reed's view, people first had to begin living in settled communities with an available food surplus before dogs and pigs could be kept in any quantity. On the other hand, the ruminants—sheep, goats, and cattle—all subsist on roughage, grass stems, leaves and so on, which are not utilized by humans for food. It would have been possible to greatly increase the food available for these species as agriculture developed, making available the by-products as forage.

■ Dogs may have been the earliest animals kept by humans, since they aided in hunting and are known to have been domesticated by Mesolithic times. The earliest date for dog remains in the Middle East is ca. 7000 B.C. from the site of Cayönu in southwestern Anatolia. Other early occurrences of the dog are from Star Carr, England, in 7500 B.C., and from Jaguar Cave, Idaho, 8450 B.C. Remains of dogs in early sites in the Middle East are rare; however, dogs

● Sheep and goats

▲ Cattle

■ The center concept

were not used for food, and their remains may have been buried rather than being scattered within the village. The dog developed from either the wolf or from a common doglike form ancestral to both dog and wolf. However, it is most probable that the ancestor was the wolf,

TABLE 12-2
Archaeological Evidence of Early Cereal Cultivation and Animal Herding in the Middle East

Sites and Stratigraphy	Approximate Dates (b.c.)	Barley	Einkorn	Emmer	Bread Wheat	Sheep	Goat	Cattle	Pig	Dog
Aegean Area										
Argissa (Thessaly), Aceramic	6,500	X		X		X	X	X	X	?
Nea Nikomedeia (Macedonia)	6,200	X	X		X	X	X	X	X	?
Knossos (Crete), Stratum X	6,100	X	X	X						
Khirokitia (Cyprus), Aceramic	6,000					X	X			
Sesklo (Thessaly), Aceramic	6,000–5,000	X		X						
Ghediki (Thessaly), Aceramic	6,000–5,000	X		X						
Anatolia										
Hacilar, Aceramic	7,000			X						?
Hacilar, Ceramic	5,800–5,000	X		X	X					?
Cayonu	7,000						X		X	X
Catal Huyuk, VI–II	7,000			X	X	X		?		
Levant										
Tell Ramad (Syria)	7,000	X		X	X					
Jericho, Prepottery Neol. A.	7,000–6,500	X		X						
Jericho, Prepottery Neol. B.	6,500–5,500	X		X						
Beidha (Jordan), Prepottery	5,850–5,600			X			X			
Amouq (Antioch) A.	5,750	X		X			X			
Mesopotamia-Khuzistan										
Ali Kosh, Bus Nordeh	5,600–6,750			X		X	X			
Ali Kosh, Ali Kosh	6,750–6,000	X		X		X	X			
Ali Kosh, M. Jaffar	6,000–5,600	X		X		X	X			
Tepe Sabz, Sabz	5,500–5,000	X		X	X					
Hassuna	5,800	X		X			X			
Egypt										
Wadi Kubbaniya	16,000	X								
Kurdistan-Kuristan										
Zawi Chemi, Karim Shahir	8,900									
Jarmo	6,750–6,500		X	X		X	X		X	X
Tepe Sarab	6,500					X	X			
Tepe Guran	6,200–5,500	X					X			
Matarrah	5,800	X		X					X	

(Based on Hole and Flannery 1967; Mellaart 1965; Reed 1959, 1961, 1969; Renfrew 1969; and others.)

with puppies less than six weeks of age being the initial domesticates.

The pig is clearly descended from the wild pig. The earliest known evidence of domestic pigs occurs at Cayonu, where they form a minor portion of the bone remains. While pigs were domesticated at least as early as 6800 B.C. (Reed 1977:546), they rarely occur in village remains in frequencies greater than 5 percent prior to Sumerian times (after 2900 B.C.). Remains of domestic pigs have also been recovered from levels at Jarmo dated 6000 B.C. The known distribution of early domestic pigs is irregular, with some areas having them much earlier than others (see Table 12-2). Flannery suggests this is due to the ecological requirements of pigs, in that they are not adapted to a pastoral herding economy. Therefore, in those regions having a steppe ecology and the practice of seasonal movements to new pastures, pigs were not favored.

● Sheep and goats as domesticates existed early, possibly even earlier than the dog, with sheep having been found at Zawi Chemi Shanidar in levels dated 8900 B.C. (Reed 1977:546). The cultivation of sheep included selection for the woolly variety. Goats were common at Jarmo. At Ali Kosh in Iranian Khuzistan, goats, and especially yearlings, are also common in levels dated 7000 B.C. (Reed 1977:564). In this particular site goats are especially important as domesticates, since they (1) occur outside their native range and (2) occur earlier than the domestic sheep.

▲ Cattle were not domesticated as early as other species, at least according to present knowledge. The earliest evidence of domestic cattle is from the site of Argissa-Maghula in Greece dated ca. 6500 B.C. Whether cattle were first domesticated in southeastern Europe rather than in southwestern Asia is still unknown. Inasmuch as cattle were domesticated later than sheep and goats, their cultivation may have been intentional, perhaps with an interest in their use as draft animals. However the earliest extant evidence of the plow is from Warka IV (Mesopo-

tamia) dated ca. 3200 B.C. The earliest cattle remains from southwest Asia, from Tepe Sabz in Iranian Khuzistan, are dated at 4300 B.C. Further studies are required to understand cattle domestication, since the early evidence is widespread and identifies no single center for their domestication.

Erick Isaac (1971:453) proposes a series of arguments supporting an agricultural origin for cattle domestication. (1) Nomadic herders use harnesses modified after those of nearby farmers. (2) No wild bovines, whose range was primarily in the area of nomadic hunters, have been domesticated. Those bovines which were domesticated lived in the same area as argicultural peoples. (3) No deer or elk species except reindeer were domesticated, and the latter were not domesticated early. (4) The feeding of captured animals was dependent upon the plant food surpluses of an agricultural people.

Charles Reed (1977:562–564) suggests that the mode of animal domestication may initially have been based on the "keeping" of puppies, piglets, lambs, and kids by little girls as pets.

Nuclear Centers

As noted above, Braidwood defines a nuclear area as "a region with a natural environment which includes a variety of wild plants and animals both possible and ready for domestication" (1967:94). The idea that certain areas offer potential for domestication while others do not is not new. ■ In 1926, the Russian geneticist N. I. Vavilov published *Studies on the Origins of Cultivated Plants*, in which he defined eight centers of domestication: (1) China; (2) the Indian subcontinent; (2a) Southeast Asia; (3) central Asia; (4) the Near East; (5) the Mediterranean; (6) Abyssinia (Ethiopia); (7) Mexico; and (8) South America: (a) the Bolivian-Peru subregion, (b) the Chilean subarea, and (c) the Brazilian-Paraguayan subarea. Today Vavilov's centers have

● The concept of noncenters
▲ The earliest evidence of domesticated grain
■ Evidence of other domesticates

been subdivided into two types, termed "centers" and "noncenters."

Jack Harlan (1971) has refined the center concept to include a small and discrete geographical area of origin having relatively few domesticates. Primary reliance is on cereal grains, with a rapid ensuing cultural development from villages, to towns, to civilization. Such centers include China, the Middle East, India, Mexico, and Peru. ● Harlan's noncenters are characterized as wide areas having indistinct boundaries and many domesticates, developed over a long period of time, with many of the latter being root crops grown in house gardens. Examples of noncenters include sub-Saharan Africa, Southeast Asia, tropical South America, and tropical Mesoamerica. In a review of this concept, Reed (1977:944) indicates that some researchers accept the noncenter theory as valid even though they may not agree that all the areas classified as noncenters by Harlan fit his own definition.

Whereas hunters and gatherers had a wide choice of foods, early farmers were more specialized and tended to rely on a more selective group of cultigens. The tremendous variety of food choices available to us today is the result of essentially 10,000 years of selective breeding and genetic manipulation. No one center provided everything, but rather, our present food base is an accumulation of many items from many centers. Of special interest, from their inception as domesticates, have been the carbohydrate-rich cereals, and while every area has its condiments, it is the cereals that have traditionally provided the bulk of the human diet. On the Eurasian landmass, for example, the Middle East produced emmer and einkorn (two wheat types) and barley. The neighboring Mediterranean

basin gave us the olive. China's contribution includes millet, soybeans, and some varieties of rice. However, the oldest date associated with rice cultivation, 6000 B.C., comes from India and Southeast Asia (Reed 1977:3). (Other specialists, for example Flannery, are only willing to state that the cultivation of rice dates earlier than 3000 B.C.) Many of our fruits had their origins in central Asia. Although not a cereal crop, five varieties of yam have Asian origins. Many of the plants that have spread widely in Africa include millet, sorghum, ground nut (peanut), and teff from Ethiopia. Africa has also contributed at least four varieties of yam and rice.

In the New World, Mexico has given the world its most productive cereal, maize, or corn, in addition to several varieties of bean and squash. In South America quinoa, manioc, additional varieties of beans, and potatoes were the main staple items domesticated.

Earliest Evidence of Domestication

With each center producing its own domesticates, the attempt at identifying the "earliest center," which implies the spread of the idea of domestication from a single center, is a meaningless exercise. On the other hand, we can comment on the early evidence by region.

In the Middle East, the early evidence comes from a number of sites. The Natufian occupation at Jericho dates to 9250 B.C. and, as we shall see in the next chapter, the Natufians were more than merely food collectors. In the Zagros mountains sheep were apparently domesticated by 8920 B.C. At Tell Abu Hureyra, Syria, three cereals—wheat, barley, and rye—were systematically exploited from 11,500 to 10,500 B.C.

The Nile Valley may have been a receptor area in which domesticated wheat, barley, sheep and goats were introduced about 5000 B.C. ▲ However, there is evidence that grain collecting

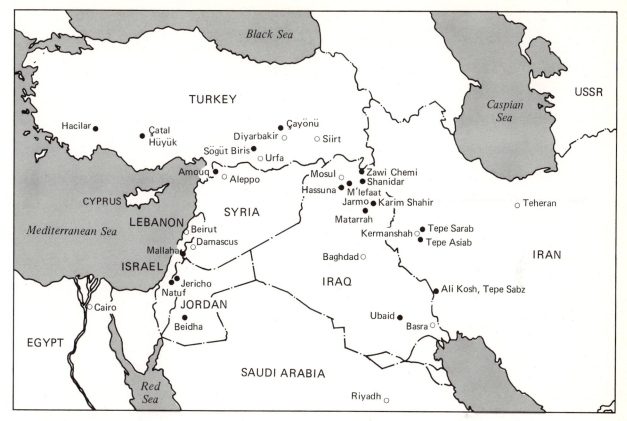

Map 12-1
Selected Archaeological Sites (solid dots)
that Show Evidence of Early Agriculture
in the Near East.

was important as early as 12,000 B.C. at Tushka near Abu Simbel and at Kom Ombo since grinding stones are common on those sites. Further, Wendorf (1979) reports radiocarbon dates of 16,000 B.C. on domesticated barley from Wadi Kubaniya in Egypt. The possibility thus exists that the eastern Sahara constituted a separate center for early grain domestication.

In North Africa at Uan Muhaggiag, cattle are dated to 5590 B.C., but the degree of their cultivation has yet to be resolved. Farther south, in the Hoggar mountains, the use of millet has been dated to between 6100 and 4850 B.C.

The West African origin of domesticated yams poses dating problems for the archaeologist. As yet we have no dates for the period of vegeculture, but Thurston Shaw suggests that the Sangoan pick (dated at between 43,000 and 13,000 B.C.) may have been used to dig wild yam (Bender 1975:216–220).

■ On the Indian subcontinent some of the earliest dates (5200 to 5000 B.C.) come from

● Chinese domesticates

▲ New World domesticates

Ghar-i-mar cave near the town of Aq Kupruk in Afghanistan. Wheat and barley seem to be the oldest domesticates there and appear to be even earlier than rice, which is dated to ca. 2300 B.C. at Lothal, north of Bombay.

In Southeast Asia there are some intriguingly early sites, such as Spirit Cave in Thailand. Here Gorman (1971:311) has recovered in levels 2 through 4 (10,000 to 6000 B.C.) evidence of bottle gourds, water chestnuts, and cucumber in a context that suggests cultivation rather than simple gathering. (Here again, Flannery disagrees, as he does not accept the earliest plant remains as "domesticated.")

In China agriculture began as early as the Yang-shao period. ● Principal crops in ancient China included rice, soybeans, millet, wheat, barley, hemp, and mulberry. Radiocarbon dates for the Yang-shao period cluster between 3000–4000 B.C., and the bristlecone pine chronology dates that culture even earlier at 4135–4865 B.C. (Ho 1977:416). Indigenous early domesticates in the Yang-shao period clearly include rice, millet, and possibly hemp. Soybeans were domesticated by historic times, 600 B.C. or earlier. The mulberry, grown for the production of silk for the ruling class, may have been cultivated as early as Yang-shao times, since a silk cocoon cut in half has been found in a Yang-shao site (Ho 1977:454). Wheat and barley seem to have been introduced into China from the Middle East in about 2000 B.C. Animal domesticates in China include the pig, dog, cattle, sheep, goat, horse, and chicken. All except the goat have been found in Yang-shao sites and therefore date to 3000 B.C. or earlier. Ho (1977:464) suggests that all these species except the goat were locally developed from indigenous wild ancestors.

The New World evidence comes from a variety of sources. ▲ MacNeish (1977) reported possible domesticates from the Infiernillo Phase (7500 to 5000 B.C.) in Tamaulipas in northeastern Mexico. These domesticates included bottle gourds, several varieties of curcubits (squash), and chili peppers. It is in the Tehuacan valley near Puebla, in south central Mexico, that the main staples are first recorded. Maize appears in the Coxcatlan Phase, beginning in 5200 B.C., with squash and beans emerging later. The remarkable aspect of the history of domestication in Mesoamerica is the fact that it took over 5,000 years of development before plant cultivation replaced hunting and gathering as the primary economic activity (Figure 18-11).

In Peru the earliest evidence of domestication indicates a very complex history. Diverse plant species were domesticated at different times and in different regions. The earliest major domesticates (Cohen 1977b:173) were the bean (8000–5500 B.C.), bottle gourd (6600–5500 B.C.), squash (5500–4300 B.C.), and cotton (4300–2800 B.C.). There are even bottle gourd fragments from the 11,000 b.c. level at Pikimachay Cave in the Ayacucho region (MacNeish 1977). While current evidence suggests that the bottle gourd, squash, and cotton were earliest in the Ayacucho region, this probably simply reflects the fact that more research on early domestication has been carried out there. With more than 100 domesticates known in ancient Peru, from both the highlands and the coast, the history of plant domestication there is undoubtedly complex. Animal domestication was much more limited in Peru, with the primary domesticates being the llama and the guinea pig.

Summary

Domestication occurred at varying times and in a number of places. Within the short span of 5,000 years (9000 to 4000 B.C.) the process was initiated in a number of areas, then elaborated and completed, with virtually nothing having been domesticated since. The ultimate importance of domestication was not the reliance on specific plants or animals but the total change in life-style that food production permitted. This change featured a sedentary way of life which led to permanent communities, larger population aggregates, and the development of craft specialists. No longer were all peoples practicing an identical behavior pattern. Specialization had become a common form of adaptation.

Whatever the causes of the development of agriculture, several other points should be kept in mind concerning Neolithic origins. (1) Considerable time was required for these changes, with new crops, at least for an extended period of up to several thousand years, being little more productive than wild resources. (2) Some peoples, perhaps due to the high productivity of wild resources in their regions, were reluctant to change from hunting and gathering to food production.

The long-term results of food production, however, were many. Two of these — population increase and the reduction of land area suitable for the new exploitative techniques — are expressed quantitatively in Figure 12-1. In the next chapter we will review how the Neolithic developed in the Middle East, the region whose Neolithic history is most completely known.

13

Neolithic Development in the Middle East

In the preceding chapter we reviewed the origins of the domestication of plants and animals in many parts of the world. We shall now review in some detail the evidence from the Middle East. This not to minimize the importance of understanding other nuclear areas, such as China, Southeast Asia or Mexico; nor is it an attempt to underrate the contributions of the latter regions to the modern world's food supply. Rather, the simple fact is that we know more about the process of domestication in the Middle East than anywhere else. ■ In addition, the Middle Eastern evidence constitutes our best extant record of how the development of food production led to the establishment of towns and the development of civilization (Map 13-1).

Synthesizing the events of any area as complex as the Middle East must be approached with some trepidation. To do this successfully requires both oversimplification and the utilization of an overall organizational theme. In the last chapter we described the multiple-era system developed by Robert Braidwood, and we shall use this model as our overall theme of organization starting with the Era of Incipient Cultivation.

Incipient Cultivators in the Levant and Syria

The Natufian

The earliest cultivators known in the Middle East are those of the Natufian culture of Palestine. Natufian remains are found in numerous caves as well as in a few open sites. Most of the findings are of stone tools. ● The major imple-

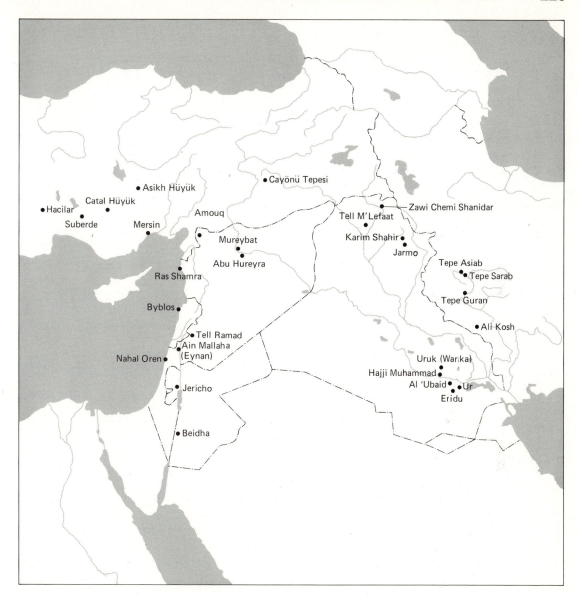

Map 13-1   Early Mesolithic and Neolithic Agricultural Sites in the Middle East.

ments suggestive of incipient cultivation are geo-metric sickle flints (microliths), showing the characteristic sheen, or polish, from the cutting of grain. Other tools include mortars and pestles, probably used for seed grinding. A rich inven-tory of bone tools includes sickle hafts, points, harpoons, fishhooks, awls, pins, needles, beads, and pendants. Food bones from the sites are typ-ical of those associated with hunting: deer, ga-zelle, bear, boar, and even leopard and hyena.

▲ Site-catchment analysis

■ Burial practices

The domestic dog has also been reported. Architecture was confined to low stone walls built in caves. Flexed burials are present, often with beads or other grave offerings.

Due to the sickle sheen found on some of the microliths, there has been a tendency to see Natufian peoples as incipient farmers who continued to hunt regularly. Vita-Finzi and Higgs (1970:1–37), using site catchment analysis (a technique which they developed), undertook the evaluation of a number of Natufian sites in a variety of settings in an attempt to define the types and locations of activities that might have been engaged in by Natufian peoples.

▲ *Site-catchment analysis* involves establishing the area which was exploited from a given site. All things being equal, the farther away a resource is from the site, the less likely it will be exploited. Beyond a certain distance it will not be economically practical to exploit the resource at all. Chisholm (1968) notes that farming people rarely go beyond 5 km, a one-hour walk, to exploit resources. Lee (1967) states that hunting peoples will rarely go beyond 10 km (a two-hour walk) for the same reasons.

Walking the distances required and using the above figures, Vita-Finzi and Higgs (1970) established a series of catchment areas and analyzed

TABLE 13-1
Natufian Site-Catchment Analysis of Coastal Sites

Site	Territory (hectares)	Marsh (percent)	Dune (percent)	Rough Grazing (percent)	Good Grazing: Potentially Arable (percent)	Arable (percent)
Nahal Oren	7,000	27	——	58	7	8
el Wad	8,000	48	7	28	5	12
Kebara	10,750	36	13	31	6	14
Iraq el-Baroud	6,700	28	——	60	7	5

TABLE 13-2
Natufian Site-Catchment Analysis of Upland Sites

Site	Territory (hectares)	Marsh (percent)	Rough Grazing (percent)	Good Grazing: Potentially Arable (percent)	Arable (percent)
Rakafet	10,800	8	45	——	47
Hayonim	9,500	——	74	9	17
Quafzeh	9,000	——	38	——	62
Shuqba	8,200	——	82	——	18
Ain Mallaha	17,500	44	29	12	15

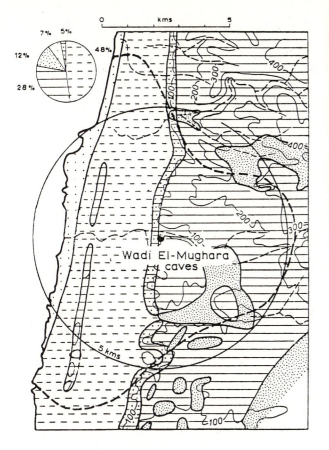

Fig. 13-1 Plot of catchment area analysis of the territory surrounding the Wadi El Mughara caves, Palestine. The method assumes a standard area of utilization from a specific site, and then the percentage of each environment zone within that catchment area is plotted on a pie graph. (Vita-Finzi and Higgs 1970.)

Fig. 13-2 Natufian structure, located on bedrock at Jericho. (Mellaart 1975: Fig. 6.)

the land use within for a series of coastal sites (Table 13-1).

The following observations are important relative to coastal sites:

1. Natufian site-catchment areas are small. (Three do not exceed 8,000 hectares within the 5 km radius.)
2. Suitable arable land does not exceed 20 percent of the total, and it lies some distance from the site.
3. Rough grazing areas would have supported either hunting or pastoralism.

In sharp contrast to the coastal sites, the upland sites show a much higher percentage of arable land as well as a substantial grazing component (Table 13-2).

Both highland and lowland sites were exploited for their animal potential on a seasonal basis. Highland sites provided grain harvests in June and July following the seasonal rains. The water resources of the lowlands (seasonal marshes) in the dry late summer and fall would have been attractive to animals. The early spring growth of vegetation on the coast and in the marsh areas would have been ideal for humans (Fig. 13-1). These potentials imply a seasonal, shifting pattern of economic reliance.

Dates for the Natufian culture include 9250 B.C. for what researchers think is the Natufian shrine at Jericho and 8650 B.C. for the Natufian material at Mureybet, Phase I (Fig. 13-2). ■ At Ain Mallaha we have evidence of round houses and storage pits, some of which were apparently

● Plant remains recovered by flotation

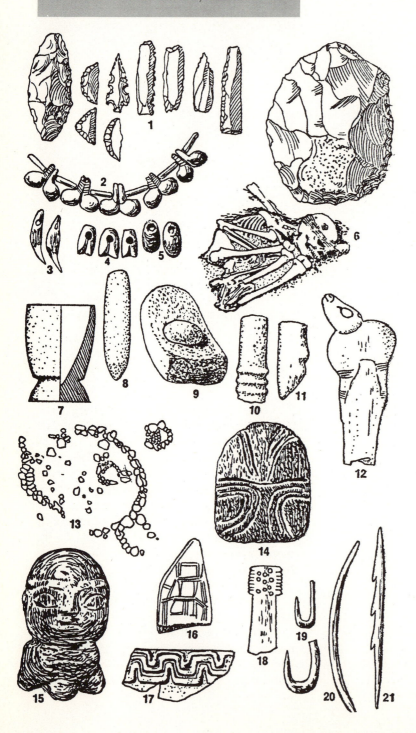

Fig. 13-3 Typical artifacts of the Natufian culture. (*1*) Blade tools; (*2*) mammiform beads on necklace; (*3*) beads of animal teeth; (*4,5*) beads; (*6*) flexed burial with shell headdress; (*7–11*) ground-stone objects; (*12*) bone animal figurines; (*13*) Natufian structure with stone foundation; (*14*) stylized figurine; (*15*) stone sculpture; (*16,-17*) design motifs; (*18*) bone or ivory wand (?); (*19*) hooks; (*20*) needle; (*21*) harpoon point. (Fairservis 1975:132.)

Fig. 13-4 Plan of Natufian settlement of Ain Mallaha. Features include round houses and storage pits, some reused for burials. The chieftain's tomb is shown at *a*, and a hearth is shown at *b*, adjacent to a mortar. (Mellaart 1975: Fig. 4.)

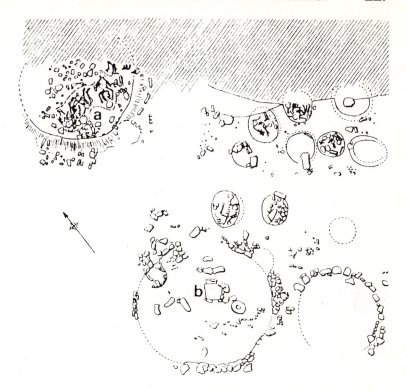

reused for burials. Burials also occur in cemeteries in both cave and open sites (Fig. 13-3). These were both primary and secondary burials. In some cases the bodies were extended and in others, tightly flexed. At Ain Mallaha an elaborate "chieftain's tomb" is located inside a house (Fig. 13-4). The tomb is 5m in diameter and 0.8m deep, with a plastered and painted parapet. It contained two skeletons, one male and one female, both of which had the legs detached. These differential mortuary practices suggest that there were distinct classes of people, with some being accorded greater importance than others.

Tell Abu Hureyra

The largest known Neolithic site in Syria, Tell Abu Hureyra, lies on the west bank of the Euphrates in northern Syria. The site covers an area 500m × 300m, with deposits averaging 5m in thickness, and contains early evidence of cereal manipulation.

The Mesolithic occupation, on the north side of the mound, lies on the edge of the Euphrates flood plain (Moore 1979:62–70). Based on artifact content, there is little to distinguish Tell Abu Hureyra from any number of so-called Mesolithic sites in the Middle East. Microliths are present, and tools made of bone are abundant. In other words, the artifacts here are roughly contemporaneous with, and resemble, those found in Natufian sites in Palestine.

● Using two flotation machines developed by workers at Cambridge University to recover plant remains and seeds, investigators at Tell Abu Hureyra were able to recover approximately 1,000 liters of plant materials. Besides peas, a wild lentil, and nuts and seeds, the remains of cereal crops were recovered. The most

▲ Genetic change must occur before we can prove species have been domesticated.

common of the latter was a primitive einkorn wheat, with wild rye and wild barley also present. Experiments with modern stands of wild einkorn wheat have established two facts: (1) simple cultivation would not genetically change the wheat, but (2) simple cultivation does disturb the natural ecology of an area. In the modern case, the wheat remained unchanged, but the disruption of the microenvironment permitted the introduction of other plants (weeds) normally associated with cultivation. At Tell Abu Hureyra three such weed plants occur, implying that the "Mesolithic hunters and gatherers" may have been cultivating at least three cereal grains and possibly some peas as well. If, when subjected to modern flotation-recovery, other Mesolithic sites also exhibit these characteristics, archaeologists may be forced to reconsider the theoretical conceptions underlying the distinctions between the Mesolithic and the Neolithic periods.

Incipient Cultivators in the Zagros Mountains

The Zawi Chemi Shanidar Phase

In the highlands west of the Tigris and Euphrates valleys, in an area known as the Zagros mountains, we have additional early evidence of domestication. Zawi Chemi Shanidar in northern Iraq is an open-air site adjacent to the Paleolithic site of Shanidar Cave. Zawi Chemi Shanidar is particularly important because it provides some of the earliest evidence of animal domestication. In level B 1, dated 8920 B.C., Perkins reports finding remains of domesticated sheep (1964:1565–1566). Although he is quick to point

out there are no morphological differences between the Zawi Chemi Shanidar sheep and wild sheep, he feels that the increased reliance on this animal and the fact that 50 percent of the remains are immature indicate a pattern of exploitation different from that exhibited by hunters.

There is some evidence of architecture, storage pits, and an elaborately developed mortuary practice at Zawi Chemi Shanidar. Microliths are still common, but there is a "heavy" lithic element of pecked and ground stone tools present. Bone implements are also common and are decorated with carvings, notches, and incised designs (Mellaart 1975:73).

The Karim Shahir Phase: ca. 8000 (?)–6500 (?) B.C.

The finds at Karim Shahir (Fig. 13-5) include numerous geometric flints but few sickle bladelets (Braidwood 1967). Grinding stones are also present. Other artifacts include stone ornaments, such as beads, pendants, rings, and bracelets. Bone tools feature simple points and needles. Two possibly animal effigies of unfired clay were also found. The kinds of plant food consumed are not known, as no vegetal remains were recovered. The bones most common are those of the species that were later domesticated: sheep, goat, cattle, horse, and wolf, but proof that domestication had already occurred at Karim Shahir or at Zawi Chemi is lacking. At Ali Kosh, another early site, the most ancient levels contain evidence of domesticated wheat and barley, with wild goats possibly having been herded.

The Era of Primary Village Farming

There is no problem in recognizing the era of primary village farming. Plants and animals at this time have become clearly domesticated. ▲ In other words, we have evidence of *genetically*

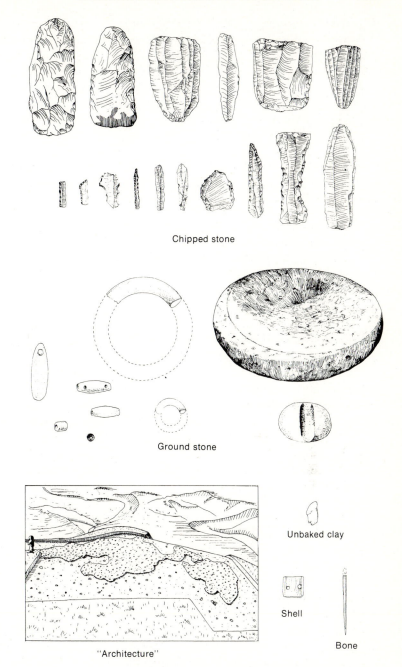

Chipped stone

Ground stone

Unbaked clay

Shell

Bone

"Architecture"

Fig. 13-5 Typical artifacts from Karim Shahir. (Braidwood 1967:107.)

induced physiological changes in both plants and animals.

The people, too, are domesticated. They have given up wandering and gathering on the landscape and have settled down in permanent villages. There is an explosive growth of craft specialties, such as pottery making; and with time, the standards of technical excellence and beauty

■ Jericho had its own domesticates.

● Hunting continued during early food production.

▲ Architecture became more elaborate.

■ Primary village farming led to a population increase.

reached are such as to suggest full-time craft specialists.

This period, the Neolithic period proper, can also be subdivided into two phases: the earlier, aceramic phase, and the later, ceramic phase. This would imply that settled village life, with a secure food supply capable of producing a surplus, is an essential precondition to craft specialization.

The Aceramic Cultures of the Levant and Syria

Aceramic refers to cultures which do not possess pottery but are Neolithic in other respects.

Pre-Pottery Neolithic A (PPNA): 8350–7350 B.C.

The reasons why Jericho, north of the Dead Sea, changed from a Natufian proto-Neolithic village of flimsy huts into a town covering 10 acres elude archaeologists. We do know, however, that there is no stratigraphic break with the Natufian, and the lithic industry seems to be a direct outgrowth of the Natufian. Additionally, there is no change in the human physical types.

At Jericho during the PPNA period, gazelle were an important dietary component. Higgs and his co-workers (1972) have argued that gazelle, among other ungulates, may have wandered in and out of domestication several times in the past (Harris 1977:225). Even if experimental steps were taken toward gazelle domestication, these efforts were not continued. In the next period, the PPNB, goats and sheep replaced gazelle. Legge (Noy, Legge, and Higgs 1973:91) suggests that the substitution may have been stimulated by the gazelle's selective diet and restricted habitat, making the animal less adaptable to domestication than sheep or goats. ■ Whether gazelle at Jericho were herded or hunted has yet to be proven, and in one sense the question is immaterial since the primary domesticates seem to be plant rather than animal. Barley, wheat, and lentils seem to have been the chief source of Jericho's wealth (Mellaart 1975:50–51).

The town was made up of round houses, each of which was approximately 4 to 5 meters in diameter and constructed of mud and brick on a stone foundation. Grain-storage rooms have also been found. After the third phase of the PPNA, fortifications appear. A stone wall 3 meters thick and 4 meters high existed, which included a tower. The tower is 10 meters in diameter and 8.5 meters high, and within it a stairway led to a water-storage system (Mellaart 1975:49). Permanent houses and defense structures attest to an increase in both population and wealth.

Jericho was abandoned in around 7350 B.C. The reason for this evacuation has yet to be determined, but we do know that it was accomplished without violence. Jericho was reoccupied in about 7000 B.C. by a people of a different cultural heritage, one that seems to have its origins to the north of Syria.

Mureybet

In Syria we have several sites with cultural inventories that closely resemble those of the Natufian of Palestine. Mureybet, on the east bank of the Euphrates, 89 kilometers southeast of Aleppo, had a Natufian-like hunting and fishing settlement. Here we can see the circular houses and bone industry typical of the Natufian culture. ● Gazelle, onager, and aurochs were hunted in equal proportion, but none of these animals seems to have been domesticated. The plant remains, and particularly the cereal grains, are among the oldest of the region. Of particular interest are the wheat and barley, which seem to be out of place ecologically unless we consider this to be a very early example of cultivation similar to that at Tell Abu Hureyra. (If true, this would indicate that cultivation may be both earlier and more widespread than previously thought.) Mureybet, Phases II and III seem to be contemporaneous with the PPNA levels at Jericho. Mureybet also seems to have been deserted prior to reoccupation by the Pre-Pottery Neolithic B culture group. The similarity (development, then abandonment, and finally reoccupation) between Mureybet and Jericho clearly indicates a widespread phenomenon.

Pre-Pottery Neolithic B (PPNB): 7000–6600 B.C.

In this period, new peoples with differing patterns of behavior replace the PPNA peoples already described. Like their predecessors, these did not have pottery; hence the designation "Pre-Pottery Neolithic B," or "PPNB." The PPNB sites are more widely distributed than those of the PPNA culture, being found not only in Palestine but also in Lebanon and Syria.

The economy was based on agriculture, utilizing wheat and barley. The wheat is a type intermediate between wild and domestic emmer. At Beidha, naked barley and wild oats are present, as well as pistachios, acorns, field peas, two kinds of wild lentils, vetch, cockscomb, and other legumes. At Jericho two-rowed hulled barley, emmer, and einkorn wheat were reported. At Tell Ramad domestic barley, emmer, einkorn, and club wheats were recovered (Mellaart 1975:66). This greater variety of cereal crops is indicative of a more secure food base.

Hunting continued to be important, with aurochs, bezoar, gazelle, wild boar, hare, jackal, and hyrax being taken. There was an increase in the frequency of domestic goats, but in many sites gazelles remained an important source of meat.

▲ Perhaps the most distinctive feature of the PPNB is its architecture, with rectangular houses replacing the round dwellings of the PPNA. This trend seems to have originated in the north and then spread southward.

The Jarmo Phase: ca. 6750 B.C.

Our next latest evidence from the Zagros mountains, following the previously discussed Karim Shahir phase, is a clear-cut example of a primary farming village. The site, named Jarmo, in the Kurdish hills of Iraq, has 27 feet of accumulated trash deposits, including a dozen layers indicative of architectural renovation. The site has been dated at 6750 ± 200 B.C., and there is thus a time gap between Karim Shahir and the full-fledged village era represented by Jarmo. What lies within this 2,000-year void has yet to be determined by archaeologists.

At Jarmo there is evidence of barley, two kinds of wheat, domestic goats, sheep, dogs, and in the latest levels, pigs. ■ The site itself covers about four acres, which indicates that the agricultural economy generated population growth. One new feature (Fig. 13-6) was that houses of several rooms were made of puddled adobe walls built on stone foundations. Stone bowls were used for food, and baking was done in clay ovens. Pottery appears in the upper one-third of the site, and in the earlier levels the appearance of pottery was presaged by clay figurines of humans and animals (Fig. 13-6). Braidwood suggests that the village looked much like modern villages in the same region. Using this present-day analogy, the 20 or so houses occupied at any one time in prehistoric Jarmo probably sheltered about 150 people. By no means were all the new cultural developments either universal or contemporaneous. For example, Sarab, a similar village in Iran, had sheep, goats, wheat, stone bowls, clay figurines, and so forth, but the houses were no more than reed huts.

● Each region has its own distinctive ceramics.

▲ The appearance of courtyards

■ Hassuna wares are widely distributed

● Naturalistic designs appear on pottery

The Ceramic Neolithic of the Levant

With the appearance of pottery in the archaeological record, investigators have a new and val-

uable tool with which to work. Since pottery styles tend to spread and change rapidly, pottery is a first-rate index fossil for delineating the spread of a culture and for documenting its changes through time. According to Mellaart (1975:227–228), most of the economies of the ceramic cultures of the Levant were based on crop-growing and domestic-animal herding. Hunting and gathering varies in importance by region. This does not mean that the types of plants being harvested or the types of animals being herded are not important. It means, rather, that most ceramic Neolithic sites have a full range of domesticated plants and animals, architecture tends to be similar, and there is little to distinguish one site from another. However, this "void" is very successfully filled by the almost infinite varieties of pottery found in the Middle East.

Byblos: Early Neolithic

Byblos, a site located on a consolidated sand dune north of Beirut in Lebanon, has small free-standing rectangular houses. The economy was based on wheat and barley (?), and domesticated animals were probably kept. ● The main cultural diagnostics are the ceramics. Pottery was highly decorated, with nail or shell impressions in pushed-up triangular or oval designs. Some examples have combed, textured surfaces. There are also monochrome burnished wares, whose colors range from grey, black, brown, and chocolate to red and buff. This is well-made, hard-fired, grit-tempered pottery of globular shape.

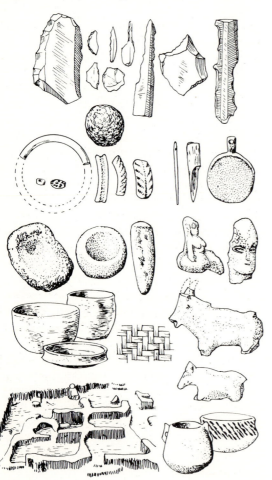

Fig. 13-6 Typical artifacts from Jarmo. *(Top row)* Flint knives, sickle blades, and scrapers. *(Second row)* stone ball; bangles of clay, bone, and shell; small beads; bone needle and point; pendant. *(Third row)* grinding stone; mortar and pestle; clay human figurines. *(Fourth row)* pottery vessels; basket weave; animal figurines. *(Fifth row)* earthen wall plan; pottery. (Faiservis 1975: 128.)

The Ceramic Neolithic Cultures of Mesopotamia

Uum Dabagiyah

In northern Mesopotamia there are two ceramic traditions: the early Iranian (Jarmo painted pottery) and the Hassuna. The Hassuna does not appear in a vacuum, but is preceded by a series of pre-Hassuna developments named after the site of Uum Dabagiyah on the Assyrian steppe of northern Iraq.

The architecture of Uum Dabagiyah is quite sophisticated. ▲ In period IV we have evidence of courtyards surrounded on three sides by blocks of storerooms, indicating that the family was the primary production unit.

Early ceramics were handmade and coil-built, with straw temper. Most wares were undecorated, but cream or white slips are sometimes found on the finer wares. A fine burnished ware was also made. In the late phases, oval vessels with rough ridges or round pitmarks inside were made. These later traits have long been considered a diagnostic characteristic of the Hassuna culture, and this ware may be ancestral to Hassuna wares.

Hassuna-Samarra-Halafian Sequence

Hassuna is often lumped into a chronological scheme that ranges from Hassuna (early), to Samarra (middle), to Halafian (late). Admittedly, all of these are Neolithic cultures, but doubts have been raised concerning the chronological implications of this simple model. Instead, we now suspect that these may be three independent and contemporaneous cultures; the Halafian in the north, Samarra in the south on the alluvial fringe, and Hassuna intermediate between the two and adapted to the rain-fed northern plain (Oates 1972:299–310).

Hassuna: 6000–5250 B.C.

The type site for this culture is Tell Hassuna southwest of Mosul (Mellaart 1975). ■ The wares have a wide distribution, with some examples being found as far away as the Syrian coast. Initially, Hassuna was characterized by monochrome cream pottery, but this later evolved into three main classes: a plain, coarse ware, a plain ware with incisions, and finally a ware with red designs painted on a cream background (Fig. 13-7).

Hassuna houses are rectangular, small, and have several rooms. Hearths and ovens are present, as are storage pits lined with bitumen.

Samarra: 5400 B.C.

Tell es-Sawwan, near Samarra, along with Choga Mami and Tell Shamshara, provides the bulk of the data on the Samarran culture and its ceramics.

● Painted and painted-and-incised variants are found together, and for the first time in the Neolithic period naturalistic animals and humans are portrayed on the pottery. This pottery was once thought to be a luxury ware but now is considered part of a distinct culture (Mellaart 1975:199). Developed forms of composition are found on the interiors of large bowls. The decorations, either chocolate brown or dark grey, are painted in a matte paint on a buff-colored surface (Fig. 13-8).

The presence of hybrid six-row barley and breadwheat is thought to indicate early irrigation.

Halafian: 5500–4700 B.C.

The Halafian is a very vigorous culture group in northern Mesopotamia, best known at Tell Ar-

▲ Polychrome pottery and evidence of trade

pachiyah near Nineveh. As farmers, these people cultivated emmer wheat, two- and six-row barley, and flax for oil. Cattle, sheep for wool, goats, and the dog were domesticated. Trade was extensive. (Mellaart 1975:156–170).

Halafian ceramics vary by period and locale. Early Halafian pottery is of apricot color, with naturalistic animals and red-and-black designs. By the middle period life forms had vanished from the cream slipped ware. ▲ In the late period we find great polychromes with elaborate centerpiece designs. The excellence of this latter phase suggests full-time potters (Fig. 13-9).

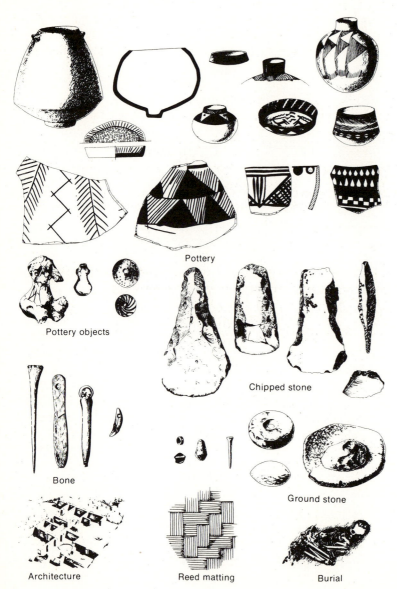

Pottery

Pottery objects

Chipped stone

Bone

Ground stone

Architecture

Reed matting

Burial

Fig. 13-7 Typical artifacts from Hassuna. (Braidwood 1967:123.)

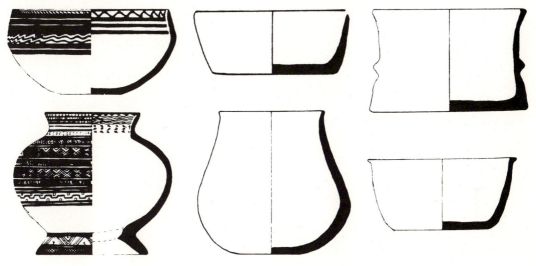

Fig. 13-8 Pottery from Tell es-Sawwan: the typical Samarran ware. (Mellaart 1975:91.)

Fig. 13-9 Typical Halafian pottery. (Clark 1977:Fig. 25.)

■ Much regional variation

● The shift from hunting to agriculture required a long time.

▲ Population increase and social stratification

■ The community becomes important.

● Appearance of craft specialists

▲ Rise of the state

The Iranian Plateau

On the Iranian plateau there are a number of Neolithic ceramic sites. These sites, although exhibiting regional characteristics, have several things in common. Their pottery tends to be thick, straw-tempered, and poorly fired. This latter trait improves through time. Dalma ware, found at Giyan, Iran, features either plain, painted, or impressed-surface treatment. Dalma ware demonstrates that the Iranian plateau was part of the Middle Eastern mainstream of development, with the late Ubaid exhibiting Dalma influence.

The site of Bog-i-no has yielded evidence for domestication, with emmer, breadwheat, and two- and six-row barley being grown. Pistachios and jujubes were collected. Sheep and goats were probably herded, but this has yet to be documented (Mellaart 1975:180).

Much more work is needed in this area, particularly if we are to understand the relationship between the Middle Eastern centers of domestication and the appearance of domesticated plants and animals in the Indus Valley and the Indian subcontinent.

Summary

As we have seen, the archaeology of the Middle East is complex, but certain themes are clear.

■ First, in a region as homogeneous as the Middle East there is tremendous interregional variation. For example, animals (sheep and goat) were first domesticated in the Zagros region, while cereal domestication came first in the Levant. ● Secondly, the shift from hunting and gathering to food production was an extended process. The people who started the process and those who subsequently were involved in it could not have had any idea as to its ultimate outcome.

We also see a dramatic increase in both the numbers and sizes of archaeological sites through time. This is indicative of population growth. ▲ By the end of the Neolithic period in the Middle East, population had grown far beyond the hunting-and-gathering carrying capacity of the land. In other words, once the process had begun, there was no turning back. Within the sites, themselves, we can see an increase in the numbers of different activities performed. We can also see the establishment of differential mortuary practices. Both trends are indicators of rising social stratification.

Storage pits can also provide insights into the social and economic organization of a society. ■ For example, if the storage pit is centrally located for easy access by the community, we infer communal effort and communal sharing. On the other hand, when storage facilities are contained within individual houses we then conclude that the family, not the community, is the primary production unit. In our survey of the Middle East we have seen the community (that is, band) replaced by the family as the primary production unit during this crucial period.

Storage also raises the possibility of surpluses. ● Surpluses can, of course, be used to support full-time craft specialists. Considering the quality of the Hassuna, Samarran, and Halafian wares, this becomes a real possibility, and by the Halafian period it is possible that entire villages did nothing but make pottery to sell and trade. A *surplus* can also be defined as storable wealth, and as such it needs protection. It is no accident that with the appearance of surpluses there is a shift from communities made up of scattered, round houses to groupings of more densely concentrated rectangular houses in more easily defended settlements. Ultimately, these settlements were fortified.

The domestication of plants and animals is an essential precursor to the rise of the state. ▲ States can develop only when certain preconditions are met. These include:

1. More intensive food production to support larger and more concentrated populations

2. The existence of surpluses to support non-food-producing specialists (The latter include religious and political leaders, who control the surpluses and who coordinate the activities of these more complex communities.)

No matter how complex the state, how esoteric the cosmology of the priests, and how diverse the craft specialties, all are dependent on the food producer and his surplus. In addition, the storage of food as wealth leads to the need to protect it from outsiders, and this is the stimulus for the rise of warrior specialists.

14

The Spread of Village Farming

Food production as a technological innovation was far-reaching in its cultural importance. After 6000 B.C. food production spread beyond its points of origin with the result that it diffused beyond the limits of the Middle East. This introduction of the Neolithic lifestyle was differential in rate, however. It diffused rapidly up major river valleys, such as the Danube, but very slowly over areas with less potential for agricultural production. Still other terrains, such as the cold, dry steppes and deserts, were outright physical barriers to the dissemination of food production. Another factor relevant to diffusion was the degree of contact among cultures.

In Europe only a few indigenous plants formed potential domesticates available for Neolithic peoples to exploit. Einkorn wheat was the only cereal native to southeast Europe, and while cattle and pigs were available, domesticated sheep and goats seem to have been imports. According to Braidwood (1967), the colonization of Europe by farmers was a combination of several processes, including (1) the actual movement of farming peoples from the Middle East; (2) the spread of objects and ideas from the Middle East beyond the actual migration routes of immigrant farmers; and (3) modifications of these objects and ideas by the indigenous European Mesolithic peoples. On the other hand, Tringham and collaborators (1980) argue for a separate European evolution after the initial introduction of agriculture, in which cultural evolution occurred in spurts.

The earliest farming communities in England and the Scandinavian countries date to some 3,000 years after the appearance of farming in Greece. ■ We thus know that the transition to

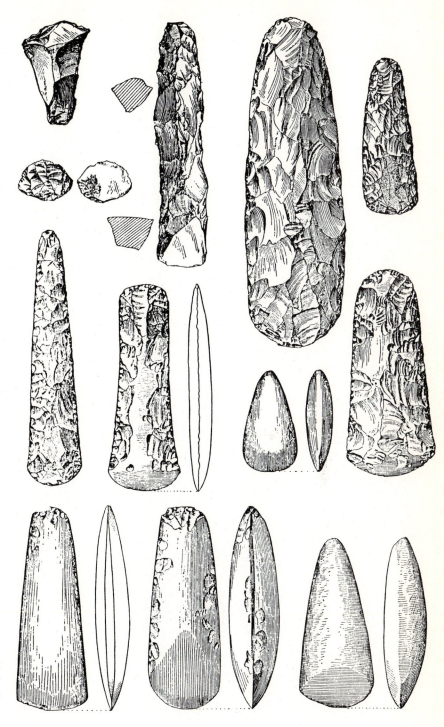

Fig. 14-1 Axes used in forest clearance, from various Neolithic sites in Britain. (Watson 1968: Plate IX.)

● The Neolithic in Turkey spread to Europe.

an agrarian way of life in Europe was gradual, and therefore the change should not be attributed to "migration." The population movement we refer to most likely consisted of small villages of farming folk moving a few miles at a time, then settling down and building a new village. Perhaps such a movement occurred only once or twice in an individual's lifetime. If we assume a generation interval of 20 years, then 150 generations (3,000 years) were required to move the 1,500 miles from Greece to Britain. This represents 10 miles per generation, or only one-half mile per year. Explanations for such movement include population pressure, the need for more fertile land, and so forth, but in fact we do not know why people moved. One of the factors inhibiting a more rapid spread of farming throughout Europe was the presence of forests. We have ample evidence from pollen diagrams that Neolithic peoples carried out major forest clearing (Figs. 14-1, 14-2). Another problem was that of adapting introduced cultigens to a new environment, a process that undoubtedly required considerable time. In the meantime, while the spread of farming and domestication across Europe was occurring, the

peoples of the Middle East continued to make further innovations.

The Anatolian Antecedents

● The early European Neolithic period, particularly that of Greece and Crete, shows a marked resemblance to that of Anatolia, the peninsula that today includes Turkey (Map 14-1). These similarities are so close that the Aegean area and Anatolia may be considered as a single cultural area. There is some scant evidence of a Mesolithic and proto-Neolithic period within this region. There existed a microlithic culture similar to the Natufian, which also had sickle blades indicative of harvesting activities.

Pre-Catal Huyuk Phase

At Hacilar in southwestern Turkey there is a small village on virgin soil which is very similar to the Pre-Pottery Neolithic (PPNB) already described. Rooms of the houses are rectangular, and the walls are of mud brick set on stone foundations. Postholes indicate the position of either awnings or fences. There is no indication of doors, and therefore entry was probably through the roof. The site is without ceramics, and no figurines have been found.

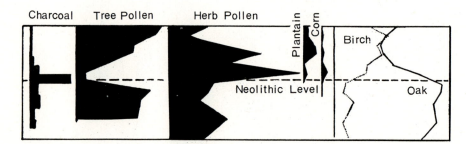

Fig. 14-2 The result of axe use—for forest clearance—is reflected in this pollen profile from Denmark. The Neolithic level is accompanied by a decrease in tree pollen, an increase in herb pollen, and a shift from oak to birch. (Clark 1952:Fig. 44.)

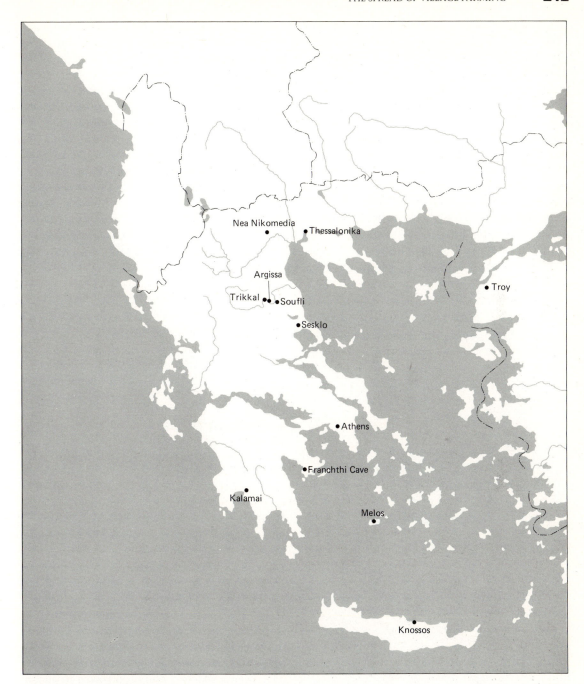

Map 14-1 Neolithic Sites in Greece.

▲ The Anatolian sequence shows a long transition from hunting to the domestication of animals.

■ Hunting was still important.

▲ Animal remains include sheep, goat, cattle, and dog. Two-row barley, emmer and einkorn (wild) wheat, and lentils make up the bulk of the plant remains. Carbon-14 dates the early phase of aceramic Hacilar to 6750 B.C.

In addition to Hacilar, there is the site known as Suberde, which dates to 6500 B.C. and which is a full-time settled hunting village. At this site 300,000 bones and pieces of bone were recovered. Of these, 25,000 were identified by species, with 9,000 attributed to either sheep or

Fig. 14-3 Reconstruction of the houses and enclosure found at Catal Hüyük. (Fairservis 1975:146.)

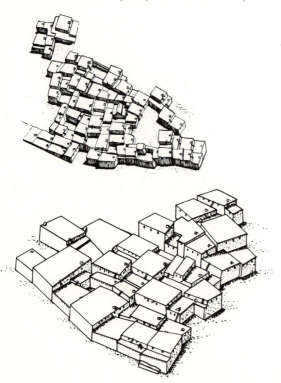

goat. Within the sheep-goat category sheep outnumbered goats 85 percent to 15 percent. The only domesticated animal found at the site was the dog. Although this is a waterside site, no fish bones were found. Other wild animals taken included jackal, fox, bear, wildcat, marten, beaver, hedgehog, and hare (Perkins and Daly 1968).

Catal Huyuk Phase

Catal Huyuk is 11 km north of Cumra on the Konya plain, and at 32 acres, it is one of the largest Neolithic sites in the Middle East. Twelve levels, dated from 7500 to 5650 B.C., are contained within the site. The C-14 dates record a continuous development (Mellaart 1967, 1975). Architecture of the site shows that each rectangular house has a storeroom and roof entry (a good defensive arrangement), and the walls were of mud brick (Fig. 14-3).

The economy was based on extensive agriculture, stock breeding, and hunting. Plants utilized included emmer, einkorn, and breadwheat, naked barley, peas, vetch, and bitter vetch. Unlike Mesopotamia, where sheep and goats were the mainstays, here cattle seem to have been the first choice, and in Catal Huyuk's heyday both domesticated cattle and sheep were herded. ■ Auroch, red deer, onager, boar, and leopard were hunted. Trade also seems to be important, and Catal Huyuk controlled the obsidian trade. Pottery appears at around 5900 B.C. and is strongly influenced by basketry designs.

Religion played a major role in the lives of the Catal Huyuk people. Forty-nine shrines distributed over nine levels were recorded by Mellaart (1967). Each building complex had a shrine, and these were superimposed one above the other (Fig. 14-4). Numerous statuettes of baked clay were found. The main deity seems to have been a goddess, who is portrayed in one of three aspects: young, giving birth, and aged. She is often accompanied by a young man or a leopard.

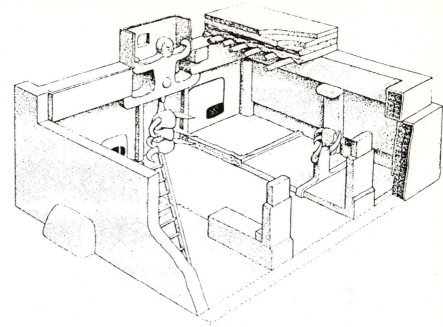

Fig. 14-4 An example of a shrine found at Catal Hüyük. These sanctuaries, within rectangular mud brick houses, contained wall paintings, plaster reliefs, and cult statues modeled in clay. Important features of these shrines are the bulls' heads, and goddesses depicted giving birth to lambs. Also shown in the wall paintings were scenes of the hunting of red deer. (Hawkes 1976:53, 57.)

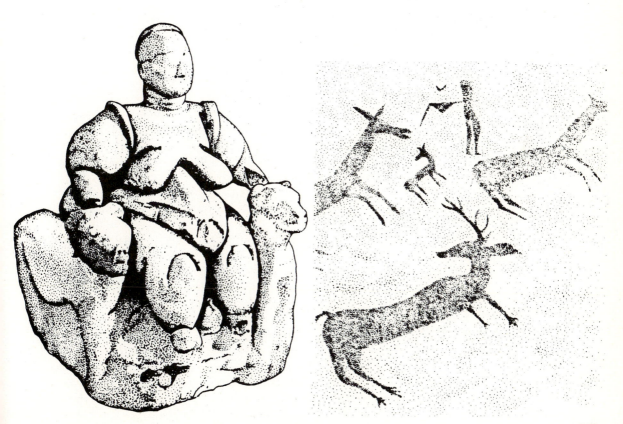

● Pottery becomes more common.

▲ A scheme for the Neolithic spread across Europe

■ The spread to the Aegean islands

● The spread to the Greek mainland

Shrine decor consists of wall painting, animal figures, and plastered reliefs, with auroch horn cores set in benches or on walls. Burial practices involved the exposure of the dead to bacterial cultures or beetles to remove the flesh from the bones, which were then wrapped in furs and placed below the floor benches of the houses. Gifts and jewelry were placed with the dead, and weapons were buried with the males.

Hacilar: 5900–5000 B.C.

The occupation at Hacilar begins where Catal Huyuk ends, providing continuity in the basic sequence of events. Hacilar, located near Burdur in southwestern Turkey, shows development in architectural style and technique. Rooms are larger than at Catal Huyuk, and the structures are two stories high.

● Pottery—thin-walled, hard-fired, and brilliantly burnished—is abundant. Fine reds, buffs, and browns were preferred colors. Representations of the fertility goddess described above are present, indicating that the religious cult survived long after Catal Huyuk had been abandoned. The inhabitants of Hacilar are believed to have used irrigation techniques to nurture their crops.

The Spread of Neolithic Farmers into Europe

▲ In 1977 Graham Clark proposed a three-phase model to describe the spread of Neolithic farmers and their food-producing techniques into Europe (Map 14-2a). Clark's first phase, the "initial" phase, is dated for the most part to the sixth millennium B.C. and is geographically restricted to Greece and the south Balkans. Phase two, the "First Expansion," is a fifth-millennium B.C. phenomenon. Geographically, the "First Expansion" phase occurs when the Neolithic spreads into two areas, the Mediterranean basin and the loess lands of central Europe. The third and final phase involves the further spread of the Neolithic into the rest of Europe.

The Initial Phase: the Aegean and Southeast Europe

■ Scattered throughout the eastern Mediterranean are a series of sites whose material content and dates indicate the Neolithic phenomenon was both early and widespread. The dates also argue for the antiquity of sea-going activity. On the island of Cyprus, Neolithic occupation at the site of Krirokitia has been dated to between 5700 and 5500 B.C. On the island of Crete at the Minoan site of Knossos, Neolithic farmers were well established by 6100 B.C. (Guilaine 1979). The Cretan farmers had Anatolian imports of domesticated sheep and goat, some cattle, pig, and dog. Emmer, einkorn, breadwheat, six-row barley, and lentils helped round out the dietary base.

Originally covering a half-acre, the site grew through time. Ceramics appear in about 5620 B.C. Although outside influence seems to be minimal, Knossos was not totally isolated since obsidian was imported from the island of Melos.

● Several sites on the Greek mainland attest to the presence of domesticated plants and animals at an early date. At Franchthi cave in the Peloponnesus overlooking the gulf of Argolis, excavation has shown human occupation extending from the Upper Paleolithic Ice Age through both the Mesolithic and Neolithic periods. The Neolithic commences at around 5900 B.C. and is marked by the sudden appearance of sheep and goats in the archaeological record. Wheat and barley also appear at about this time. The sudden advent of domesticated plants and animals would argue for an influx of new people. Stone axes attest to early forest clearance. Where pottery appears it is a non-wheel-made, undecorated variety.

On the Greek plains of Thessaly there are a series of Neolithic sites: Argissa Magula, Sesklo, and Soufli. Only Argissa Magula has provided datable material (6200–6000 [?] B.C.). The Thessalian farmers grew emmer and einkorn wheat,

two- and six-row barley, and oats. Peas, lentils, vetch, pistachio, acorns, and wild olives were also utilized. When pottery appears, it is a deepred or red-brown, grit-tempered, burnished ware. At a later time red-and-white designs appear.

Still further north in Macedonia, 60 km west of Thessaloniki, lies the site of Nea Nikamedia. Its date of 6220 B.C. makes this site one of the earliest in Europe, and it, too, has the Anatolian domesticates. Houses at Nea Nikemedia, like those in Thessaly, are square structures, with

Map 14-2a The Spread of the Neolithic into Europe.

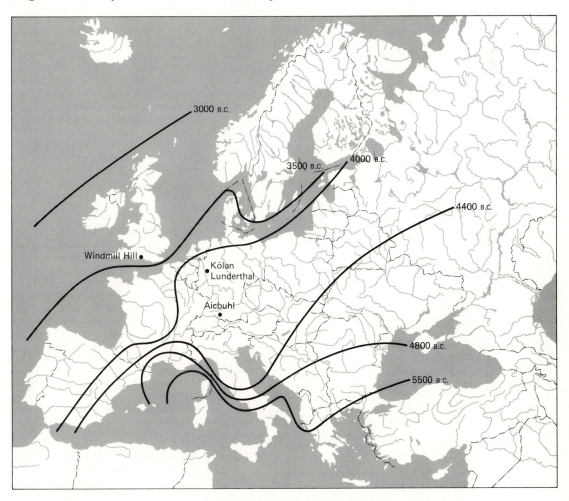

▲ Villages stabilize in size

■ We can trace the Neolithic spread by means of pottery.

the larger ones being used as cult edifices. Rectangular houses are common in both southeastern Europe and Anatolia. However, those at Nea Nikamedia and Thessaly are free-standing, individual structures instead of the grouped contiguous apartment blocks of the Middle East. This dichotomy persists in the Balkan area, with some Neolithic characteristics obviously being Anatolian (Middle Eastern) and some uniquely European.

Lower-Danubian Farmers

Farming spread outward from the Aegean to Bulgaria, Yugoslavia, Hungary, and Romania, a principal route being the Danube valley. Since in each country this Neolithic manifestation has unfortunately been given a separate name, we are consequently faced with an impossible terminology too confusing to mention.

These Neolithic groups share many characteristics, such as pottery, housing, and burial practices. In their pottery, three types can be defined: a thick, coarse, orange ware, a grey or buff ware, and a fine, hard, well-fired variety. Within these categories are regional variants in surface treatment and form. Clay anthropomorphic figures are also present, as in Greece and Anatolia. Clay stamp seals are also common in all. Houses range in shape from rectangular to almost square. Two main construction techniques were used (Fig. 14-5). The first involves construction of a framework of thin, vertical posts which were then packed in clay. The wattle-and-daub method was also used, in which the vertical posts are interwoven with thin lathes and then packed in mud. At Karanovo there is evidence that walls were plastered and painted.

Roofs were also different, being pitched instead of flat. (This is not supposition, for preserved models of house types clearly illustrate the pitched feature.) Among the causes of these changes was the environment, since housing developed in the arid Middle East had to be adapted to the colder, wetter European climate. Another characteristic in common between the eastern European and Middle Eastern settlements was the formation of tells, in which the layered sequence of prior settlements forms a mound such as that at Karanovo. ▲ Typical villages were of 50 to 60 houses, with a population in the vicinity of 300. Piggott (1965:47–49) estimates that the amount of grain consumed by such a group would require a total cropland of about 430 acres, or about 7 acres per family.

The mixed economy combined shifting cultivation with the keeping of cattle, sheep, goats, and pigs. Hunting and fishing were also important. Einkorn wheat and millet, both of which are indigenous to the region, were cultivated. The agricultural system was probably of the slash-and-burn type: the clearing and planting of small plots within a forest for several years, followed by several years of fallowing before replanting. Crops were stored in small clay-lined silos. Hunting was done with slings, and fishing with nets. Agricultural implements included an adaptation of the Middle Eastern type of sickle. Grains were processed with grinding stones, and ovens were used for baking. Trade indicates the existence of an intervillage and regional communication system. Major items traded were ornaments of *Spondylus* shell from the Mediterranean and obsidian from Hungary and Transylvania.

The First Expansion: Eastern Europe

Farming at first spread up the Danube into central Europe and later to the north and west. A major attraction was the deep loess soils so favorable to agriculture. We may view this diffusion of agricultural peoples as a colonization, and it was marked with forest clearance.

■ The expansion is clearly indicated by the proliferation of a diagnostic pottery. Vessel

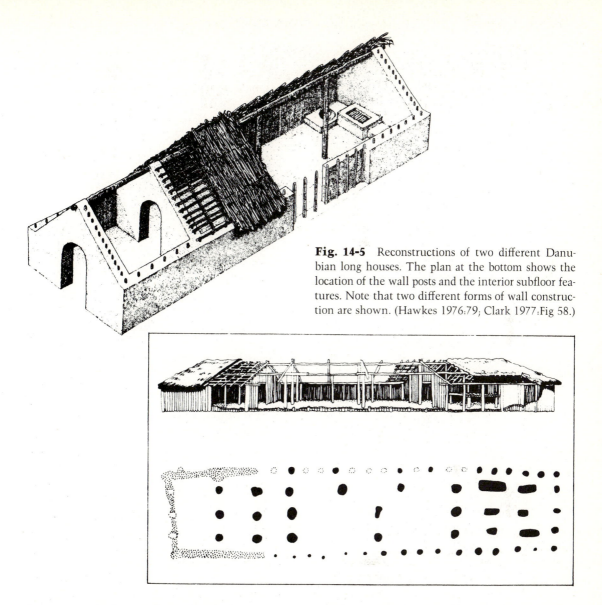

Fig. 14-5 Reconstructions of two different Danubian long houses. The plan at the bottom shows the location of the wall posts and the interior subfloor features. Note that two different forms of wall construction are shown. (Hawkes 1976:79; Clark 1977:Fig 58.)

forms were fairly simple, hemispherical bowls and round-bottomed flasks. The pottery was decorated with linear bevels arranged in spirals or spiral-meanders, design elements which give the culture its name: Linear-banderkeramic (LBK). This expansion has also been called the "Danubian I" period and is dated to between 4500 and 4200 B.C. LBK ceramics are widely distributed, ranging from Hungary to the Oder estuary, and from northern France and Holland to the Ukraine. In spite of the large areas involved, the Danubian I (LBK) settlements are remarkably uniform. This latter feature is probably due to the rapidity of the culture spread, the causes of which in turn are probably linked to explosive population growth and shortages of land suitable for farming.

Pigs, goats, sheep, and cattle were kept, but these do not seem to have been major sources of food. Also neglected were the hunting resources of the region. These farmers practiced slash-and-burn agriculture, planting barley, beans, lentils, peas, flax, and three kinds of wheat (einkorn, emmer, and hexaploid). The major agricultural

> ● A new kind of house
>
> ▲ Regional adaptation to local conditions
>
> ■ The impressed-pottery culture spread along the Mediterranean coast.
>
> ● Copper appears in Europe.
>
> ▲ The Swiss lake dwellings

tool was the hoe. *Spondylus* shells used as bracelets remain popular and are found even in northern France.

● Another innovation was the introduction of the longhouse. Villages included up to 20 such structures. These were large (18 to 22 feet wide and 30 to 130 feet long), with gabled halls and walls of wattle-and-daub construction. Villages contained from 200 inhabitants to perhaps 600. The occupants of the longhouses were probably some form of extended family. No matter what the exact social form, it must have differed considerably from the small house settlements of the lower-Danubian farmers.

In the Danubian II period (the latter half of the lineal expansion) the longhouses are replaced by smaller rectangular structures. This implies social or economic changes in the basic unit of production. ▲ Greater regional variation shows up in both the ceramic and tool inventories, indicating adaptation to local conditions. During this period hunting becomes more important, and in the west the appearance of fortified sites argues for land competition.

The First Expansion: the Mediterranean

■ At the same time along the Mediterranean coast there was an east-to-west spread of a separate tradition — the "impressed pottery" culture, known by a distinctive ware indented with the serrated edge of a cardium shell.

The pressed wares are believed to have had their origins in the eastern Mediterranean, in southern Turkey and Syria, and they later appear in the Balkans and along the Adriatic coast of Italy. In the western Mediterranean, pottery sites are found in Sicily, Malta, Elba, and Sardinia, on the Italian coast, and westward to the southern coast of France. Later, inpressed pottery appears in Spain and Portugal. The distribution of the culture is almost exclusively coastal, with most sites being located within 50 miles of the coast.

The economy of this culture featured the herding of sheep, goats, and cattle. These people also cultivated barley, hunted, and fished. The bow and arrow was their principal hunting weapon. Trading by sea, especially of obsidian from the Lipari islands, near Sicily, was another important economic pursuit. The initial Neolithic immigrants to the region probably amalgamated with the indigenous Mesolithic peoples to produce this distinctive regionally oriented culture.

The Second Expansion: Eastern Europe

During the Second Expansion period in eastern Europe new elements appear within the basic farming economy. ● For example, copper ornaments, although initially rare, through time become more plentiful due to increased demand. Pottery with red-and-white pigment designs appears during this period. Wood-and-mud houses were grouped in small villages, which were sometimes fortified.

In northern Europe settlement by farmers was late (for example, after 3000 B.C. in Denmark). The region was cold, damp, and was not particularly favorable to agriculture; therefore farming was not introduced until after all of central and southern Europe had been occupied. The first farmers in the north tried the same agricultural practices that had been perfected farther south, but with little success. The subsequent farmers of the region went through several periods of economic adjustment before

Fig. 14-6 Reconstruction of a Bronze Age Pile Village, 2200–1100 B.C. (Photograph courtesy of H. Bachelmann.)

suitable crops, such as barley and rye, and the techniques for their cultivation were adopted. Meanwhile, at the same time cultural developments in the Middle East had progressed to the level of true urbanism.

The Second Expansion: Western Europe

After 4000 b.c., Neolithic culture spread inland to France, Switzerland, and the Italian lake district (Phillips 1975:75–111). ▲ In this region the settlements are termed "lake dwellings" (Fig. 14-6). When initially discovered, such pile dwellings built along lake shores were thought to represent villages built over water. Subsequent research indicates that most were originally built on boggy ground along lake shores (for example, Aichbühl in Württemburg). Frequently, subsequent peat growth has covered the village remains so that today they are found within bogs. A major feature of such sites is their excellent preservation of materials, including perishable artifacts. Each house of approximately 10 feet × 20 feet included two rooms and a porch and probably sheltered a nuclear family. A maximum of 65 houses is known for such villages,

with a population estimated at from 120 to 370 (Piggott 1965:58).

Cultural manifestations assigned to this tradition in Western Europe extend from Spain to Britain. Basic traits include lumpy pots, lakeside villages, considerable hunting and stock breeding, the mining of flint (Fig. 14-7), and the use

Fig. 14-7 Reconstruction drawing of the mining of flint at the Neolithic quarry of Grimes Graves, Norfolk, England. (Courtesy of Ministry of Public Building and Works, England.)

249

■ By 3000 B.C., Europe had developed its own distinctive Neolithic economic system.

of axes rather than adzes. Wheat was grown, and the domestic animals were cattle and pigs, along with a few sheep. Carts, drawn by draft animals, were used on wooden roadways (Fig. 14-8). Axes were manufactured in what amount to actual factories. Burials were important, and the typical pattern was simultaneous, collective burials under earthen mounds as long as 300 feet. The bones or cremated bones of the dead were heaped together at the wider end of the mound on top of a low platform of chalk or within a pile of flint nodules. The total number of burials is small, 25 being the maximum number contained in one mound. These burials, to judge from their associated mounds, probably represent the interments of chiefs and their families.

The portrayal we have attempted of early agriculturalists in Europe is that of a peasant society containing marked intergroup similarities but also simultaneously indicative of several different sets of influences or cultural patterns. In other words, agricultural life in Europe was diffused in several directions and according to several patterns.

■ By the third millennium B.C. the European agriculturalists were subsisting through the cultivation of wheat, barley, peas, lentils, beans, apples, and flax: The seeds of the latter were used

Fig. 14-8 A Neolithic roadway constructed of timbers dated 2300 B.C. (Photograph courtesy of John Coles.)

for food and the fiber used in textiles and basketry. Cattle were kept and were fed leaves of the elm tree, among other foods. A further development of this time was the building of monumental, stone-lined, chambered tombs indicative of a major religion (one which we will discuss in Chapter 16).

By 2500 B.C., the close of an era in European prehistory, the agricultural colonization had ended and peasant farmers were established throughout Europe. Simultaneously, in northern and western Europe there continued in existence nonagricultural hunters and fishers, a tradition which persisted for several millennia. Meanwhile we have in the Middle East the development of civilization, the first harbingers of which — copper implements — appear in the Mediterranean by 2500 B.C.

The Spread of the Neolithic to India

The spread of primary village farming into the Indian subcontinent appears, at first, to be a straightforward proposition. Since we know, for example, that wheat, barley, and the various millets were not native to India and that the earliest evidence for their domestication occurs in the Middle East, we assume that primary village farming and all that it entails spread into India from the latter area.

The earliest Neolithic evidence on the subcontinent known to date comes from the preceramic site of Mehrgarh near the Belon river in central Pakistan (Jarrige and Meadow 1980:122–133). Dating back to the sixth millennium B.C., this settlement consisted of multiroomed mud brick units separated from one another by open spaces.

Impressions of cereal grains found in mud debris indicate the presence of two-rowed hulled barley, six-rowed barley, emmer and einkorn wheat, and breadwheat. This implies that Pakistan was a very early center of plant domestication. It is also possible to see at Mehrgarh the shift from wild-animal to domesticated-animal dependence, with sheep, goats, and cattle being the prime domesticates.

The site of Mehrgarh is reminiscent of the Middle East but might equally well have derived from an Afghanistani origin. For example, at Ghari-mar (Snake Cave), Ghar-i-asp (Horse Cave), and Dara-i-kur (Cave of the Valley) in northern Afghanistan we have evidence for an early sheep-goat association and possibly for cattle. This association is of considerable antiquity (14,665 B.C.) and these domesticable species constituted 80 to 89 percent of the collections (Perkins 1972: 73). Another possibility is that of an indigenous development of food production which at an early data also adopted domesticated animal species introduced from the Middle East. It may well be possible, as Shaffer (1978) argues, that Afghanistan was part of a core area of domestication which fostered plants and animals similar to those of the Middle East.

Regardless of point of origin, once domesticates were introduced into the subcontinent, the pattern of subsequent spread is fairly clear. Wheat and barley, spreading from northwest to southeast, reach the Indus valley and the plains of the Ganges by 2500 B.C. (see Map 14-2b). By 1000 B.C. wheat was being grown as far south as the Godavari river in the central Deccan plateau. Barley, spreading more slowly, reached the central Deccan plateau by 500 B.C. (map 14-4; Vishnu-Mittre 1977).

Rice seems to have radiated from two points on the subcontinent. On the west coast rice is dated to 2300 b.c. at Lothal on the Bay of Cambay, spreading inland and southward down the Konkani coast. In the east rice is dated to 1500 B.C. at Bairdipur in the Garhjat Hills. Its cultivation spreads from there to the northwest on the plains of the Ganges. The nature and direction of the initial diffusion of rice growing seems linked to the presence of Monsoon-deposited rainfall. On the other hand, almost 2,000 years were required for rice cultivation to spread into the dryer areas of India (Map 14-3).

● Middle Eastern domesticates are introduced into the Nile Valley.

In northern Baluchistan the Kile Ghul Mohammad wares are replaced by Zhob pottery. The Zhob potters decorated their wares with friezes of humped cattle with long legs, a feature reminiscent of that found at Hissar and Siyalk in western Iran.

The succeeding Nal potters dropped the cattle motif from their repertoire. Nal pottery has a highland distribution and consists of polychrome wares. On the other hand, Amri pottery, dated to 2400 B.C., was restricted to the lower foothills and the Indus valley and features both geometric designs and delightful animals. Di-

Map 14-2b The Spread of Wheat and Barley into the Indian Subcontinent. (after Vishu-Mittre)

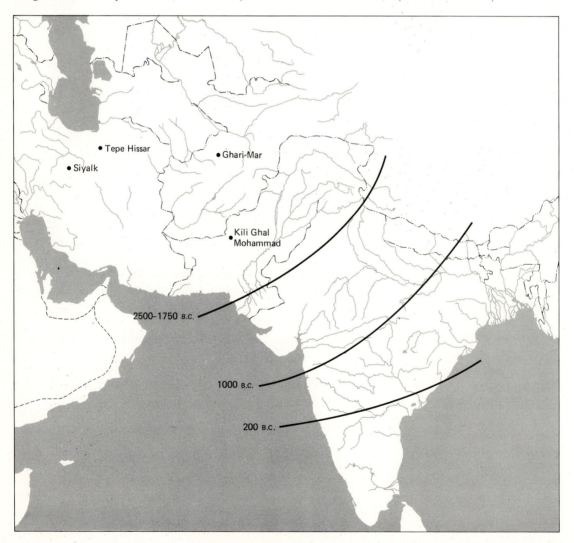

rectly descended from the Nal potters is the Kulli group, a common motif of which is cattle, or oxen, tied to a tree. This ware, found as far away as Abu Dhabi on the Persian Gulf, clearly attests to pre-Harrapan Sumerian contact between the Indus valley and the valleys of the Tigris and Euphrates and to the importance of cattle to these peoples. This contact with the Middle East assumes great importance after 2300 B.C. with the establishment of the civilization of the Indus valley.

The Spread of the Neolithic into Africa

● In spite of the possibly early domestication of barley at Wadi Kubbaniya in Egypt some 18,000

Map 14-3 The Spread of Rice into the Indian Subcontinent. (after Vishu-Mittre)

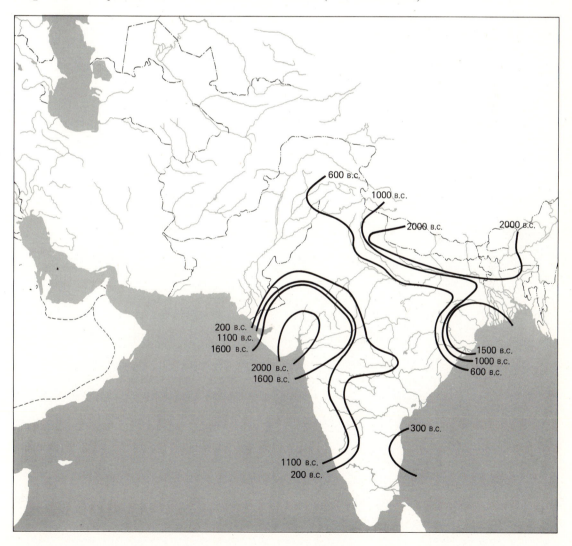

▲ Neolithic traits spread westward along the North African coast.

■ The Sahara—possibly an independent center of domestication.

years ago, as revealed by excavations of Fred Wendorf and others (1979), current evidence supports the idea of the introduction of domesticates into Egypt from the Middle East at a much later date. Middle Eastern cereals appear in the Fayum of Egypt at 5000 B.C. Goat, sheep, pig, and cattle are present but their degree of domestication is not known. There are no traces of housing, but basket-lined silos have been found.

In all probability, the Fayum people were incipient cultivators who followed their herds, returning annually to plant and harvest their crops. The shift to settled life came quickly. By 4000 B.C. the village of Merimde, located on the western edge of the Nile Delta, covered an area of 180,000 square meters and had an estimated human population of 16,000 (Hoffman 1979). Houses with plastered floors in arrangements along a curving street suggests that there was central planning. Merimde is not unique, for similar settlements have been found at El Omri south of Cairo and at Deir Tasa, Badari, and at Hammamiya in upper Egypt.

Between 3800 and 3600 B.C. objects of value (e.g., ivory combs) make their appearance in the

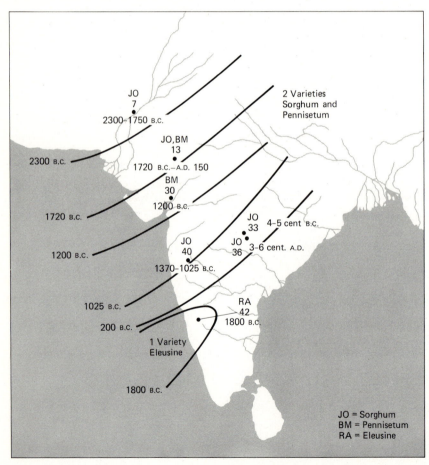

Map 14-4 Geographic Distribution with Dates of the Spread of Millets in the Indian Subcontinent. (after Vishnu-Mittre)

archaeological record. The large numbers of human figurines and carved animals present are probably indicative of a religious cult. By 3600 B.C. statues and zoomorphic vessels appear, attesting to a growing artistic tradition. Gold and lapis lazuli were being used for ornaments. Evidence for conquest and the political domination that led ultimately to the unification of Egypt into a single nation-state is provided by the Narmer palette. (On this stone Narmer is portrayed in the typical conquering-pharaoh pose, which indicates the appearance of civilization.)

In sharp contrast to the developments in Egypt is the site of Es Shaheinab near Khartoum in the Sudan. By 3200 B.C. this site was inhabited by hunters and gatherers who also utilized pottery, a Neolithic trait. ▲ In addition to spreading up the Nile, Neolithic traits spread westward along the Mediterranean coast. At the coastal cave site of Haua Fteah in Libya, domestic sheep and goat appear at 5000 B.C. (McBurney 1967). However, the stone tools recovered show no stylistic break with the tools of the preceding hunting tradition. This persistence of Mesolithic tool types and technologies is a major feature of the North African Neolithic.

By the fourth millennium B.C., Neolithic traits are found in the Maghreb. Here, on the Algerian plateau, Neolithic culture may be divided into two parts. The first, typical of the desert, is characterized by rock art and by small amounts of pottery; the second has a more northerly distribution, abundant pottery, and no arrowheads. The main domesticates seem to be sheep and goat, but domesticated cattle have been found at Uan Muhuggiag dating to 5590 B.C.

Well to the south in the central Sahara harpoon points and fishing gear have been recovered. The pottery found here closely resembles that found at Es Shaheinab, while arrowheads closely resemble those of the Fayum. Similar specimens have been dated to 5950 B.C. at Dungul Oasis (Hester and Hobler 1969). ■ This evidence lends support to the idea that the Sahara served as a potential center of domestication. Further documentation is the fact that at the higher elevations of the mountainous portions of the Saharan region, wild cereal plants are still found. In addition, the rock art portrays the herding of cattle. With postglacial climatic changes and the drying out of the Saharan region, these early efforts at domestication were ultimately doomed to failure.

South of the Sahara, in West Africa, the Neolithic development had a different history. Agriculture may have emerged as early as the fifth millennium B.C. In Sierra Leone, Ghana, and Nigeria, an apparent change in the economy is dated as early as 3000 B.C.; however, to term this food production may not be warranted at this time. As a basic staple, the yam spread throughout the length of the West African rain forest and southward into the northern portions of the Congo basin. The appearance of horticulture is indicated by the presence of pottery and ground and polished stone axes used in forest clearance. However, we do not know when this spread occurred. In East Africa, it is also possible that forest clearance in the Lake Victoria basin dates to as early as the first millennium B.C. Since it is certain that there were no large herds of domesticated animals present (the tsetse fly would have precluded this) most meat must have been derived from hunting.

In sharp contrast to West Africa, the East African grasslands have long been the home of pastoralists. They and their long-horned cattle may have moved into Nubia from the Sahara in around 2500 B.C. They then moved southward into the Horn of Africa, and subsequently into Kenya. Recent early dates on bovids reported from Kenya and dating to about 10,000 B.C. are now thought to be remains of eland, and thus were probably wild rather than domesticated (Wendorf 1980).

Africa is linked to the development of an iron-working technology and the southward spread of Bantu-speaking peoples. Basically these were people who worked iron, lived in villages

● A Mesolithic economy with pottery

▲ Slash-and-burn agriculture and millet and domesticated animals

■ Painted pottery

● Growth in village size

(smaller earlier, larger later), and who made pottery, kept livestock, and grew cereals. They were present in Zambia and Malawi around 2,000 years ago, according to radiocarbon dates. They were present in Zimbabwe, Rhodesia, between A.D. 300 and 1000 and had migrated south of the Limpopo River before A.D. 900.

The Far East

There is no evidence to support the idea that Neolithic farming spread into Asia from the West. On the contrary, the evidence strongly argues for a local, independent development of a Neolithic life-style, based on the domestication of indigenous species of plants and animals.

The Neolithic of China*

The Early Neolithic: 7000–4000 B.C., and Possibly Earlier

Throughout China a number of sites have come to light that fit into the early Neolithic period. In general, these locations exhibit mixed characteristics, such as the presence of cord-marked pottery and polished stone axes, which we associate with Neolithic culture. On the other hand, most of these sites seem to be located along the banks of rivers and streams or along the sea coast. In other words, there is a heavy exploitation of fish and molluscs. ● Therefore, while the artifact inventory looks "Neolithic," the

*After Chang (1977) and Rawson (1980).

economic base is of a "Mesolithic" type. An Xianrendong, Jiangxi (Hsien-jen-tung, Kiangsi), cord-marked pottery in China has been dated to 6875 (± 240) B.C., but corded ware in Japan dates to as early as 9000 B.C. (Jomon phase) and to 7000–8000 B.C. along the Thai-Burmese border. Based on these comparisons, cord-marked pottery may ultimately be revealed to have existed earlier in China.

There is some speculation that the southern cord-marked-pottery makers were cultivators. Botanists agree that taro and yams were among the earliest cultigens in Southeast Asia, another cord-marked pottery area, and the range of these undoubtedly extended into southern China. It is obvious that much more work will be necessary to eliminate the many ambiguities as to Neolithic origins and to more firmly date the early Neolithic period in these areas.

The Late Neolithic: 4430–2065 B.C.

THE YANG-SHAO (YANG SHAO) CULTURE: 4000–1620 B.C.

The best known of the late Neolithic cultures in China is the Yang-Shao culture of the Huang Ho river valley. Later, the Yang-Shao spreads into adjacent areas. ▲ Subsistence of the Yang-Shao peoples was based on the cultivation of millet and domesticated animals, primarily the pig. They lived in villages and practiced slash-and-burn agriculture. Villages were moderate in size, rarely exceeding 20,000 square meters. At Banpocun (Pan-Po-T'sun) for example, we have a village approximately 200 meters long and 100 meters wide. The houses at Banpocun were fairly permanent (Fig. 14-9). Most of these structures were 3–5 meters in diameter and were either square, rectangular, or round. In the center of the village was a large communal house 20 meters × 12.5 meters in size. Houses were clustered on the western side of the village, while the eastern portion had pottery kilns. A cemetery north of the site contained only adults, whereas children were buried in urns between houses. Large ditches separated the living areas from the cemetery area. These ditches were intentionally constructed and divide the site into subunits. Any other function they may have had is unknown.

Pottery was both handmade and molded (Fig. 14-10). ■ Ritual ware consisted of polished red-and-black bowls and basins with painted red or black designs. The painted designs featuring an-

Fig. 14-9 Houses of Neolithic age found at Banpocun (Pan-Po-T'sun) Pan P'o Ts'un, China. The houses were of circular or rectangular form with thatched roofs and walls of poles and mud. (Hawkes 1976:79.)

Storage vessel, Pan P'o Ts'un, China

Polished stone adze, Pan P'o Ts'un, China

Fig. 14-10 Typical implements found in the Chinese Neolithic villages. The storage jar was probably used to store grain, and the adze could have been used either for woodworking or field cultivation. (Hawkes 1976:75.)

imals, fish, and masks are diagnostic of the Yang-Shao culture.

THE LONGSHAN (LUNGSHAN) CULTURE: 2600–1523 B.C.

The Longshan culture is partially contemporary with and ultimately replaces the Yang-Shao culture. Geographically, it is found in the lower Huang Ho valley. Villages tend to be located on the upper stretches of tributary streams, usually within sight of a hill and of one another. Longshan villages are larger than their Yang-Shao counterparts, ranging in size from 600 to 360,000 square meters. The average size is around 90,000 square meters. ● Larger village size and greater village density indicate an increased population density, which ultimately sets the stage for expansion.

Pottery—a wheel-made, thin-walled blackware—is the main diagnostic trait of the Long-

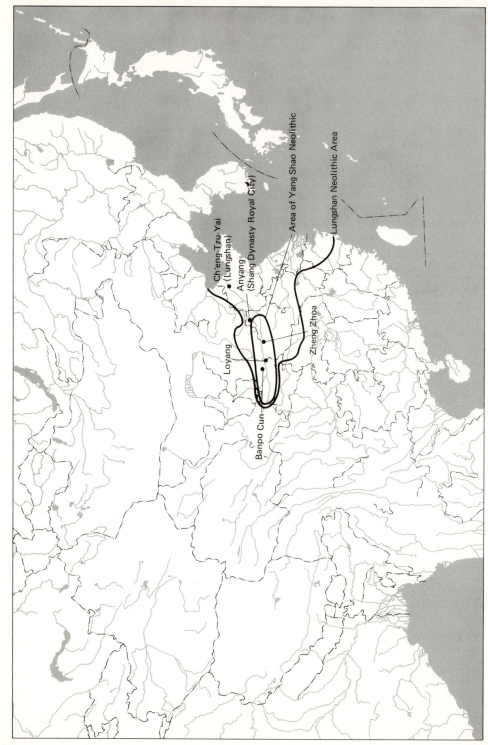

Ch'eng-Tzu-Yai
(Lungshan)

Anyang
(Shang Dynasty Royal City)

Area of Yang Shao Neolithic

Lungshan Neolithic Area

Loyang

Zheng Zhoa

Banpo Cun

Map 14-5 Neolithic and Later Cultures of China. (after Chang)

▲ Undecorated pottery

■ The earliest pottery in the world

● Cultivation of rice

shan period. ▲ This product is undecorated, with angular contours and a high polish. In sharp contrast to the painted wares of the Yang-Shao, no painted pottery is found in the Longshan.

The Longshan spread beyond the core area of the Huang Ho valley, and in that movement it diffused new ideas and techniques of food production. In the new areas we find essentially Neolithic cultures which exhibit traits resembling but not identical to those of the Longshan. These cultures have been lumped together under the convenient rubric "Longshanoid," and they are found in coastal China and in the Yangtse valley to the south of the Huang Ho.

The Neolithic in Japan

The prehistoric period in Japan is traditionally divided into four periods: the Pleistocene Paleolithic, the Jomon, the Yayoi, and the Kofun.

The exact time at which Japan was first occupied during the Pleistocene is still being debated by scholars. Estimates of the date of initial settlement range from as early as 100,000 years ago to as late as 30,000 years ago. Fumiko Ikawa-Smith, in a recent article (1980), opts for a date of 50,000 years ago. While the early dates tend to raise some skepticism, the recent discovery of obviously early material in Korea, at Choen-Kok-Li (Serizawa 1980), certainly argues for an early date. The Korean material, which is still undated, resembles Lower Paleolithic finds of considerable antiquity in other parts of the world. Obviously, much more work needs to be done in Korea, in nearby Siberia and Manchuria, and on the Japanese archipelago before this problem can be finally resolved. Much of the following discussion is drawn from Bleed (undated ms., 1972, 1974, 1978).

The Jomon Period: 11,000–300 B.C.

The Jomon period, named for its distinctive cord-marked (Jomon) pottery, is often equated with Neolithic manifestations found elsewhere. Certainly the presence of pottery and polished stone implements argues for this assignment. ■ Jomon ceramics are the earliest dated wares known anywhere in the world, and those at Fukui Cave are dated at 10,750 ± 500 B.C. On the other hand, evidence for systematic cultivation by Jomon peoples is at best tenuous.

Ecologically, Japan is most complex and diverse, and the 10,000 or more sites attributed to the Jomon culture are scattered throughout a variety of environmental settings. For example, some 2,500 sites are coastal kitchen middens, where the emphasis is on the exploitation of maritime resources. Forested inland areas rich in oak were exploited for their acorns and other nuts. The presence of a buckwheat grain in a Jomon site has been offered as evidence of cultivation, and Peter Bleed, using flotation techniques, has recovered numerous plant remains. However, the extent to which Jomon peoples were cultivators has yet to be resolved. Late in the Jomon period nut exploitation became quite intense, and questions as to whether or not nut-bearing trees were cultivated have also been raised. In general, the Jomon period seems to be one of local subsistence adaptation over which a generalized pottery style seems to have been superimposed.

The Yayoi Period: 300 B.C.–A.D. 300

The Yayoi period forms the basis of traditional Japanese society. Yayoi peoples were wet-rice cultivators who used stone and brass tools. Bronze was also used for manufacturing mirrors, bells, and weaponry.

● The basic subsistence pattern is one of rice cultivation in flooded fields. However, hunting,

▲ The Middle East was the most important center for domestication.

fishing, and gathering continued and certainly formed an important dietary component. The Yayoi period is also characterized by forest clearance, indirect evidence of the growing expansions of cultivation as well as an indication of increasing population size.

To some degree the various communities were integrated politically into a single political state, but was this due to the efforts of the descendants of the Yayoi rice farmers or to the efforts of horse-riding invaders? This is another question which has yet to be resolved. The idea of invaders is not far-fetched, and it is believed that the cultivation practices, weaving, and the use of Dolmen burials were introduced into the islands from the continent.

The Kofun Period:
A.D. 300–A.D. 600

The Kofun period is named after its key-shaped burial mounds. These tombs normally range in size from 10 to 20 meters in diameter, but some are more than 300 meters in size. The tombs are thought to contain the remains of ancient chiefs who were leaders of small, independent political units. Iron swords, helmets, and suits of armor recovered from the tombs attest to the military orientation of these early chieftains. Bronze mirrors and earthenware representations of warriors, animals, and houses (called Haniwa) have also been recovered from these tombs. While the power of the chieftains seems to have been based on ritual authority, the larger tombs clearly attest to the fact that these leaders commanded a sizable labor force. There is a decline in tomb construction that correlates well with the building of Buddhist temples in the succeeding historic period.

The Spread of the Neolithic in the Pacific Area

By the time Neolithic manifestations (that is, domesticated plants and animals) had spread into the Pacific, the continent of Australia had long been occupied. There are numerous sites which date within the 30,000-to-40,000-year range, and some estimates extend to 50,000 years ago. These early dates argue strongly for effective sea transport far earlier than originally surmised, since the subcontinent has not been linked to Southeast Asia since the early Pleistocene.

Once Australia was peopled, there began the inevitable process of adapting to the many local environments. Despite regional variations produced by this adaptation, the occupants of the subcontinent were always hunters and gatherers with an essentially Paleolithic life-style.

On the other hand, to the north of Australia lie the island groupings collectively called Melanesia: New Guinea, New Britain, and New Caledonia. In these islands domesticates were extensively exploited by as early as 5,000 years ago, and in New Guinea this phenomenon may be even earlier.

The initial expansion into the Pacific is marked by the appearance of a sand-tempered pottery known as Lapita ware. Designs included geometric forms, stamped while the medium was still plastic. Lapita ware dates to between 3,000 and 2,000 years ago. Since Lapita has essentially a maritime distribution, it is reasonable to assume that the latter can be equated with the presence of the double-hulled canoe, a major factor in the spread of peoples and domesticates throughout the islands.

The basic domesticates include coconut, breadfruit, and taro. On coral islands coconuts assume major importance, while breadfruit and taro remain relatively unimportant. Conversely, on volcanic islands it is taro and breadfruit which are important. Domesticated animals carried to the islands include chickens, pigs, and dogs.

Polynesia seems to have been settled from Melanesia starting at about 2,000 years ago. By A.D. 250 colonists had reached Hawaii, by a.d. 210, Easter Island, and by A.D. 1000 they had settled New Zealand.

Summary

▲ Although many areas of the world have contributed to the international food supply, such as the important New World domesticates — corn, beans, squash, and potatoes — the plants and animals domesticated in the Middle East have had a major impact. In Europe, for example, with the exception of the olive and an Italian millet, the staple food base was, and is, based on plants and animals whose domestic origins lie in the Middle East. From Europe these domesticates were transferred into the New World, where they continue to thrive. Along with rice in India, Middle Eastern domesticates provide the nutritional base for much of central Asia.

Africa has also been the home of many domesticates, but plants domesticated in Africa, with the exception of millet, sorghum, and yams, did not appreciably spread beyond their points of origin during the Neolithic. Again, the plants and animals that have spread widely in Africa seem to be of non-African origin.

The spread of the Neolithic life-style has had a major impact on most of the key ecological regions of the world. Humans cleared land, destroyed natural cover, and drove many species, both plant and animal, into extinction in their never-ending quest for new areas to farm. Once begun, the Neolithic life-style spread rapidly throughout the world until there remain today only a few areas (i.e., Arctic tundra and desert) wherein people do not practice farming as their principal means of subsistence. In addition, the Neolithic system of food production was the necessary economic foundation for the rise of the great city states and empires — the subject of our next chapter.

15

The Development of Civilization

■ Civilization has a similar history of development in several parts of the world.

● A sequence of developmental periods

What is Civilization? Some Definitions

One of the most fascinating problems in archaeology deals with the causes of civilization and with why it appears when and where it does.

Civilization may be defined as a level of cultural attainment normally marked by the presence of writing, monumental architecture, and a stratified social system. It is also described in superlative terms, especially in reference to artistic achievement. Other definitions cite the rise of a true state as being the most characteristic attribute of civilizations. ■ What is fascinating is that in several major regions of the world, including Mesopotamia, coastal Peru, Mesoamerica, and China, cultures progressed through a similar sequence of levels. Thus civilization would appear to be the evolutionary result of a certain set of enabling or permissive conditions. Julian Steward (1971) has identified these evolutionary levels as follows: The era of Incipient Agriculture is followed by a Formative era. ● The sequence we term "civilization" begins with a Florescent era and is followed by the era of Militarism, Fusion or Conquest, and Cyclical Empires (Map 15-1).

The Formative Era

In examining the usage of these terms, Robert M. Adams (1971:574) applies the term *Formative* to those cultures which possess neither full-time craft specialists nor substantial concentrations of wealth. Most Neolithic societies fit a Formative classification. Adams also presents a set of formal definitions (1971:589). Whereas the

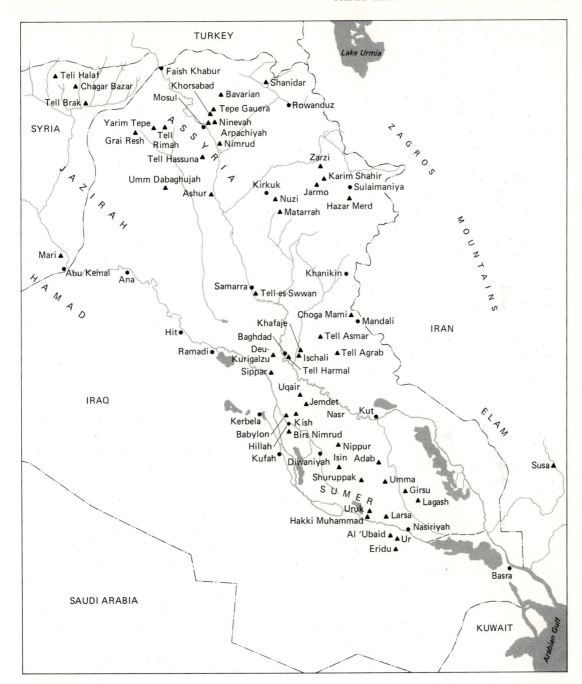

Map 15-1 Important sites in the Middle East of the Formative, Florescent, and Dynastic Eras. (After Lloyd)

▲ The Formative era defined

■ The Florescent era

● The Dynastic era defined

▲ Developments leading to the Florescent era in Mesopotamia

■ Painted animals

● Temples

latter are based primarily on the Mesopotamian evidence, they also can be generally applied to other regions. ▲ The Formative is defined as follows:

> Adoption and spread of typical upland village subsistence pattern, and perhaps, also, spread of its corresponding forms of social organization. Sedentary agriculture, with digging-stick and hoe cultivation of wheat and barley, domestication of sheep, goats, and probably cattle. Ceramics were crafted. Communities remained small and relatively uniform in size and composition but increased in number, spreading into the alluvium with the introduction of irrigation techniques. A "fertility cult," was present.

The Florescent Era

The *Florescent* era (Adams 1971:574) is characterized by the coherence of several periods of growth during which a distinctively civilized pattern of living emerged out of a folk village substratum. ■ The formal definition, based on Mesopotamian data, includes the following (Adams 1971:590):

> *Florescent.* Emphasis shifted to the lowlands with the development of plow-irrigation agriculture. Expansion of technology and appearance of full-time craft specialization; introduction of potter's wheel, cart and chariot, sail, copper metallurgy, early phases in the development of writing. Rapid growth in concentration of surpluses, largely in hands of priestly hierarchies, with consequent

building of monumental religious structures in town-urban centers. Beginnings of warfare.

The Dynastic Era

The *Dynastic* or *Militaristic* era features little change in subsistence patterns, with some elaboration in crafts. The major changes were the rise of militarism and the assumption of political power by secular authorities. Major characteristics of the era include increased control over the supply and production of goods and the growing importance and privileges of the ruling class. The latter are marked by the construction of palaces, special tombs, and the accumulation and conspicuous consumption of luxury goods. Population increase led in part to the wars of conquest and the rise of empires.

● Adams (1971:590) defines the Dynastic era as follows:

> Separation and institutionalization of secular-political and religious-economic controls in true urban centers—the appearance of kingship and the city-state. Emphasis on fortifications and growing importance of warfare, culminating in Sargonic conquests. Slow growth of private capital in trading and manufacturing, but at the end of the era temples probably still dominated the economic life. Rationalization and expansion of handicraft production; bronze metallurgy, refinement of cuneiform script.

This is the period of the city and city-state, with pyramids, temples, and palaces constituting a political and religious center.

Ancient civilizations in the Old World are numerous and range from the famous to the obscure. The earliest developments were in the valleys of major rivers such as the Tigris, Euphrates, Nile, Indus, Yangtze, and Huang Ho. Later civilizations developed in Anatolia, Greece, Italy, Tunisia, Sudan, Ethiopia, and Arabia. There is no opportunity here to describe each of these civilizations in detail. As examples, however, we will summarize the Mesopotamian sequence, and those of Egypt, the Indus Valley, and North China.

The Florescent Era: The Mesopotamian Sequence

The initial steps in the Mesopotamian development are the Jarmo, Hassuna, and Halafian assemblages discussed previously. These make up the Formative era, which is ultimately terminated by the Early Ubaid period. ▲ The Ubaid developments lead into the next major era, the Florescent.

The Early Ubaid Period (4500–3500 B.C.)

Perhaps the most important single event in the Ubaid period was the shift to irrigation agriculture. The agricultural system in the southern alluvial plains requires planting in September or October, with the major growth period awaiting the melt-water runoff the following April and May. During planting, the streams were at a low level, which required that the ditches be dug deeply to permit irrigation. Because the threat of silting of the canals was constant, large forces of organized labor were required to maintain the irrigation system. With irrigation came greater reliance on vegetables, dates, fish, and centralized herds.

Painted pottery is a prime diagnostic of the Ubaid period. ■ Plants, animals, and sweeping curves add a bit of life to the standard triangles, stripes, and cross-hatched designs. Ubaid pottery has a wide distribution in the Tigris and Euphrates valleys. In addition, more than 40 Ubaid sites are now known in the northeast province of Saudi Arabia (Masry 1975), Qatar, and Bahrain (Oates et al. 1977:221–234).

● At Eridu, Ubaid builders constructed temples of mud brick set in clay mortar. These edifices are constructed on a monumental scale and are indicative of the rise of a priestly class (Fig. 15-1). Certainly at Eridu the most imposing early

Fig. 15-1   Aerial view of the Elamite ziggurat located between Shulte and Shuster, Iran. The massive size of the artificial mound and its surrounding wall are clearly visible. (Courtesy of Aerofilms, Ltd.)

▲ Permanent urban settlements

■ Craft specialists

● Temples increase in size and complexity.

▲ A priestly class

■ Size of settlements

● Writing appears

▲ The cylinder seal

architecture is the temple complex, and there is a good possibility that other early Sumerian city sites will have Ubaid-period religious structures underlying their later architecture.

At this point we should clarify the nature of the archaeological data available. ▲ The Florescent era witnessed the rise of major permanent urban settlements, with structures of mud brick. These towns featured continuous occupation over a long period, with subsequent settlements being built on the remains of earlier ones. The result was a typical Mesopotamian feature: the tell, a hill constituted of layer upon layer of stratified urban remains (Fig. 15-2). With the tells being up to 63 feet in height (for example, Ras Shamra) and containing up to 30 distinct cultural layers, it is possible for the archaeologist to reconstruct a nearly continuous record of Mesopotamian civilization.

The Warka/Protoliterate Period (3500–2900 B.C.)

■ Advances in social organization in the Florescent era included increasing numbers of craft specialists. For example, the manufacture of copper into simple implements by casting is known from an Early Ubaid level at Tepe Gawra. During the subsequent Warka and Protoliterate periods we have the introduction of smelting and the use of closed molds. From this time on, copper weapons and ornaments increase in frequency, and the smith is increasingly a craft specialist. In addition, the potter's wheel was

introduced during the Warka period. Whereas the economy continued to be based on intensive agriculture, the tendency was toward increasing specialization by profession through time.

● Temples continued to grow in size and complexity; therefore stone masons, setters of mosaic, architects, and so forth were needed as full-time artisans. (As an example of the need for such specialists, it has been estimated that the A Zigguart at Warka took 1,500 men five years to build.) The temples are the most impressive features of the time, and a correspondingly great amount of archaeological attention has been devoted to their study. These structures were built of mud brick set occasionally on stone foundations. Part of the underlying foundation consisted of remains of earlier buildings. These mound foundations gave the temples their commanding setting, overlooking the entire community. A flight of steps led up to the long central room which had an offering table at one end and a broad platform at the other. Flanking the central room were smaller rooms. From the latter, ladders led to a higher story and from there to the roof. The temple's exterior was ornamented with projections and recesses.

Although the temples were of obvious importance, there is some doubt as to the nature of their function in the society. However, the temple buildings were known to have been used to store the communities' surplus crops. ▲ Since there is little evidence of any other centralized authority, the priests were the logical class capable of directing the large-scale irrigation projects. It has not even been determined at what point the role of the priesthood became a full-time specialty, but almost certainly this occurred within the Florescent era.

■ The size of settlements is not well known. One estimate of the population of Jemdet Nasr is 2,800. During this period population increased more rapidly in the southern alluvial plains, and communities were larger there than in the uplands of the north. Extensive trade was carried on between the two regions, but by this time the

Fig. 15-2 Ground-level view of the tell at Eridu, Mesopotamia, a stratified mound of occupational levels. On top *(bottom)* is the ziggurat built about 2000 B.C. by Ur-Nammur. (Beek 1962:33.)

major developments were originating in the alluvial south, primarily as a result of its tremendous agricultural productivity.

● Writing appeared during the Protoliterate period, about 3,200 B.C. The earliest examples of writing included accounts of quantities of goods, but before long the method was expanded to include lists of gods and other esoteric matters. The Mesopotamian system of writing in clay with a stylus, with the fired clay tablets then providing a permanent record, is a fascinating study in itself. The invention of writing is one of the major developments of civilization, since it provides a form of communication between generations which is not dependent upon the spoken word. With writing came records and accounts and thus the ability to assess taxes and all of the other responsibilities assigned to the individual by a centralized government. While such matters are not an unmixed blessing, it is clear how dependent upon writing civilization must be.

▲ We should also note here the development of the cylinder seal (Fig. 15-3). Small cylinders of stone or pottery were decorated with recessed figures which, when the cylinder was rolled upon damp clay, left a permanent impression. Seals were used as indications of ownership of the property belonging either to individuals or to the temples. Another possible function of seals was their representation of the owner in a religious sense, bearing a type of magical rela-

■ The Dynastic era in Mesopotamia

● Shift to the rule of kings

▲ Crafts production becomes more standardized.

■ The appearance of bronze

Fig. 15-3 Impressions made from Sumerian and Akkadian cylinder seals. *(Top)* A contest scene dated about 2650 B.C.; *(bottom)* a mythological scene, dated about 2300 B.C. (Courtesy of the British Museum.)

tionship to the owner's personality. Seals are among the most common artifacts of this period.

In summary, the Mesopotamian Florescent era possessed a society with strong economic controls, probably exercised by a theocracy, with developing urbanism and external trade relationships. The degree of private ownership is debatable. The most obvious candidate for political authority and the ownership of surplus property would be the temple and its associated priesthood.

The Early Dynastic Period (2900–2255 B.C.)

■ The Dynastic era reflects numerous developments which are more the result of social and political influences than of changes in the economic base. Therefore, the economy was not the important cause of events that it had been in prior eras; instead, we may view the economy as a constant. ● The important changes include a shift from theocratic rule to the secular rule of kings. This transition was accompanied by the appearance of palaces and royal tombs. The concept of royal privilege carried with it elaborate tombs, some with use of the true arch, containing valuable offerings. The latter included costly statuary, metal vessels, and even chariots. The concept of the intentional burial of wealth reveals that status was related to conspicuous consumption; and the afterlife needs of the ruler took precedence over the daily needs of his living constituents.

▲ Crafts continued to be elaborated, but the emphasis was on increased production rather than on acquiring new manufacturing tech-

niques or materials. ■ One exception was the development of bronze. Metallurgy consists of a set of highly specialized skills and techniques and is based on a very accurate knowledge of certain physical and chemical properties of substances. Metallurgy does not include the use of metals, such as gold and copper, which existed in a natural state and therefore were used in antiquity. Metallurgy consists of the knowledge that pure metals can be obtained from the ores, oxides, or sulphides of metals through the use of heat in a process called smelting. Secondly, metals so obtained are fusible and thus can be cast or formed into a variety of useful shapes. Thirdly, even when cold, many metals are still malleable and can be shaped. Finally, metallurgy depends on the knowledge that metals can have their characteristics changed by heating and cooling. If a metal is too brittle, heating and gradual cooling can soften it, whereas heating and quenching hot metal in cold water can harden it (a process called tempering). Perhaps the ultimate in metallurgical knowledge is alloying, which involves the combining of two or

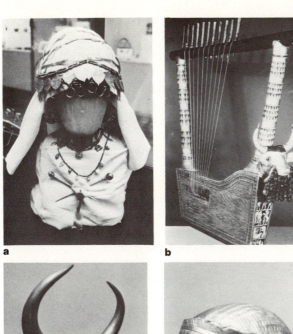

Fig. 15-4 Contents of the royal tombs at Ur. (*a*) Queen's headress; (*b*) harp; (*c*) gold vessels; (*d*) bull's-head ornament, probably from a harp; (*e*) helmet. [a, d, e] Courtesy of the British Museum; [b, c] courtesy of the University of Pennsylvania Museum.)

more metals to produce a new metal with characteristics that are different from those of the original materials. For example, copper, which is soft, is mixed with either tin or arsenic, both of which are brittle, to produce the alloy bronze. The latter is harder than copper and more malleable than either tin or arsenic.

Subsidiary skills required to make metals include prospecting, mining, and the transport of ores, which are not evenly distributed throughout the world. Metallurgy also requires high temperatures, which in turn requires knowledge of how to make charcoal and how to produce the high drafts needed to reduce the ores to metals. Commonly used devices include bellows and blow tubes. The adoption of metals and the acquisition of metallurgical knowledge seem to have been gradual, since along with craft specialization there was a segregation of craft products, with metal and stone being used for royal vessels (Fig. 15-4) and pottery being increasingly limited to the common people.

● The appearance of urbanism

▲ Sumer—one of the earliest civilizations.

■ Empires and city-states

● Steps in the development of urbanism

▲ Civilization does not depend upon the use of metal.

● Perhaps as important as any other single element at this time was the increase in population and increase in the density of settlement to the level of true urbanism. Sites covered up to 700 acres, and the populations of individual cities reached 20,000 to 30,000. The increase in the size of cities was the result both of actual population increase and of population *concentration* for purposes of defense. Warfare was, after all, a major feature of the period. A key factor leading to warfare included population increase, which possibly expanded to the limit of available resources. Early conflicts were fought by armies made up of craft guilds directed by their foremen, who in turn were responsible to palace officials. The lack of concern for permanent conquest of adjacent territories came to an end with the accession of the Akkadian Dynasty. After that date (2370 B.C.) major empires were established.

So far we have discussed the development of civilization as a series of stages, each with its primary characteristics. While this method has merit from the standpoint of classification, it tends to omit the human element. Civilization did not develop in a preordained manner dictated by some superorganic aspect of culture. Rather, it was the result of innovations made to solve the intimate problems in the daily lives of people, and we owe it to these people to give credit for their accomplishments by describing them in greater detail.

▲ The earliest of these civilizations was that of the Sumerians, peoples of the alluvial southern plains of Mesopotamia (Figure 17-6). The early development of Sumer, represented archae-ologically by period IV at Uruk and at Jemdet Nasr, begins at about 3200 B.C. These were levels representing true civilization, for they possessed writing, large irrigation projects, and other criteria which are accepted as evidence of civilization. The basic political unit of the Sumerians was the city-state, a territory of varying size with the city at its center as a religious, political, and administrative hub. The cities themselves consisted of mud brick buildings surrounded by city walls. Within the city the dominant structures were the temples and ziggurats (actually, artificial mountains of brick, the basis of the concept of the Tower of Babel). The city limits enclosed several square miles, and populations are estimated at from 50,000 to 100,000, with Ur as possibly the largest city. There were 15 to 20 of these city-states, and each extended its control over adjacent lands. The cities were economically interdependent but politically autonomous, and thus the conflicts among cities, while common, were not serious. The Sumerians provide our earliest written records of education, law, government, medicine, agriculture, philosophy, ethics, wisdom, and history (Kramer 1959). The Sumerian city-states came to an end with their conquest by Sargon of Akkad in 2370 B.C.

The Akkadian Period and Beyond (2370-2255 B.C.)

Under the leadership of Sargon, the kingdoms and city-states of Akkad and Sumer were united, and new emphases emerged. ■ The empire launched by Sargon lasted through several reigns, and Sumer as well as northern Mesopotamia were incorporated into one political unit. However, Sargon's empire ultimately collapsed under external pressure originating on the Iranian plateau.

The rest of Mesopotamian history is one of cities such as Babylon and Assur establishing kingdoms, expanding into empires that incorporated most if not all of Mesopotamia, and then collapsing as a result of external pressure and internal dissensions.

The City

Urbanism is a process intimately linked to the rise of civilization. In Mesopotamia the growth of urbanization has been analyzed in order to isolate the processes at work. Several major features are cited by Adams (1973) as relevant. ● The growth of urbanism in Mesopotamia was differential both in the time of its appearance and its duration, and several patterns of development are evidenced. In the pre-urban period, during which the pattern was less varied, settlements were of types labeled small towns, villages, and hamlets and were evenly distributed over the landscape. The next step was the depopulation of much of the alluvial plain, with people shifting to residence in the cities. The emphasis was on forced or persuaded resettlement. The settlements did not nucleate due to population growth, although the population was increasing. What occurred was a politically motivated restructuring of the existing society. In Adams's view this modification was artificial and was carried out for the benefit of a small oligarchy with a strong political motivation. Thus the actual size of the cities may reflect the political organization rather than any inherent environmental facts.

Life in the city had disadvantages for the common citizen, since he was subject to demands for communal labor in agriculture and in the construction of public buildings. He also paid taxes and was subject to military conscription. A final detrimental factor was the increase in urban epidemic disease. One result of the negative effects of urbanism was that the individual citizens remained in the city under at least partial duress and, further, did not truly participate in many of the social institutions associated with urban life. Nonetheless, the trend toward urban-

ism was very strong with the result that by the Dynastic period nearly a quarter of all settlements in Mesopotamia were cities.

The Mesopotamian Accomplishments

The Mesopotamian economy was based upon intensive-irrigation agriculture of grain crops. This was the time during which the maximum agricultural potential of the region was attained. Subsequently, the productivity of the region deteriorated, owing to the increase in evaporated salts in the soil. Probably the major feature of the economy was the degree of organization and control of the irrigation system. Such control in the production of food was essential to the development of urbanism and the support of crafts specialists.

In this chapter we have ignored the archaeological subdivision termed the "Bronze Age." Although bronze was an important commodity and its appearance provides a useful archaeological index fossil, the major developments of the times were in the social and political realm. ▲ We should therefore comprehend that while bronze containers, weapons, and other implements were functionally useful, they do not in themselves bring about the important characteristics of civilization; that is, urbanism, political autonomy, and such. The Sumerians were capable craftsmen in metal, having learned to alloy tin and copper to produce bronze at about the beginning of the Dynastic period. They are credited with the invention of the closed mold and the lost-wax technique of casting, which appeared in about 2500 B.C. They also worked in gold, silver, and lead, and after 3000 B.C. they manufactured in iron on a small scale. Since metal ores do not occur in Mesopotamia, an elaborate system of trade relations with Asia Minor, Syria, Cappadocia, Oman, and Afghanistan was necessary. Besides metals, items of trade included lapis lazuli, shells, cedar, pine, and stone

■ Other features of Mesopotamian civilization

● The development of Egyptian civilization is an enigma.

▲ The Dynastic era appears suddenly.

■ Middle Eastern influence in Egypt

for statuary. The Sumerians are also credited with the invention of the wheel. First used in turning pottery, the wheel had been adapted to use on carts by 3000 B.C. The earliest writing dates to Uruk IV (3200–3100 B.C.), as documented by the finding of 500 to 600 clay tablets. Largely pictographic, these early tablets functioned as inventories or receipts of products.

a

b

c

Fig. 15-5 Mesopotamian architecture and sculpture: (*a*) From Nineveh, a wounded lioness: the scene celebrates the hunting prowess of Ashurbanipal, king of Assyria, 668–630 B.C. (*b*) the towers on the west side of the Ishtar gate at Babylon, showing the sculptures in relief 604–562 B.C. (*c*) the man-headed, winged bulls from Khorsabad, Iraq, flanking the entrance to the central portal: shown as found during excavation, these date to the Assyrian period, ca. 722–705 B.C. ([*a*] Courtesy of the British Museum; [*b,c*] Courtesy of the Oriental Institute, the University of Chicago.)

■ Among the myriad other Sumerian accomplishments are the plow, sculpture (Fig. 15-5) in the round (i.e., three-dimensional); calendars; and a system of mathematics, including a method of dividing the circle. The Sumerians wove garments, built boats, brewed beer, made music on harps, raced chariots, and maintained an elaborate religion. Each city probably had a patron deity as well as a pantheon of gods, to whom the temples were dedicated. Built of plano-convex-shaped adobe bricks, some temples were as large as 245 by 100 feet, with the associated ziggurat standing even taller. The Sumerians produced the world's first civilization, and we shall find evidence of the spreading influence of cultural ideas from Sumer as we review the developments of other early civilizations.

Civilization in Ancient Egypt

Egypt has been termed the "Gift of the Nile," which is both accurate and redundant, for in most respects the Nile Valley and Egypt are identical. Geographically, the situation is little different today from the time of the pharaohs. Approximately 97 percent of the modern nation consists of uninhabited desert, which through time has functioned to isolate the Nile Valley from other regions nearby. Our concepts of the life of Ancient Egypt are based on the world-famous remains consisting primarily of tombs and temples dedicated to the gods or to the royal family. The way of life of the common people is still inadequately known, although we have wall paintings and other evidence from the tombs of the nobles. ● We also know less than we would like of the origins of ancient Egyptian civilization.

It is possible, with some stretching, to fit Egypt into the Formative-Florescent-Dynastic model used for Mesopotamia. Obviously, the earlier Neolithic manifestations previously described fit rather well into the Formative period, while the later, pharaonic Egypt fits equally well into the Dynastic portion of the model. The problem is to determine just what fits into the Florescent period. It is standard archaeological opinion that plant and animal domestication were introduced from the Fertile Crescent. These introductions first appear in the Badarian, Amratian, and Naqadan cultures, which date from about 4000 B.C. or even earlier. These "Predynastic" cultures were the antecedents of the Dynastic civilization, and they were peopled by village dwellers with a mixed economy featuring hunting, fishing, farming, and animal husbandry (Map 15-2). Through studies of the pottery Sir Flinders Petrie was able to demonstrate that these Predynastic peoples were in fact the direct ancestors of the first Dynasty. Thus in Egypt we go directly from the Predynastic to the Dynastic period. ▲ Archaeologically, there must still be omissions in the record since the appearance of the Dynastic manifestations seems abrupt, with little advance notice that a major civilization had been developing (Map 15-3).

Narmer, the first pharaoh of the First Dynasty, unified Egypt into one nation, a land which traditionally had been divided into Upper and Lower Egypt (Emery 1961). The First Dynasty, which began about 3200 B.C., introduced royal tombs of great size, writing, stone vessels, and artifacts of both copper, bronze and ivory (15-6). Such manifestations imply a long progression, but here the archaeological record is inadequate. This "missing" but implied period of development may constitute at least part of the Florescent stage defined earlier.

One explanation is that the development of Egyptian civilization occurred in the Nile Delta and has subsequently been covered by thick layers of alluvium. ■ Another hypothesis is that the ideas leading to civilization radiated outward from Sumer and influenced such indigenous cultures as the Egyptian Predynastic, thereby leading to a rapid development. Probably, both explanations have a basis in fact. With respect to the Delta theory one line of evidence cites the fact that in hieroglyphics the symbols for right and left are the same as those for west and east.

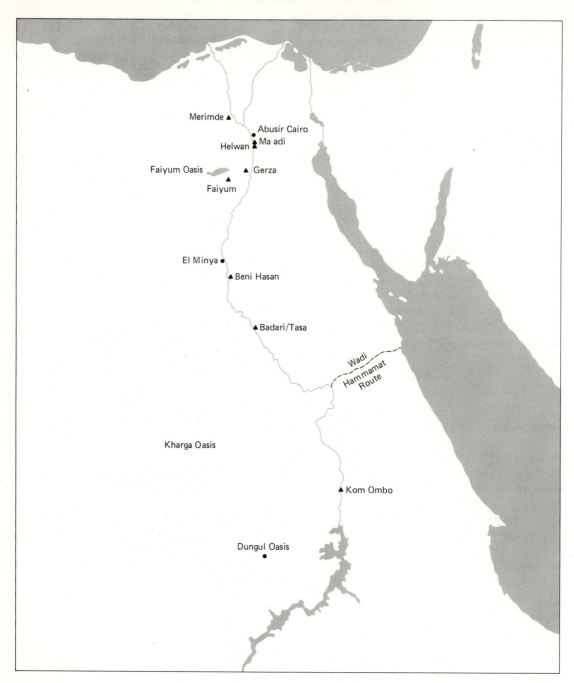

Map 15-2 Sites of Predynastic Egypt.

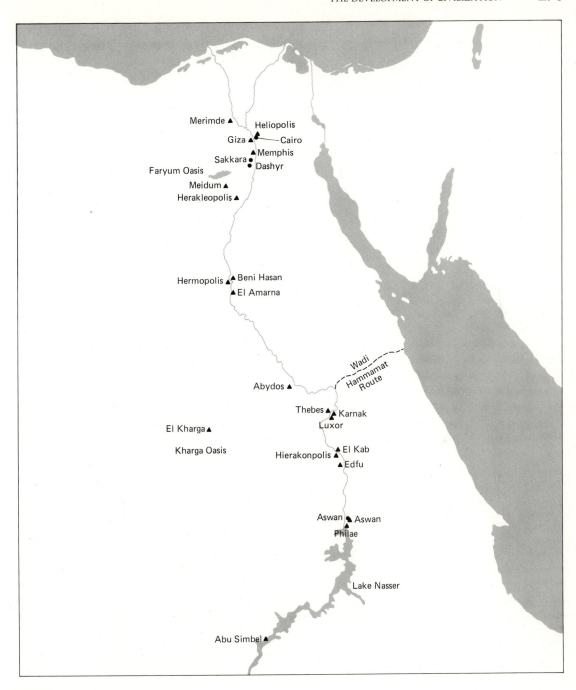

Map 15-3 Sites of Dynastic
Egypt.

● Central aspects of Egyptian civilization

▲ The Egyptians lived in villages, not cities.

■ We know much about the everyday life.

This suggests an origin of Egyptian writing in the Delta, with a cultural orientation facing upstream. Archaeological evidence of Sumerian influence includes three cylinder seals from the Uruk period. Subsequently, the Egyptians engraved their own seals. Some engravings feature Mesopotamian art styles. (For example, a Gilgamesh type of culture hero is shown on an ivory knife handle from Begel-el-Arak.) Finally, the introduction of mud brick dramatically changed Egyptian architecture. Writing is the other major trait with Sumerian priority.

The Early Dynastic period is subdivided into (1) the Archaic period (Dynasties I and II, (3200–2700 B.C.) and (2) the Old Kingdom (Dynasties III–VI, 2700–2160 B.C.). The archaeological record gives little evidence that the Archaic was a developing civilization. On the other hand, we know that during the Archaic period there was political turmoil and religious unrest (Emery 1961). (For example, the royal tombs at Saqqara were burned and long-established, popular gods such as Set were downgraded and replaced by deities associated with the sun.) It might be reasonable to include the Archaic period in the Florescent stage as well as the little-known Predynastic development already described above.

By the beginning of the Old Kingdom (Egyptian Dynasties III through VI) the pharaoh ruled supreme. Further, since he was considered to be a living god, he also exercised divine supremacy. His authority was supreme in the region from the first cataract at Aswan northward to the Mediterranean. It was during the Old Kingdom that the largest pyramids in Egypt were built. These are clearly a testimony to the pharaoh's power and to the ability of the state to undertake large-scale public works early in the Dynastic period.

● Certain themes persist in Egyptian history. The first theme is that of the long succession of dynasties (33 in all) lasting for the better part of 3,000 years, during which art, literature, engineering, and science remain remarkably constant after their initial development in the Archaic and Old Kingdom periods. The second theme is one of extended periods of strong central authority followed by temporary collapses

Fig. 15-6 An ivory statuette of an early (1st Dynasty) Egyptian Pharoah wearing the crown of upper Egypt and the dress worn by kings at their jubilee festivals, 1st Dynasty, about 3100 B.C. (Courtesy of the British Museum.)

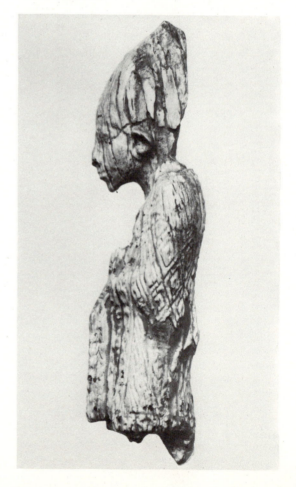

Fig. 15-7 Aerial view of the great pyramids at Giza, Egypt, just west of modern Cairo. Also present are rows of mastaba tombs and numerous other features not visible in this photo, including the Sphinx and subsurface chambers for the solar boats. (Courtesy of Aerofilms, Ltd.)

and then the reestablishment of strong central authority. Finally, Egypt always has had a strong interest in the Middle East, and particularly Palestine. During the Old Kingdom cedar from Lebanon was imported for use in coffins and for shipbuilding. Later, external threats to Egypt's security came from the Middle East. It is thus no accident that during the New Kingdom period, when Egypt was a world power, her empire was expanded through conquest to include the Middle East.

The Egyptian Life-Style

▲ The Egyptians differed from the Sumerians in many ways. The Egyptian population lived in villages rather than in cities, and although Egypt was densely populated, it was not in a strict sense urban. (At least we have limited evidence of true cities.) The populace was well-organized, as enormous quantities of labor were required to build the pyramids and other public works. For

example, thousands of workers must have been necessary to build the pyramid of Cheops which contains 2 million blocks weighing up to 15 tons apiece (Fig. 15-7). However, although population density was high, it was essentially distributed over many peasant-farming villages strung along the Nile rather than in urban centers.

Evidence of life in Ancient Egypt is derived from several sources. First, there are the buildings themselves—the pyramids and other tombs, temples, forts, and domestic dwellings. ■There are paintings on tomb walls, bas-relief carvings, and the small models of aspects of everyday life in wood or clay which made up part of the tomb offerings. Because so much of what we know about the life-style of the ancient Egyptians is derived from tombs and tomb paintings, there is the tendency to assume the Egyptians had a morbid fascination with death. Nothing could be further from the truth. Tomb building, mummification, and all the accompanying rituals had only one purpose: the preser-

277

● Temples had specialized functions.

▲ Tombs ranged from simple to elaborate.

vation of the body (and hence of the soul) so that the dead could continue throughout eternity those activities and pastimes they had enjoyed in life.

The towns evolved from small, walled units which in early times were circular and which later were rectangular. Within the town walls, the house blocks had segregated uses. A few sites approach urbanism. For example, at Tell el Amarna there were rows of three-room house blocks with streets between them. Near the pyramid complexes rows of small uniform houses were built for the occupancy of the workers. At Giza these were of brick and were of identical size, 164 square meters per unit. The lack of interior furnishings and trash suggests that these units were kept clean in response to a royal decree.

Middle-class houses from the Third Dynasty feature a vestibule, a small closet, a hall, living room, and a bedroom. The models from the tombs feature several house types, the simplest of which is a rectangular enclosure of several rooms with an awning at the rear. Another type has two stories with terraces in front. There is an associated courtyard, with a water basin, an oven, and grain bins. The roofs were of vaulted brick, windows were small and high, and at the top of the roof were small ventilation cupolas. There were granaries formed by rows of domed mud bins. The bins were filled at the top and had a small trapdoor at the bottom for the removal of the grain. Rows of pottery jars were set in racks for food and water storage. Latrines were built within the houses. Houses of the Middle Kingdom consisted of large rectangular units with many rooms facing onto a street; also associated were enclosed courtyards. Analysis of the change in house type through time would provide one means of studying changes in family composition in Ancient Egypt through time.

The temples held a core position in the religious life of the people. Because of the concern of each pharaoh to dedicate new temples during his reign, these came to dominate the daily life of the common people as well. ● Several forms of temples were built, each of which had a specialized function. These included cult temples, sun temples, and mortuary temples. The cult temples were dedicated to a specific god, who was represented by a statue of gilded wood or stone placed at the rear of the temple. The building plan was rectangular, symmetrical, and divided into three parts. Major associated features included courtyards with rows of support columns (the hypostyle hall), an inner sanctuary with only one door (which was manned by a priest), and pylon-type gateways (Fig. 15-8). Another feature was a crypt for valuable offerings. A solar boat for the use of the pharaoh in his afterlife journey (Fig. 15-8) was also a common addition. Sun temples were rectangular-walled structures open to the sky. There was no cult statue and therefore no need for a sanctuary. There was an altar and frequently an obelisk, a stone monument symbolic of the sun's rays.

Mortuary temples were the scene of mortuary services. The typical arrangement consisted of a building termed a "valley portal," located at the edge of the Nile. Leading from this portal was a causeway to the mortuary temple several hundred meters distant. The mortuary temple was adjacent to the pyramid tomb, and the features of the former included a false door facing east with an offering table behind it for the food needed in the afterlife. Facing the table was a statue of the deceased. More elaborate decorations within the temple included wall murals illustrating the daily life of the deceased.

▲ Tombs were of three types. In general order of appearance from early to late, they include mastabas, pyramids, and rock-cut tombs. The mastaba was a rectangular superstructure

Fig. 15-8 Details of Pharonic civilization. (Photographs courtesy of Philip M. Hobler.)

A pylon or massive city gate, carved in bas relief illustrating the deeds of the Pharoah who had it built.

Remnants of a hypostyle hall with one massive papyrus column standing to its original height, Temple of Karnak, Luxor.

Bas relief carving from the wall of a tomb.

Facade of the temple of Nefertari cut into the bedrock sandstone at Abu Simbel.

(Left) Subtarranean crypt which contained a solar boat at the pyramid complex of Giza, near Cairo. (Right) Nubian slaves with ropes tied around their necks. Bas relief carving from the main temple built by Ramses II at Abu Simbel.

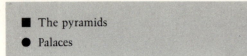

■ The pyramids
● Palaces

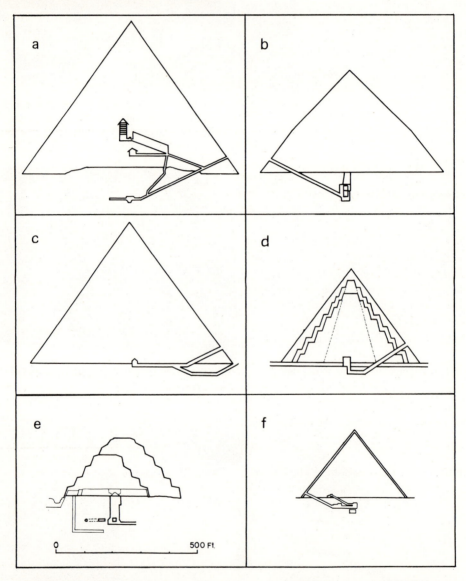

Fig. 15-9 Profiles of the largest and best-known ancient Egyptian pyramids. All drawn to the same scale, they illustrate details of construction and the complex of galleries used for burials. (*a*) Great Pyramid of Cheops; (*b*) Bent Pyramid at Dashur; (*c*) Pyramid of Chephren; (*d*) Pyramid at Meidum; (*e*) Step Pyramid at Saqqara (the earliest true pyramid); (*f*) Pyramid of Mycerinus.

built of massive brickwork and surrounded by an enclosing wall. The burial chamber was initially inside but later was expanded into an underground substructure with a central chamber surrounded by storage compartments. The early mastabas were designed with a single burial chamber, but later two chambers were common. By the Fourth Dynasty the mastabas were situated at the western desert edge of the Nile and arranged in orderly rows.

■ Pyramids are the most impressive tombs build in Ancient Egypt. Since they are also the best known, there is less need to describe them in great detail. These massive structures with a variety of internal features have led to Edwards's (1961) specialized text on the subject. The pyramids were built of huge stone blocks set closely together. Sir Flinders Petrie measured the gap between blocks as averaging 1/50th of an inch. The typical slant of the pyramid exterior is 52°. Within each pyramid was a tunnel leading to a burial chamber. Other features include false tunnels and chambers to distract tomb robbers (Fig. 15-9). The actual construction relied on mass labor and use of simple tools. According to Badawy (1966:52):

> The technical excellence of the masonry owes more to the ability of the craftsmen than to the use of mechanical devices more elaborate than sledges hauled up ramps, windlasses and pulleys for lifting and transporting, adzes, chisels, saws, drills, and polishing stones for dressing and finishing the stone blocks.

The dimensions of the larger pyramids are enormous (Fig. 15-7) and are among the wonders of the world. The development of the pyramids can be traced from the early stepped form, such as that at Saqqara, to a unique specimen at Dashur (the Bent Pyramid, with its two separate angles of incline), and finally to the true pyramidal form first exemplified at Meidum (Fig. 15-9). By the fifth and sixth Dynasties pyramids were smaller and less well built. Although they continued to be constructed during the New King-

dom, they were no longer a royal prerogative, and the pharaohs were buried in rock-cut tombs.

Rock-cut tombs were developed at the end of the Old Kingdom and were first used by the nobles. These feature greater security than mastabas and even more than pyramids, since the entrance may be more easily concealed. During the New Kingdom the royal tombs as well as those of the nobles were cut into the living rock. The necropolis at Thebes, located on the west bank of the Nile, is the best-known burial area, with the pharaohs buried in the Valley of the Kings (Fig. 15-10), their families in a nearby valley, and between the two an area reserved for tombs of the nobles.

Badawy (1966:55) describes a New Kingdom royal tomb as follows:

> It consists of a slightly slanting corridor with three offset stretches flanked by niches; passing through an antechamber, the corridor is intercepted by shafts and ends in a sarcophagus chamber.

● Badawy's (1966:31) description of the palaces of Amenhotep III provides a glimpse of the nature of these structures.

> In the so-called palace of the king the official quarters feature a few columned audience halls, each with a throne on a dais along the east wall, a staircase to the upper floor or terrace, a large central hall with two rows of columns arranged symmetrically with four separate suites for *harim* ladies on each side and a royal suite at the rear (south). The kitchens are in a separate block between this palace and another one to the south. Paintings and decorative moldings in applique lavishly cover the walls with scenes from official life or with images of the household genius Bes; floors are decorated with the representation of pools, plants, and birds, and ceilings have rows of flying vultures and geometric patterns. Each suite in itself forms a complete dwelling based on the tripartite plan and featuring a front columned vestibule, a central hypostyle hall with a canopied throne, a closet, a bedroom and a robing room.

▲ Ancient India featured cities.

The above complex covered an area of 350 by 270 meters and featured a T-shaped lake connected to the Nile.

A final type of public structure was the fort. Constructed of mud brick, its walls followed the natural contours of a defensive location. Within the walls were public buildings, granaries, barracks, and a temple. A further refinement was the inclusion of bastions in the walls.

We have confined our description to the major features of Egyptian civilization, especially the monumental remains. Much has necessarily been omitted, as, for example, the burial

ceremonies and the mummification process. The elaborate crafts included the carved painted wooden sarcophagi, the tomb furniture, jewelry, and monumental stone statuary. All attest to the complexity of material culture. For details of these findings numerous well-illustrated popular works on the subject are available.

Civilization in the Indus Valley

In the Indus Valley region, within what are now the modern nations of India and Pakistan, another major civilization arose after 2500 B.C.

Fig. 15-10 The tomb of Seti I in the Valley of the Kings, west of Luxor, Egypt. (Leacroft and Leacroft 1963:11.)

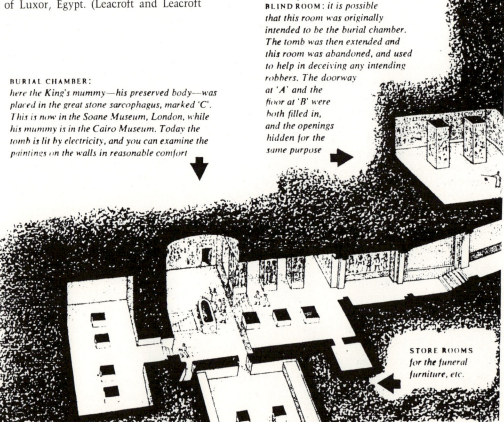

BURIAL CHAMBER:
here the King's mummy—his preserved body—was placed in the great stone sarcophagus, marked 'C'. This is now in the Soane Museum, London, while his mummy is in the Cairo Museum. Today the tomb is lit by electricity, and you can examine the paintings on the walls in reasonable comfort

BLIND ROOM: *it is possible that this room was originally intended to be the burial chamber. The tomb was then extended and this room was abandoned, and used to help in deceiving any intending robbers. The doorway at 'A' and the floor at 'B' were both filled in, and the openings hidden for the same purpose*

STORE ROOMS *for the funeral furniture, etc.*

(Fairservis 1975) (Map 15-4). Two of the major centers were at Mohenjo-daro and Harappa, and the latter is the name given to this culture. The origins of the Indus civilization are not clear, but they seem to be based primarily on local developments. We also infer that cultural ideas spreading outward from Sumer may have shaped developments in the Indus Valley.

We cannot apply the Formative-Florescent-Dynastic model to the Indus Valley culture since we do not have solid evidence of its origins. Furthermore, we do not know the nature of its religious orientation or of its political structure. Such evidence is probably present in the script, since this was a literate society, but this script has not yet been deciphered.

▲ The major cities are urban (Fig. 15-11), with large, rectangular house blocks joined into larger contiguous units separated by streets. The public buildings, such as the communal granaries, baths, assembly halls, and religious structures, were frequently segregated into a separate area termed a "citadel." We perceive many cultural elements here which, while not identical to Sumerian traits, are similar. These include seals, mud brick architecture, wheeled carts, stone statuary, and the art of casting in bronze. Even the division of cities into residential areas and ceremonial centers has Sumerian counterparts. Major features in the Indus sites are the grid pattern of the streets, the use of built-in garbage containers, and brick-lined drains in the

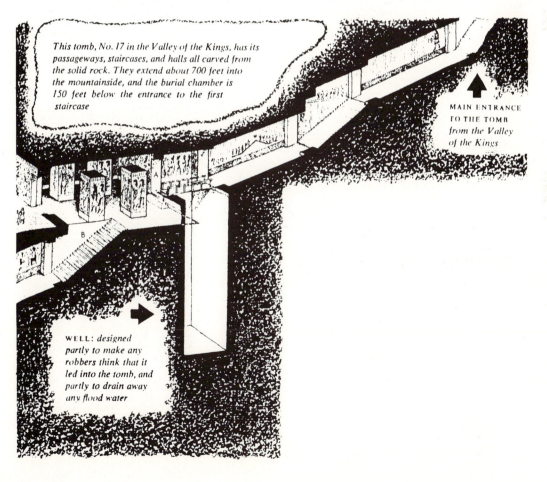

This tomb, No. 17 in the Valley of the Kings, has its passageways, staircases, and halls all carved from the solid rock. They extend about 700 feet into the mountainside, and the burial chamber is 150 feet below the entrance to the first staircase

MAIN ENTRANCE TO THE TOMB from the Valley of the Kings

WELL: designed partly to make any robbers think that it led into the tomb, and partly to drain away any flood water

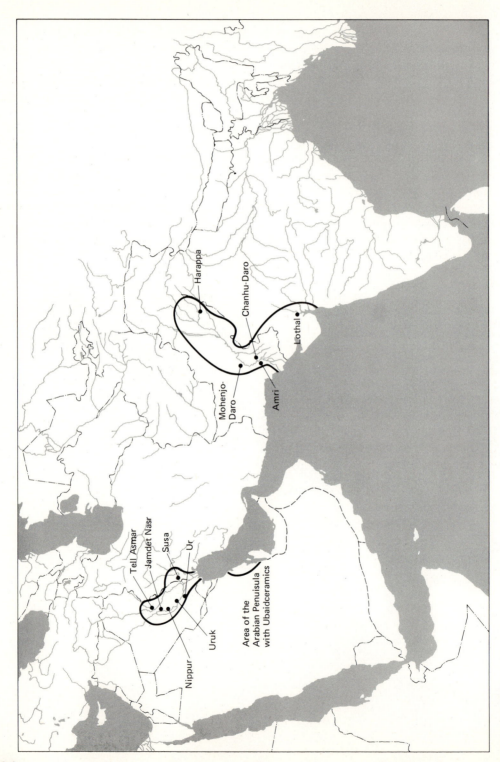

Map 15-4 Distribution of the Indus Valley Civilization with its main sites.

Harappa

Chanhu-Daro

Lothal

Mohenjo-Daro

Amri

Tell Asmar

Jamdet Nasr

Susa

Ur

Uruk

Nippur

Area of the Arabian Penuisula with Ubaidceramics

streets. There were bathrooms in the houses. The houses themselves were somewhat monotonous in their regularity.

Another major difference concerns the geographic spread of Indus civilization. The cities were not restricted to a small area, as in Sumer and Ancient Egypt. Instead, the 70 or so major Indus sites extended over an area of 1,500 km from north to south. This represents a half-million square miles, which easily makes it geographically the largest of the ancient civilizations.

The economy featured the familiar Middle Eastern crops plus some interesting Asian additions. These people grew wheat, six-rowed barley, sesame, dates, melons, cotton, and peas. Domestic animals included cattle, ass, horse, buffalo, and camel. We might point out here that the camel, today considered one of the diagnostic characteristics of Egypt, was actually domesticated in western Asia and was introduced into the Nile Valley in about 500 B.C. by the Persians.

The archaeological importance of the Indus civilization may be assessed in several ways. The ruins themselves are massive and are a clear indication of a major urban population. Within the centers, craft specialists were at work pro-

Fig. 15-11 Plans of the major cities of the Harappan civilization, Mohenjo-daro, Hapappa, and Kalibangan, with a detail of the former showing streets and nucleated houses indicative of urbanism. (Schwartsberg, J. E. 1978.)

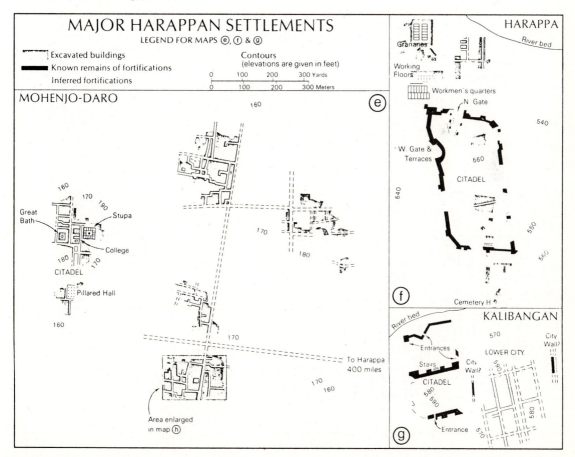

■ Bronze implements were common.

ducing seals, pottery, and bronzes, as well as continuing an industry in well-made, stone-bladed tools. ■ The copper and bronze implements included tanged knives, axe and chisel blades, mirrors, fishhooks, spear and arrow points, a range of jars, vases, bowls, and even a handled pan of skillet form (Fig. 15-12). The bronze vessels were similar in form to the pottery vessels.

The Indus Valley civilization is very similar to modern Asian city-based societies wherein large cities are surrounded by small settlements. For example, Mohenjo-daro and Harappa each covered several hundred hectares, whereas their surrounding hamlets rarely exceeded 10 hectares (25 acres) in area. There are no intermediate-sized cities in this culture (15-13).

The major concerns of the Indus civilization seem to have been internal rather than being focused on external conquest and expansion. According to Daniel (1968:114, Figure 9), trade, although widespread, was limited to small objects, including pottery, seals, beads, and other small artifacts. While these items have been found as

(Fig. 15-11 continued.)

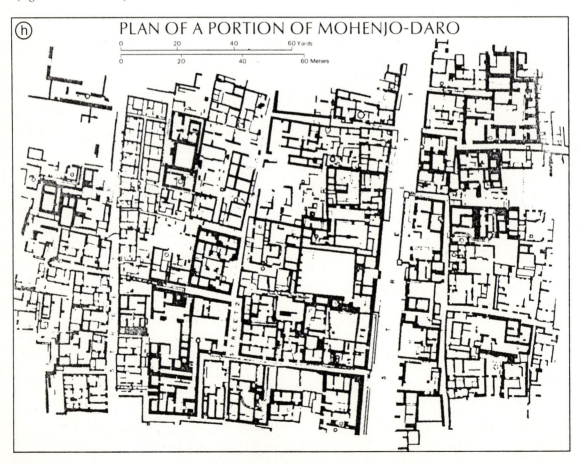

PLAN OF A PORTION OF MOHENJO-DARO

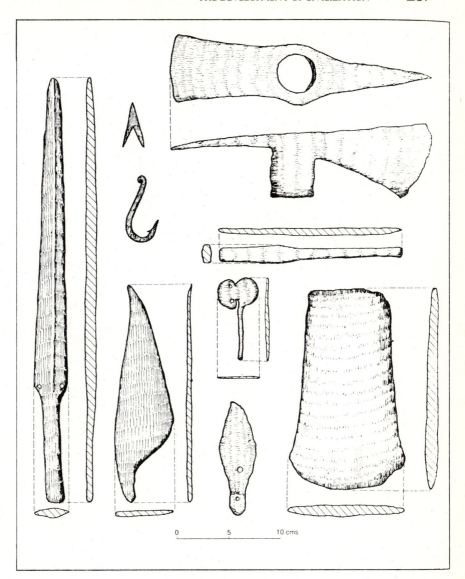

Fig. 15-12 Copper and bronze weapons and tools from Mohenjo-daro. (Schwartsberg, J. E. 1978.)

far away as northern Iraq, they are all indicative of limited trade and thus of technological independence.

Another characteristic of this society is that although it developed suddenly, once established, there was little further cultural change. We are impressed with the cultural uniformity over a long period of time, including the standardization of brick form and size. The sites themselves possess little individuality, and it is not certain that the major sites functioned as true capitals or city-states. Uniformity and conservatism are also evident in the crafts.

After a period of decline marked by reuse of bricks and less city planning, the Indus Valley culture disintegrated in about 1900 B.C. Possible causes cited for its collapse include repeated flooding by the Indus, course alterations in the

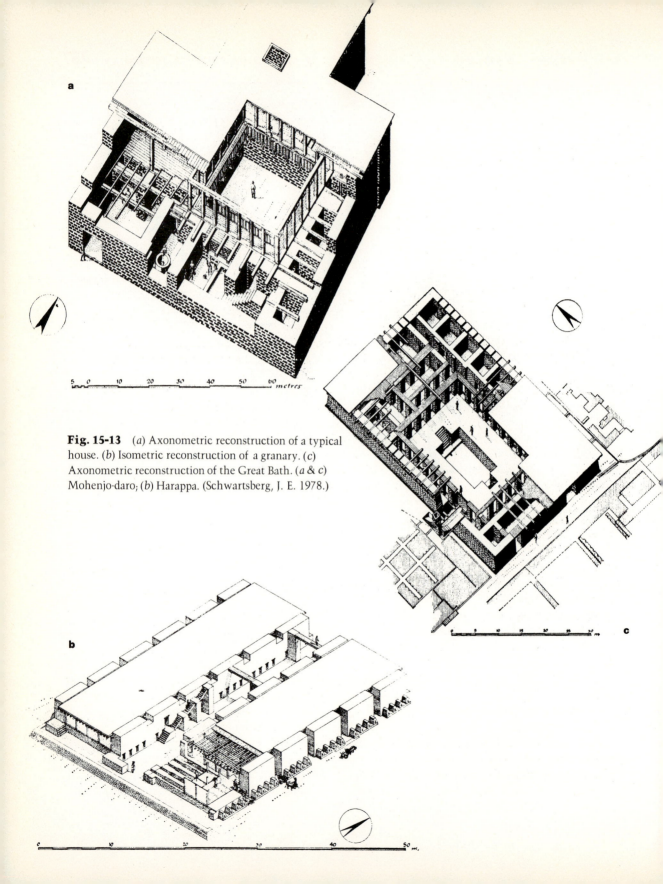

Fig. 15-13 (*a*) Axonometric reconstruction of a typical house. (*b*) Isometric reconstruction of a granary. (*c*) Axonometric reconstruction of the Great Bath. (*a* & *c*) Mohenjo-daro; (*b*) Harappa. (Schwartsberg, J. E. 1978.)

● Scapulimancy with oracle bones

river, and invasion of Indo-European-speaking peoples from the northwest—the Aryans. Further archaeological research is required before these causal factors can be properly evaluated.

Civilization in Ancient China

The earliest civilization in China, the Shang, (Shang) is found in the Valley of the Huang Ho ("Yellow River") and dates to between 1600 B.C. and 1026 B.C. The Shang civilization is a direct outgrowth of the preceding Neolithic farming-village culture, and ultimately it in turn was supplanted by the feudalistic Zhou (Chou) period (1027–256 B.C.). Once again, we have a situation in which the Formative-Florescent-Dynastic model is applicable with some degree of success. Again for clarity, we would place the various Chinese Neolithic cultures in the Formative stage, the Shang Bronze period in the Florescent stage, and the feudal Chou period in the Dynastic stage. Unfortunately, the archaeological record is not quite this clear-cut. While the main outline holds true, there are traits and characteristics of the late Neolithic that would have to be placed in the Florescent stage and some aspects of the Shang obviously fit into the Dynastic stage.

Shang Dynasty: The Age of Bronze (1523–1027 B.C.)

The Shang Dynasty is marked by the appearance of urbanism, bronze casting, writing, and human sacrifice. Shang people lived in large walled cities, such as Anyang (Anyang). They were ruled by kings who possessed chariots and elaborate cast-bronze vessels, owned slaves, and were buried in elaborate tombs.

The economy was agricultural, exploiting the rich valley floor. Major crops were millet, rice, and wheat. There was a variety of others as well: broad beans, water chestnut, peanut, sesame, melon, peach, and sour date (Chang 1973:527). Domestic animals were cattle, pig, sheep, dog, chicken, and horse. In addition, silkworms were kept, and clothing was woven of silk as well as of hemp.

Truly unique items, of which at least 100,000 examples have been recovered, are inscribed bones and tortoise shells covered with writing ideographs (Fig. 15-14). ● These specimens were used in the ancient art of scapulimancy or fortune telling (Chou 1979). In producing these oracular objects, a hot-pointed piece of metal was applied to a pit that had been specially cut on the inscribed side of the bone. As a result, cracks appeared on the back of the object. The cracks so generated were then interpreted by fortune-tellers. It has been suggested that the shape of the prepared pit might have governed to some degree the form of the cracks and thus the pre-

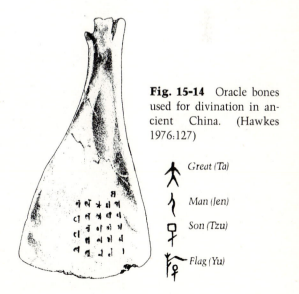

Fig. 15-14 Oracle bones used for divination in ancient China. (Hawkes 1976:127)

Great (Ta)

Man (Jen)

Son (Tzu)

Flag (Yu)

▲ Royal tombs

■ How did Shang bronze casting originate?

dictions. Most of the answers requested could be given in terms of yes or no. In any event, these oracle bones were used for predicting weather, the fate of crops, other agricultural matters, and military concerns. They were also consulted to resolve all of the private matters of the king, including questions concerning his health, the health of his family, the future, and so on. Daniel (1968:130) relates the example of Kin Wu-ting, who even consulted the oracle to determine which of his ancestors was responsible for his toothache.

▲ Eleven elaborate and complex royal tombs with human sacrifices have been recovered at Anyang (Figs. 15-15, 15-16). These cruciform tombs vary in size, with the largest being just a little over 100 meters in length. Each consists of a square pit with an access ramp leading to the

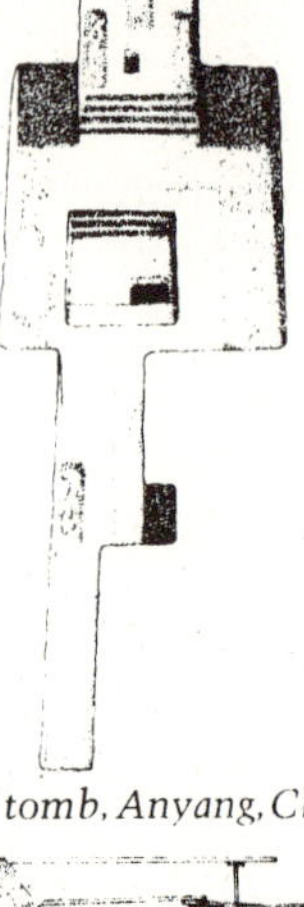

Fig. 15-15 Plan of a royal tomb Anyang, China, and a reconstruction of a Shang period house. (Hawkes 1976: 131.)

Royal tomb, Anyang, China

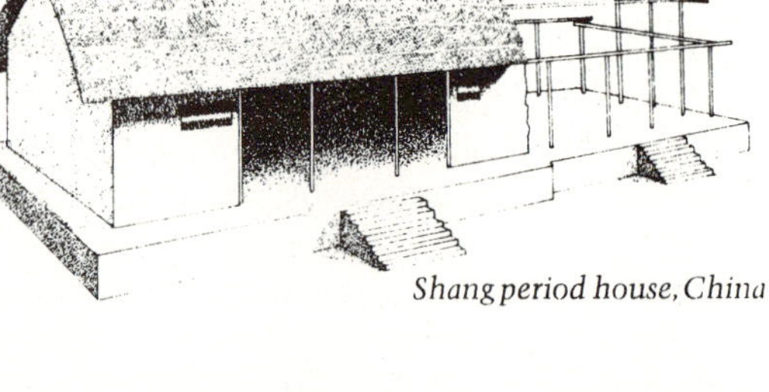

Shang period house, China

Fig. 15-16 Example of a Shang/Chou dynasty chariot burial. The wooden portions of the chariots had rotted away, but the archaeologists were able to perserve the impressions in the soil as they were found. The museum building was then constructed around the find. (Photograph courtesy of H. M. Wormington.)

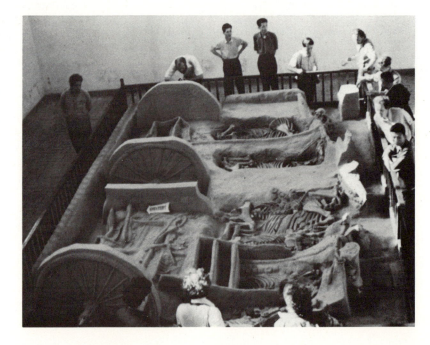

central burial. John Hay (1973:62–63) has described the construction of such a tomb:

When the king died, a great pit was marked out, 45 1/2 feet (14 metres) long and 39 feet (12 metres) wide. The earth from its excavation was brought out along two ramps, cut progressively into the northern and southern sides. In later burial custom the southern side had ritual priority. This must have been so even in Shang times, for when the pit was nearly 15 feet (4.7 metres) deep, the northern ramp was no longer used. With access from the south the pit was continued to a total depth of 23 feet (7.2 metres). In the centre of its floor a small "waist pit" was dug. This gateway to the underworld was then protected by the sacrificial burial of an armed warrior. Over his body a wooden floor to the main tomb chamber was laid. On this were placed four great beams to form a rectangle in the pit. The space between these beams and the sides of the pit was then filled with earth and pounded firm. This was repeated with a further eight sets of beams, thus building a massive wooden chamber, 8 1/2 feet (2.5 metres) deep, surrounded by a platform of pounded earth. Presumably at this stage the king's corpse, already encoffined, was lowered into the chamber and surrounded with royal treasure. Above him the chamber was roofed with timbers, elaborately carved, inlaid and painted.

The king departed with terror in his train. On the platform of beaten earth around his chamber were laid the corpses of many compelled to follow. In the Wu-kuan-ts'un tomb twenty-four skeletons were found on the west side and seventeen on the east. They were accompanied by many objects, those on the west more ornamental and those on the east more warlike, and the skeletons must be female and male respectively. Probably they were of the king's own household, for they clearly have their own rank. The one in the centre of each side is principal, accompanied by many bronze, jade and bone objects and even a sacrificial dog. They, like some of the others, were buried in a coffin. These unfortunates must have been dispatched with care beforehand, for unlike many sacrificial burials, the corpses had been decently laid to rest.

The two entrance ramps were now protected by four dogs at the lower end of each. Higher up both ramps three pits were dug to receive sixteen horses, the ready-bridled teams for eight chariots. Between the horses squatted two armed warriors. Still the terror was inexorable, witnessed in reverse by the archaeologists. Over the array of corpses the pounding of earth began again. Many other animals, especially monkeys and deer, were buried in the process. Men were decapitated and their heads were placed in successive layers of pounded earth. Thirty-four skulls were found, all facing the centre. South of the tomb, seventeen exactly ordered subsidiary graves were located. They contained 160 headless skeletons and were unaccompanied by any objects. The connection with the skulls seems obvious and suggests that a majority of skulls has not been found. If so, at least 249 people were sacrificed to the king's after-life.

At one time the beautiful cast-bronze vessels for which the Shang Dynasty is famous posed a real problem for archaeologists. The earliest bronzes recovered came from the site of Anyang, and the artistic standard achieved by the Shang metalworkers has never been exceeded. ■ The problem was simple: Where and how did Shang bronze casting originate? It seemed to burst upon the scene as a fully developed technical skill and as a fully mature art style (Fig. 15-17). Consequently, various diffusionist models were developed to explain the origins of Shang-bronze technology. In 1950, a Shang site earlier than Anyang was recovered at Zheng Zhou (Cheng-Chou), and it now appears that there was a local development of bronze working based on a highly advanced ceramic technology. In other words, bronze casting was a gradual development out of Longshan and early Shang ceramic efforts.

Zhou (Chou) Dynasty: The Iron Age (1027–2211 B.C.)

The Zhou Dynasty replaced the Shang Dynasty in 1027 B.C. This was not a gradual supplanting, nor was it the collapse of one dynasty followed by the rise of another. Rather, it was sudden replacement by conquest.

● Civilization develops in a consistent pattern.

The Zhou Dynasty is characterized by warfare, agriculture, industry, and the philosophical underpinnings of historical China as we know it. (The great philosopher Confucius [551–579 B.C.] lived during the Zhou period.) The origins of the Zhou are very hazy, but originally these people were probably derived from the Shang. The Zhou had their great cities, but unlike the Shang, who fortified only their palaces, the former fortified the entire city.

Geographic origins of the Zhou seem to lie in the west, particularly in the Wei He valley. This period, when the Zhou capitol city was located in Shaanxi (Shensi) province, is called the "western Zhou." After 771 B.C. the capitol was shifted to Luoyang" (Lo yang) in Henzn (Honan). This later period is known as the "eastern Zhou." The shift from west to east seems to be due to

nomadic pressure in the west, and portions of the Great Wall were built during the Zhou period as a defense against the nomadic invasion.

The Zhou emphasis on war is also reflected in its chariot burials. Chariot burials are not unique to the Zhou, and in fact they were also quite common in the Shang. However, unlike Shang two-horse chariots, the Zhou chariots had four horses, were lighter, and were more graceful. In both the Shang and Zhou periods horses and drivers were buried with their chariots. Weapons, and particularly the ge (ko) dagger-axe, abound in Zhou burials.

Basic Themes in Chinese Civilization

If any theme persists in Chinese prehistory and history it is that of continuity. For example, the earliest writing found in China, that used by the scapulimancers of the Shang, is directly ances-

Fig. 15-17 Bronze ritual wine vessels of the late Shang dynasty, eleventh century B.C. (Photographs courtesy of the Metropolitan Museum of Art, Rogers Fund, 1943.)

tral to modern Chinese and can be read by modern Chinese scholars without specialized training.

Further, pottery found in Neolithic kitchens indicates that the Neolithic diet was similar to the modern Chinese diet. In fact, virtually every ceramic form found in the Neolithic kitchen is also found in the modern Chinese kitchen so that no modern chinese cook has a problem in recognizing the functions of the Neolithic pottery.

In China dynasties come and go, but the picture that emerges is one of continuous growth and elaboration on a few basic themes.

Summary

● Civilization has developed in different areas and at different points in time, but in every case each area shows a generally similar *sequence* of development. First, there is a concentration of population. Second, this concentration usually occurs in fertile river valleys. Third, in each case there are firmly established food staples capable of producing a surplus. Fourth, these surpluses, once available, are channeled into support for full-time specialists, such as craftsmen, artisans, religious specialists, and ultimately political and military specialists. The food surpluses also lead to the rise of urbanism. Finally, a concomitant of urbanism is the appearance of militarism and of cyclical empires.

It would seem that once a stable food base capable of producing a surplus is established, then population nucleation inevitably follows. By the same token, once nucleation occurs civilization is more likely to develop than not. Where civilization did not follow a Formative period the lack of its development seems related to environmental limitations on the achievability of a food surplus. On the other hand, where civilization appears without a preceding Formative era, it may be identified as having been introduced from another region which had already developed a civilization.

16

The Transition to History*

Introduction

At this point in our narrative we need to pick up the leftover pieces of Old World prehistory to fit them into an orderly scheme. As mentioned previously, the later they are in time, the more varied and complex the cultures extant. There were also differential rates of cultural change. Cultural innovations were rapid in the Middle East, while other areas, such as northern and western Europe, changed more slowly. In part, cultural lag reflects the limited and slow acceptance of traits introduced from other regions. These developments should be viewed not as necessarily indicating resistance to change but as cultural adaptations to local conditions. ■ In Europe there were long-established hunting-and-fishing economies which were successful. Therefore, the adoption of cultivated plants and animals during the Neolithic was a slow process marked by intermittent acceptance by the indigenous hunting-and-gathering peoples and by crop failure due to environmental limitations (Tringham et al. 1980). Similar adaptive trends may be perceived with the introduction of bronze implements, and later those of iron.

Throughout this period, beginning as early as 4500 B.C. (Renfrew 1971:68–69) and lasting until the Roman conquest of Gaul and Britain, we perceive both change and continuity in European society. We have mentioned continuities in economy. Other long-standing traditions included trade. Early trade items included flint

*In this chapter and in Chapter 17 we have converted radiocarbon dates to agree with the radiocarbon recalibration. All other dates stand as is. This revision was necessary, for the recalibrated dates have clearly indicated that previously held views of cultural diffusion were in error.

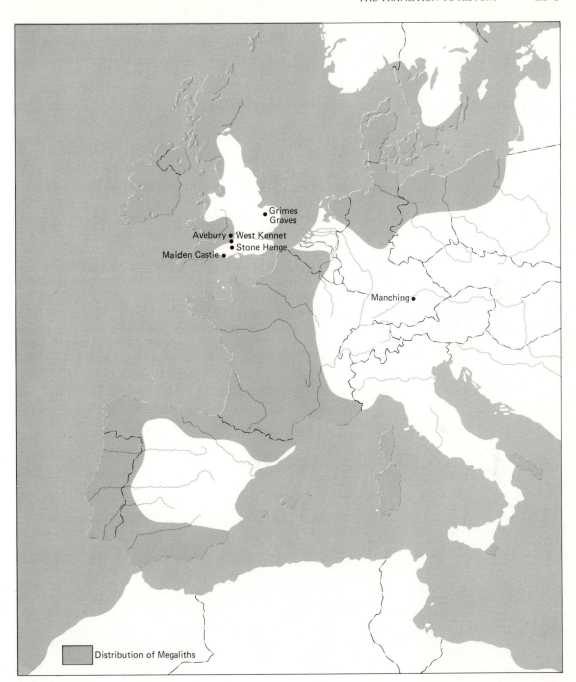

Map 16-1 Distribution of Megalithic Monuments in Europe with the Location of Important Sites.

● Megalithic monuments

▲ Sequential patterns of movement of peoples and traits across Europe

■ A pattern of coexistence — peasants to the north and civilization along the Mediterranean.

● The colder European climate favored cultivation of barley, flax, peas, beans, rye and oats.

▲ A balanced economy

axes, amber, and gold. Later on, slaves, leather, salt and salted-meat products, and possibly bronze were traded southward into the classical world in exchange for manufactured products, especially wine.

Another long-standing tradition involved the construction of monumental collective tombs (i.e., gallery graves and chamber tombs). These gigantic stone structures, dating as far back as the Neolithic period and continuing into the Bronze Age (Daniel 1980), were an outgrowth of the large Neolithic earthen barrows of an earlier

period (Map 16-1). ● The Megalithic tombs are, of course, closely related to and part of a religious tradition whose visible manifestations consisted of large stone structures — menhirs, alignments, and huge monuments, such as those of Avebury (Fig. 16-1) and Stonehenge (Figs. 16-6 to 16-9). Later in the period all of this engineering expertise was applied to the construction of immense hillforts. These facts of continuity document the presence of a unique European adaptation — a continuing peasant society which, while exposed to numerous influences from the centers of civilization, went its own way. V. Gordon Childe has summarized these events in *The Prehistory of European Society* (1958). ▲The narrative he presents, along with those of most other authors on the subject (Hawkes and Hawkes 1949; Braidwood 1967; Piggott 1965; Clark 1952, 1977), outlines a pattern of sequential movements of peoples across the European continent and the British Isles, each bringing a distinctive set of culture traits: bell beakers, battle axes, food vessels, hero burials, cremations,

Fig. 16-1 A Megalithic monument, the henge at Avebury, aerial view. (Courtesy of Ministry of Works, Crown Copyright.)

urnfield burials, bronze, iron, and hill forts.

We must bear in mind that during this same interval there developed the major civilizations of southern Europe: the Cretan, the Mycenaean, the Etruscan, the Phoenecian, the Greek, and finally the Roman. The cultural complexity of these societies is staggering, for they featured codified laws, state religions, monumental sculpture and architecture, standing armies, political institutions (with some still in effect today), fine arts, and the writing of history and poetry — an almost unending list of accomplishments. It is not our goal here to review these civilizations as their study lies within the field of classics rather than in prehistory. ■Their presence on the southern fringe of Europe provided a constant input of cultural ideas northward and furnished a market for products traded southward. The unique quality of the cultures of northern and central Europe is evidence of the strength of the indigenous peasant society. These "crude barbarians" (so termed by their civilized neighbors) had the cultural integrity to lead their lives in their own fashion.

Subsistence

The economy of northern Europe featured a mixed reliance on the hunting and gathering of wild foods with the addition of cereal agriculture. Originally this featured the clearing of the forested loess lands for growing wheat and barley. Later these cultigens spread northward with the result that environmental selection favored rye and oats, which were better adapted to damp and cold. Millet was also an early European cultigen, as were flax and apples. The land was cultivated by means of a two-field method, with fallowing between crops. ● Another aspect of the system involved the rotation of cereal crops (which exhaust the soil of nitrogen) with legumes, peas, beans, vetches, and lentils (all of which enrich the soil). The thin scatter of potsherds found on the old fields suggests that vil-

Fig. 16-2 Patterns of ancient fields. (Courtesy of J.K.S. St. Joseph and the Committee for Aerial photography, University of Cambridge.)

lage debris and manure were spread on the fields for fertilizer. The fields were small, and cultivation was by the individual family (Fig. 16-2).

The earliest domesticated animal was the dog, first used by Mesolithic humans in the hunt. As hunting continued in importance, the dog retained its position. The addition of domesticated food animals and crops did not replace hunting and gathering, but instead allowed the economy to feature a greater variety of resources. People relied on stable domesticated food resources, with the secondary availability of wild foods during poor crop years. ▲ The result was a balanced economy without the specialization and reliance on a few crops, the development of large food surpluses, and other features characteristic of the Middle East. The economy thus encouraged cultural stability in the form of continuing peasanthood, rather than change leading toward population increase, urbanism, and ultimately civilization.

According to Clark (1952:117), we do not have reliable information concerning the rela-

■ Domestic animals

● A shifting pattern of cultivation

▲ Long-established trade routes

■ Wheeled carts

● A variety of house types

▲ Huge Megalithic monuments

tive frequency of the various domestic animals kept. ■ The domesticates included cattle, sheep, pig, horse, and in the north, reindeer. Clark does state that through time in temperate Europe there was a decline in the frequency of pig and cattle with a corresponding increase in sheep and horses. He correlates this change with an increase in forest clearance.

Agricultural techniques employed slash-and-burn forest clearing, then the cultivation of small fields with hoes and digging sticks. ● The practice of forest clearing, planting, and fallowing was further modified by the frequent shifting of villages. The existing houses were abandoned, and the people moved elsewhere to clear new fields and build new houses. Estimating the population at 5 individuals per house and from 50 to 60 houses per village, we derive an average village population of 300 (Piggott 1965:47).

A major invention now attributed to these peasant peoples was the rotary grinding mill, or quern, which spread from northern Europe to the Classical world.

Trade

The evidence of trade with the Mediterranean Classical world documents the degree of interaction tempered with cultural selection that was in effect. The peasants of northern Europe did not seek to acquire all the luxuries available, nor did they slavishly copy all that they were exposed to. The major items acquired from the Mediterranean world were ornaments and objects manufactured of metal, especially weapons and armor. Traded in exchange were amber, tin, gold, copper, and salt.

The distribution of items distinctive of Mycenaean culture, dating from the fourteenth or fifteenth century B.C., throughout continental Europe documents the extent of the trade in effect at that time. ▲ The routes by which such trade was implemented had undoubtedly been in existence for several thousand years by Mycenaean times. With respect to the acquisition of rare natural resources, continental Europe lay within the sphere of Mediterranean influence. However, the peasant tribes remained culturally aloof, continuing their own life-style and integrating those trade items they acquired into their own system of values. We cannot therefore attribute the noncivilized nature of these tribes to cultural isolation from the civilized world. It is obvious that these peoples were aware of the nature of civilization and simply chose to continue their peasant existence. Environmental limitations may have been of some importance, but the evidence from trade suggests that cultural selection was of equal significance. After the seventh century B.C. a major trade item from the Mediterranean was wine, as evidenced by the vessels in which it was imported as well as those for serving it.

Transport

■ Wheeled transport by wagon or cart was the typical mode in prehistoric Europe. The wheel had been invented in Mesopotamia prior to 3000 B.C., and its use had spread across Europe by 2500 B.C. Early wheels were solid, being either single pieces of wood or discs made from planks. There were two forms of vehicles, the two-wheeled cart and the wagon with four wheels. There is also archaeological evidence of corduroy roads of logs, built as early as 2500 B.C. The use of wheeled vehicles required proper terrain, not too hilly or boggy. Central and northern Europe possessed these qualities, with the result that wheeled vehicles aided the frequent moves of the peasant farmers. Another aspect of this innovation was the associated rise in the importance of draft animals, both oxen and horses with their harness trappings. In Celtic times there was a shift from the heavier wagons to the lighter, two-wheeled war chariots. (After 500 B.C. the typical warrior's or chief's grave includes the chariot.) The appearance of spokes in the last few centuries B.C. likely derives from the need for lighter, faster chariots.

The *gauge* of wagons, the distance between the wheels, was established at between 3 feet 6 inches and 3 feet 9 inches, a tradition that extends from the time of Ur in Mesopotamia down to the Hallstatt wagons of the fifth and sixth centuries B.C. The later Iron Age La Tene wagons shifted to a gauge of 4 feet 8 1/2 inches, a cultural legacy still in use today. (This dimension is the standard railroad gauge.) Archaeological evidence for these gauges is provided by wheel ruts preserved in numerous European sites. In northern Europe there was a continuation in the use of the vehicles developed in earlier periods — the sledge, wooden dugout, and skis.

Villages and Housing

Archaeology is especially satisfactory as a technique for the recovery of information about prehistoric housing. We can recover evidence of house types and village patterns, from which we can then estimate population. Covering the last four millennia B.C., we have from Europe large quantities of village remains available for study.

● The variety of housing is impressive. There is evidence of oblong houses with porches, oval-shaped palisade units built of timber, rectangular and square one-room units, stone units, timber-framed structures with mud walls, pile dwellings, and so on. The majority of these structures feature either log or post construction and are arranged in villages of from 15 to 75 houses with populations of 100 to 400. This pattern was a long-standing one based on living close to one's farmland. The buildings

within the village were segregated by use into houses, barns, granaries, and sheds for livestock. The houses frequently had dual use, with one part serving as a stable for livestock, a pattern still used in rural Europe. Houses measured from 10 by 15 feet to 15 by 30 feet, and the number of acres cultivated by the village was several hundred. A Linear Pottery village, for example, with a population of about 400, would farm 600 acres (Piggott 1965:52).

Religion

The earliest evidence of religion within this period, beginning in about 4300 B.C. (Renfrew 1971:69), consists of enormous stone-lined, chambered tombs (Figs. 16-3, 16-4). ▲These are evidences of a religious cult termed *Megalithic*, which featured the construction of numerous monuments built of large individual stones. We

Fig. 16-3 A Megalithic monument, the West Kennet Long Barrow, Wiltshire, England. (Courtesy of Ministry of Works, Crown copyright.)

■ The spread of a religious cult

● Types of tombs

▲ The henges

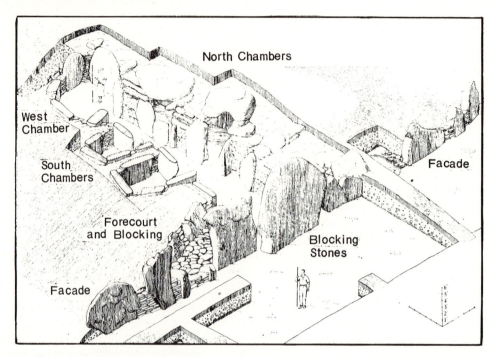

Fig. 16-4 Plan of the West Kennet Long Barrow, a chambered tomb dating from the third millennium B.C. (Piggott 1965:Fig. 30.)

Fig. 16-5 The stone alignment at Carnac, Brittany, France. There are 1099 menhirs arranged in 11 parallel rows. (Courtesy Editions de'art Jos.)

have little besides these monuments to document the nature of this cult, which was in vogue for 1,000 to 2,000 years over most of western Europe. The monuments include a variety of forms, not all of which are tombs. There are large areas covered with parallel rows of individual stones placed a few meters apart. These "stone alignments" are best known from Brittany in France (Fig. 16-5). There are also enormous single stones termed *menhirs*, which were erected perhaps as shrines. Another variety of construction, the *trilithon*, features the capping of one or two vertical stones with a horizontal stone. A final type of monument consists of circular alignments of individual stones or trilithons to form an outdoor shrine or temple. These are the henges, the most famous of which, Stonehenge, we will discuss in greater detail below. There is no doubt that a major religious cult must have directed the efforts necessary to quarry and erect the stones, weighing up to 40 tons apiece, which undoubtedly required much of the free time of the society. According to Piggott (1965:60), more than 5,000 Megalithic tombs are known in France, 3,500 in the Danish islands, and 2,000 in the British Isles.

Earlier explanations of the origins of this cult held that it was the result of diffusion from the center of civilization in the eastern Mediterranean. Renfrew's revision (1971) of European chronology, based on the recalibration of radiocarbon dates, indicates that the monuments are earlier than originally thought. They also are earliest in Brittany, thus disproving any supposed diffusion from an Aegean source. It is more likely that they originated first in western Europe.

Although the archaeological evidence is inadequate, we can make some general statements about the cult. ■ The objects within the tombs are those of the local cultures; thus we are not dealing with a single culture but instead with the spread of a cult which had its own independent ethic. The spread of this religion was described by Childe (1958) as colonization or mis-sionization by groups of Megalithic saints, who introduced the religious concepts and determined who was to be buried within the tombs. Childe noted in France the presence of two different levels of tombs: those for the Megalithic chiefs and inferior ones for the native Neolithic peasants. Surely burial in these tombs was a great honor, as the number of burials within a tomb ranged from approximately 8 to 40. The tombs were likely the property of specific social groups, with burial reserved to the members of one family or larger kin group. Clark (1977:136) also notes the maritime distribution of the megalithic monuments, particularly the collective tombs, and attributes their possible spread to fishermen following schools of hake and mackerel from the deep waters south of the British Isles to the shallower waters of the north.

● Tombs are of two general formats: (1) the passage grave, with a passage leading to a multi-chambered polygonal or circular room, and (2) the gallery grave, without the separate entry passage but having instead an elaborate entrance to an oblong burial chamber.

Some of the tombs are decorated with carved or painted designs. Most of the designs are geometric in spiral, curvilinear, and rectilinear patterns. Another form of decoration consists of the symbolic representation of a female deity, a type of mother-goddess. Inasmuch as some of the goddess representations are associated with those of axes, it is also thought this figure may have had some connection with warfare.

▲ The henges stand as the greatest examples of the Megalithic builder's skill, and of these, Stonehenge in Wiltshire, England, is the most outstanding (Figs. 16-6 to 16-9). Harold Edgerton (1960:848–849) has ventured a reconstruction of the building techniques used at Stonehenge:

Stonehenge architects chose to build with gray sandstone slabs called sarcens, which they quarried on the Marlborough Downs. . . . Here on the Marlborough Downs about 1500 B.C., toilers lever an embedded sarcen from the earth. Their fellows,

■ The sequence of construction of Stonehenge

risking crushed arms or legs, thrust timbers under the stone. With the slab clear of the ground, workmen begin to shape it by heating the line of an intended cut with firebrands. Others then douse the stone with cold water to inflict internal stress. Finally, men batter the sarsen by simultaneously dropping 50-pound stone mauls. Four maul hurlers, standing on animal skins to save feet from blistering, await their foreman's shout. With arm raised, he delays until an assistant marks the target line, which still steams from its fire-and-water bath.

The maul hurlers then threw their stones on the line until the unwanted portion of the stone had been sheared off. The quarrying was only a minor portion of the total effort involved. The quarried sarsens were then hauled on a wooden sledge over log rollers the 24 miles to the Stonehenge construction site. While long rows of workers pulled on the ropes attached to the sledge, other laborers would run relays, placing the recently used log rollers in front of the advancing sledge. Once at the site, the stones were set by rolling them into position with the lower third of the stone over a pit dug to receive it. The top of the stone was elevated with levers

until the bottom portion slid into the pit (Fig. 16-7a). The setting of the lintel stones was even more difficult, for this required the inching forward of the stones up some sort of inclined plane made of log cribbing until the stone could be aligned atop the vertical slabs (Fig. 16-7b). The size of the task can be appreciated in light of the fact that replacing some fallen lintels in 1958 required the aid of a 60-ton crane. The major circle of stones at Stonehenge once included 30 stones set in a ring 97 1/3 feet across. The individual sarsens were up to 20 feet in height and weighed 40 to 50 tons. Further evidence of the skill of the builders is provided by the fact that the lintels were fitted to the uprights with mortise and tenon joints and the lintels were fitted together with a tongue-and-groove joint.

Outside of the circle of sarsens were two rings of holes which held smaller stones termed "bluestones." These weighed up to 4 tons, but the amazing fact is that they were transported from quarries up to 250 miles away. Another feature of interest (Fig. 16-8) is an enclosing earthwork circle. Around its inside perimeter are 56 symmetrically placed small pits, some of which are filled with cremated bone. Also around the perimeter are upright station stones. The entrance features three uprights set in a line, with parallel earthworks flanking them. At

Fig. 16-6   View of Stonehenge, Wiltshire, England, showing the trilithons at ground level. (Courtesy Ministry of Works, Crown copyright.)

Raising the sarsens

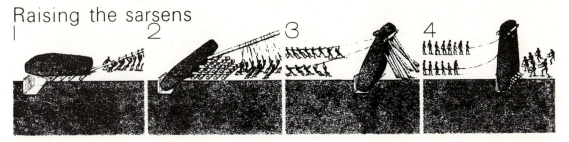

Fig. 16-7 Reconstruction of the method of construction at Stonehenge. (*above*) Raising the sarsens; (*below*) raising the lintels. (Atkinson 1978:33.)

Raising the lintels

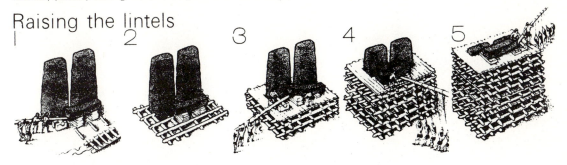

the point where the entrance meets the earthen circle are two additional uprights. The overall meaning of Stonehenge has been lost in antiquity. In recent centuries it has formed an important part of the Druid religion, wherein each June solstice ceremonies are conducted at the site. However, we have no evidence that the Druids actually built this monument.

■ Stonehenge was built in three stages of construction (see Fig. 16-8) (Atkinson 1956). Stage I, begun in about 2500 B.C. according to radiocarbon-dated features, included the enclosing ditch and embankment, the heel stone and its flanking embankments, the four station stones, and the 56 Aubrey holes. Named for the man who first studied them, the Aubrey holes are 2 1/2 to 6 feet in diameter and from 2 to 4 feet in depth. Forming a circle 288 feet in diameter, they are filled with chalk rubble and, frequently, cremated human bones. The second stage of construction, begun about 2350 B.C., included the setting up of the 82 bluestones in two

rows, each stone about 6 feet apart. Stonehenge III is the final stage, which includes the most dramatic portions of the monument as it is preserved today. Beginning in about 2000 B.C. and continuing until 1900 B.C., this last building phase included the construction of the sarsen circle, the placement of five trilithons, a horseshoe of bluestones, and, exterior to the sarsens, two circles of holes termed "Y" and "Z" holes. The total amount of construction time required was enormous. Hawkins (1965:73) has provided an estimate of the days of labor required (Table 16-1).

Stonehenge has been likened to an outdoor temple, which function it might well have served, even if the rites were held there infrequently. One novel interpretation of the use of the monument derives from research by Gerald Hawkins (1965), who has provided a series of reconstructions of astronomical sightings that may be taken by aligning the various stones with the positions of the sun, moon, stars, and planets. On

Period I
about 2800 BC

Period II
about 2100 BC

Period IIIa
about 2000 BC

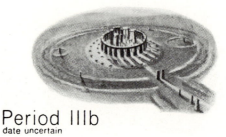

Period IIIb
date uncertain

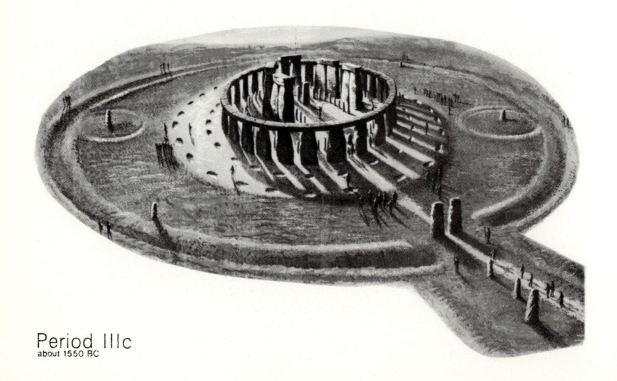

Period IIIc
about 1550 BC

TABLE 16-1
Minimum Work Total in Man-Days

Digging ditch, making bank: 3500 cubic yards, at 1 yard per man-day	3500
Carrying for above	7000
Digging 5000 cubic yards for Avenue banks, leveling, survey, etc.	6000
Carrying for above	12,000
Transporting 80 bluestones, average weight 4 tons,	
24 miles by land at 100 men per stone, 1 mile per day	192,000
216 miles by water at 10 men per stone, 10 miles per day	17,280
Erecting Stonehenge II at 20 man-days per stone	1600
Transporting 80 sarsens average weight 30 tons,	
20 miles by land at 700 men per day	1,120,000
Dressing, shaping sarsens: 3 million cubic inches of rock powder at 50 cubic inches per man-day	60,000
Cutting with stone axes, hauling 300 logs for lattice tower, 2000 rollers, at 1 man-day per log	2300
Making 60,000 yards of hide rope at 1 man-day per yard	60,000
Erecting Stonehenge III at 200 man-days per stone	16,000
TOTAL MAN-DAYS	1,497,680

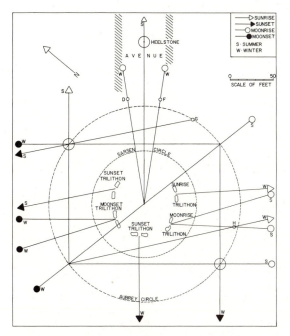

Fig. 16-9 The astronomical sightings possible, utilizing the Stonehenge monument in its Period III form. (After Hawkins 1965:Fig. 12.)

Fig. 16-8 Reconstruction of the principal stages of construction at Stonehenge, which extended from approximately 2800 B.C. to 1550 B.C. (Atkinson 1978:20–21.)

the basis of a computerized program, Hawkins asserts that the monument functioned as a type of computer used in astronomical observations. No correlations were observed for the stars and planets, but 10 sun and 14 moon positions were noted, with an average error of 1.5 degrees. The probability of such correlations being due to chance is less than one in a million (Hawkins 1965:172). The lines of sight plotted are illustrated in Figure 16-9. The more than 200 such monuments known typically feature circles, often with flattened sides.

Other authors, principally Thom (1967, 1971), Hutchinson (1972), and Cowan (1970), have reviewed the reasons for Megalithic monuments and their methods of construction. Their interpretations of the details of these structures include ascribing to their makers a rudimentary knowledge of trigonometry, use of a standard length of measurement, the Megalithic yard of 2.72 feet, use of a flexible compass, and even a set of beliefs leading toward Pythagorean mathematics. Certainly such evidence provides proof of the ability of Megalithic humans to think in abstract terms.

Following the Megalithic period, the primary evidence of religion consists solely of grave of-

● The introduction of copper to Europe

▲ The spread of copperworking

■ The continuum from bronze to iron

● The flat-grave people

ferings; and later, just prior to the Roman conquest, a formalized religion—that of the Druids—can be distinguished. (This sect will be discussed in our overview of the Celtic world.)

Metalworking

Until now the main emphasis of this chapter has been on the continuity and the persistence of local traditions, even under the impact of new ideas and influences from the so-called civilized world. ● On the other hand, copper metallurgy may have been independently invented in southeast Europe, and certainly central Europe must be considered an innovative leader in bronze technology. At this point we shall revert to the more conventional approach of dealing with archaeological evidence and consider developments in western Europe, eastern Europe, and finally central Europe. The earliest indigenous items, dating to before 2500 B.C., are found in the Vinca culture of the Balkans, where they antedate the appearance of copper work in the Aegean (Renfrew 1971:69). Between 4500 and 3000 B.C. the techniques of metalworking had spread to most of eastern Europe. The earliest implements were shaft-hole axes, spiral arm rings, copper discs, spiral beads, and flat axe blades. These items were traded northward as far as Denmark.

Copper metallurgy was also present in western Europe but at a later date. ▲ The spread of copper metallurgy in western Europe can be attributed to two basic complexes or groups. The first, variously labeled "Globular Amphora," "Corded Ware," "Single Grave," "Battle Axe" or "Boat Axe" peoples, attests to a period of inbound emigration and turmoil. These newcomers, thought to be Indo-Europeans, brought with them wheeled vehicles, domesticated horses, and copper metallurgy.

The second group or complex is the Bell Beaker people, named after the distinctive bell-shaped pot or cup found in their graves. Archery equipment (bow guards) is also part of the funerary equipment of this group. Bell Beaker folk were above all migratory traders, spreading cultural traits across western Europe. Evidence of their culture has been found in Spain, Brittany, England, Ireland, central Europe, and southern France, and traces have also been found in Italy, Sardinia, and Sicily. There are two schools of thought concerning Bell Beaker origins. One school favors a Spanish origin for these dynamic people, whereas the other argues for an eastern European beginning. They used copper, and it is believed that their smiths, with their knowledge of casting, traveled with the trading bands.

TABLE 16-2
Chronology of European Bronze and Iron Age Cultures

Date	Period	Culture
500 B.C.–A.D. 0	Late Iron Age	La Tene
730 B.C.–480 B.C.	Early Iron Age	Hallstatt
1250 B.C.–730 B.C.	Late Bronze Age	Urnfield
1450 B.C.–1250 B.C.	Middle Bronze Age	Tumulus
1800 B.C.–1450 B.C.	Early Bronze Age	Unetice (or Flat-Grave)

(Dates are approximate and vary by geographical region. Adapted from Coles and Harding 1979)

Whether their skills included mining and smelting is not known. Their metallurgical techniques included the use of the simple open mold rather than the closed valve type. In any event, their activities stimulated the use of bronze in Europe, with the exploitation of tin from Cornwall and copper from Ireland and England. Their efforts also included the introduction of goldworking and its extraction from Irish sources.

After this initial contact with copper and copper metallurgy the peoples of western Europe, with the exception of a few isolated areas, seem to have lost interest in large-scale metallurgy. The items that do appear are the result of trade. It is not until the Middle Bronze Age (post 1500 B.C.) that large numbers of bronze objects start appearing in graves in the West.

The Shift to Bronze in Eastern Europe

The Chalcolithic — or copper-using — cultures of eastern Europe were replaced by bronze-using cultures in Bulgaria, Rumania, and parts of Hungary. These new groups show strong affinities with the cultures that used bronze in Anatolia. In this early period metal objects are fairly rare, but by the Middle Bronze Age locally made metal objects are quite common, and large hoards of bronze objects have been recovered from this period. Bronze weapons appear in large numbers, indicating an emphasis on warfare and the rise of a warrior class. Objects and remains also show strong influences from central Europe.

Archaeological Evidence of Bronze from Central Europe

Like most Bronze Age cultures of both eastern and western Europe, those of central Europe are known mostly from grave goods. In other words, many cemeteries, in contrast to only a few settlements, have been excavated. Part of this problem is undoubtedly due to earlier interests in obtaining objects for museum display as opposed to obtaining knowledge for its own sake. It is only recently that archaeological interests have shifted to studies dealing with subsistence, environment, and ecology. The archaeological subdivisions of the Bronze Age of central Europe are therefore based on changes in mortuary practices.

The Bronze Age Cultural Sequence

The term "Bronze Age," as used here, like the later term "Iron Age," denotes a general period of technological achievement within which there are numerous chronological periods and geographic variants which have been defined. ■ In central Europe it is possible to establish a fairly neat chronological sequence as one can see in Table 16-2.

When this chronological scheme was originally established it was considered highly probable that the Unetician flat-grave people were replaced by a Tumulus building folk and that the Tumulus builders were superseded by the cremation-oriented Urnfielders. Now authorities are not so certain that this is the case. In fact, the three are believed now to be one people who changed their mortuary rites. In Europe there are literally hundreds of local variations in styles and forms of the various periods subsumed under the general rubric of either Bronze or Iron Age. For clarity's sake we have opted to present a simplistic sequence of Unetice, Tumulus, and Urnfield, and so on. (For persons especially interested in the European Bronze Age Coles and Harding [1979] is particularly recommended as a starting point.)

Unetice Period: 1800–1450 B.C.

● Although its origins are confused, the Unetice is the best known and the most typical of the Early Bronze Age cultures of central Europe.

▲ The Unetice people controlled trade.

■ Graves covered with earthen mounds

● Urnfields — the cemeteries with cremations in pottery vessels.

▲ Archaeologically, the Celtic Iron Age is divided into the Hallstatt and La Tene periods.

Unetician subsistence was based on both stock breeding and agriculture. Hoe farming continued from the preceding period, but the ox-drawn plow was almost certainly in use as well. The presence of linear scars on ancient fields indicates plowing, sometimes in criss-cross patterns. The dating of plow furrows is not easy, but in some instances dated barrows (burial mounds) have preserved beneath them just such furrows (Piggott 1965:150). The plow was of wood, with a single foot or sole and a long beam attached to the yoke of oxen. There is still controversy as to whether metal shares were used, since replaceable wooden shares have been found. However, the use of iron shares dates at least as early as the Roman period. The use of the plow and the use of bronze sickles for harvesting seems to have produced a quantum jump in food production.

The Unetician people also controlled the central European copper and tin sources and the production and trans-shipment of bronze, as well as that of gold and amber. ▲ Such control of trade and production made this a wealthy society, a fact attested to in the grave finds of richly decorated daggers with engraved blades. Gold wire was also used for ornaments.

Unetician graves are flat graves (that is, without mounds or other superstructures). However, toward the end of the Unetician period low mounds, or barrows, built of earth or clay and covered with stone were constructed. Most of the surviving mound-covered graves are found on nonarable land, while the so-called flat graves are usually located on arable land. Consequently, the flatness of the "flat graves" may be due to extensive plowing over the millennia. As a result the sharp cultural and chronological distinctions between the Unetice period and the succeeding Tumulus period based on mortuary practices may simply be derived from evidence from graves which have been subsequently altered by plowing. Unetician graves are simple oval pits, with hollowed-out tree trunks used as coffins. There is a general orientation to the east.

Tumulus Period: 1450–1250 B.C.

There is total continuity between the Tumulus and Unetice periods. Both occupied the same territory, both used the same cemeteries, and both had the same economic base. The major differences are the change in mortuary patterns late in the period noted above and a change in the area of residence to southeastern Europe. Although the Tumulus peoples initially occupied the same geographical area as the preceding Unetice period, there is a later geographical expansion into southeastern Europe, particularly into the Hungarian plain and into western Transylvania.

■ It is, of course, the Tumuli or mounds that cover the graves that give this culture its name. The body was placed in a coffin or in a log chamber, which rested either on a pavement of stone slabs or on a layer of white sand. Offerings of young cattle often accompany the corpse. Above this structure, a barrow of earth was raised and surrounded by a ring of stones. Differential sizes of the graves and wealth offerings indicate the social positions of the occupants.

Tumulus folk were fond of ornamentation. Male burials were accompanied with long pins, daggers, axes, swords, knives, and often razors. Female burials also have pins, which were used to fasten woolen cloaks. Bracelets, arm rings, bead necklaces, and finger rings also accompanied female burials.

Some traces of cloth have survived. The most common was a standard fabric of loosely woven wool. There was also a fine material, made from specially selected and prepared long woolen fibers, which was restricted to scarves and belts.

Urnfield Period: 1250–730 B.C.

With the Tumulus expansion into southeastern Europe, contact was made with the Urnfields, a people whose mortuary rites centered on cremation. ● Urnfield takes its name from the large cemeteries of cremation burials in which the ashes were placed in pottery vessels or funerary urns. The latter practice spread very rapidly throughout the areas associated with the Tumulus peoples, thus implying that we are dealing not only with Urnfield peoples but also with the diffusion of the practice of cremation to other groups such as the Tumulus people.

More than just a change in mortuary practice sets this late Bronze Age group apart, however. First, the Urnfield smiths mastered the techniques of sheet-metal manufacture, a more efficient method than casting for the manufacture of helmets, shields, and vessels. This change is not revolutionary in nature but is a logical outgrowth of a constantly expanding technology. Secondly, there is a dramatic and concurrent expansion of Urnfield people into western Europe.

Between 1000 and 900 B.C. the Urnfield people had penetrated into northern Italy (Terremare culture) and onto the Mediterranean islands. By 1000 B.C. Urnfields occurred east of the Rhine, and by 750 B.C. they appear in southern France. Ultimately, they spread into Belgium, the Netherlands, Spain, and the British Isles.

The Iron Age—the Celtic World

With the end of the Urnfield culture we find ourselves in a rather unique position in the study of prehistory. Our subjects are no longer anonymous makers of pottery and metal implements but are identified in historical accounts. Ancient records from the Classical world and place-name studies in western Europe clearly indicate that these were the Celtic peoples.

▲ The Celtic Iron Age is subdivided into the Hallstatt and La Tene archaeological periods. In general the Hallstatt period differs little from the preceding Late Bronze Age Urnfield society, with one exception. Iron is the main metal being worked; and it duplicates the same tool types and forms of the Bronze Age (Fig. 16-10), except that swords, for example, are much larger, taking advantage of iron's greater tensile strength.

Mortuary practices also changed. There are now high-status four-wheeled wagon burials (Fig. 16-12), and interments placed near fortified centers (Fig. 16-11) which contain urns and jars traded in from Greek and Etruscan workshops. In the succeeding La Tene period high-status burials include two-wheeled chariots.

During the La Tene period there is a shift from thrusting to slashing weapons, and we also have the founding of large fortified trading centers or towns, called Oppida, many of which have survived as modern cities.

Celtic Political Structure

The structure of the society of rural Europe is known from archaeology as witnessed by the wagon burials of heroes or chieftains (Fig. 16-12) as well as from the historical writings of Julius Caesar, Tacitus, and others. The basic social unit was the tribe, or tuath, a small group ruled by a local chieftain below whom was a level of nobility made up of warriors. A third class included the craftsmen, priests, and poets. According to Roman writers (who may have been prejudiced), basic features of the society were barbarism, love of warfare, idleness, boasting, and feasting, when its citizens were not engaged in endemic intertribal warfare.

Celtic Warfare

The practice of war by the Celts is known from the inclusions of weapons and chariots in burials, but of even greater detail are the historical accounts from Roman sources. We may infer

Fig. 16-10 Objects of metal dating to the Iron Age. (*a*) A Celtic bronze flagon from Lorraine, early 4th century B.C.; (*b*) bronze shield in La Tene style from the Thames at Battersea, first century B.C.; (*c*) torc of electrum from the Snettisham treasure, first century B.C.; (*d*) the decorated back of the bronze Desborough Mirror, first century B.C.; (*e*) bronze helmet from the Thames at Waterloo Bridge, first century B.C. (Courtesy of the British Museum.)

Fig. 16-11 La Tene burial at Pernant, Aisne, France, with associated grave offerings. (Photo courtesy of Gilbert Lobjois.)

Fig. 16-12 Wagon grave in plank-built chamber, showing remains of wagon, position of male and female burials, grave goods, etc. Hallstatt D. culture, sixth century B.C. (Piggott 1965:Fig. 101.)

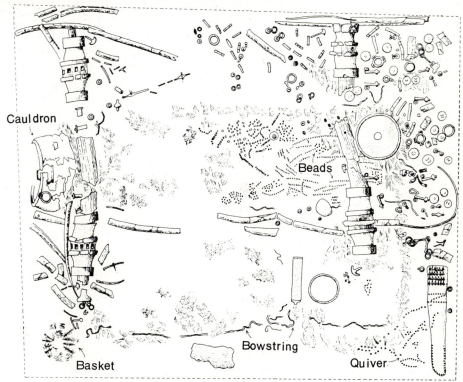

warfare from the swords, spears, shields, helmets, and rare body armor recovered archaeologically. However, it is from the historical sources that we obtain our knowledge of the place of warfare in the society and of the tactics employed. The appearance of horse trappings has led some authors to infer the use of cavalry, but in fact the horse was more typically ridden to provide access to the battlefield, with the contest consisting of individual clashes on foot.

■ With the transition from Hallstatt to La Tene culture in about the fifth century B.C., we have the rise of chariot warfare. The following is a description of a chariot-warrior chieftain in action (Powell 1963:106–107):

> It may be deduced that the initial purpose of the chariot warrior was to drive furiously towards and along the front of the enemy ranks to instill terror by sight, and by the delivery of missiles, no less than by the tremendous noise that was kept up by shouting, horn blowing, and beating on the sides of the waggons drawn up to the flanks or in the rear. The warriors then descended from their chariots, which the charioteer held in readiness for a quick retreat if need be, while the warrior, with casting spear, or drawn sword, stood out to deliver a challenge to an opposing champion. The challenge was evidently in a set formula of boasts of prowess, and perhaps of lineage, incorporated in a war song. Indeed, a kind of frenzy was probably worked up. In inter-tribal fighting, it would appear that the main body of troops became involved only after this phase of individual contest, and perhaps only if one side had become certain of success in a general melee. The course of events against Roman armies must have involved the whole body of fighting men more directly, and it led to considerable modification in battle order.

The archaic mode of individual challenge, and encounter by champions, recalls the scenes in the *Iliad*, and the Celts were indeed the inheritors of that tradition which had long become outmoded south of the Balkans and of the Alps.

In Caesar's account of chariot warriors, he states that they ran up the pole between the horses, or at least intimidated the enemy with their agility.

The average Celtic warrior fought on foot with armament consisting of a cutting sword, one or two spears used for casting, and a long, oval shield of wood with iron fittings. A unique feature was the warrior's appearance in battle naked, which was intended as an appeal for magical or supernatural protection. The horsemen practiced the decapitation of foes, whose heads were displayed hung from the horses' bridles and were eventually taken home for show. By the first century B.C. the sling, obtained from Mediterranean sources, had made its appearance as a weapon of war. One result of the use of slings was the restructuring of the hilltop forts to include multiple ramparts.

The final accolades given to the successful warriors were the feasts and gifts provided by the king. ● Celtic feasts were renowned for gluttony and indulgence in drinking. These affairs were socially structured, with the best portions rigidly allocated by rank, including the presentation of the boar's head to the charioteer.

▲ The other major evidence of warfare is defensive: the hilltop forts, which became common after 1000 B.C. The basic feature of their construction was a timber-framed rampart covered with earth (Fig. 16-13). The fortress was located on a prominent hilltop, with the rampart defenses surrounding its perimeter. Piggott (1965:204) cites the fact that the amount of timber required was substantial; for example, one small fortress utilized all the 9-inch timbers to be cut at one time from 60 acres of forest. The timbers were placed both vertically and horizontally and were secured with iron nails. A unique

Fig. 16-13 Aerial view of Maiden Castle. (Courtesy of Aerofilms, Ltd.)

aspect of these forts was that many of the ramparts are preserved today in vitrified form, as a result of firing. Such firing had previously been thought to be part of the construction process. However, the modern view is that all fired walls were the result of enemy attack. Constructional features present include the use of protruding bastions along the wall, in-turned gateways, enclosure of springs, flanking guard chambers along gateways, and, late in the period, multiple ramparts.

The larger hill forts, termed Oppida by the Romans, functioned as tribal centers. One of the largest of these, at Manching, Bavaria, encloses an area about 1 1/2 miles in diameter. Within these fortresses were houses, streets, workshops, grain-storage pits, and pastures for livestock. The primary use of the hill fort was for refuge in time of attack, with the typical peasant living in and farming near his village.

Celtic Religion

■ Druidism and Druids are prime components of Celtic religion. There is no evidence that Druidism is descended from the Megalithic religion. The ancient Druids were practitioners of magic and ritual, and in Ireland they also bore arms. They foretold events through revelations supposedly received while in a trance. They also made votive offerings to trees and water bodies. The majority of these offerings consisted of sprinkling the blood of sacrificed animals, but humans were also occasionally sacrificed. The Druids memorized the transmitted oral literature and believed in an afterlife, as witnessed by the inclusion of numerous burial offerings. Their sacrifices were organized according to the concepts of earth, fire, and water, as symbolized in offerings made by hanging, burning, and drowning. Druids were important in secular matters, for they were advisors to the kings. There is little evidence that they functioned as a true intelligentsia, since they neither wrote history nor served as philosophers, but the Celtic world possessed a strong oral tradition. Our knowledge of the Druids comes from the writings of their Roman contemporaries, and we therefore know their practices in much greater detail than if we had to rely solely on archaeological evidence.

The Celtic Twilight

It was inevitable that the Classical world of Rome and the culture of the Celts would collide. ● Rome never forgot that Celts had sacked the Eternal City in 387 B.C.; and the Celts of north-

▲ The Roman conquest of Maiden Castle

■ History replaces prehistory in Europe.

● Modern people experiment with an Iron Age life-style.

ern Italy remained a threat until the Battle of Telamon in 225 B.C., when Rome finally triumphed. In 58 B.C. a series of political crises in Gaul (modern France) led Julius Caesar to intervene in Celtic life in Gaul, giving Rome control over vast sources of raw materials and the markets for their finished products. Later, of course, Roman armies conquered Britain as well.

▲ At this point in our discussion, there seems no more appropriate way to dramatize the end of this period than to describe the Roman conquest of Maiden Castle between A.D. 43 and 47. Sir Mortimer Wheeler (1943:61–63) has reconstructed the events from the archaeological findings:

> Approaching from the direction of the Isle of Wight, Vespasian's legion may be supposed to have crossed the River Frome at the only easy crossing hereabouts—where Roman and modern Dorchester were subsequently to come into being. Before the advancing troops, some 2 miles away, the sevenfold ramparts of the western gates of Dunium towered above the cornfields which probably swept, like their modern successors, up to the fringe of the defences. Whether any sort of assault was attempted upon these gates we do not at present know; their excessive strength makes it more likely that, leaving a guard upon them, Vespasian moved his main attack to the somewhat less formidable eastern end. What happened there is plain to read. First, the regiment of artillery, which normally accompanied a legion on campaign, was ordered into action, and put down a barrage of iron-shod ballista-arrows over the eastern part of the site. Following this barrage, the infantry advanced up the slope, cutting its way from rampart to rampart, tower to tower. In the innermost bay of the entrance, close outside the actual gates, a number of huts had recently been built; these were set

alight, and under the rising clouds of smoke the gates were stormed and the position carried. But resistance had been obstinate and the fury of the attackers was roused. For a space, confusion and massacre dominated the scene. Men and women, young and old, were savagely cut down, before the legionaries were called to heel and the work of systematic destruction began. That work included the uprooting of some at least of the timbers which revetted the fighting-platform on the summit of the main rampart; but above all it consisted of the demolition of the gates and the overthrow of the high stone walls which flanked the two portals. The walls were now reduced to the lowly and ruinous state in which they were discovered by the excavator nearly nineteen centuries later.

> That night, when the fires of the legion shone out (we may imagine) in orderly lines across the valley, the survivors crept forth from their broken stronghold and, in the darkness, buried their dead as nearly as might be outside their tumbled gates, in that place where the ashes of their burned huts lay warm and thick upon the ground. The task was carried out anxiously and hastily and without order, but, even so, from few graves were omitted those tributes of food and drink which were the proper and traditional perquisites of the dead. At daylight on the morrow, the legion moved westward to fresh conquest, doubtless taking with it the usual levy of hostages from the vanquished. . . . into this ash a series of graves had been roughly cut, with no regularity either of outline or of orientation and into them had been thrown, in all manner of attitudes—crouched, extended, on the back, on the side, on the face, even sitting up—thirty-eight skeletons of men and women, young and old; sometimes two persons were huddled together in the same grave. In ten cases extensive cuts were present on the skull, some on the top, some on the front, some on the back. In another case, one of the arrowheads already described was found actually embedded in a vertebra, having entered the body from the front below the heart. The victim had been finished off with a cut on the head. Yet another skull had been pierced by an implement of square section, probably a ballistabolt. The last two and some of the swordcuts were doubtless battlewounds; but one skull, which had

received no less than nine savage cuts, suggests the fury of massacre rather than the tumult of battle — a man does not stay to kill his enemy eight or nine times in the melee; and the neck of another skeleton had been dislocated, probably by hanging. Nevertheless, the dead had been buried by their friends, for most of them were accompanied by bowls, or in one case, a mug for the traditional food and drink. More notable, in two cases the dead held joints of lamb in their hands — joints chosen carefully as young and succulent. Many of the dead still wore their gear: armlets of iron or shale, an iron finger-ring, and in three cases bronze toe-rings, representing a custom not previously, it seems, observed in prehistoric Britain but reminiscent of the Moslem habit of wearing toe-rings as ornaments or as preventatives or cures of disease. One man lay in a double grave with an iron battle-axe, a knife and, strangely, a bronze earpick across his chest. The whole war cemetery as it lay exposed before us was eloquent of mingled piety and distraction; of weariness, of dread, of darkness, but yet not of complete forgetfulness. Surely no poor relic in the soil of Britain was ever more eloquent of high tragedy. . . .

Thereafter, salving what they could of their crops and herds, the disarmed townsfolk made shift to put their house in order. Forbidden to refortify their gates, they built new roadways across the sprawling ruins, between gateless ramparts that were already fast assuming the blunted profiles that are theirs today. And so, for some two decades, a demilitarized Maiden Castle retained its inhabitants, or at least a nucleus of them. . . .

The above event is symbolic in that it represents the head-on collision of two different cultural systems: Celtic Europe and the Classical world of Rome. This conflict continued for four centuries after the fall of Maiden Castle, but the latter is representative of many similar events. The cultural systems in contact were no longer able to live in peaceful and symbiotic coexistence. ■ From this time on the European events which follow pertain to history rather than to prehistory.

In 1977 the British Broadcasting Company undertook an unusual experiment. ● Using 12 adults and 3 children carefully screened from thousands of applicants, the BBC attempted to reconstruct life in the Celtic Iron Age (Green 1978). The participants were given training in pottery making, metalworking, and weaving, as well as in basic survival training in the recognition of edible wild plants and dangerous poisonous plants. They were provided with some basic hand tools, a few tents for immediate shelter, seed grain for farming, as well as 2 dogs, 3 cows, 4 pigs, 9 goats, 25 sheep, 40 chickens, and some bees.

Leaving behind the world of television, telephones, bluejeans, and supermarkets, their job was to live a Celtic life-style for one year. These people wove their own cloth and made clothes, fed themselves, made their own tools, and built their own shelter and farm buildings. It took 14 weeks to build and thatch a communal roundhouse 48 feet in diameter and 30 feet high, and the structure was a remarkable success in one of England's colder winters.

The group had 10 acres of pasture and 5 acres of cultivated land to work with. On the cultivated portion they grew wheat, barley, oats, peas, and beans. They were equally successful in their husbandry efforts: their goats produced 16 kids; their cattle, 4 calves; and their sheep, 16 lambs. They were able to support their animals over the winter with three and one-half tons of hand-harvested hay. The animals were able to produce sufficient meat, hides, and hair for the dietary and clothing needs of the community.

Without clocks, radios and television it was not surprising that the pace of these people's lives slowed down. Most activities were concentrated in the daylight hours, and in the winter they felt tired if they did not have a full 12 hours' sleep.

An experiment such as this is neither archaeology nor even experimental archaeology, but it does give flavor and life to otherwise lifeless objects such as those recovered from the Celtic Iron Age.

PART IV

CULTURAL DATA REVEALED BY ARCHAEOLOGY—THE NEW WORLD

Once the New World had been occupied, population soared and in a comparatively short time humans had spread throughout the western hemisphere. Since all environments found on earth, except the antarctic, are located in the western hemisphere, it should not be surprising that the most diverse sorts of adaptation to environmental conditions have occurred there. These adaptations ranged from those of the Arctic and tundra of the north to those of the hot and humid tropical rain forests of Amazonia.

Once groups of people had settled into their environmental niches, development similar to that found in the Old World occurred. In New World studies we use a slightly different system to describe the various levels of cultural complexity. This approach was developed by Gor-

■ A stage classification of New World cultures

● Lithic stage

▲ Archaic stage

■ Formative stage

● Classic stage

▲ Postclassic stage

don Willey and Phillip Phillips in their monumental synthesis *Method and Theory in American Archaeology*, published in 1958. ■ Willey and Phillips define a series of stages, five in all, which are typical of New World cultures. The stages, ranging from early to late, are termed Lithic, Archaic, Formative, Classic, and Postclassic. This is a generalized sequence referring to all New World developments, and in fact most culture traditions did not participate in every one of these stages. Often, cultures within a region developed until a level was reached at which environmental limitations became significant. On the other hand, some cultures remained at essentially the same level over long periods of time. There are even examples of change from one particular stage to a later, more simplified one. The stage concept is nonetheless useful, and we shall use it here.

● In the Willey-Phillips classification, the *Lithic stage* refers to the culture of the earliest Americans. This encompasses both the presumed earliest unspecialized core and flake industries and those featuring advanced technology in stoneworking, including the blade technique, bifacial flaking, and the fluting of projectile points. They state that the *"Lithic is the stage of adaptation by immigrant societies to the late glacial and early postglacial climatic and physiographic conditions in the New World"* (Willey and Phillips 1958:80). The earliest manifestations in every region of the New World may be assigned to this Lithic stage, even though such remains in a few areas, such as the Amazon Basin, are extremely rare.

▲ The next stage in our sequence, the *Archaic stage*, is defined as *"the stage of migratory hunting and gathering cultures continuing into environmental conditions approximating those of the present"* (Willey and Phillips 1958:107). The Archaic was initiated after the extinction of the Late Pleistocene megafauna and was terminated in many regions by the transition to a full-fledged agricultural economy. In between these two dramatic end points, the Archaic is marked by regional adaptation to local food resources of every possible type. In those situations such as the Great Basin, California, and the Northwest Coast, where agriculture was never important, Archaic cultures continued in existence until the time of historic contact. In terms of the technology, the most important criteria of the Archaic were the rise in importance of grinding and polishing in stone-tool manufacture and the use of basketry. In those areas where agriculture did develop, the Archaic subsistence pattern was replaced by the rise of the Formative stage.

■ The New World *Formative stage* is partly the equivalent of the Old World Neolithic. Willey and Phillips (1958:146) define the Formative *"by the presence of agriculture, or any other subsistence economy of comparable effectiveness, and by the successful integration of such an economy into well-established, sedentary village life."* They further cite the fact that such societies typically feature pottery making, weaving, stone carving, and a specialized ceremonial architecture. As Willey and Phillips also state, "These elements are not linked to American agriculture through any inner causality. . . ." (1958:146). (In a later chapter, in which the Formative is discussed in detail, we shall attempt to factor out these interrelationships.)

● The *Classic stage*, according to Willey and Phillips, is defined more in terms of qualitative factors than quantitative ones. The Classic features *"excellence in the great arts, a climax in religious architecture, and a general florescence in material culture"* (Willey and Phillips 1958:182). Another factor of overriding importance is the rise of urbanism. The Classic fits our definition of civilization, for it includes monumental public architecture, a calendrical system, writing, pervasive art styles, widespread trade in luxuries, a class or even caste system, a formal pantheon of gods, and a priestly oligarchy. The Classic stage did not develop throughout the New World but was restricted to Mesoamerica and the Andean region. One reason for this limited geographic range was environmental, other, social and political factors were also likely significant.

▲ The *Postclassic stage* featured mass production of crafts, strong political control by secular leaders, urbanism, military expansion, and conquest. *"The Postclassic stage in Middle America and Peru is marked by the breakdown of the old regional styles of the Classic stage, by a continuing or increased emphasis upon urban living, and, inferentially, by tendencies toward militarism and secularism"* (Willey and Phillips 1958:193). In two cases, the Aztec and the Inca, Postclassic empires were terminated by European conquest.

We have reviewed the stage classification of Willey and Phillips as an introductory scheme preparatory to our further review of New World data. The authors of this scheme contemplated additional subdivisions such as an Early and Late Archaic, Preformative, and so on, since the individuality of specific cultures made their assignment to one of the five major stages a gross oversimplification. They further recognized that other cultures could reasonably be categorized as "belated" or "marginal." However, for our purposes we will follow the basic outlines of the five major stages as defined. In order to more fully communicate the evolution of culture through these stages in the New World we have included maps of the culture areas for the different time periods (Figures 18-1 and 18-2).

Within the later stages, we further identify regional adaptations which we term *culture areas*. The culture-area concept is adapted from its anthropological use relative to modern aboriginal or ethnographic cultures. The concept proposes that for areas of similar environment, the cultures living therein tend to develop similar economic adaptations, having more culture traits in common than they share with societies lying outside their common area. According to this concept, as applied to archaeology, one influencing factor is that through time environments change in terms of climate, flora, and fauna. These environmental factors along with those of a cultural nature (e.g., innovations, the diffusion of culture traits, conquest, and such) lead to modifications of the boundaries of the archaeological culture areas through time. Since there is nonetheless an inherent integrity in the cores of these areas the culture-area concept may be validly used in archaeology.

There is, further, a historical framework for each of the distinctive cultural-environmental adaptations which we term a culture area. With respect to two of our defined stages, the Lithic and the Archaic, our frame of reference is continental in scope. We therefore do not define archaeological culture areas for those stages. Our culture areas (Figs. 18-1 to 18-3) refer to adaptations which have occurred later in the record, when the cultural adaptations were regional in scope.

Within each culture area we utilize the concept of *cultural tradition*, the definition of which (Willey and Phillips 1958:37) is *"a (primarily) temporal continuity represented by persistent configurations in single technologies or other systems of related forms."* Such traditions, presented in phase-sequence diagrams, form a major archaeological method of describing past cultures as complexes of traits persisting through time.

In our choice of the Willey-Phillips scheme of stages we do not intend to imply any degree of evolutionary determinism. There is no sequence of steps through which any specific culture has been *ordained* to evolve. Each cultural tradition was the result of internal change or innovation coupled with externally produced change or diffusion. These factors led to the development of a technology, social structure, and subsistence system which were adapted to the specific environments inhabited. Thus, each culture must be viewed as a historical result of all of these factors rather than the outcome of any preconceived sequence of evolutionary steps. Therefore, when we group such cultures into stages we deliberately emphasize their similarities and deemphasize their differences. The result is the lumping of somewhat differing manifestations into large, catchall subdivisions. Here, we use the stage system of classification as a convenient teaching aid albeit in full knowledge of the range of variation that exists in the individual cultures included in any given stage. Having explained this methodology, let us proceed with how and when the New World was first occupied.

■ Proof of the early inhabitants of the New World is difficult to obtain.

17

The Early Occupation of the Americas

Introduction

The quest for the remains of the earliest Americans is one of the most exciting topics in all of New World archaeology. ■ The problem lies not in finding evidence of human occupation but in proving that those remains are truly early. At present no sites dating appreciably earlier than 12,000 B.C. are universally accepted by specialists. Problems associated with proof include (1) demonstrating that suspected stone implements were in fact made by humans rather than being formed by accidents of nature; (2) recognizing as artifacts objects of bone that were intentionally broken for use as tools; (3) identification of bone accumulations, blackened areas, and other manifestations as being due to human activities; (4) demonstrating that artifacts, bone beds, and so on are in fact associated with early dates; and (5) proving that the dates themselves are not in error.

Recognition of early tools is central to the entire issue of the earliest occupation of the New World, since pieces of stone may come to resemble true artifacts as the result of alteration by natural causes. Termed *geofacts*, these specimens may have been flaked by rolling during flash floods; by spalling as the result of changes in temperature; by being washed over cliffs; and even as the result of compression in the soil (Stanford 1979:148). Further complicating the issue is the fact that many bona-fide artifacts were tools of expediency, quickly made or utilized without modification for tasks at hand; and therefore the archaeologist may find that bona-fide tools are no better formed than other specimens which were produced by natural actions. The way to distinguish between items which

TABLE 17-1
Sites in the New World Thought to Be Very Early

Site (Authenticity of Artifacts in Doubt)	Age	Problems
Calico Hills, California	30,000 years to possibly 500,000 years	Geologists believe deposits are very old. Stone "tools" may be naturally flaked.
El Bosque, Nicaragua	32,000 years	Stone "tools" may be naturally flaked.
San Diego area, California	Third interglacial	Stone "tools" may be naturally flaked.
Scripps Campus, La Jolla, California	19,550 ± 700 B.C.	Campsite may be associated with later C-14 date of 5420 ± 100 B.C.
Friesenhahn Cave, Texas	Early Wisconsin(?)	Specimens of both stone and bone are not accepted as "tools."
Medicine Hat, Alberta	25,000 years	Stone "tools" may be naturally flaked.
Potter Creek Cave, California	Late Pleistocene	Bone "tools" may be naturally polished.
Tule Springs, Nevada	Springs active 40,000 and 12,000 years ago	C-14 date of 21,800 B.C. was from a mixed sample. Bone "tools" may have been polished by spring action.
Rancho La Brea, California	Estimated at between 9000 and 32,000 B.C.	Bones exhibit "cuts" which "could" be due to human activity.
American Falls Reservoir, Idaho	30,000 years	Marks on bones could be natural.
Trail Creek, Alaska	13,050 ± 280 B.C. to 15,750 ± 350 B.C.	Bones were possibly broken by people.
Copperton Site, Oklahoma	15,625 ± 550 B.C. to 18,450 ± 450 B.C.	Bones were possibly broken by people.
Santa Rosa Island, California	35,550 B.C. 27,750 ± 3000 B.C. 9850 ± 800 B.C.	Deeply buried deposits difficult to excavate and evaluate. Blackened areas may be hearths. There are no well-made stone artifacts.
San Miguel Island, California	Probably similar to finds on Santa Rosa Island.	Artifacts not in proven association with bones. No artifacts found *in situ*.

Site (human remains not well dated)	Age	Problems
Laguna Beach Skeleton, California	15,200 ± 1470 B.C.	Shells below find date 6350 ± 80 B.C.
Los Angeles Skeleton, California	23,600 years	Minimal-sized sample of the skull was dated.
Taber, Alberta	32,000 years to 60,000 years	Dated by geologic correlation of beds dated elsewhere.

Site (Undoubted Artifacts)	Age	Problems
Black's Fork, Wyoming	Possibly 9–10,000 years	Primitive nature of tools due to inclusion of quarry debris.
Spanish Diggings, Wyoming	(?)	Includes quarry debris.
Tolchaco Complex, Arizona	(?)	Includes quarry debris.
China Lake, California	Claimed to be 25,000–45,000 years.	
Lewisville, Texas	35,050 B.C.	Clovis pt. may be intrusive. "Hearths" may be wood rats' nests. C-14 date may be contaminated.

TABLE 17-1

Site (Undoubted Artifacts)	Age	Problems
Sheguiandah Site, Ontario, Canada	30,000 years	Artifacts may have been transported by glaciers. Age of lower levels in doubt.
Old Crow Flats, Yukon	25,050 ± 2000 B.C. (date on bone-fleshing tool)	Some researchers feel bones were broken or shaped into tools by later peoples.
Meadowcroft Rockshelter, Pennsylvania	11,290 ± 1010 B.C. to 15,225 ± 975 B.C. (dates on hearths)	Dates may have been contaminated by groundwater. M. Wormington (personal communication) accepts the Meadowcroft dates, while noting that some researchers still do not. For a discussion favoring the acceptance of the dates, see Adovasio and colleagues (1980). For reasons against their acceptance, see Mead (1980) and Haynes (1980).
Wilson Butte Cave, Idaho	13,050 ± 800 B.C. 12,550 ± 500 B.C.	Cuts on bone possibly made by people. Artifacts associated, but dates may be on intrusive bones.
Fort Rock Cave, Oregon	11,310 ± 720 B.C.	Artifacts include a mano—not normally thought to be so early.
Pasika Complex, British Columbia	Thought to be pre-12,000 years	Crudeness of tools does not prove great age.
Valsequillo area, Mexico	25,000–40,000 years (uranium date) 19,900 ± 850 B.C. and 33,050 B.C. (shell dates); over 35,000, but no earlier than 600,000 years (hydration date)	Artifacts alleged to have been planted. Archaeologists do not accept very old geologic dates.
Tlapacoya, Mexico	22,050 ± 4000 B.C. 20,450 ± 2600 B.C.	Association of artifacts with dated charcoal not proven.
Muaco, Venezuela	14,425 ± 400 B.C. 12,350 ± 500 B.C.	Bones and artifacts of different time periods mixed in spring deposits.
Taima Taima, Venezuela	12,490 ± 435 B.C. 11,060 ± 280 B.C. 8340 ± 90 B.C.	Artifacts occur between the dated layers.
Rancho Peludo, Venezuela	11,965 ± 200 B.C.	All levels contain pottery.
El Abra Rockshelter, Colombia	10,450 ± 160 B.C.	Artifacts may be associated with the date.
Pikimachay Cave, Peru (Paccacaisa level)	17,650 ± 3000 B.C. 18,250 ± 1000 B.C. 14,100 ± 1200 B.C.	Artifacts are so crude there is some question they were made by humans.
Ayachucho level	12,200 ± 180 B.C.	There seems to be no problem. This is the earliest dated occupation level in the New World which every authority is willing to accept as valid.

● The earliest migrants to the New World were *Homo sapiens sapiens.*

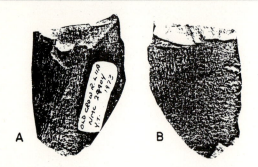

Fig. 17-1 Bone tools and flakes thought to be both of human manufacture and very early in the New World. *(Top)* *(a)* Dorsal surface of mammoth bone flake; *(b)* ventral surface of same flake. *(Bottom)* *(a)* Side view of a spirally fractured bison metapodial; *(b)* close-up of *(a)*; *(c)* front view of *(a)*; *(d,e)* bone cores. (Bonnichsen 1978:Fig. 7-8.)

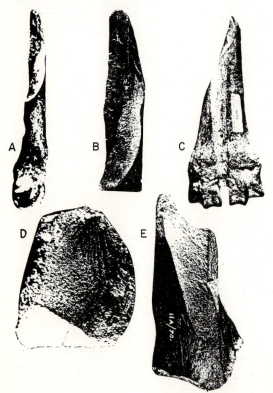

are of human manufacture and those that are not is to demonstrate that the site in question presents irrefutable evidence of human presence (i.e., butchered bones, charcoal, and quantities of tools or flaking debris). Such comprehensive proof is usually lacking in sites that are thought to be very early, and the earlier the sites appear to be, the fewer the remains normally present. This problem is so severe that recognized authorities examining the same specimens often disagree as to whether such tools are in fact made by humans.

These problems in site identification have led to a long list of supposedly early locations, all of which, for one reason or another, are in dispute. Presented in Table 17-1 is a list of these localities with their associated findings and the reasons why the latter remain in question. (Locations of the sites are shown in Map 17-1, and examples of bone flakes, bone tools, and stone implements typical of these early sites are illustrated in Figure 17-1.) What is clear at this time is that while probably not all these sites are due to human activity, some of them will sooner or later become accepted as proof that early Americans occupied the New World prior to the last major glacial advance more than 25,000 years ago.

Peopling of the New World

● In contrast to the Old World, where we have both cultural and physical evidence of human evolution from primate ancestors, in the New World we only have evidence of *Homo sapiens sapiens* possessing an advanced culture of a level which can be termed *Upper Paleolithic.* Thus, humans occupied the New World at a date late in their total overall cultural history, bringing with them a culture as evolved as that of their Old World contemporaries. However, once in the New World, the culture of these early migrants rapidly adapted to the specific environments present (Map 17-2).

Map 17-1 Very Early
Sites in North America.
(after H.M.Wormington)

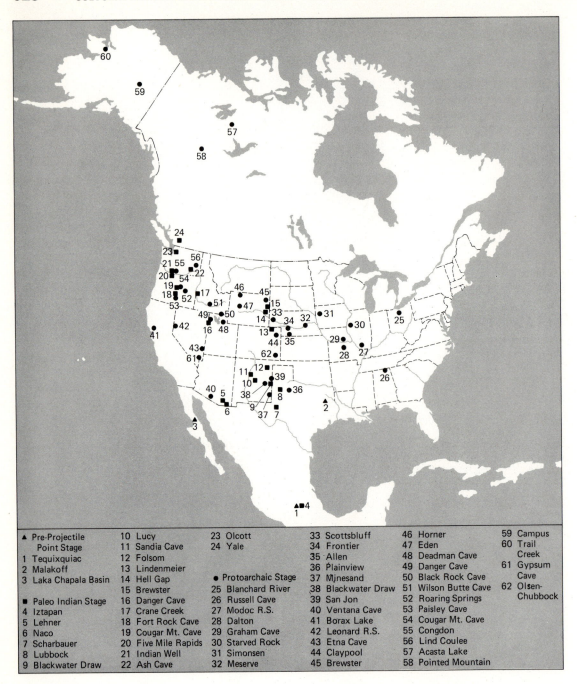

▲ Pre-Projectile Point Stage	10 Lucy	23 Olcott	33 Scottsbluff	46 Horner	59 Campus
1 Tequixquiac	11 Sandia Cave	24 Yale	34 Frontier	47 Eden	60 Trail Creek
2 Malakoff	12 Folsom		35 Allen	48 Deadman Cave	61 Gypsum Cave
3 Laka Chapala Basin	13 Lindenmeier	● Protoarchaic Stage	36 Plainview	49 Danger Cave	62 Olsen-Chubbock
	14 Hell Gap	25 Blanchard River	37 Mjnesand	50 Black Rock Cave	
	15 Brewster	26 Russell Cave	38 Blackwater Draw	51 Wilson Butte Cave	
■ Paleo Indian Stage	16 Danger Cave	27 Modoc R.S.	39 San Jon	52 Roaring Springs	
4 Iztapan	17 Crane Creek	28 Dalton	40 Ventana Cave	53 Paisley Cave	
5 Lehner	18 Fort Rock Cave	29 Graham Cave	41 Borax Lake	54 Cougar Mt. Cave	
6 Naco	19 Cougar Mt. Cave	30 Starved Rock	42 Leonard R.S.	55 Congdon	
7 Scharbauer	20 Five Mile Rapids	31 Simonsen	43 Etna Cave	56 Lind Coulee	
8 Lubbock	21 Indian Well	32 Meserve	44 Claypool	57 Acasta Lake	
9 Blackwater Draw	22 Ash Cave		45 Brewster	58 Pointed Mountain	

Map 17-2

▲ Pre-Projectile Point Stage

1 Pozo de Muáco	12 Aceguá
2 Manzanillo	13 Potraro Sucio
3 Chocó	14 Carro de Montevideo
4 Garzón	15 Playa Verde
5 Gatchi I	16 Taltal
6 Jose Vieira	
7 Gruta de Wabeto	
8 Barracão	
9 Quarai	
10 Catalán	
11 Ampajango	

■ Paleo-Indian Stage

17 El Jobo
18 Lauricocha Caves Level I
19 Quebrado de Camarones
20 Zuniquena
21 Lagoa Santa Caves
22 El Totoral

● Protoarchaic Stage

23 El Inga
24 Lauricocha Caves, Levels II & III
25 Ichuña Rock Shelter
26 Ongamira Cave
27 Ayampitín
28 Intihuasi Cave
29 **Palli** Aike Cave
30 Fell's Cave

▲ Various migration theories

■ Migration via the Bering Strait

The majority of archaeologists accept the view that humans entered the New World by means of a movement across the Bering Strait, either at times of lowered sea level, when a land bridge was present, or during the winter, when passage over ice would have been possible. ▲ There are other theories relative to the peopling of the New World, but these primarily relate to later periods. For example, Greenman (1963) has outlined a northern Europe-to-Greenland-to-northeastern North America route, which would have required boats. Pottery from Ecuador dated 2500 B.C. features attributes similar to those of Jomon pottery of Neolithic Japan, leading Meggers, Evans, and Estrada (1965) to suggest a direct sea migration from Japan then. The Aleutian island chain forms another suitable route. There is also the possibility of South Atlantic crossings, reenacted by Thor Heyerdahl in his famous voyages in Ra I and II, the papyrus reed boats built according to Ancient Egyptian designs. We will not debate here the merits of these particular theories. At this point we are interested in the earliest migrations to the New World, and all evidence points to the Bering Strait as the initial point of entry.

There is also ample evidence of later movements of peoples into the New World, and thus there is no need to think of a single migration with irreversible effects. Early migrations probably included nonprojectile-point, pebble-tool users as well as specialized big-game hunters who utilized an Upper Paleolithic type of tool inventory. Later documented migrations include a culture pattern represented by microblades, an Aurignacian-like blade-using culture, and even later, about 3000 B.C., the arctic specialization which we know as Eskimo culture.

There is also evidence of later movements from the New World back to Siberia; therefore, the crossing of the Bering Strait was not a rare, unidirectional event. Such crossings must have occurred many times during the course of daily life in the region, since a similar environment is present on both sides of the Strait. In addition, this steppe ecology extended over much of North America, including portions of what is now the northern tier of U.S. states. Thus the peopling of the New World was a logical process which culminated in permanent occupation of the areas south of the Late Wisconsin ice border. Probably these early peoples initially entered the New World following herds of mammoth and other late Pleistocene big game as part of their normal migratory hunting life-style (Fig. 17-2). Their continuation on into previously unoccupied areas should therefore not be viewed as an intentional activity but rather as a simple expansion of their hunting territory.

A Migration Hypothesis

■ Earlier versions of the Bering Strait migration theory emphasized the presence of a land bridge at the Strait as a result of lowered sea level during a glacial maximum (Figure 17-3). However, the recent discovery that Australia (which is separated from the mainland of Asia by an enormously deep oceanic trough and which was not linked to Asia during any glacial event) was peopled as early as 32,750 years ago (R. Berger 1978; White and O'Connell 1979) has changed our thinking. Since Australia could only have been occupied as the result of the use of boats, crossing the Bering Strait equally might not necessarily have required the presence of a land bridge. This being the case, we can be more flexible in our thinking with respect to the initial migration to the New World. For example, in the first edition of this text, we developed the point of view that the time of an early migration was determined by (1) the presence of a land bridge at Bering Strait and (2) the presence of an open, unglaciated passageway, the trans-Canada corridor, between the two major Canadian glaciers, the Laurentide and the Cordilleran ice sheets (Fig. 17-4).

Fig. 17-2 The Late Pleistocene megafauna of the New World. Another species typical of the circumpolar Arctic tundra, the woolly rhinoceros, for reasons not yet understood never crossed Bering Strait to become part of the New World fauna. The giant bison probably became extinct prior to human population of the New World, although new finds continue to suggest greater antiquity for initial human entry into the New World. (Martin and Guilday 1967:Fig. 13-8)

● A migration hypothesis

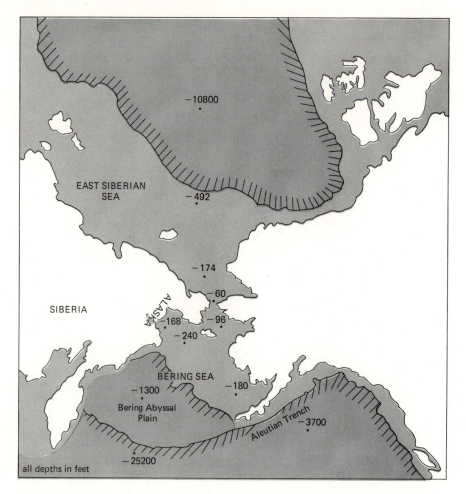

Fig. 17-3 The Land Bridge at Bering Strait at its maximum extent (shown in light gray).

● This hypothesis (Hester 1976:304–306) was presented as follows:

Any consideration of migrations would seem to be based on the primary variable of migration rates of the game animals that were being followed and hunted. In the present case, the primary animal was the mammoth. Analysis of the environmental needs of the mammoth should give us some clues

as to movements of these animals in response to advances and retreats of Late Wisconsin glaciers.

Stomach contents of mammoths preserved in frozen ground in Siberia indicate that these mammoths were subsisting on a diet of young shoots and cones of fir, pine, birch and willow leaves and a broad variety of boreal meadow and tundra herbs, mosses, and grasses. If we may assume that these were the type of mammoth that early hunt-

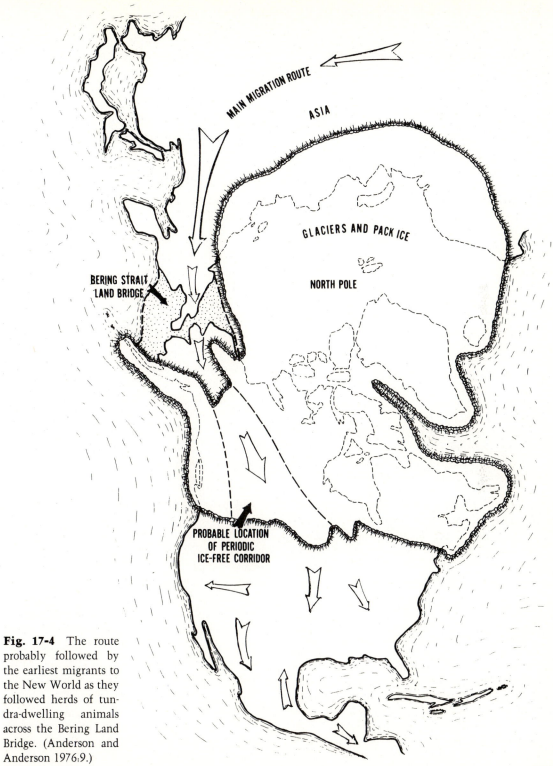

Fig. 17-4 The route probably followed by the earliest migrants to the New World as they followed herds of tundra-dwelling animals across the Bering Land Bridge. (Anderson and Anderson 1976:9.)

331

▲ The trans-Canada corridor may not be as important as we once thought.

ers followed into the New World then it is possible to conceive of these mammoths following such an environmental zone (termed Taiga-Tundra) from Siberia into Alaska through Canada and into the United States with the dependent hunters in close attendance. The time necessary to accomplish this migration need not have been great as the mammoth were almost certainly moving in direct relationship to the glacial advances and retreats, which we know to have been rapid. The natural path of this migration would conform closely to the northern boundary of the boreal forest belt of Canada and the eastern United States, an important corridor for migrations from earliest times to the present. The movements of these prey animals would have been governed by movements of the Late Wisconsin continental glaciers. In this respect two factors acting in opposition to each other are of importance: 1. Increasing glaciation would result in the lowering of sea level thus creating a land bridge across the Bering Strait. 2. Increasing glaciation would result in the coalescence of the Cordilleran and Laurentide Ice Sheets thus blocking any possible migration route between Bering Strait and the United States. The combination of these factors clearly indicates that conditions suitable for migrations across Bering Strait continuing southward to the United States during the Late Wisconsin must have been infrequent and of short duration. Haynes has presented the view that such an opportunity only occurred once, about 12,000 years ago. We believe that several such opportunities existed during the Late Wisconsin.

If we may reconstruct the kind of glacial regimen providing both dry land at the Bering Strait and along a trans-Canada corridor between the Cordilleran and Laurentide Ice Sheets, it would appear to be either: 1. During a glacial advance which had lowered sea level sufficiently to permit crossing but had not progressed to the point where the Cordilleran and Laurentide Ice Sheets had coalesced. 2. During a glacial retreat which had melted sufficient ice to form a corridor but had not yet inundated the Bering Strait.

Details of these advances and retreats with the favorable times for migration are presented in Figure 17-5.

▲ The trans-Canada corridor is no longer considered as important as when the above migration hypothesis was written. At the American Quaternary Association meeting in 1978 in Edmonton, Alberta, an entire symposium was devoted to a review of the trans-Canada corridor problem. The reasons presented for the diminished significance of the trans-Canada corridor were as follows:

1. It may not have been closed, except briefly.
2. It may not have posed as much of a barrier to migration as previously thought.
3. The documentation of pre-Llano (12,000-year-old) sites has proceeded to the point that we have reasonable evidence that people had occupied the New World at places such as Old Crow Flats in the Yukon and Pikimachay Cave, Peru, prior to the last major climax of the Wisconsin glaciation. Such sites, with their evidence of 20–26,-000-year-old occupation, make the lockstep theory cited above seem unduly rigorous.
4. Migration may have occurred down the western coast of Canada (Fladmark 1978).

Two conclusions stem from the accumulating evidence for the presence of early migrants more than 20,000 years ago. The Old Crow Flats material implies that it would be possible for early migrants to wait out a glacial advance while they occupied the unglaciated Yukon refugium. Then, after deglaciation or during an interstadial, they could have migrated to the south. At the same time, the early dates from Pikimachay Cave suggest that an even longer time scale may be appropriate, with the earliest migration dating to an interglacial period. If so, then the trans-Canada corridor is a side issue insofar as identifying the time and mode of the earliest migration is concerned.

A final word concerns even earlier evidence. Some implements from the site at Dry Creek in

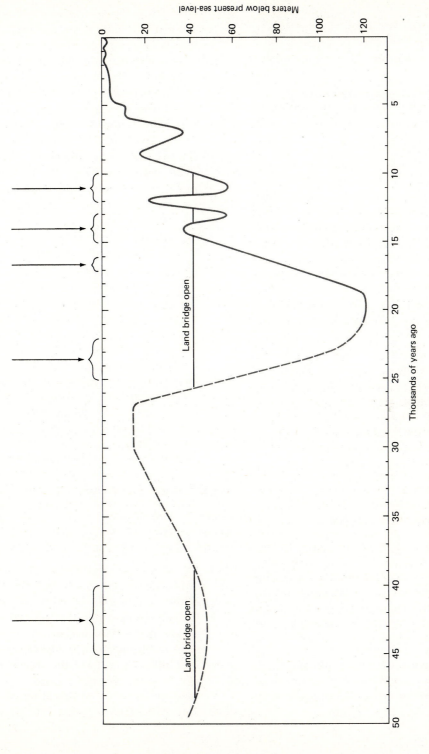

Fig. 17-5 Graph of sea level at Bering Strait. Arrows and brackets illustrate times of possible migrations. (Compiled from Hopkins [1967:Fig. 4] and Müller-Beck [1967:Fig. 2].)

■ Migration depended upon following herds of tundra-dwelling animals.

● The earliest migrants probably were Upper Paleolithic peoples.

▲ The early migrants, few in number, entered a vacant environmental niche of enormous size.

Alaska are of forms that, if found in the Old World, would certainly be classified as Mousterian. Further, Alan Bryan reports the presence of a skull cap from Lagoa Santa Cave in Brazil which is very similar to that of a Neanderthal (Bryan 1978:318). These slight indications suggest that it is not inconceivable that the earliest Americans may date back to the Middle Paleolithic. However, actual proof of this has yet to be established.

To date, a considerable body of data has been acquired from more than 400 known sites that include nearly every country in the New World. Thus the question of the origins and dispersal of early peoples in the New World has proceeded beyond the point where we need actively to seek additional sites, except for the earliest time level. Needed now are synthetic schemes which will lead to an orderly understanding of known data as well as provide an organizational framework for new data as they are acquired.

Environmental Factors

While there are still numerous gaps in our knowledge, we may delimit our study of early migrants to the New World through a combination of major facts known to be either plausible or implausible. These findings fall into two categories, the first of which—environmental factors—is presented below.

1. Although not an absolute requirement, we believe the major New World migrations occurred during times of a land bridge at the Bering Strait (between Siberia and Alaska). The latter formed several times in association with periods of glacial advance.

2. Throughout the time of human entry, Beringia featured a tundra environment.

3. The ice-free areas of Alaska and the Canadian Yukon served as a refuge for humans and animals during times of glacial advance. These areas have been ice-free for the last 30,000 years as a result of high-latitude aridity caused by the glacial accumulation in the Laurentide and Cordilleran Ice Sheets to the south (England and Bradley 1978).

4. During times of glacial advance, the Laurentide and Cordilleran glaciers merged. During times of glacial retreat an ice-free area, the trans-Canada corridor, is believed to have formed between these two glacial masses.

■ 5. During the Pleistocene, North America was invaded by large numbers of Eurasian herd-dwelling mammals, the so-called *Pleistocene megafauna*, and we may assume that hunters followed soon after.

6. During periods of glacial advance, there was a southward displacement of vegetal zones and a corresponding northward shift of these zones in times of glacial retreat.

Cultural Factors

Based on the available evidence, the second major category of knowledge of early New World peoples consists of cultural factors:

1. No cultures specifically identified as Lower or Middle Paleolithic have ever been found in the New World.

2. Human remains from the New World are all assigned to *Homo sapiens sapiens* and date to within the last 30,000 years. (At least this is true for those specimens for which we have verified dates [Protsch 1979].)

3. Migrants to the New World via Beringia first had to adapt to life in higher latitudes. In the Old World, most of such prior adaptations are of Middle Paleolithic age (ca. 70,000–30,000 years ago), although Bordes (1978) states that the earliest Paleolithic adaptation to the colder European climates may date back 200,000 years.

4. The majority of early New World peoples were specialized hunters, a life-style which did not develop until the Middle Paleolithic.

● **5.** The life-style of specialized hunters such as those of the Upper Paleolithic includes a nomadic following of the game herds, or at least seasonal movements adjusted to concentrations of game.

6. Inasmuch as several different early cultural traditions are known in the New World, we may postulate the occurrence of several early migrations rather than a single origin. (However, the presence of distinct traditions could also be the result of postmigration regional adaptation.)

7. By 8000 to 9000 B.C., there were many different cultures present in the New World, each with a locally adapted economy.

Cultural Evolution in the New World

Integrating the above facts and assumptions into a cohesive whole requires that we deal in generalities rather than specifics. The occupation of the New World was part of the worldwide expansion of humans into the higher latitudes which occurred during Middle and Upper Paleolithic times. Claims of great antiquity of early remains in America (50,000–100,000 years) are probably excessive in that prior to entry into the New World, humans had to have adapted to the colder climates of the higher latitudes. In addition, we should expect to find ancestral cultures in Siberia. Evidence to date suggests that Paleo-

lithic peoples *(Homo erectus)* did not live north of 50° N. in Europe and 40° N. in China. The distribution of the Neanderthals is essentially the same (Howell 1965:74, 124). Radiocarbon dates on Pleistocene sites in Siberia range from 39,050 to 9385 B.C. (Klein 1971:141), all dates of Upper Paleolithic age. Cultures cited as possible Siberian antecedents include Diuktai, dated 33,000 to 31,000 B.C., and Mal'ta-Afontova (Mochanov 1978). Most evidence suggests that occupation of the New World was accomplished by the modern humans, *Homo sapiens sapiens*, after they had developed a life-style based upon exploitation of game herds in a tundra environment. Movement into the New World was therefore part of the worldwide expansion of humans into previously unoccupied regions.

We assume that these early migrants were few in number. ▲ In addition, the concept of solitary bands entering an unoccupied habitat of enormous extent at several times provides one explanation for the cultural diversity to be perceived at the 8000–10,000 B.C. time level. Cultural evolution (or adaptation) to the various New World environments was rapid and was facilitated by band isolation. This view also helps to explain our difficulty in identifying specific Old World cultural antecedents of New World industries. Movements of peoples, once south of the ice border, would have been governed to some degree by the presence of physiographic features and vegetation zones. We can thus infer migration routes and population movements in response to shifts in these zones.

A final consideration is the *mode* of population movements. Martin (1973) has presented an argument for the "wave" theory of migration. His view envisions a population "front" of approximately 40 persons per 100 km^2, traveling like the crest of a wave inexorably southward at a speed that moved the front from Edmonton, Alberta to Tierra del Fuego within 1,000 years (Fig. 17-6). Behind this front, however, population density would have been much less. An al-

■ Common elements in the classification schemes

● The Core Tool-Chopper migration

ternative view is that of the band splitting typical of modern-day hunter-gatherers, which occurs when population density reaches about 30 percent of land carrying capacity (Lee and DeVore 1968). Owing to the cultural diversity present at the 8000–10,000 B.C. time level, we favor the band-splitting mode as more appropri-ate than the wave theory of a single massive migration.

The Cultural Inventory

Early sites in the New World are hereby arbitrarily defined as those dated earlier than 8,000 years ago. This large, lumped-together category includes sites of varying complexity of cultural content, varying associations (geological, floral, and faunal), and varying degrees of authenticity

Fig. 17-6 Movement of early hunters in the New World as the "crest of a wave." As extinction of local fauna occurred, the "wave" moved southward. (Martin 1973:Fig. 2.)

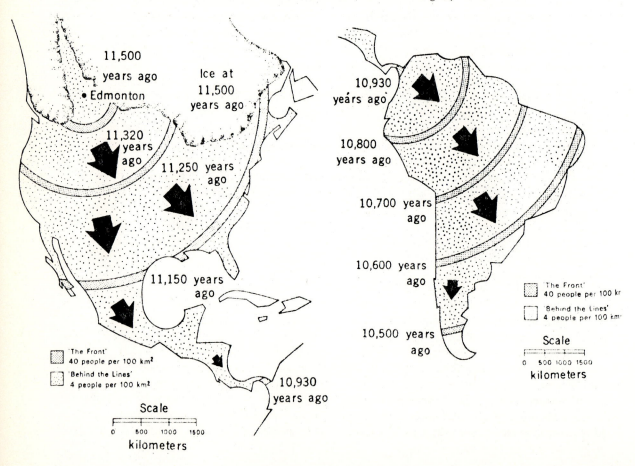

TABLE **17-2**
New World Cultural Chronologies according to Various Authorities

Age B.C.	Krieger (1964)	Willey (1966) North America	Willey (1971) South America	MacNeish (1971)
6000	Proto-Archaic Stage	Desert Tradition, Archaic Tradition; Northwest Microblade Tradition	Andean Hunting-Collecting Tradition	Specialized Point Tradition
8000	Paleo-Indian Stage	Old Cordilleran Tradition, Big-Game-Hunting Tradition	Old South American Hunting Tradition, East Brazilian Upland Tradition	Blade, Burin, Leaf-Point Tradition
10,000		Hypothetical Origins	Biface Tradition, Chopper Tradition	Flake and Bone Tool Tradition
18,000	Pre-Projectile Point Stage	Problematical Pre-Projectile Point Horizon	Flake Tradition	Core Tool Tradition

of stratigraphic position, accuracy of dating, and acceptability of "artifacts."

It is no wonder then that authorities have had difficulty in classifying these diverse manifestations into a comprehensive scheme. Major researchers who have dealt at some length with this so-called pre-8000-year-old level are Alex Krieger, Gordon Willey, and Richard MacNeish. Both Krieger and MacNeish have attempted a single scheme encompassing the entire New World. Willey's classifications are separate for North America and South America, although he indicates their interrelationships. In Table 17-2 we have attempted to correlate these three classifications with one another.

Integration of New World Classifications

The synthetic schemes proposed by Krieger, Willey, and MacNeish differ in detail but possess major elements in common. It is these common elements which aid our attempt to order our thinking about early peoples in the Americas. Although such an overview suffers from overgeneralization, it provides the advantage of being so broad in scope that individual new finds are not likely to prove it to be erroneous in major

features. ■ Several major agreements among the various schemes are as follows:

● **1.** Evidence at several sites suggests that the earliest migrants possessed a Core Tool-Chopper-Nonprojectile Point complex of implements which are specifically not related to the Acheulean-Mousterian cultural tradition of the Old World. Instead, they may be derived from the Chopper-Chopping Tool tradition of Southeast Asia and China, as MacNeish suggests (Fig. 17-7). Inasmuch as this Core Tool tradition is early in the New World and is not related to the Old World Upper Paleolithic, it seems our best evidence of the earliest Americans. These remains do *not* imply a culture adapted to a tundra environment and life in a cold climate. It thus seems reasonable to suggest that such early migrants from Asia may have made their way northward to the Bering Strait during a warmer interval, an interglacial or interstadial. There is no need, however, to evoke great age for these remains. According to the climatic data recovered from the Camp Century ice core, substantial warm intervals occurred between 17,000 and 21,000 B.C., between 29,-

▲ The Upper Paleolithic blade-using migrants

■ The first culture adapted to the New World

● A late survival of the Core Tool tradition

500 and 31,500 B.C., and yet earlier between 35,000 and 42,000 B.C. (Flint 1971:Fig. 16–13). Why should archaeologists refer loosely to the antiquity of occupation in the New World as being possibly "50,000 to 100,000" years of age when more recent dates are tenable? (Figure 17-7 illustrates the possible times and routes of this migration.)

2. The next migrants to the New World were the cold-adapted, specialized big-game hunters with cultural affinities derived from the Old World Upper Paleolithic. ▲ These migrants possessed flake and blade industries with traits of Mousterian affinity as well as those of generalized Upper Paleolithic type. Specific traits typical of European industries (e.g., Aurignacian, Gravettian, etc.) do not occur. This fact suggests that the New World migrants were an off-shoot of Siberian cultures that had diverged culturally prior to the advent of the European specialized Upper Paleolithic industries. Here is where we may lump Willey's Flake tradition with MacNeish's Flake and Bone Tool tradition and the Blade, Burin, and Leaf-Point tradition. These three traditions have in common generalized late

Fig. 17-7 Hypothetical reconstruction of the Chopper Tool migration to the New World.

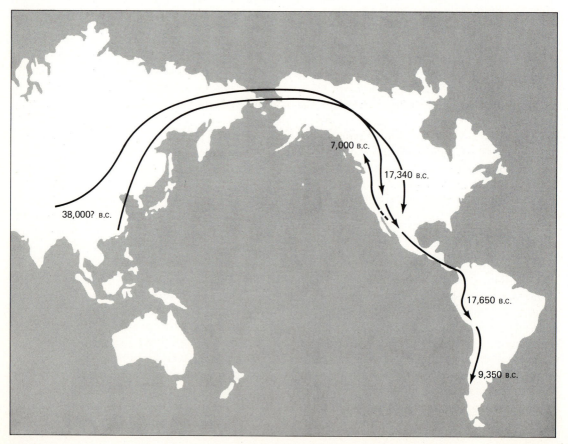

Mousterian-Upper Paleolithic affinities. They thus represent our current evidence of the second group of New World migrants (Fig. 17-8). The validity of each of these as a separate tradition awaits the accumulation of new evidence. They may represent separate waves of migrants or sequential evolutionary steps in a single major tradition which could be termed "New World Upper Paleolithic."

■ **3.** The Paleo-Indian tradition, with its distinctive life-style, fluted projectile points, and relatively high population density, represents a New World cultural adaptation. These peoples possessed hunting techniques adapted to New World environmental conditions as well as new types of stone implements evolved from generalized Old World antecedents. They represented the first "American" culture.

● **4.** The Old Cordilleran tradition seems the best candidate for a late survival of the early core tool users, with the addition of bifacially flaked bi-points. This culture co-existed with the Paleo-Indian tradition, and the differences in their cultural inventories implies separate histories over a very long time. The presence in South America of a Core Tool-Chopper tradition followed by the Andean Biface horizon is a situation highly analogous to that in North America. Unfortunately, the former is not well known, perhaps due to our long-standing fixation on Paleo-Indian remains. Future re-

Fig. 17-8 The Late Mousteroid-Upper Paleolithic migration to the New World.

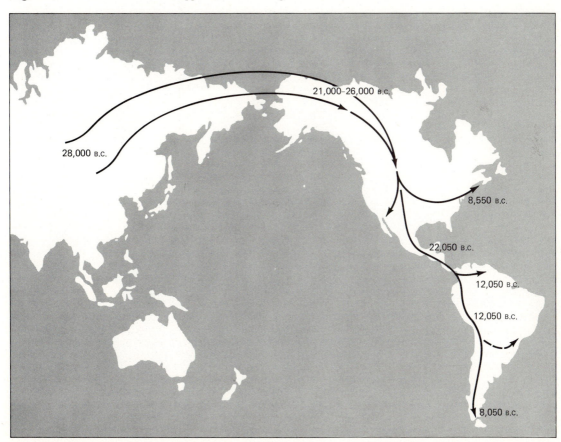

▲ The Microblade migration

search will undoubtedly help clarify the evolution of this major cultural tradition. Owing to a different economic orientation, the Core Tool tradition may have been spreading back northward (Fig. 17-7) as the Paleo-Indians were expanding to the south (Fig. 17-8).

5. At least one post-Pleistocene dispersal is documented, that of the Northwest Microblade tradition. This is a Mesolithic-type industry found earliest in northern Japan between 10,000 and 14,000 B.C. (Hayashi 1968; Kobayashi 1970; Morlan 1967a,

1967b). ▲ Successive isochronic lines have been plotted from radiocarbon-dated sites (Fig. 17-9) documenting the steady movement of microblade manufacture from Alaska to the south and east between 9000 B.C. and A.D.1. Müller-Beck (1967:402) further perceives cultural similarities between the Aurignacoid industry at Mal'ta and the Aleutian site at Anangula (6500 B.C.). He thus postulates during this same post-Pleistocene interval an Aurignacoid migration into northern North America (Fig. 17-10).

In summary, three major traditions have been identified. The earliest was the Core Tool-Chopper tradition, which was followed by the New World Upper Paleolithic tradition, which in turn was suc-

Fig. 17-9   The Microblade migration to the New World.

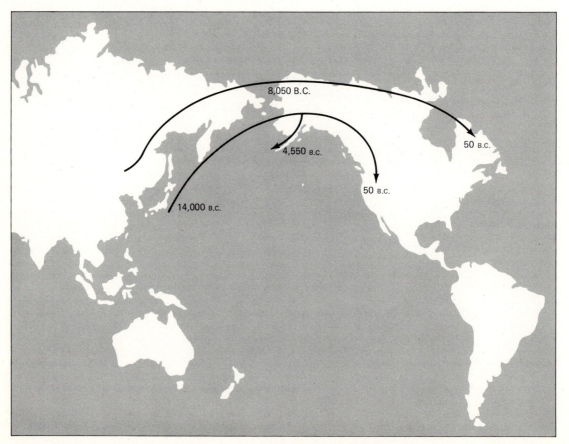

ceeded by the Microblade tradition. We may term the latter culture a "New World Mesolithic" tradition. A fourth movement of less extent, identified by Müller-Beck, consists of a late arrival of Siberian Upper Paleolithic cultures of Aurignacian affinities.

Migration Routes

The suitability of routes taken by the early migrants was conditioned by topography and the extent of glaciation. In North America, the unglaciated portion of central Alaska as well as the Arctic coastal plain north of the Brooks range provided alternative routes to the interior. Migrations across Canada from north to south are typically portrayed as extending along the MacKenzie River valley through the corridor between the Cordilleran and Laurentide Ice Sheets into the continental United States. Within that region the primary route is assumed to lie east of the Rocky Mountains, continuing southward into the Cordillera Central of Mexico. Offshoots of the main route undoubtedly extended to the east and west. An alternative route is suggested by Fladmark (1978) as extending from Alaska through Canada and down the west coast. Evidence of any migrants in Central America is still minimal, yet there exists abundant evidence that such migrants did reach South America. Recently, evidence of Clovis

Fig. 17-10 The Aurignacoid migration to the New World.

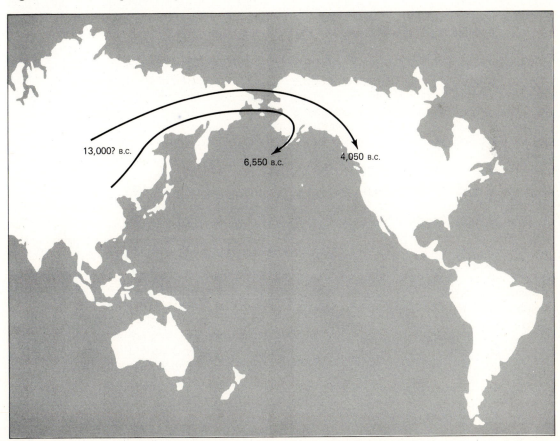

■ The Andean chain—a migration route 3,000 miles in length.

● The Core Tool tradition existed through numerous climatic fluctuations.

▲ The Upper Paleolithic migrants evolved into the Paleo-Indian tradition.

materials has been reported from highland Guatemala, so the documentation continues to accumulate.

In South America we have a unique geographical setting. The Andean mountain chain extends most of the length of the continent. ■ Thus, for nearly 3,000 miles, early migrants could have moved from north to south within the same environmental zone or zones. One result is that north-to-south migration would not have required any modification in economy. On the other hand, a shift of 100 miles or so to the east or west of the Andean range would have required such a readaptation. Possible exceptions to this situation would have been eastward movement into the Venezuelan plains and the east Brazilian uplands. (These concepts of migration routes are integrated with our discussion of early cultural traditions in Figures 17-7 to 17-10).

Environmental Adaptations

Core Tool-Chopper Tradition

The Paccacaisa complex of crude stone tools from highland Peru was associated with a warm, forested environment which shifted to a cold grassland late in the period. Associated fauna were horse or camel and sloth. The Chopper tradition of Venezuela was associated with a climate cooler and wetter than that of today. The region featured forests and savanna grasslands populated with mastodon, horse, and sloth. The Old Cordilleran tradition featured hunting, fishing, and plant collecting, and thus had a mixed economy rather than a specialized one. The later

portion of the Old Cordilleran tradition extended into the Altithermal, a warmer, ● dry interval, and adapted to such a climate. ● To summarize these disparate data; the Core Tool-Chopper tradition persisted over a long time through repeated climatic fluctuations and must be viewed as a culture of considerable economic flexibility.

New World Upper Paleolithic Tradition

Upper Paleolithic-type cultures in the New World were Taiga-Tundra adapted, specialized big-game hunters who, as they moved southward, became hunters of the Great Plains, gallery forests, eastern deciduous woodlands, altiplano, forested savanna, and savanna grasslands. These people thus demonstrated flexibility in adapting to differing environmental niches, while continuing in their adherence to big game hunting. ▲ This culture, culminating in the Paleo-Indian tradition, consists of the first specifically adapted New World peoples. Their specialization led to cultural extinction with the advent of the climatic changes accompanying the Altithermal.

Since several hundred sites are known and many have been excavated, the Paleo-Indian tradition is the best-known early New World culture. As a result, we have a more complete understanding of its economy and life-style. The basic environmental adaptation is best known from sites such as Clovis, Dent, and Lindenmeier in the Great Plains. However, sites are also common in the eastern United States and data indicate that these sites are not only numerous but more varied than those in the West. In addition, Meadowcroft and Dutchess Quarry caves date earlier than the western Clovis manifestations. Since it has been described in detail, we will present a review of the Plains adaptation as it is known (Wendorf and Hester 1962):

The Paleo-Indian cultural tradition on the Great Plains was adapted to the utilization and exploita-

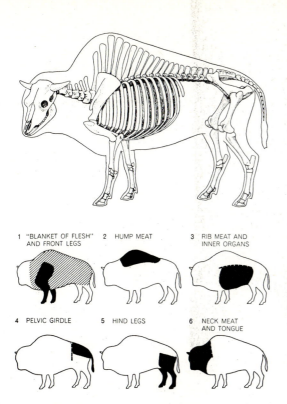

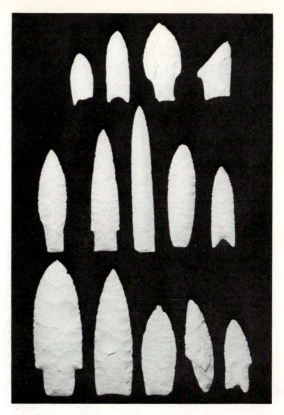

Fig. 17-11 Reconstruction of the butchering methods used by the Paleo-Indian hunters at the Olsen-Chubbock site. The black areas illustrate specific "butchering units" that were identified by the excavator from the piles of bones at the site. (Wheat 1967:52.)

Fig. 17-12 Examples of Paleo-Indian artifacts. *(Top from left)* Folsom point; Plainview point; Stemmed point, Patagonia; Cody knife *(Middle from left)* Hell Gap point; Scottsbluff point; Eden Valley point; Agate Basin point; Jimmy Allen point *(Bottom from left)* Alberta point; Clovis point; Brown's Valley point; Saudia point; Saudia point (fluted, Lucy site). (Grady photograph.)

tion of a savanna grassland with abundant permanent water in small ponds and streams. . . . The stream valleys sheltered galleries of juniper and oak in the valleys and along the bottoms. On this savanna landscape moved large herds of giant bison and smaller groups of other Pleistocene forms now extinct.

The correlation between type of site and site situation is striking . . . campsites tend to occur on ridges, dunes, or hills which overlook either a stream channel or a pond at a distance of several hundred yards to a mile. Kill sites tend to occur either at the edge of former ponds or stream channels.

Attributes of a camp site include hearths, discarded food bones, chipping debris, and a full

chipped and flaked tool complex [Figs. 17-11, 17-12]. . . . The food bones are normally disarticulated and are occasionally split and charred. Seeds, grinding stones, and storage or cooking pits are rarely present. Activities identified with campsites include food preparation, working of hides, and tool manufacture. The high proportion of point bases over point tips, a common attribute of campsite lithic collections, is suggestive of repair of weapons.

Kill sites are characterized by animal skeletons, frequently in high numbers, with the associated projectile points utilized to kill them plus a limited number of chipped and flaked butchering tools in-

343

■ Paleo-Indian butchering techniques

● A massive Late Pleistocene extinction removed 31 genera of large animals without replacement. Were human hunters responsible?

Fig. 17-13 River of Bones resulting from a Paleo-Indian stampede of bison across a small arroyo: the Olsen-Chubbock site in southeastern Colorado. (Courtesy of Joe Ben Wheat.)

cluding some of bone. Often preferred portions of the animals are missing. These body parts, presumably, were cut out and taken back to nearby campsites, though hearths are occasionally present indicating that some of the kill was consumed or smoked on the spot.

One basic hunting pattern, reconstructed as follows, represents a majority of all the sites surveyed. The campsite was situated so that animals in the vicinity could be observed as they came for water. Once observed, the animals were stalked and killed as they were drinking in a stream or pond. The number of animals killed by this technique ranged from one to about thirty. Both mammoth and bison were hunted by this method.

A second pattern is the stampede ... the animals in this case being bison which were driven into an arroyo, a stream, or over a cliff, where many of the animals were crushed or drowned. The number of animals killed by this technique occasionally was as high as several hundred. ...

The location of the projectile points in the carcasses indicates an identical method of killing for both mammoth and bison. The spears were aimed at the thoracic region with the intent to penetrate the heart, spinal cord or other vital parts. ...

The absence of an emphasis on the hunting of horses and the absence of mammoth traps suggest that we are studying hunting techniques specifically adapted to New World conditions rather than techniques transferred from an Old World tradition.

■ Our best evidence for Paleo-Indian butchering techniques comes from the Olsen-Chubbock site in Eastern Colorado. At this site approximately 190 bison were killed by stampeding across a small arroyo (Fig. 17-13). Of the bison killed, approximately 75 percent were completely butchered and 16 percent were partially butchered. The task would have required 100 people about two and a half hours or 50 people a half-day. Ten men could have completed the task in about two days (Wheat 1972:116).

In his analysis Wheat, assuming that 50 percent of the usable meat was preserved by drying, estimates the size of the participating group of early hunters as follows. His estimate is 36,560 pounds of usable meat, which could have been eaten by 50 persons in 73 days, 100 persons in 37 days, 150 persons in 24 days, or 200 persons in 18 days. If 100 persons had 100 dogs, the consumption could have taken place within 22 days (Wheat 1972:122). While not precise, such estimates help us to understand the possible kill-utilization patterns that the Paleo-Indians may have employed. (The sequence of butchering of an individual bison is illustrated in Figure 17-11.)

A study of sites by time period for the Llano Estacado (Texas and New Mexico) revealed 13 sites of Clovis age, 29 of Folsom, and 39 of the Parallel Flaked or Plano horizon period. Many of these were multicomponent sites, suggesting a continuation of the same land-use pattern through several thousand years (Wendorf and Hester 1975). The site data also imply a steady population increase through time.

Analysis of stone types utilized for tool manufacture at Blackwater Draw, New Mexico, and the location of the stone quarries has led to the inference that the Paleo-Indian social group, probably a small band or an extended kin group, ranged over an area with a radius of 90 to 120 miles, with the radius of the territory utilized from a single campsite ranging from 3.6 to 18.6 miles. Band size was estimated at six families totaling 25 members, 5 to 10 of whom served as hunters (Hester and Grady 1977:92–94). Through time the Paleo-Indian tradition featured changes in tool inventory and in the animals hunted.

A New World Mesolithic Tradition?

The concept of a New World Mesolithic tradition is not a particularly sound one. Certainly, there was an expansion of microblade users into northwestern North America, but their economy may have featured a greater degree of hunting specialization than was the case with Old World Mesolithic peoples. Although the later Eastern Archaic tradition (to be discussed in the next chapter) featured a mixed hunting-gathering economy of generalized Mesolithic type, culturally this was a separate New World evolutionary unit not historically related to the Old World Mesolithic. Perhaps the major conclusion to be reached from this observation is that by the Postglacial period cultural evolution in the New World had gained momentum to the point that any new migrants were rapidly acculturated or assimilated and hence quickly adapted to New World environments. Current evidence suggests that the population of early New World migrants was initially small but then rapidly increased after their arrival, owing to the availability of food resources in previously unexploited environmental niches. In any event, site-density data indicate that any migrants entering the New World after 9000 B.C. would have found numerous guides to show them the way or numerous occupants already exploiting the better environments.

Late Pleistocene Extinction

One of the most dramatic events to occur at any time during the tenure of humankind on earth is the widespread extinction of the Late Pleistocene mammalian fauna. Martin (1967) has reviewed the problem in some detail. According to this analysis, the extinction was rapid, occurring between 13,000 and 6000 B.C. The areas where this occurred include North America and South America, New Zealand, Australia, and Madagascar. The extinction primarily affected the large herd-dwelling mammals of more than 50 kilograms adult weight (Fig. 17-2). With their primary hosts so removed, the extinction broadened to include the associated carnivores, scavengers, commensals, and parasites.

● The loss of 31 genera of large herbivores in North America alone documents the scope of this prehistoric ecological catastrophe. What is even more impressive, as it contrasts with earlier periods of extinction, is that most of these animals were not superseded by other species mals were not superseded by other species adapted to their ecological niche. In many cases these niches have remained empty to the present, and thus we have a case of extinction without replacement. Also of unique quality is the fact that the small mammals did not suffer a corresponding reduction but continued in existence to become our modern fauna. Only the modern bison, elk, deer, mountain sheep, caribou, mountain goat, and musk-ox remain as large herbivores, and these species average considerably less in body weight then their Late Pleistocene predecessors. Further unique features cited by Martin are that the large oceanic mammals did not become extinct, nor did appreciable numbers of species of plants. Thus the Late Pleistocene mammalian extinction is unique and imbalanced.

Martin further poses the question: Why did extinction occur when it did? If the extinction was related to climatic change, why did it occur after the fauna had survived several previous glacial and interglacial periods? Martin explains this unique pattern of extinction as the result of prehistoric overkill by early hunters, but this hypothesis cannot be verified easily. Certainly, early peoples hunted many of the animals which became extinct. On the other hand, numerous other genera which became extinct have not been reported in association with artifacts, implying that these, at least, were not hunted by humans. Other explanations that have been offered (Martin and Wright 1967) include stress brought about by climatic changes, disease, and out-of-phase mating patterns. These issues have not yet been resolved, but from our perspective, as we trace the cultural development of early peoples in the New World, the extinction of the Late Pleistocene fauna was and is highly significant. It meant these early Americans could no longer survive as specialized big game hunters, regardless of whether they had been primarily responsible for the extinction. And by this time it had become necessary to modify the economy in ways that will be examined in the chapter which follows.

18

The Development of New World Cultures

Following the initial peopling of the New World was a period of filling up of the available environmental zones (Figs. 18-1, 18-2). This expansion was rapid and undoubtedly was accompanied by a low population density. Once established, however, early New World cultures began to undergo population growth with increasing specialization and adaptation to specific New World environments. The first major focus on regional adaptation is what we term the *Archaic stage*. The earliest Americans had followed a life-style based on gathering and migratory big game hunting. Later Americans took up farming and a sedentary life-style. In between those adaptations was the Archaic, a distinctive life-style lasting for thousands of years.

The Archaic Stage

■ The concept of an Archaic stage, divided arbitrarily by Griffin (1979:226–239) into early (8000–6000 B.C.), middle (6000–4000 B.C.) and late (4000–1000 B.C.), has shifted in recent years from a concern with the types of artifacts utilized to an emphasis on life-style and ecological adjustment. One reason for this has been the development of a greater understanding of the nature of the Archaic. Previously, when cultures were viewed primarily in terms of their artifactual inventory, the Archaic appeared to be a bewildering maze of local cultures, here using fish weirs, nets, fishhooks, and such, there using choppers and grinding stones. Attempts at chronological ordering through reference to artifact types were frustrated by the wide variety of artifact forms as well as by the limited change of

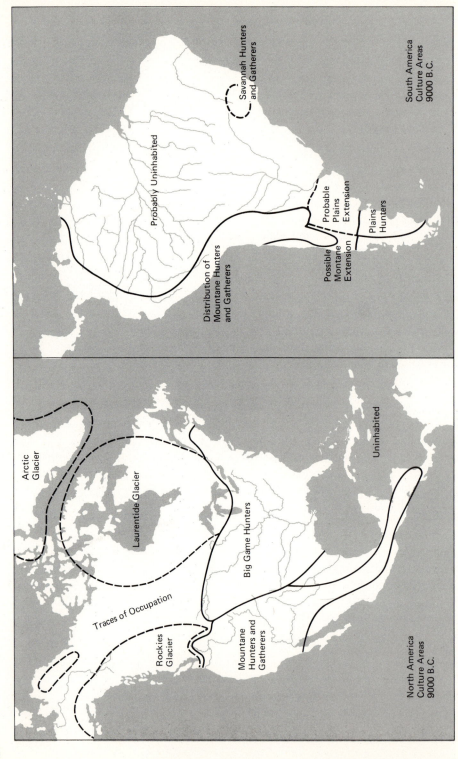

Fig. 18-1 New World culture areas at 9000 B.C. (Modified from Sanders and Marino 1970:Fig. 2.)

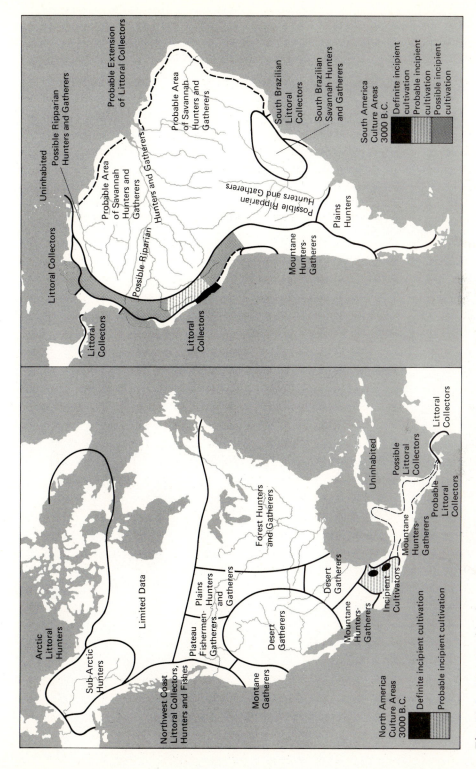

Fig. 18-2 New World culture areas at 3000 B.C. (Modified from Sanders and Marino 1970.Fig. 3.)

349

these through time. A further problem concerned the chronological overlap between early Archaic cultures (as early as 8000 B.C.) and late Paleo-Indian manifestations (as late as 6000 B.C.). If the Archaic had evolved from the Paleo-Indian tradition, then why was there such an overlap in age? Was this due to errors in dating, or could the Archaic represent direct descendants of an earlier non-Paleo-Indian tradition? Further problems derived from attempts to define the Archaic in negative terms. (For example, it did not possess either pottery or agriculture.) As a result of these problems, the Archaic stage became the focus of a special conference at the So-

ciety for American Archaeology meetings in 1955, and a publication growing out of that meeting (Byers 1959) led to the present concept of a continent-wide Archaic stage.

The latter concept refers to the Archaic stage as dominated by hunting-gathering societies, each exploiting its local environment with a breadth and intensity of resource utilization previously unknown in the New World. These societies exploited the plant kingdom, especially in the gathering of seeds. Shellfish were collected where available in quantity, fishing became important, and no species of small mammal was ignored. As the ecological niches were

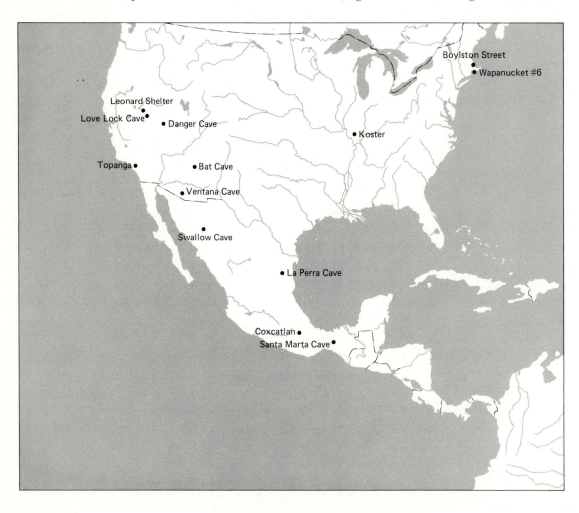

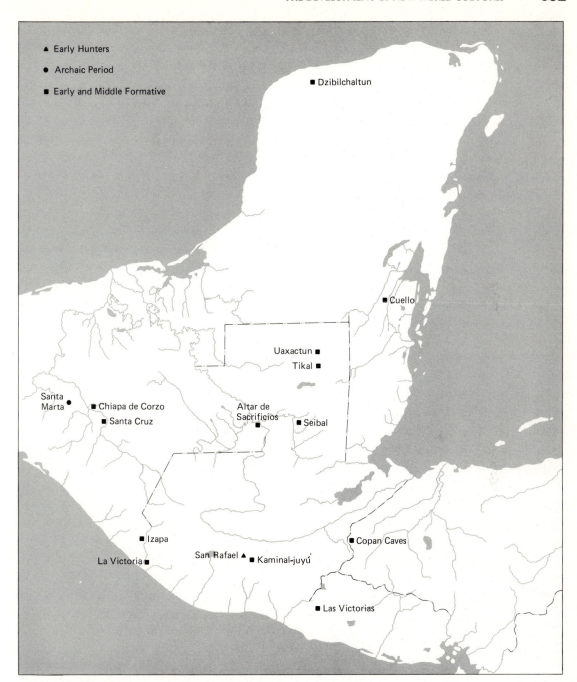

▲ Early Hunters

● Archaic Period

■ Early and Middle Formative

■ Dzibilchaltun

■ Cuello

Uaxactun ■

Tikal ■

Santa
Marta ●   ■ Chiapa de Corzo
        ■ Santa Cruz

Altar de
Sacrificios
        ■   ■ Seibal

■ Izapa

San Rafael ▲   ■ Copan Caves

La Victoria ■   ■ Kaminal-juyú

■ Las Victorias

Map 18-1a&b Archaic Sites in North America. (After Russell and Meadowcroft)

● Archaic peoples were semisedentary.

systematically explored for utilizable resources, the tool inventory became increasingly varied and to some degree specialized, although numerous multipurpose tools were also in vogue (Fig. 18-3).

● Other characteristics of the Archaic adaptation included a band-type social organization made up of small related groups of people with a semisedentary life-style. Termed *restricted wandering* (Beardsley et al. 1955), this pattern emphasized seasonal movements of the band

Fig. 18-3 Fish trap constructed of rock walls located at the mouth of a salmon spawning stream. At high tide the walls inundated. At low tide the fish are trapped behind the walls. (Photo courtesy of J. Anthony Pomeroy.)

from one known food resource or harvest to another. The required mobility limited the quantity of cultural items that could be acquired or transported. Campsites tended to be revisited as the group moved in a yearly cycle. However, the necessity to move in order to acquire adequate food at all seasons of the year inhibited the kinds of cultural developments that are associated with a fully sedentary life. In the Archaic, then, we have the formation of a life-style which tended to reinforce itself. The Archaic need for mobility as well as the ability of the economy to meet current needs tended to slow the rate of cultural change. For these reasons, some Archaic societies lasted into the historic period. For example, in the Great Basin cultures exhibited homeostasis (a state of nonchange in which all parts of the system are in harmony) over 9,000 to 10,000 years, a balanced adaptation to scarce but stable multiple resources (Jennings 1968:136–137). Owing to regional diversity in environments, it has been possible to define separate resource utilization patterns for the Archaic. We thus have the Primary Forest Efficiency of the eastern United States, the Coastal Adaptations of the Atlantic Seaboard, the Desert Culture of the Great Basin, and others.

Primary Forest Efficiency (Caldwell 1958) is defined as a mixed reliance on forest products (nuts, berries, fruits, and seeds, each harvested in turn) in conjunction with the hunting of deer and small mammals as well as use of riverine resources, primarily fish and the freshwater mussels. Caldwell describes this pattern as one of harmonious balance between humans and their environment, with increasing specialization and diversity in the tool inventory through time. Although seasonal shifts in resource harvests were the rule, the site types suggest there were base camps utilized for part of the year interspersed with use of small temporary seasonal-harvest camps. By 2000 B.C. there had developed strong linkages in the cultural patterns of all eastern Archaic peoples. Furthermore, they had reached the maximum population possible with the Archaic economy. Archaic productive efficiency included the utilization of all natural resources, not just foods. For example, fiber was used extensively in matting, basketry, nets, sandals, and cordage. The resulting products led to efficiency in fishing, trapping, winnowing, storage, and transport.

Following the final retreat of the Wisconsin glaciation there was a gradual replacement of tundra and boreal forest by mixed oak deciduous forests as the climate zones shifted to the north during the Postglacial. In contrast to the closed pine boreal forest, this new forest biome was rich in plant food (nuts, seeds, etc.) and in animals (white-tail deer, bear, elk, small mammals, birds, turtles, etc.), and the streams and coasts provided fish and shellfish. Migratory birds were also present in large numbers. With such resources at their disposal it is not surprising that Archaic cultures were present in eastern North America and that they are viewed as being adaptations to this new Postglacial environment.

In general, sites tended to be larger in size and to occur in greater frequency than in the preceding Paleo-Indian period, thereby indicating larger populations. This increased population density may be attributed to the greater carrying capacity of the Postglacial environment.

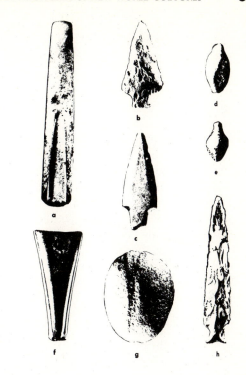

Fig. 18-4 Boreal archaic tools from coastal sites in Maine. (*a, f*) Gouge; (*b, h*) chipped point; (*c*) slate point; (*d, e*) plummets; (*g*) grooved bolas stone. (*c, d, g, h*) early Boreal; others, late Boreal. (After Byers, 1959.)

Early Archaic: 8000–6000 B.C.*

The *Early Archaic* represents the period when the region acquired vegetation similar to that present when the first Europeans arrived (Griffin 1978:227). Most of our information on the Early Archaic comes from the margins of northeast America, particularly from locations like Modoc Rock Shelter and the Koster site in Illinois. On the other hand the amount of information on Early and Middle Archaic cultures is sparse for Indiana and Ohio and almost absent for New York and New England. In fact there is a south-to-north gradient in which site frequency increases from south to north from the Early Archaic (rare) to the Late Archaic (abundant). Both Fitting (1969) and Ritchie (1969, 1971) argue that Archaic penetration of the northeast is correlated with the northward advance of the deciduous forest and the concurrent retreat of the boreal pine forest during the hypsithermal climatic episode (Funk 1978:22–23). This "gap" in the archaeological record of the Early Archaic and Middle Archaic has been attributed to the low carrying capacity of the boreal pine forest (Fig. 18-4). In other words, there are few sites because food resources were also few and far between. Griffin (1978), on the other hand, feels that the "gap" is due to the failure of investigators to devote adequate time and re-

*After Funk 1978:16–27.

▲ The Boylston Street Fish Weir

sources to the search for Early and Middle Archaic sites.

Both points of view may be correct. Certainly, sites do exist that have Early Archaic components. Sheeprock Rock Shelter in Pennsylvania has occupancy dated to 6920 ± 320 B.C. This layer is situated immediately above a layer containing Kirk corner-notched points which have been dated to 7000 B.C. in the southeastern United States. The middle levels produced untyped, stemmed points and untyped corner-notched points which are attributed to the Early and Middle Archaic periods. Other scattered sites in New York, New Jersey, Pennsylvania, and New Hampshire partly confirm Griffin's hypothesis of the Early and Middle Archaic penetration of the northeast, but the overall scarcity of sites for these periods may still be due to the limited resource potential of the region.

Middle Archaic: 6000–4000 B.C.

By the Middle Archaic period the vegetal cover had assumed a completely modern appearance. Concurrently during this period Indian expansion reached its northernmost limits both in the interior and on the coast (Griffin 1978:229).

In southern New England, Dincauze (1971) has identified the Neville complex, characterized by large, straight-based Neville points, and the Stock complex (stemmed-point forms). Neville and Stock have the earliest ground and polished stone tools in the northeast (6000–5000 b.c.) and seem to parallel development farther south in North Carolina.

Some of the Middle Archaic sites are spring fishing stations, located where spawning anadromous fish could be caught. To date, we have only evidence of riverine and lake-margin sites. The extent to which sea resources were exploited is unknown thus far, since sea-oriented sites are presently submerged. The available evidence supports the basic idea of people involved in diverse economic activities on a seasonal basis.

The Late Archaic: 4000–1000 B.C.

The best available evidence of the Archaic and its life-styles comes, of course, from the Late Archaic period (Tuck 1978:28–39). Here, for the first time, cohesive complexes can be identified. During the Late Archaic, for example, we can see the nature of the ecological adaptations in which contemporary groups inhabiting differing locales exhibit different patterns of behavior. What we are dealing with is broad regional adaptations in which the impact of local environments can be perceived. (In a sense, these local adaptations can be viewed as variations on a theme.) During this period houses appear for the first time (Fig. 18-5), skill in grinding and polishing stone reaches a high degree of development, and long-distance trade is established along the water routes.

Within the northeast several regional complexes have been identified. These include the Mixed Prairie-Hardwood area of the midwest, the Lake Forest area, the Maritime area, and the Mixed Forest areas of the northeast. These regional groups are followed by a general transitional period in which steatite bowls, early ceramic vessels, and thick soapstone gorgets all make their appearance. Points tend to be broad-stemmed, foreshadowing those of the succeeding Woodland period.

In the Mixed Prairie-Hardwood area the best evidence of local adaptation comes from the Koster site in southern Illinois. Here deer, elk, beaver, bear, raccoon, fox, and squirrel were taken, as were turkeys, pigeons, fish, and shellfish. In general these people made their living by hunting, fishing, and collecting.

In contrast, the Lake Forest adaptations occurred in a biome distinguishable from the boreal forest to the north and the deciduous forest to the south. Communication was based on the use of the water bodies, lakes and rivers. Hunting of raccoon, cottontail, deer, and gray squirrel was common in the Lake Forest region. Fish were significant as well. A unique aspect of the period is the Maritime Archaic burial cult, featuring multiple burials with associated stone and bone implements.

Caribou were the dominant Cervidae of the Maritime region, which included northern New England, the maritime provinces of Canada, Newfoundland, and Labrador. In the southern portions of this region caribou gave way to moose and elk. However, the most important resources came from the sea, and several varieties of seal as well as walrus, porpoise, and various species of whale were available for exploitation. In the spring and summer the maritime peoples exploited the coasts for their resources, both mammal and fish. ▲ An outstanding site is the Boylston Street Fish Weir found during excavations for a building in Boston in 1913. The weir was constructed of sharpened wooden stakes of 4 to 16 feet in length which had been driven into a bed of blue clay 16 feet below modern sea level. Obviously, sea level then was lower since the weir would have been between the high-

and low-tide lines, with the tops of the stakes under water at high tide. The 65,000 stakes, placed about 2500 B.C., had bundles of brush wedged between them to make a fence impenetrable to the fish trapped within. The two acres of area enclosed within the weir could have provided an enormous fish catch under favorable conditions. On the west coast of Canada, modern Indians used somewhat similar traps made of stone until about 40 years ago. They stated that traps of this sort could provide up to 400 salmon in a single day's catch, a total of about 2,000 pounds.

In the Mixed Forest areas of the northeast south of New Hampshire, in the oak, hickory, chestnut, deer, and turkey biome, we have a pat-

Fig. 18-5 Lodge floor plans found at Wapanucket No. 6, Massachusetts. (Jennings 1968:Fig. 4-10.)

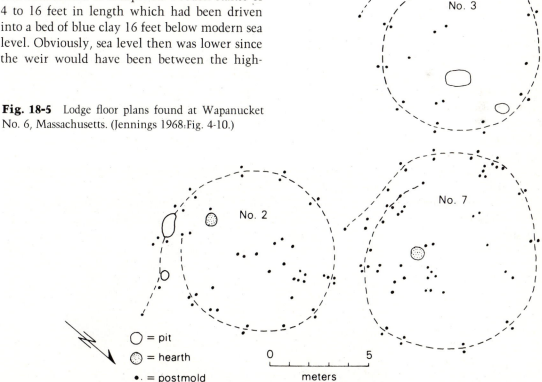

■ Adaptation to a desert environment

● Adaptation to gathering seeds and acorns

▲ Adaptation to the seacoast

tern of seasonal-resource exploitation. In general, there was year-round coastal occupancy, which was complemented by inland hunting on a seasonal basis. With the first snows these Archaic peoples moved inland to take migratory caribou. The rest of the winter was spent in hunting solitary caribou, beaver, and so on, until spring.

The Desert Culture

Widespread in the American Southwest, the Great Basin, and northern Mexico was the Archaic manifestation termed the Desert Culture (Jennings and Norbeck 1955). ■ The economy was specialized to acquire a living in a semiarid region characterized by numerous varieties of cactus, desert grasses, and shrubs. At varying altitudes, the tree species included mesquite, juniper, pinon, and, on the highest mountains, pine, spruce, and fir. Since surface water was rare to nonexistent and vegetation sparse, the carrying capacity of the environment for flora, fauna, and

humans was low. The economic specializations practiced were seed gathering and the use of traps and snares to acquire small mammals, reptiles, and birds. The culture pattern is best known from numerous stratified dry cave sites in the Great Basin: Danger Cave, Ventana Cave, Lovelock Shelter, and Leonard Shelter. In the Great Basin the transition to an Archaic economy occurred early, with the extinction of the Late Pleistocene fauna occurring by about 9000 B.C. The same economy, as represented by the culture of the Paiute Indians, persisted into the historic period of the nineteenth century A.D.

The Desert Culture is also noted for its wealth of preserved perishable artifacts and food remains (Fig. 18-6). The dry cave environments of the sites provide the best record of a total lifeway we have preserved from the Archaic period. The settlement pattern indicates a sparse population which utilized caves and rock shelters. The economy featured nonsedentary seasonal gathering keyed to intensive exploitation of all available resources. The artifact inventory relied on a wide variety of implements made from wood, bark, and fiber, such as baskets, netting, matting, sandals, and so on. Even duck decoys were made from reeds.

The primary characteristic of the Desert Culture was the seasonal movement of its people in

Fig. 18-6 Perishable artifacts typical of the Desert Culture. (Photograph courtesy of Philip M. Hobler.)

order to exploit ephemeral food resources. This pattern of activity was first described by Julian Steward (1938). Archaeologically, Steward's model of seasonal exploitation has been tested in the Reese Valley of Nevada by D. H. Thomas (1972, 1973) and by Grady (1976, 1980) in the Piceance Basin of Colorado. In the Reese Valley Thomas clearly demonstrated a pattern of riverine zone exploitation coupled with utilization of the distant but complementary Pinyon-juniper zone. Grady's work in the Piceance Basin also demonstrated a pattern of seasonal-resource exploitation. In this case, however, the latter are distributed by marked altitudinal differences, and the major integrative device is the annual movement of the basin's mule deer herd. Both patterns were typical of the Desert Culture. We shall return to the Desert Culture later, because it was upon this cultural and economic base in the states of Tamaulipas and Puebla, Mexico, that plant domestication developed.

The California Sequence

Prehistorically, California is a region dominated by Archaic cultures. Within the borders of the state there existed three major economic systems. In the desert regions of southeastern California the cultural pattern was essentially that of the Desert Culture. ● The Topanga culture (Fig. 18-7) and the poorly defined San Dieguito complex (Lipe 1979:336) are examples of desert-based, seed-gathering groups which featured a chipped and flaked stone tool inventory in addition to reliance on the metate and mano used in the grinding of the seeds collected.

Farther north, in the Central Valley region, the economic staple was the acorn. Here the acorn was utilized into the historic period with little change in artifact inventory between that of the early peoples and of the later occupants (Fig. 18-8). A major cultural adaptation was the use of mortars cut into bedrock, with pestles used in the preparation of acorns. The latter were ground to a powder and leached to remove the tannic acid before being made into cakes,

porridge, and other foods. Other food resources were birds, fish, deer, and elk.

▲ Coexisting with the Desert adaptations were a series of coastal variants, which used resources of the littoral environment. Major resources were shellfish, especially the California abalone and mussels. Sea mammals hunted included the sea lion, sea otter, seal, and dolphin. A final major staple was deep-sea fish, including barracuda, tuna, and swordfish. Evidence from the coastal middens illustrates the prolific resources available. Typical of the central or coastal Californian cultures was the fact that the abundance and stability of the food resources led to population expansion and the establishment of permanent settlements. These factors permitted California to experience one of the highest population densities known for prehistoric peoples not utilizing agriculture.

California societies had the following social features, as inferred from their cultural remains (Meighan 1959:303). The largest political unit was the village, extending in population up to several hundred persons. Social distinctions existed, as indicated by the preferential treatment given to a few burials within each village, but it is thought that such class distinctions were based on personal recognition of individuals rather than on heredity. Warfare was prevalent, and trophy heads were taken. However, no defensive sites are known. Trade over long distances was common, with one of the favored routes carrying the trade of marine shells to the southwestern cultures of Arizona and New Mexico. Charmstones, quartz crystals, and sucking tubes present in Californian cultures imply that a shaman-directed, curing-oriented religion was practiced.

Somewhat similar littoral-resource users lived to the north, from California throughout the Northwest Coast of the United States to southern Alaska. We will not describe these cultures in detail here; however, a study by Conover (1978) provides perhaps the most detailed analysis available of the food-resource utilization of such peoples (Fig. 18-9).

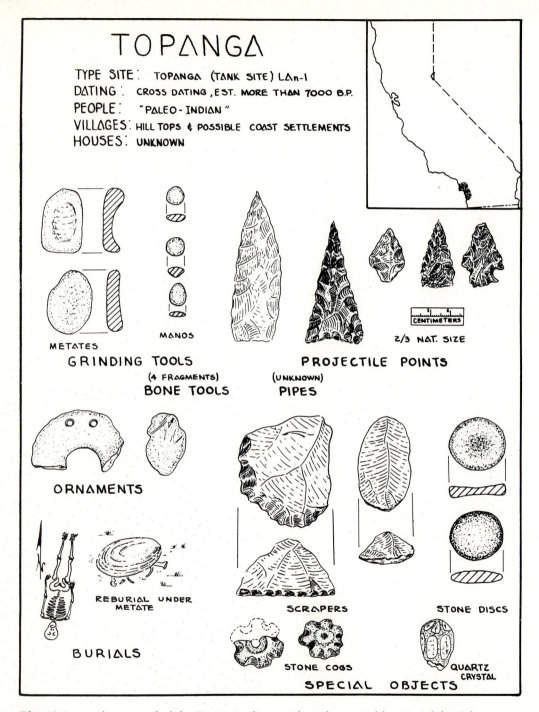

Fig. 18-7 Artifacts typical of the Topanga culture, early gatherers and hunters of the California desert and coast. (Meighan 1959:Fig. 1.)

Fig. 18-8 Artifacts typical of the Late California Central Valley cultures. (*a*) early Canaliño to 2000 B.P. (*b* [*see page 360*]) A.D. 1000–1860 (Meighan 1959:Fig. 14-7.)

LATE CANALIÑO

TYPE SITE: MESCALITAN ISLAND
DATING: PROTO-HISTORIC (EARLY CANALINO TO 2000 B.P.)
PEOPLE: BROADHEADS
VILLAGE LITTORAL & ISLAND
HOUSES LARGE DOME SHAPED & RUSH COVERED
DRAWINGS AFTER ORR, 1943; ROGERS, 1929.

MORTARS & PESTLES
GRINDING TOOLS

SPEARHEAD   2/3 NAT. SIZE
CENTIMETERS
PROJECTILE POINTS

FISH HOOKS
SHELL

SPANGLES & PENDANTS

MARKERS

LIMPET SHELL

PIPES

BEADS

ORNAMENTS

REBURIALS WITH WHALE BONE
BURIALS

COMAL

ARROW-SHAFT
STRAIGHTENER

WOVEN SEAGRASS

BASKET

SANDSTONE BOWL

SHELL BEAD INLAY
IN ASPHALTUM

TARRING
PEBBLES

STEATITE OLLA

WHALE EFFIGIES

STONE DISH

PAINT MORTARS
& STONE BOWL

OLIVELLA INLAY
SANDSTONE BOWL

SPECIAL   OBJECTS

B

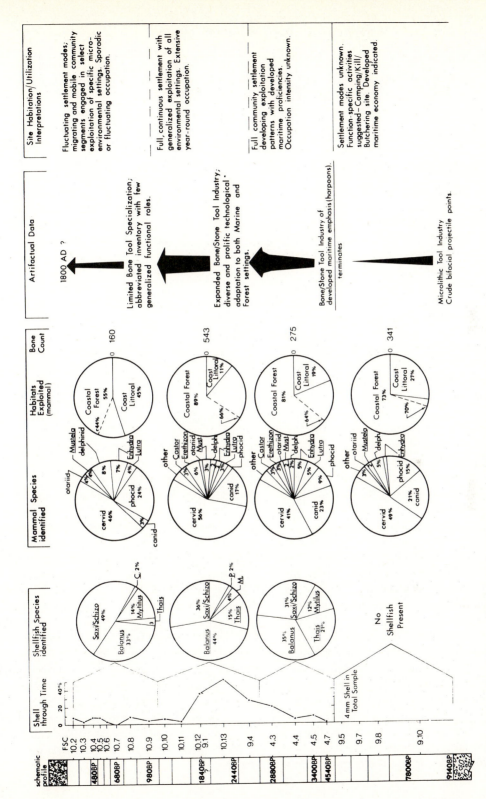

Fig. 18-9 Summary of prehistoric resource utilization on the Northwest Coast, Namu, British Columbia. (Conover 1978:Fig. 49.)

■ The search for the origins of corn

● The Tehuacan Valley of Puebla has produced the earliest evidence of domesticated corn.

The Rise of Agriculture in the New World

The development of agriculture as a primary subsistence economy in the New World is linked especially to two plants: corn and beans. Although numerous other domesticates — and we shall review those later — were developed, it was corn that became the New World staple. Due to its prehistoric importance, primitive corn also has great significance for archaeologists in their search for cultural origins, being in a sense a "Holy Grail" pursued by archaeologists and botanists alike. ■ The search for the beginnings of corn was not easy, for aboriginally, corn was grown from the Dakotas all the way southward to central Chile. Somewhere within this vast heartland of the New World lay the point of origin, but its location required more than 20 years of research. A primary problem was that the remains of the corn plant were perishable, therefore limiting the search to those dry cave sites where such fossils would be preserved.

The history of this quest has been related by Richard S. MacNeish both in print (MacNeish 1967:3–13) and by means of a color film, "The Origins of Corn in Mesoamerica." The first breakthrough was the discovery of primitive corn cobs at Bat Cave, New Mexico, in 1948. These finds by Herbert Dick were submitted to Paul Mangelsdorf, a botanist at Harvard, for study and were subsequently verified as being ancestors of modern corn. Their age was established by radiocarbon at 2,000 to 3,000 years B.C. Simultaneously, MacNeish was finding early corn at LaPerra cave in Tamaulipas state, in northeastern Mexico. Later work in Tamaulipas suggested to MacNeish that the corn there was not the earliest domesticated. However, the Tamaulipas specimens led him to shift his search farther southward.

In 1958 MacNeish explored caves in Guatemala and Honduras but found no corn. In 1959 MacNeish and Frederick Peterson excavated Santa Marta Cave in Chiapas, but their finds of corn pollen there were not old enough to suggest that corn had been originally domesticated that far south. Thus the search had narrowed: As far as MacNeish was concerned, the homeland of corn had to lie between Tamaulipas and Chiapas.

A study of suitable environments for the early domestication of corn suggested that three regions were most probable: southern Oaxaca, the Rio Balsas region of Guerrero, and the Tehuacan Valley of Puebla. In 1959 and 1960 MacNeish visited numerous caves in Puebla and Oaxaca, eventually selecting Coxcatlan Cave in the Tehuacan Valley as the most promising. On January 27, 1960, excavations revealed a tiny corn cob about an inch in length. ● A month later this specimen was dated by C-14 at 3610 ± 250 B.C., the earliest corn found up to that time. The next step was the formation of the Tehuacan Valley project of the R. S. Peabody Foundation. This expedition was to consist of three years of study in the region, with the goal of documenting the transition from an Archaic hunting-and-gathering economy to a fully agricultural one. The project was interdisciplinary, requiring analysis of the natural environment as well as specialized studies of all the recovered ancient cultigens, such as corn, beans, squash, amaranth, and so on. Other experts studied the food bones, prehistoric feces, prehistoric irrigation systems, and geology. The objectives of this undertaking were formidable, for within Mesoamerica a wide variety of plants and animals had been known to the Archaic inhabitants in their intensive use of all available resources. (For example, the range of plants eventually cultivated in Mesoamerica includes more than a hundred species.)

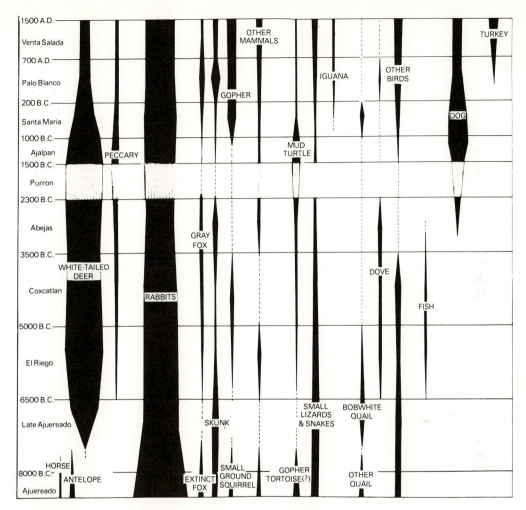

Fig. 18-10 Changing exploitation of faunal species through time by the prehistoric inhabitants of the Tehuacan Valley, Puebla, Mexico. (Flannery 1967:Fig. 95.)

Detailed studies by Flannery (1967) of the fauna in the Tehuacan Valley sites illustrate (Fig. 18-10) the mixed reliance on a wide variety of food animals. Identification of the other major components of the diet was achieved through a combination of studies, including analysis of dry vegetal parts, pollen, food bones, and coprolites.

Still to be resolved, however, is the problem of the ancestry of corn (maize). A core sample taken in Mexico City produced "maize pollen" at a depth of 200 feet dating to 80,000 years ago. This date was, of course, long before humans were present in the Valley of Mexico and has been offered as proof that modern maize is descended from wild corn rather than from various wild grasses, such as teosinte (Mangelsdorf 1980). On the other hand, Beadle (1980a) states that maize pollen and teosinte pollen are indistinguishable from one another, even under the electron microscope. Secondly, Beadle (1980b)

▲ The shift to domestication was a slow process.

argues on the basis of botanical and genetic grounds (i.e., fruit, case, and chromosome count) that teosinte is the wild ancestor of corn. Sears (1981) states that it is just possible the depth of the corn pollen in Mexico City may be due to the subsidence of the lake bottom rather than to great age. Regardless of how this argument is ultimately resolved, corn (maize) is the basic staple upon which New World civilization was built.

The Tehuacan Valley Sequence

MacNeish (1964 a & b) was able to identify and establish nine periods in the Tehuacan Valley chronological sequence (Table 18-1).

In the early Ajuereado and El Riego phases, the emphasis is on hunting and plant collecting. By the El Riego period the people of the valley were all sowing the plants that later became domesticates (e.g., squash, avocados, and chiles).

The Coxcatlan phase (5200–3400 b.c.) was one of acquisition of new plants. While the way of life was much the same as in the El Riego phase, plants such as maize, chiles, avocados, and gourds were present early. Later came ama-

ranth, three kinds of beans, and yellow zapotes, and by the end of the period, black and white zapotes. Maize makes its first appearance during this phase, and domesticates account for approximately 14 percent of the total dietary intake.

During the succeeding Abejas period sedentary village life first appears along with more plants, such as new varieties of pumpkin. Maize has crossed with teosinte and formed a new hybrid. The increase in domesticate productivity is reflected in the fact that by this period domesticates account for 30 percent of the dietary base.

The Purron phase is not well known, but pottery makes its first appearance in the Tehuacan Valley at this time. The fact that this phase is not well known is frustrating, since the following Ajalpan phase is characterized by full-time agriculturalists, and this transition to full-time agriculture is not clearly understood.

As mentioned earlier, MacNeish excavated a series of cave sites in Northern Mexico, and by the period 7000–5000 b.c. (the Infiernillo phase) bottle gourds used as containers, chili peppers as a condiment, and pumpkins used as food are all present. Maize does not appear until after 3000 b.c., and when it does, it is of two varieties. The picture that emerges is one of multiple centers of domestication. Maize appeared approximately 2,000 years earlier in the Tehuacan Valley, but pumpkins, chiles, and squash emerged earlier in

TABLE 18-1
Chronology of Cultural Periods and Agricultural Development in the Tehuacan Valley

Site	Dates	Economy
Venta Salada	700–A.D. 1500	Full-time agriculture
Palo Blanco	200 B.C.–A.D. 700	Full-time agriculture
Santa Maria	1000 B.C.–200 B.C.	Full-time agriculture
Ajalpan	1500 B.C.–1000 B.C.	Full-time agriculture
Purron	2300 B.C.–1500 B.C.	Shift to an agricultural threshold
Abejas	3500–2300 B.C.	70 percent hunting, 30 percent collecting
Coxcatlan	5000–3500 B.C.	Plant collecting-hunting, appearance of domestication
El Riego	6500–5000 B.C.	Deer-hunting emphasis
Ajuereado	8000–6500 B.C.	So-called big game hunting: horses, antelope

the Tamaulipas region than in the Tehuacan Valley. ▲ These results indicate that the transition from an Archaic economy to an agricultural one (Fig. 18-11) was slow, requiring more than 5,000 years. In addition, it was broad-based, with many different species of cultigens and wild plants being relied upon. Far from being a revolution, the development of plant cultivation in the New World was a gradual process in an economy already broadly based on the widespread utilization of all available resources.

The development of plant cultivation in the New World has received considerable study. Mangelsdorf, MacNeish, and Willey (1964) cite a number of requisite conditions for this development. One factor was that of great diversity in the natural vegetation. Also, the region should impose hardships upon its inhabitants, causing acquisition of adequate foodstuffs to require intensive conscious effort. (Thus the most likely regions for cultivation would be semiarid, with distinct annual dry and rainy seasons.) A final

Fig. 18-11 The transition to an agricultural economy as reflected in the frequency of plant and animal remains found in the caves in the Tehuacan Valley. (MacNeish 1967:Fig. 186.)

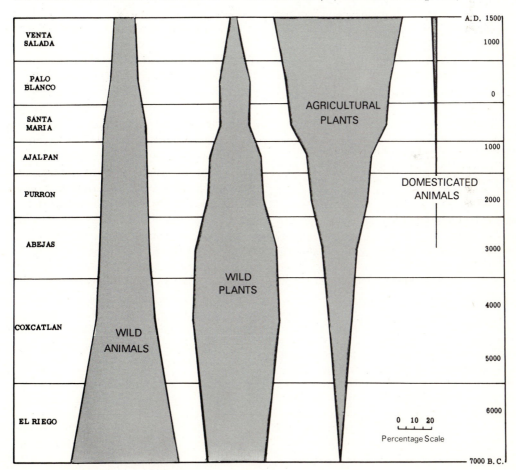

■ Domestication on the coast of Peru appeared in a fishing economy.

factor is of course the nature of the cultural exploitative patterns which were developed by the Archaic peoples.

Flannery (1971) has developed an explanatory model for the cultural adaptation to plant cultivation. In the studies of Mesoamerican food remains a number of facts have been isolated: (1) Certain plants and animals, whether wild or domesticated, were always more important than others. (2) The use of these species required a procurement system which also permitted the continued survival of the species. (3) Use of these resources depended upon seasonality and scheduling.

In arid Mesoamerica Flannery perceives six major procurement systems utilizing maguey, cactus fruit, tree legumes, wild grass, white-tailed deer, and cottontail rabbit. The exploitative pattern (Flannery 1971:91–92) is reconstructed as follows:

> In the late dry season and early rainy season, there is a period of peak abundance of wild plant foods. These localized resources were intensively harvested, and eaten or cached as they came to maturity; this appears to have been a "macroband" activity. Because "all hands" participated in these harvests, little deer hunting was done; instead the Indians set traps in the vicinity of the plant-collecting camp, an activity which does not conflict with intensive plant harvests the way deer hunting would.
>
> In the late fall and winter, most plants have ceased to bear fruit, but deer hunting is at its best. Since this is the mating season, male deer (who normally forage by themselves) fall in with the does and fawns, making the average herd larger; and since this is also the season when the deciduous vegetation of the highlands sheds its leaves, the deer can be more easily followed by hunters. As the dry season wears on, however, the deer grow warier and range farther and farther back

into the mountains. This is the leanest time of the year in terms of plant resources, and it was evidently in this season that man turned most heavily to plants available year round, like the root of the Ceiba (which can be baked like sweet manioc) or the heart of the maguey plant (which can be roasted). These appear to have been "microband" activities.

> By chewing roots and maguey hearts, the pre-ceramic forager managed to last until the late spring growing season, at which point he could wallow in cactus fruit again. Essentially, his "schedule" was keyed to the seasonal availability of certain wild plants, which climaxed at those times of the year which were best suited for small-game-trapping. He scheduled his most intensive deer hunting for the seasons when big plant harvests were not a conflicting factor.

Having defined above the Archaic economy practiced in the semiarid highlands of Oaxaca and Puebla, Flannery goes on to suggest a model as to how this system might have been modified to include plant cultivation. The term proposed by Flannery is *positive feedback*, consisting of original accidental deviations which through time gradually made possible an increasing reliance on certain plants. In Mesoamerica the most important of such deviations were genetic changes in corn and beans. In beans, for example, such changes included increased permeability in water, rendering them easier to cook, and limp pods (in contrast to brittle pods, such as mesquite), which made their harvest easier. Corn increased its size, hybridized with its close relatives, lost the glumes, and increased the number of kernels. In addition, corn and beans together supplement each other nutritionally—another form of positive feedback. In Flannery's terms (1971:95), this positive-feedback network acted as follows:

> The more widespread maize cultivation, the more favorable genetic changes, the greater the yield, the higher the population, and hence the more intensive cultivation. There can be little doubt that pressures for more intensive cultivation

were instrumental in perfecting early water-control systems, like well-irrigation and canal-irrigation.

Another aspect of the system was that the formulation of a formal planting season and harvesting season interfered with those economic activities previously scheduled for those times of the year. Therefore, spring harvests of natural crops of wild plants, prickly pear, and organ cactus and fall harvests of acorns, fruits, and guaves would have been reduced due to lack of available labor. Rainy-season hunting of deer and peccary were also curtailed. One other feature of the cultivated plant harvests and planting would have been augmentation of band size and length of time spent together in one location. According to Niederberger (1979), such resource-use scheduling had led to a sedentary life-style in central Mexico as early as 6000 B.C. This sedentism is a direct causal factor of our next major cultural development, the Formative stage, which is discussed in the next chapter.

Domestication in South America

So far in this section we have not discussed the Archaic cultures of South America. In some aspects, the process of domestication there is remarkably similar to that already described for Mesoamerica. In other respects, however, it is dramatically different. In both areas the process was long and drawn out, and in both no one geographical locale acted as a center from which all domesticates radiated outward. On the other hand, the domestication process in Mesoamerica tended to emphasize plant utilization, whereas in South America the emphasis was more balanced, with both plants and animals being exploited.

In contrast to Mesoamerica, where few preceramic sequences are known, many are known from Peru (MacNeish 1977:755). These sequences clearly establish the existence of a highland-lowland dichotomy in which dramatically different subsistence activities were occurring in both the coastal-lowland regions and in the highlands.

Early Peruvian Coastal Adaptations

■ Clear evidence for domestication appears on the coast around 5000 B.C. during the Lower Archaic period (Lumbreras 1974:37). The coastal evidence is derived from a series of midden deposits, the best known of which are those at Chilca and Encanto. Encanto is a complex of 13 sites located near the Bay of Ancon. Lanning (1963) describes the ecological setting on the nearby Lomas (hills), which features a winter fog-nurtured vegetation. Therefore the Lomas are vegetated in the winter, but totally barren in the summer. This lack of summer resources implies a transhumant pattern of seasonal exploitation in which the Lomas occupants probably moved into the uplands for the summer or to the seashore in order to harvest coastal resources.

The development of agriculture on the Peruvian coast is not well understood. Certainly, the gathering economy practiced on the Lomas during the Archaic period would have provided a knowledge of specific harvests—a situation somewhat analogous to the incipient cultivation that originated in the "hilly-flanks" zone in the Middle East. However, in Peru the development of agriculture on the coast is best documented in the coastal villages, which had populations ranging up to 3,000 persons and which relied primarily upon the harvesting of fish, shellfish, sea mammals, and birds and only secondarily upon cultivated plants. The earliest domesticates appear in Preceramic Period VI and date in the interval between 3000 and 2500 B.C. These plants included cotton, the bottle gourd, squash, and achira (a starchy root). Slightly later, corn,

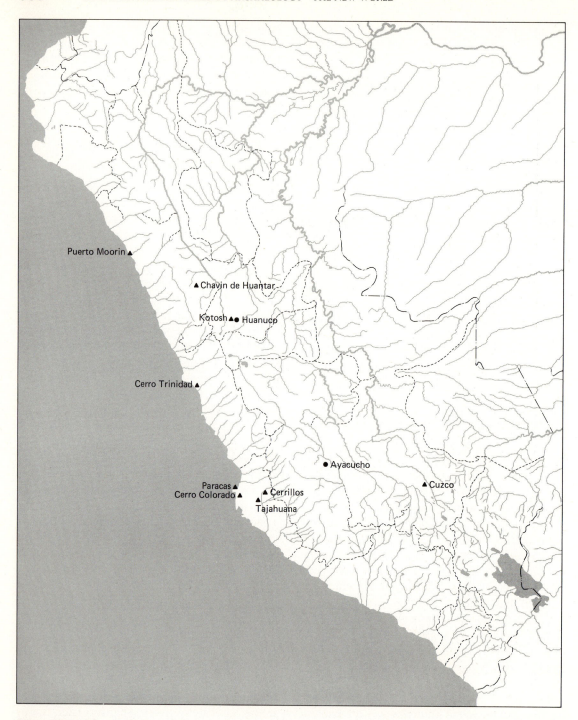

Puerto Moorin ▲

▲ Chavin de Huantar

Kotosh ▲● Huanuco

Cerro Trinidad ▲

● Ayacucho

▲ Cuzco

Paracas ▲
Cerro Colorado ▲   ▲ Cerrillos
▲ Tajahuana

Map 18-2a&b Archaic and Formative Sites in South America. (After Lumbreras)

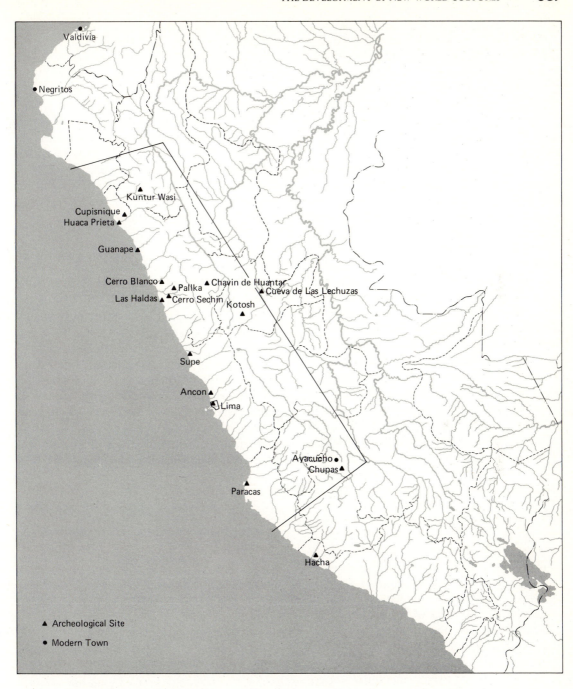

Valdivia

Negritos

Kuntur Wasi

Cupisnique
Huaca Prieta

Guanape

Cerro Blanco Pallka Chavin de Huantar
Las Haldas Cerro Sechin Cueva de Las Lechuzas
Kotosh

Supe

Ancon
Lima

Ayacucho
Chupas

Paracas

Hacha

▲ Archeological Site

● Modern Town

● Domestication in the Andean highlands appeared in a hunting-and-gathering economy.

▲ Early domesticated plants on the Peruvian coast were squash, beans, and cotton.

beans, and peanuts appear (Cohen 1977:225–230).

Given the Peruvian coastal reliance on marine resources as the primary economy, the shift to agriculture must have depended on somewhat different factors than those of importance in the Middle East. Lischka (1975) presents a hypothesis for the development of domestication, citing as the single most influential factor the periodic southward movement of El Niño, a warm countercurrent which moves southward from Ecuador every 20 to 50 years. The dramatic effects of El Niño include a massive die-off of marine life coupled with heavy rains on the normally arid Peruvian coast. According to Lischka's theory, El Niño forced temporary reliance on land resources, which included potential domesticates. The effects of El Niño lasted several years and included a rise in the water table in the coastal valleys, an increase in the productivity of the Lomas zone, and conditions suitable for an increase in the productivity of any domesticates being cultivated. With population increase, through time the villages were forced to rely increasingly on cultivation since their numbers were too great to simply return to a gathering life-style on the Lomas during the years immediately after El Niño. Other aspects of the coastal adaptation were centered on Peru's marine resources. Certainly mollusc and small fish make up the bulk of the midden debris, but at Encanto, incipient agriculture is suggested by the presence of squash and zapallos.

One hundred kilometers to the south, at the site of Chilca, there lived a community of approximately 100 families (Engel 1964), although Lumbreras (1974) feels the latter figure may be

too high. These people lived in small circular or semicircular houses, usually with conical superstructures of 2.4 meters in diameter erected over a pit 35 centimeters in depth. Treatment of the dead is represented by simple interments with distinctive mortuary goods, usually two woven mats. The mats, or, in some cases, mantles with fringe, are woven from rushes. There is some evidence of ritual. In one grave eight mortuary bundles were recovered from below a layer of ash. The ash contained both burned human and animal bone, suggesting the possibility of ritual cannibalism or human sacrifice.

Early Archaic Highland Adaptations

● In the highland areas of Peru, there is evidence of domestication from several sites. Of particular significance are the 12 sites excavated in the Ayacucho region (MacNeish 1971; MacNeish, 1977). Although MacNeish has recovered evidence of the earliest occupation of South America (20,000 B.C.) and has demonstrated a long period of hunting and gathering over the millennia, only a few of his later periods evidence domestication of plants and animals (Table 18-2).

TABLE 18-2
Chronology of Cultural Periods and Agricultural Development in the Ayacucho Region, Peru

Period	Dating, B.C.	Economy
Cachi	3150–1800 B.C.	
Chihua	4600–3150 B.C.	First appearance of corn
Piki	5850–4600 B.C.	Collecting, hunting, some planting
Jayawa	7150–5850 B.C.	Trapping and plant collecting
Puente	9050–7150 B.C.	Trapping and plant collecting

(MacNeish 1977)

Subsistence patterns of the Puente phase can be divided into wet-season and dry-season activities. The main thrust of wet-season activities seems to have been the trapping of small mammals (particularly guinea pigs) and plant collecting. Seeds suitable for grinding have been found in the wet-season manifestations of this period. Large numbers of bones of small animals, and particularly those of guinea pigs, suggest that the latter may have been tamed. Certainly, the trapping or collecting of animals was important.

Change occurs during the Piki phase. Small-band hunting is still the main dry-season activity; however, hunting is rare during the wet season. In this season the main activity seems to have been trapping, plant collecting, keeping guinea pigs, and possibly the planting and harvesting of seed crops (MacNeish 1977:776). This pattern was certainly not restricted to the Ayacucho region since domesticated beans have also been found at Guitarrera Cave (Kaplan, Lynch, and Smith 1973). MacNeish notes a tendency for wet-season camps to be slightly larger than dry-season camps.

Upper Archaic Coastal Adaptations

Lumbreras (1974) equates the Upper Archaic period with a time of village horticulture. Again, we have the highland-lowland dichotomy. In the lowlands despite the great variation among sites there is an overall homogeneity. For example, sites tend to be located near the seashore or near freshwater springs far from the region's torrential streams. During this interval the winter fog-supported vegetation in the Lomas zone was drying up, thus stimulating a move to more permanently watered areas.

The earliest site identifiable with the Upper Archaic period is that of Huaca Prieta on the north coast. The site is dated by C-14 to 2500 B.C. ▲ Whether Huaca Prieta was permanently or seasonally occupied has not been determined.

Several variations of squash, beans, cotton, chili peppers, the root plant achira, and various fruits have been found there.

Between 2000 and 1300 B.C. the large numbers of sites which existed on the coast had a number of characteristics in common: an absence of pottery; the presence of cotton; similar levels of textile technology; and a common subsistence pattern. Differences among these sites include: degree of refinement in agricultural methods; differential growth rate of the sedentary life-style; and the progressive addition of new traits (Lumbreras 1974). Remains of terrestrial mammals are present in small numbers in these coastal villages, but the primary emphasis of the economy is apparent in the marked increase in large sea mammals, particularly seals. Whales were also utilized but were probably taken stranded on the beaches rather than being hunted. Shellfish were a major component of the coastal diet.

It is within this cultural pattern, featuring a coastal subsistence with a mixed economy including domesticated plants, that the first evidence of permanent ceremonial structures appears. At Las Haldas, the oldest pyramids have been found, the most important being 465 meters long, seven platforms high, and dating to 1844 ± 80 B.C. (Lumbreras 1974).

Upper Archaic Highland Adaptations

The Upper Archaic manifestation at Ayacucho occurs in the Chihua and Cachi phases, dated at 4600–3150 B.C. and 3150–1800 B.C., respectively. MacNeish (1977) sees these entities as contemporaneous with the lowland Encanto and Chilca complexes found on the coast. If this is the case, it implies that domesticates were a prime resource earlier in the highlands than on the coast. In the period from 5600 to 4500 B.C. (as inferred from the Encanto complex) there is a shift to molluscs and fish as a food resource. Later, dur-

■ Corn appears in Peru.

ing the Early Horizon and Early Intermediate periods (to be discussed subsequently), sea-mammal resources decrease in importance with an associated increase in the exploitation of domesticated guinea pigs and llamas.

■ It was during the Upper Archaic (Chihua phase 4600–3150 B.C.) that maize made its first appearance in Peru. This grain seems to be ancestral to the most primitive form of corn known today, called "Confite Morocho" (MacNeish 1977:780), and it also is closely related genetically to the Mexican Nal-Tel variety.

Summary

In both Mesoamerica and South America the shift from a hunting-and-gathering life-style to an economy based on domesticates was a long process. In both cases there were seemingly multiple centers for domestication coupled with a good deal of interregional and intraregional exchange. In the New World as in the Old, the establishment of a sedentary life-style based on a food surplus produced by domesticates seems to have been an essential requirement preceding the rise of civilization.

19

The Formative Cultures of the New World

Introduction

It was during the Formative period that new and exciting things began to happen in the New World. These new developments ultimately led to the establishment of civilization in the Americas. Before considering the nature of these innovations, we first shall review what is meant by the term Formative.

■ In their definition of the *Formative*, Willey and Phillips stress the appearance of agriculture and the resultant development of a sedentary life-style. However, James Ford, in his classic work *A Comparison of Formative Cultures in the Americas*, takes issue with the Willey-Phillips definition. According to Ford (1969:5), in both Mesoamerica and Peru agriculture was practiced centuries before other Formative-trait complexes, such as ceramics or polished stone tools, became common. Ford is also critical of the concept of "sedentary life occurring early" and chooses instead to view this "sedentism" as a process that required time to develop. Ford also points out that some of the earliest pottery (dated 3200 ± 150 B.C.) occurs in a matrix of coastal shellfish-gathering cultures on the Ecuadorian coast (Meggers 1979, Fig. 7) where, according to Meggers, Evans, and Estrada (1965:167–168), it was probably introduced from Japan. They view the actual introduction of pottery as resulting when a boatload of Japanese sailors or fishermen of the Jomon culture were blown off course by a typhoon and then eventually drifted across the Pacific to land at Valdivia, Ecuador (Fig. 19-1). These new arrivals then presumably introduced pottery making to the local residents, using indigenous raw materials. While there are similarities between Jomon and

● The Formative includes agriculture, a settled village life, and pottery.

▲ The village was the primary social unit.

■ Ceremonial centers appear.

● Pottery appears between 2000 and 3000 B.C.

the early Ecuadorian ceramics, critics have noted numerous problems of correlation. For example, the currents of the Pacific Ocean are such that the trip of the Japanese could not have been made in less than 556 days. This does not take into consideration problems posed by climate and sheer survival. Additional objections to the hypothesis question (1) the parallels between the Jomon and Ecuadorian ceramics; (2) the ac-

Fig. 19-1 Route of the hypothesized introduction of Jomon-type pottery from Japan to the coast of Ecuador. (Meggers, Evans, and Estrada 1965:Fig. 103.)

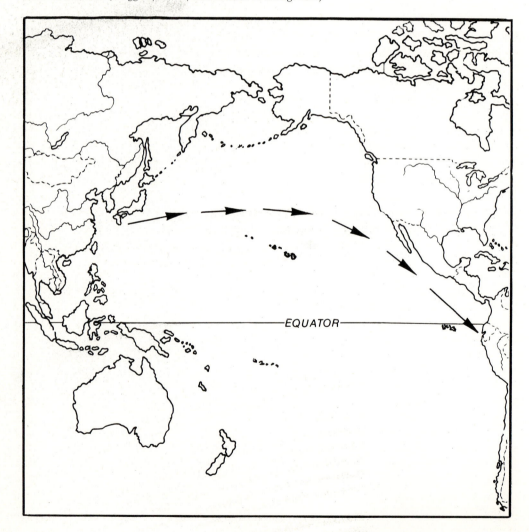

curacy of the report itself; (3) the presence of ceramics at Puerto Hormiga, Colombia, which may be as early or earlier than the Valdivia material; and (4) finally, the presence of ceramics at Valdivia that apparently precede the Jomon-like material found in the Valdivia A Levels (McEwan and Dickson 1978:362–367). It has nonetheless been accepted that Valdivia features the oldest known pottery in the New World.

● We view the Formative as the rise of agriculture, a settled village life, and pottery. This was a period within which a series of developments came to be associated together; a process requiring considerable time. However, the reasons for the development of Formative culture were undoubtedly complex. There occurred a series of parallel independent developments, region by region, coupled with a widespread communications network along which ideas, objects, and their associated behavioral patterns were diffused. The cultural complexity of this movement is enormous, and to explain the details of the New World Formative cultures would require a separate text.

Important Formative developments occurred not only in Peru and Mesoamerica but also in the eastern United States, southwestern United States, Central America, and Colombia. Belated or marginal Formative cultures (as they are termed by Willey and Phillips [1958]) are known from the Great Plains river valleys, the Guianas, Ecuador, the mouth of the Amazon, and the southern Andes southward to central Chile. The primary hallmark of the Formative is a reliance on domesticated plants as the economic mainstay. Even in Mesoamerica, such reliance developed late, no fully agricultural economy being extant until 1500–1000 B.C. In Mesoamerica, in contrast to the Old World Neolithic, domesticated animals were never particularly important as food resources. The Mesoamerican and southwestern domesticated animals included the dog (eaten in Mesoamerica), turkeys, parrots (kept for their feathers), and stingless bees. Peruvian domesticated animals were primarily highland species, with the llama, alpaca, and vicuna being kept for their wool and meat and used for the transport of goods but not for riding. One other domesticate, the guinea pig, was eaten, and guinea pig dung was also utilized for fertilizer.

▲ Settlement patterns featured the village as the basic unit. Small clusters of individual houses, located adjacent to the fields, were the rule. Basic house types included above-ground mud, stone, or wattle-and-daub-walled units with roofs of thatch or poles, grass, and earth. The typical village consisted of 6 to 10 such units. Not far away was the ceremonial center, built and used by the members of several such villages. Ceremonial centers were not universal, for within the Formative there was considerable cultural variation. ■ The highest development of ceremonial centers occurred in Mesoamerica, where the center featured flat-topped, platform mounds (pyramids) surmounted by a temple. These pyramids were arranged around a rectangular, open ceremonial plaza which often included vertically set, carved stone slabs, or stelae, which were placed to commemorate specific dates and to record dynastic events. Frequently the date of erection was inscribed on these slabs. Other associated features included tombs, mosaic floors, carved stone altars, and residences for the priests.

The Mesoamerican Formative Stage

The period between 2000 B.C. and A.D. 300 in Mesoamerica is known as the Formative stage or the "Preclassic" period.

The Early Formative

● Pottery appears in the Tehuacan Valley (Purron phase) and at Puerto Marques (Pox phase) on the coast of Guerrero prior to 2300 B.C. Hammond (1977) reports pottery at Cuello, Belize,

▲ Representational modeling in pottery

■ Figurines appear.

dating to 2000 B.C. in an Early Formative context. An even earlier date, 3200 B.C., may also be valid, but more work is needed to determine whether or not this phase was Formative or Archaic.

By 1500 B.C. ceramics and settled village life were widespread. At Altamira during the Barro phase (1600–1500 B.C.) we have the earliest pottery retrieved to date from the Pacific coast. This was followed in the same area by the Ocos phase (1500–1000 B.C.), and Ocos material is known from at least 20 sites. The basic settlement pattern seems to have been one which integrated land suitable for farming with the rich resources provided by the lagoon-estuary environment. M. D. Coe (1960) suggests a South American origin for the ceramics found at Ocos since these seem quite similar to those found in the Chorrera phase at Guayaquil, Equador.

TLATILCO

Tlatilco, one of the earliest known settlements in the valley of Mexico, poses several problems for the prehistorian. The village, dating to as early as 1200 B.C., was located west of Lake Texcoco and covered an area of some 160 acres. Not much is known about the village since most of it has been destroyed by brickworkers. However, 340 burials have been excavated, many of which contain lavish grave goods. Some of the latter are reminiscent of the coastal Olmec, which will be discussed later.

▲ At Tlatilco we have modeled ceramics depicting armadillo, oppossum, wild turkey, bear, frog, rabbit, fish, duck, and turtle (Coe 1977:60). Bones of deer and waterfowl also attest to the variety present in the Tlatilco subsistence base. Tlatilco ceramics can be divided into two types: large, hollow and small, solid vessels. A curious

aspect of these works is the representations of deformed people and those with split faces. The latter often portray a skull and half of a face, possibly illustrating the division of life and death so common to the Mexican cosmology.

The Middle Formative

The villages of El Arbolillo and Zacatenco are located on the ancient beach lines of Lake Texcoco and therefore represent a lake-shore adaptation. Both villages covered several acres, and refuse deposits indicate a lengthy occupation. Although the residents were permanent agriculturalists, the enormous number of deer bones and bones of aquatic birds clearly indicate that hunting was a major dietary source.

■ Thousands of fragments of female figurines have been found at the sites and throughout the valley as well. Most of these are nude or at best painted, and these probably functioned as household deities. Burials are found beneath the floors of houses or in cemeteries. Grave goods include a few pots and implements and sometimes jade beads placed in the mouths of the deceased.

The Early and Middle Formative periods together represent the establishment and spread throughout much of Mesoamerica of the basic farming village. In a sense, these villages became the basic building blocks of Mesoamerican culture and civilization. No matter how elaborate or complex the succeeding cultural manifestations became, they were supported by the peasant village and its agricultural subsistence base.

The Late Formative Period

It is during the Late Formative that we see the first evidences of the cultural elaboration referred to above, since it was during this period

Map 19-1 Formative and Preclassic Sites in Mesoamerica and South America. (After Adams and Lumbreros)

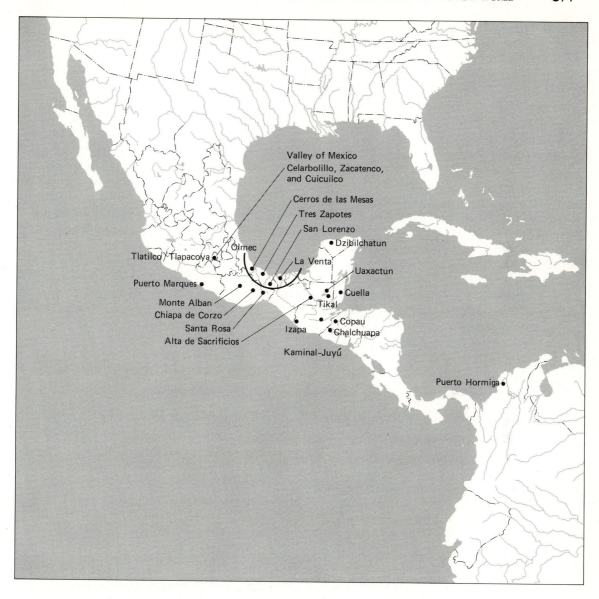

Valley of Mexico
Celarbolillo, Zacatenco,
and Cuicuilco

Cerros de las Mesas

Tres Zapotes

San Lorenzo

Olmec

Dzibilchatun

Tlatilco / Tlapacoya

La Venta

Uaxactun

Puerto Marques

Cuella

Monte Alban

Tikal

Chiapa de Corzo

Santa Rosa

Copau

Alta de Sacrificios

Izapa

Chalchuapa

Kaminal-Juyú

Puerto Hormiga

● Hieroglyphic writing appears.

▲ Monumental carving in basalt

that the temple-pyramid complex made its first appearance. The earliest temples were thatched-roof structures similar to the houses found in the valleys, but unlike the houses, these early edifices were set on low, earthen platforms. By the latter part of the Late Formative these platform structures had become the nuclei of enlarged villages and ceremonial centers such as Cuicuilco, south of what today is Mexico City.

At Cuicuilco, a round platform 387 feet in diameter and consisting of four stone-faced tiers rising to a height of 70 feet supported a cone-shaped structure of an additional 20 feet in height. Access to the top of the latter was provided by two ramps on either side. Volcanic activity in the valley seems to have terminated the

occupation at Cuicuilco, but we must not overlook the dramatic rise of Teotihuacan (to be discussed in the next chapter) as a factor which contributed to the abandonment of Cuicuilco.

The Olmec: 1500 B.C.–100 B.C.

Up to this point the development of the Formative is one in which Neolithic-like villages spread and became more complex. The later in time, the more aspects of civilization are present.

In what is one of Mesoamerica's least promising environments, the north coast of the Isthmus of Tehuantepec, in an area of hot, humid, lagoons and swamps, we have the development of what many would term a true civilization. Here, as in other areas, there were ceremonial centers; but associated with these centers in the Olmec culture we have evidence of a degree of cultural complexity unique in the New World at this date.

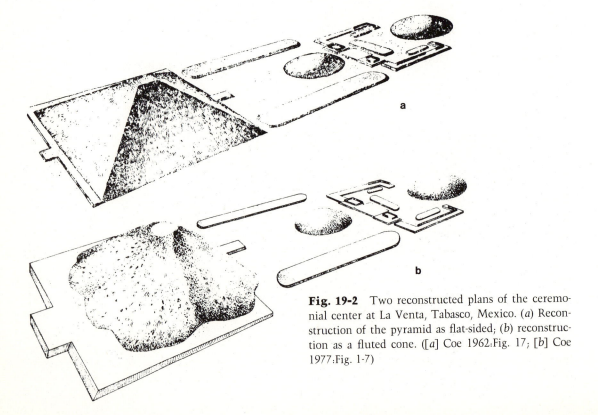

Fig. 19-2 Two reconstructed plans of the ceremonial center at La Venta, Tabasco, Mexico. (*a*) Reconstruction of the pyramid as flat-sided; (*b*) reconstruction as a fluted cone. ([*a*] Coe 1962:Fig. 17; [*b*] Coe 1977:Fig. 1-7)

TABLE 19-1
Olmec Cultural Periods

Olmec I	1500–1200 b.c.
Olmec II	1200–400 b.c.
Olmec III	400–100 b.c.

The Olmec can be subdivided into three basic periods (Table 19-1). According to Adams (1977) during Olmec I we are dealing with an Ocos-like culture. Olmec II is broken down into two subphases: the San Lorenzo (1200–900 B.C.) and the LaVenta Horizon (900–400 B.C.). This scheme recognizes the priority of San Lorenzo, its destruction, and the ultimate rise in power of the site of LaVenta, Tabasco (Fig. 19-2), from 1300 to 600 B.C. ● LaVenta is located on an island in the Tonala River, and it is here that hieroglyphic writing, the use of stelae, and the building of a formalized ceremonial center appear for the first time in Mesoamerica. The site consists of earthen mounds rebuilt or added to in layers. Within the mounds but covered with earth are floor mosaics of blocks of serpentine in the form of jaguar masks (Fig. 19-3). Presumably these masks were buried immediately after dedication. Other important features are an enclosure formed by vertical basalt columns and a tomb enclosure formed by the same type of columns. ▲ In addition to the beautifully carved stelae weighing up to 50 tons (Fig. 19-4), the impressive monuments include great, carved stone human heads (Fig. 19-5) which weigh up to 15 tons and portray a distinctive people with down-curving mouths, shown wearing a type of helmet. Most impressive is the fact that the basalt quarry for these stones lay 60 miles upstream. Presumably the sculpted stones were floated to their positions by means of rafts during times of high water.

The Olmec art style—of which the jaguar motif, ceramic "babies" (Fig. 19-6), and jade carvings were all a part—has a wide distribution and has been found in contexts as far away as Guatemala. How this spread occurred is open to de-

Fig. 19-3 Jaguar-mask mosaic of serpentine blocks laid within the southwest platform and then immediately buried under layers of soil at the formative site of La Venta, Tabasco. (Drucker, Heizer, and Squier 1959:Plate 16.)

bate. The Olmec are known to have been heavily involved with trade, but whether some form of "missionary" effort is also indicated has yet to be determined. In summary we can say that this interval saw the rise of sedentary village life, the establishment of a religious theocracy, the building of ceremonial centers, and the development of crafts, including carving in jade, pottery making, and such. Other developments included a growth in population, an increase in the size of ceremonial centers, and a codification of beliefs, especially in religion, with the establishment of a pantheon of gods and a specialized priesthood. Religious beliefs were expressed in architecture, art, and in other avenues of knowledge, including astronomy and calendrical notation. These ideological concepts constitute a distinctive characteristic of Mesoamerican culture, and they cannot be explained as the inevitable result of

Fig. 19-4 Large stela from La Venta, Tabasco, Mexico. (Hester photograph, courtesy of Mexican National Museum of Anthropology.)

the adoption of an agricultural economy. These were unique developments in New World culture history, and they occurred during the Formative. The later Classic cultures amplified the basic Mesoamerican culture pattern but did not alter its configuration.

The South American Formative Stage

The Andean sequence constitutes a series of major cultural developments somewhat paralleling those of Mesoamerica. We have in the An-

Fig. 19-5 One of the great stone heads, weighing several tons, from La Venta, Tabasco, Mexico. (Courtesy Mexican National Museum of Anthropology.)

Fig. 19-6 A figurine from the Olmec culture of southeastern Mexico. Human figurines are one of the hall-marks of the Mesoamerican Formative period. (Grady photograph, courtesy of Denver Art Museum)

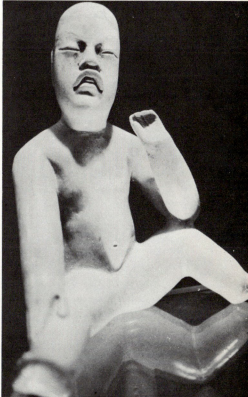

■ Horizon styles—a Peruvian hallmark.

● The Andean regions

▲ Agriculture begins at 2500 b.c.

■ Pottery appears.

● Chavin—the first Horizon style.

dean region, especially in Peru, a sequence that begins with Preceramic periods, evolving into a period of experimentation with plant domestication and leading to full-fledged irrigation agriculture. This sequence can be subdivided into the major categories of Archaic, Formative, Classic, and Postclassic.

The close similarity between the Andean developments and those of Mesoamerica has led in part to Julian Steward's definition (1957) of the concept of multilinear evolution, in which similar cultural patterns evolve in regions with similar environmental and historical factors. The Andean pattern is so close to that of Mesoamerica in chronology, general cultural evolution, and even in cultural details—species of plants cultivated and design styles—that the possibility of direct historical contacts between the Mesoamerican and the Andean areas cannot be ignored. On the other hand, positive proof that such contacts occurred is lacking.

■ A basic integrative factor present in Andean archaeology is the feature termed a *Horizon style*. Horizon styles are decorative elements which occur together in a variety of media such as pottery, stone sculpture, weaving, bone carving, and metalwork. A further feature of these styles which makes them of incalculable archaeological value is the fact that they are noted for their rapid spread and brief duration in time. Horizon styles are therefore useful as chronological markers, serving to correlate local archaeological cultures one with the other. Through time from early to late, the major Horizon styles are Chavin, White on Red, Negative Painted, Tiahuanaco, Huari, Interlocking, and Inca.

They are most common on pottery but are also present in weaving, metalwork and other crafts. In brief, a Horizon style is distinctive in form, widespread geographically, and of brief duration. Horizon styles further serve to provide Andean archaeology with a portion of its unique quality.

The Andean region is dominated by the Andean mountain chain, rising to 20,000 feet near the equator and diminishing in elevation both to the north and the south. The central area within which most of Andean culture developed includes Peru and portions of Ecuador and Bolivia. ● This may be subdivided into six major regions (Map 19-2): the North, Central, and Southern Highlands, and the North, Central, and South Coasts. The highlands include the mountains, high plateaus, and mountain valleys, all primarily at elevations of 9,000 feet or above. There the climate is equitable, with adequate rainfall in the lower portions. The climate changes to a cold steppe regime at heights of 11,000–14,000 feet, and higher still lie alpine tundra and snowfields. The coastal region is desert. Rainfall occurs inland in the mountains and returns to the sea by means of a series of 40 or more short, steep, parallel river valleys. The combination of no rain on the coast and availability of surface water only in the valleys early led to dependence on irrigation. A further bonus is the preservation of perishable materials. The coastal aridity permits the recovery, through archaeological methods, of as complete a record of a prehistoric life-style as found anywhere in the world. Only Egypt, Mesopotamia, and the American Southwest have similarly optimal conditions for preservation coupled with an outstanding culture.

Our discussion of Andean culture history will attempt to follow the basic Archaic, Formative, Classic, and Postclassic scheme used so far to integrate the New World data. However, these particular terms are not specifically employed in South American archaeology. Instead, we have the scheme proposed by Lumbreras

(1974:13), who structures the sequences using the Willey-Phillips (1958) terms Lithic, Archaic, and Formative for the hunter-gatherer, incipient agriculture, and early pottery-making village epochs, respectively, followed by the Regional Developmental period, the Huari Empire, the Period of Regional States, and the Empire of Tawantinsuyu (more widely known as the "Empire of the Inca").

The Andean Farming Tradition

In the Andes we have the development of a strong Formative cultural pattern. The extent to which this development was the result of influences from Mesoamerica is still under investigation. ▲ Agriculture began in the Farmer-Fisherman period, after 2500 B.C. By 1000 B.C. the Andean farming tradition was fully established and formed the economic basis for all later Andean cultural developments. This tradition featured intensive agriculture of valley bottomlands watered by irrigation.

The Formative period in Andean South America is dated to between 1800 B.C. and A.D. 100. Lumbreras (1974:49) further subdivides the Formative into these stages: the Lower Formative, consisting of non- or pre-Chavin manifestations; the Middle Formative, consisting of the Chavin culture; and the Late Formative, consisting of cultures derived from both Chavin and non-Chavin antecedents.

The Lower Formative

■ The Lower Formative is marked by the appearance of pottery. In some areas, such as Huaca Prieta, the pottery is so primitive that it may have been independently invented. Without attempting to take into account the seemingly unending varieties of Peruvian ceramics, we can say that their variety and technological excellence increases through time. During the Lower Formative there is also evidence of in-

creasing ceremonialism, with the appearance of ceremonial structures. Some of these structures are artificial mounds constructed of clay and stone in the shape of animals, possibly cats.

The Middle Formative: The Chavin Period

The earliest Pan-Peruvian cultural manifestation, the Chavin culture, occurred within the Middle Formative (900–200 B.C.). ● The Chavin (named after the typesite, Chavin de Huantar, in the Northern Highlands), is marked by a Horizon style of the same name (Fig. 19-7). In the highlands the Horizon style is present in stone sculpture and other media, and on the coast it is present in pottery as well as in weaving and metalwork. The style consists of abstract, repeated, curvilinear representations of a feline or anthropomorphized feline. The single uniformly present diagnostic feature is overlapping canine teeth. Other stylistic elements include men, demons, jaguars, eagles, serpents, caimans, and other beasts (Willey 1971:116; Lumbreras 1974:57–80). Another feature is eyes in which the pupils are located at the top of the orbit. The style is bilaterally balanced with repeated elements that are clearly intended as decorative rather than representational. (An analogy that comes to mind are the Buddhas with many arms typical of North India and adjacent China.) The style is contemporaneous with the Olmec culture of the Mesoamerican Formative, in which the jaguar-mouth art motif figured prominently. It is tempting to suggest a historical connection on this basis, but in fact the similarities between the two styles are more general than specific.

An even more suggestive correlation with Mesoamerica may be made with the carved vertical stone slabs set around the temple at Cerro Sechin in the Casma valley in northern Peru (Fig. 19-8). The age of the site is uncertain, but it is assigned by Willey (1971:112) to the Prechavin period. At Cerro Sechin these slabs have been deeply carved with individual human fig-

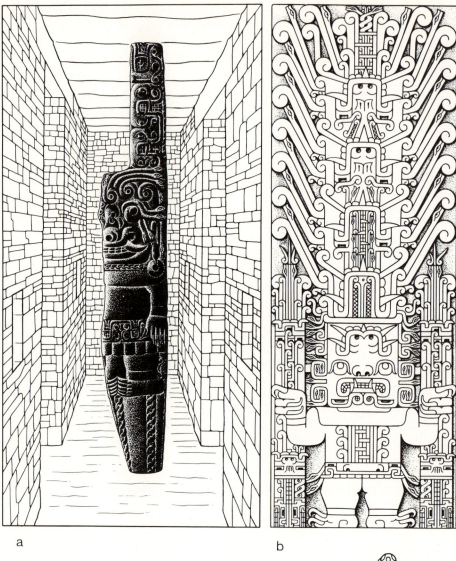

Fig. 19-7 The Chavin Horizon style in different media. (*a*) The Lanzon, a stone column in the interior of the main building at Chavin de Hauntar; (*b*) drawing of the carving on the Raimondi stone, also from Chavin de Hauntar, (*c*) a pottery vessel from the Paracas peninsula. (Willey 1971:Figs. 3-38, 3-39, 3-40.)

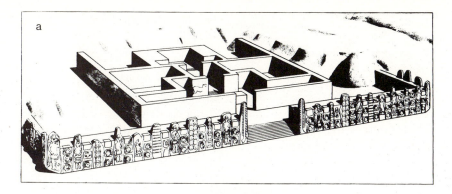

Fig. 19-8 Striking stylistic similarities between South America and Mesoamerica in the Formative period. (*a*) The temple at Cerro Sechin, Casma Valley, Peru, showing placement of the bas relief figures; (*b*) details of the figures at Sechin; (*c*) detail of one of the figures, termed "Danzantes," from Monte Alban, Oaxaca. ([*a*] and [*b*] Willey 1971:Figs. 3-30, 3-31; [*c*] Hester photograph.)

▲ Realistic modeling on pottery

■ Temples made of adobe brick appear.

ures in profile. The similarities between these figures and the Danzantes of Monte Alban, Oaxaca, which are of similar age (to be discussed later), is indeed striking (Fig. 19-8c), especially since such carved slabs are rare in both Mesoamerica and the Andean area. The Sechin style features warriors or dignitaries carrying maces, seminude or dismembered men, and geometric elements (Willey 1971:112).

Bennett and Bird (1964) have applied the term *Cultist* to the Chavin period, for they infer that the art style was associated with the peaceful dissemination of a religious cult which became nearly pan-Andean in scope. The period is marked by a rather sudden flowering of culture. The crafts include outstanding pottery, weaving, and even metalworking. There is evidence in the refuse deposits and cemeteries of a population increase. The appearance of temples signifies a formalized religion as well as a social organization capable of scheduling the construction of public buildings. The appearance of the art style was sudden and without obvious antecedents, unless it is traceable to Cerro Sechin. The style was superimposed upon a number of local cultures, each of which was evolving toward similar cultural goals, all of which shared the common Andean farming tradition. Location of sites in places later abandoned as too swampy or too arid implies that agricultural techniques were as yet imperfectly developed.

In his discussion of cultural innovations, Willey (1971:115) is impressed with the developments during the Middle Formative (1800–900 B.C.). Cited are the appearance of plant cultivation, increase in the number of sites, and florescence in crafts and ceremonial structures. However, Willey is unwilling to assert that all these

developments were the logical outgrowth of agriculture. For example, sedentism and the increase in population had been initiated by the coastal-fishing and shellfish-gathering peoples, and thus there was already in effect a social tradition of communal living prior to the development of agriculture. Food debris from Chavin sites, especially from coastal middens, reveals reliance on seafoods as well as on the peanut, warty squash, and avocado. There is a strong possibility that both the dog and the llama were domesticated.

The most outstanding architectural manifestation is the site of Chavin de Huantar. At an elevation of 10,000 feet in the northern highlands of Peru, the Chavin ceremonial complex covers an area of 210 square meters. The site constructions consist of a series of rectangular platform mounds with remains of rectangular buildings on top. The platforms contain within them stone-slab-lined galleries and rectangular rooms on three levels connected by stairways and inclines. Interior ventilator shafts carry air to underground galleries and rooms. The exterior facing stones were well-cut pieces of granite. Also attached to the platform exterior was a set of human and animal heads sculpted in the round in the Chavin Horizon style and tenoned into the wall. Other stone sculptures at the site include a cornice carved with figures in relief, and carved stone slabs set into the exterior walls, lintels, and columns. Set within one of the galleries inside the platform is the Great Image or Lanzon (Fig. 19-7), a carved stone slab of prism form. It is a bas-relief of an anthropomorphic figure with the Chavin-style fangs, hair represented by snakes, ornaments in the ears, and a necklace and girdle of combined serpent-jaguar faces. The Great Image is presumed to have represented a supreme deity deliberately placed in a setting calculated to inspire awe.

The Chavin style changes through time, with the Great Image being an early, more representational figure. The Raimondi Stone (Fig. 19-7) is typical of the later, more abstract style. Accord-

Fig. 19-9 One of the earliest major temples from the Peruvian Formative period at the site of El Paraiso or Chuquitanta on the central coast. The walls are of unshaped stones laid up without the use of mortar. (Hester photograph.)

ing to John Rowe, Chavin de Huantar included, in addition to the ceremonial center, an associated residential area, and several nearby villages. Presumably, these villages shared in the maintenance and use of the ceremonial center.

The best-known Chavin pottery is that from the North Coast Cupisnique culture. Typically, the pottery ranges from black to brown and is highly polished. It features the unique Peruvian vessel form, the stirrup-spouted vessel, so typical from this period and throughout the entire Peruvian ceramic tradition. ▲ Cupisnique ware is famous for its realistic modeling of plants, animals, humans, and buildings, a tradition in pottery which continued throughout the Peruvian cultural sequence and which provides a wealth of information about the prehistoric Peruvian life-style. Cupisnique pottery is common and is usually intact, for vessels were placed in graves as burial offerings. Other decorative techniques include the use of zoned decoration, incising, punctations, and other surface manipulations.

The coast sites also possess temples (Fig. 19-9) which, although of lesser size than Chavin de

Huantar, are nonetheless impressive. ■ Adobe, made into bricks of conical form, was the major building material. Typical platforms were as much as 170 meters square and 30 meters in height, having as decoration adobe sculptures in the Chavin style. Some of these sculptures were painted. Domestic architecture consisted of simple, thatch-roofed houses of adobe built on circular and rectangular platforms. Metalworking appears at this time on the North Coast. Manufacturing techniques were limited to soldering, hammering, annealing, and repoussé decoration. Items were of thin gold and include crowns, ornaments, ear spools, tweezers, and pins found as grave offerings. The repoussé decoration is clearly in the Chavin style.

Chavin influence is seen elsewhere, as in the Paracas pottery of the South Coast. The excellently made Paracas wares also include evidence of a non-Chavin tradition. Important ceramic traits are the double spout and bridge bottle, red-slipped decoration, negative painting, whistling bottles, and polychrome-painted decoration. Paracas burials include excellent examples of weav-

387

● Evidence of weaving

▲ Development of ceramic styles

■ Many Formative elements from Mesoamerica were introduced into North America.

ing, and the painted pottery designs and those of the textiles are similar.

● The spindle whorl and heddle loom are the first weaving implements to appear. All weaving was in cotton and included plain weave, tapestries, weft stripes, fringes, tassels, and embroidery. Clothing included belts, breechclouts, a head cloth, and feather headdresses. Ornamentation was not limited to clothing but featured body painting as well as rings, bracelets, ear plugs, and necklaces of bone, turquoise, lapis lazuli, shell, gold, and iron pyrites. Personal beauty was also enhanced by artificial skull deformation.

In review we may categorize Chavin culture as based upon a settled farming way of life which had presumably originated at an earlier date. The presence of separate, identifiable cultural patterns, such as the Paracas pottery, is indicative of local autonomy. The Chavin religion, about which little is known, was the only unifying element in the Andean area, and its influence was limited to the far North Coast, Central Coast, and Northern Highlands. It is not well represented on the South Coast, although some Paracas pottery shows the Chavin influence (Willey 1971: Figs. 3-51, 3-52). The absence of fortifications implies the peaceful spread of a religious cult based upon worship of an anthropomorphized feline deity. There was no overall political unity, and the social organization consisted of family units organized into small villages. The major integrative force in the society was its religion.

The Upper Formative

This is the period described by Bennett and Bird (1964) as the "Experimenter" period. According to Bennett and Bird, it was during the Experimenter period that perfection was acquired in crafts, building, and agricultural methods. Perhaps the deliberate intention to *experiment* which they imply is overstated; nonetheless, this was the time of achievement of control over the environment through irrigation farming. The period was marked by two Horizon styles in pottery: White on Red and Negative Painted.

THE WHITE-ON-RED AND NEGATIVE PAINTED HORIZON STYLES

The Salinar and Gallinazo pottery styles, which typify the White-on-Red Horizon on the North Coast, continue the previous incised decoration which often outlines the white-painted areas. Appliqué is also used. The Chavin motif is no longer present, and designs are instead simple geometric lines and dots. ▲ Life modeling continues, and two new vessel forms are introduced: the handle-and-spout bottle and the figure-handle-and-spout vessel. Stirrup-spout vessels continue in vogue.

Gallinazo pottery has some elements of the White on Red style but more commonly features the Negative Painted style. The latter utilizes a resist-dye painting in which a dull black paint contrasts with the lighter base color of the vessel. In this style the designs are outlined in black on the base color. Modeling is even more common than in the Salinar pottery. Inasmuch as Gallinazo cultural levels are stratigraphically above those of the Salinar culture, it is apparent that the change from the White-on-Red Horizon to the Negative Painted Horizon also is indicative of a chronological difference in the two styles. Salinar house types continued to be built on platform mounds or terraces, with the house walls of conical adobes. Some rooms were agglutinated into small compounds. Small, flat-topped platform mounds scattered throughout the valley probably served as local worship centers. On the tops of nearby hills, walled fortifications represent the earliest evidence of warfare recorded in ancient Peru.

The main site at Gallinazo is considerably larger than that of previous communities. The total site area ranges from 2 to 6 square kilometers, depending upon different archaeologists' criteria for how concentrated the population is to be included. The total population is estimated at 5,000 to 10,000 persons living in clusters of adobe apartments, although Wendell Bennett, the excavator, estimated that 20,000 rooms occur within the area adjacent to the ceremonial center. The latter is dominated by a pyramid 25 meters in height associated with smaller pyramids, platforms, and a walled courtyard. Gallinazo probably served as the capital of its valley, the Viru, with numerous other small settlements within the valley being occupied simultaneously. The Salinar-Gallinazo sequence is the cultural antecedent of the great Mochica civilization of the North Coast, one of the most outstanding cultures ever to exist in aboriginal America and a culture which we shall review in the next chapter.

The Formative in North America

Perhaps the single most important fact about the Formative in North America is that the cultures to the north lagged behind Mesoamerican developments. In fact, no culture group in North America ever evolved beyond the Formative stage.

■ Northern cultures did not develop the wealth of cultural detail characteristic of the

Fig. 19-10 Plan of the great Mississippian culture center at Cahokia, Illinois. (Morgan 1980:50.)

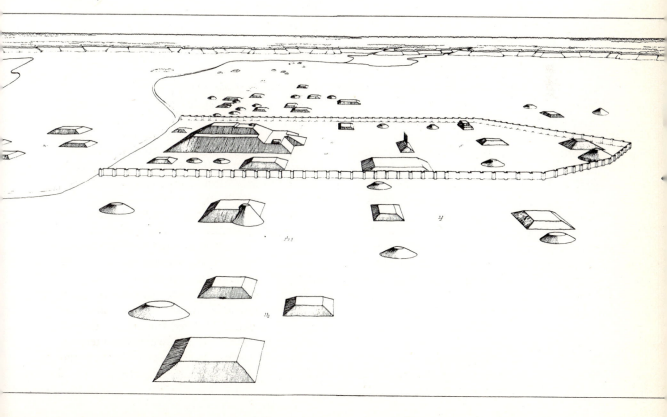

Fig. 19-11 Symbols of the Southern cult: human hands, hearts, skulls, bones, serpents, and the taking of heads. (Willey 1966:304, 307.)

Mesoamerican societies and, in addition, numerous culture traits can be traced back to the south, indicating that Mesoamerica functioned as a major center of diffusion. For example, in the southwestern United States there were Mesoamerican-type introductions, such as ballcourts, the use of irrigation, pyrite mirrors, copper bells, and certain ceremonial parallels (e.g., priests' costumes, belief in the feathered serpent, the use of feathers, and even the presence of pyramids). In the eastern United States we have the northward spread of temple mounds after a.d. 700. These were earthen flat-topped mounds of pyramidal form with temples on top (Fig. 19-10). A later feature was a religious complex, termed the "Southern" cult, which included many symbols

of Mesoamerican affinity-hands, skulls, human bones, and priests in costume, some with trophy heads (Fig. 19-11). Introduced as domesticates into both regions from Mesoamerica were corn, beans, and squash.

Another feature which must be taken into account in the study of the North American Formative cultures is that of environmental limitation. The Southwest is semiarid, and the availability of rainfall in sufficient quantity for agriculture was a continuing problem, so much so that the Puebloan religion became focused on rainfall propagation. However, Southwestern cultures did attain a Formative level of accomplishment (Figs. 19-12, 19-13, 19-14).

Fig. 19-12 Aerial photograph of the five-story Pueblo Bonito, Chaco Canyon, New Mexico. The rectangular rooms were living and storage units; the round rooms were the ceremonial "kivas." (Courtesy of Hardwick and Associates.)

Fig. 19-13 Network of prehistoric roads linking the major sites in Chaco Canyon with other major Chacoan sites located to the northwest (for example, the Salmon and Aztec ruins) and to the southwest (for example, Kin Bineola, Kin Klizhin, and Kin Yda). The roads to the east probably led to Pueblo Pintado. (Anderson and Anderson 1976:49.)

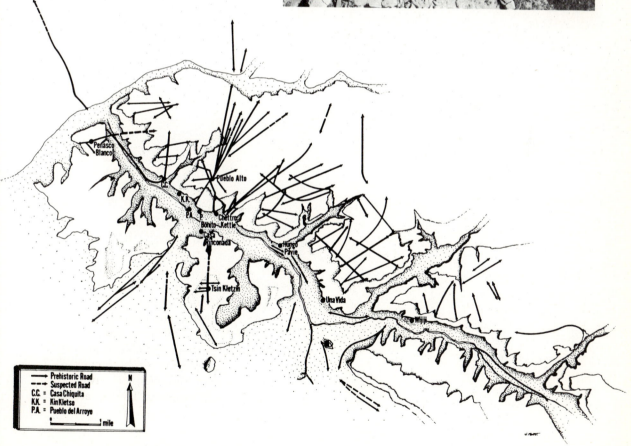

III Banded

IV Slab

II Chinked

I Local

III Banded

Fig. 19-14 Details of the differing styles of Chacoan masonry. (Anderson and Anderson 1976:5.)

In the Great Plains region the soil available for agriculture was limited to the river-valley bottoms. The land used today for production of a major portion of the world's supply of wheat and corn, the rolling plains uplands, was unavailable to the prehistoric Great Plains inhabitants. They were unable to farm the uplands with the agricultural tools at their command, the digging stick and bison scapula hoe, but they did farm the easily cultivated, well-watered valley bottoms. It was not until the introduction of the moldboard plow in the nineteenth century A.D. that the upland sod could be effectively broken. In the eastern United States, south of Massachusetts, the primary emphasis was on farming supplemented by hunting. This economic pattern was capable of supporting large population centers. North of Massachusetts, owing to environmental limitation there was the persistence of an archaic type of mixed-resource economy.

Ceremonialism was also present in North America. In the eastern United States the ceremonial centers, which consisted of specialized burial areas with burial mounds and enclosing earthen embankments, were associated with major population centers such as Cahokia. The latter has been estimated to have had a maximum population of 40,000 to 50,000 (Fig. 19-10). In the Southwest the ceremonial room, the kiva, was located within the village (Fig. 19-12).

Summary

The Formative period is an extremely varied one, ranging geographically from North America through Mesoamerica to South America. Chronologically, it occurred early in Mesoamerica and South America and late in North America. The Formative is marked by the establishment of settled villages founded on a reasonably secure agricultural base. This base was sufficiently productive to support full-time specialists, particularly priests, along with the construction of specialized and often quite large ceremonial structures. Writing and high levels of achievement in the arts, government, and religion all have their origins and initial developments in the Formative period.

20

The Classic Period in the New World

The Classic Achievement in Mesoamerica

The transition from the cultures of the Formative stage (Mesoamerican Preclassic period) to those of the Classic period was gradual. The classic was marked more by superlatives—in architecture, thought, writing, crafts, and so forth—rather than by the appearance of new phenomena. ■ The Classic achievements represent a cultural florescence, stunning in their magnificence and variety. In this chapter we will attempt to outline the major features of the Mesoamerican Classic and its South American counterpart.

An understanding of the Classic achievement can be gained from simple statements concerning the magnitude of the sites considered. In Mesoamerica, for example, Teotihuacan was an urban complex covering eight square miles, with a population estimated to be as large as 100,000 to 200,000. As another example, the site of Monte Alban in Oaxaca has a central plaza the size of a modern football field surrounded by a complex of buildings all of which are located on the top of a mountain. The site has been undergoing annual excavation and restoration for more than 40 years and much still remains to be done.

Urbanism and Settlement Patterns

In central Mexico one word sums up the Classic period: urbanism, as represented at Teotihuacan. Long recognized as an urban center, recent studies conducted on the Teotihuacan mapping project reveal the growth of the city period by pe-

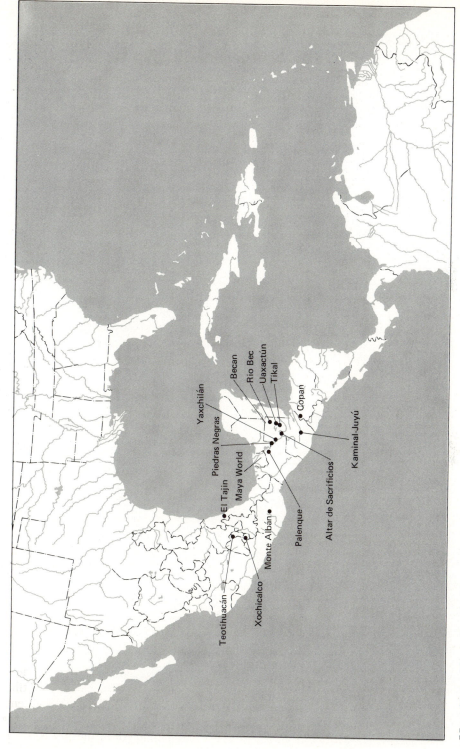

Map 20-1 Classic Sites in Mesoamerica.

395

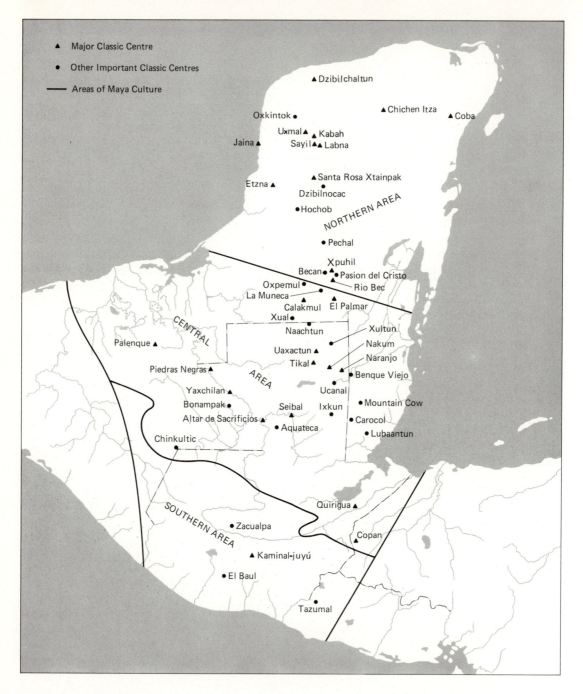

▲ Major Classic Centre

● Other Important Classic Centres

── Areas of Maya Culture

▲ Dzibilchaltun

▲ Chichen Itza

▲ Coba

Oxkintok ●

Uxmal ▲ ▲ Kabah

Jaina ▲ Sayil ▲▲ Labna

Etzna ▲ ▲ Santa Rosa Xtainpak

Dzibilnocac

● Hochob

NORTHERN AREA

● Pechal

Xpuhil

Becan ● ▲▲

Pasion del Cristo ▲

Oxpemul ● ● Rio Bec

La Muneca

Calakmul ▲ ▲ El Palmar

Xual ●

Naachtun ● Xultun ▲

CENTRAL

Uaxactun ▲ Nakum ▲

Palenque ▲ Tikal ▲ Naranjo ▲

AREA

Piedras Negras ▲ ● Benque Viejo

Yaxchilan ▲ Ucanal ●

Bonampak ● Seibal Ixkun ● Mountain Cow

Altar de Sacrificios ▲ ▲ ● Carocol

● Aquateca ● Lubaantun

Chinkultic ●

Quirigua ▲

SOUTHERN AREA ● Zacualpa

● Copan

▲ Kaminal-juyú

● El Baul

▲ Tazumal

● Teotihuacan—the first city in the New World

riod. ● Teotihuacan is unique in that it was built according to an overall city plan. It was laid out within a central-valley location surrounded by low mountains. The layout features a major north-south street, the Street of the Dead, which runs the full length of the city. Other major structural units include an east-west street, a ceremonial center with many major pyramids and temples (Fig. 20-1), and an extensive residential district made up of clustered one-story apartments. There were more than 2,000 such apartment compounds within the city during its

maximum extent. Two opposing structures, the Ciudadela and Great Compound, face each other at the intersection of the Street of the Dead and the east-west avenue. These structures are believed to have formed the bureaucratic, ceremonial, and commercial center of the ancient city. The overall impression of a basic city plan is supported by the recent detailed mapping, and planning was certainly present throughout the city and not just in the central core area.

The residential units were set off into *barrios*, or neighborhoods, some of which featured segregated housing for craft specialists. The religious structures associated with these compounds imply that the local residents cooperated in ritual activities. Population in the apartment complexes is estimated at from 20 to 100 persons

TABLE 20-1
Teotihuacan Developmental Sequence

Valley of Mexico Sequence (after Price [1976])	Teotihuacan Sequence	Dates, Years	Main Events
Late Horizon	Metepec	Late Classic A.D. 750–900	Population fairly stable to late in period, then rapid decline in numbers. Collapse followed by appearance of a series of centers of smaller size.
Middle Horizon	Xolalpan	Early Classic A.D. 200–750	Period A.D. 450–650. Population peaked at 125,000, possibly 200,000.
	Tlamimilolpa		Population doubles, with further expansion into Mesoamerica. Increasing urbanization.
Upper First Intermediate	Miccaotli	Late Formative A.D. 1–200 or Late Pre-Classic	Collapse of Cuicuilco. Valley integrated into a single political economic system.
	Tzacualli		Conquest of north and central Texcoco chiefdoms.
	Ticoman IV		Teotihuacan controls only its local valley, planning of center underway.
		(After Culbert [1979:408–409])	(After Sanders, Parsons and Logan [1976:175–176])

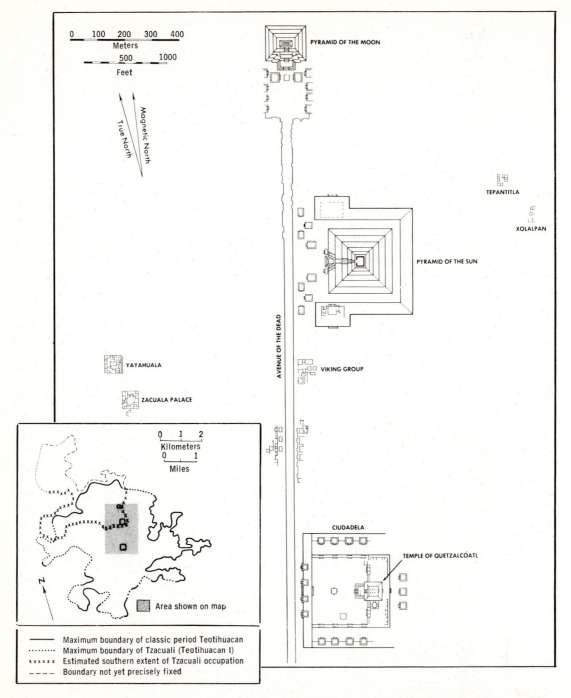

Fig. 20-1 *(Left)* Plan of the urban center of Teotihuacan, Mexico, during the Classic period. *(Right)* Aerial photograph of the same area. ([*Left*] Willey 1966:Fig. 3-40. [*Right*] Millon 1973:Fig. 4.)

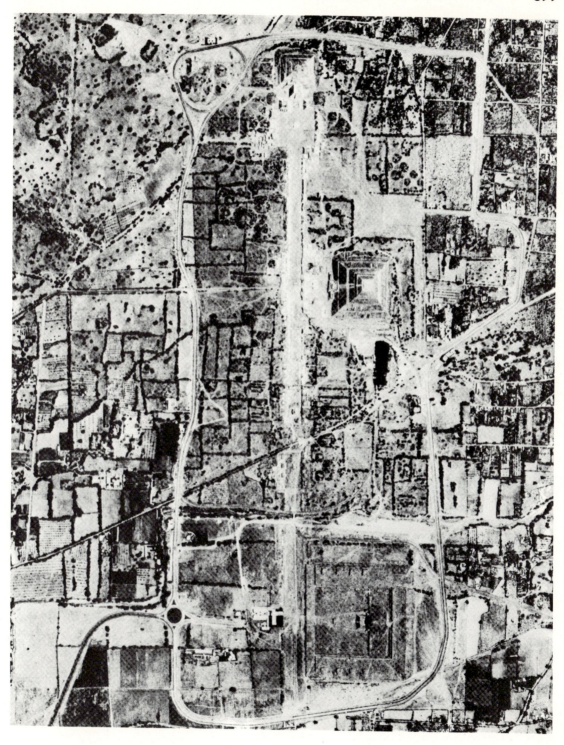

per compound, a group likely related by kinship. Many of the workshops were for obsidian, others being for ceramics, stone, figurines, lapidary work, and work in basalt and slate.

Another major function of the city was as a marketplace and center for long-distance trade. The combination of trade, religious ceremonials, and workshops led to an intense urbanization unique in Mesoamerica. Millon (1970) estimates the population to have been 75,000 at minimum, with 125,000 being more probable and 200,000 not entirely unlikely. Teotihuacan was the most urbanized city in Mesoamerica during the Classic, and its power and influence were equally impressive. It was not until the rise of the Aztec in the Postclassic period that a comparable urban center existed. (The development of Teotihuacan is summarized in Table 20-1.)

The Teotihuacan art style is apparent in polychrome tripod cylindrical pottery jars, jars and lids painted with a fresco technique, wall murals, stone ornamental carving on pyramid risers, pottery figurines, carved stone human masks, and giant, rather stiff human figures carved of stone. (This carving consisted of the crude rounding of the square stone blocks, so that we can somewhat facetiously speak of sculpture "in the square.") Teotihuacan art, at least the smaller pieces, was widely distributed. For example, the tripod cylinder jars were traded as far as Guatemala. A major artistic element in Teotihuacan art was the portrayal of deities, especially Tlaloc, the rain god, and Quetzalcoatl, the plumed serpent. Humans and animals were

Fig. 20-2 The Pyramid of the Sun at Teotihuacan as seen from the Pyramid of the Moon. The platform mounds in between, fronting on the Street of the Dead, are excellent examples of the Talud-Tablero style of architecture so prevalent at the site. (Hester photograph.)

Fig. 20-3 A stone carving of Quet-zalcoatl, the plumed serpent, on the front of a pyramid at Teotihuacan. Quetzalcoatl was a principal deity of the Central Mexican Classic period. (Grady photograph.)

realistically portrayed. One major mural in the Temple of Agriculture depicts crops being distributed to the gods.

▲ Architecture in central Mexico featured a style of pyramid facade best typified at Teotihuacan but also present over much of highland Mesoamerica. Termed the *Talud-Tablero* style, it features a stepped temple platform, the steps of which consist of a sloping riser surmounted by a vertical riser with a rectangular recess (see Fig. 20-2). The center front of the pyramid features a stairway flanked by steeply sloping abutments. This is the architectural style so common at Monte Alban and other urban centers of this region. Decorative elements at Teotihuacan feature carved stone heads of the feathered serpent (Fig. 20-3) and various deities set into the wall recesses of the pyramids.

Map 20-1 presents a set of maps locating the major sites by period and region. At least 100 population centers may be considered major, and hundreds more were of lesser size and importance. Cultural chronologies have been worked out for many of the major regions of Mesoamerica. In addition to those of Teotihuacan, the best-known and most impressive Classic culture in the valley of Mexico are the Zapotec culture of the valley of Oaxaca and the Mayan culture of the Guatemalan highlands and the Yucatecan lowlands.

Oaxaca

In Oaxaca the major site at Monte Alban represents a Classic continuation of the enormous ceremonial center established there during Preclassic times. Preclassic art at Monte Alban is noted for the spectacular bas-relief carvings on stone slabs of nude men in dancing positions, the so-called Danzantes. Classic art at Monte Alban is best represented by the pottery urns of seated deities. Also present are stelae carved with figures and hieroglyphs. Tombs placed in terrace platforms and under patios have fresco murals featuring hieroglyphs, gods, and humans. Pottery vessels in a variety of forms—spouted jars, floreros, candeleros, and cylinder jars—show considerable Teotihuacan influence. After Monte Alban III b, the Late Classic period, the site was abandoned except as a burial place. The reasons for the abandonment of the Late Classic centers such as Monte Alban are still not fully understood (Sabloff and Willey 1967).

Vera Cruz

In the Vera Cruz region there existed a distinctive culture, termed Totonac. The principal site,

■ Elaborate crafts are typical of the Classic cultures.

● The Maya—the leaders of Mesoamerican civilization

El Tajin, near Papantla, features at least 60 major pyramidal mounds, the most famous of which, the Temple of the Niches, has been restored. The exterior of this pyramid is covered with small square recesses which are somewhat like windows architecturally. There are 365 of these niches, which implies a correlation between this temple and the 365-day tropical year. El Tajin was influenced by the lowland Mayan architectural style with its corbeled arches and elaborate roof combs. Most distinctive of Vera Cruz art are the pottery figurines with their famous smiling faces. ■ Other arts include the elaborate stone carving on small unique items such as mirror backs, yokes, hachas, and palmas (Fig. 20-4). The following interpretation of the use of these unique items is provided by Gordon Willey (1966:143):

> The yokes, palmas, and hachas probably represent stone replicas of wooden paraphernalia used in the ceremonial ball game. Yokes, which are large horseshoe-shaped affairs, were worn around the waist of the players as protective belts and the long thin, paddle-shaped palmas were apparently fitted into the fronts of these belts. Just what function the hachas performed is less certain; perhaps they were court markers or scoring devices used in the game. These hachas, or "thin-stone heads" as they are sometimes called, are approximately life-sized human heads or faces in profile. They were widely traded in southern Mesoamerica over routes that extended far beyond the borders of Central Vera Cruz into the Isthmus of Tehuantepec and down the Pacific Coast of Guatemala.

The Mayan World

The earliest intellectual developments in Mesoamerica, including the calendar and hiero-

Fig. 20-4 Stone carvings typical of the Classic Huastec culture, Vera Cruz, Mexico: *(left)* palma; *(right)* hacha. (Hester photographs, courtesy of Mexican National Museum of Anthropology.)

glyphic writing, occurred at the Preclassic (Formative) Olmec sites of San Lorenzo and La Venta and at the Oaxacan site of Monte Alban. ● Nonetheless, by Classic times the Maya of the Guatemalan highlands and lowlands had become the acknowledged leaders of Mesoamerican thought, knowledge, and science.

Prior to the detailed archaeological excavation programs of the twentieth century, there was nearly a century of explorer and antiquarian interest in Mesoamerican ruins. The Mayan country was a focal point inasmuch as the jungle was filled with "lost cities," any of which could provide new and unique finds. Explorations, which continue today (e.g., the recent site surveys in Belize and elsewhere in Honduras by Dennis Puleston, Normand Hammond, Gary Pohl and others), began in 1839 with the landing at Belize, Honduras, of John Lloyd Stephens, a New York lawyer, accompanied by Frederick Catherwood, an English illustrator. Stephens had in 1837 published a travel book about his visit to Arabia and Palestine, and the trip to Central America was undertaken in the hope of writing about the ancient cities to be found there. Eventually published in two volumes, Stephens's *Incidents of Travel in Central America, Chiapas, and Yucatan* (1843) provides the earliest detailed descriptions of ancient Mayan ruins. Catherwood's accompanying illustrations are priceless because they are uniquely accurate copies of the ancient buildings and monuments with their then-undecipherable hieroglyphs. At the time Catherwood was copying these monuments, most European illustrators were adapting aboriginal peoples and archaeological findings in their illustrations to fit artistic concepts derived largely from the ancient Classical world. In addition to their amazing accuracy, Catherwood's illustrations provide us with a record of the condition of the ruins prior to modern restoration.

During the last half of the nineteenth century explorers and students expanded existing knowledge of the ancient cities of Mesoamerica, for the most part without undertaking major ex-

cavations. These pioneers made known to the world the ancient splendors present in the Central American jungles (Wauchope 1965, Deuel 1967). The wealth of the Mayan culture was so overwhelming that the Carnegie Institution established a major program of study under the leadership of Sylvanus Morley, and for more than 30 years various Mayan sites were studied in detail. The largest sites, which included Uxmal, Chichén Itzá, Tikal, and Copan, were termed "metropolises" by Morley and Brainerd (1956). Centers of the second class, which they called "cities," numbered approximately 20. The Carnegie efforts resulted in major excavations at most of these sites. The results include not only studies of the entire cities but detailed excavation reports of individual buildings (Morris 1931; Ruppert 1935).

Past archaeological research has focused on problems dealing with site location, chronology based on the calendrical dates, architectural studies and building reconstruction, ceramic seriation, radiocarbon dating and the calendrical-correlation problem, detailed site mapping, urban developments, studies of economy, and studies of social organization. Current research interests in the Mayan world include studies of settlement patterns, political relationships, subsistence, epigraphy, and shifting populations.

Mayan Writing

Due to the destructive acts of the Spanish following their conquest of Mexico in 1521, little of ancient Mayan writing can be translated. Long after the passing of the Classic period, the local Maya retained their codices and many of the old traditions. The Spanish, however, ordered these "works of the devil" burned, with an enormous resultant loss of traditional Mayan knowledge. Currently, with the aid of computers, major efforts at deciphering the known inscriptions are underway. Experts differ as to what is recorded in the glyphs. J. Eric Thomp-

▲ The hieroglyphs not only record dates and astronomical events but also the political history of the ruling elite.

son, a leading scholar of Mayan epigraphy, has asserted that the inscriptions deal only with time, astronomy, ceremonies, gods, and astrological matters. ▲ Tatiana Proskouriakoff (1960, 1961, 1963, 1964) suggests that the glyphs also contain the dynastic succession of the hereditary elite and other historical events. Her work has clearly established that the stelae so common in major Mayan sites are genealogical records of an elite ruling class. As Adams (1977:153) points out, "the sumptuously dressed individuals are not, as once thought, priests-impersonators of gods, or gods themselves, or mythical beings engaged in mythically significant events." Instead we are dealing with real people involved in real events. No longer do we see the Mayan elite as being contemplative individuals, totally absorbed in manipulating and contemplating dates on their complex calendar. At Bonampak and at Mul-chic near Uxmal, murals undoubtedly recording historical events show warfare, slaughter, and even head-hunting. Individuals such as "Bird-jaguar" of Yaxchilan and his defeated foe, "Jeweled-skull," have emerged from the mists of time to take their rightful places as historical figures.

The Mayan Calendar

A major feature of Mayan knowledge was astronomy, which has been preserved for us by means of calendrical notations on the carved stelae as well as in the few surviving codices. Astronomically derived calendars include the 365-day tropical year, a lunar calendar based on the 29 + -day lunar cycle, and a calendar that correlated five 584-day revolutions of Venus with eight 365-day years. A further refinement was the correlation of the 13-month, 20-day month,

260-day Tzolkin with the 365-day year. This set of correlations resulted in a term of 52 years, called the calendar round. The latter possessed all the possible position variations in day and month names before the two sets of correlated day names and numbers returned to the point of origin.

Mayan dates were expressed in what is termed the Long Count or Initial Series calendar (Fig. 3-8). The Maya dealt in elapsed time, with all time being reckoned from a mythical point of origin based on astronomical calculations. This origin was 3113 B.C., a date believed to be prior to the beginnings of Mayan culture. Units of time were counted by means of a vigesimal system — that is, based on units of 20. The various segments of elapsed time are given in Table 20-2 (Morley 1946:276).

TABLE 20-2
Mayan Units of Time

20 kins	=	1 uinal or 20 days
18 uinals	=	1 tun or 360 days
20 tuns	=	1 katun or 7,200 days
20 katun	=	1 baktun or 144,000 days

The Long Count was inscribed with the introductory glyph followed, from top to bottom and left to right, by the various glyphs for the units of elapsed days (baktuns, katuns, tuns, uinals, and kins) since the last great cycle, with these in turn being followed by other glyphs with astronomical meanings. Adjacent to each time-unit glyph is a number in the bar-and-dot system signifying the number of elapsed baktuns, katuns, and so on. Each date is additive: For example a date of 9.3.3.14.0 would read 9 baktuns, 3 katuns, 3 tuns, 14 uinals, and 0 kins. Thus we would add $9 \times 144{,}000 + 3 \times 7{,}200 + 3 \times 360 + 14 \times 20 + 0 \times 1$ to obtain the number of elapsed days since the last great cycle (Coe 1977:58).

The Mayan City and Its Environs

Constituting the central feature of Mayan cities are the civic and ceremonial structures faced with cut-stone, limestone masonry. These buildings include large pyramids and platform mounds of earth-and-rock fill. The pyramids with temples on top are often high and steep, and even with the decay of centuries they are impressive indeed (Fig. 20-6).

Other major buildings included the ball courts, palaces, and rarely, round buildings, some of which were astronomical observatories. Basic to the ceremonial center design was a rec-tangular plaza surrounded on three or four sides by pyramids and platform mounds. Through time these central plazas grew by accretion until they formed a type of acropolis. Proskouriakoff (1946) has provided a reconstruction of this type of development for structure A-V at Uaxactun, where eight successive stages of construction are revealed. Other features of ceremonial centers include causeways, stelae placed at the base of stairways and fronting on a plaza, and in Yucatan, natural wells called cenotes, many of which were sacred places into which offerings were made. Evidence suggests that the inhabitants of the residential units, the palaces, almost certainly were a hereditary elite. The common peo-

Fig. 20-5 Aerial view of the Mayan ceremonial center at Copan, Honduras. Even though partially covered by dense vegetation, numerous mounds are clearly visible. (Courtesy of Hardwick and Associates.)

■ Superlative architectural development

● Ridged fields—a technique to utilize swampy land for agriculture

ple lived in small villages scattered throughout the farmlands, although many also lived within the major centers. Villages were groups of one-room, thatched structures frequently built on small earthen or stone platforms.

Fig. 20-6 Masterpieces of Mayan architecture of the Classic period. (*a*) The Pyramid of the Magician at Uxmal, Yucatan; (*b*) the palace and Temple of the Inscriptions at Palenque, Campeche, Mexico; (*c*) an aerial view of temples 1 and 2 and the North and South Acropolis at Tikal, Guatemala. ([*a*] and [*b*] Horace E. Day photograph. [*c*] Hester photograph.)

ARCHITECTURE

■ Architecturally, the Mayan buildings are superlative. Many were specialized for religious functions and therefore did not need to be spacious or hospitable. Major general features of the religious buildings were that they were thick-walled, built atop massive pyramidal platforms, and featured little interior space, the rooms being dark, narrow, and high-ceilinged (Fig. 20-6). Above the rooms extended an extraordinarily heavy stone roof, made necessary due to a lack of knowledge of the true arch. The Maya used the corbeled arch made of stones cantilevered toward the center, which necessitated enormous quantities of stone. Above the roof line were intricate decorative features, including roof combs, flying facades, and sculptured friezes. Within the temples occasionally were decorative panels,

a

b

c

such as those in the Temple of the Foliated Cross at Palenque.

At the Temple of the Inscriptions at Palenque, a burial chamber was located beneath the pyramid, with a stairway leading to the temple above. Within the chamber a sarcophagus with a sculptured lid enclosed the burial of a priest or king named Pacal, the face of which was covered by a beautiful jade mosaic mask. Undoubtedly, more such royal tombs remain to be discovered since Pacal's tomb is not the only one known.

A current controversy concerns the degree of urbanism of the major Mayan ceremonial centers and the origins of Mayan civilization (Adams 1977). Earlier arguments have asserted that the economy was based on the milpa system, a practice of clearing small fields which were farmed for two or three years and then abandoned for six to eight years. This system, which is the one used in the area today, leads to a dispersed settlement pattern. Thus if the milpa method was utilized prehistorically, then the major centers could not have been urban. Recent studies at Tikal, Dos Aguadas, and Barton Ramie, among others, reveal population estimates of from 575 to 1600 persons per square mile, while the modern density is 25 to 100 persons for the same unit area (Culbert 1974:41–42). William Haviland (personal communication) estimates there were 40,000 commoners living in Tikal at the time of its greatest extent. While the evidence is not yet complete, it would now seem that Mayan cities were cities in the strict sense of the word, and if this is true subsistence practices in addition to the milpa system must have been employed to support these urban complexes. Culbert (1974:47–51) has suggested that the elite may have enforced a shorter fallowing cycle, which would have increased yields by 28 percent at the expense of a 60 percent increase in labor.

It is now known that the Maya devoted considerable effort to obtaining a secure and adequate food supply. ● They built canals, reservoirs, and ridged fields in swamps (Adams 1980), and they also constructed terraces and check dams to provide arable land and regulate the flow of water. Pockets of highly productive land were aggressively exploited, and now specialists are even discussing the possibility of long-distance trade in foodstuffs (Harrison and Turner 1978; and the 1979 Maya Subsistence Conference). The cultivation of other foods besides corn could have increased the total agricultural yield. Possible crops include yams, sweet potatoes, manioc, the breadnut, and edible leaves (Brewbaker 1979). In addition, recent research at Coba suggests that orchards were maintained within Maya cities to produce fruit, bark, resin, and fiber (Folan et al. 1979).

The major causes of the rise of the Mayan civilization identified at an archaeological conference held in 1974 included population growth, intrasocietal and intersocietal competition and conflict, occupational specialization, and the development of new forms of sociopolitical integration. One argument continues concerning the relative importance of trade versus warfare. Meanwhile, yet another causal factor, ideology, has not as yet been clearly assessed (Adams 1977b).

A concept that has died a timely death is the hypothesis that Mayan cities, like Greek city-states, were totally independent entities. Recent studies of the glyphs indicate there were marriages between the ruling elites of the various major centers, and an innovative but somewhat controversial study by Marcus (1973) emphasizes the organization of the Mayan settlements into an hierarchical network. According to emblem glyphs, the four regional capitals in A.D. 730 were Copan, Tikal, Calakmul, and Palenque. In A.D. 849 the four capitals were Seibal, Tikal, Calakmul, and Motul de San Jose. The four capitals fit the Mayan concept of the universe, which was divided into four directions and a center, each with its own color, flora,

▲ Volcanism influenced Mayan migrations.

■ The Mayan civilization collapses.

fauna, and deities. Each regional capital or "super site" was linked to a series of secondary centers, yielding a hexagonal settlement pattern (Fig. 20-7). The secondary centers in turn had their own satellites in a similar configuration. This pattern, while based on cosmological considerations, was also partly the result of functions to be provided by the centers: travel and transport. Marcus further suggests that since the hexagonal patterns are of unequal sizes, the relationship may have been based on population rather than on geographic area. The organization within each quadrant featured a five-tier hierarchy of capital, secondary center, tertiary center, village, and hamlet.

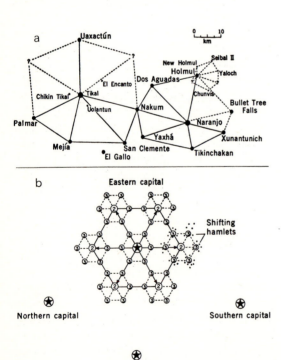

Art

Mayan art was truly Classic in the sense that it was omnipresent and elaborate. Media included wall murals within tombs and temples, bas-relief carvings in stone, modeled pottery, mosaic stone plaques, mosaic stone friezes on buildings, polychrome-painted pottery, and painted hieroglyphic books called codices.

Decorative features of Mayan art include the elaborate costumes of jaguar skins, feathers, and jade ornaments worn by the priests. Depicted were rulers, soldiers, war captives, and occasionally women. The art style is curvilinear and flowing, featuring zoomorphs, plants, and water elements intertwined with the human figures and deities. Other elements include monster figures and monster masks. Priests are shown with the characteristic sloping profile from the end of the nose to the top of the head, an effect achieved in life by head binding with the resultant frontal deformation of the skull. The hieroglyphs were also highly artistic. The decorative motifs on pottery were similar to those of the wall panels. Favorite subjects were monkeys, serpents, jaguars, humans, birds, and monsters. Bands of glyphs on pottery were used as decorative borders, some of these being pseudoglyphs rather than having symbolic meaning. A major feature of pottery and mural painting was the portrayal of humans in profile. Scenes from daily life occur on the best-known murals, one of which features a battle scene and the other a seacoast fishing village. Other murals, of which those at Bonampak are best known, illustrate religious ceremonies.

Fig. 20-7 A hypothetical reconstruction of Mayan settlement patterns. (*a*) Relationships between Tikal and its secondary centers; (*b*) schematic diagram illustrating the general hexagonal nature of Mayan settlement, extended to include the tertiary centers and shifting hamlets (circled stars: regional capitals; 2s: secondary centers; 3s: tertiary centers; dots: shifting hamlets). (Marcus 1973:Figs. 6 and 8.)

TABLE 20-3
Historical Development of the Maya

Period	Date	Events
Late Classic	A.D. 600–900	A period of cultural elaboration and population growth. Greater numbers of ceremonial centers, and an increase in architecture. Last third of period (A.D. 800–900) featured a decline that led to desertion or near desertion. Collapse occurred earlier in south than in the north.
Classic Hiatus	A.D. 534–593	Marked drop in stelae carving and a slackening of ceremonial construction as a phenomenon. This was more pronounced in the south, particularly in the Peten.
Early Classic	A.D. 250–600	Appearance of initial series dates. Stelae cult spreads, with much evidence for calendric validation of ruling autocracy.
Proto-Classic	50 B.C.–A.D. 250	Introduction of ceramic traits from Salvadorian-Guatemalan highlands—a period of florescence.
Late Preclassic	350 B.C.–50 B.C.	A rise in population density, regional diversity, and the appearance of social organization that is usually associated with civilization.

(After Willey 1977:383–423)

Historical Development of the Classic

The Classic was a time of development of great regional cultures such as the Maya, Zapotec, and Totonac. Several major themes emerge, such as the role and rule of a hereditary elite, ceremonialism, commerce, and warfare. The Classic period lasted from A.D. 250 to A.D. 900, and can be divided into three parts: Early Classic (A.D. 250–600), the Classic Hiatus (A.D. 534–593), and the Late Classic (A.D. 600–900) (Willey 1977:383–423; Table 20-3).

Migration may have been a major stimulus to development of the Mayan Classic. ▲ Sheets (1979) argues for large-scale abandonment of the southeastern Mayan highlands of El Salvador and Guatemala during the Late Preclassic due to a violent eruption of the volcano at Ilopango which totally devastated the area within a radius of 100 kilometers. Survivors moved northward and appeared as refugees in the lowlands of Guatemala and Belize.

Prior to the eruption, the southeastern highlands would surely have been a major distribution center for trade between the Maya area and Mexico to the north. With the eruption and the consequent shifting of populations northward, Tikal became the major trading center of the Mayan world. Certainly, the influx of peoples into the lowlands had a major impact on the Classic development.

■ After A.D. 900 the building of major centers, the carving of stelae (at least dated ones), and other evidences of the Classic culture came to an abrupt end throughout the southern portion of the lowland region. Migration, since it may have contributed to the evolution of the Classic period, may equally have been a factor in its collapse. Originally archaeologists felt this collapse was followed by a mass movement of the Maya to Sayil, Kabah, Uxmal, and other cities to the north in Yucatan. However, recent workers are of two opinions on this issue. Some support the migration concept, whereas others believe the northern cities witnessed a similar decline of the Classic culture. Thus far this question remains unresolved.

Reasons for the Mayan downfall are not yet understood. Various theories advanced are a re-

● Local valley cultures, each distinctive in crafts but all excelling in technique

volt against the elite, foreign invasions, a breakdown in the trade network, environmental limitations of the slash-and-burn system, inadequate soils to support a large population, a regional water shortage, and a corn blight. The most plausible hypothesis might be a combination of several such causes (Culbert 1974), although Hamblin and Pitcher (1980), having tested all of these hypotheses mathematically, favor class warfare as the most probable cause of the Classic collapse. In any event, the Mesoamerican Classic, for whatever reasons, was at an end.

The Classic Achievement in South America

The Classic period in Andean South America was a time of excellence and superlatives. Arts and crafts reached such high standards of artistic excellence that Bennett and Bird (1964) felt compelled to call it the "Mastercraftsmen" period. Lumbreras (1974) prefers the term "Regional Developmental Period" and dates it from 100 B.C. to A.D. 700. In a sense both labels are correct and useful. Obviously, Bennett and Bird are emphasizing the high standards of artistic and technical excellence, while Lumbreras underscores the regional variety in arts and crafts which was also typical of the period (Map 20-2).

● Unlike the Chavin horizon of the Middle Formative, in which we saw the spread of a dominant and all-pervasive artistic style, during the "Regional Developmental Period" each of the local Peruvian valleys developed its own style. In some areas ceramics predominated, in others, textiles; but everywhere the emphasis was on technical quality and artistic skill. And surprisingly enough, the pursuit of excellence did not seem to limit quantity.

Pottery making was an advanced craft, featuring modeled, painted, and mold-made ceramics in profusion. The latter, due to their realistic detail, offer some of the most valuable evidence for cultural reconstruction to be found anywhere in the world. From ceramics we have details of social and political organization, religious practices, house types, disease, and sexual practices.

Weaving was an equally important craft. Peruvian textiles, preserved by virtue of having been buried in graves dug in the dry sands of the desert coast, are among the best-known textiles from any prehistoric or even historic culture. In terms of the technical proficiency displayed in the types and fineness of weaves, colors, and patterns, these textiles are unsurpassed. Weaving was done in cotton and wool, and everyday garments as well as specialized wrappings for burial bundles were made. Male attire consisted of a breechclout belt, slit-neck shirt, shawl, and a headband. Females wore a wrap-around dress with a belt, a headband, a shoulder shawl, and bags with carrying straps.

Ornaments and implements were made of metals, including gold, silver, copper, bronze, tin, and electrum. Metalworking technique included casting, soldering, gilding, and the use of filigree. Ornamentation featured body painting, tattooing, skull deformation, inlaying of teeth, and the wearing of earplugs, noseplugs, and necklaces. Minor crafts were wood carving, the carving and painting of gourds, basketry, and the manufacture of ornaments and implements in shell, stone, and bone.

Lumbreras (1974) has identified several regional cultures that fit into this period. These include the Gallinazo (300 B.C.–A.D. 300), the Mochica (A.D. 100–800), the Recuay (?–A.D. 800), the Lima (A.D. 200–800), the Nazca (A.D. 100–800), the Huari (A.D. 700–1100) and the Tiahuanaco (A.D. 100–1200), plus a series of little-known regional-culture groups whose existence is evidenced primarily by a distinctive ceramic style. Lumbreras is also quick to point out the rather ambiguous nature of the Gallinazo cul-

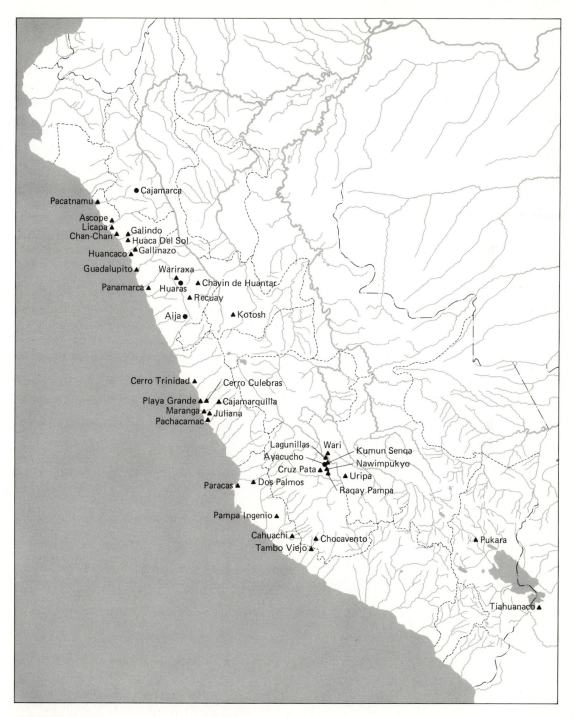

Map 20-2 Classic Sites in South America. (After Lumbreros.)

ture, which we have already described in a For-mative setting. The Gallinazo certainly possesses Formative affinities (e.g., White-on-Red ce-ramics), but these are associated with "Nega-tive" painted wares. The latter technique better fits into our Regional Development, or "Master-craftsmen," period.

We have chosen three of the above Regional Cultures — the Mochica, Nazca, and Tiahuan-aco — for a more detailed discussion in an at-tempt to give an impression of the richness and variety of the Andean Classic period.

The Mochica Civilization: A.D. 100–800

We could rely upon Mochica ceramics as the sole source of information and still be able to re-construct a creditable version of the life-style of these people. The modeled ceramics are so real-istic and reveal such a wealth of detail, in com-bination with the realistically painted pottery, that a glimpse is afforded into every aspect of an-cient Mochica culture (Figs. 20-8, 20-9). With

their main site at Moche, the Mochica expanded beyond their home valley to dominate the North Coast, becoming the inheritors of the North Coast cultural traditions. The themes ev-ident in pottery, mural art, and fortifications imply that expansion was based upon the actual conquest of adjacent valleys.

Architecture featured massive adobe brick ceremonial structures, the most impressive of which, the Huaca del Sol at Moche, is a terraced and truncated pyramid 228 by 136 meters with a maximum height of 41 meters. The Huaca del Sol functioned as a platform for one or more temples, while the nearby Huaca de la Luna, a terraced platform abutting a hillside, included residences which probably belonged to the rul-ing elite.

The Mochica were highly concerned with personal status. Portrait-head vessels record the actual countenances of individuals, each of whom may be identified as to his real-life im-portance due to the geographic distribution of his particular portrait vessels. In addition, status was further indicated by the type of headdress

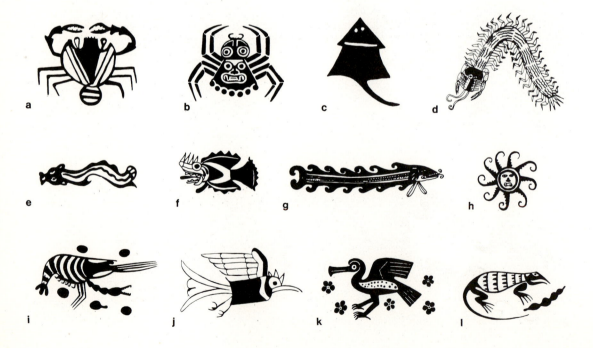

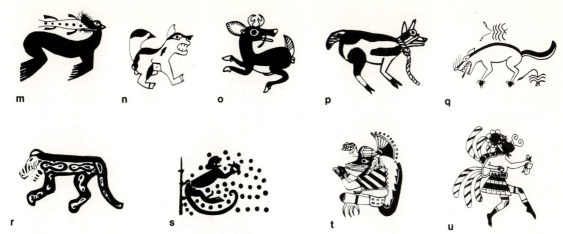

Fig. 20-8 Painted depictions on Mochica pottery. While realistic in concept, Mochica paint-ing has its own distinctive symbolism. Illustrated are various animals and scenes: (*a*) crabs; (*b*) spiders; (*c*) rays; (*d*) centipedes; (*e*) catfish; (*f*) bonitos; (*g*) barracudas; (*h*) octopuses; (*i*) crayfish; (*j*) hummingbirds; (*k*) Muscovy ducks; (*l*) lizards; (*m*) sea lions; (*n*) dogs; (*o*) deer; (*p*) llamas; (*q*) foxes; (*r*) felines; (*s*) monkeys; (*t*) iguanas; (*u*) dragon flies; (*v*) line of warriors; (*w*) sea lion hunt. (Donnan 1976:37–41.)

a

b

c

d

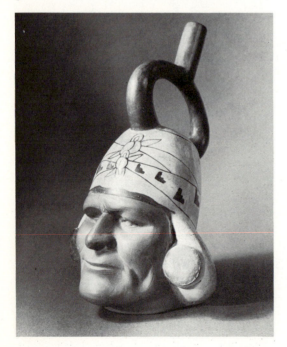

e
f
g
h

Fig. 20-9 a–h; i–l on page 416.

i

j

k

l

▲ Mochica culture is well known to us because every phase of life is illustrated on pottery.

■ Nazca pottery features some of the best polychrome ware ever made.

worn. Mochica society was male-dominated and militaristic. ▲ Other aspects of Mochica society delineated by molded ceramics include types of animals, plants, demons, houses, and scenes from daily life, including sexual practices, hunting, fishing, the punishment of prisoners, religious rites, and burial scenes. As a further ramification, some painted vessels bear scenes of men carrying small bags of beans marked with crosses and dots. It has been suggested that the beans may have served as symbolic ideographs, which if not an actual language, could have functioned as memory aids in the transmission of messages.

Grave offerings provide a wealth of cultural objects. Graves have been found on top of pyramids, in cemeteries, and in locations adjacent to the farmed portions of valleys. Graves were rectangular pits with the burials placed inside, in an extended position. Some grave pits were roofed with adobe bricks. Offerings placed in graves differed according to the status of the individual interred. Burial items included the stirrup-spouted vessels, ornaments of gold, copper, silver, and inlaid bone. For the first time there was the widespread use of metal in utilitarian implements as well as in ornaments. Copper was used for axes, spears, helmets, and for the points of digging sticks. Metalworking techniques included alloying, casting, and gilding.

Fig. 20-9 Depictions in Mochica modeled pottery, showing cultivated plants, styles of dress, and familiar animals: (*a*) warty squash; (b) pacae; (*c*) portrait vessel; (*d*) woman nursing a child; (*e*) portrait vessel; (*f*) warrior with a war club; (*g*) crayfish; (*h*) owl; (*i*) fox; (*j*) frog; (*k*) terrapin; (*l*) head of a deer. (Donnan 1976:Figs. 4, 8, 37, 81, 82, 84, 85, 87, 89, 93, 94, 108.)

Mochica achievements constitute a major regional culture, with a strong political organization as well as the infinite variety and accuracy of modeled ceramics. No other ancient culture surpassed the skill of the Mochica in the manufacture of modeled pottery.

Nazca Culture: A.D. 100–800

The South Coast is known for the development at this time of a culture termed *Nazca*, after a valley of the same name. ■ An outgrowth of the preceding Paracas culture of the same region, the Nazca is world-famous for its polychrome-painted ceramics. Nazca ceramic decorations include designs present on textiles found on the famed Paracas mummy bundles, among which are a cat-demon, and bird, fish, and animal designs. Nazca pots are known to have as many as 11 colors, although 4 or 5 are most common — red, black, white, gray, orange, and shades of each. Among the major vessel forms is the double-spouted bottle with a bridge between the spouts and open bowls. The Nazca area is also famed for its textiles, which were specially manufactured to be used as mummy wrappings and which featured a wide variety of weaves, including brocade, double cloth, tapestry, gauze, lace, and weft stripe. These textiles are among the highest in quality ever manufactured in the world at any time. Woven of llama wool and cotton, the fabrics feature a background color of black, red, or green, with embroidered designs in the same elements as the pottery. The weaving is further enhanced by the wide range of dyes used; 190 shades, or hues, are known.

Architecture and settlement patterns of the South Coast Nazca are less well known, owing to the focus of the excavators on the recovery of burials from cemeteries. Large towns or cities did exist at this time. For example, at Cahuachi, in the Nazca Valley, a platform was surmounted with a temple of wedge-shaped adobes, and

● Tiahuanaco—a major ceremonial center located at an elevation too high to occupy on a year-round basis

Tiahuanaco: A.D. 100–1200

Tiahuanaco is a major ceremonial center located on the eastern side of Lake Titicaca. The site is situated on the altiplano at an elevation of 14,000 feet (Lumbreras 1974:139), and because this elevation is too high for most crops except quinoa, potatoes, and oca, there must have been considerable reliance on herding. ● The environmentally limited economy was probably responsible for the site construction pattern and use: This place was probably not a residential center for the populace. Archaeologists believe that it was constructed at intervals, perhaps during religious pilgrimmages, at which time the regional population accumulated materials which were used during the rest of the year by a small group of skilled construction workers. This project was never finished, and the building of sections at intervals would explain the

nearby is a ridge covered with walled courts and rooms. Perhaps the best-known Nazca features are the strange patterns or drawings on the ground made by removing stones from the surface (Fig. 20-10). The patterns are thought to be of Nazca origin, since they are of design elements common to the ceramics and textiles. The motifs include primarily geometric elements and animal figures. Their abstract design and large size, necessitating an aerial vantage point to best perceive them in their entirety, have led recent authors to ascribe to them mystical meanings, and even to attribute their construction to extraterrestrial beings.

Fig. 20-10 Aerial photo of one of the marvelous outlined figures (a hummingbird) on the plains of Nazca, South Coast of Peru. (Hester photograph.)

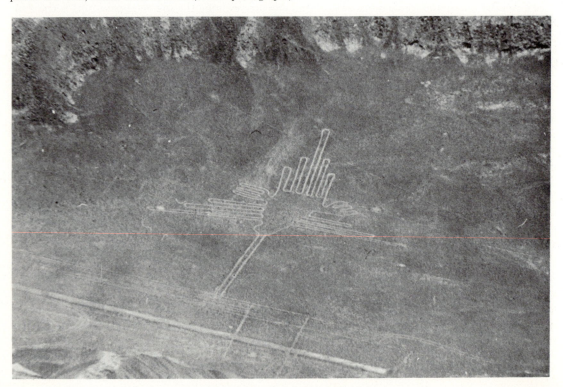

Fig. 20-11   The famous monolithic gateway at Tiahuanaco. (Willey 1971:Fig. 3-90.)

presence of structural units which are internally organized but are not arranged into an overall site plan.

There are four major structural units and several smaller ones. The largest consists of a natural mound made into a pyramid 210 meters square and 15 meters high, on top of which are house foundations. Associated is a water reservoir, which may also have served as a fortress. Another unit features a stone-faced earthen platform 135 by 130 meters with an inner courtyard. The other structural units are similar but smaller. There are associated stone statues and monolithic gateways. Carving in the round is suggested, but actually the technique employed consists of bas-relief carving on four sides of slabs weighing up to 100 tons. The extremely impressive gateways (Fig. 20-11), which were made by carving a doorway through giant stone slabs, are decorated with friezes of bas-relief carving in the Tiahuanaco style. This Horizon

style features stiff human figures, pumas, and condors carved in profile. The largest gateway, called the Gateway of the Sun, has positioned above its opening a deity called the Gateway God. The figure, facing frontward and clasping a staff in either hand, is a variant of the anthropomorphic deity, with a headdress of snakes and a jaguar-style mouth.

While our knowledge of the Tiahuanaco culture is somewhat limited, we do know something of its architectural use of stone. Stone for sculptures and construction was imported from quarries 5 kilometers distant. Building blocks were fitted together by cutting notches or grooves into their edges, then fitting copper T- or I-shaped clamps into the grooves. Some of the decorative carved heads were separately carved and then tenoned into walls. Building stones were further finished by the grinding of their surfaces. Ceramics are well fired and highly polished. Principal vessel forms include flaring-

▲ The Tiahuanaco Horizon style

sided goblets, open bowls, and bowls with annular bases. Although as many as eight colors of paint were used, most pottery is black, white, and red.

In the Highlands, sites of Tiahuanaco culture are represented by cemeteries, stone building units, and stone sculpture. Sites on the coast are represented primarily by cemeteries. It is from the coast, where preservation is of such high degree, that we have most of the evidence of Tiahuanaco textiles. The latter are well made, especially the tapestries, and their decoration also includes use of the Tiahuanaco Horizon style.

Several styles of burial were employed. On the Central Coast the interments are in pits, and mummies are wrapped in special garments, with an attached mask of clay, metal, or wood. South Coast burials are in large pottery urns, and in the Highlands burials were placed in boxes lined with stone slabs.

Lumbreras identifies three post-Formative phases for Tiahuanaco (Phases III, IV, and V). In Phases III and IV, the so-called Classic intervals, the Tiahuanaco culture seems centered in the Lake Titicaca region with some possible expansion to the north. Phase V sees an expansion to the east, west, and south, and downward into the coastal areas (Lumbreras 1974:139). The expansion northward certainly influenced the Huari culture, which then in turn began its main consolidation and expansion. (The expansion of Huari is part of the Andean Postclassic period and will be discussed in the next chapter.) The Tiahuanaco expansion to the east, west, and south was apparently the result of military and political actions and is marked by the spread of the Tiahuanaco Horizon style.

▲ The Horizon style is present in stone carving, architecture, and ceramics. In ceramics the style is manifested in polychrome painting in white, black, and red (Fig. 20-12). Ceramics are

Fig. 20-12 Ceramic vessel typical of the Tiahuanaco-Wari horizon style. (Hester photograph, courtesy the Inca Museum.)

highly polished with a red slip and designs outlined in black. The basic stylistic feature is a standing anthropomorphic deity facing forward and clasping a staff in each hand. The overlapping canine teeth recur as a motif, and other motifs are the heads of birds and animals, the profiled running human figure wearing a cape and a bird mask, repeated profile figures of pumas and condors, and repeated geometric designs, circles, dots, and crosses. The design style is frequently stylized to the point that the deity figure is represented only by the face, the body being made up of geometric elements.

Summary

Certain themes are prevalent in Andean prehistory. We know, for example, that religion was practiced under the leadership of priests, who were responsible for organizing all ritual. Most ceremonies were agricultural in nature, and another major focus was upon the burial rites. The latter featured a public ceremony in which the corpse was wrapped in burial clothing and then entombed along with the appropriate offerings.

We know also that transportation was difficult because within a few miles the terrain ranged from sea level to 20,000 feet. Some of the highest areas (those above 15,000 feet) were utilized for mining. Major transport was on foot, with the llama as the principal beast of burden. On the open sea sailing rafts with centerboards were used, and boats of tied bundles of reeds were common on the highland lakes.

Intensive agricultural production supported a large population, which lived in permanent houses. The latter were built of both stone and adobe brick. The village was the basic social and political unit, and each had its own headman and worked as a cooperative labor force. Villages were organized into larger political units which through time became increasingly larger in size and complexity. Class distinctions were important and were based on wealth and political influence. Late in the tradition these distinctions crystallized into a true caste system.

Warfare was an organized activity conducted by a specialized warrior class with military leaders. Implements of war included the spear thrower, spear, club, sling, shield, bow and arrow, and bolas. The practice of warfare relied on use of spies, blockades, the storming of fortresses, and fighting in formation. However, during the Classic period, warfare, while important, did not lead to the formation of the type of large heterogeneous empire which was so characteristic of the Postclassic period.

21

The Postclassic Period in the New World

The Postclassic Transition in Mesoamerica

The shift from the Classic to the Postclassic period is marked by a series of dramatic events, the most dramatic of which is the abandonment of the greatest city in Mesoamerica, Teotihuacan. The collapse of this great city may have had a domino effect, since other Classic sites such as Monte Alban also fell into disuse. Even the Maya were not immune to the effects of this collapse, and there was a major shift of cultural emphases and population out of the Classic Maya lowlands northward into Yucatan.

■ If the transition to the Postclassic is marked by the disintegration of the Classic cultures, the abandonment of some of the major centers, outbound emigration, the cessation of temple building and the creation of monumental sculpture, it is also marked by the appearance of the Chichimecs, the tribes from the north. Although these peoples did not cause the collapse of the Classic cultures, they were able to take advantage of the existing internal weaknesses in the system. The Postclassic was therefore a time of cultural change in which the established order was replaced by chaos, out of which grew a new culture type with new centers, a new kind of leadership, and a new social organization. Major changes included a shift to militarism and violence, with new gods of war enshrined. These deities, due to their violent nature, required increasing sacrifices, especially human ones, for their appeasement. With the advent of the Postclassic the center of cultural development shifted to central Mexico, whereas the Maya lowlands never totally recovered from the Classic collapse. Throughout Mesoamerica

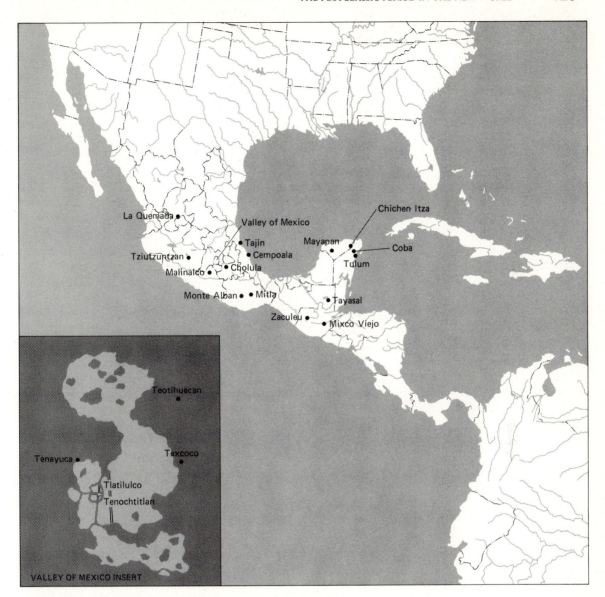

Map 21-1 Mesoamerican Archaeological Sites and Regions.

then, the old traditions were altered but not completely severed. Many traditions did continue, although modified, and the new emphases probably were much more important to the rulers, priests, and warriors than to the common people.

The Chichimecs were former Desert Culture hunters and gatherers, living on the northern frontier of Mesoamerica in a situation analogous to that of the barbarian Germanic tribes on the frontier of Rome. Through time and in ways which can only be surmised, these peoples became knowledgeable in the patterns of Mesoamerican civilization. They moved southward, possibly because drought forced them out of their homeland, settled down, and took up Mesoamerican farming practices. One late group of Chichimecs, known to us as the Aztec, first appeared in the Valley of Mexico about A.D. 1300 and settled next to civilized peoples known as Culhuas. The Aztec initially served as mercenary soldiers for the Culhuas and—more parallels with Rome—within a hundred years came to dominate them. But we are ahead of our story, for there were numerous significant Postclassic developments prior to the rise of the Aztec.

The Early Postclassic:
A.D. 800–1168

TULA OF THE TOLTECS

The earliest of the Chichimecs to make significant contributions were the peoples we know as the Toltec. They settled at Tula, Hidalgo, in about A.D. 856 (Dutton 1955:247), when they built a substantial city on a bluff for reasons of defense (Fig. 21-1). The city center occupies about one square kilometer, with numerous mounds scattered over the adjacent hills. While undoubtedly important, Tula was not an urban center of the scope of Teotihuacan. Its architecture, which is a continuation of the *talud-tablero* tradition of central Mexico, features two major

pyramids flanking a central patio. Adjacent to the pyramids are unique additions in the form of a colonnade and a structure with more such columns (appropriately named the Palace of the Columns). To the north is a second plaza with an I-shaped ball court along its north side.

According to Dutton (1955:246), the architecture of Tula, constructed to impress rather than to endure, was poorly built. Large rocks without mortar were utilized as the central nucleus of the walls, and the weakness of the internal structure led to considerable damage and subsequent repair through time. Wall decorations were of stucco and sculpted stone relief. The sculptural tradition included a style which was bold but lacking in detail and hence lacking in realism. Bas-relief carving was used extensively on the stone columns and pyramid walls. Especially diagnostic of Toltec sculpture are the famous caryatid figures. These, by definition, are human figures used as support columns. The figures at Tula (Fig. 21-2) are those of a Toltec warrior.

Other items unique to Toltec architecture are the Atlantean figures and standard bearers (Fig. 21-2). The former consist of small human forms 30 inches in height with arms upstretched which were used as support columns for altars. The standard bearers possess cupped hands with a hole drilled through for the staff of a flag. At Tula one standard bearer was positioned at each end of the 131-foot-long wall adjacent to Pyramid B. Decorative friezes on this wall depict a serpent devouring a human skeleton (hence its assigned name, the Serpent Wall). Other frieze elements repeated on the tablero sections (vertical portions) of the wall and the pyramid walls are eagles or vultures devouring human hearts, human skulls, squared spirals, jaguars, and monster masks.

The square warrior columns of the same height as the caryatids were also in four sections. Each column has similar elements on each of its sides: warriors, a collection of weapons such as atlatls or darts, a symbol representing a "terres-

Fig. 21-1 Tula of the Toltecs. *(Above)* Reconstruction drawing of the main plaza at Tula. *(Below)* The major pyramid at Tula, showing the use of carytids and rows of columns. ([*Above*] Courtesy of the Mexican National Museum of Anthropology. [*Below*] Courtesy of Philip M. Hobler.)

● A Toltec migration

▲ The Aztec conquer their neighbors in the Valley of Mexico.

Fig. 21-2 Sculptural details at Tula: *(Bottom-left)* Caryatids; *(right)* standard bearer; *(left)* Atlantean figures. (Hester photographs, courtesy of Mexican National Museum of Anthropology.)

trial belt" symbolized by an eye and an upper mandible, and finally a panel combining the warrior, war equipment, and the terrestrial belt. (We have described the Tula architectural features in some detail since they also occur at the Mayan site of Chichén Itzá, some 600 miles to the southeast.)

After the Spanish Conquest, the Aztec related to Spanish historians the legends of their people and those of other central Mexican groups. According to these legends, soon after the founding of Tula, there arose two factions. One followed the political leader (or king) Topiltzin, who was dedicated to the peaceful god Quetzalcoatl, the feathered serpent. The other faction swore allegiance to Tezcatlipoca, the "Smoking Mirror," the new god of war and death. The adherents of Tezcatlipoca were victorious, and Topiltzin and his followers were driven out of Tula in about A.D. 987. ● According to legend, they traveled to the south and east, where they set sail with the promise to return. Although we are not sure that Topiltzin was the Mexican leader who conquered Yucatan—a fact mentioned in the Mayan histories—we can identify Mexican ar-

chitectural elements in Yucatan, especially at Chichén Itzá (Fig. 21-7).

After the defeat and exodus of Topiltzin and his followers, the Toltecs who remained at Tula assumed cultural and military leadership of central Mexico, where their empire continued for 200 years until it also was destroyed violently in about A.D. 1156 or 1168 (Coe 1966:120).

The Late Postclassic and Protohistoric: A.D. 1168–1521

THE AZTEC EMPIRE

The Aztec were another of the Chichimec tribes who left their hunting-and-gathering desert existence to settle in the Valley of Mexico, that great central Mexican center of culture from Preclassic times to the present. Legends hold that the Aztec began their wanderings in about A.D. 1168 (Vaillant 1950:97). At first they lived on an island in a lake in western Mexico. On the nearby shore in a cave they acquired their god Huilzilopochtli, whom they then carried with them on their wanderings. According to the annals, the Aztec or Tenochcas were among the last of these tribes to enter the Valley of Mexico. They are described as quarrelsome, cruel, unfaithful to their word, and women stealers. They were also brave, disdaining death and practicing warfare as a means of livelihood. Their garments were of palm fiber and their sandals of straw — truly an impoverished wardrobe — and they moved from place to place within the Valley of Mexico, eventually settling on Chapultepec Hill, where they took up farming.

Life during the thirteenth century in the Valley of Mexico included a delicate balance of power among the various tribes. Alliances were formed at times in order to curb aggressive neighbors. The Tenochcas took part in these affairs and became noted for their prowess in warfare. In one battle in which the Culhuas and Tenochcas fought the Xochimilcas, the former were successful and took many prisoners. When Coxcox, the Culhua chief, asked the Tenochcas why they had taken no prisoners, the Tenochcas pointed out that 30 of the prisoners had had an ear cut off and that they possessed the missing ears. The prestige so acquired led the Tenochcas to ask for Coxcox's daughter in marriage to their chief. Their wish granted, the overjoyed Tenochcas sacrificed the girl to their gods. The ceremony, to which they invited the girl's father, involved a priest wearing the girl's skin in impersonation of a nature goddess. Needless to say, Coxcox was horrified and with his warriors drove out the Tenochcas, who fled to an island in the middle of Lake Texcoco which was already a refuge for dissidents from the mainland. As a result of these events, which took place sometime between 1299 and 1323 (Bernal 1963:89), the city of Chapultepec was abandoned and a new site, Tenochtitlan, was founded on the island in the lake (Fig. 21-3). After the establishment of Tenochtitlan the Aztec petitioned the Culhuas for a chief, a wish which was granted. ▲ They then allied themselves with the Tepanecs against the Culhuas, whom they destroyed in 1367. In 1428 the Aztec turned on the Tepanecs and with the assistance of Texcoco and the Tacuba destroyed forever the power of the Tepanecs of Azcapotzalco. In 1434 the Aztec-Texcoco-Tacuba alliance was formed, uniting the most powerful cities into the political unit which we know as the Aztec Empire. However, this empire was never as well integrated or as dominant as the Inca Empire in Peru. For example, the Aztec were unable to subjugate some of their close enemies, among whom were the Tarascans 40 miles to the west of Tenochtitlan and also the Tlascallans in Puebla state.

Aztec Life

The Aztec, in a series of political maneuvers, assumed the role of legal descendants of the Culhuas, the valley group who claimed to be the direct descendants of the Toltecs of Tula. By

■ Chinampas—the secret of the Aztec farming economy

● Trade

▲ Social classes

■ Aztec gods were bloodthirsty.

these political acts the Aztec purported to continue the Toltec traditions, and many Aztec cultural traits can in fact be traced to Toltec origins. (The architecture, for example, especially at Tenayuca shows strong Toltec affinities.)

■ The Aztec economy featured an extremely productive farming system utilizing rafts (chinampas) which were built in the lake and then covered with earth and muck from the lake bottom. Through time the chinampas gradually became permanently fixed to the lake floor. Other major aspects of the Aztec economy relate to the strategic location of Tenochtitlan. Situated in the center of the lake and ringed with cities on the mainland, the city formed a natural trade center. Transport was by canoe as well as by means of five causeways which connected Tenochtitlan to the mainland. ● Trade extended widely beyond the city to the farthest extent of the empire. A special group of merchants, the

pochteca, traveled as far as Panama and the American Southwest on trading missions. Due to their opportunities to observe and trade with distant tribes, the pochteca also served as messengers and spies. Within the city major crafts included jewelry making, pottery manufacture, the working of feathers into garments, and metalworking. These goods had their primary market among the aristocracy.

Aztec social organization was based upon a system of clans called *calpulli*. The common people belonged to the calpulli, and each group had lands specifically farmed by its own members. Each of the 20 clans also had its own temple and market. (An intriguing thought is the possibility that this system was a legacy from the ancient civilization at Teotihuacan.) ▲ Social classes included slaves, who were primarily prisoners of war and comprised the lowest class; next, the common people; and finally the professionals (the warriors, bureaucrats, artisans, merchants, and priests). Service to the state was rewarded with special status, and even merchants were so dignified. Most notable were the warrior orders, the eagle and jaguar knights (Fig. 21-4). Rule was by an emperor selected from a royal lineage by a council of high officials. The emperor was considered semidivine and was ac-

Fig. 21-3 Reconstruction of the main square of Tenochtitlan. In the rear center are the twin temples dedicated to the bloodthirsty god Huitzilopotchtli. (Hester photograph, courtesy of Mexican National Museum of Anthropology.)

Fig. 21-4 An Eagle knight, member of an Aztec military society. (Hester photograph, courtesy of Mexican National Museum of Anthropology.)

corded considerable autonomy. All of the officials had large private land holdings from which they received income, and tribute was exacted from subject tribes. Warfare provided the most common method of achieving status. Our knowledge of Aztec life and customs is based on records dating to soon after the Spanish Conquest and hence is *historical* rather than *archaeological*. The most important reference is the Florentine codex, which provides numerous illustrations of the various aspects of Aztec culture (Dibble and Anderson 1957).

Aztec Religion

The integrative mechanism within Aztec society—the beliefs and justification for the major areas of activity—was derived from the religion. ■ The Aztec not only emphasized the typical Postclassic focus on violence and death but in-

tensified this aspect into an obsession with fulfilling the dictates of bloodthirsty gods. The primary deities were Huitzilopotchtli, Quetzalcoatl, and Tezcatlipoca, but the Aztec pantheon provided a wealth of deities hardly equaled by any other society known to history. According to Vaillant (1944), there were "3 great gods, 4 creative deities, 15 fertility gods, 6 rain gods, 3 fire gods, 4 pulque gods, 12 planetary and stellar gods, 6 earth gods, 6 variants of the great gods, and 4 others (Fig. 21-5). There were also gods of death, the day hours, night hours, days and weeks."

The religion was based upon the concept that Huitzilopotchtli, the sun or giver of life, must be nourished by human blood. Sacrifice was carried out by black-garbed priests who practiced penance by slashing their own ears with obsidian knives to provide blood. Human sacrifices were carried out in the front of the temples on the tops of the pyramids. Stone boxes containing fire received the hearts of the sacrificial victims, whose bodies were then thrown down the steps of the pyramids. The total number of sacrifices eventually required is staggering. In one three-day ceremony late in the Aztec reign, 40,000 individuals were sacrificed and their skulls displayed on the skull rack or Tzompantli. Recent research suggests that the sacrifices were not only ceremonial but also provided protein, as the bodies of the victims were eaten. Another method of sacrifice consisted of a gladiatorial contest between a captured warrior armed with a dummy weapon of feathers (instead of obsidian blades) and an Aztec knight armed with real weaponry. This encounter took place upon the circular stone of Tizoc to which the captive was tied. There was apparently a sharing of beliefs among neighboring tribes, since captives believed that such a death was glorious and that the sacrificed would be united with the god Huitzilopotchtli. Other major religious features were the ceremonial rebuilding of the pyramids and the destruction of all household items at the end of each 52-year cycle.

● The Aztec capital lies beneath modern Mexico City.

▲ Outnumbered, the Spanish were better organized than the Aztec.

■ Toltec influence at Chichén Itzá

Fig. 21-5 The recently discovered Aztec sculpture of the moon goddess found at the site of the Templo Major in Mexico City. (*a*) The entire monument, as discovered; (*b*) detail of the face of the goddess. (Horace E. Day photographs.)

Aztec Archaeology

Contrary to what might be expected, we do not have a wealth of archaeological materials available from the Aztecs. ● This is due primarily to the systematic destruction of Tenochtitlan by Cortez, who then rebuilt his capital on the ruins of the city. Subsequent excavations for building foundations and the recent subway system have revealed fragmentary evidence of the ancient Aztec splendor (Fig. 21-5). Some of the best-preserved Aztec remains lie outside the former capital city at Tenayuca, and at Malinalco, where a temple was cut into the living rock. Also notable are the canals for gardens and baths cut into bedrock near Texcoco by its famous ruler Nezahualcoyotl.

Aztec pottery consisted of a series of black-on-orange types derived from the Mazapan wares of the late Teotihuacan-Toltec era. Aztec stone carving is spectacular in its conception. Known sculptures emphasize representational, three-dimensional depictions of the various deities, boxes for sacrificed hearts, the famous calendar stone (which details the Aztec concept of the cosmos), the sacrificial altars, and so on. Perhaps most impressive is the moon goddess (Fig. 21-5).

The Spanish Conquest

Cortez landed on the coast of Vera Cruz in 1519, having been since an early age one of the band of disinherited, gold-hungry, religiously inspired adventurers known to history as *conquistadores.*

Rapacious, without fear, and believing that their mission to conquer and convert the Indians was divinely sanctioned, such men were destined to achieve military miracles in the New World.

The Spanish arrived at a time most propitious for attack. The neighboring tribes, long oppressed by the Aztec with their demands for tribute and sacrificial victims, were ready for revolt. Furthermore, the Aztec leader Montezuma was seeking guidance from his soothsayers. Numerous ill omens had been noted: a column of fire seen at midnight, the destruction of a temple by lightning without thunder, sudden waves on the lake, among others. Most impressive was a bird, caught by hunters, with a mirror on its head in which Montezuma perceived an army of armed men mounted on the backs of deer.

In addition to opportune timing, the Spanish had on their side the advantages of military aims and techniques. The Aztec fought for ceremonial reasons and with the primary goal of taking prisoners for sacrifice. ▲ The Spanish forces were disciplined and, moving from point to point upon orders, they achieved superiority of arms wherever they went. Although the Spanish forces were pitifully small, Cortez achieved a psychological advantage by burning his ships so that his men had no choice but to advance. He further met an Indian woman named Malinche on the coast, who became his mistress and interpreter and through whom he learned of the desires for revolt. Cortez marched inland, joined by allies from Cempoala, the Totonac capital, and by the Tlaxcalans. Vacillating and indecisive, Montezuma permitted the Spanish to enter Tenochtitlan, where they were quartered in part of the royal palace. The Spanish reciprocated by kidnapping the Aztec emperor, who was soon afterward killed either by the Spanish or by his own people (the record is unclear). In the subsequent great Aztec uprising, known as the Noche Triste, the Spanish were driven from the city, with severe fighting occurring at breaks in the causeways made by the Aztec. More than two-thirds of the Spanish were killed. Retreating to Tlaxcala, they rested and were reinforced with new troops from Cuba. Over a period of seven months they built an armada of 13 small boats and the following year returned to Tenochtitlan with 50,000 Tlaxcalan allies. In a great battle fought on the lake the Aztec in canoes were no match for the Spanish. Their valiant leader, Cuahtemoc, was captured, and on August 13, 1521 the Aztec surrendered.

The Maya Postclassic

The Postclassic period in the Mayan world can be divided into an early phase characterized by strong Mexican influence and a late phase without Mexican influence.

The Mexican period at Chichén Itzá dates from A.D. 987 to 1187. In the traditional histories of the Maya, the so-called Books of Chilam Balam, preserved since the Spanish Conquest, there are references to the arrival in Yucatan of a man named Kukulcan ("Feathered Serpent") in about the year A.D. 987. There is some confusion about the date, owing to use of the Mayan Short Count at this time. Since each Short Count cycle always ended on the same day events on specific dates in the Short Count system could refer to more than one possible true date, separated by 256¼ years. If we accept the A.D. 987 dating of Kukulcan's arrival, then his party could have been the displaced group of Toltecs led by Topiltzin. The major events are recorded in wall murals in the Temple of the Warriors (Fig. 21-6). The Toltec arrived by sea, and in the first mural they are shown offshore in boats scouting a Mayan seaside village. A second mural illustrates a battle on the water, with the losing Maya on rafts and the Toltec in canoes. The next mural shows the battle on land, where fighting takes place in the houses and temples. There the Maya are defeated again, and their leaders are sacrificed. The Toltec then imposed leadership on northern Yucatan. ■ Their capital city was established at Chichén Itzá, where the new architectural style represented a combination of the old northern Mayan Puuc style and the Toltec elements. Columns became important, being used inside rooms to provide greater interior space. Colonnades nearly identical to those at Tula (Fig. 21-7) were added. Further additions included the decorative friezes of repeated skulls, serpents, and such.

Specific major structures of the Mexican period are the giant pyramid dedicated to Kukulcan, the "Castillo" (Fig. 21-7), and the Temple of the Warriors, a structure similar to the Pyramid B complex at Tula but even larger. Inside the Temple of the Warriors is another smaller temple, the Temple of the Chacmool. A most interesting feature of the latter structure is that within it is an altar in Toltec style set upon Atlantean figures. Curiously, these figures were set

several inches into the floor as though they had been too tall for use in the smaller interior temple. This fact has led to speculation that possibly the altar with its Atlantean figures had actually been transported from Tula by the Toltec to be reinstalled at Chichén Itzá. Proof that such in fact happened could rest on mineralogical identification of the stone utilized. Other major buildings of the period include the beautiful ball court, the largest in Mesoamerica, flanked by temples within which are murals and bas-reliefs depicting Toltec life and scenes of battle.

A further Toltec contribution to Mayan life was the intensification of human sacrifice and the introduction of the Tzompantli, or skull platform, which supported racks upon which the heads of the sacrificed were placed. The platform itself is decorated with a frieze of skulls im-

Fig. 21-6 Battle scene from the wall mural in the Temple of the Warriors, Chichén Itzá, Yucatan. This is likely an actual historical record of the conquest of the Maya by Topiltzin and his followers from Tula. (Morley and Brainerd 1956:Plate 25.)

a

b

Fig. 21-7 Architectural splendor of the Mexican period at Chichén Itzá. (*a*) Chac mool and rattlesnake column at the entrance to the Temple of the Warriors; (*b*) wall ornament on the Temple of the Warriors, consisting of a mask of Chac, the rain god, within a snake's mouth; (*c*) view of the Temple of the Warriors from the Castillo; (*d*) view of the Castillo from the Temple of the Warriors. (Hester photographs.)

c

d

● The Maya civilization disappears.

▲ The appearance of political expansion

paled on stakes. Human sacrifice was also accomplished by the throwing of humans alive into the sacred cenote, which was a continuation of a pre-Toltec practice. According to Bishop Landa, one typical time for such sacrifices was during drought. The cenote has been dredged, and from study of the skeletons recovered we now know that most of the victims were adult males, although children and women were also sacrificed. A wealth of other sacrifices, including gold and jade ornaments, pottery, and copal incense, has been recovered from the cenote. One further indication of sacrifice consists of reliefs on the ball court depicting the decapitation of a ball player. (One can only assume that playing the ball game was a very serious matter indeed.)

Another diagnostic trait of the Mexican period is the presence of a specific type of glazed pottery termed Plumbate ware. Plumbate was unique in its non-central-Mexican point of origin. Manufactured in kilns near the Guatemala-Chiapas border, it was widely traded throughout the Yucatan peninsula and effectively serves as a chronological marker.

According to the chronicles, Chichén Itzá was abandoned on the Short Count date of Katun 6 ahau (correlated with A.D. 1224), and from that time the Toltec were no longer important in Mayan history.

The Late Postclassic at Chichén Itzá

Following the Mexican period in Yucatan we have the legendary migrations of the Itzá. In their wanderings the Itzá moved across Yucatan to Lake Peten Itzá, then eastward to Belize. They then turned north under the leadership of a man known as Kukulcan II. In Katun 4 ahau (A.D. 1224–1244) they reached Chichén Itzá, which they proceeded to occupy as squatters. They

founded the city of Mayapan in Katun 13 ahau (A.D. 1263–1283), which after A.D. 1283 became the capital of Yucatan. The city was an urban community consisting of numerous houses built on platform mounds within an enclosing city wall. Inside the wall were approximately 2,000 houses with 11,000 to 12,000 inhabitants. The city was without an internal plan.

The Late Postclassic in Yucatan is marked by strife between the ruling families. The last such revolt at Mayapan in Katun 9 ahau (A.D. 1441–1461) resulted in the destruction and abandonment of the city. The Itzá left Yucatan and wandered back to Lake Peten Itzá, where they established a new capital at Tayasal on an island in the lake. Here they remained, continuing the Mayan traditions in a limited way until they were conquered by the Spanish much later. The Postclassic in Yucatan had no such dramatic ending as the conquest of the Aztec. ● The Maya simply drifted farther and farther into the jungle to be lost to history, and they were much more difficult for the Spanish to ultimately subdue. In place of the Itzá dynasty in Yucatan there were left 16 rival city-states, all weak and faltering in their ability to continue basic Mayan traditions yet ready to war with one another. This situation existed until the Spanish Conquest, at which time we pick up the story of the Mayan culture from the writings of Bishop Landa and other historical sources. Even though the Classic Mayan culture, religion, and so forth had been greatly reduced, the people still had in their possession the ancient hieroglyphic codices. Thus the single most dramatic event of the Spanish-Mayan confrontation was the public burning of these documents. Owing to the Spanish zeal in eradicating these "works of the devil," only three have survived.

The South American Postclassic

Three of Lumbreras's periods fit within the Postclassic. These are the Huari (Wari) Empire period (A.D. 700–1100), the Regional State period

(A.D. 100–1400) and the Empire of Tawantin-suyu (A.D. 1430–1532), usually referred to as the Inca Empire.

The period A.D. 700–1100 marks a turning point in Andean archaeology. No longer were the regional cultures content to remain within their own valleys, developing their own styles in crafts, practicing their own religions, and largely ignoring the endeavors of the other regional cultures in the nearby valleys. In this period there developed an attempt at imperialism similar to that of the Mochica at an earlier date. Two cultural centers—Tiahuanaco, in the Southern Highlands at the southern end of Lake Titicaca, and Huari in the Central Highlands—extended their cultural influences outward by colonization and conquest. Bennett and Bird (1964) termed the period *expansionist*, which is certainly appropriate. With more complete archaeological knowledge it would be possible to identify in this period antecedents of the later Inca expansion. ▲ The period featured the manipulation of man-hour units and the political organization and subjugation of peoples.

It is important to distinguish between Tiahuanaco, as already described in Chapter 20, and the term "Tiahuanacoid." The latter term refers to the spread of material that is, to quote Lumbreras (1974:151), "'derived from,' 'similar to,' or 'Tiahuanaco-like.'" It is now felt that these various "Tiahuanacoid" manifestations in both the coastal zones and the highlands were due to the expansion of the Huari (Wari) Empire.

Huari

Huari archaeology is not very well known, due primarily to the late recognition of its importance as a cultural center. Much of the Huari sphere of influence was interpreted previously as Tiahuanacoid since Huari materials incorporate elements derived from the Tiahuanaco style. According to Willey (1971:160–161), we may infer from ceramics the following developments in the Huari region. Tiahuanaco influences first appear at Conchopata, a shrine near Huari. Votive urns at Conchopata feature depictions of the Gateway God plus additional elements which are locally distinctive. Willey suggests that missionaries from Tiahuanaco introduced these religious concepts into the Central Highlands. Lumbreras points out that while the Conchopata material reflects Tiahuanaco motifs, it is obviously of local manufacture. The Tiahuanaco style at Huari gives rise to a ceramic style known as Robles Moqo. Conchopata and Robles Moqo are diagnostic of the Huari I period. Huari II is another ceramically based period, and here we have the appearance of the so-called coastal Tiahuanaco variants, Vinaque, Atcaro, and Pachacamac. In any event, these became the styles associated with the local rulers. Vinaque pottery, which features the derived Tiahuanaco-style deities and animals, is most common in spouted bottles, keros, beakers, face-neck jars, and anthropomorphic jars. Most evidences of Huari influence are indicated in ceramics by a fusion of Huari elements with those (Nazca, Pachacamac, Mochica, and so forth) of the prior local style. At the end of the Vinaque period the city of Huari was abandoned, possibly as a result of attack, and the Huari influence was then superseded by a reassertion of local regional cultures.

Viewed primarily from the perspective of ceramic analyses, the Tiahuanaco-Huari influences can be described as, first, the introduction of new ideas with little change in the prior cultural patterns. A second phase embodied dramatic change in both old and new ideas, with subsequent fusion of the two. Finally, there was the development of new styles out of the fused elements, followed by some reassertion of the old local styles. We may infer that major social changes accompanied the pottery changes. These changes are most evident on the North Coast where Mochica settlements and religious centers were abandoned and new cities built inside poured-adobe, rectangular-walled compounds. The building of walled urban communities is a practice which came to dominate the succeeding phase, the Regional State period.

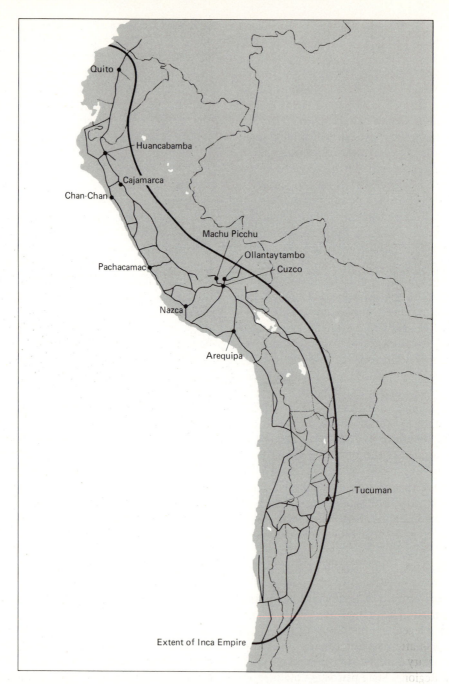

Map 21-2 Postclassic sites in South America.

> ■ The Chimu—an empire on the North Coast of Peru
>
> ● Chan Chan—a great urban center

At the site of Huari are complexes of buildings whose basic plan consisted of thick-walled, rectangular enclosures containing streets, plazas, and platforms, all of which in turn were entirely surrounded by thicker and higher walls (Lumbreras 1974:161). This configuration seems to foreshadow the developments of major centers such as Chan Chan in the succeeding Regional State period. If Huari was a state based on hierarchical structure, as Isbell and Schreiber (1978:372–389) argue, then it is fair to ask questions about lines of communication. Lumbreras (1974:162) places the origins of the great aboriginal road system in the Huari period. Admittedly, this system was added to and expanded by later empires and kings.

The Regional State Period

■ After A.D. 1000 the major developments in Andean prehistory shifted back to the North Coast, the location of the great Chimu kingdom. At its greatest expansion the latter extended 600 miles from north to south. Other kingdoms of this period are less well known: the Cuismanu of the Central Coast, the Chuquismancu located farther south, and the Chincha of the South Coast. In the highlands we have the earliest evidence of the Inca as a regional culture at Cuzco. In the Southern Highlands there is a continuation of a local culture at Tiahuanaco. It is from this time period that we have our earliest historical records—legends transcribed from the Inca by the Spanish after the Conquest.

Termed "City Builder" by Bennett and Bird (1964), the Regional State period is noted for the rise of local city-states in all of the Andean subregions. Major features expressed in all these cultures are: planned urban communities, population increase, strong political organization, mass production of crafts with attendant decrease in artistic skills, and a concern for the manipulation of large amounts of labor through the authority vested in the government. Our review of this period will consider only the Chimu kingdom as an example.

CHAN CHAN AND THE CHIMU KINGDOM

● The Chimu capital at Chan Chan, located in the arid Moche Valley only a kilometer from the sea, is the largest and most impressive city of the period (Fig. 21-8). Chan Chan is made up of nine residential units or compounds. These quadrangles are enclosed by walls which extend to a height of 9 or more meters. Within the very thick compound walls, which are a combination of poured adobe and adobe brick (Fig. 21-9), are residential areas, the largest of which is 375 by 480 meters. The enclosed structures include gabled houses, sunken gardens, stone-lined water reservoirs, courtyards, small rooms, streets, pyramids, stairways, terraces, and tombs. Interspersed among the nine quadrangles lay irrigated fields, cemeteries, small buildings, and reed marshes. The size and decoration of the dwelling units plus grave contents indicate that the Chimu were powerful and wealthy. A major function of the quadrangles was to provide housing for the ruling class, with possible use also as mortuary complexes for dead Chimu kings (Moseley and Mackey 1973:318–345).

Despite the size of the city, in which monumental architecture extends over more than 20 square kilometers, the population may not have been excessively large, perhaps in the range of 25,000 to 30,000 (Moseley 1975:219–225). In other words, the city is of the type Schaedel (1951) terms *Urban Elite Center*, which included the functions of political administrative center, religious center, and urban-life center. Some other sites, which lacked the elaborate courtyards and fine residences, provided the more ordinary housing of the common people.

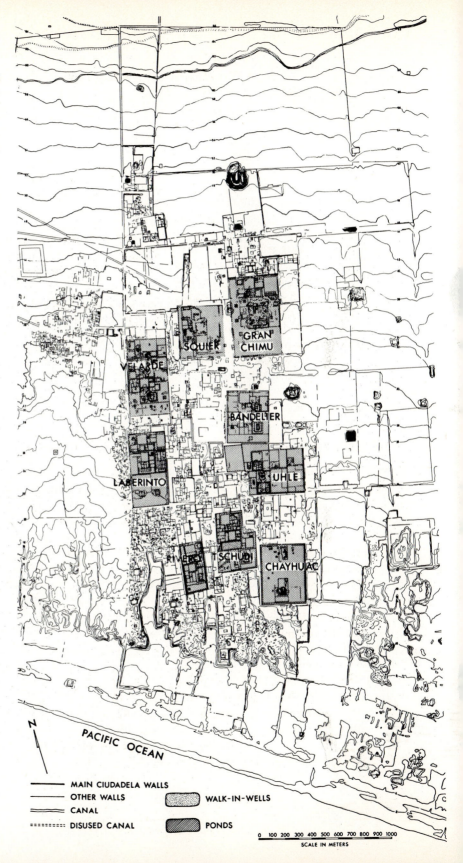

Fig. 21-8 Plan of the great Chimu capital at Chan Chan on the north coast of Peru. There are nine massive adobe-walled compounds, within which are located residences, tombs, cemetaries, gardens, and water reservoirs. (Moseley 1975:Fig. 1.)

SQUIER

GRAN CHIMU

VELARDE

BANDELIER

LABERINTO

UHLE

RIVERO TSCHUDI

CHAYHUAC

N

PACIFIC OCEAN

— MAIN CIUDADELA WALLS
— OTHER WALLS
CANAL
DISUSED CANAL

WALK-IN-WELLS

PONDS

0 100 200 300 400 500 600 700 800 900 1000
SCALE IN METERS

Fig. 21-9 Compound wall at Chan Chan. (Hester photograph.)

It is assumed that these *Urban Lay Centers* were tributary to and under the political authority of the Urban Elite Centers, of which Chan Chan was the largest and finest.

Major features typical of Chan Chan are the arabesque murals carved in the adobe walls (Fig. 21-10). The decorations are geometric in concept, even though they include repeated figures of men, deities, and animals. It has also been suggested that the quadrangles had further social connotations; that is, that they functioned as barrios, semiautonomous units based on kinship or craft specialization. The parallels with the residential areas at Teotihuacan suggest that a similar urban pattern was in effect. From this

Fig. 21-10 Wall sculpture at Chan Chan. (Hester photograph.)

▲ The Inca consolidated all of the Andean region into a single empire.

■ The Inca Horizon style

period we have evidence of a highway system which may have actually been initiated during the period of the Huari Empire. This system, which was augmented and maintained by the Chimu, finally became part of the later and much more famous Incan road network.

Chimu pottery is a mold-made blackware which, in the forms and style of the vessels, represents a continuation of the earlier Mochica-modeled tradition. Chimu ceramics on the other hand, due to their emphasis on mass production, represent a major reduction in ceramic skills. The focus is on quantity rather than quality. The forms—the stirrup-spout vessels, figure-bridge-spout types, and the modeled houses, humans, animals, and so on—are continuations of earlier North Coast pottery themes. Chimu art is well known, owing to the excellent preservation within the burials. There are patterned textiles, painted textiles, wood carvings and metalwork. The latter features silver and gold used for ornaments and domestic service; in addition, quantities of the new alloy, bronze, came into widespread use at this time for weapons and utilitarian implements.

One outstanding feature of the Central Coast is the famous fortress of Paramonga. Although militarism was not as important here as in the Mesoamerican Postclassic, it was nonetheless present. The later Inca were not responsible for the introduction of militarism into the Andean region, but simply perfected an existing militaristic tradition. Other cultures of the Regional State period are less well known. These cultures—the Chincha, Ica, Rimac, and many other valley peoples—were subjugated by the Inca in their imperial expansion.

Tawantinsuyu: The Inca Empire, A.D. 1430–1523

The political organization the Spaniards destroyed in Peru in 1532 was called Tawantinsuyu, its capital was Cuzco, and its ruler was called "Inca" (Lumbreras 1974:217). It is by this latter name that the culture of Tawantinsuyu is better known.

The geographic extent of the Inca Empire is known, but its population has been variously estimated at from 1.5 million to 6 million. A major unknown factor is the population reduction caused by the Spanish Conquest, which could have reached 90 percent of the Preconquest population. The census of 1571 reported 1.5 million, but the population may have exceeded 3.5 million during the height of the empire. Between 1250 and 1532, 12 Inca rulers are known, but the first 8 were legendary. (The latter probably refer to a local Cuzco ruling clan.) Known reigns begin in 1438 with the ninth Inca; therefore the empire lasted only 94 years. ▲ The conquest of Andean tribes and the establishment of the empire occurred primarily after 1470. Expansion was brought about through the desire for economic gain and in order to strengthen the ruling class. Victory was due to superior organization and numerical superiority on the battlefield. After the capture of a particular region a census would be taken and a relief map modeled in clay. Villages were often moved *en masse* as a means of reducing the possibility of revolt. Sometimes new Inca rulers were installed, but often local rulers were retained, their sons being taken as hostages to Cuzco. Then the new areas were connected by roads to the existing empire.

During the Inca period there was little change in the prior agricultural economy. The first ground was broken for planting when the priests felt it was propitious. Personal service was taxed, with the people farming the lands of the church and state. Taxes were in terms of manpower labor units, and the labor system was

a pyramid with the ruling family at the top. Inca foods are the same as those of the local Indians today: corn and potato soup, corn bread, corn beer, and dried llama meat. The food surplus of each district was stored in state granaries and used to support the aristocracy, priests, the army, and all public laborers.

The society featured two basic castes: (1) the Inca, the original conquerors and rulers of conquered territory and (2) the commoners. Privileges were very important, and the upper class controlled all high posts, performed no labor and received all of the education.

Inca Archaeology

Inca materials mark the end of all archaeological sequences. Inca is the third Horizon style to cover the entire Peru-Bolivia region. Most areas have both purely Inca-style artifacts and Inca-influenced local materials. The Cuzco area was the main center of the culture, a fact confirmed archaeologically as well as historically. Ceramics are the best Inca diagnostic trait, but textiles, metalwork, and architecture were also well made. Textiles and ceramics seem to be the result of mass production. The building style suggests an emphasis on organized unit labor (Fig. 21-11).

Little is known of the origin of the Incan art style because excavations have not revealed much material ancestral to Inca. According to tradition, the Inca occupied the Cuzco region for at least three centuries. The period from 1200 to 1438 is termed *Early Inca*. Burials of this period were flexed and cloth-wrapped, and they were placed in beehive-shaped masonry tombs with corbeled vaults. Few Early Inca objects of metal have survived, but bone is common, as are slate knives. The ceramics have carelessly painted linear and geometric designs in black, white, and red.

The *Late Inca* archaeological period covers the era of political expansion. Most artifacts and ruins pertain to this period; thus it is the best known. ■ The art style features repeated geometric elements. In pottery distinctive vessel forms include shallow dishes with lugs, tall flower-pot-shaped vases with an everted rim, and the most distinctive form, the aryballoid jar. The latter was a large, round-bodied form with a long, narrow neck, an everted rim, and two handles on the body to support a carrying strap.

The Inca Achievement

The 90+ years of the Inca Empire formed the most significant period in the history of Andean culture. During this era the entire Andean culture was given a new orientation, which has continued to the present. Thus modern Peruvian Indian history and culture begin with Pachacuti, the founder of the Inca Empire, rather than with the Spanish Conquest. At the time of the Inca conquest the area was populated by a large number of small tribal groups who shared many elements of culture but who also differed from one another in numerous ways. The Inca eliminated most of the differences by unifying the language, life-style, and institutions of a vast region. (For example, today five-sixths of all Indians speak Quechua, the Incan language). The continuity of Incan administrative structure was more an inevitable result than an intentional policy on the part of the Spanish. Thus there is today a feeling of solidarity among the Andean Indians, who share a belief in a common cultural heritage — a true Inca legacy.

The Spanish Conquest

The end of the Inca Empire was presaged by a period of civil war. The Inca (ruler), Huayna Capac, who came to power in about 1493, continued his father's work of organizing and consolidating the empire. He conquered lands to the north and extended the empire to the northern border of what today is Ecuador. Huayna Capac

Fig. 21-11 Inca architectural and masonry styles. *a.* Panoramic view of Machu Picchu. (Hester photograph.) *b.* Agricultural terraces at Machu Picchu. (Hester photograph.) *c.* Monolithic masonry at the Inca fortress of Sacsahuaman, showing a stone with 10 angles. Note the close fit of the joints. (Photograph courtesy of Ken Kirkwood.)

died in 1527 without naming a successor, and his death was followed by five years of civil war. In that same year, 1527, Pizarro's first expedition reached Tumbez, the northernmost Incan settlement on the coast.

The story of Pizarro's conquest has strong parallels with that of Cortez in Mexico, and it is clear that the methods that had worked in Mexico were also employed in Peru. However, Pizarro's first expedition was marked with perhaps even greater heroism than any achieved in Mex-

ico. The expedition was formed in Panama and sailed down the coast. It touched at Tumbez, and for the first time the Spanish learned what they had previously only dared hope — that the Inca were fabulously wealthy in gold and silver. The expedition proceeded to spend the winter on a small dry island off the coast. After a brief time its members sought to convince Pizarro that they should return to Panama. Pizarro drew a line in the sand and enjoined all who would follow him in conquering Peru to step across it.

Twelve men did, and the rest sailed away to Panama. Pizarro's group nearly starved during the winter, living mostly on crabs. However, their determination encouraged the partners of Pizarro in Panama to fund another expedition the following spring.

In the meantime, since Huayna Capac had died without a successor, the Inca Empire plunged into civil war. Huascar, Huayna's eldest son, was the obvious choice, and the high priest at Cuzco crowned him as the Inca since the rule of descent was that the emperor choose as his successor his most competent son by his principal wife. Atahualpa, another son of Huayna, assumed governance in the north at Quito. Feeling that he should have been named Inca, Atahualpa initiated a revolt against Huascar. The ensuing war ended in a battle near Cuzco with the victory of Atahualpa's forces and the capture of Huascar, who soon afterward was put to death by drowning. The news of the victory reached Atahualpa in Cajamarca at about the same time as Pizarro arrived there.

The Spanish followed a plan similar to that previously utilized by Cortez. Initially accepting the hospitality of the Inca, they then captured him and held him for a ransom set at a roomful of gold and silver. A trial was held, and Atahualpa was convicted of crimes of idolatry. He was given the choice of accepting Christianity and being mercifully executed by garroting or of being burned at the stake. Atahualpa chose the former. Owing to the recent civil war there was still no clear heir to the throne, and the Inca Empire was thus left without legal leadership. All power resided in the Inca, and since that position was vacant the Spanish quickly and easily seized the entire empire.

22

Other New World Cultures

■ After 3000 B.C. the New World features regionally adapted cultures.

The record of human occupation of the New World after 3000 B.C. shows increasing specialization, region by region, based on more intensive utilization of local resources. Such specialization, with increasing adaptation to local environments, resulted in the divergence of local cultures from one another. ■ For data after 3000 B.C. it is no longer possible to categorize continentwide stages. We must instead rely on the concept of *culture area*, the tendency within each major geographic region for cultures to be more alike and somewhat distinct from cultures of surrounding regions.

Major regional specializations identified by 3000 B.C. in North America include Arctic Littoral Hunters, Subarctic Littoral Hunters, Northwest Coast Littoral Hunters, Fishers and Gatherers, Plateau Fishermen-Gatherers, Desert Gatherers, Plains Hunter-Gatherers, Plains Village Farmers, Southwestern Farmers, Eastern Farmers and Hunter-Gatherers, Montane Hunter-Gatherers, Incipient Cultivators (in Mexico), and Littoral Collectors (Fig. 18-2). South American data are less well known, but identified economic strategies specific to regions at 3000 B.C. include Littoral Collectors, Riparian Hunter-Gatherers, Montane Hunter-Gatherers, Savanna Hunter-Gatherers, and Plains Hunters (Fig. 18-2); (Meggers and Evans 1979).

By 1000 B.C. the situation had changed to include new centers of incipient cultivation in the North American Southwest and the Mississippi River Valley. Farming was by this time widespread in Mesoamerica. In South America there had developed a farming tradition in the Andean region as well as a distinct tropical-farming pattern (Fig. 22-1). Major changes after A.D. 300 include expansion of the areas farmed in both

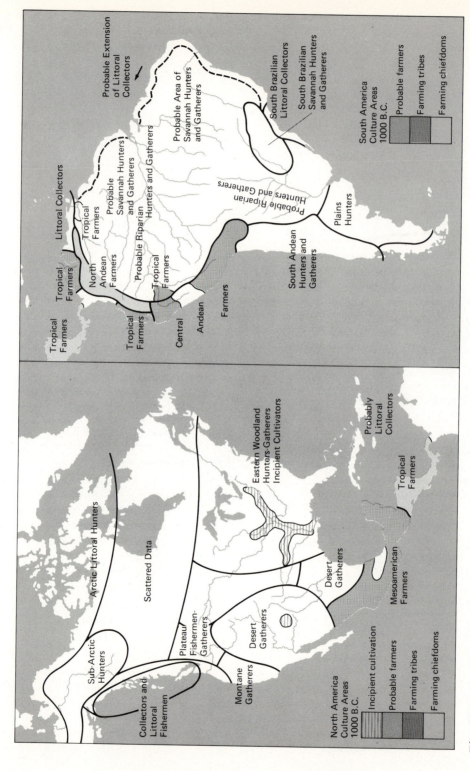

Fig. 22-1 New World culture areas: North and South America at 1000 B.C. (Modified from Sanders and Marino 1970:Fig. 4.)

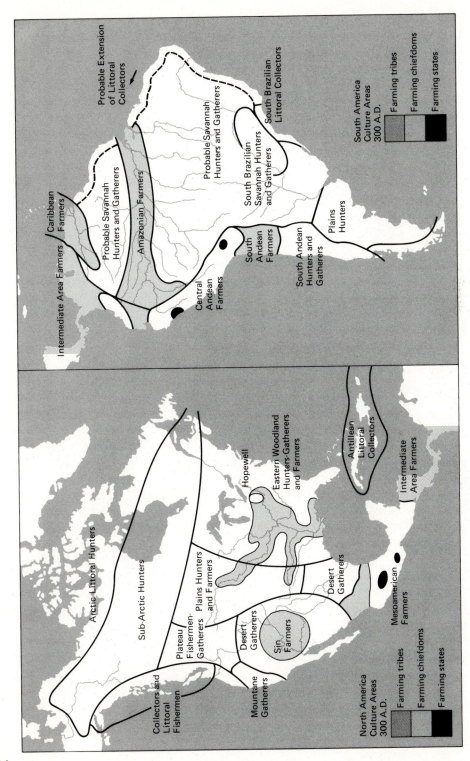

Fig. 22-2 New World culture areas: North and South America at A.D. 300. (Modified from Sanders and Marino 1970:Fig. 5.)

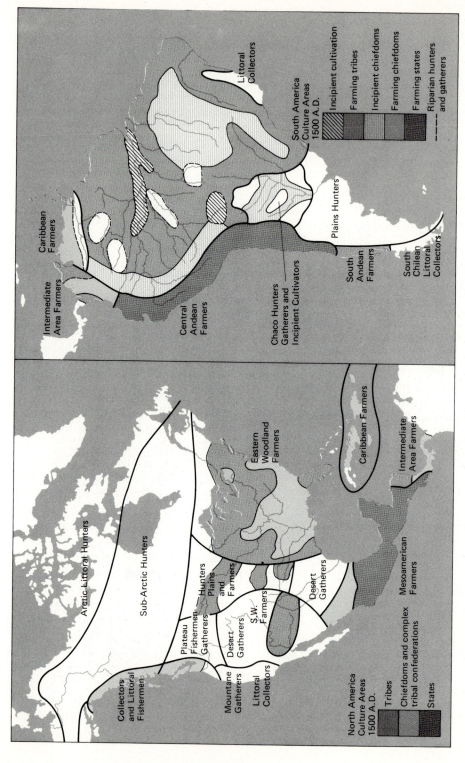

Fig. 22-3 New World culture areas: North and South America at A.D. 1500. (Modified from Sanders and Marino 1970:Fig. 6.)

● The Eskimo Tradition

▲ Athabaskans inhabited the Canadian interior.

■ A varied economy supported a high level of culture on the Northwest Coast.

North and South America and widespread settlement of the Caribbean Islands by Littoral Collectors (Fig. 22-2).

By A.D. 1500 the areas farmed had expanded to the limits of the environments suitable for cultivation. This expansion progressed through time as the former hunters and gatherers adopted farming. By A.D. 1500 (Fig. 22-3) we can view the New World hunters and gatherers as those peoples occupying areas unsuitable for farming. Most of these hunting-gathering peoples remained at a stage of cultural complexity similar to that of the pre-3000 B.C. Archaic Stage. Exceptions to this trend include the Northwest Coast of North America, where the intense productivity of the open sea, littoral, and coast forest provided a food surplus and thus fostered the development of a complex culture (Hester and Nelson 1978). The Great Plains of North America, with its enormous carrying capacity of buffalo, permitted a similar food surplus (Wedel 1979). That culture, exploiting the great herds, is an example of a cultural stage termed Climax Hunting (Hester 1962). In both of these examples the food-getting mechanisms were highly efficient, rivaling the productivity of farming as an economy. While admittedly brief, this summary provides a unifying conceptual framework for all New World prehistorical data. We will now proceed to a brief description of these economic adaptations. Those adaptations which have been discussed in earlier chapters will not be repeated here. The latter include Desert Gatherers, Incipient Cultivators, Mesoamerican Farmers, Eastern Forest Hunter-Gatherers, and Andean Farmers.

North America

Arctic Littoral Hunters

Early in Arctic prehistory we have a somewhat poorly known manifestation represented by a Mesolithic-type industry utilizing microblades. Although our evidence concerning the economic adaptation of these peoples is scanty, what is available suggests that they were inland hunters of caribou and, farther south, of deer.

● After about 3000 B.C. we have the initiation of the Eskimo Tradition with its specialization for life on the Arctic littoral. Eskimo resource utilization included the hunting of sea mammals from boats and through holes in the ice. The species hunted were primarily the walrus and seal. Other reliance was on whaling, fishing, and the trapping of small mammals, hunting of birds, and gathering of sea-bird eggs. Food resources were adequate to support a sparse population, but the adaptation for survival required an intense knowledge of game habits, the weather, and ice conditions. Also necessary were efficient game-taking devices, the most important of which was the socketed, detachable, toggling-harpoon head attached to a line with floats. The use of this composite weapon provided both the killing and retention capability necessary to hunt and retrieve sea mammals. The intense winter cold required warm permanent houses of sod, stone, bone, and driftwood construction heated by seal-oil lamps. Other adaptations to cold included use of tailored fur clothing and the consumption of large amounts of animal fat. Survival was further achieved through the use of dogsleds in winter, with overnight stops in easily built snow igloos. Winter villages were permanent and were located on the coast. The summer dwellings were portable skin tents, permitting movement into the interior for hunting at the time of the annual caribou migration. Social organization was clearly limited by the nonavailability of a food surplus. Bands

were small and were governed by a headman. The possibility of winter isolation and starvation led to practices of abandonment of the aged and, rarely, to cannibalism.

Subarctic Littoral Hunters

South of the Tundra the interior of Canada features boreal forest. Poor in natural resources, this area has seemingly always featured a sparse population. The major food resource was the caribou, whose annual pattern of migration made kills at certain spots at certain times of the year likely. Major hunting techniques included use of the bow and arrow combined with stalking. Other food-getting procedures relied on traps or snares. Archaeological evidence is scanty and is comprised of small collections of implements from widely scattered sites. ▲ Ethnographic information indicates that these peoples, the Athabaskans, as well as the Cree, Montagnais, and Naskapi, adapted to the cold winters through the use of log houses, snowshoes, and dog toboggans. Summer living featured the use of bark houses, bark canoes, and a migratory life combining hunting with the gathering of berries and other plant foods.

Northwest Coast Littoral Hunters, Fishers, and Gatherers

The Northwest Coast environment is characterized by heavy coastal rain forest and an extensive highly involuted coastline. Food resources available to the prehistoric inhabitants were many and were easily obtained. Beginning as early as 2500 B.C. and continuing to the nineteenth century A.D., the economy was one of mixed reliance on fishing at the mouths of salmon streams during the annual spawning season; shellfish gathering; the inland hunting of deer, caribou, moose, and mountain goat; bottom fishing for cod and halibut in the shallow bays;

and the offshore harpooning from boats of sea lions, seals, porpoises, and larger whales. Subsistence was varied, emphasizing seasonal harvests some of which required seasonal transhumance. Examples include seaweed gathering, fur-seal hunting, and fishing at the mouths of the salmon streams.

Houses were large, rectangular dwellings built of posts and split planks obtained from the local straight-grained red cedar. Extended families lived within these 30-by-60-feet structures. When the village moved, the planks of the houses were sometimes taken along. During the winter season — a period of almost incessant cold rain — life focused on wood carving and an elaborate ceremonial calendar. Such noneconomic activities could be afforded due to the wealth of stored food. Salmon and clams were smoked, and strips of halibut were dried. Herring eggs and fish oil were stored in wooden boxes for later consumption. ■ The wealth of food available on the Northwest Coast permitted the growth of one of the most highly developed nonagricultural cultures anywhere in the world. The technology associated with food getting included dugout canoes, fish weirs, fish lines with composite hooks, harpoons, fixed-barbed-point spears, dip nets, and rakes used for pulling surface-schooling fish into canoes.

The Littoral Collectors of California were more limited in their resources than the peoples who lived farther north. Major resources included deep-sea fish, sea birds, and shellfish, especially abalone and crabs (Elsasser 1978).

Inland, the California Montane food collectors specialized in the gathering of acorns and pine nuts. The abundance of wild-grass seeds and nuts was such that a high population density was possible, and bands lived in permanent villages. Collecting expeditions went out from the villages to harvest the local wild plants. Even though the carrying capacity of the land was high in terms of nonagricultural productivity, band size was nevertheless limited to a few

● In the Interior Plateau hunter-gatherers adapted to a riverine life-style.

▲ The Plains Hunter-Gatherers hunted buffalo.

■ Village farmers settled the Plains river valleys.

● Corn, beans, and squash supported the Southwestern Farmers.

▲ Irrigation was practiced in southern Arizona.

■ In the Eastern Woodlands hunting and gathering was replaced by agriculture.

hundred persons. Social organization included fraternities; however, California bands did not have as complex a social organization as those of the Northwest Coast. Through time California cultures continued an Archaic stage subsistence pattern.

Plateau Fishermen-Gatherers

Basic environmental resources in the Interior Plateau region included the annual salmon run, sturgeon, deer, and the root of the camas plant. In the higher mountains elk, mountain goat, and bighorn sheep were also available. ● Fishing by netting or the spearing of salmon swimming upstream formed the base of a long-term economy in the region, dating back to about 9000 B.C. Associated artifacts include bone points, ground-edge cobbles, and bipoints typical of the Old Cordilleran Culture. Between 5000 and 1000 B.C. Plateau prehistory is poorly known. After A.D. 500 there appears a regional culture distinctive of the area. Termed the Northwest Riverine Tradition, this culture featured permanent villages in the river valleys and a major reliance on fishing. The tool inventory included a complex of ground-stone woodworking tools, probably introduced from the north after 1000 B.C. Other trends through time include increasing trade with the Northwest Coast

littoral peoples and the introduction of specific Northwest Coast traits, including house types and burial patterns.

Plains Hunter-Gatherers

Plains cultures possessed a nomadic life adjusted to reliance on the migratory herds of buffalo. This pattern emerged during the Paleo-Indian period. There is a Plains Archaic period, but sites are few and during the period human occupation was at a minimum. Later occupation, from 3000 to 500 B.C., featured the use of rock shelters and open campsites. The artifact inventory included chipped-stone skin-dressing tools as well as bone fleshers. The primary food animals included buffalo, deer, antelope, birds, reptiles, and freshwater mussels. Site features are limited to fire hearths and excavated storage pits. ▲ A typical hunting technique was the use of the stampede to drive herds of buffalo over a cliff, the so-called buffalo jump. The migratory bison hunter's life-style is best known to us from historical accounts rather than from archaeological investigations. An eyewitness account of one such group was recorded by Castañeda, the chronicler of Coronado's expedition of 1539–1541 (Hammond and Rey 1940:186):

After seventeen days of travel, I came upon a rancheria of the Indians who follow these cattle. These natives are called Querechos. They do not cultivate the land, but eat raw meat and drink the blood of the cattle they kill. They dress in the skins of the cattle, with which all the people in this land clothe themselves, and they have very well-constructed tents, made with tanned and greased cowhides, in which they live and which they take along as they follow the cattle. They have dogs which they load to carry their tents, poles, and belongings.

Plains Village Farmers

The majority of the archaeology of the Plains is derived from the sedentary riverine villages of

the Missouri River drainage. These settlements developed during A.D. times after the introduction of corn horticulture. ■ Farming was conducted in small plots in the valley bottoms, and the villages were constructed on the first terrace above the river. Houses were of the earth-lodge type and featured a semisubterranean excavated floor, wooden support posts, and a cribbed log superstructure, with the entire dwelling then covered with earth. Villages ranged from a few houses up to a maximum of 200. Another feature common to these sites was the widespread use within and between the houses of bell-shaped, undercut storage pits. Community labor was used in the excavation of defensive moats around the villages and the erection of a wooden palisade, sometimes featuring bastians. The economy was mixed, with fall hunts for buffalo augmenting the garden produce.

Southwestern Farmers

Following its development in Mesoamerica, plant cultivation utilizing specific cultigens spread northward into the Southwest. ● Although the earliest occurrences of corn in the Southwest date to 3000 B.C., the corn, beans, and squash agricultural economy did not substantially alter the Southwestern life-style until the first centuries A.D. The initial pattern established was that of small sedentary villages made up of semisubterranean to subterranean pithouses. Pottery was introduced, and a distinct Southwestern cultural tradition was formed. Later developments included the use of a separate and architecturally distinct subterranean structure, used for religious ceremonies, the kiva. After about A.D. 1000 the house type changed to the pueblo, a series of surface units made up of contiguous masonry rooms. In the northern Southwest between A.D. 1100 and 1300 there occurred a climax in architecture, with large villages containing up to 3,000 people living in multistory units of up to five stories.

The social organization and culture of these people has persisted to the present and is characterized by a strong religion which emphasizes keeping in harmony with nature through ceremonies and prayers for rain. Individual aggressiveness is minimized, and the relationships among individuals are highly structured according to their roles as members of numerous secret societies which cross-cut kin groups.

▲ In southern Arizona the initial settlements were confined to the major river valleys and featured the use of irrigation with a major system of canals. The infusion of Mexican traits was strong, and besides the food plants, included iron-pyrite mosaic mirrors, copper bells, carved stone palettes, and pottery styles. There was much trade in shell bracelets and other shell ornaments. Architectural introductions include the ball court and even flat-topped pyramidal mounds. The Hohokam culture, as it is termed, flourished from about 300 B.C. to A.D. 1400, after which the large settlements were abandoned. The probable cause of abandonment was the silting-up of the canals and progressive salinization of the fields. At the height of the occupation the canals were up to 75 miles in length and 30 feet in width, and the maintenance of a system of this magnitude would certainly have required community control of labor. Nonetheless, there is no evidence of the cultural attributes we ascribe to civilization, and we must therefore view the Hohokam culture as another manifestation of the New World Formative stage.

Eastern Farmers and Hunter-Gatherers

In Chapter 18 we described the economy of the Archaic peoples of the Eastern Woodlands of the United States. Termed Primary Forest Efficiency, this economy focused on a mixed reliance on the hunting and gathering of a wide variety of locally available foods. ■ Late in the Archaic Period, after 2500 B.C., there occurred the introduction of limited cultivation of plants

● A burial cult featured burial mounds with elaborate burial offerings.

▲ Temple mounds appear.

■ South American hunter-gatherers occupied marginal environments.

and the use of pottery (Chomko and Crawford 1978). After these introductions these previously semisedentary peoples began to live in permanent villages along the major river valleys. These later occupants have been classified into two major cultural traditions: the Woodland Tradition (1000 B.C.–A.D. 700) and the Mississippian Tradition (A.D. 700–1700).

The Woodland Tradition has as its major distinguishing characteristic the use of a gray, friable pottery, surface-decorated with cordmarking or impressions of fabrics. The cordmarking was done with a cord-wrapped paddle while the clay was still damp. Vessel forms were simple, consisting primarily of globular jars with pointed bottoms. Other major features were burial mounds and earthworks, which were associated with an elaborate pattern of ceremonial treatment of the dead. The most outstanding developments of this cultural pattern are known from the Ohio River Valley.

During the earlier portion of this tradition, termed Burial Mound I (1000–300 B.C.), the economy featured cultivation of sunflower, marsh elder, squash, gourd, and chenopod. Gordon Willey (1966:268) states that corn found in a Burial Mound II context (300 B.C.–A.D. 700) indicates a long period of antecedent development. Therefore although not found in Burial Mound I levels, corn was probably grown at that time. A recent and unexpected date on corn from the Koster site in southern Illinois suggests that it may date from as early as 5000 B.C. in the region.

● The most distinctive Burial Mound I culture is that termed Adena, an outgrowth of Late Archaic burial ceremonialism. The Adena featured clusters of conical burial mounds of up to

20 meters in height surrounded by earthen enclosures of up to 100 meters in diameter. Within the mounds were rectangular log tombs placed within a pit. Inside the tombs were two or three extended burials covered with red ochre. Sometimes the tombs were burned before being covered with the earthen mound. Another burial pattern featured cremation in clay basins. With both types, elaborate offerings of grave goods were included. The artifacts consisted of ground and polished stone celts, gorgets, boatstones, effigy pipes, and stone tablets with carved, curvilinear designs. Ornaments of copper as well as copper axes were used. Villages were simple pole-and-thatch structures grouped in clusters of from two to five. Probably several such villages supported a single burial complex.

The Burial Mound II period is best known from the Hopewell culture, which is also well represented in the Ohio River Valley. Hopewell constitutes a continuation of the Woodland cultural pattern, being more elaborate than the Adena. The major deviations from Adena consist of the burial rites. Furthermore, the Hopewell culture was disseminated widely into adjacent regions—an expansion viewed as having been exercised by an elite. Certainly, social stratification is evident in the Hopewell burial patterns. Three-fourths of the dead were cremated, whereas burial in log tombs was reserved for a minority. The log tombs held enormous quantities of grave goods, including thousands of freshwater pearls, chipped arrowheads, effigy pipes, copper ornaments, and sheet-mica cutouts in the form of heads, hands, swastikas, animal claws, and geometrics. The earthworks were larger and more elaborate than those of the Adena culture, including areas of up to 100 acres with walls of up to 5 meters in height. Another new feature was the fortification of hilltops. Hopewell culture emphasized wealth conspicuously consumed in its burial ceremonies. Many of the objects so sacrificed were made from materials traded over great distances, such as copper from Michigan, obsidian from Wyoming, silver

from Ontario, galena from Illinois, mica from North Carolina, marine shells from the coasts of Florida, and chalcedony from North Dakota (Griffin 1980:375). The Hopewell culture may thus be viewed as indicative of a cultural climax, although there is no evidence of urbanism and the overall level of attainment is that of the Formative stage.

The Mississippian tradition (A.D. 700–1700) is not a simple continuation of Woodland traits. The differences between the former and latter cultures suggest that major influences had spread up the Mississippi Valley from Mesoamerica. Although intervening areas in northern Mexico and southern Texas show little evidence of such cultural transmission, the new traits are definitely of Mesoamerican affinity. These introductions include rectangular, flat-topped platform mounds arranged around rectangular, open plazas. ▲ Called *temple mounds*, these structures served as bases for both temples and the houses of the chiefs. The structures themselves were of pole and thatch. The largest community known is Cahokia (Fig. 19-10), located within the suburbs of the present city of St. Louis. Numerous mounds are known, the largest of which, Monk's Mound, measures 200 by 300 meters by 30 meters in height. According to Willey (1966:298), 80 mounds are known within a 3-to-4 mile radius, and approximately 200 smaller mounds are estimated to have been destroyed by recent plowing. Studies at Cahokia by Melvin Fowler have been concerned with the mapping of the entire site from early aerial photographs, estimating its maximum population (perhaps as much as 40,000 at its peak), and the excavation of incredibly elaborate burials featuring large numbers of individuals with enormous quantities of burial offerings, all interred in accompaniment to other persons of obviously high status.

The Mississippian culture spread up the river systems into Wisconsin and southeastward as far as Tennessee, Alabama, and Georgia. In these remote locations the Mississippian communities feature palisaded earthworks and appear to represent intrusive communities surrounded by other peoples still practicing a Woodland lifestyle. The Mississippian featured as one of its dominant elements the Southern cult, which has been mentioned previously as a possible extension of Mesoamerican ceremonialism. The end of the Mississippian tradition is marked by a smooth transition to the cultures of the historic tribes of the Southeastern United States. Whereas numerous cultural traditions persisted into the historic contacts of DeSoto and others, the period of cultural florescence began to wane after A.D. 1200. Nonetheless, as late as A.D. 1700, the Natchez, a stratified society of nobles and commoners, maintained ceremonial centers with temple mounds and burial mounds.

South America

Our knowledge of South American prehistoric economic systems is less than that for North America. Few sites outside the Andean region have been excavated in detail. Three primary economies may be isolated: hunting-gathering, incipient-agriculture, and tropical-forest slash-and-burn agriculture.

Hunters and Gatherers

■ Primary areas where hunting and gathering were practiced included the savannas, the deciduous forests of the Brazilian and Guianan highlands, and the pampas. Typical subsistence patterns included the hunting of deer and guanaco with the bow and the bolas, the gathering of wild seeds, roots, and other plants, fishing done with the bow, and coastal shellfish gathering. Shelters were sometimes caves; otherwise windbreaks made of skins were used. The camps were occupied only as long as food was locally available. Due to the meager cultural inventory and the added difficulty of site location in areas now densely vegetated, most site data are limited to

● In the Amazon culture is limited to simple village farmers, who shift their fields every few years.

tools of chipped stone, bone, and shell. The largest social groups were the bands of guanaco hunters in the pampas, where the availability of game permitted habitation by groups in excess of 100 individuals. Elsewhere, the low carrying capacity of the Amazonian tropical-forest environment limited population. The tropical-forest pattern featured seasonal camps along the rivers with a rainy season dispersal of smaller groups who moved out into the savanna grasslands for collecting purposes.

Incipient Cultivators

The tropical-forest pattern described above was modified by the addition of limited cultivation, primarily of bitter manioc. The use of cultigens was simply added to the already established hunting-and-gathering economy. Villages were small, probably consisting of several extended families. Pottery features soft gray to brown surface-textured wares.

Tropical-Forest Slash-and-Burn Agriculturalists

According to Meggers (1954), the Amazonian tropical forest, evaluated in terms of its agricultural potential, is a limiting environment which only permits or gives rise to cultures existing at a subsistence level. The agricultural system is based on the cutting and burning of small areas to prepare plots for planting. Major crops are manioc, and in A.D. times, corn. ● Villages were small, located on the river banks, and were frequently moved as the fields were exhausted after four to six years. There was no permanent architecture and no elaborate social organization or religion. Transportation was by dugout canoe on the network of rivers. The pottery continues the tradition of incised decorated wares. Other artifacts include basketry, textiles, and implements of ground stone. The mixed hunting-and-gathering economy was also continued. Fishing employed the use of poison. The house type was pole-and-thatch and included single family units as well as large rectangular communal houses. There was some preference for secondary burial in pottery urns. For the most part, archaeological evidence for tropical agriculturalists dates to after A.D. 500, although knowledge is rapidly increasing. For example, Meggers (1979) cites a cool, dry interval of 4,000 to 2,000 years ago as the single most probable cause of the widespread occupation of the Amazon by pottery-bearing peoples. Lathrap (1970) goes even further to propose that intensive agriculture was practiced in the Amazon by 5,000 years ago, causing a population increase which in turn led to continuous outward migration. In about A.D. 500 there began the spread of tropical agricultural peoples to the Antilles, where they replaced the earlier shellfish-gathering littoral inhabitants termed Meso-Indians.

In general, we may summarize South American cultures in all those areas lying beyond the Andean chain as possessing little in the way of elaborate social organization, architecture, and crafts.

PART V

THE FUTURE OF ARCHAEOLOGY

At this point in the text, we have completed a summary of human physical and cultural evolution as we know it so far. However, our knowledge of the past is limited by our reliance on archaeological concepts and techniques as well as by our reliance on two other aspects — the availability of trained personnel and the availability of sites suitable for study. In the following chapter, we will discuss the training required of a professional archaeologist. In addition, we will review how sites are being protected today so that they may be studied in the future. And finally, we discuss what you can do to aid in this cause.

23

The Nature of Modern Archaeology

Archaeology as a Profession

The traditional roles of archaeologists are two: the archaeologist as museum curator and researcher, and the archaeologist as instructor and researcher in an academic setting. Recent years have seen the rise of the full-time contract archaeologist, who recovers information from sites threatened with destruction as a result of modern construction projects. If you are interested in becoming a professional archaeologist, these are the principal positions which might be available to you. The opportunities for employment are of course governed by the current tradition of training and education in archaeology.

One does not start at the "bottom" and work step-by-step toward the "top" of the archaeological profession—at least, not if we consider field excavation as the "bottom." The reason for this seeming injustice is that field excavations require the application of learned *skills*. The field excavator is a skilled technician who, without additional education, will forever remain at the level of a field foreman. Such a position is marginal at best, not well-paid, and has no built-in opportunities for advancement. Traditionally, positions in field archaeology are filled on a temporary basis by graduate students who are simultaneously working toward advanced degrees. The technician in field excavations is further limited by the fact that archaeology is a scholarly discipline requiring knowledge of concepts and direct involvement in the pursuit of scientific inquiries. The archaeologist must be able to formulate scientific problems, develop hypotheses, and establish methodologies for test-

ing the validity of theories. It is in this area that the typical amateur archaeologist falls short, for archaeology is not the location and collection of prehistoric objects but the pursuit of knowledge of past lifeways through application of a scientific methodology.

There are too few available jobs in the field of archaeology for an individual to risk ending his or her formal education after attaining simply a B.A. degree in archaeology. The few jobs available for the person with a Bachelor's degree are short-term salvage situations offering no permanent career opportunities. (Recently, archaeology has begun to be offered in secondary schools, and thus some teaching positions may become available at that level as well [Cotter 1979].) Therefore, the route to advancement as a professional archaeologist requires education at the graduate level. A Master's degree is the minimum qualification for professional status, and for many positions a Ph.D. is required. It is necessary to decide early to undertake such graduate study due to the increasingly higher requirements for admission to graduate schools. To be admitted to graduate school today, without special additional qualifications, an overall undergraduate grade-point average of at least B or preferably higher is required. A further qualification is maximum possible excavation experience while still an undergraduate. Most large universities operate some type of field school in archaeology during the summer. Even if tuition is required, it is to your advantage to enroll in such a program. If you do well on your first dig, then you stand a chance of being selected in later seasons as an excavation supervisor or laboratory assistant, both of which are salaried positions.

After deciding on archaeology as a career, what is the next step? Archaeology in most American universities is offered within the overall discipline of anthropology. You would thus elect a major in anthropology. Most such programs require courses in cultural anthropology, physical anthropology, and anthropological linguistics in addition to the courses in archae-

ology. An average major of 30 to 36 credit hours may require up to 20 hours of general anthropological course work, with the balance to be made up of electives in archaeology. Additionally, you should be able to acquire six hours of these electives by participation in one of the summer field schools. Other alternatives are the offerings of Classical archaeology in departments of Classics, Oriental languages, or Near Eastern languages.

In other countries, archaeology may be organized differently within a university setting. For example, in Canada at both the University of Calgary and Simon Fraser University archaeology constitutes a separate department. In European universities, prehistory is frequently offered as a separate major. If you are currently enrolled in a small college or university in the United States which does not offer a major in anthropology, you should consider transferring to one that does. Otherwise, even after being admitted to graduate school with your B.A. degree you may immediately have to make up 18 to 20 hours of undergraduate requirements in anthropology. If it is necessary to transfer, the best way to locate a suitable university is to go to the university library or the registrar's office and read the curriculum offerings of university catalogs. You should read the degree requirements and review the courses offered to enable an optimal selection. It is probable that within your own state there is a university with a program suitable to your needs. A further aid is the *Guide to Departments of Anthropology*, published annually by the American Anthropological Association.

Once you have obtained your graduate degree, what kinds of positions are available? Teaching posts in junior colleges, four-year colleges, and, rarely, universities may be obtained with a Master's degree. Increasingly, however, the job market is catering to candidates with the Ph.D., which means that the competition for positions is becoming more intense. Today, about three-fifths of all individuals with advanced degrees in anthropology hold university or college teaching positions and of these about 20 percent

specialize in archaeology. Currently, there is little opportunity for teaching anthropology in high schools. However, with trends of increasing specialization in secondary education, in the future archaeology may be introduced into the high school curriculum. Once you have prepared for a teaching career you can learn about jobs available through attendance at professional meetings, where there is an opportunity to discuss the positions being offered with representatives from those departments seeking personnel. The largest of these recruitment centers is held in conjunction with the annual meeting of the American Anthropological Association.

According to the *Guide to Departments of Anthropology* (1979), there are at present 4,869 professional anthropologists employed by 337 academic departments, 13 research departments, and 57 museums in North America. These same departments have a total of 7,205 graduate students and 16,106 undergraduate majors enrolled. In the academic year 1978–79 394 students were graduated with the Ph.D. degree, 931 with the Master's, and 4,440 with the B.A. In 1972 the same guide listed 3,300 professional anthropologists. Therefore these figures, while incomplete, suggest that as long as professional employment is tied directly to college-level teaching, the opportunities for a career in anthropology are limited. If we accept Charles Frantz's (1972) estimate that 20 percent of all anthropologists specialize in archaeology, there is presently a national total of fewer than 1,000 professional archaeologists. Currently there are only 500 members of the Society of Professional Archaeologists. While the Society of American Archaeology has more than 4,000 individual members, their enrollment includes many student and amateur members.

John Rowe (1954:230–231) has summarized the field of archaeology as a profession, and we quote part of his discussion here:

> Archaeology is a field of pure research, like astronomy or history. It is not economically profitable to anyone nor are its results normally useful to business and industry. Consequently, there are no jobs for archaeologists in the sense that there are jobs for accountants or even for research chemists and engineers. Furthermore, it is difficult to raise funds to finance research projects in archaeology, even on a small scale, because the subject has little or nothing to offer to business, to national defense or even to public entertainment. It is an unlikely field in which to look for solutions to modern social problems and hence has no appeal for reformers.

> It is important to emphasize the economic difficulties of archaeology as a career because they are not always obvious to people whose imagination is fired by reading of archaeological discoveries or by visiting museums and ancient ruins. Employment opportunities for people trained as professional archaeologists are few and the salaries comparatively low. At the same time it is a field that requires thorough training and usually a Ph.D. degree (i.e., three to five years of graduate work after the normal four years of college). No one should plan to make a career of archaeology unless he is so deeply interested in it that he is not really concerned about how much he is going to earn.

Rewriting the same article later, Rowe (1961:49) again stresses the privations attendant upon a career in archaeology.

> The best positions open to archaeologists are those as college and university teachers or museum curators, and such jobs are strictly limited in number. Only the larger colleges and universities teach archaeology, and relatively few museums can afford to have research men on their staffs. In these jobs, of course, the archaeologist is expected to devote a substantial part of his time to teaching or to the care and exhibition of collections, and his research has to be carried on very largely in his spare time, evenings, weekends, and during vacations. Archaeologists do not work bankers' hours. Field trips, except for work on local sites, require leave, and if the archaeologist has a family to support it must usually be leave with pay. Few universities or museums can afford to be liberal with leave of this kind.

The funding of archaeological research was also discussed by Rowe (1961:50):

> It may be noted that research on historic monuments and sites of actual or potential public interest is a kind of "applied archaeology," because it increases the resources of the tourist business. Nevertheless, the private businesses which profit from increases in the tourist trade have contributed little directly to the support of the archaeological work which makes local sites intelligible and interesting to the visitor. Work of this kind tends to be regarded as a responsibility of government, like the provision of bathing facilities at public beaches.
>
> American archaeologists whose field of interest lies outside the United States depend on research grants made by foundations or on the generosity of private benefactors for funds to pay the expenses of their field work. The money is usually raised in the name of the university or museum for which the archaeologist works, and, as we have noted, the institution must provide a leave of absence for the time he will be in the field. Occasionally an American archaeologist will enter the service of a university or museum in the country where his research interest lies in order to have more frequent opportunities for doing field work. Such service is a valuable experience, but it is likely to be difficult to arrange, since in most other countries there are even fewer positions for trained archaeologists than there are in the United States, while there is certainly no lack of local candidates for the positions.

Since 1961 the situation with respect to jobs in research archaeology has improved considerably. There are and have been available since 1960 substantial sums for research grants and salvage contracts. In fact, during the 1960s archaeological research has experienced a heyday in the availability of funds which was part of national support of all scientific endeavors. Archaeological research grants in amounts of $20,000 to $100,000 were common, and several projects had budgets of $300,000 to $400,000. The return to more limited funding was initiated in about 1970 in conjunction with the overall downturn in business and the Nixon Administration's program to cut back governmental expenditures in higher education, research, and development. However, at present the need for rescue archaeology continues.

The personal qualities required of the professional archaeologist are also spelled out by Rowe (1954:232). These statements are as true today as they were in 1954.

> Because most jobs in archaeology involve either university teaching or museum work, a prospective archaeologist should have the temperamental qualifications for one or the other of these types of work and should plan his studies with the kind of position he wants in mind. A general requirement for research in any field is intellectual curiosity, an interest in asking questions and looking for answers to them. This curiosity should be combined with impartiality and suspicion of conclusions presented without fair discussion of the evidence. Archaeological field work demands some special qualifications. An archaeologist should be able to stand considerable amounts of physical discomfort without its interfering with his work or making him excessively irritable; he should be a methodical and systematic worker; and he needs some degree of manual dexterity. Above all he should have patience. Most of the time an archaeological excavation is dull routine, and the work goes very slowly. Some spectacular discoveries may be made, of course, but they are likely to be a lot less frequent than the disappointments.

The training of a professional archaeologist is a lengthy process requiring the acquisition of a variety of skills. To paraphrase Rowe (1961:51–53), the student needs to be able to write well, should possess competence in foreign languages, should be skilled in map making, photography, typing, mechanical drawing, and field surveying. What we are saying is that professional training in archaeology requires additional skills other than those concerned with locating and excavating sites, lab study of artifacts, and re-

search writing. The archaeologist in the field must be a "jack of all trades." He or she has to be able to repair trucks, build a latrine, repair plumbing, negotiate with local ranchers, cook, administer first aid, balance the budget, and serve as psychological counselor to his crew. A second responsibility is the need to understand something of the ancillary disciplines that are so important to archaeology — geology, palynology, paleontology, geochronology, and others. Only with such knowledge can the archaeologist design the site-excavation plan to enable the recovery of data important to these disciplines. Furthermore, the researcher should also be able to understand the contributions these data can make to specific cultural research problems. Therefore, in order to become suitably trained, the archaeologist needs graduate-level study in a variety of other disciplines. Only after these requirements have been met will the student be prepared to accept the responsibility of being a modern archaeologist.

The acquisition of the skills we have described can only be obtained through a combination of academic studies and actual field experience. Most universities offer a summer excavation program, and it is here that the student can learn the distinctions between archaeology as an academic discipline and as a field science. Other opportunities for field experience may be obtained by joining a weekend dig sponsored by a local amateur society, or rarely, the pressure for fast action on a salvage program may provide direct employment as an unskilled digger. If you wish to learn more about archaeology as a profession you should contact your local amateur society and university. Only by becoming acquainted with the archaeologists in those groups can you become informed as to the training opportunities they have available.

Professional archaeologists fill several different kinds of roles. This discussion has been broadly divided into teaching and research activities, which may be further subdivided as follows (Table 23-1). A general discussion of roles and opportunities is also presented in Rowe (1961).

Salaries for professional archaeologists have improved in recent years in line with the improvement in the salaries of all university professors. Currently, museum assistants may be either hired on a basis of $3 to $4 per hour, or at an annual salary of up to $8000 per year. Field archaeologists, depending upon their qualifications, receive salaries from $800 per month for short-term contracts to as much as $18,000 annually. State archaeologists' salaries are on an annual basis and range from $15,000 to $25,000. Museum curators' and professors' salaries are based on academic qualifications, seniority, and experience. The salary range is from about $15,000 to more than $30,000 for professors with less than five years' experience to those with 25 to 30 years' experience, respectively. According to Frantz (1972:210) anthropologists earned a median salary in 1967–1968 of $12,200 for the nine-month academic year. Current figures would be in the vicinity of $20,000 to $22,000 for median salaries. Museum directors' salaries vary widely, depending upon the size of the museum. Accordingly, one can expect a range of from $15,000 to $35,000.

Since 1970 the major change in archaeology has been the development of *public archaeology*. Originally initiated as the salvage of sites threatened by construction projects, public archaeology has expanded to include the inventorying of all sites on federally owned and state-owned lands, the evaluation of such sites for their significance, and their preservation whenever possible by a variety of means. Methods of site preservation include changing the area to be affected by a project, realignment of right of ways, and covering over the endangered site with earth. If none of these measures can be exercised, the site is then *mitigated* (the term used for the recording of details and the salvage of all possible data). The initial step is the mapping of sites; site map-

TABLE 23-1
Professional Archaeological Roles and Activities

Role	Activities Required	Degree Required
1. University Professor	Prepare courses, lectures, grade exams, participate in departmental and university committee meetings. Serve on thesis advisory committees, give public lectures. Publish scientific research papers, attend scientific conferences and present papers. Direct a summer field school. Conduct individual research. Write research proposals and raise funds. Direct research projects and supervise personnel.	Ph.D.
2. College Professor	Engage in all activities listed above except those tied directly to a graduate-studies program.	M.A.–Ph.D.
3. Junior College Professor	Prepare courses, lecture, grade exams, serve on committees. Possibly direct a summer field program. Sometimes also teach allied fields, such as sociology or history. Research opportunities and responsibilities are usually less than at university and college levels, with teaching load greater.	M.A.
4. Museum Director	Supervise and administer all programs and personnel in a museum. Major responsibilities are fund raising and maintenance of "political" contacts. May also originate and direct research.	Ph.D.
5. Museum Curator	Conduct individual research, publish scientific papers, and present papers at scientific conferences. Occasionally, teach a course, if affiliated with a college or university. Design and supervise installation of exhibits. Supervise cataloging and maintenance of collections. Raise funds, design research projects, and direct research.	M.A.–Ph.D.
6. Museum Assistant	Catalog specimens, maintain files, repair specimens, store and maintain collections. Conduct preliminary analysis of specimens as part of laboratory research.	B.A.
7. State Archaeologist	Negotiate for salvage contracts. Either supervise or subcontract salvage work. Maintain files on all site-location data in the state. Supervise budgets, hire personnel, visit salvage projects and maintain close contact with all archaeology currently underway in the state. Conduct individual research; prepare and publish scientific reports. Review environmental impact statements.	M.A.–Ph.D.
8. Field Archaeologist	Direct the excavation of sites. Supervise laborers, select site areas to be excavated, and keep all records, photos, and maps resulting from excavations.	B.A.–M.A.
9. Contract Archaeologist	Privately employed, the contract archaeologist essentially manages a small business firm. Bid on contracts, prepare proposals and budgets, hire and supervise field archaeologists and lab technicians. This role is primarily that of an entrepreneur, and the contract archaeologist may rarely actually participate in field work.	B.A., M.A., or Ph.D.

ping from surface indications, mapping with airborne, remote-sensing equipment, mapping using ground-penetrating radar or electrical resistivity devices, and underwater mapping through the use of side-scanning sonar and magnetometers. Excavation is the data-recovery technique commonly used when sites must be destroyed by the project activities. Sites to be excavated are selected through reference to the site-survey information and, on large projects where not all sites can be excavated, by sophisticated sampling methodologies.

Authority for such programs within the United States includes the Federal Antiquities Act of 1906, the Historic Sites Act of 1935, the Reservoir Salvage Act of 1960, the National Historic Preservation Act of 1966, the National Environmental Policy Act of 1969, Executive Order 11593 of 1971, the Archeological Salvage Act of 1974, the Archeological Resources Protection Act of 1979, and the Historic Preservation Act of 1980. It is not our intent here to detail all the provisions within this body of legislation. Such coverage is presented by McGimsey (1972); King (1978); King, Hickman, and Berg (1977); Talmadge and Chester (1977); Schiffer and Gumerman (1977); McGimsey and Davis (1977); and others. Furthermore, a series of bureaucratic procedures has been developed with which the various state and federal construction agencies must comply before archaeological sites deemed significant may be mitigated. The entire set of procedures is complex, and we need not concern ourselves here with them.

What is significant for our review here is the fact that public archaeology has led to a flurry of archaeological mitigation within the United States to the extent of now providing employment for several thousand persons on a year-round basis. Many states have organized councils of professional archaeologists, most of whom are employed in contract archaeology, and membership in these councils approaches 100 in many states. There are also the field laborers, who on some large projects may number from

100 to 200. Therefore we may state that during the 1970s the number of persons doing professional archaeology has doubled or even tripled. Contract work does not provide a secure and continuing career with retirement benefits, health insurance, and so forth, but it has offered employment in the field to the extent that archaeology in the United States is currently experiencing a period of extremely rapid growth. How long this will continue under the current economic recession is not predictable. In addition, the administration of President Reagan may well focus more on the development of resources than upon the protection of environmental values. Nonetheless, we face a growth in energy development during the next decade in accompaniment with which we may expect an associated growth in contract archaeology. Thus whereas the future for academic positions would appear to be one of slow decline owing to reduction in college enrollments, contract archaeology may well continue to provide expanding opportunities.

Archaeology as a Hobby

Archaeology as a hobby can be divided into two major realms: (1) the study of archaeology as a subject through visits to museums and sites, and through reading various site reports and popular books and (2) the collecting of artifacts from sites. The amateur archaeologist pursues archaeology as a hobby for many of the same reasons that people everywhere pursue their hobbies. It is an interesting, absorbing, leisure-time activity which can combine scholarly research with outdoor exercise and the thrill of a treasure hunt. Amateur archaeologists may be classified into two groups, the scholarly amateurs and the pot hunters or plunderers. The collecting of prehistoric artifacts without their accompanying provenience data is analogous to the collecting of bottle caps or matchbook covers; it amounts to

the senseless accumulation of trivia. On the other hand, the looter, who digs for objects to sell, not only destroys sites but forever destroys archaeological information. In many instances such pillagers violate not only our antiquities laws but also transgress our moral responsibility to preserve the human heritage. Many people fit neither category, being neither serious amateurs nor looters but simply curious persons who will pick up an arrowhead or a potsherd if they find one. These individuals are not to be condemned but instead should be educated to recognize the value of what they have found.

Serious amateur archaeologists usually belong to a local society which has monthly meetings, sponsors field trips, may publish a newsletter, and occasionally sponsors a weekend excavation. By joining such a group the interested amateur can become part of a larger organization which fosters the same interests as his or her own. Amateur archaeologists tend to belong to one of several groups in our society. Often these are retired individuals looking for something interesting to do with their spare time. Another major category consists of the businessman, lawyer, or other professional who seeks interests outside his or her profession for relaxation and diversion. Such persons can frequently make great contributions to ongoing archaeological projects by providing their expertise on a voluntary basis.

Organized amateur societies provide numerous services to professional archaeologists and to the profession of archaeology in general. Foremost among these is the provision of an organized body of interested citizenry who can act in a concerted manner to influence antiquities legislation, sponsor a drive to preserve a particular site, support scientific publication, and locate sites. An effective local society provides the liaison between professional archaeologists and the general public. Occasionally in the United States (but commonly in England) amateur societies become highly proficient in archaeological skills, excavating sites and reporting their find-

ings in a scientific manner. When amateur archaeology is carried out at this level it provides an important adjunct to the limited work that can be funded and directed by professionals. In every situation where an amateur is investigating sites there is one cardinal rule to be observed. If anything is removed from the site it should be recorded so that when studied later it will have documented provenience.

Examples of work by amateur archaeologists range from indiscriminate surface collecting and the pillaging of buried sites to the scientific recovery of total site information. A classic example of uncontrolled amateur pillaging was the selling of permits at $10 a day by the city of Boulder, Colorado to individuals to dig for old bottles at the A.D. 1870–1890 former city dump. This ill-conceived, unsupervised project was abruptly terminated when a cavein killed one of the excavators.

One other major subject which should be covered in any discussion of amateur archaeology is the permission to investigate sites. Sites on federal and state lands are in most states protected by law, with permission to collect from or excavate such sites being granted by a supervisory federal or state agency. Normally, such permission is granted only to qualified professional archaeologists. Therefore the interested amateur should first determine who owns the land he or she wishes to investigate. If these lands are in private ownership then permission may be obtained from the land owner.

We are now living in a time of realization that our cultural and environmental resources are not inexhaustible but are in fact quite limited and fragile. The greatest service any amateur archaeologist can perform is to join the state and national movements to conserve our prehistoric heritage. At present construction projects endanger more sites than existing resources in time, funds, and trained personnel are capable of salvaging. What is needed is a national campaign to identify those sites not currently endangered in order to preserve them for future generations.

Threats to the Past and the Need for Preservation

During the 1970s we witnessed the culmination of certain processes that have intensified steadily since the end of World War II. These processes relate to all types of land modification, as associated with economic development: the construction of highways, dams, pipelines, electrical transmission lines, the drilling of oil wells and gas wells, strip mining for coal, copper, and uranium, the construction of subdivision housing, urban renewal, and harbor dredging. The list is endless and it represents major and permanent alterations of the landscape. An associated, if inadvertent, result of these activities is the destruction and threatened destruction of archaeological sites. Sites may be destroyed by the direct impact of a construction project, such as the removal of earth for use in the fill of a dam. Equally, sites may be destroyed as the result of the indirect impacts resulting from a project. A site may be subjected to erosion due to land modification nearby, or the site may be made more accessible to looters simply through road construction or the filling of a lake. All of these effects have increased at a fantastic rate during the past four decades, with the cumulative result that by the early 1970s archaeologists were beginning to fear that all evidences of the past were soon to be obliterated (Davis 1971, 1972).

Economic development is, of course, a worldwide phenomenon and as a result rescue archaeology has been performed not only within the United States but also in connection with the Aswan Dam, the Euphrates Dam, the Kainji reservoir, as well as pipelines, transmission lines, and so forth in Canada, Mexico, and other nations. The problems facing the efforts to protect and preserve archaeological resources are therefore worldwide. The above concerns have led to the birth of a new movement in archaeology: the conservation movement. We have seen the formation of a new society, the American Society for Conservation Archaeology, and the development of what is called Cultural Resource Management. Cultural resource management means that archaeologists and agency planners are now as concerned with site avoidance and site preservation as they are with data recovery from sites through excavation. The site that is preserved today may be our only source of information in the future. The concern, then, is with managing cultural resources, since they are nonrenewable and once destroyed, are lost forever. What is important is the entire resource base, which

> means the totality of information sources that can be used to understand past human activities. This base includes not only cultural remains, such as artifacts, structures, features, activity areas, and so forth, but any parts of the natural and cultural environments that were either used or modified by peoples in the past or which can aid in understanding the basic relationships between people and their environment in the past. Another element of the resource base exists at the level of spatial relationships—among materials at a site, among sites, and between sites and aspects of the natural environment. *The resource base, then, is not just the sum of specimens and sites, but includes networks of interrelationships that potentially can contribute another magnitude of information. In other words, the whole is greater than the sum of its parts.* (McGimsey and Davis 1977:27)

Cultural resource management has therefore led to a joint effort among archaeologists and state and federal agency officials to maximize the potential of these resources through prudent management. For example, site mitigation is not simply a one-step salvage operation based on excavation but in fact includes: "(1) avoidance of the destruction or disturbance of cultural resources; (2) active measures for resource preservation or minimization of effect; (3) investigation or the conservation of information through

adequate study of the resources before they are destroyed" (McGimsey and Davis 1977:29). A further recognition has been the broadening of the concept of cultural resources to include not only archaeological sites but also historic structures, historic districts, neighborhoods, folkways, social institutions, belief systems, sacred places, and the like.

Hand in hand with this redefinition of cultural resources has been the initiation of regulations and programs by the various agencies and national governments to identify, record, protect, and preserve cultural resources. We are still far from the ideal of managing all our cultural resources, for thousands of sites, especially archaeological ones, are as yet unlocated, owing to the lack of comprehensive programs for site inventory. Nevertheless, the tide has turned from the uncontrolled, unnoticed, wanton destruction of sites on an ever-increasing scale to the current concern for site location, evaluation, preservation, and protection. Whereas today there are definite programs in cultural resource management in effect, a state of emergency still exists. This is due to the ever-increasing number of land modification projects coupled with a still inadequate supply of trained cultural resource managers. Furthermore, many federal agencies have woefully inadequate budgets for cultural resource management, and many state agencies have no budget at all.

The future of archaeology, then, is not safe but is still under attack, and it is up to each of us to do what we can to locate sites and ensure that they receive proper management in a cultural resource program. You may ask what any interested citizen can do, and the answers are several. You can join an amateur society which helps to locate and record sites. You can report any site evidence you find individually directly to the office of the State Archaeologist in your state. And especially, you can report any circumstance in which you observe archaeological resources actually being destroyed by construction. Some agencies are still not fully in compliance with National Historic Preservation Acts, and therefore the report of any citizen can be the first step in ensuring that a particular agency will be more conscientious in its approach to cultural resources. The help of all individuals is needed in these efforts, for the rate of site destruction still exceeds the capability of professional archaeologists to mitigate all of the sites that are currently threatened. With our combined vigilance, there can and will be archaeology in the future.

REFERENCES

Chapter 1

BELZONI, G., 1820, *Narrative of the Operations and Recent Discoveries within the Pyramids, Temples, Tombs, and Excavations in Egypt and Nubia*, 2 vols. London: J. Murray.

CAMDEN, W., 1586, *Britannia.*

CLARK, J. G.D., 1969, *Archaeology and Society: Reconstructing the Prehistoric Past.* New York: Barnes & Noble.

COTTRELL, L. (ed.), 1960, *The Concise Encyclopedia of Archaeology.* New York: Hawthorn.

DANIEL, G., 1962, *The Idea of Prehistory.* London: Watts.

———, 1967, *The Origins and Growth of Archaeology.* New York: Crowell. (Paperback ed., Baltimore: Penguin.)

DEUEL, L., 1967, *Conquistadors without Swords: Archaeologists in the Americas.* New York: St. Martin's Press.

FRERE, J., 1800, "Account of Flint Weapons Discovered at Hoxne in Suffolk," *Archaeologia* Vol. 13: 204–205.

GETTY, J. P., 1965, *The Joys of Collecting.* New York: Hawthorn.

HARRISON, W. H., 1838, *A Discourse on the Aborigines of the Valley of Ohio.* Columbus: Historical Society of Ohio.

HEIZER, R., 1962, *Man's Discovery of His Past: Literary Landmarks in Archaeology.* Englewood Cliffs, N.J.: Prentice-Hall.

HESTER, J. J., P. M. HOBLER, and J. RUSSELL, 1970, "New Evidence of Early Roads in Nubia," *American Journal of Archaeology* Vol. 74: 386–389.

HOLE, F., and R. HEIZER, 1969, *An Introduction to Prehistoric Archaeology*, 2ed. New York: Holt, Rinehart and Winston, Inc.

———, 1973, *An Introduction to Prehistoric Archaeology*, 3ed. rev. New York: Holt, Rinehart and Winston, Inc.

INGERSOLL, E., 1874, *New York Tribune.*

JEFFERSON, T., 1944, *The Life and Selected Writings of Thomas Jefferson.* A. KOCH and W. PEDEN (eds.). New York: Modern Library.

LHWYD, E., 1707, *Archaeologia Britannia.*

LYELL, C., 1863, *The Geological Evidences of the Antiquity of Man*, 2d American ed. Philadelphia: Lippincott.

———, 1872, *Principles of Geology*, 11ed., 2 vols. New York: Appleton.

MORGAN, L. H., 1877, *Ancient Society or Researches in the Lines of Human Progress from Savagery through Barbarism to Civilization.* New York.

SCHLIEMANN, H., 1884, *Troja. Results of the latest researches and discoveries on the site of Homer's Troy and in the heroic tumuli and other sites made in the year 1882.* New York: Harper and Brothers.

SQUIER, E. G., 1877, *Peru Illustrated. Incidents of Travel and Exploration in the Land of the Incas.* New York: Hurst and Co.

SQUIER, E. G., and E. H. DAVIS, 1848, *Ancient Monuments of the Mississippi Valley.* Washington, D.C.: Smithsonian Institution.

STEPHENS, J. L., 1843, *Incidents of Travel in Central America, Chiapas, and Yucatan*, 2 vols. New York: Harper & Row. (Reprint of one volume: *Incidents of Travel in Yucatan*, with introduction by V. Von Hagen [ed.]. Norman, Okla: University of Oklahoma Press, 1962.)

TYLOR, E. B., 1881, *Anthropology.* London.

VON HUMBOLT, A., 1814, *Researches Concerning the Institutions and Monuments of the Ancient Inhabitants of America, with Descriptions and Views of Some of the Most Striking Scenes in the Cordillieras*, 2 vols. (French title cited in text.) London: Longmans.

USSHER, J., 1650, *Annals of the Ancient and New Testament.*

WORSAAE, J. J. A., 1849, *Primeval Antiquities of Denmark.* London.

Chapter 2

BROTHWELL, D., and E. S. HIGGS, 1970, *Science in Archaeology.* New York: Praeger.

CLARK, J. G. D., 1977, *World Prehistory in New Perspective*, 3ed. Cambridge, England; New York: Cambridge University Press.

CLAUSEN, C. J., A. D. COHEN, C. EMILIANI, J. A. HOLMAN, and J. J. STEPP, 1979, "Little Salt Spring, Florida: A Unique Underwater Site," *Science* 203, No. 4381: 6090614.

COLE, S., 1965, *The Prehistory of East Africa.* New York: Mentor.

EDWARDS, I. E. S., 1972, *The Treasures of Tutankhamun*. Catalog for the Tutankhamun exhibit, sponsored by the Trustees of the British Museum. London: *The Times* and *The Sunday Times*.

FRANKEL, DAVID, 1979, *Archaeologists at Work: Studies on Halaf Pottery*. London: British Museum.

GEORGI, CARL E. (ed.), 1978, *The Ice Age—When Did It Begin and Has It Ended?* Transactions of the Nebraska Academy of Sciences, Vol. VI. Lincoln, Neb.

HOLE F., and R. HEIZER, 1973, *An Introduction to Prehistoric Archeology*, 3ed. rev. New York: Holt, Rinehart and Winston, Inc.

LEAKEY, M. D., 1967, "Preliminary Survey of the Cultural Materials from Beds I and II, Olduvai Gorge, Tanzania," W. W. Bishop and J. D. Clark (eds.), *Background to Evolution in Africa*. Chicago: University of Chicago Press.

———, 1979, "Footprints in the Ashes of Time," *National Geographic*, 155: 446–457.

OAKLEY, K. P., 1972, *Man the ToolMaker*, 6ed. London: British Museum.

SCHIFFER, M. B., 1976, *Behavioral Archaeology*. New York: Academic Press.

SEMENOV, S. A., 1964, *Prehistoric Technology*. English edition (Russian edition, 1957). London: Barnes & Noble.

WATSON, W. (with additions by G. G. SIEVEKING), 1968, *Flint Implements: An Account of Stone Age Techniques and Cultures*, 3ed. London: British Museum.

WENDORF, F., 1968, *The Prehistory of Nubia*, 2 vols. Dallas: Southern Methodist University Press.

WILLEY, G. R., and P. PHILLIPS, 1958, *Method and Theory in American Archaeology*. Chicago: University of Chicago Press.

WILSON, M. (ed.), 1974, *Applied Geology and Archaeology: The Holocene History of Wyoming*. Laramie: Geological Survey of Wyoming.

Chapter 3

AITKEN, M. J., 1968, "Thermoluminescent Dating in Archaeology: Introductory Review," in D. J. McDougall (ed.), *Thermoluminescence of Geological Materials*. New York: Academic Press, pp. 369–378.

BADA, J. L., and P. M. HELFMAN, 1975, "Amino Acid Dating of Fossil Bones," in *World Archaeology*, Vol. 2.

BANNISTER, B., 1969, "Dendrochronology" in Brothwell and Higgs, 1969, pp. 191–192.

BROTHWELL, D., and E. HIGGS, 1969, *Science and Archaeology*, 2d. ed. New York: Praeger.

COOK, S. F., 1946, "A Reconstruction of Shell Mounds with Respect to Population and Nutrition," *American Antiquity* 12:51–53.

COSGROVE, H. S., and C. B. COSGROVE, 1932, "The Swarts Ruin," *Peabody Museum Paper* 15, No. 1.

COX, A., 1969, "Geomagnetic Reversals" *Science* 163, No. 163, No. 3864:237–245.

DEETZ, J., 1967, *Invitation to Archaeology*. New York: Doubleday.

DeGEER, G., 1912, "A Geochronology of the Last 12,-000 Years," *Proceedings of the 11th International Geological Congress*. Stockholm, 1912, pp. 241–258.

———, 1940, *Geochronologia Suecica Principles*. Stockholm: Avenska Vetenskapsakademiens, Handlingar, Vol. 18, No. 6.

FERGUSON, C. W., 1972, "Dendrochronology of Bristlecone Pine Prior to 4000 B.C." Paper presented at the International Radiocarbon Dating Conference, Wellington, New Zealand.

FRANKEL, D., 1979, *Archaeologists at Work: Studies on Halaf Pottery*. London: British Museum.

GIFFORD, E. W., 1916, "Composition of California Shellmounds," *University of California Publications in American Archaeology and Ethnology* 12:1–29.

GROOTES, P. M., 1978, "Carbon-14 Time Scale Extended: Comparison of Chronologies," *Science* 200, No. 5337:11–15.

HARE, P. E., 1974, "Amino Acid Dating–A History and an Evolution," *MASCA Newsletter* 10:4–7.

KENNEDY, G., and L. KNOPF, 1960, "Dating by Thermoluminescence," *Archaeology* 13:137–148.

LLOYD, S., 1963, *Mounds of the Near East*. Edinburgh: Edinburgh University Press.

LLOYD, S., and F. SAFAR, 1945, "Tell Hassuna," *Journal of Near Eastern Studies* IV, Fig. 5.

MICHELS, J. W., 1973, *Dating Methods in Archaeology*. New York and London: Academic Press.

MORLEY, S., and G. BRAINERD, 1956, *The Ancient Maya*, 3ed. Stanford, Calif.: Stanford University Press.

SMILEY, T. L. (ed.), 1955, *Geochronology*. Tucson: University of Arizona Press.

STUIVER, M., C. J. HEUSSER, and I. C. YANG, 1978, "North American Glacial History Extended to 75,000 Years Ago," *Science* 200, No. 4337:16-21.

STUIVER, M. and P. D. QUAY, 1980, "Changes in Atmospheric Carbon-14 Attributed to a Variable Sun," *Science* 207, No. 4426:11-19.

STUCKENRATH, R., JR., W. R. COE, and E. K. RALPH, 1966, "University of Pennsylvania Radiocarbon Dates IX," *Radiocarbon* 8:348-385.

SUESS, H. E., 1965, "Secular Variations of the Cosmic-Ray Produced Carbon-14 in the Atmosphere," *Journal of Geophysical Research* 70:5950.

VAILLANT, G. C., 1935, "Excavations at El Arbolillo," *American Museum of Natural History Anthropological Papers* 35, Part 2.

WALKER, A., and R. F. LEAKEY, 1978, "The Hominids of East Turkana," *Scientific American* 239(2):44-56.

Chapter 4

ADAMS, R. E. W., 1980, "Swamps, Canals, and the Locations of Ancient Maya Cities," *Antiquity* LIV: 206-214.

BARKER, P., 1977, *Techniques of Archaeological Excavation*, New York: Universe Books.

CLARKE, D. L., 1968, *Analytical Archaeology*. London: Methuen.

DANCEY, W. S., 1981, *Archaeological Field Methods, an Introduction*. Minneapolis: Burgess Publishing Co.

DEUEL, L., 1973, *Flights Into Yesterday*. Harmondsworth, Middlesex, England: Penguin Books Ltd.

HAGGETT, P., 1965, *Locational Analysis in Human Geography*. London: Edward Arnold.

HESTER, T. A., R. F. HEIZER, and J. A. GRAHAM (eds.), 1975, *Field Methods in Archaeology*, 6th ed. Palo Alto, Calif.: Mayfield.

JUDGE, W. J., E., J. I. EBERT, and R. K. HITCHCOCK, 1975, "Sampling in Regional Archaeological Survey," in Mueller, 1975.

KING, T. F., 1978, *The Archaeological Survey: Methods and Uses*. Washington, D.C.: Heritage Conservation and Recreation Service, U.S. Department of Interior.

MILISAUKAS, S., 1973, "The Need for a Common Language of Measurements," *American Antiquity* 38(1):1-2.

MUELLER, J. W. (ed.), 1975, *Sampling in Archaeology*. Tucson, Ariz.: University of Arizona Press.

St. JOSEPH, J. K. S., 1966, "Air Photography and Archaeology," in J. K. S. St. Joseph (ed.), *The Uses of Air Photography*. London: John Baker.

———, 1972. Personal Communication.

STONE, K. H., 1960, Appendix in John H. Roccoe, "Photointerpretation in Geography," in *Manual of Photographic Interpretation*. Fallschurn, Va.: American Society of Photogrammetry.

WHITTLESEY, JULIAN H., 1967, "Balloon Over Sardis," *Archaeology* 20(1):67.

———, 1970, "Tethered Balloon for Archaeological Photos," *Photogrammetric Engineering* 36(6):181.

———, 1975, "Elevated and Airborne Photogrammetry and Stereo Photography," in Elmer Harp, Jr. (ed.), *Photography in Archaeological Research*. Albuquerque, N.M.: University of New Mexico Press.

Chapter 5

CHANG, K. C., 1958, "Study of the Neolithic Social Grouping: Examples from the New World," *American Anthropologist* 60:298-334.

CHISHOLM, M., 1968, *Rural Settlement and Land Use*. London: Hutchinson University Library.

CHORLEY, R. J., and P. HAGGETT, 1967, *Models in Geography*. London: Methuen.

CHRISTALLER, W., 1966, *Central Places in Southern Germany*, trans. C. W. Bashin. Englewood Cliffs, N.J.: Prentice-Hall.

CLARKE, D. L., 1968, *Analytical Archaeology*. London: Methuen.

CLARK, J. G. D., 1952, *Prehistoric Europe: The Economic Basis*. London: Methuen.

———, 1953, "The Economic Approach to Prehistory," *Proceedings of the British Academy* 39:215-238.

———, 1972, *Star Carr: A Case Study in Bioarchaeology*, Addison-Wesley Module. Reading, Mass.: Addison-Wesley.

COE, M. D., and K. V. FLANNERY, 1964, "Microenvironments and Mesoamerican Prehistory," *Science* 143:650–754.

DEETZ, J., 1967, *Invitation to Archaeology*. New York: Doubleday.

GRADY, J., 1980, *Environmental Factors in Archaeological Site Locations*, BLM Cultural Resource Series No. 9, Denver, Colorado.

GREENHUT, M. L., 1956, *Plant Location in Theory and Practice*. Chapel Hill, N.C.: University of North Carolina Press.

HAGGETT, P., 1965, *Locational Analysis in Human Geography*. London: Edward Arnold.

HAMMOND, N. D. C., 1972, "Locational Models and the Site of Lubaantun: A Classic Maya Centre," in D. L. Clarke, (ed.), *Models in Archaeology*. London: Methuen.

HARRIS, M., 1971, *Culture, Man, and Nature*. New York: Crowell.

HAURY, E. et al., 1955, "An Archaeological Approach to the Study of Cultural Stability," in R. Wauchope (ed.), *Seminars in Archaeology*, Society for American Archaeology, Memoir 11:31–58.

HESTER, J. J., 1962, "A Comparative Typology of New World Cultures," *American Anthropologist*, 64(5):1001–1015.

HESTER, J. J., and J. GRADY, 1977, "Paleoindian Social Patterns on the Llano Estacado," in Eileen Johnson, (ed.), "Paleoindian Lifeways," *The Museum Journal* XVII:78–96.

HIGGS, E. S., 1972, *Papers in Economic Prehistory*. Cambridge: Cambridge University Press.

———, 1975, *Paleoeconomy*. Cambridge: Cambridge University Press.

HODDER, I. R., 1972, "Locational Models and the Study of Romano-British Settlements," in D. L. Clarke (ed.), *Models in Archaeology*. London: Methuen.

HOLE, F., and R. F. HEIZER, 1969, *An Introduction to Prehistoric Archaeology*, 2ed. New York: Holt, Rinehart and Winston, Inc.

KRIEGER, D. A., 1953, Comment in S. Tax et al. (eds.), *An Appraisal of Anthropology Today*. Chicago: University of Chicago Press.

MARCUS, J. 1973, "Territorial Organization of the Lowland Classic Maya," *Science* 180:911–916.

MEGGERS, B. J., 1954, "Environmental Limitation on the Development of Culture," *American Anthropologist* 56(5):801–824.

MELTZER, D. J., 1979, "Paradigms and the Nature of the Change in American Archaeology," *American Antiquity* 44(4):644–657.

PLOG, F., and J. N. HILL, 1971, "Explaining Variability in the Distribution of Sites," in G. J. Gumerman, (ed.), *The Distribution of Prehistoric Population Aggregates*. Prescott, Ariz.: Prescott College Press.

SHARER, R., and W. ASHMORE, 1979, *Fundamentals of Archaeology*. Menlo Park, Calif.: Benjamin/Cummings.

STEWARD, J. H., 1938, "Basin-Plateau Aboriginal Sociopolitical Groups," *Bureau of American Ethnology Bulletin* 120. Washington, D.C.: Smithsonian Institution.

THOMAS, D. H., 1972, "A Computer Simulation Model of Great Basin Shoshonean Subsistence and Settlement Patterns," in D. L. Clarke (ed.), *Models in Archaeology*. London: Methuen.

———, 1973, "An Empirical Test for Steward's Model of Great Basin Patterns," *American Antiquity* 38:155–176.

TRIGGER, B. G., 1968, Determinants of Settlement Patterns," in K. C. Chang (ed.), *Settlement Archaeology*. Palo Alto, Calif.: National Press Books.

TYLOR, E. B., 1871, *Primitive Culture: Researches into the Development of Mythology, Philosophy, Religion, Language, Art, and Custom*. London: J. Murray.

VITA-FINZI, C., and E. S. HIGGS, 1970, "Prehistoric Economy in the Mt. Carmel Area of Palestine: Site Catchment Analysis," *Proceedings of the Prehistoric Society* 36(1–37).

WEBER, A., 1957, *Theory of the Location of Industries*. English Edition.

WILLEY, G. R., 1953, "Prehistoric Settlement Patterns in the Viru Valley, Peru," Bureau of American Ethnology Bulletin 155. Washington, D.C.: Smithsonian Institution.

WILLEY, G. R., 1966, *An Introduction to American Archaeology*, Vol. 1: *North and Middle America*. Englewood Cliffs, N.J.: Prentice-Hall.

———, 1971, *An Introduction to American Archaeology*, Vol. II: *South America*. Englewood Cliffs, N.J.: Prentice-Hall.

WILLEY, G. R., and P. PHILLIPS, 1958, *Method and Theory in American Archaeology*. Chicago: University of Chicago Press.

WITTFOGEL, K. A., 1955, "Developmental Aspects of Hydraulic Societies," in *Irrigation Civilizations:*

A Comparative Study. Washington, D.C.: Pan American Union.

Chapter 6

Anonymous, 1979, "Biology, Behavior and Environment in Human Evolution," *Mosaic* 10(2):2–11.

Birdsell, J. B., 1975, *Human Evolution*, 2d ed. New York: Hougton-Mifflin Co.

Boule, M., and H. V. Vallois, 1957, *Fossil Men*. London: Thames and Hudson.

Brace, C. L., H. Nelson, and N. Korn, 1971, *Atlas of Fossil Man*. New York: Holt, Rinehart and Winston, Inc.

Broderick, A. H., 1963, *Father of Prehistory; the Abbé Henri Breuil: His Life and Times*. New York: Morrow.

Butzer, K. W., 1969, "Geological Interpretation of Two Pleistocene Hominid Sites in the Lower Omo Basin," *Nature* 222:1138–1140

———, 1971, *Environment and Archaeology*, 2d ed. Chicago: Aldine-Atherton.

Day, M. H., 1965, *Guide to Fossil Man*. Cleveland: World Publishing.

de Lumley, H., and M. de Lumley, 1979, "L'Homine de Tautavel, le Premier Européen Connu," in *Dossiers de l'Archéologie 36*, Juillet (July).

Emiliani, C., 1966, "Paleotemperature Analysis of Caribbean Cores p 6304–8 and p 6304–9 and a Generalized Temperature Curve for the Past 425,-000 Years," *Journal of Geology* 74:109–126.

Falk, D., 1980, "Language, Handedness, and Primate Brains: Did the Australopithecines Sign?" *American Anthropologist* 82(1):72–78.

Haggett, P., 1965, *Locational Analysis in Human Geography*. London: Edward Arnold.

Harris, J. W. K., 1980, "Early Man," in A. Sherratt (ed.), *The Cambridge Encyclopedia of Archaeology*, New York: Crown; Cambridge: Cambridge University Press.

Harrisson, R. 1972, "The Prehistory of Borneo," *Asian Perspectives* XIII.

Howells, W. W., 1977, "Hominid Fossils," in *Paleoanthropology in the Peoples Republic of China*. Washington, D.C.: National Academy of Sciences.

Isaac, G., 1978, "The Food-sharing Behavior of Proto-human Hominids," *Scientific American* 238(4):90–108.

Johanson, D. C., and T. D. White, 1979, "A Systematic Assessment of Early African Hominids," *Science* 203, No. 4378:321–330.

Jolly, A., 1972, *The Evolution of Primate Behavior*. New York: Macmillan.

Kitahara-Frisch, J., 1980, "Apes and the Making of Stone Tools," *Current Anthropology* 21(3):359.

Leakey, M. D., and R. E. F. Leakey (eds.), 1978, *Koobi Fora Research Project*, Vol. 1, *The Fossils and an Introduction to Their Context*. Oxford: Oxford University Press.

Malez, M., F. H. Smith, J. Radovcic, and D. Rukavina, 1980, "Upper Pleistocene Hominids from Vindija, Croatia, Yugoslavia," *Current Anthropology* 21(3):365–366.

Peters, C. R., 1979, "Toward an Ecological Model of African Plio-Pleistocene Hominid Adaptations," *American Anthropologist* 81(2):261–278.

Rightmire, G. P., 1979, "Implications of Border Cave Skeletal Remains for Later Pleistocene Human Evolution," *Current Anthropology* 20(1):23–35.

Trinkhaus, E., and W. W. Howells, 1979, "The Neanderthals," *Scientific American* 241(6):118–133.

Von Koenigswald, G. H. R., 1962, *The Evolution of Man*. Ann Arbor: University of Michigan Press.

Washburn, S., 1978, "The Evolution of Man," *Scientific American* 239(3):194–208.

Watson, R. A., and P. J. Watson, 1969, *Man and Nature*. New York: Harcourt Brace Jovanovich.

Chapter 7

Biberson, P., 1961, "Le Paléolithique Inferior de Maroc Atlantique," *Service des Antiquités du Maroc* 17.

Bishop, W. W. and J. R., Clark, 1967 *Background to Evolution in Africa*. Chicago and London: University of Chicago Press.

Clark, J. D., 1970, *The Prehistory of Africa*. New York: Thames & Hudson Ltd.

Coles, J. M., and E. S. Higgs, 1969, *The Archaeology of Early Man*. Baltimore: Penguin.

COPPENS, Y., 1976, "The Great East African Adventure," *Centre National de la Research Scientifique* 3:2.

COPPENS, YVES, et al., 1976, *Earliest Man and Environments in the Lake Rudolf Basin.* Chicago: University of Chicago Press.

DART, R., 1955, "Cultural Status of the South African Man-Apes," *Annual Report.* Washington, D.C.: Smithsonian Institution.

————, 1957, "The Osteodontokeratic Culture of *Australopithecus Prometheus,*" Memoir Transvaal Museum, South African Republic.

FALK, DEAN 1980, "Language, Handedness, and Primate Brains: Did the Australopithecines Sign?" *American Anthropologist* 82(1):72–78.

FREEMAN, L. G., Jr., 1977, "Paleolithic Archaeology and Paleoanthropology in China," in W. W. Howells and P. J. Tsuchitani (eds.), *Paleoanthropology in the People's Republic of China.* Washington, D.C.: National Academy of Sciences, pp. 79–113.

HARRIS, J. W. K., 1980, "Early Man," in *The Cambridge Encyclopedia of Archaeology.* A. Sherratt (ed.), pp. 62–70. New York: Crown Publishers, Cambridge University Press.

ISAAC, C. L., J. W. K. HARRIS, and D. CRADER, 1976, "Archeological Evidence from the Koobi Fora Formation," in Yves Coppens, F. C. Howell, G. D. Isaac, and R. E. F. Leakey (eds.), *Earliest Man and Environments in the Lake Rudolf Basin,* pp. 533–551. Chicago: University of Chicago Press.

ISAAC, G. L., 1976, "Plio-Pleistocene Artifact Assemblage from East Rudolf, Kenya," in Coppens et al., 1976, pp. 552–564.

JURMAIN, R., H. NELSON, H. KURASHINA, and W. A. TURNBAUGH, 1981, *Understanding Physical Anthropology.* St. Paul, Minn.: West Publishing Co.

KRETZOI, M., and L. VERTES, 1965, "Upper Biharan (Intermindel) Pebble-Industry Occupation Site in Western Hungary," *Current Anthropology* 6:74–87.

LEAKEY, L. S. B., 1970, Personal Communication.

LEAKEY, M. D., 1967, "Preliminary Survey of the Cultural Material from Beds I and II, Olduvai Gorge, Tanzania," in W. W. Bishop and J. D. Clark (eds.), *Background to Evolution in Africa.* Chicago: University of Chicago Press, pp. 417–446.

MASON, R. T., 1962, *Prehistory of the Transvaal: A Record of Human Activity.* Johannesburg: Witwatersrand University Press.

OAKLEY, K. P., 1972, *Man The Toolmaker,* 6ed. London: British Museum.

OHEL, M. Y., 1979, "The Clactonian: An Independent Complex or an Integral Part of the Acheulean?" *Current Anthropology* 20(4):685–726.

STEKELIS ,M. 1966, *Archaeological Excavations at Ubeidiya 1960–1963.* Jerusalem: Israel Academy of Sciences and Humanities.

STILES, D., 1979, "Early Acheulean and Developed Olduwan," *Current Anthropology* 20(1):126–129.

TRINKAUS, E., and W. W. HOWELLS, 1979, "The Neanderthals," *Scientific American* 241(6):118–133.

WALKER, A., and R. E. F. LEAKEY, 1978, "The Hominids of East Turkana," *Scientific American* 239(2):44–56.

WASHBURN, S., 1978, "The Evolution of Man," *Scientific American* 239(3):194–208.

Chapter 8

BORDES, F., 1961, "Typologie Du Paléolithique Ancien et Moyen," Memoir 1, *Publications de l'Institute de Préhistoire de L'Université de Bordeaux.* Bordeaux: Delmas.

————, 1968, *The Old Stone Age,* World University Library. New York: McGraw-Hill.

CLARK, J. D., and C. V. HAYNES, JR., 1970, "An Elephant Butchery Site at Mwanganda's Village, Karonga, Malawi, and Its Relevance for Paleolithic Archaeology," *World Archaeology* 1(3):390–411.

de LUMLEY, H., 1969a, "A Paleolithic Camp at Nice," *Scientific American* 220:42–59.

————, 1969b, "Une Cambine Acheuleunne dans la Grotte du Lazaret (Nice)," *Memoirs de la Soci.ete-Prehistorique Francaise,* Tome 7.

de SONNEVILLE-BORDES, 1967, *La Prehistoire Moderne.* Perigueux: P. Fanlac.

EDWARDS, S. W., 1978, "Nonutilitarian Activities in the Lower Paleolithic: A Look at the Two Kinds of Evidence," *Current Anthropology* 19(1):135–317.

HOWELL, F. C., et al., 1965, *Early Man.* New York: Time/Life Books.

ISAAC, G. L., 1971, "The Diet of Early Man: Aspects of Archaeological Evidence from Lower and Middle Pleistocene Sites in Africa," *World Archaeology* 2(3):278–299.

———, 1977, *Olorgesailie: Archaeological Studies of a Middle Pleistocene Lake Basin in Kenya.* Chicago: University of Chicago Press.

LEE, R. B., and I. DEVORE (eds.), 1968, *Man the Hunter,* Chicago: Aldine.

OAKLEY, K. P., 1972, *Man the ToolMaker,* 6ed. London: British Museum.

SAMPSON, C. G., 1974, *The Stone Age Archaeology of Southern Africa.* New York and London: Academic Press.

WATSON, W. (with additions by G. G. SIEVEKING), 1968, *Flint Implements: An Account of Stone Age Techniques and Cultures,* 3ed. London: British Museum.

Chapter 9

Anonymous, 1979, "On the Emergence of Language," *Mosaic* 10(2):39–45.

ABLE, O., 1926, "How Neanderthal Man Hunted Cave Bears," *Natural History* 26(3):252–256.

BINFORD, L. R., and S. R. BINFORD, 1966, "A Preliminary Analysis of Functional Variability in the Mousterian of Levallois Facies," *American Anthropologist* 68, 2(2):238–95.

BORDES, F., 1968, *The Old Stone Age.* New York: McGraw-Hill.

———, 1972, *A Tale of Two Caves.* New York: Harper & Row.

BORDES, F., and D. de SONNEVILLE-BORDES, 1970, "The Significance of Variability in Paleolithic Assemblages," *World Archaeology* 2, No. 1:61–73.

BORDES F., and F. PRAT, 1966, "Observations sur les Faunes du Riss et du Würm I," *L'Anthropologie* 69:31–46.

BUTZER, K., 1971, *Environment and Archaeology,* 2ed. Chicago: Aldine-Atherton.

CLARK, J. D., 1979, "Radiocarbon Dating and African Archaeology," in R. Berger and H. Suess (eds.), *Radiocarbon Dating.* New Haven, Conn.: *American Journal of Science,* pp. 7–31.

CLARKE, D. L., 1972, "Models and Paradigms in Contemporary Archaeology," in D. L. Clarke (ed.), *Models in Archaeology.* London: Methuen.

FAIRSERVIS, W. A., 1975, *The Threshold of Civilization: an Experiment in Prehistory.* New York: Scribner's.

FREEMAN, L., 1980, "The Development of Human Culture," in Sherratt A., *The Cambridge Encyclopedia of Archaeology,* Trewin Copplestone Publishing Ltd., pp. 79–86.

LAVILLE, M., 1973, "The Relative Position of Mousterian Industries in the Climatic Chronology of the Early Würm in the Perigord," *World Archaeology,* 4(3):321–338.

MCBURNEY, C. B. M., 1950, "The Geographical Study of the Older Paleolithic Stages in Europe," *Proceedings of the Prehistoric Society* 16:163.

OAKLEY, K. P., 1972, *Man the ToolMaker,* 6ed. London: British Museum.

PEYRONY, D., 1934, "La Ferrassie-Mousterien, Perigordien, Aurignacian," *Prehistoire III:1–92.*

SAMPSON, C. G., 1974, *The Stone Age Archaeology of Southern Africa.* New York and London: Academic Press.

SHERRATT, A. (ed.), 1980, *The Cambridge Encyclopedia of Archaeology.* England Trewin Copplestone Publishing Ltd.

SOLECKI, R. S., 1963, "Prehistory in Shanidar Valley, Northern Iraq," *Science* 129(1551):179–193.

———, 1971, *Shanidar: The First Flower People.* New York: Knopf.

WATSON, W. (with additions by G. G. SIEVEKING), 1968, *Flint Implements: An Account of Stone Age Techniques and Cultures.* 3ed. London: British Museum.

Chapter 10

BORDES, F., 1968, *The Old Stone Age.* New York: McGraw-Hill.

BORDES, F., 1972, *A Tale of Two Caves.* New York: Harper and Row.

BUTZER, K. W., 1964, *Environment and Archaeology: An Introduction to Pleistocene Geography.* Chicago: Aldine.

CATON-THOMPSON G., 1952, *Kharga Oasis in Prehistory.* London: University of London, the Athlone Press.

CLARK, J. G. D., 1977, *World Prehistory in New Perspective*, 3ed. Cambridge, England; New York: Cambridge University Press.

COLES, J. M., and E. S. HIGGS, 1969, *The Archaeology of Early Man*. Harmondsworth, Middlesex, (England): Penguin.

CORNWALL, I., 1970, *Ice Ages: Their Nature and Effects*. London: John Baker.

de HEINZELIN, J., 1962, "Ishango," *Scientific American* 206(6):105–116.

EISELEY, L., 1955, "The PaleoIndians: Their Survival and Diffusion," in *New Interpretations of Aboriginal American Culture History*, 75th Anniversary Volume, Anthropological Society of Washington, Washington D.C.

FAIRSERVIS, W. A., Jr., 1975, *The Threshold of Civilization: An Experiment in Prehistory*. New York: Scribner's.

FORBES, A., Jr., and T. R. CROWDER, 1979, "The Problem of Franco-Cantabarian Abstract Signs: Agenda for a New Approach," *World Archaeology* 10(3):35–366.

FREEMAN, L., 1980, "The Development of Human Culture," in A. Sherratt *The Cambridge Encyclopedia of Archaeology*. Trewin Copplestone Publishing Ltd.

HAWKES, J., 1976, *The Atlas of Early Man*. New York: St. Martin's Press.

INSKEEP, R. R., 1979, *The Peopling of Southern Africa*. New York: Barnes & Noble.

LEROI-GOURHAN, A., 1967, *Treasures of Prehistoric Art*. New York: Abrams.

———, 1968, "The Evolution of Paleolithic Art, *Scientific American*, 218(2):59–79.

MARSHACK, A., 1972, *The Roots of Civilization*. New York: McGraw-Hill.

———, 1979, "Upper Paleolithic Symbol Systems of the Russian Plain: Cognitive and Comparative Analysis," *Current Anthropology* 20(2):271–311.

McBURNEY, C. B. M., 1960, *The Stone Age of Northern Africa*. Baltimore: Penguin.

———, 1967, *The Haua Fteah (Cyrenaica) and the Stone Age of the Southeast Mediterranean*. Cambridge: Cambridge University Press.

OAKLEY, K. P., 1972, *Man the ToolMaker*, 6ed. London: British Museum.

WATSON, W. (with additions by G. G. SIEVEKING), 1968, *Flint Implements: An Account of Stone Age Techniques and Cultures*, 3ed. London: British Museum.

Chapter 11

BORDAZ, J., 1970, *Tools of the Old and New Stone Age*. Garden City, N.Y.: Natural History Press.

BUTZER, K., 1971, *Environment and Archaeology*, 2ed. Chicago: Aldine-Atherton.

CLARK, J.D., 1959, *The Prehistory of Southern Africa*. London: Pelican.

———, 1970, *The Prehistory of Africa*. New York and Washington: Praeger.

CLARK, J. G. D., 1952, *Prehistoric Europe, The Economic Basis*. London: Methuen.

———, 1967, *The Stone Age Hunters*. New York: McGraw-Hill.

———, 1975, *The Earlier Stone Age Settlement of Scandinavia*. New York: Cambridge University Press.

———, 1977, *World Prehistory in New Perspective*, 3ed. Cambridge, England; New York: Cambridge University Press.

HAWKES, J., 1965, *History of Mankind, Cultural and Scientific Development*, Vol. I, Part I, *Prehistory*. New York: Mentor Books.

———, 1976, *The Atlas of Early Man*. New York: St. Martin's Press.

KLEIN, R. G., 1977, "Ecology of Early Man in Southern Africa," *Science* 197:115–126.

OAKLEY, K. P., 1972, *Man the ToolMaker*, 6ed. London: British Museum.

SAMPSON, C. G., 1974, *The Stone Age Archaeology of Southern Africa*. New York and London: Academic Press.

SREJOVIC, D., 1972, *Europe's First Monumental Sculpture: New Discoveries at Lepenski Vir*. New York: Stein and Day.

TRINGHAM, R., 1971, *Hunters, Fishers and Farmers of Eastern Europe, 6000–3000* B.C. London: Hutchinson University Library.

WENDORF, D. F., 1968, *The Prehistory of Nubia*, Vol. 2. Dallas: Southern Methodist University Press.

WERNICK, R., 1975, "Danubian Minicivilization Bloomed before Ancient Egypt and China," *Smithsonian* 5:34–41.

ZEUNER, F. E., 1958, *Dating the Past: An Introduction to Geochronology*, 3ed. London: Methuen.

Chapter 12

BENDER, B., 1975, *Farming in Prehistory, from Hunter-Gatherer to Food-Producer.* New York: St. Martin's Press.

BINFORD, L. R., 1968, "Post-Pleistocene Adaptations," in S. R. Binford and L. R. Binford (eds.), *New Perspectives in Archaeology*, Chicago: Aldine, pp. 313–341.

BRAIDWOOD, R. J., 1967, *Prehistoric Men*, 7ed. Glenview, Ill.: Scott, Foresman.

CHILDE, V. G., 1929, *The Most Ancient East.* London: Routledge and Kegan Paul.

——, 1953, "Old World Prehistory: Neolithic," in A. L. Kroeber (ed.), *Anthropology Today.* Chicago: University of Chicago Press, pp. 193–210.

COHEN, M. N., 1977, *The Food Crisis in Prehistory.* New Haven and London: Yale University Press.

——, 1977b, "Population Pressure and the Origins of Agriculture: An Archaeological Example from the Coast of Peru," in Reed, 1977, pp. 135–177.

FLANNERY, K. V., 1965, "The Ecology of Early Food Production in Mesopotamia," *Science* 147: 1247–1256.

——, 1968, "Archaeological Systems Theory and Early Mesoamerica," in B. J. Meggers (ed.), *Anthropological Archaeology in the Americas.* Washington, D.C.: Anthropological Society of Washington.

——, 1971, "Origins and Ecological Effects of Early Domestication in Iran and the Near East," in Streuver, pp. 50–79.

GORMAN, C. F., 1971, "The Hoabinhian and After: Subsistence Patterns in Southeast Asia during the Late Pleistocene and Early Recent Periods," *World Archaeology* 2:300.

HARLAN, J. R., 1971, "Agricultural Origins: Centers and Non-Centers," *Science* 174:468–474.

HARLAN, J. R., and D. ZOHARY, 1966, "Distribution of Wild Wheats and Barleys," *Science* 153:1074–1080.

HAWKES, J., 1976, *The Atlas of Early Man.* New York: St. Martin's Press.

HO, P. T., 1977, "The Indigenous Origins of Chinese Agriculture," in Reed, 1977, pp. 413–484.

HOLE, F., and K. V. FLANNERY, 1967, "The Prehistory of Southwest Iran: A Preliminary Report," *Proceedings of the Prehistoric Society* 32:147.

ISSAC, E., 1971, "On the Domestication of Cattle," in Stuart Struever (ed.), *Prehistoric Agriculture.* Garden City, New York: Natural History Press, pp. 451–470.

LUBBOCK, J., 1865, *Prehistoric Times.* London.

MACNEISH, R. S., 1977, "The Beginnings of Agriculture in Central Peru," in Reed, 1977, pp. 753–801.

MELLAART, J., 1965, *Earliest Civilizations of the Near East.* London: Thames and Hudson.

MEYERS, J. T., 1971, "The Origins of Agriculture: An Evolution of Three Hypotheses," in Struever, pp. 101–121.

REED, C. A., 1959, "Animal Domestication in the Prehistoric Near East," *Science* 130:1629.

——, 1961, "Osteological Evidence for Prehistoric Domestication in Southwestern Asia," *Zeitschrift für Tierzuchtung and Zuchturngsbiologie* 76:31.

——, 1969, "The Pattern of Animal Domestication in the Prehistoric Near East," in Ucko and Dimbleby, p. 361.

——, 1971, "Animal Domestication in the Prehistoric Near East," in Struever, pp. 423–450.

——, 1977, "A Model for the Origin of Agriculture in the Near East," in Reed, 1977, pp. 544–567.

——, 1977, "Origins of Agriculture: Discussion and Some Conclusions," in Reed, 1977, pp. 879–953.

——, 1977, *The Origins of Agriculture.* The Hague: Mouton.

RENFREW, J., 1969, "The Archaeological Evidence for the Domestication of Plants: Methods and Problems," in Ucko and Dimbleby, p. 149.

STRUEVER, S. (ed.), 1971, *Prehistoric Agriculture.* Garden City, N.Y.: Natural History Press.

UCKO, P. J., and G. W. DIMBLEDY (eds.), 1969, The Domestication and Exploitation of Plants and Animals. London: Duckworth.

VAN ZEIST, W., 1969, "Reflections on Prehistoric Environments in the Near East," in Ucko and Dimbleby, pp. 35–46.

VAVILOV, N. I., 1926, *Studies on the Origin of Culti-*

vated Plants. Leningrad: Institute de Botanique Appliquée et d'Amélienations des Plantes.

WENDORF, D. F., et al., 1979, "Use of Barley in the Egyptian Late Paleolithic," *Science* 205:1341–1347.

WRIGHT, H. E., Jr., 1977, "Environmental Change and the Origin of Agriculture in the Old and New Worlds," in Reed, 1977, pp. 281–318.

ZEUNER, F. E., 1963, *A History of Domesticated Animals*. London: Hutchinson.

Chapter 13

BRAIDWOOD, R. J., 1967, *Prehistoric Men*, 7ed. Glenview, Illinois: Scott, Foresman.

CHISHOLM, M., 1968, *Rural Settlement and Land Use*. London: Hutchinson University Library.

CLARK, J. G. D., 1977, *World Prehistory in New Perspective*, 3ed. Cambridge, England; New York: Cambridge University Press.

FAIRSERVIS, W. A., Jr., 1975, *The Threshold of Civilization: An Experiment in Prehistory*. New York: Scribner's.

HARRIS, D. R., 1977, "Alternative Pathways Toward Agriculture," in Reed, pp. 179–244.

HIGGS, E. S. (ed.), 1972, *Papers in Economic Prehistory*. Cambridge, London, and New York: Cambridge University Press.

LEE, R. B., 1967, "Kung Bushman Subsistence: An Input-Output Analysis," in A. P. Vayda (ed.), *Environment and Cultural Behavior*. Garden City, New York: Natural History Press.

MELLAART, J., 1975, *The Neolithic of the Near East*, New York: Scribner's.

MOORE, A. M. T., 1979, "A Pre-Neolithic Farmers' Village on the Euphrates," *Scientific American*, 241(2):62–70.

NOY, T., A. J. LEGGE, and E. S. HIGGS, 1973 "Excavations at Nahal Oren, Israel," *Proceedings of the Prehistoric Society*, 39.

OATES, J., 1972, "Prehistoric Settlement Patterns in Mesopotamia," in P. J. Ucko and G. W. Dimbleby (eds.), *Man, Settlement and Urbanism*. London: Duckworth.

PERKINS, D., 1964, "Prehistoric Fauna from Shanidar, Iraq," *Science* 144:1565.

REED, C. A. (ed.), 1977, *The Origins of Agriculture*. The Hague: Mouton.

VITA-FINZI, D., and E. S. HIGGS, 1970, "Prehistoric Economy in the Mount Carmel Area of Palestine: Site Catchment Analysis," *Proceedings of the Prehistoric Society* 36:1.

Chapter 14

BLEED, PETER, n.d.. Draft manuscript for Japanese National Encyclopedia.

——, 1972, "Yayoi Cultures of Japan: An Interpretive Summary," *Arctic Anthropology* Vol. IX(2).

——, 1974, "Patterns and Continuity in Protohistoric Japan," *Arctic Anthropology* Vol. XI (supplement).

——, 1978, "Origins of the Jomon Technical Tradition," *Asia Perspectives* Vol. XIX(1).

BRAIDWOOD, R. J., 1967, *Prehistoric Men*, 7 ed. Glenview, Ill.: Scott, Foresman.

CHANG, KWANG-CHIH, 1977, *The Archaeology of Ancient China*, 3d ed. New Haven: Yale University Press.

CLARK, J. G. D., 1952, *Prehistoric Europe: The Economic Basis*. London: Methuen.

——, 1977, *World Prehistory in New Perspective*. Cambridge: Cambridge University Press

GUILAINE, J., 1979,, "The Earliest Neolithic in the West Mediterranean," *Antiquity* Vol. LIII (204):22–30.

HAWKES, J., 1976, *The Atlas of Early Man*. New York: St. Martin's Press.

HESTER, J. J., and P. M. HOBLER, 1969, *Prehistoric Settlement Patterns in the Libyan Desert*, University of Utah Anthropological Papers, No. 92. Salt Lake City: University of Utah Press.

HOFFMAN, M. A., 1979, *Egypt Before the Pharaohs: The Prehistoric Foundations of Egyptian Civilization*. New York: Knopf.

IKAWA-SMITH, F., 1980, "Current Issues in Japanese Archaeology," *American Scientist* 68:134–145.

JARRIGE, J. F., and R. H. MEADOW, 1980, "Antecedents of Civilization in the Indus Valley," *Scientific American* 243 :12,122–5.

McBURNEY, C. B. M., 1967, *The Huah Fteah (Cyrenaica) and the Stone Age of the Southeast Mediterranean*. Cambridge, England: Cambridge University Press.

MELLAART, J., 1967, *Catal Huyuk, a Neolithic Town in Anatolia*. New York: McGraw-Hill.

———, 1975, *The Neolithic of the Near East*. New York: Scribner's.

PERKINS, D., Jr., 1972, "The Fauna of the Aq Kupruk Caves: A Brief Note," in L. Dupree (ed.), "Prehistoric Research in Afghanistan (1959–1966)," *Transactions of the American Philosophical Society* Vol. 62, Pt. 4.

PERKINS, D., Jr., and P. DALY, 1968, "A Hunter's Village in Neolithic Turkey," *Scientific American* 219 (1968):96–106.

PHILLIPS, P., 1975, *Early Farmers of West Mediterranean Europe*. London: Hutchinson.

PIGGOTT, S., 1965, *Ancient Europe from the Beginnings of Agriculture to Classical Antiquity*. Chicago: Aldine.

RAWSON, J., 1980, *Ancient China: Art and Archaeology*. London: British Museum.

REED, C. A. (ed.), 1977, *The Origins of Agriculture*. The Hague: Mouton.

SERIZAWA, C., 1980, "Choen-Kok-li." Paper read at University of Nebraska, Lincoln, Nebraska, March 1980.

SHAFFER, J. G., 1978, "The Later Prehistoric Periods," in F. R. Allchin and N. Hammond (eds.), *The Archaeology of Afghanistan*. New York, London, San Francisco: Academic Press.

TRINGHAM, R., D. Krstic, I. KAISER, and B. VOYTEK, 1980, "The Early Agricultural Site of Selevac, Yugoslavia," *Archaeology* 33(2):24–32.

VISHNU-MITTRE, 1977, "Changing Economy in Ancient India," in Reed, pp. 569–588.

WATSON, W. (with additions by G. G. SIEVEKING), 1968, *Flint Implements; An Account of Stone Age Techniques and Cultures*, 3. ed. London: British Museum.

WENDORF, D. F., et al., 1979, "Use of Barley in Egyptian Late Paleolithic," *Science* 205:1341–1347.

———, 1980, Personal communication.

Chapter 15

ADAMS, R. M., 1971, "Developmental Stages in Ancient Mesopotamia," in S. Struever (ed.), *Prehistoric Agriculture*. New York: Natural History Press, pp. 572–590.

———, 1973, "Patterns of Urbanization in Early Southern Mesopotamia," in R. Tringham (ed.), *Urban Settlements*. Andover, Mass.: Warner Modular Publications.

BADAWY, A., 1966, *Architecture in Ancient Egypt and the Near East*. Cambridge, Mass.: M.I.T. Press.

BEEK, M. A., 1962, *Atlas of Mesopotamia*. London: Thomas Nelson.

CHANG, K. C., 1973, "Radiocarbon Dates from China: Some Initial Interpretations," *Current Anthropology* 14(5):525–528.

CHOU, H. H., 1979, "Chinese Oracle Bones," *Scientific American* 240(4):100–109.

DANIEL, G., 1968, *The First Civilizations*, Apollo edition. New York: Crowell.

EDWARDS, I. E. S., 1952, *The Pyramids of Egypt*. Harmondsworth, Middlesex, England: Penguin.

EMERY, W. B., 1961, *Archaic Egypt*. Harmondsworth, Middlesex, England: Penguin.

FAIRSERVIS, W. A., Jr., 1975, *The Roots of Ancient India*, 2ed. Chicago: University of Chicago Press.

HAY, J., 1973, *Ancient China*. London: Bodley Head.

KRAMER, S. N., 1959, *History Begins at Sumer*. Garden City, N.Y.: Doubleday Anchor Books.

LLOYD, S., 1978, *The Archaeology of Mesopotamia*. London: Thames and Hudson.

MASRY, A. H., 1975, *An Introduction to Saudi Arabian Antiquities*. Department of Antiquities and Museums, Ministry of Education, Kingdom of Saudi Arabia.

OATES, J., T. E. DAVIDSON, D. KAMILLI, and H. McKERRELL, 1977, "Seafaring Merchants of Ur," *Antiquity*, Vol. LI, No. 204:221–234.

PIGGOTT, S., 1961, *The Dawn of Civilization*. New York: McGraw-Hill.

STEWARD, J. H., 1971, "Some Implications of the Symposium," in S. Struever (ed.), *Prehistoric Agriculture*. New York: Natural History Press.

WHEELER, M., 1961, "Ancient India: The Civilization of a Subcontinent," in S. Piggott (ed.), *The Dawn of Civilization*. New York: McGraw-Hill.

Chapter 16

ATKINSON, R. J. C., 1956, *Stonehenge*. Harmondsworth, Middlesex, England: Penguin Books.

———, 1978, *Stonehenge and Neighboring Monuments*. Department of the Environment, London.

BRAIDWOOD, R. J., 1967, *Prehistoric Men*, 7ed. Glenview, Ill.: Scott, Foresman.

CHILDE, V. G., 1958, *The Prehistory of European Society*. Baltimore: Penguin.

CLARK, J. G. D., 1952, *Prehistoric Europe: The Economic Basis*. London: Methuen.

——, 1977, *World Prehistory in New Perspective*. Cambridge, England: Cambridge University Press.

COLES, J. M., and A. F. HARDING, 1979, *The Bronze Age in Europe*. London: Methuen.

COWAN, T. M., 1970, "Megalithic Rings: Their Design Construction," *Science* 168:321–325.

DANIEL, G., 1980, "Megalithic Monuments," *Scientific American*, 242(1):78–90.

EDGERTON, H., 1960, "New Light on an Old Riddle, Stonehenge," *National Geographic Magazine* 117(6):346–366.

GREEN, T., 1978, "Modern Britons Try the Iron Age, Find They Like It," *Smithsonian Magazine*, 9(3):80–87.

HAWKES, C., and J. HAWKES, 1949, *Prehistoric Britain*. Harmondsworth, Middlesex, England: Pelican.

HAWKINS, G., 1965, *Stonehenge Decoded*. New York: Doubleday.

HUTCHINSON, G. E., 1972, "Long Meg Reconsidered," *American Scientist* 60:24–31, 210–219.

PIGGOTT, S., 1965, *Ancient Europe from the Beginnings of Agriculture to Classical Antiquity*. Chicago: Aldine.

POWELL, T. G. E., 1963, *The Celts*. London: Thames and Hudson.

RENFREW, C., 1971, "Carbon 14 and the Prehistory of Europe," *Scientific American* 225(4):63–72.

THOM, A., 1967, *Megalithic Sites in Britain*. London: Oxford University Press.

——, 1971, *Megalithic Lunar Observations*. Oxford: Clarendon Press.

TRINGHAM, R., D. KRISTIC, T. KAISER, and B. VOYTEK, 1980, "The Early Agricultural Site of Selevac, Yugoslavia," *Archaeology* 33(2):24–32.

WHEELER, R. E. M., 1943, *Maiden Castle*. London: Dorset.

Chapter 17

ADOVASIO, J. M., J. D. GUNN, J. DONAHUE, R. STUCKENRATH, J. E. GUILDAY, and K. VOLMAN, 1980, "Yes, Virginia, It Really Is That Old: A Reply to Haynes and Mead," *American Antiquity* 45(3):588–595.

ANDERSON, D., and B. ANDERSON, 1976, *Chaco Canyon*, Globe, Arizona: Southwest Parks and Monuments Association.

BERGER, R., 1978, "Thoughts on the First Peopling of America and Australia," in Bryan, pp. 23–24.

BONNICHSEN, R., 1978, "Critical Arguments for Pleistocene Artifacts from the Old Crow Basin, Yukon: A Preliminary Statement," in Bryan, 1978, pp. 102–118.

BORDES, F., 1978, Preface in Bryan, pp. v–vi.

BRYAN, A. L., (ed.), 1978, *Early Man in America from a Circum-Pacific Perspective*. Occasional Paper No. 1 of the Department of Anthropology, University of Alberta. Edmonton, Canada: Archaeological Researches International.

BUTZER, K. W., 1971, *Environment and Archaeology*, 2ed. Chicago: Aldine.

CALDWELL, J. R., 1958, *Trend and Tradition in the Prehistory of the Eastern United States*. Washington, D.C.: American Anthropological Association, Memoir No. 88.

ENGLAND, J., and R. S. BRADLEY, 1978, "Past Glacial Activity in the Canadian High Arctic," *Science* 200 (4339):265–270.

FLADMARK, K. R., 1978, "The Feasibility of the Northwest Coast as a Migration Route for Early Man," in Bryan, pp. 119–128.

FLINT, R. E., 1971, *Glacial and Quaternary Geology*. New York: Wiley.

GREENMAN, E. F., 1963, "The Upper Paleolithic of the New World," *Current Anthropology* 4(1):41–91.

HAYNES, C. V., 1980, "Paleoindian Charcoal from Meadowcroft Rockshelter: Is Contamination a Problem?" *American Antiquity* 45(3):582–587.

HAYASHI, K., 1968, "The Fukui Microblade Technology and Its Relationships in Northeast Asia and North America," *Arctic Anthropology* V(1):128–190.

HESTER, J. J., 1976, *Introduction to Archaeology*. New York: Holt, Rinehart and Winston.

HESTER, J. J., and J. GRADY, 1977, "Paleoindian Social Patterns on the Llano Estacado," in E. Johnson (ed.), *Paleoindian Lifeways*, pp. 78–96, The Museum Journal XVII. Lubbock, Tex.: West Texas Museum Association.

HOPKINS, D. M., 1967, "The Cenozoic History of Beringia—a Synthesis," in D. M. Hopkins (ed.), *The Bering Land Bridge*. Palo Alto, Calif.: Stanford University Press, pp. 451–484.

HOWELL, F. C., 1965, *Early Man*. New York: Time/Life Books.

KLEIN, R. G., 1971, "The Pleistocene Prehistory of Siberia," *Quaternary Research* Vol. 1 (2):pp. 133–161.

KOBAYASHI, T., 1970, "Microblade Industries in the Japanese Archipelago," *Arctic Anthropology* Vol. VII: 38–58.

KREIGER, A., 1964, "Early Man in the New World," in J. D. Jennings and E. Norbeck (eds.), *Prehistoric Man in the New World*. Chicago: University of Chicago Press.

LEE, R. B., and I. DeVORE, 1968, *Man the Hunter*. Chicago: Aldine.

MacNEISH, R. S., 1971, "Early Man in the Andes," *Scientific American* 224(4):36–46.

MARTIN, P. S., 1967, "Prehistoric Overkill," in Martin and Wright, pp. 75–120.

———, 1973, "The Discovery of America," *Science* 179:969–974.

MARTIN, P. S., and J. E. GUILDAY, 1967, "A Bestiary for Pleistocene Biologists," in Martin and Wright, pp. 1–66.

MARTIN, P. S., and H. E. WRIGHT, Jr., (eds.), 1967, *Pleistocene Extinctions: The Search for a Cause*. New Haven, Conn.: Yale University Press.

MEAD, J. I., 1980, "Is It Really That Old? A Comment about the Meadowcroft Rockshelter, 'Overview'," *American Antiquity* 45(3):579–582.

MEGGERS, B. J., C. EVANS, and E. ESTRADA, 1965, *Early Formative Period of Coastal Ecuador*, Smithsonian Institution Contributions to Anthropology No. 1, Washington, D.C.

MOCHANOV, I. A., 1978, "The Paleolithic of Northeast Asia and the Problem of the First Peopling of America," in Bryan, p. 67.

MORLAN, R., 1967a, "The Preceramic Period of Hokkaido: An Outline," *Arctic Anthropology* Vol. IV(1):164–220.

———, 1967b, "Chronometric Dating in Japan," *Arctic Anthropology* IV(2):180–211.

MÜLLER-BECK, H., 1967, "On Migrations of Hunters Across the Bering Land Bridge in the Upper Pleistocene," in D. M. Hopkins (ed.), *The Bering Land Bridge*. Palo Alto, Calif.: Stanford University Press, pp. 373–408.

PROTCH, R., 1979, "New Absolute Dates on Upper Pleistocene Fossil Hominids from America," in R. Berger and H. E. Suess (eds.), *Radiocarbon Dating*. Berkeley, Los Angeles, London: University of California Press, pp. 69–75.

STANFORD, D., 1979, "Afterword: Resolving the Question of New World Origins," in R. L. Humphrey and D. Stanford (eds.), *Pre-Llano Cultures of the Americas: Paradoxes and Possibilities*, pp. 147–150.

WENDORF, D. F., and J. J. HESTER, 1962, "Early Man's Utilization of the Great Plains Environment," *American Antiquity* 28(2):159–171.

———, 1975, *Late Pleistocene Environments of the Southern High Plains*, Publication No. 9 of the Fort Burgwin Research Center. Dallas: Southern Methodist University Press.

WHEAT, J. B., 1967, "A Paleo-Indian Bison Kill," *Scientific American* 216(1):44–52.

———, 1972, "The Olsen-Chubbock Site: A Paleo-Indian Bison Kill," *Memoirs of the Society for American Archaeology*, No. 26.

WHITE, J. P., and J. F. O'CONNELL, 1979, "Australian Prehistory: New Aspects of Antiquity," *Science* 203(4375):21–28.

WILLEY, G. R., 1966, *An Introduction to American Archaeology*, Vol. I. Englewood Cliffs, N.J.: Prentice-Hall.

———, 1971, *An Introduction to American Archaeology*, Vol. II. Englewood Cliffs, N.J.: Prentice-Hall.

WORMINGTON, H. M., n.d., *The Ancient Hunters and Gatherers of the Americas*. In press. New York: Academic Press.

Chapter 18

BEADLE, G. W., 1980a, "The Ancestry of Corn," *Scientific American* 242(1):112–119; 1980b, "Letter," *Scientific American* 242(4):8.

BEARDSLEY, R. K., et al., 1955, "Functional and Evolutionary Implications of Community Patterning," in R. Wauchope (ed.), *Seminars in Archaeology*. Society for American Archaeology, Memoir No. 11.

BYERS, D. S., 1959, "An Introduction to Five Papers on the Archaic Stage," *American Antiquity* 24:229–232.

BYERS, D. S. (ed.), 1967, *The Prehistory of the Tehuacan Valley*, Vol. 1, Austin: University of Texas Press.

CALDWELL, J. R., 1958, *Trend and Tradition in the Prehistory of the Eastern United States.* American Anthropological Association, Memoir No. 88. Washington, D.C.

COHEN, M. N., 1977, *The Food Crisis in Prehistory: Overpopulation and the Origins of Agriculture.* New Haven and London: Yale University Press.

CONOVER, K., 1978, "Matrix Analysis," in J. J. Hester and S. M. Nelson (eds.), *Studies in Bella Bella Prehistory.* Department of Archaeology, Simon Fraser University, Publication No. 5:67–99. Burnaby, British Columbia.

DINCAUZE, D. F., 1971, "An Archaic Sequence for Southern New England," *American Antiquity* 32(2):194–198.

ENGEL, F., 1964, "El Preceramico sin Algodon en la Costa del Peru," *35 Congresa Internacional de Americanistas, Actas y Memorias* 3:141–152. Mexico.

FITTING, J. E., 1969, "Settlement Analysis in the Great Lakes Region," *Southwestern Journal of Anthropology* 25(4):360–377.

FLANNERY, K. V., 1967, "The Vertebrate Fauna and Hunting Patterns," in Byers, 1967, pp. 132–188.

———, 1971, "Archaeological Systems Theory and Early Mesoamerica," in S. Struever (ed.), *Prehistoric Agriculture.* New York: Natural History Press, pp. 80–100.

FUNK, R. G., 1978, "Post-Pleistocene Adaptations," in Trigger, pp. 16–27.

GRADY, J., 1976, *Preliminary Report on the Excavation of "Square S" Rock Shelter (5RB271), Rio Blanco County, Colorado.* Craig, Colo.: Bureau of Land Management District Office.

———, 1980, *Environmental Factors in Archaeological Site Locations.* Bureau of Land Management, Denver, Colorado, Cultural Resource Series, No. 9.

GRIFFIN, J. B., 1978, "The Midlands and Northeastern United States," in Jennings, 1978, pp. 221–279.

JENNINGS, J. D., 1968, *Prehistory of North America.* New York: McGraw-Hill.

———, 1978, *Ancient Native Americans*, San Francisco: Freeman.

JENNINGS, J. D., and E. NORBECK, 1955, "Great Basin Prehistory: A Review," *American Antiquity* 21:1–11.

KAPLAN, L., T. F. LYNCH, and C. E. SMITH, 1973, "Early Cultivated Beans *(Phaseolus vulgaris)* from an Intermountain Peruvian Valley," *Science* 179:76–77.

LANNING, E., 1963, "A Preagricultural Occupation on the Central Coast of Peru," *American Antiquity* 28:360–371.

LIPE, W. D., 1979, "The Southwest," in Jennings, 1979.

LISCHKA, J. J., 1975, *Periodic Catastrophism on the Peruvian Coast.* Paper presented at the annual meeting of the Society for American Archaeology.

LUMBRERAS, L. G., 1974, *The Peoples and Cultures of Ancient Peru.* Washington, D.C.: Smithsonian Institution Press.

MacNEISH, R. S., 1964a, "The Origins of New World Civilization," *Scientific American* 211(5):29–37.

———, 1964b, "Ancient Mesoamerican Civilization," *Science* 143:531–537.

———, 1967, "A Summary of Subsistence," in Byers, 1967.

———, 1971, "Early Man in the Andes," *Scientific American* 224(4):34–46.

———, 1977, "The Beginning of Agriculture in Central Peru," in C. A. Reed (ed.), *The Origins of Agriculture.* The Hague: Mouton.

MacNEISH, R. S., A. Nelken-Terner, and I. W. Johnson, 1967, *The Prehistory of the Tehuacan Valley*, Vol. 2: *The Nonceramic Artifacts.* Austin: University of Texas Press.

MANGELSDORF, P. C., 1980, Letter in Response to G. W. Beadle, 1980, *Scientific American* Vol. 242(4):8.

MANGELSDORF, P. C., R. S. MacNEISH, and G. R. WILLEY, 1964, "Origins of Middle American Agriculture," in R. J. Wauchope and R. C. West (eds.), *Handbook of Middle American Indians*, Vol. 1. Austin: University of Texas Press, pp. 427–445.

MEIGHAN, C. W., 1959, "California Cultures and the Concept of an Archaic Stage," *American Antiquity* 24:289–305.

NIEDERBERGER, C., 1979, "Early Sedentary Economy in the Basin of Mexico," *Science* 203(4376):131–142.

RITCHIE, W. A., 1969, *The Archaeology of New York State*, Rev. ed. Garden City, N.Y.: Natural History Press.

———, 1971, "The Archaic in New York State," *New*

York State Archaeological Bulletin 52(July):2–12.

SANDERS, W. T., and J. MARINO, 1970, *New World Prehistory*. Englewood Cliffs, N.J.: Prentice-Hall.

STEWARD, J. H., 1938, *Basin-Plateau Aboriginal Sociopolitical Groups*. B.A.E. Bulletin 120. Washington, D.C.

THOMAS, D. H., 1972, "A Computer Simulation Model of Great Basin Shoshonean Subsistence and Settlement Patterns," in D. L. Clarke (ed.), *Models in Archaeology*, pp. 671–704. London: Methuen.

——, 1973, "An Empirical Test for Steward's Model of Great Basin Patterns," *American Antiquity* 38:155–176.

TRIGGER, B. G., 1978, *Handbook of North American Indians*, Vol. 15. Washington, D.C.: Smithsonian Institution.

TUCK, J. A. 1978, Regional Cultural Development, 3000 to 300 B.C.," in Trigger, pp. 28–43.

Chapter 19

ADAMS, R. E. W., 1977, *Prehistoric Mesoamerica*, Boston: Little, Brown.

ANDERSON, D., and B. ANDERSON, 1976, *Chaco Canyon*. Globe, Ariz.: Southwest Parks and Monuments Association.

BENNETT, W., and J. BIRD, 1964, *Andean Culture History*, 2d ed. New York: Natural History Press.

COE, M. D., 1960, "Archaeological Linkages with North and South America at La Victoria, Guatemala," *American Anthropologist* Vol. 62:363–393.

——, 1967, *Mexico*. Mexico: Ediciones Lara.

——, 1977, *Mexico*, 2ed. New York: Praeger.

DRUCKER, P., R. HEIZER, and R. J. SQUIER, 1959, *Excavations at La Venta, Tabasco, 1955*, B. A. E. Bulletin 170. Washington, D.C.: U.S. Government Printing Office.

FORD, J. A., 1969, *A Comparison of Formative Cultures in the Americas*. Washington, D.C.: Smithsonian Institution Press.

HAMMOND, N., 1977, "The Earliest Maya," *Scientific American* 236(24):116–133.

LUMBRERAS, L. G., 1974, *The Peoples and Cultures of Ancient Peru*. Washington, D.C.: Smithsonian Institution Press.

McEWAN, G. F., and D. B. DICKSON, 1978, "Valdivia, Jomon Fishermen and the Nature of the North Pacific: Some Nautical Problems with Meggers, Evans, and Estrada's (1965) Transoceanic Contact Thesis," *American Antiquity* 43(3):362–376.

MEGGERS, B. J., 1979, "Climate Oscillation as a Factor in the Prehistory of Amazonia," *American Antiquity* 44(2):252–266.

MEGGERS, B. J., C. EVANS, and E. ESTRADA, 1965, *Early Formative Period of Coastal Ecuador: The Valdivia and Machallilla Phases*. Washington, D.C.: Smithsonian Institution Press.

MORGAN, W. N., 1980, *Prehistoric Architecture in the Eastern United States*. Cambridge, Mass. and London: MIT Press.

STEWARD, J. H., 1957, *Theory of Culture Change*. Urbana, Ill.: University of Illinois Press.

WILLEY, G. R., 1966, *An Introduction to American Archaeology*, Vol. I: *North and Middle America*. Englewood Cliffs, N.J.: Prentice-Hall.

——, 1971, *An Introduction to American Archaeology*, Vol. II: *South America*. Englewood Cliffs, N.J.: Prentice-Hall.

WILLEY, G. R., and P. PHILLIPS, 1958, *Method and Theory in American Archaeology*. Chicago: University of Chicago Press.

Chapter 20

ADAMS, R. E. W., 1977, *Prehistoric Mesoamerica*. Boston: Little, Brown.

——, 1980, "Swamps, Canals, and the Locations of Ancient Maya Cities," *Antiquity* LIV, p. 206.

BENNETT, W., and J. BIRD, 1964, *Andean Culture History*. Garden City, N.Y.: Natural History Press.

BREWBAKER, J., 1979. Personal communication.

COE, M. D., 1977, *Mexico*, 2ed. New York: Praeger.

CULBERT, T. P., 1974, *The Lost Civilization: The Story of the Classic Maya*. New York: Harper & Row.

——, 1979, "Mesoamerica," in J. D. Jennings (ed.), *Ancient Native Americans*. San Francisco: Freeman.

DEUEL, L., 1967, *Conquistadors without Swords: Archaeologists in the Americas*. New York: St. Martin's.

DONNAN, C. B., 1976, *Moche Art of Peru*. Los Angeles: Museum of Cultural History, U.C.L.A.

FOLAN, W. J., L. A. FLETCHER, and E. R. KINTZ, 1979, "Fruit, Fiber, Bark, and Resin: Social Organization of a Maya Urban Center," *Science* (204) 4394:697–701.

HAMBLIN, R. L., and B. L. PITCHER, 1980, "The Classic Maya Collapse: Testing Class Conflict Hypotheses," *American Antiquity* 45(2):246–267.

HARRISON, P. D., and B. L. TURNER II, 1978, *Pre-Hispanic Maya Agriculture*. Albuquerque, N.M.: University of New Mexico Press.

LUMBRERAS, L. G., 1974, *The Peoples and Cultures of Ancient Peru*. Washington, D.C.: Smithsonian Institution Press.

MARCUS, J., 1973, "Territorial Organization of the Lowland Classic Maya," *Science* 180:911–916.

MILLON, R. 1970, "Teotihuacan: Completion of Map of Giant Ancient City in the Valley of Mexico," *Science* 170:1077–1082.

MILLON, R. (ed.), 1973, *Urbanization at Teotihuacan, Mexico*, Vol. I: *The Teotihuacan Map*. Austin, Tex.: University of Texas Press.

MORLEY, S., 1946, *The Ancient Maya*. Stanford, Calif.: Stanford University Press.

MORLEY, S., and G. BRAINERD, 1956, *The Ancient Maya*, 3d ed. Stanford, Calif.: Stanford University Press.

MORRIS, E. H., 1931, *The Temple of the Warriors at Chichen Itza, Yucatan*. Carnegie Institution of Washington Publications, No. 406. Washington, D.C.

PRICE, B. J., 1976, "A Chronological Framework for Cultural Development in Mesoamerica," in E. R. Wolf (ed.), *The Valley of Mexico*. Albuquerque, N.M.: School of American Research, University of New Mexico.

PROSKOURIAKOFF, T., 1946, *An Album of Maya Architecture*. Carnegie Institution of Washington Publications, No. 558. Washington, D.C.

———, 1960, "Historical Implications of a Pattern of Dates at Piedras Negras, Guatemala," *American Antiquity* 25:454–475.

———, 1961, "The Lords of the Maya Realm," *Expedition* 4:14–21.

———, 1963, "Historical Data in the Inscriptions of Yaxchilan I," *Estudios de Cultural Maya* 3:149–167.

———, 1964, "Historical Data in the Inscriptions of Yaxchilan II," *Estudios de Cultural Maya* 4:177–201.

RUPPERT, K., 1935, *The Caracol at Chichen Itza*. Carnegie Institution of Washington Publications, No. 454. Washington, D.C.

SABLOFF, J. A., and G. R. WILLEY, 1967, "The Collapse of Maya Civilization in the Southern Lowlands: A Consideration of History and Process," *Southwestern Journal of Anthropology* 23:311–336.

SANDERS, W. T., J. R. PARSONS, and M. H. LOGAN, 1976, "Summary and Conclusions," in E. R. Wolf (ed.), *The Valley of Mexico*. Albuquerque, N.M.: School of American Research, University of New Mexico Press.

SHEETS, P. D., 1979, "Maya Recovery from Volcanic Disasters Ilopango and Ceren," *Archaeology* 32(3):32–42.

STEPHENS, J. L., 1843, *Incidents of Travel in Central America, Chiapas, and Yucatan*, 2 vols. New York: Harper & Row.

WAUCHOPE, R., 1965, *They Found the Buried Cities*. Chicago: University of Chicago Press.

WILLEY, G. R., 1966, *An Introduction to American Archaeology*, Vol. I: *North and Middle America*. Englewood Cliffs, N.J.: Prentice-Hall.

———, 1971, *An Introduction to American Archaeology*, Vol. II: *South America*. Englewood Cliffs, N.J.: Prentice-Hall.

———, 1977, "The Rise of Maya Civilization: A Summary View," in R. E. W. Adams (ed.), *The Origins of Maya Civilization*. Albuquerque: School of American Research, University of New Mexico Press.

Chapter 21

BENNETT, W., and J. BIRD, 1964, *Andean Culture History*, 2ed. New York: Natural History Press.

BERNAL, I., 1963, *Mexico Before Cortez*. New York: Doubleday.

COE, M. D., 1966, *The Maya*. London: Thames and Hudson.

DIBBLE, C. E., and A. J. O. ANDERSON (trans.), 1957, *Florentine Codex, Parts V and VI*, No. 14. Salt Lake City: School of American Research, University of Utah.

DUTTON, B. P., 1955, "Tula of the Toltecs," *El Palacio* 62(7–8):195–251.

ISBELL, W. H., and K. J. SCHREIBER, 1978, "Was Huari a State?" *American Antiquity* 43(3):372–389.

LUMBRERAS, L. G., 1974, *The Peoples and Cultures of Ancient Peru*. Washington, D.C.: Smithsonian Institution Press.

MORLEY, S., and G. BRAINERD, 1956, *The Ancient Maya*, 3ed. Stanford, Calif.: Stanford University Press.

MOSELEY, M. E., 1975, "Chan Chan: Andean Alternative to the Preindustrial City," *Science* 187 (4173):219–225.

MOSELEY, M. D., and C. J. MACKEY, 1973, "Chan Chan, Peru's Ancient City of Kings," *National Geographic* 143(3):318–345.

SCHAEDEL, R., 1951, "Major Ceremonial and Population Centers in Northern Peru," in *Civilizations of Ancient America*. Selected Papers of the XXIX International Congress of Americanists. Chicago: University of Chicago Press.

VAILLANT, G. C., 1944, *The Aztecs of Mexico*. Harmondsworth, Middlesex, England: Pelican.

———, 1950, *The Aztecs of Mexico*. Suffolk: Pelican.

WILLEY, G. R., 1971, *An Introduction to American Archaeology*, Vol. II: *South America*. Englewood Cliffs, N.J.: Prentice-Hall.

Chapter 22

CAMPBELL, J. and L. S. CORDELL, 1975, "The Arctic and Subarctic," in S. Gorenstein (ed.), *North America*, St. Martin's Series in Prehistory. New York: St. Martin's Press.

CHOMKO, S. A. and G. W. CRAWFORD, 1978, "Plant Husbandry in Prehistoric Eastern North America: New Evidence for its Development," *American Antiquity* 43(3):405–408.

ELSASSER, A. B., 1978, "Development of Regional Prehistoric Cultures," in R. F. Heizer (ed.), *Handbook of North American Indians*, Vol. 8: *California*. Washington: Smithsonian Institution Press.

FORBIS, R. G., 1975, "Eastern North America," in S. Gorenstein (ed.), *North America*, St. Martin's Series in Prehistory. New York: St. Martin's Press.

GRIFFIN, J. P., 1980, "Agricultural Groups in North America," in A. Sherratt (ed.), *The Cambridge Encyclopedia of Archaeology*. Trewin Copplestone Publishing Ltd.

HAMMOND, G. P., and A. REY, 1940, *Narratives of the Coronado Expedition 1540-1542*. Albuquerque: University of New Mexico Press.

HARP, ELMER, JR., 1978, "Pioneer Cultures of the Sub Arctic and the Arctic," in J. D. Jennings (ed.), *Ancient Native Americans*. San Francisco, Calif.: Freeman.

HESTER, J. J., 1962, "A Comparative Typology of New World Cultures," *American Anthropologist* 64(5):1001–1015.

HESTER, J. J. and S. N. NELSON (eds.), 1978, *Studies in Bella Bella Prehistory*. Simon Fraser University Publication No. 5. Burnaby, B.C.

LATHRAP, D. W., 1970, *The Upper Amazon*. New York: Praeger.

LIPE, W. D., 1978, "The Southwest," in J. D. Jennings (ed.), *Ancient Native Americans*. San Francisco, Calif.: Freeman.

MEGGERS, B. J., 1954, "Environmental Limitation on the Development of Culture," *American Anthropologist* 56:801–824.

———, 1979, "Climatic Oscillation as a Factor in the Prehistory of Amazonia," *American Antiquity* 44(2):252–266.

MEGGERS, B. J., and C. EVANS, 1978, "Lowland South America and the Antilles," in J. D. Jennings (ed.), *Ancient Native Americans*. San Francisco, Calif.: Freeman.

SANDERS, W. T., and J. MARINO, 1970, *New World Prehistory*. Englewood Cliffs, N.J.: Prentice-Hall.

WEDEL, W., 1978, "The Prehistoric Plains," in J. D. Jennings (ed.), *Ancient Native Americans*. San Francisco, Calif.: Freeman.

WILLEY, G. R., 1966, *An Introduction to American Archaeology*, Vol. I: *North and Middle America*. Englewood Cliffs, N.J.: Prentice-Hall.

Chapter 23

Anonymous, 1979, *Guide to Departments of Anthropology*. Washington, D.C.: American Anthropological Association.

COTTER, J. L., 1979, "Archaeologists of the Future: High Schools Discover Archaeology," *Archaeology* 32(1):29–35.

DAVIS, H. A., 1971, "Is There a Future for the Past?" *Archaeology* 24:300–306.

———, 1972, "The Crisis in American Archaeology," *Science* 176:267–272.

FRANTZ, C., 1972, *The Student Anthropologist's Handbook: A Guide to Research, Training, and Career.* Cambridge, Mass.: General Learning Press.

KING, T. F., 1978, *The Archeological Survey: Methods and Uses.* Washington, D.C.: Cultural Resource Management Studies, HCRS, U.S. Department of Interior.

KING, T. F., P. P. HICKMAN, and G. BERG, 1977, *Anthropology in Historic Preservation: Caring for Culture's Clutter.* New York: Academic Press.

McGIMSEY, C. R., III, 1972, *Public Archaeology.* New York: Seminar Press.

McGIMSEY, C. R., III, and H. DAVIS, 1977, *The Management of Archaeological Resources: The Airlie House Report.* Special Publication of The Society for American Archaeology. Washington, D.C.

ROWE, J., 1954, "Archaeology as a Career," *Archaeology,* Vol. 7:229–236.

———, 1961, "Archaeology as a Career," *Archaeology,* Vol. 14(1), 45–55.

SCHIFFER, N. B., and G. GUMERMAN (eds.), 1977, *Conservation Archaeology.* New York: Academic Press.

TALMADGE, V., and O. CHESLER, 1977, *The Importance of Small Surface, and Disturbed Sites as Sources of Significant Archeological Data.* Washington, D.C.: Cultural Resource Management Studies, National Park Service, U.S. Department of the Interior.

Chapter 8 (addition)

SHIPMAN, P., W. BOSLER and K. L. DAVIS, 1981, "Butchering of Giant Geladas at an Acheulian Site." *Current Anthropology,* Vol. 22 (3): 257–264. University of Chicago Press.

ISAAC, G. Ll. 1977, *Olorgesailie: Archeological Studies of a Middle Pleistocene Lake Basin in Kenya.* Chicago, Ill.: University of Chicago Press.

INDEX

Page numbers in italic denote illustrations.

ACKNOWLEDGMENTS

1-1, 1-2: J. Hester, P. M. Hobler, and Russell, "New Evidence of Early Roads in Nubia," *American Journal of Archaeology*, Vol. 74:386-389 (1970). **1-3, 15-17:** Metropolitan Museum of Art. **21-2, 21-3, 21-4, 1-4, 19-4, 19-5,** and **20-4:** J. J. Hester photo, courtesy of the Mexican National Museum of Anthropology. **1-7, 2-6, 2-7, 2-8, 2-9, 2-10, 3-6, 4-3, 4-8, 19-8c, 19-9, 20-2, 20-6c, 20-10, 21-7, 21-9, 21-10, 21-11a & b:** J. J. Hester photos. **2-1, 7-5, 7-11, 8-3, 9-4, 10-2, 10-4, 10-5, 11-9:** K. P. Oakley, *Man the Tool-Maker*, 6th ed. (1972), Trustees of the British Museum (Natural History). **2-2, 9-2, 9-3, 10-1, 14-1:** W. Watson (with additions by G. G. Sieveking), *Flint Implements: An Account of Stone Age Techniques and Cultures*, 3 ed. (1968), Trustees of the British Museum. **1.5:** L. Cottrell, *The Concise Encyclopedia of Archaeology*, © Hawthorn Books, Inc. (1960). **1.6:** Originally published in Schliemann, H., 1884, *Troya. Results of the latest results and discoveries on the site of Homer's Troy and in the heroic tumuli and other sites made in year 1882.* (New York: Harper and Bros.). **2-3, 10-3, 11-10, 13-9:** G. Clark, *World Prehistory* (1977), Cambridge University Press. **2-5:** Trustees of the Museum 1959. **3-1,** Map 15-1: S. Lloyd, *Mounds of the Near East*. (1963) Edinburgh: Edinburgh University Press. **3-4, 3-13:** J. W. Michels, *Dating Methods in Archaeology* (1973) Academic Press, Inc. **3-5:** Brothwell and Higgs, *Science in Archaeology* (1969) Thames and Hudson, Ltd. **Table 3-1:** *Australian Archaeology*, D. J. Mulvaney (ed.), p. 93 (Australian Institute of Aboriginal Studies, Canberra, 1972). **3-7:** Stuckenrath, et al. "University of PA. Radiocarbon Dates IX," *Radiocarbon 8* (1966) 348-385. American Journal of Science. **3-8:** H. E. Suess, *Journal of Geophysical Research*, Vol. 70 p. 5950 (1965) © by American Geophysical Union. **3-9, 21-6:** S. G. Morley and G. W. Brainerd, *The Ancient Maya*, 3 ed. © 1946, 1947, and 1956. Stanford University Press. Courtesy of the Board of Trustees of the Leland Stanford Junior University. **3-10:** National Geographic Society. **3-11:** V. Bucha, "Intensity of the Earth's Magnetic Field during Archaeological Times in Czechoslovakia, "*Archaeometry 10:* Fig. 10. By permission of Cambridge University Press. **3-12:** R. L. Fleischer et al. *Tracks of Charged Particles in Solids* (1965) *Science*, 149:383-393, Fig. 13. American Association for the Advancement of Science. **4-1:** Office of the Colorado State Archaeologist. **4-2:** W. S. Dancy, *Archaeological Field Methods* (1981) Burgess Publishing Co. **4-4:** J. W. Mueller, *Sampling in Archaeology* Tucson, Arizona: University of Arizona Press (1975). **4-5, 16-2:** J. K. S. St. Joseph and the Committee for Aerial photography, University of Cambridge. **4-6, 4-9, 8-2, 17-12, 20-3:** J. Grady photos. **4-7, 15-5b & c:** Oriental Institute, University of Colorado. **5-1, 5-3, 5-6, 5-8:** R. J. Sharer and W. Ashmore, *Fundamentals of Archaeology*. Menlo Park, California, The Benjamin/Cummings Publishing Co., Inc. (1979). **5-4:** M. Haury, "An Archaeological Approach to the Study of Cultural Stability," Society for the American Archaeology from *Memoirs of the Society for American Archaeology* Vol. 22 1956. **5-5:** J. J. Hester "A Comparative Typology of New World Cultures," *American Anthropologist* 64(5):1001-1015 1962. **5-9:** I. R. Hodder "Location Models and the Study of Romano-British Settlements," in D. L. Clarke (ed.), *Models in Archaeological London*, Methuen (1972). **6-1:** J. B. Birdsell, *Human Evolution*, 2 ed. New York: Houghton Mifflin Co, (1975). **Table 6-2, 9-10, 9-11, 11-1:** K. W. Butzer, *Enviroment and Archaeology*, 2 ed. Chicago: Aldine-Atherton (1971). **6-2, 6-4, 6-5, 6-6, 6-7, 7-7, 8-1, 9-9, 10-10, 15-3, 15-4, 15-5a, 15-6, 16-10:** Trustees of the British Museum (Natural History). **6-3:** *The Illustrated London News*, London Electrotype Agency. **6-8:** Courtesy of Maurice P. Coon and Wayland Minot (photographer). **6-9:** C. L. Brace, H. Nelson, N. Korn, and M. L. Brace, *Atlas of Human Archaeology* 2 ed. Holt, Rinehart and Winston (1971). **6-10:** Musée del'Homme. **7-1:** Y. Coppens, *Earliest Man and Environments in the Lake Rudolf Basin*. Chicago: University of Chicago Press (1976). **7-2, 7-4, 7-6:** Dexter Press slides. **7-3:** M. D. Leakey, *Olduvai Gorge Vol. III*. Cambridge University Press (1972). **7-8, 7-9:** J. D. Clark, *The Prehistory of Africa*, New York: Thames & Hudson Ltd. (1970). **Table 7-1:** J. M. Coles and E. S. Higgs, *The Archaeology of Early Man*. Baltimore: Penguin Press (1969). **7-10, 20-9b, d & k:** American Museum of Natural History. **8-4:** G. L. Isaac, *Olorgesailie: Archaeological Studies of a Middle Pleistocene Lake Basin in Kenya*. Chicago: University of Chicago Press (1977). **8-5:** de Sonneville-Bordes, *La Prehistoire Moderne*, Per-

igueux: P. Fanlac (1967). **8-6, 10-8, 13-3, 13-6, 14-3:** W. A. Fairservis, *The Threshold of Civilization: An Experiment in Prehistory*, Scribner's (1975). **8-7:** H. de Lumley, "A Paleolithic Camp at Nice," *Scientific American* 220:42-59, W. H. Freeman & Co. (1969). **9-1 (left/ right), 9-8:** A. Sherratt, *The Concise Cambridge Encyclopedia of Archaeology*, Trewin Copplestone Publishing Ltd. (1980). **9-6:** M. Laville, "The Relative Position of Mousterian Industries in the Climatic Chronology of the Early Würm in the Perigord," *World Archaeology*, 4(3):321-338 (1973). **10-9, 11-12, 11-13, 12-2, 12-4, 14-4, 14-5, 14-9, 14-10, 15-14, 15-15:** J. Hawkes *The Atlas of Early Man*, St. Martin's Press (1976). **14-7, 16-1, 16-3, 16-6:** Ministry of Public Buildings and Works, England. **15-1, 15-7, 16-13:** Courtesy of Aerofilms Ltd. **15-8, 18-6, 20-1 (bottom):** Philip M. Hobler (photographer). **15-10:** H. Leacroft and R. Leacroft, *Buildings of Ancient Egypt*, William R. Scott Inc. (1963). **15-6:** Courtesy of H. M. Wormington. **16-5:** Editions de'Art Jos. **16-11:** Courtesy of Gilbert Lobjois. **17-13:** Courtesy of Joe Ben Wheat, **18-3:** Courtesy of J. Antony Pomeroy. **19-6:** J. Grady photograph courtesy of the Denver Art Museum. **20-6a & b, 21-5:** Horace E. Day. **20-9a & l:** Dr. and Mrs. Franklin D. Murphy. **20-9c & f:** Art Institute of Chicago. **20-9e:** Field Museum of Natural History. **20-9c:** Boyer Fund, Logan Museum of Anthropology. **20-9H:** Museum of Cultural History. **20-9I:** Larry and Judi Anderson. **20-9j:** Mr. & Mrs. Donald H. McClelland. **20-12:** J. J. Hester photograph courtesy of the Inca Museum. **20-1 (top):** Mexican National Museum of Anthropology. **21-11c:** Courtesy of Ken Kirkwood. **9-7:** D. L. Clarke, "Models and Paradigms in Contemporary Archaeology," in D. L. Clarke (ed.), *Models in Archaeology*. Methuen (1972). **9-12:** F. Bordes and F. Prat "Observations sur les Faunes du Riss et du Würm I," *L'Anthropologie* 69:31-46 (1966). **10-6, 10-7:** A. Leroi-Gourhan, *Treasures of Prehistoric Art*, Abrams (1967). **10-11:** F. Bordes, *A Tales of Two Caves*, Harper & Row (1972). **Table 11-1, 11-5, 14-2:** J. G. D. Clark, *Prehistoric Europe, The Economic Basics*, Methuen & Co. Ltd. (1952). **11-2:** F. Zeuner, *Dating the Past*, Methuen & Co. Ltd. (1958). **11-3, 11-4, 11-11, 11-9:** G. Clark, *The Earlier Stone Age—Settlement of Scandinavia*, Cambridge University Press (1975). **11-6, 11-7:** J. G. D. Clark, *The Stone Age Hunters*, McGraw Hill (1967). **11-8:** J. Bordaz, *Tools of the Old and New Stone Age*. Natural History Press (1970). **Table 11-3, 13-7, 13-5:** R. J. Braidwood, *Prehistoric Men*, 7 ed. Scott Foresman & Co. (1967). **Table 11-4:** J. Hawkes, "History of Mankind, Cultural and Scientific Development," Vol. I, Part I, *Prehistory*. New York: Mentor Books. (1965). **12-3:** K. V. Flannery, "The Ecology of Early Food Production in Mesopotamia," *Science* 147:1247-1256 (1965). **12-1:** K. V. Flannery, "Origins and Ecological Effects of Early Domestication in Iran and the Near East," in Streuver, pp. 50-79 (1971). **Table 12-1:** F. E. Zeuner, *A History of Domesticated Animals*, London: Hutchinson (1963). **Table 12-2:** F. Hole and K. V. Flannery, "The Prehistory of Southwest Iran: A Preliminary Report," *Proceedings of the Prehistoric Society* 32:147 (1967). **13-1:** D. Vita-Finzi and E. S. Higgs, "Prehistoric Economy in Mount Carmel Area of Palestine: Site Catchment Analysis," *Proceedings of the Prehistoric Society* 36:1 (1970). **13-2, 13-4, 13-8:** J. Mellaart, *The Neolithic of the Near East*. New York: Schribner's (1975). **14-6:** Courtesy of H. Bachelmann. **14-8:** Courtesy of John Coles. Map **14-4:** Vishnu-Mittre, "Changing Economy in Ancient India," in Reed, pp. 569-588. (1977). **Map 14-5:** Kwang-chih, Chang, *The Archaeology of Ancient China*, 3 ed. New Haven: Yale University Press (1977). **15-2:** M. A. Beek, *Atlas of Mesopotamia*. London: Thomas Nelson (1962). **16-7, 16-8:** R. J. C. Atkinson, *Stonehenge and Neighboring Monuments*. Department of the Environment, London (1978). **16-9:** G. Hawkins, *Stonehenge Decoded*. New York: Doubleday (1965). **Table 16-2:** J. M. Coles and A. F. Harding, *The Bronze Age in Europe*. London Methuen & Co. Ltd. (1979). **17-2:** P. S. Martin and J. E. Guilday, "A Bestiary for Pleistocene Biologists," in Martin and Wright, pp. 1-66 (1967). **17-4, 19-13, 19-14:** D. Anderson and B. Anderson, Chaco Canyon, Globe, Arizona: Southwest Parks and Monuments Associations. (1976). **17-5:** D. M. Hopkins, "The Cenozoic History of Beringia—a Synthesis," in D. M. Hopkins (ed.), *The Bering Land Bridge*, Palo Alto, CA.: Stanford University Press, pp. 451-484 (1967). **17-5:** H. Müller-Beck, "On Migrations of Hunters Across the Bering Land Bridge in the Upper Pleistocene," in D. M. Hopkins (ed.), *The Bering Land Bridge*, Palo Alto, CA.: Stanford University Press, pp. 373-408 (1967). **17-6:** P. S. Martin, "The Discovery of America," *Science*

179:969-974. (1973). **7-11:** J. B. Wheat, "A Paleo-Indian Bison Kill," *Science American* 216(1):44-52. (1967). **17-1:** R. Bonnichsen, "Critical Arguments for Pleistocene Artifacts from the Old Crow Basin, Yukon: A Preliminary Statement," in Bryan, 1978, pp. 102-118. (1978). **Map 17-1:** H. M. Wormington, *The Ancient Hunters and Gatherers of the Americas.* In Press. New York: Academic Press (n.d.). **18-1, 18-2, 22-1, 22-3:** W. T. Sanders and J. Marino, *New World Prehistory.* Englewood Cliffs, New Jersey: Prentice-Hall (1970). **18-4:** J. D. Jennings, *Prehistory of North America,* New York: McGraw-Hill (1968). **18-5:** J. D. Jennings, *Ancient Native Americans.* San Francisco: Freeman and Co. (1978). **18-7, 18-8:** C. W. Meighan, "California Cultures and the Concept of an Archaic Stage," *American Antiquity* 24:289-305 (1959). **18-9:** K. Conover, "Matrix Analysis," in J. J. Hester and S. M. Nelson (eds.), *Studies in Bella Bella Prehistory.* Department of Archaeology, Simon and Fraser University, Publication No. 5:67-99. Burnaby, British Columbia (1978). **18-10:** K. V. Flannery, "The Vertebrate Fauna and Hunting Patterns," in Byers, 1967, pp. 132-188. (1967). **18-11:** R. S. MacNeish, "A Summary of Subsistence," in Byers 1967. **Map. 18-2a & b, Map 20-2:** L. G. Lumbreras, *The Peoples and Cultures of Ancient Peru.* Washington, D.C.: Smithsonian Institution Press. (1974). **Table 18-2:** R. S. MacNeish, "The Beginning of Agriculture in Central Peru," in C. A. Reed (ed.), *The Origins of Agriculture.* The Hague: Mouton (1977). **19-1:** B. J. Meggers, C. Evans, and E. Estrada, *Early Formative Period of Coastal Ecuador: The Valdivia and Machallilla Phases.* Washington, D. C.: Smithsonian Institution Press. (1965). **Map 19-1:** R. E. W. Adams, *Prehistoric Mesoamerica,* Boston: Little, Brown (1977). **19-2a:** *México.* México: Ediciones Lara (1967). **19-2b:** *México,* 2 ed. New York: Praeger. (1977). **19-3:** P. R. Drucker; R. Heizer and R. J. Squier, "Excavations at La Venta, Tabasco, 1955, *B.A.E. Bulletin* 170. Washington, D.C.: U.S. Government Printing Office (1959). **19-7, 19-8a & b:** G. R. Willey, *An Introduction to American Archaeology,* Vol. II: South American. Englewood Cliffs, New Jersey: Prentice-Hall (1971). **19-10:** W. N. Morgan, *Prehistoric Architecture in the Eastern United States.* Cambridge, Mass. and London: MIT Press. (1980). **19-11, 20-1 (left):** G. R. Wiley, *An Introduction to American Archaeology, Vol. I: North and Middle America.* Englewood Cliffs, New Jersey: Prentice-Hall (1966). **19-12, 20-5:** Hardwick and Associates. **20-1 (right):** R. Millon, *Urbanization at Teotihuacan, Mexico, Vol. I: The Teotihuacan Map.* Austin, Texas: University of Texas Press (1973). **20-7:** J. Marcus, "Territorial Organization of the Lowland Classic Maya," *Science* 180:911-916 (1973). **Table 20-3:** G. R. Willey, "The Rise of Maya Civilization: A Summary View," in R. E. W. Adam (ed.), *The Origins of Maya Civilization.* Albuquerque: School of American Research, University of New Mexico Press (1977). **20-8, 20-9:** C. B. Donnan, *Moche Art of Peru,* Los Angeles: Museum of Cultural History, U.C.L.A. (1976). **20-11:** G. W. Willey, *An Introduction to American Archaeology, Vol. II: South America.* Englewood Cliffs: Prentice-Hall (1971). **21-8:** M. E. Moseley, "Chan-Chan: Andean Alternative to the Preindustrial City," *Science* 187 (4173):219-225 (1975). 2-4: F. Hole and R. F. Heizer, An Introduction to Prehistoric Archaeology, 3 ed. (1965, 1969, and 1973), Holt, Reinhart and Winston.